CORNERSM

JAM

ABOUT THE AUTHORS

Alex Elliott-Howery and Jaimee Edwards run the
Cornersmith Cooking School in Sydney, where they
teach traditional kitchen skills for modern cooks,
highlighting the importance of seasonal eating and
reducing food waste. Their mission is to empower
home cooks to make less wasteful, more delicious
meals every day.

Previous books include *Cornersmith*,
Cornersmith Salads and Pickles and *Use It All*,
also published by Murdoch Books.

THE FOOD SAVER'S A-Z

THE ESSENTIAL CORNERSMITH KITCHEN COMPANION

**Alex Elliott-Howery
& Jaimee Edwards**

murdoch books

Sydney | London

Published in 2022 by Murdoch Books, an imprint of Allen & Unwin

Murdoch Books Australia
83 Alexander Street, Crows Nest NSW 2065
Phone: +61 (0)2 8425 0100
murdochbooks.com.au
info@murdochbooks.com.au

Murdoch Books UK
Ormond House, 26–27 Boswell Street, London WC1N 3JZ
Phone: +44 (0) 20 8785 5995
murdochbooks.co.uk
info@murdochbooks.co.uk

For corporate orders and custom publishing, contact our business development team
at salesenquiries@murdochbooks.com.au

Publisher: Jane Morrow
Editorial Manager: Virginia Birch
Creative direction: Megan Pigott
Cover and text design: Northwood Green
Editor: Nicola Young
Illustrations: Mirra Whale
Production Director: Lou Playfair

ISBN 978 1 92235 198 2 Australia
ISBN 978 1 91166 853 4 UK

 A catalogue record for this
book is available from the
NATIONAL LIBRARY OF AUSTRALIA   National Library of Australia

A catalogue record for this book is available from the British Library

Typeset by Midland Typesetters, Australia
Printed by C & C Offset Printing Co., Ltd

OVEN GUIDE: You may find cooking times vary depending on the oven you are using. For fan-forced
ovens, as a general rule, set the oven temperature to 20°C (35°F) lower than indicated in the recipe.

TABLESPOON MEASURES: We have used 20 ml (4 teaspoon) tablespoon measures. If you are using a
15 ml (3 teaspoon) tablespoon add an extra teaspoon of the ingredient for each tablespoon specified.

10 9 8 7 6 5 4 3 2 1

MIX
Paper | Supporting
responsible forestry
FSC   FSC® C008047
www.fsc.org

*The authors and publishers acknowledge that we meet and work on the traditional lands
of the Cammeraygal, Gadigal and Wangal people of the Eora Nation and pay our respects
to their elders past, present and future.*

**TO ALL COOKS
EVERYWHERE WHO ARE
DOING THEIR BEST TO
REDUCE FOOD WASTE**

CONTENTS

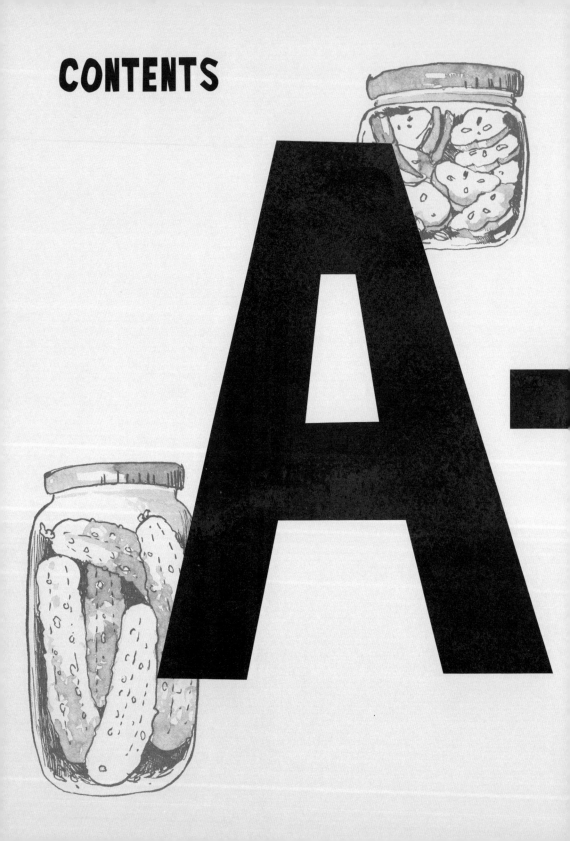

A-

INTRODUCTION

We're all too familiar with the daily struggle of putting meals on the table that tick all the boxes: yummy, affordable, nutritious, low-waste food that will be enjoyed by everyone and not end up in the bin. We know the food choices we make can play an important role in alleviating environmental problems, reducing food waste, avoiding excess packaging, managing budgets and building healthy bodies, but we also know it's not an easy feat.

As enthusiastic self-taught cooks and experienced teachers at the popular Cornersmith Cooking School, we have been discussing, experimenting with and refining our kitchen skills over 16 years of friendship and professional collaboration. When each of us had small children, we committed to preservative-free this, wholemeal that, and everything – including the Vegemite – was made from scratch. We turned ourselves inside out being the most wholesome and eco-conscious (if not the most boring) citizens on the planet.

Now we both have bigger kids who are bringing home Slurpees, the cooking school has expanded and life has got busier, more complicated and more expensive. We can't 'homestead' from city kitchens when we come home at 6 pm. At the same time, the stakes of the climate emergency are higher, and we know that now, more than ever, community and individual change matters. We haven't given up on the home-made everything, but we've learned how to cut corners, focus our priorities and develop 'hacks' for both sanity and sustainability.

While we both still love a day spent bottling tomatoes, we're now much more into perfecting quick tips and tricks that will keep kitchen scraps out of the bin and recipes that are versatile enough to stretch over a few dinners.

When our last cookbook, *Use It All*, came out in 2020 we were surprised and delighted by its success. The feedback made us realise that people in households of all kinds want to change their habits in the kitchen. We had discussions with readers and our cooking school students about the obstacles to reducing food waste, and for many it's simply that the wisdom of 'what to do with the thing' has been lost. So we looked to the cooks from less wasteful times for lessons in resourcefulness and thrift – rustic meals, wartime rations – to really learn for ourselves and show readers how to make the very most out of every ingredient.

This book is a look into our own fridges and pantries, fruit bowls, freezers and gardens, to see the ways we manage the food that comes into our kitchens. It's not about lifestyle or Instagram perfection. It's about real people cooking good, simple, affordable food while also making better environmental choices.

We want to encourage you to be a more confident and instinctive cook, to take creative liberties with what you have and what you like. This book is to be used as a guide, as though we're there with you in your kitchen, reminding you to look at what you already have rather than head to the shops. The layout is an A–Z ingredient manual, designed to help you use up anything you're sick of looking at or that's going to go bad next week. We'll show you how half a jar of tomato paste can be turned into dinner, just how many things you can do with a tired broccoli head, how delicious cauliflower leaves and leek tops actually are, and how never to throw away cooked pasta or rice again. You'll find advice on what ingredient goes with what, ways to store food properly for longer life, quick ideas for what to do with awkwardly small amounts of something, waste hacks, ingredient swaps, preserving tips and, of course, the answers to that endless question, 'What's for dinner?'

Our recipes are simple but delicious. We use minimal ingredients and basic cooking techniques to feed ourselves, our families and friends with ease. This book will save you time and money while bringing resourcefulness back into your kitchen.

Remember, you don't need to be perfectly sustainable – even small changes will make a difference. We hope these pages help.

Alex & Jaimee

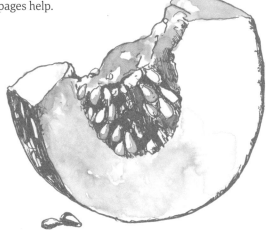

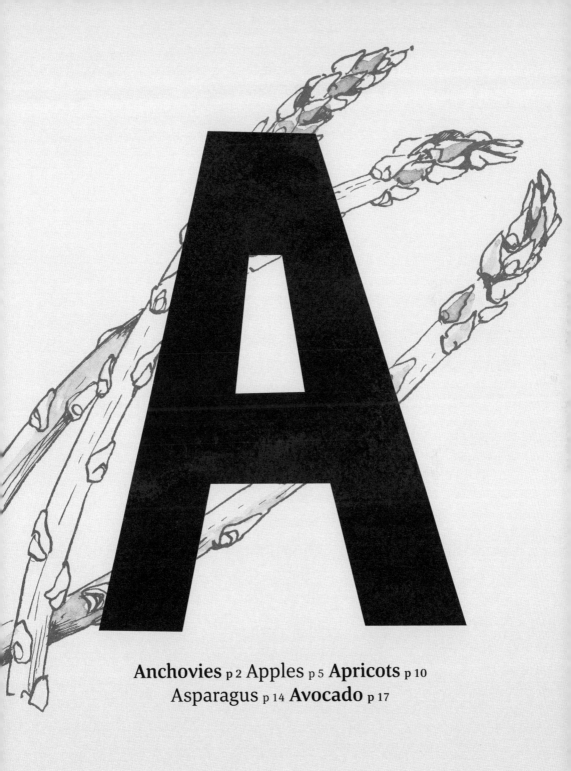

Anchovies

Ah, anchovies ... the great divider of palates. You might love them or hate them, but many people have half a jar of anchovies rattling around in their fridge. Intensely salty, these preserved little fishies can add a depth and complexity to dishes that can be hard to identify, even for the haters.

Go with Olive oil, butter, onions, garlic, chilli, capers, fennel, lemons, bitter salad greens, beetroot, brussels sprouts, cabbage, cauliflower, tomatoes, capsicum (pepper), eggplant (aubergine), zucchini (courgettes), potatoes, olives, bread, eggs, cheeses, sage, warm spices like cinnamon and allspice, coconut cream

Storage Unopened, a jar of anchovies will last 1 year in the pantry. Once opened, keep anchovies in the fridge; they'll be at their best for 3–4 months, but honestly, they're so salted that they'll still last for years.

Substitutes If you don't have anchovies, try replacing their intense salty flavour with these punchy options: a dash of fish sauce, capers, worcestershire sauce, preserved lemons or salted olives.

Some ideas for finishing the anchovy jar

* Combine a few chopped anchovies with capers and currants and stir them through left-over cooked rice or couscous, adding olive oil and plenty of herbs for a meal for one. Heat this up in a small saucepan or eat cold as a grain salad.
* Add chopped anchovies to the Niçoise Salad of Sorts (p 39).
* Add some thinly sliced anchovies to roasted beetroot just before serving, for extra richness.
* After you've eaten all the anchovies in the jar, drizzle the left-over anchovy oil on toast and top with fresh tomato or a boiled egg. Or drizzle anchovy oil over garlic bread to make it extra rich. You could also add a splash to a salad dressing.
* Anchovies in the fridge and pasta in the pantry mean either Puttanesca (p 71) or Parsley Pasta Sauce (p 199) is on the menu tonight.

✴ ***Quick tapenade*** Finely chop pitted olives with a few anchovy fillets, mixing in ground black pepper, a squeeze of lemon juice, a few chilli flakes and olive oil. Serve with fish or cheese. For a full Tapenade recipe, see p 310.

Anchovy butter
MAKES 150 G (5 OZ)

Sorry, not sorry, if you're among the uninitiated, to introduce you to the world of compound butters. They're basically butter mixed with something intensely flavoured – savoury or sweet – to give you even more reason to love butter. This anchovy butter will turn tomatoes on toast into something worth inviting friends over for, while putting a generous slice on a cooked steak, letting it melt and eating it with a very simple green salad and a martini is as close to perfect as life can get. We also love Herby Compound Butter (p 192) and Lemon-flavoured Butter (p 240).

In a small bowl, mix 120 g (4¼ oz) unsalted softened butter, about 25 g (1 oz) drained then finely chopped anchovies, and a pinch each of cayenne pepper, ground cinnamon and ground black pepper (or whatever you have that will make it yummy and spicy). Once combined, keep in an airtight container in the fridge for 3–4 weeks or the freezer for up to 3 months.

Comfort pasta sauce
SERVES 4

This recipe is a version of one of Marcella Hazan's pasta sauces. It's a perfect way to use those few last anchovies, adding richness to otherwise very basic ingredients. Our families crave this household favourite whether spirits are high or low.

Place a medium saucepan over medium heat, and melt 100 g (3½ oz) unsalted butter. Add 1 small diced onion, 4 finely chopped garlic cloves and 4–6 chopped anchovies. Sauté for 5–7 minutes, then add 400 g (14 oz) tinned crushed tomatoes. Reduce the heat to low and simmer gently, covered, for 15 minutes. Blitz to a rich orange sauce using a hand-held blender. Serve with any pasta.

Cheat's caesar salad dressing

MAKES ½ CUP (125 ML)

The beauty of this dressing is that it really does use up bits and bobs from the fridge. If you have most of the ingredients for the dressing, all you need is a cos lettuce and salad is served. Of course this dressing is also great with other salads, and even on grilled (broiled) chicken, boiled potatoes or poached eggs.

Finely chop 3 anchovies and 1 garlic clove, then smash together with the flat of your knife. Transfer to a bowl and mix with 1 tbsp lemon juice, 1 tsp worcestershire sauce and 1 tsp mustard. In another bowl, mix ½ cup (120 g) mayonnaise and ¼ cup (25 g) grated parmesan, then add the anchovy mixture and whisk to combine. If too thick, loosen with 1–2 tbsp water. Keep in the fridge for up to 1 week.

TO MAKE A QUICK CAESAR SALAD

Grab a cos lettuce, tear it up, throw it in a bowl, top with 3 chopped hard-boiled eggs and 1 handful of Croutons (p 51), and drizzle with the dressing.

Apples

Is there anything more annoying than half an apple? There is not. After many years of raising children, we've both become experts in using up apples that have one tiny bite taken from them. If you're in the half-eaten fruit years, we see you; if not, we encourage you to think about apples as more than a snack. They're salad, dessert, condiment and everything in between.

Go with   Beetroot, pumpkin (squash), brussels sprouts, cabbage, carrots, celery, radishes, daikon, turnips, fennel, kohlrabi, silverbeet (Swiss chard), butter, cheeses, pork, bacon, ham, nuts, sunflower seeds, sesame seeds and tahini, berries, rhubarb, quince, pears, persimmons, dried fruit, brandy, maple syrup, honey, cloves, allspice, cinnamon, coriander seeds, horseradish, ginger, rosemary, thyme, sage

Storage   Apples will keep in a fruit bowl on the kitchen counter for about 5 days. For longer storage, refrigerate them for 2–3 weeks. Once an apple has been cut, it will last longer if covered in water with a squeeze of lemon juice mixed in.

Substitutes   Hard pears can be used instead of apples as their texture is similar, but you might want to amp up the seasoning, as the flavour is much milder. Poached quince, rhubarb and pear can replace apples in cooked dishes or baking.

Some ideas for the apples in the fruit bowl

* When roasting pumpkin (squash), sweet potato, fennel or onions, throw in some unpeeled apple chopped to a similar size to the vegetables.
* Sauté apple and cabbage in butter for the perfect complement to a sausage or baked potato. See Sautéed Cabbage (p 67), adding 1 thinly sliced apple to the shredded cabbage.
* Make a toastie with good cheese, thinly sliced apple and a little chutney or mustard.
* Quick-pickle (p 473) thinly sliced apple for salads and cheese boards. »

* Get baking – try the Seedy Breakfast Muffins (p 371), replacing some or all of the pumpkin (squash) with grated apple.
* Make a batch of jam or a jelly. Apples have very high pectin levels, so adding 1–2 apples to fruity jams will help them set. Add them to the Rhubarb Jam in the Foolproof Jam recipe (p 389) or make the Rosemary and Apple Jelly (p 209).
* **Stuffed apples** Core wrinkly old apples, stuff them with butter, brown sugar and nuts, and bake at 180°C (350°F) until soft and caramelised, about 30 minutes.

Apple salad is a thing
SERVES 4 AS A SIDE

Apples are crunchy, tart and sweet, and they're not just for desserts and lunchboxes. Try making them the base of a simple salad and never look back. The best way to prepare them is to leave the skin on and cut them into fine matchsticks (google it if you don't know how). From there just add green leaves from the fridge or garden to pull together an interesting salad. We like using a bitter leaf like rocket (arugula), but if you have something milder on hand, go ahead. Chopped herbs such as parsley or basil work well too.

Cut 2 unpeeled apples into matchsticks and place in a bowl. Season with a little salt. Tear some green leaves into smallish pieces and add to the apple. Throw in some toasted nuts or the Seedy Salad Mix (p 409), and toss with a simple vinaigrette made by mixing 1 tbsp olive oil, 1 tsp dijon mustard, ½ tbsp white wine vinegar and a big pinch of sugar. Or if you're feeling adventurous, dress with Egg Yolk Dressing (p 154).

Roast apple and sage stuffing
STUFFS 1 CHICKEN

A stuffing that's as good as the roast meat it stuffs is a non-negotiable – otherwise, what's the point? This stuffing is rich, herby and perfect for less than crisp apples. Feel free to experiment with other fruits, like apricots, plums or pears. If you don't have sage, use another fresh herb of your choice but just add it in, skipping the frying step.

Preheat the oven to 180°C (350°F). Core 2 large unpeeled apples, cut into large cubes and arrange in a baking tray. Drizzle with 1 tbsp olive oil and season with salt and pepper. Roast for 20 minutes or until caramelised at the edges.

Heat 2 tbsp olive oil or butter in a frying pan over medium heat, then fry 1 small handful of sage leaves until crisp. Remove from the heat and stir in the roasted apple and ¼ cup (30 g) chopped pecans (or almonds or walnuts), mixing well. Grate the zest of 1 lemon into the mix, then add plenty of salt and pepper and 1 tsp of your favourite ground spice (or to taste).

Use this to stuff a chicken or turkey or a pork roast. If you're the sort of eccentric who likes to eat stuffing on its own, spread it out in a pie dish, cover with foil and roast for 30 minutes.

Simple stewed apples
SERVES 3–4

This dish can be enjoyed on its own, served with custard or yoghurt, or used as a filling for pies, crumbles, crepes or on top of pancakes. Other fruits stew well too, so try this method with rhubarb, pears and stone fruits. Don't be put off by floury apples – this recipe will disguise any inadequacies.

Peel and chop 3 apples, saving the cores and skins for a batch of Apple Scrap Vinegar (p 9). Melt 2 tsp butter in a saucepan over medium heat. Immediately add the apple before the butter browns. Add 1 tsp ground cinnamon, 2–3 tbsp white (granulated) sugar and a splash of water. Bring to a simmer, cover, then reduce the heat to low and cook down for 8–10 minutes. If the fruit is too liquidy, remove the lid and cook off the excess juices.

Jaimee's apple bake
MAKES 1 x 24 CM (9½ IN) CAKE

This easy cake-type dessert is Russian in origin. It has the classic flavours of apple and cinnamon – and the major Russian food group of sour cream. It's almost like a teacake. Feel free to replace the apples with other fruits like apricots, peaches, pears, cherries or blueberries.

Preheat the oven to 180°C (350°F) and grease a round 24 cm (9½ in) spring-form cake tin generously with butter. Core 750 g (1 lb 10 oz) apples (about 5 apples), chop into small pieces and drizzle with the juice of 1 lemon to stop them from browning. Beat 125 g (4½ oz) caster (superfine) sugar, 4 egg yolks and ½ cup (125 g) sour cream until frothy. Sift in 1 cup (150 g) plain (all-purpose) flour, 1 tsp ground cinnamon, the apples and a pinch of salt. Mix well. Whisk 4 egg whites to stiff peaks and fold into the mixture. Transfer to the tin and bake for 30 minutes. Serve warm with single (pure) cream.

Apple pie filling for bottling or freezing

MAKES 2 x 750 ML – 1 LITRE (27–35 OZ) JARS

Having apple pie filling on hand means you're minutes away from having a pie in the oven. All the hard work is done; all you need to do is roll out pastry, add the filling and bake. Fill your pantry with jars of this mix over the winter months, when apples are crisp, flavoursome and cheap. Use it for pies, turnovers and crumbles, but also with porridge, yoghurt or ice cream. It freezes really well, so pour into 4 cup (1 litre) containers and freeze for up to 3 months. The recipe makes enough for 2 small pies, but feel free to halve, double or triple.

Peel 2 kg (4 lb 8 oz) apples of your choice (the tarter the better), then core and cut into 1 cm (½ in) slices. (Don't throw away the peels and cores – use them up with the Apple Scrap Vinegar and Pectin Stock recipes opposite.) Pop the apple slices into a bowl of water with a squeeze of lemon juice to stop them going brown. Bring a pot of water to the boil and blanch the apple slices for 1 minute. Remove them from the water with a slotted spoon and set aside in a bowl. (Let the water cool, then use it to water your plants.)

Combine 1½ cups (375 ml) water, ¾ cup (165 g) caster (superfine) sugar, 1 tsp ground cinnamon and a big squeeze of lemon juice in a saucepan. Warm over low heat until the sugar dissolves. Add the blanched apple slices, then increase the heat to medium, bring to a simmer and cook for a few minutes, until the mixture thickens a little.

Transfer to airtight containers or jars and store in the fridge for 1 week or the freezer for up to 3 months.

FOR THE PRESERVERS

If you're into preserving, you can bottle this mix to enjoy all year round. Using tongs, pack the cooked apple slices into hot sterilised (p 501) 750 ml – 1 litre (27–35 oz) jars, then cover with the cinnamon-y water from the saucepan, making sure the apples are well covered in liquid. Remove air bubbles by carefully inserting a clean butter knife or chopstick to push them out or burst them, then seal and heat-process (p 502) for 30 minutes. Once cool, squirrel away in the pantry for up to 6 months.

TO MAKE AN APPLE PIE

Empty the apple into a saucepan, holding back some of the liquid if it's too watery. Warm over medium heat and slowly sprinkle in ½ tbsp cornflour (cornstarch) or 1 tbsp plain (all-purpose) flour. Stir in gently and let the mixture boil for a few minutes to thicken. Allow it to cool before adding to the pastry; for a crumble, pour it straight into the dish.

APPLE PEEL AND CORES

Apple scrap vinegar

Making your own vinegar at home is easy, and this fruit scrap vinegar recipe uses apple or pear cores and skins. We make a batch of this after we've cooked an apple pie or chutney, and it honestly takes 5 minutes. Use this vinegar for salad dressings or a dipping sauce, as a quick-pickling liquid or to add a little acidity to dishes that need a lift.

Add skins and cores to a large jar or crock and just cover with water, cup by cup. For each 1 cup (250 ml) water add 1 tbsp caster (superfine) sugar and 1 tbsp raw apple cider vinegar. Cover with muslin or a clean Chux and secure with a rubber band or string. Leave on the benchtop for a few weeks until it's a little bubbly and smells and tastes like cider. Strain out and discard the scraps. Pour the liquid back into the jar, cover with muslin again and leave on the bench until it turns into vinegar (it will taste acidic, tart and fruity). The warmer the weather, the quicker this will happen. Once you're happy with the taste, strain into a clean bottle, then seal and store in the fridge. It will keep for a really long time.

Pectin stock

This is an excellent recipe for our jam-making friends. You need pectin to make a well-set jam, but instead of buying commercial pectin, why not have a go at making your own? Then, when you're making jam, replace the water in the recipe with pectin stock. It will last for 2 weeks in the fridge or you can freeze it for up to 3 months. Keep in mind that the pectin will lose a little of its strength if frozen.

After making an apple pie or relish (see 'What's in the Fruit Bowl' Relish, p 333), save your skins and cores. Feel free to add any other high-pectin fruits or citrus peel you have on hand. Put your scraps in a saucepan and just cover with water. Simmer gently for 30–45 minutes, then strain into jars or containers, allow to cool and store in the fridge or freezer.

To make jam, see the Foolproof Jam recipe on p 389.

Apricots

A good apricot is a rare and wonderful thing. When you do come across them, buy a kilo or two. Their floral sweetness, with a hint of sharp acid, makes them an obvious choice for dessert, but apricots definitely have an affinity for savoury pairings too.

Go with	Almonds, blueberries, chocolate, cardamom, ginger, rosemary, oranges, vanilla, cheeses, butter, cream, dark chocolate, coconut, cumin, meats, mustard, bitter greens, pepper
Storage	To ripen apricots, store on the benchtop, putting them in a paper bag if you want to speed things up. Once perfectly ripe, eat them straight away or store in the fridge for 2–3 days.
Substitutes	Instead of apricots you can use peaches or nectarines in most recipes. The flavour will be subtly different, of course, but still delicious. Be sure to check out the peaches section (p 331) for more recipes.

Some ideas for using ageing apricots

* Squish overripe apricots onto toast with ricotta and honey or brown sugar. Or turn them into a jammy toastie in a sandwich toaster.
* When slow-cooking lamb or pork, add 4–5 halved apricots with cardamom and allspice (a nice change from prunes).
* Stuff a chicken with ripe apricots, nuts and garlic, or make the Roast Apple and Sage Stuffing (p 6), replacing the 3 apples with 6–8 apricots. Cook the apricots for less time, around 10–15 minutes, until they begin to brown.
* Make a rustic summer fruit pie using the Fig Crostata recipe (p 163). It's the perfect way to use up squishy apricots and the last few scrapings from the jam jar. Sprinkle with chopped rosemary before baking, and serve with vanilla ice cream.

Apricots can be rescued by grilling

If, despite your best intentions, your apricots went wrinkly in the fridge, grill (broil) them.

Brush with a neutral-flavoured oil like grapeseed or sunflower oil, then cook under a hot grill (broiler) for 3–4 minutes each side or until golden and starting to caramelise. The riper the fruit the less cooking time needed. You can also grill fruits on a hot barbecue, or in a chargrill pan or even a very hot frying pan.

If you're thinking of throwing grilled (broiled) fruits into a salad, season them lightly with salt and pepper and a squeeze of lemon juice after grilling. If they're destined for sweetness, drizzle with honey, maple syrup or a sprinkling of sugar, and serve with single (pure) cream.

Apricot, rocket (arugula) and pepita salad
SERVES 4 AS A SIDE

This is a lovely fragrant combination of ingredients, a late-summer version of the classic pear, rocket and parmesan salad. Use your ripe, blushing apricots for this one.

Put 3–4 big handfuls of rocket or other bitter green leaves in a salad bowl and sprinkle with a little salt and ground pepper. Cut 4 apricots into quarters or sixths and add to the leaves. Using a vegetable peeler, shave 12 parmesan ribbons over the ingredients and add a handful of toasted pepitas (pumpkin seeds). Drizzle with your good oil and best vinegar. Give it a light toss with clean hands and grind some more pepper on top.

Apricot chicken
SERVES 4

An update on the 1970s dinner-party favourite. This version uses fresh apricots, rosemary, mustard and apple cider vinegar for a quick family dinner. It's an easy way to use up less than perfect stone fruits. Feel free to mix apricots, peaches and nectarines.

Brown 500 g (1 lb 2 oz) chicken thighs in a frying pan over medium heat for 4 minutes on each side, then remove from the pan and set aside. Add a little oil to the pan and sauté 1 sliced onion for 5 minutes or until soft. Add 3 sliced garlic cloves, 1 tbsp chopped rosemary, ¼ cup (55 g) brown sugar, 1 tbsp apple cider vinegar and 2 tbsp dijon mustard, then cook, stirring constantly, for another 1–2 minutes. Add 6 roughly chopped apricots (no need to peel), ½ tsp salt and some ground pepper, then simmer until the apricots have softened. Add the chicken thighs, mixing well to coat them in the apricot glaze. Cover and simmer for 10–15 minutes or until the chicken is cooked through. Serve with couscous or rice and a leafy green salad.

Savoury roasted fruits

SERVES 4 AS A SIDE

Roasting fruits is a great way to empty a fruit bowl. By adding salt and pepper, and a little liquid such as wine, stock or even a splash of vinegar, you will deepen the intensity of flavour. Serve roasted fruits with grilled (broiled) or roasted meats, toss them through green leaves or cooked grains or pulses such as brown rice, chickpeas or barley, or serve with fancy cheese and wine.

Preheat the oven to 180°C (350°F). Arrange 500 g (1 lb 2 oz) – or whatever amount needs using up – of halved and stoned apricots cut side up in a baking tray, adding an onion cut into wedges if you'd like. Drizzle with 2–3 tbsp olive oil and season with plenty of salt and pepper. Sprinkle with 1 tbsp caster (superfine) sugar and 1–2 tsp ground spices (e.g. cumin, cinnamon, cardamom), then mix well with clean hands to coat the fruits evenly. Add a little moisture if you'd like – a few knobs of butter, a generous splash of wine, stock or vinegar – then roast for 20–30 minutes, shaking the tray every now and then, until the apricots are golden.

Poached apricots

If you have a few apricots and some spices rattling around, it might not seem like much, but you're well on your way to a fancy breakfast or dessert. If you have more apricots you can double or triple the recipe. Follow the Four Ways to Poach Pears recipe (p 336), but use lighter spices – a few slices of fresh ginger, cardamom pods, some vanilla or even a splash of rosewater. If you want to poach in a boozy syrup, replace the red wine in the pear recipe with white wine or rosé or even left-over sparkling wine. Serve poached apricots with ice cream, French Toast (p 51), porridge or Baked Rice Pudding (p 392).

Apricot and ginger jam

Apricot jam is a real treat, and this is a recipe for using an abundance of beautiful apricots. You can spread it liberally on buttered toast, but it's also wonderful as a filling for sponge cake or as a glaze for pork chops. Follow the Foolproof Jam recipe (p 389), using 1 kg (2 lb 4 oz) apricots and ¼ cup (50 g) grated fresh ginger.

Home-made dried apricots

Dried apricots are often full of sulfites and the sulfite-free ones are incredibly expensive. If you find yourself with a glut of apricots, try the simple Drying Fruits method (p 357).

See cherries, peaches and plums for ideas with other stone fruit.

Asparagus

Unless you're a keen gardener, you don't really find yourself with too much asparagus, do you? It's one of those ingredients that we intentionally buy and then maybe don't have enough ideas about how to eat. The answer is to keep it pretty simple. Asparagus is best eaten as close to being picked as possible. That said, unless you grow it you will always be eating asparagus long after it's been picked. That also means there's no way on this earth you can justify buying out-of-season asparagus flown in from overseas in the middle of winter. Buy asparagus in spring, prepare it a few simple and delicious ways, and then miss it for the rest of the year.

Goes with	Cream, cheeses, butter, eggs, almonds, sesame seeds, pasta, mayonnaise, mustard, garlic, soy sauce, ham and bacon, tofu, capers, chives, parsley, thyme, dill, tarragon, spring onions (scallions), green beans, snow peas (mange tout), spinach
Storage	To store asparagus, take off the rubber bands that usually hold the bunches of spears together. The spears won't last longer than 2 days. If you're going to eat them within a day, store them in a glass with the ends in a little water. If you want to make them last another day, store them in a clean cloth or reusable plastic bag in the fridge. Freeze the woody ends for making stock.
Substitutes	Broccoli stems make a good substitute for asparagus in a cooked dish. If you need to use something else in place of raw asparagus, try thinly sliced celery or green beans.

Some ideas for eating every last asparagus spear

* Use a bean slicer or slice vertically for very thin strips to throw raw into salads.
* Serve grilled (broiled) with a soft-boiled egg, chopped capers and good toast.
* Stir-fry with minced (ground) pork and lots of finely chopped ginger.
* Char then toss through pasta with a little bacon or prosciutto or Home-made Bacon Bits (p 23), olive oil, lemon juice and chilli flakes.
* Blanch then add to crunchy green leaves and sliced avocado for a very simple green salad. Dress with Classic Mustard Vinaigrette (p 283) or Orange Vinaigrette (p 316).
* Try the Spring Greens Medley (p 341) – it's a delicious way to clean out all the greens in the fridge, especially asparagus that's seen better days.
* Make Japanese-style Sesame Greens (p 40) with chopped asparagus spears.

Blanched or grilled (broiled) asparagus

Asparagus is best lightly blanched in well-salted water or charred on a hot barbecue grill or in a hot pan – see Charred Green Beans (p 39) for cooking tips. Grill or blanch your asparagus, then lay on a platter, see what you have in the fridge and top with any of the following:

* a drizzle of sesame oil and soy sauce, and a scattering of toasted sesame seeds
* finely chopped bacon or prosciutto and plenty of olive oil, pepper and herbs
* orange zest and juice, chilli flakes and red wine vinegar
* mayonnaise, lemon and tarragon
* Cheat's Caesar Salad Dressing (p 4)
* lashings of Anchovy Butter (p 3).

Asparagus stir-fry

Asparagus stir-fried to perfection is so simple and delicious that it should make an appearance on the table once a week during spring. Serve with grilled (broiled) fish and a glass of wine. Use the Stir-fried Celery method (p 87).

Asparagus soup

We dream of eating this for dinner once the children move out. Follow the same method as for Green Soup (p 440), using asparagus instead of green leaves. A little tarragon would make this extra lovely. And don't forget to save the woody green ends for making stock (see below).

Asparagus omelette

This is a very nice meal if you're dining alone. It's light and easy but in no way feels lonely. Have it for an al fresco dinner or as a Sunday breakfast. Follow the Two-egg Omelette recipe on p 150, adding charred or lightly blanched asparagus, a little goat's cheese and plenty of ground black pepper.

Quick-pickled asparagus

When the season is here, make a few jars of this for the fridge. The spears are great thinly sliced through a green salad, served on crusty bread with creamy cheese or on an antipasto board. Follow the method in the Quick-pickling recipe (p 473), adding a peeled garlic clove, a few strips of lemon peel and a thyme sprig or a bay leaf to each jar. Allow them to sit for a week or so before eating.

Woody asparagus end stock

Put the asparagus ends in a saucepan, and for every 1 bunch's worth of ends (about a handful) add 1 cup (250 ml) water, ¼ tsp salt, some peppercorns, a small thyme or tarragon sprig (or a bay leaf), and 1 crushed garlic clove. Bring to the boil over medium heat, then reduce the heat to low and simmer for 10–15 minutes. Strain and use the stock to make an asparagus soup (above) or spinach soup (p 392). If not using immediately, freeze the stock for up to 3 months.

Avocado

Café staple and millennial icon, avocados are everywhere. They're the healthy green butter of our dreams, but demand for avocado is high, so to ensure they are a sustainable crop, go easy on just how many you smash. Autumn is their peak season, so enjoy them then and don't let stray halves get lost in the fridge.

Goes with	Citrus fruits, mango, pineapple, mint, tomatoes, corn, coriander (cilantro), chives, parsley, lettuce, cashews, pepitas (pumpkin seeds), sunflower seeds, fish, bacon, ham, chicken, blue cheese, cottage cheese, chilli, cumin, quinoa, mayonnaise, sour cream, chocolate, Vegemite
Storage	Keep a ripe uncut avocado in the fridge for up to 3 days. Unripe avocados will never ripen in the fridge, so pop them on the benchtop and they will ripen in 2–3 days. Store cut avocado, with a squeeze of lemon juice on the exposed surfaces, in an airtight container in the fridge for 2–3 days.
Substitutes	Hmmm ... substitutes for avocado are tricky. Texturally they are like bananas, but please don't make banana guacamole! And seriously, we both tried to make banana bread with avocado but the kids weren't fooled for a minute. Avocados really are their own thing. What they are good for in terms of substitutes is adding a non-dairy creamy element to cooking. So think of using avocado instead of butter or cheese in sandwiches or burgers.

Some ideas for dressing up smashed avocado

Smashed avocado is a breakfast classic for a good reason; it's about the most perfect thing you can eat to start your day – just add toast. To make a good thing even better, and because amping up the flavour will also help make your avocados go further, try adding any of the following:

* finely diced preserved lemon
* finely chopped garlic and chopped mint
* thinly sliced green chillies, chopped coriander (cilantro) leaves and lime juice »

* wasabi and mayonnaise
* feta and lemon juice
* diced cucumber and parsley
* toasted seeds
* Vegemite.

Avocado dressing

MAKES ABOUT 1 CUP (250 ML)

This luxurious dressing can be used in multiple ways. Try it over leafy greens or roasted carrots, use it in wraps or burgers, drizzle it over fish, or even use it as a dip.

In a food processor combine 1 avocado, 2 tbsp tahini, about ¼ cup fresh herbs (such as coriander/cilantro, oregano, parsley or dill), 2 garlic cloves and a pinch of salt. Blitz until smooth, then add 1½ tsp ground cumin, 1 tsp chilli powder or flakes, the juice of 1 lime and ¼ cup (60 ml) water. Blitz again until everything is well combined and you have a smooth green sauce.

Avocado salsa

MAKES ABOUT 2 CUPS (500 G)

This salsa is a must-have on the table when serving tacos, tortilla chips or grilled (broiled) fish.

Very finely dice ½ red onion and gently mix with 2 diced avocados, 1–2 jalapeno chillies (or other fresh chillies) and the leaves from 1 bunch of coriander (cilantro). Season with salt and pepper to taste and add the juice and zest of 1 lime.

'What needs using up' guacamole

Tacos, burritos and nachos appear often in our houses. And they're usually a mishmash of what's in the fridge. If we have ripe avocados then guacamole makes an appearance. This isn't so much a recipe as a reminder to use up bits and pieces.

Mash avos in a good-sized bowl – sometimes it's two or three avos, sometimes it's only half, and everyone gets a spoonful on their taco. Add something acidic – lime or lemon juice is ideal, but a little splash of vinegar will do the trick if there's no citrus to hand. If you have a little sour cream, cream cheese or yoghurt that needs using up, add 1 tbsp, then add finely chopped garlic if you have it, and some chopped fresh or pickled chillies or a pinch of chilli flakes for a kick.

Often ½ finely diced tomato makes its way in, or that little bit of onion we don't know what to do with, the last of the coriander (cilantro) leaves or very thinly sliced coriander stems. Mix gently and serve.

Chicken and avocado soup

This soup is inspired by the flavours of Mexico – the home of the avocado. There's a lightness to it and it's best enjoyed at the beginning of autumn, when avocados begin to appear and the last of the tomatoes are still around. This soup is also a good way to use up left-overs from a roast or poached chicken.

Follow the Left-over-chicken Soup recipe (p 106), replacing the 2 cups vegetables with 2 cups (440 g) diced tomatoes. After pouring in the stock, add the shredded chicken and 1 diced firm avocado. Warm through, then garnish with coriander (cilantro) leaves. Remove from the heat, allow everything to sit for 5 minutes, then serve with a squeeze of lime juice.

BROWN AVOCADO

One of the hardest questions to answer in our cooking classes is what to do with too many avocados or brown avocados. The truth is there's not a lot you can do to make avocados last longer or to preserve them in any way. And while there's nothing wrong with brown avo, no one wants to spread it on their toast or eat greying guacamole.

Some ideas for hiding brown avocado so it gets eaten

Try one of the recipes over the page, or these hot tips:
* Mash really well and add to beaten eggs before scrambling. It's almost like adding a dash of cream. Add plenty of chopped herbs to turn it into green eggs of sorts.
* Bake with it – by adding dark sugar and unsweetened cocoa powder you can hide all the ugly brown bits. Sneak this combination into baked recipes, such as replacing some of the butter in brownies or a chocolate cake.

Pretend Nutella with half a brown avo
MAKES ABOUT ¼ CUP (60 ML)

You can absolutely spread this on toast and give it to the kids for breakfast. Just don't try to trick anyone over five years old.

Mash ½ brown avo very well with a fork, then mix in 1 tbsp unsweetened cocoa powder, 2–3 tsp brown sugar and a little dash of vanilla. Keep mixing until everything is combined. Spread on toast and top with slices of banana.

Rice, greens and half-an-avo fritters
MAKES 6, SERVES 2–3

We make use of half a brown (or green) avo by using it as an egg replacement here and there. These fritters usually have two eggs, but you can replace one with half an avo that needs using.

In a small bowl, mash ½ avocado, then add 2 eggs and whisk until creamy and smooth. In another bowl combine 1 cup (185 g) cooked rice, 1 cup thinly sliced greens (kale, spinach, cabbage or fennel), ½ cup chopped herbs, 1 chopped small chilli, 1 finely chopped garlic clove and ½ tsp salt. Add the avocado mix to the rice mix and combine. Heat ¼ cup (60 ml) oil in a frying pan and drop in dollops of the mixture (2–3 tbsp) to make 4–6 fritters. Fry on each side for 2–3 minutes and serve immediately. Yummy with some sour cream and chilli jam.

B

Bacon

One rasher of bacon can go a long way when it comes to lending its salty and smoky flavour to a dish. Its fats will also melt into whatever you're cooking. Try buying smaller amounts from good-quality butchers selling free-range meat, then use it more like a condiment than a hero ingredient.

Goes with   Beans, peas, lentils, pasta, eggs, cheddar, avocado, asparagus, potatoes, sweet potato, pumpkin (squash), corn, onions, leeks, cabbage, sauerkraut, brussels sprouts, kale, kohlrabi, silverbeet (Swiss chard), parsnips, mushrooms, sage, rosemary, basil, apples, bananas, grapes, maple syrup, honey, whisky

Storage   If you're buying bacon in a sealed packet it will keep, unopened, in the fridge until its expiry date. Open packets, or bacon bought from the butcher, need to be eaten within 5 days. Remove the bacon from its packaging and transfer to an airtight container. To freeze raw or cooked bacon for up to 1 month, wrap it in foil, then seal in an airtight container or baking paper.

Substitutes   Parmesan rinds and a little smoked paprika, a little miso paste in soups, haloumi cheese, speck, prosciutto or even ham.

Some ideas to use up a bacon rasher or two

✱ Sauté some chopped bacon with your Mirepoix (p 314) – finely diced onion, carrot and celery – to make a smoky base for non-vegetarian stews and hearty soups. Cut everything the same size and sauté low and slow with plenty of olive oil.

✱ Add to Odd-knobs Mac 'n' Cheese (p 101) before it goes in the oven. Heat 1 tsp oil in a frying pan over medium heat and fry 1 rasher of bacon. Into the melting bacon fat, throw 4 sage leaves and fry until crispy. Remove the bacon and sage from the pan, then chop and add to the cheesy pasta mix before it goes in the oven.

* As a base for a tasty stir-fry or fried rice, add 1 chopped bacon rasher to a hot wok with 1 chopped onion.
* Add to your home-made Baked Beans (p 37).
* When you're barbecuing fresh sardines or other oily fish, scatter cooked and chopped bacon on top and serve with a tomato salad.
* If there are only one or two rashers of bacon left, fry them, chop them up and add to a potato salad (p 362), a caesar salad (p 4) or a lentil stew (p 246).

Home-made bacon bits

Those weird bright-red bacon bits from the shop aren't bacon, but we know there's a very real taste for them on a baked potato with sour cream. Make this home-made version instead and you won't be disappointed. You can also scatter them over salads, eggs or pasta, or into lentil or vegetable soups, and they're a good way to make a few rashers go further.

Preheat the oven to 180°C (350°F). Lay the bacon on a baking tray, sprinkle with a good amount of ground black pepper and a little paprika, and bake for 15–20 minutes, until the bacon is very crispy. Drain the bacon on paper towel until completely cool. You can either chop the bacon into small pieces or pulse it in a food processor until crumbly. Serve right away or transfer to an airtight container and store in the fridge for up to 5 days. Add to hot dishes like pasta bakes or refresh in a hot pan to sprinkle on top of eggs and soups.

Bacon and maple syrup
MAKES ABOUT ½ CUP (125 ML)

This syrup is a bit spicy, a bit salty and a bit sweet, adding so much flavour to pan-fried vegetables and meats. Try it with sweet potato, pumpkin (squash), potatoes or cauliflower wedges, or chicken thighs or pieces of fish.

In a frying pan over medium heat, fry a chopped bacon rasher for 2 minutes or until brown, then add ½ cup (125 ml) maple syrup, ½ tsp salt, ½ tsp ground black pepper, 1 tsp paprika and, if you feel like it, a pinch of cayenne pepper. Let it bubble gently for a few seconds. Add a knob of butter and let the syrup thicken a little, then add up to 500 g (1 lb 2 oz) sliced vegetables, chicken thighs or fish fillets, turning often so the sugars don't burn. You can also use the mix to cook pork chops, pieces of fish, chicken thighs, slices of pumpkin or sweet potato.

Bananas

Oh, the old brown banana debacle. It's a weekly occurrence in most households and we're here to help. Although the world doesn't need another banana bread recipe, we've included one because it's shockingly easy and surprisingly tasty. But there's more than one way to mash an old banana, and this section will shine a light on a few options, including what you can do with a black banana.

Go with	Coffee, chocolate, caramel, coconut, brown sugar, honey, warm spices, dried fruits, ginger, lemongrass, kiwi fruit, passionfruit, pears, cherries, pineapple, limes, coriander seeds, dark spirits, bacon, chilli, dairy products, oats, nuts and nut butters
Storage	Store unripe bananas in the fruit bowl. Once ripe they can go in the fridge up to 7 days. The skins will go brown but the flesh inside will ripen more slowly. To freeze, don't leave them in the skins, even if you're really tired. Peel and chop, then pop them in an airtight container.
Substitutes	Other ripe tropical fruits, like mango and papaya, would be your best flavour and texture substitutes for bananas. In baking you can replace one mashed banana with ½ cup (125 ml) apple sauce or Simple Stewed Apples (p 7), or a very ripe mashed pear. And if you're into using avocados in baking, you could definitely swap them with bananas and vice versa. If you're in the midst of baking and are one egg short, experiment with using a banana as a binding agent: use half a mashed ripe banana to replace one egg. It won't give exactly the same result, but it will be better than finding your keys and going to the shops.

Some ideas for using up an abandoned banana or two

* Make jaffles (sealed toasted sandwiches) with banana slices, chocolate buttons and a sprinkle of cinnamon; banana, ricotta and honey; nut butter, banana and raisins; or, if you're feeling adventurous, banana, cheddar and chilli jam.
* Grill (broil) them. Cut off the stalks and then, leaving the skin on, cut the banana in half lengthways. Sprinkle each half with brown sugar and ground warm spices (like cinnamon, nutmeg or allspice). Line the grill (broiler) pan with baking paper and cook the banana halves for 5 minutes or until they turn golden brown and start to bubble. Remove from the skin and serve with yoghurt or ice cream.
* Add to curries. It sounds insane but it's really good – and bananas *are* used in Caribbean curries to balance out the heat. We've tried adding a ripe banana to a chicken curry and to a potato curry. The results were subtle and sweet and not strange at all.
* Make banana and coconut sambol. Gently mix a sliced banana, 1 tbsp desiccated (shredded) coconut and 1 tbsp lime juice. Serve with spicy curries.
* Whiz frozen banana in a food processor and it strangely turns into ice cream. Add a dash of cream or yoghurt and a splash of maple syrup for a creamier texture and taste. See the Kiwi Fruit Whip recipe (p 227) for more details.
* ***Banana porridge*** Roughly chop a spotty old banana and put it in a small saucepan with ½ cup (125 ml) water, ½ cup (125 ml) milk of your choice, a splash of maple syrup, 1 tbsp honey and, if you like, a pinch of ground cinnamon. Bring to a simmer, and give the banana a good mash with a fork. Add ½ cup (50 g) oats and another ½ cup (125 ml) water and simmer, stirring often, until thick and oozy. Makes one big bowl or two smaller serves.
* ***Home-made dried banana chips*** See Drying Fruits (p 357) for method and tips.

Banana sauce for desserts
MAKES 1 CUP (250 ML)

Caramelly and banana-y – pour this over vanilla ice cream and top with toasted peanuts if you're craving a banana split. It's also yummy drizzled over puddings, cakes or French Toast (p 51).

Melt ¼ cup (65 g) butter in a small saucepan over medium heat. Add ¼ cup (60 g) brown sugar and 2 tbsp maple syrup or honey, and mix well. Add a big pinch of ground cinnamon and simmer gently, stirring often, for 2 minutes. Add 2 overripe mashed or puréed bananas and a little pinch of salt. Feel free to add a generous splash of whisky if you want. Cook for another 1–2 minutes, until thick and glossy. Serve warm or pour into a container and keep in the fridge for a week or so.

Black banana jam

This recipe is in our last book, *Use It All*, but it's so helpful that we had to include it here as well. It's so good on waffles, French Toast (p 51), crepes and wholewheat crackers with cheddar. It also works with defrosted bananas if you need to deal with too much banana mass in the freezer.

Mash 3–4 overripe bananas and pop in a saucepan with the zest and juice of 1 orange or lemon, a splash of natural vanilla extract if you have it (or a pinch of ground cinnamon), ⅓ cup (75 g) brown sugar and 100 ml (3½ fl oz) water or juice. Place over low heat and stir until the sugar dissolves. Increase the heat to medium and simmer for 10–15 minutes, until thick, glossy and a rich brown. If you're feeling fancy, add a pinch of salt (it will taste like salted caramel) or a splash of whisky or rum. Spoon into a clean jar or airtight container, seal well and store in the fridge for a few weeks.

Banana ketchup
MAKES 3 CUPS (750 ML)

Don't knock it till you've tried it. This condiment is huge in the Philippines, where it's served with fried rice, chicken dishes and grilled (broiled) eggplant (aubergine). You can use it as you would other ketchups and sauces – on sausages, fries, meatloaf and fish fingers – and it's perfect for using up overripe bananas.

In a food processor or blender, put 3–4 sliced ripe bananas (about 350 g/12 oz), 1 roughly chopped onion, 3 garlic cloves, a 3 cm (1¼ in) knob of fresh ginger if you have it, 1–2 chopped chillies or 1 tsp chilli flakes if you want some heat, ⅓ cup (80 ml) apple cider vinegar or white wine vinegar and ½ tsp salt. Blitz until smooth. Heat 2–3 tbsp vegetable oil in a saucepan and add the banana mix, another 1 cup (250 ml) vinegar, 1 tbsp soy sauce, ⅓ cup (75 g) brown sugar, 1 tbsp mixed ground spices (whatever you have in the pantry – cinnamon, allspice, ginger, cloves, nutmeg, pepper). Simmer for 20–30 minutes over low heat, adding 2–3 tbsp water if the ketchup gets too thick or starts to stick to the pan. Once it's thick and glossy, pour into bottles, seal well and store in the fridge for up to 1 month. If you want to store this in the pantry for up to 2 years, pour hot into hot sterilised jars or bottles (p 501), seal and heat-process (p 502) for 15 minutes.

Simplest banana bread

We've included this easy four-ingredient base recipe because it can be made with mashed banana, left-over mashed roast pumpkin (squash), stewed apples (p 7), overripe pears or a combination of whatever you have that needs using up. Don't expect the oil-heavy café version. This is a simple and clean banana bread that's great toasted and spread with lots of butter.

Make it fancier by adding ½ cup chopped nuts or dried fruits, or 1 tsp ground warm spices like cinnamon, allspice or nutmeg with the flour.

Preheat the oven to 180°C (350°F) and line a 25 cm (10 in) loaf (bar) tin with baking paper. In a large bowl, mix 4 overripe mashed bananas (about 450 g/1 lb), ½ cup sugar of your choice and 2 beaten eggs. Sift in 1½ cups (220 g) self-raising flour and fold through, being mindful not to over-mix. Transfer the batter to the tin and bake for 40 minutes or until a skewer inserted in the middle comes out clean.

BANANA SKINS

Our honest opinion is that banana skins are best placed in the compost. Having said that, if you're truly committed to using it all, banana skins are definitely edible. While they can be used in baking recipes (we're not convinced), they're better in curries and stews. Check out Nigella Lawson's banana skin curry (it sort of tastes like eggplant/aubergine). Alex has made a pretty delicious banana skin relish, though – follow the 'What's in the Fruit Bowl' Relish recipe (p 333), replacing some or all of the fruit with blanched banana skin.

Give non-organic banana skins a good wash before using, as they're often coated in pesticides, then bring a big pot of water to the boil and blanch them for 1 minute to soften the fibres. Drain well.

And if you have staghorn ferns growing, you can feed them your (unblanched) banana skins.

Barley

Barley is so rosy-cheeked, hair-in-plaits wholesome it has never really had enough glamour to become on trend. But you know what – it's chewy, nutty and terribly good for the gut, and therefore should not be overlooked. One of the best things about barley, though, is that it soaks up a lot of liquid, so a near-empty bag of barley can grow to feed the household.

Goes with	Potatoes, pumpkin (squash), celery, onions, leeks, cabbage, kohlrabi, beetroot, mushrooms, leafy greens, parsley, nuts, cumquats, cream, milk, yoghurt, mild cheeses
Storage	Store uncooked barley in an airtight container in the pantry for up to 1 year. Cooked barley should be stored in an airtight container in the fridge for 3–5 days. You can freeze cooked barley and store it for 1 month.
Substitutes	Arborio rice makes a good substitute for barley as it has a similar creamy consistency once cooked. Otherwise most grains will stand in barley's place in recipes.

Some ideas for using barley

* Add cooked barley to the Spiced Lamb and Chickpea Pie Filling (p 233) instead of chickpeas.
* Mushrooms and barley are made for each other. Top cooked and buttered barley with Mushroom Ragu (p 279), or replace the brown rice in the Brown Rice, Mushroom and Spinach Soup (p 392) with cooked barley.
* **Barley salad** Yes please. Make the Big Grain Salad (p 379) even more wholesome by replacing the quinoa with barley, or use barley instead of buckwheat in the Buckwheat Salad (p 63).

Barley risotto
SERVES 2

Mix up your risotto game by switching to barley. You'll end up with a bowl that's nourishing and comforting for those times you need it. It might take about an hour, so don't make it when you're in a rush.

Heat 2 tbsp oil or butter in a heavy-based saucepan over medium heat. Add 1 diced brown onion and sauté until translucent, then add 2 chopped garlic cloves and the picked leaves of 1 thyme sprig if you have it. Stir in ½ cup (100 g) pearled barley and ½ cup (125 ml) white wine or ½ cup (125 ml) water with a squeeze of lemon juice. Stir until the barley absorbs all the liquid, then add 3 cups (750 ml) chicken or vegetable stock, one ladleful at a time, making sure the liquid is absorbed between each ladleful, stirring often (but thankfully not as much as a risotto made with rice). This might take about 1 hour. Once the barley is tender but still chewy, add the zest of 1 lemon, ¼ cup (25 g) grated parmesan, plenty of salt and ground black pepper to taste, and 1 medium handful of chopped fresh herbs such as parsley.

The best barley side – one dish, three meals
MAKES 3 CUPS (ABOUT 440 G)

A recipe that uses up those last grains in the jar is music to our ears. This recipe is the best because not only does it use ½ cup (100 g) uncooked barley (or buckwheat or rice), but it can be used as a side dish, a stuffing for a roast chicken or to fill cabbage rolls. Double it and you've got the beginnings of three meals this week.

Start by cooking ½ cup (100 g) barley in a large saucepan of water for about 30 minutes, until tender but still a little bitey. Drain and set aside. In the same saucepan, heat 2 tbsp olive oil and add 1 diced small onion, 3 chopped garlic cloves, 1 tsp caraway seeds, celery seeds or dill seeds and ½ tsp each of salt and pepper. If you have a carrot or celery stalk that needs using, dice it and pop it in the pan too. Sauté for 7–10 minutes. Add 1½ cups (about 220 g) of the cooked barley and ½ cup (80 g) sauerkraut or chopped pickles. Cook until everything is heated through, then add more salt and ground pepper to taste. Remove from the heat and add the chopped leaves of 1 bunch of dill, parsley or tarragon, or whatever herbs you have in the fridge.

TO USE YOUR BARLEY MIX
- Serve with sausages or grilled (broiled) meat. For a meat-free option, we eat this dish with wilted greens on the side and throw toasted nuts over everything as a complete meal.
- Stuff a chicken, field mushrooms or capsicums (peppers).
- Make Cabbage Rolls (p 68).

Wally Rath's barley vegetable soup

SERVES 6

Wally Rath was Jaimee's mum's adoptive father. He was an old-fashioned Irish Australian who only knew how to cook two dishes: the perfect scrambled eggs (the trick is to cook the eggs over very low heat in a saucepan) and this soup. It's simple fare, to say the least, but it's comforting and will practically make you Irish. Make a batch using the last few things in the fridge and eat it all week.

Chop 1 kg (2 lb 4 oz) mixed winter vegetables such as carrots, parsnips, potato, cauliflower (not pumpkin/squash or sweet potato because they will go mushy) into 1 cm (½ in) pieces and add to a large saucepan or stockpot with ½–1 cup (100–200 g) uncooked pearled barley. Cover with 6–8 cups (1.5–2 litres) stock, and season generously with salt and plenty of ground pepper. Cook for about 40 minutes, until all the vegetables are very tender and the barley is cooked through. Using a potato masher, mash the vegetables roughly. Don't use a blender, as this soup is supposed to be chunky. Cook for a further 5 minutes, then taste and adjust the seasoning. Serve with a drizzle of cream if you'd like.

Lemon barley water

You will have seen the cordial version of this in the supermarkets, but that's a far cry from this old-fashioned health drink. This version is high in folate, copper and magnesium, and is said to be detoxifying, but the real bonus is that it uses up that last bit of barley.

Place ⅓ cup (70 g) barley in a large saucepan with 4 cups (1 litre) water and a little pinch of salt. Cover and bring to the boil over medium heat, then reduce the heat to low and simmer for 50 minutes. Strain into a jug, add the juice of 1 lemon and 1 tbsp honey, and stir to dissolve. Once cool, store a jar or bottle in the fridge for up to 4 days.

TO USE THE MUSHY LEFT-OVER BARLEY

- Mix it into a stuffing.
- Add it to a soup.
- Use it as a binding agent for meatballs, patties and fritters.
- Make it into a porridge by adding some milk, honey and a knob of butter, and simmering for a few minutes.

Beans, broad

Broad beans are a sure sign that spring has arrived. They have the grassy flavour of green runner beans but with more substance. Yeah, you have to slip the beans from their skins, but really, this amount of effort (and reward) only comes around once a year, so stop putting it off, put on a podcast, sit down and get to work.

Go with   Almonds, walnuts, pine nuts, sultanas, mint, parsley, basil, chives, dill, garlic, onions, olive oil, butter, soft cheeses, bacon, ham

Storage   You can keep broad beans that are still in their pods wrapped in a clean tea towel (dish towel) in the fridge for 2–3 days. Podded beans must be eaten immediately, or blanched, cooled and frozen for up to 3 months.

Substitutes   Large white beans have a similar texture, and small fresh peas are a good substitute for flavour.

How to prepare Unless you have very fresh and very young broad beans, you will need to
broad beans   double-peel them. To do this, remove the beans from their large outer pod. Bring a pot of salted water to the boil, blanch the beans for 1–2 minutes, then strain, refresh under cold water and, when cool enough to handle, slip the outer skin right off.

Some ideas for using broad beans

* Add them to soups. Make a springtime minestrone soup (p 36) with broad beans, zucchini (courgettes) and plenty of fresh herbs.
* Broad beans, peas and asparagus will brighten a chicken noodle soup – see Left-over-chicken Soup (p 106).
* Cooked broad beans work in a similar way to cooked peas. Head to p 339 and check out the peas recipes. »

* Add broad beans to the Spring Greens Medley (p 341) for a bright green side.
* Toss peeled and cooked broad beans (previous page) in olive oil with lemon zest, chilli flakes and plenty of salt and pepper. Add this to hot buttered pasta with handfuls of chopped fresh herbs and dollops of ricotta.

Broad bean mash

SERVES 4 AS A DIP OR SIDE

Make this bright green dip to eat with flat breads (p 168) and Grilled Zucchini (p 497). You could try this same mash with fresh or defrosted frozen peas.

Prepare 500 g (1 lb 2 oz) broad beans as on the previous page. Put half the beans in a food processor with a handful of picked mint leaves, 1 tbsp olive oil and a big pinch of salt. Blitz until smooth, then add the rest of the beans and ¼ cup (25 g) grated parmesan, and pulse a few times to keep the mash chunky. Scoop into a serving bowl.

Broad bean salad

SERVES 2, OR 4 AS A SMALL SIDE

All the effort here is in shelling the beans, then all you have to do is pull it all together and enjoy with a cold dry white wine, feeling rather smug. If you can't be bothered to double-peel broad beans, this salad is yummy with cooked or tinned white beans.

Prepare 1 kg (2 lb 4 oz) broad beans as on the previous page. Place the beans in your prettiest bowl, season with salt and pepper, and add 1½ cups chopped fresh soft herbs, like dill or parsley. Dress with Classic Mustard Vinaigrette (p 283) and add about 50 g (1¾ oz) soft cheese, such as goat's curd, ricotta or burrata, to finish.

Ful medames with fresh broad beans

SERVES 2–3

Traditionally ful medames is made from dried broad beans (also called fava beans). It's eaten all across the Middle East with different interpretations. Making it with fresh broad beans is definitely deviating from tradition, but this version is so good that we just might be forgiven. Take note that if you don't have enough broad beans or only have the patience for a small amount of podding, then use 1 kg (2 lb 4 oz) broad beans and 1 cup frozen (140 g) or fresh (155 g) peas.

Prepare 2 kg (4 lb 8 oz) broad beans as on p 31. Dry-roast 2 tsp cumin seeds or ground cumin (whichever you have) in a saucepan over low heat until aromatic. Add ¼ cup (60 ml) olive oil, 4 sliced garlic cloves, ½ tsp salt and lots of ground pepper, then sauté for 30 seconds. Add the broad beans – and peas, if using – and mix well. Add just enough water to cover the beans, then pop the lid on the saucepan. Simmer over low heat for about 30 minutes, until the beans are very soft. You may need to add more water during cooking to keep everything soupy.

Meanwhile, hard-boil 2–3 eggs, then peel, cut into quarters and set aside. When the beans are done, mash them a little using a fork, then add the juice of ½ lemon and stir through. Adjust the seasoning as needed. Serve in bowls, topped with a boiled egg and plenty of chopped parsley, with delicious bread on the side (such as the Flotsam and Jetsam Flat Breads, p 168).

BROAD BEAN PODS

So you did it. You shelled all those beans and now you have a mountain of broad bean pods. Yes they can go into the compost or worm farm, *but* have you ever made your own country-style wine *and* did you know you can make it using broad bean pods? This is a genius way to use empty pods, and obviously knowing how to make your own booze is an important survival skill.

Broad bean pod wine

To try this, you'll have to buy some wine yeast and yeast nutrients specially from an online wine-making store.

Bring about 8 cups (2 litres) water to the boil in a large saucepan. Add the empty pods from 1 kg (2 lb 4 oz) broad beans, 1 kg (2 lb 4 oz) white (granulated) sugar, the juice and zest of 2 oranges and 1 lemon, and a handful of sulfite-free dried apricots (p 13). Boil for about 30 minutes. Allow to cool, then strain the liquid into a 12–16 cup (3–4 litre) glass jar or food-grade bucket cleaned with boiling water. Add 1 cup (250 ml) strongly brewed green tea, 8 g (generous ¼ oz) wine yeast and 4 g (generous ⅛ oz) yeast nutrient. Cover, keep out of direct light and allow to ferment for about 8 days, regularly opening the top of the jar or bucket to allow gas to escape. Once the brew tastes dry (i.e. no longer sweet), pour into clean glass bottles and seal (it will be a bit cloudy, but don't worry) and leave for 6 months to 1 year. Drink cold like a white wine.

Beans, dried or tinned

You should probably have at least two tins of beans or a bag of dried beans in the cupboard at all times. The best thing about beans is that they can help you turn whatever is in the pantry or fridge into a meal. One egg? A little stock? Half a jar of passata (puréed tomatoes)? A bit of celery? Add some beans and suddenly something's happening. It's this approach to cooking that makes for a sustainable kitchen. Don't run to the shops every time you can't think of what to cook. Instead, open up the pantry and deal with that quarter-full bag of beans.

Go with	Stocks, robust oils, hard cheeses, yoghurt, tahini, beef, lamb, bacon, eggplant (aubergine), tomatoes, capsicum (pepper), zucchini (courgettes), potatoes, carrots, corn, silverbeet (Swiss chard), spinach, onions, garlic, celery, chilli, parsley, mint, coriander (cilantro), mustard seeds, coriander seeds, cumin, paprika, bay leaves, oregano, rosemary, sage
Storage	Store dried beans in an airtight container in the pantry for years. Store unused cooked or opened tinned beans in an airtight container in the fridge for 3–4 days.
Substitutes	No, not all beans taste the same – of course they don't. But let's get real, you can swap nearly any kind of bean with another and still be able to make the recipe of your choosing.

How to decide on tinned vs dried

Tinned is easy, but dried is cheaper and more sustainable. There, that's the difference. Try to get into the habit of going to the bulk shop (if there's one near you) and buying dried beans. But of course the truth is that we end up buying tins when we're in a hurry, or we forgot, or had other things to do. Here's a very rough conversion and some advice for soaking and cooking to help make it easier:

* As a general rule of thumb, dried beans double in volume once soaked and cooked.
* About ½ cup (around 100 g/3½ oz) dried beans, once soaked and cooked, will give you about the same amount as the drained contents of a 400 g (14 oz) tin.
* A 400 g (14 oz) tin of beans gives about 240 g (8½ oz) drained beans.
* Cooking times and soaking requirements for dried beans are different. Red kidney beans definitely need to be soaked before cooking at a boil. They are toxic otherwise.
* Dried beans take 40 minutes to 1½ hours to cook, depending on their size and whether they've been soaked first.

Some ideas for a tin of beans or last half-cup of dried beans

* Turn salad into a meal. Combine a tin of beans with cooked rice, couscous or barley, and add lots of fresh herbs and capers or something pickled. Use the pickle brine and a splash of olive oil to make the dressing.
* Add a tin of beans or a handful of cooked beans to your next tray of roasted vegetables. Coat the beans with a little oil, season well and tip them into the roasting tray for the last 5–10 minutes of cooking.
* Try the 'No Food Processor? No Worries' Mashed Hummus or the crispy Oven-roasted Chickpeas (both on p 109) with white beans or kidney beans instead of chickpeas.
* Follow the Simple Chickpea Stew recipe (p 110), using white beans or red kidney beans instead of the chickpeas.
* For nachos or burritos, drain tinned black beans or red kidney beans and fry in a hot oiled frying pan with diced onion, chopped garlic, some spice mix 4 (p 420) and plenty of salt.
* **Beans and greens** Sauté some chopped bacon, then throw in roughly chopped spinach and sauté until wilted. Add a tin of black-eyed peas or white beans, then cook until everything is hot but still brightly coloured. Add salt, squeeze some lemon juice on top and lunch is served.
* **Pasta e fagioli** Cook any short type of pasta, strain and return to the pot. Add drained tinned beans and Comfort Pasta Sauce (p 3) or your favourite tomato-based pasta sauce and lots of parmesan.

Bean mash
SERVES 2

You can make a simple meal of a bean mash if you add a side salad, some flat breads and maybe a few pickles. Or spread on toast with a few green leaves for breakfast or lunch.

Heat 2 tbsp oil in a medium saucepan and gently cook 2 chopped garlic cloves and ½ tbsp chopped rosemary, oregano or sage. Add 1 cup cooked white beans or 400 g (14 oz) drained tinned white beans and a big pinch of salt, then cook for 2–3 minutes, until thick. Mash with a fork, adding another 1 tbsp oil, a squeeze of lemon juice and 1 tbsp water. If you're making this with soaked and cooked beans, you may need an extra splash of water or oil, depending on how soft the beans are.

Simplest minestrone soup
SERVES 4

You can't go wrong with a minestrone soup. Roughly speaking, it's a thick vegetable soup of many descriptions. This very simple version makes use of whatever vegetables you have around. Serve with crusty bread and be happy that you made a meal this good in about half an hour.

Heat ⅓ cup (80 ml) olive oil in a largish saucepan over medium heat, then add 500 g (1 lb 2 oz) thinly sliced vegetables like zucchini (courgettes), green beans, broccoli, cauliflower and fennel, with 2 chopped garlic cloves and 1 tsp each of salt and pepper. Stir and leave to cook for 2–3 minutes. Add 400 g (14 oz) drained tinned beans (or ½ cup dried beans, soaked and cooked) and about 6 thyme sprigs. Cover with 4 cups (1 litre) beef, chicken or vegetable stock and 400 g (14 oz) tinned tomatoes or a 400 g (14 oz) jar of passata (puréed tomatoes). If you have an old parmesan rind hanging around, chuck it in the pot. Reduce the heat to medium–low and cook, covered, for about 30 minutes. Serve in bowls with a very generous amount of grated parmesan.

If you have any left-over minestrone, you can turn it into Ribollita (p 53) the next day by adding grilled (broiled) stale bread and plenty of shredded cavolo nero, kale or spinach.

Chilli con carne
SERVES 4

When Jaimee visits her mum Margie, she still asks her to make this. You can tone down the heat or amp it up according to taste. Serve it over rice with sour cream, coriander (cilantro) and lime.

In a large saucepan or stockpot, heat 2 tbsp oil and sauté 1 diced red onion and 2 finely chopped garlic cloves until soft. Add 500 g (1 lb 2 oz) minced (ground) beef and cook until browned all over. Add 1 tsp salt, 2 tsp ground cumin, 2 tsp ground coriander, 1½ tsp chilli flakes, 1 cinnamon stick, ½ cup (125 g) tomato paste (concentrated purée), a few squares of dark chocolate, 400 g (14 oz) tinned red kidney beans (or ½ cup/95 g dried beans, soaked and cooked), 400 g (14 oz) tinned tomatoes and about 1½ cups (375 ml) stock (or at a pinch, use water, increasing the spices and salt to compensate). Cover and simmer over low heat for 40–50 minutes.

Baked beans
SERVES 4

Baked beans are for breakfast, lunch or dinner. They're as good cold as they are hot. They're a side, or perfect in a toastie, on a baked potato or as the main event. Nail a baked beans recipe and you probably won't ever buy the stuff swimming in sweet tomato sauce again.

Preheat the oven to 170°C (325°F). In a cast-iron pot or casserole dish, heat 2 tbsp oil or butter and sauté 1 diced onion until soft and sweet. If you like, add some diced smoked sausage, bacon or speck. Add 400 g (14 oz) drained and rinsed tinned white beans (or ½ cup white dried beans, soaked and cooked), 400 g (14 oz) tinned chopped tomatoes, about 1 cup (250 ml) water or stock to make it soupy, a parmesan rind or two if you have them, 1–2 tbsp something sweet – like brown sugar, maple syrup or honey – and 1 tsp salt. Cover, transfer to the oven and bake for 40–60 minutes, until reduced and delicious. Season with plenty of salt and pepper, and serve.

Beans, green

Green beans are excellent to have in the fridge. They're so reliable and versatile, and we're yet to come across someone over three who doesn't like them. They can be a side, a quick stir-fry or sauté; they can be added to soups like Simplest Minestrone (p 36) or Wally Rath's Barley Vegetable (p 30), made into a complete salad, or charred, slow-cooked, pickled or fermented. When they're in season and cheap, buy a big bag, store them well and eat them every night. While they're lovely and fresh, eat them raw in salads or lightly blanched in salty water. As they get a little older, stir-fry or char them. Then, when they've really seen better days, at the very end of the week, or even the week after, make one of the slow-cooked dishes over the page.

Go with   Tomatoes, broccoli, kale, wombok (Chinese cabbage), daikon, turnips, fennel, peas, asparagus, zucchini (courgettes), lentils, basil, chives, dill, mint, tarragon, parsley, spring onions (scallions), garlic, chilli, ginger, cumin, fennel seeds, star anise, miso, sesame seeds and tahini, parmesan, feta, tofu, toasted nuts, lemons, preserved lemon, olives, olive oil

---

Storage   To help your green beans last longer in the fridge, store them unwashed in an airtight container for 1 week. Once your beans have gone limp or have dried out, use them for cooked dishes; low, slow cooking hides a multitude of sins.

Substitutes   Green beans can be replaced with other green crunchy vegetables – broccolini, broccoli, asparagus, fennel.

Some ideas for making the most of those last green beans

✳ Stir-fry them. Follow the Stir-fried Celery recipe (p 87), using green beans instead of celery. Keep it simple with just green beans, garlic and plenty of pepper.

✳ Blanch beans in boiling water and drain well. While they're warm, add olive oil, plenty of salt, crumbled feta or 2–3 tbsp ricotta, and a big handful of whatever herbs you have.

✳ Thinly slice them lengthways and add them raw to slaws and salads.

✳ Ferment them using the Fermented Carrots recipe (p 78).

✳ Pickle them using the Italian-style Preserved Green Beans (over the page) or Basic Vegetable Pickling (p 472) recipe.

✳ ***Niçoise salad of sorts*** Combine boiled baby potatoes, quartered boiled eggs, blanched green beans, some olives and cherry tomatoes. Dress with your best olive oil, salt and pepper, and plenty of lemon juice. Add tuna, or anchovies if you like. Dress this salad while the potatoes and beans are still warm.

Garlicky, cheesy roasted green beans

The best side to make to use up as little as a handful or as much as half a kilo (a pound), this works well for the beans you forgot to eat last week. You can try this same method with broccoli, cauliflower or asparagus.

Preheat the oven to 200°C (400°F). Wash and dry your green beans and pop them in a bowl. Coat with olive oil, salt and pepper, plenty of crushed garlic and grated parmesan. Roast for 10–15 minutes, until the beans are tender and a little charred. Feel free to dress them up with cayenne pepper, chilli flakes and/or cumin seeds before roasting.

Charred green beans

A hot dry pan and a lightly oiled but heavily seasoned vegetable is a winning combination. While fresh is always best, this cooking method helps disguise any age spots.

In a bowl, coat beans in a little oil and plenty of salt and pepper. Char them in a very hot dry frying pan until tender and a little blackened. The trick is to only do one layer of beans at a time and not rush to turn them, letting them blacken a little first. While they're still warm, coat with 2–3 tbsp of either pesto, harissa paste, chilli paste or toasted sesame seeds.

Japanese-style sesame greens
SERVES 2 AS A SMALL SIDE DISH

This is a really lovely way to make a small amount of vegetables a little bit special – the sesame seeds add nuttiness and a little protein. You can follow the same method for spinach, asparagus or broccoli.

Chop 200–250 g (7–9 oz) green beans into bite-sized pieces on a sharp angle. Blanch in generously salted water until just tender. Strain, run under cold water and set aside to dry. In a small frying pan, dry-roast 2 tbsp sesame seeds until golden and transfer to a mortar or bowl. Give them a bash with the pestle or crush them with the back of a spoon until they form a chunky paste. Add 1 tbsp soy sauce, 2 tsp caster (superfine) sugar and a pinch of salt, and mix well. Pop the beans in a bowl and coat well with the sesame dressing – it won't seem like enough, but keep mixing. Serve right away, although it also lasts well in the fridge for 1–2 days.

Really easy green bean curry
SERVES 3–4

Learn to make a simple vegetable curry by heart. It's quicker and cheaper than Uber Eats, it uses up what's in the fridge, and you've got lunch for work the next day. We love a one-vegetable curry, like green beans, but feel free to use this method with the hodgepodge that's left in the crisper.

Sauté 1 sliced onion in a little vegetable oil in a saucepan or frying pan over medium–high heat until softened. Add a few finely chopped garlic cloves or 1 tbsp grated fresh ginger if you have it, and a few curry leaves or 1 tbsp curry powder (we're very fond of Keen's brand). If you have mustard seeds or fenugreek seeds, add 1 tsp. Saute briefly, then add up to 400 g (14 oz) green beans (or any veg), ¾ cup (185 ml) coconut milk and ½ tsp salt. Simmer until the beans are cooked through. Add a squeeze of lemon or lime juice and some coriander (cilantro) leaves if you have them, and serve.

Italian-style preserved green beans
MAKES ABOUT 2 x 500 ML (18 OZ) JARS

Green beans pickle and ferment really well, making an excellent addition to salads and antipasto plates. The recipe for these Italian-style preserved green beans was taught to us by an elderly neighbour; they're cooked in a sweet vinegar mix and then covered in oil. It's a lovely preserving method for other vegetables too, such as broccoli, charred capsicums (peppers), eggplant (aubergine) and zucchini (courgettes). Don't expect these to taste like a pickle; they're less acidic, but they will add more flavour to a meal than a plain green bean. We use these to instantly dress up a salad – toss them through a niçoise salad (p 39), or a potato salad (p 362), serve them with a cheese plate or add them to a shared lunch spread.

In a large saucepan, bring to the boil 1 cup (250 ml) water, 1 cup (250 ml) white wine vinegar, 2 tsp salt and ⅓ cup (75 g) white (granulated) sugar. Add 500 g (1 lb 2 oz) green beans and 4 peeled garlic cloves, then reduce the heat and simmer, covered, for 5 minutes. Strain and allow the beans to dry completely.

If you want to store them in the pantry, sterilise 2 × 500 ml (18 oz) jars or 3 × 350 ml (12 oz) jars (p 501). Otherwise they can be stored in a clean jar or airtight container in the fridge.

In each jar put 1 tbsp black peppercorns, 2 tsp dried or fresh woody herbs (such as rosemary, oregano or thyme), 1 tsp chilli flakes and 1 whole peeled garlic clove or strip of lemon peel. Pack the beans into the sterilised jars and completely cover with sunflower, vegetable or olive oil or a combo – you'll need about 300 ml (10½ fl oz) oil for each 500 ml (18 oz) jar. Seal the jars and store in a cool, dark place for up to 3 months. Allow to sit for at least 1 week before eating. Once opened, store in the fridge and use within 3 months.

Green beans and grains
SERVES 3–4 AS A SIDE

This is another great way to cook ugly old green beans: one pot, huge flavour. This version is a simplified riff on a Turkish recipe from Musa Dagdeviren. It's so simple and delicious, with few ingredients. Traditionally it's made with burghul (bulgur), but it's also good with white rice, quinoa or couscous. Feel free to add crushed garlic or ground cumin or paprika with the onions if you'd like. Serve with grilled (broiled) meats, falafel and haloumi cheese. And in summer try it with sliced zucchini (courgette), eggplant (aubergine) or okra.

In a heavy-based saucepan over medium heat, sauté 1 sliced onion in 2–3 tbsp olive oil until soft and sweet. Add 2–3 tbsp tomato paste (concentrated purée), up to 500 g (1 lb 2 oz) green beans cut into thirds and 1 tsp salt, then sauté, stirring often, for at least 10 minutes. Make a well in the centre of the beans and add 50 g (1¾ oz) uncooked grain of your choice and just under 1 cup (250 ml) water or stock. Reduce the heat to low and cook, covered, for 30 minutes. Remove from the heat, fluff up the grains, mixing them through the beans, then put the lid back on and let it rest for 10 minutes.

Beetroot

D-rama. Beetroot make a show of themselves, all over your hands and the bench when you prep them, but they deserve our full attention. At once earthy-tasting and sweet, beetroot are hearty – and if used wisely, one bunch can feed a modest-sized household. Don't forget that beetroot are root-to-leaf eating. Soup, salad and a pickle in one vegetable – well worth the bloody mess.

Goes with   Carrots, pumpkin (squash), kohlrabi, parsnips, dill, tarragon, parsley, barley, buckwheat, sour cream, ricotta, butter, almonds, hazelnuts, walnuts, sunflower seeds, tahini, ginger, garlic, honey, horseradish, sauerkraut, apples, pears, oranges, pomegranate, anchovies, vinegar, mustard, black pepper

---

Storage   Treat a bunch of beetroot as two separate vegetables. Separate the leaves and stems from the roots and store separately. Wrap the leaves and stems in a clean damp tea towel (dish towel) or clean Chux and pop in a reusable plastic bag. They will stay fresh for a week in the fridge. Store the unwashed roots wrapped in a clean cloth bag in the crisper for up to 10 days.

Substitutes   Consider other root vegetables, like carrots, celeriac, sweet potato or turnips. To replace leaves, use spinach, silverbeet (Swiss chard) or sweet potato leaves. If you're after the colour, crunch and sweetness of beetroot, but only have cabbage (obviously red would be even better), then go ahead and use it in salads and slaws.

How to boil or roast beetroot

Trim and scrub the beetroot.

To boil, place in a large saucepan or stockpot with a pinch of salt. Cover and bring to the boil, then reduce the heat and simmer until the beets can be pierced easily with a knife. Drain.

To roast, place in a small ovenproof dish so the beets fit snugly, and drizzle a little oil over them. Cover with foil and roast at 200°C (400°F) for 40 minutes. Allow to cool.

Once the beets are cooked, slip the skins off with your hands. Beautiful ruby beetroot jewels will be revealed. Dress with good-quality olive oil, salt and pepper and your finest vinegar, or try one of the ideas below. Store in the fridge for up to 5 days.

FLAVOUR IDEAS FOR ROASTED OR BOILED BEETS

* Combine dressed beets, soft-boiled eggs, smoked fish and chives.
* Mix chopped roasted beets, toasted nuts, crumbled feta and parsley.
* Serve with sour cream, dijon mustard and dill.
* Combine with grapes roasted using the Roasted Cherries method (p 103), adding plenty of chopped herbs.
* Add the zest and juice of 1 orange and season with more olive oil, salt and lots of ground black pepper.
* Make your potato salad pink by adding roasted beets, capers and plenty of chopped dill. See the Anything-goes Potato Salad variations on p 362.

Some ideas for using every last beet

* Make a back-of-the-fridge beet dip. When your forgotten beets have lost their lustre, roast them until sweet and soft, then peel and blend them with olive oil, garlic, salt, a splash of vinegar and some ground coriander. Eat on toast with boiled eggs for breakfast, or in pitta bread for lunch.
* Peel and slice some raw beetroot and pickle them following the Basic Vegetable Pickling recipe (p 472). Beetroot like warm spices such as juniper berries, caraway seeds, black pepper and fresh ginger.
* Turn the Seedy Breakfast Muffins (p 371) red using raw grated beets, and throw in a handful of chocolate chips and poppyseeds.
* *Raw beetroot salad* Make a salad by combining 1 raw beetroot and 1 raw carrot, both grated or cut into matchsticks, with 2–3 tbsp diced pickles, and stirring through ¼ cup sour cream (65 g) or yoghurt (70 g) and plenty of salt and pepper. If you happen to have it, add 1 tbsp freshly grated horseradish.

Whole-bunch-of-beets kraut

MAKES 1 x 750 ML (27 OZ) JAR

Not really a sauerkraut as there's no cabbage here, but we are using the method and making a fermented beet kraut that you can eat in the same way as a sauerkraut: on sandwiches, in salads and alongside grains, potatoes and roasted vegetables or meats. It's a great way to use the whole bunch of beetroot – roots, stems, leaves and all. This is not a beginner's ferment, not because it's difficult, but because the high sugar content of beetroot means they ferment quickly and can go slimy if you don't keep your eye on them. Make this in winter when beetroots are in season and fermentation takes a little longer. Allow for a maximum of three days to ferment before transferring to the fridge.

Cut the stems off about 4 beetroot, then scrub the roots and wash the leaves and stems. Thinly slice the stems, shred the leaves and put both in a bowl. Grate the roots into the bowl. Add 3 tsp salt and 2 tbsp of any of the following: dill seeds, grated horseradish or finely chopped garlic, black peppercorns or mustard seeds. Mix well. Using clean hands, massage all the ingredients until everything is quite wet and your hands are purple. Fill a 750 ml (27 oz) jar (or a few smaller jars), making sure liquid is covering the surface of the beets.

Follow the fermenting steps in the Basic Sauerkraut recipe (p 66).

Ugly-beetroot borscht

SERVES 4

There are as many borscht recipes as there are households across Eastern Europe. This one is the lazy version of Jaimee's grandmother's borscht. It's good to keep in mind when you've forgotten that bunch of beetroot in the fridge.

In a large saucepan or stockpot heat 2 tbsp butter or vegetable oil over medium heat, then sauté 1 diced onion, 1 diced carrot and 3 finely chopped garlic cloves, stirring often so as not to brown the onion or garlic. Meanwhile, wash and scrub 3 large or 4 small beetroot. If the beets are big or gnarly, peel them. Chop the beetroot into smallish chunks, add to the pot and give everything a good stir. Add 6 cups (1.5 litres) of your choice of stock, then reduce the heat to low and simmer, covered, for about 40 minutes, until the beetroot is soft. Add ½ cup (140 g) sauerkraut and blitz everything with a hand-held blender. Serve hot with a generous dollop of sour cream and a handful of chopped dill.

Raw grated beet salad

Tasty, fast and economical. One beet serves one or two, so scale up depending how many you're feeding. Feel free to add half a grated apple or a lonely carrot or radish if they're in the fridge and need using up.

Peel beets (and any other root veg) and grate into a large bowl. Finely grate a knob of fresh ginger or horseradish or some garlic into the beets, then season generously with salt and pepper, a splash of vinegar, a squeeze of lemon or orange juice and a drizzle of olive oil. Taste and add more of what's needed. Gently toss parsley or dill leaves through, and if you have any toasted seeds, sprinkle them on top to serve.

Beet relish

MAKES ABOUT 3 x 300 ML (10 OZ) JARS

This is a good recipe for when you've bought a bunch of beets and have no idea what to do with them. It's simple to make, uses the whole bunch including stems, and lasts for many months in the fridge. Serve on sandwiches, burgers and steaks, or with cheese or falafel.

In a medium saucepan, heat ¼ cup (60 ml) sunflower or other vegetable oil over medium heat. Add 1 thinly sliced onion and the thinly sliced beet stems, and sauté until soft, sweet and pink. Add 3–4 peeled and grated raw beets, 1 grated apple (leave it out if you don't have it, or replace it with 1 cup/75 g shredded cabbage), 1½ tsp ground pepper and 2–3 tbsp grated fresh ginger or 1–2 tsp ground cumin. Add 1 cup (250 ml) red wine or apple cider vinegar, ½ cup (110 g) caster (superfine) sugar and 1 tsp salt. Stir until the sugar dissolves, reduce the heat to low, then simmer for 20 minutes or until the relish has begun to thicken, adding a little water if it starts to dry out. It will keep in clean jars or an airtight container in the fridge for a really long time.

BEETROOT LEAVES AND STEMS

Beet leaves are generally hacked off and chucked away. If they're in good nick from the shops or you've grown them at home, make sure you hang onto them and use them like other leafy greens. Beets are closely related to silverbeet (Swiss chard), so their leaves can be treated in the same way. Little tender leaves are lovely in salads, bigger leaves are great in spinach pies, and the big old tough guys can either be stir-fried or blanched and sautéed, or you can try turning them into chips (see over the page).

Stir-fried beet leaves

SERVES 2 AS A SIDE

Beetroot leaves can stand in for any green leaf. This is a bold statement, but we're sticking by it. You can use them in place of spinach as well as bok choy. In this recipe we mix things up by stir-frying beet leaves with Thai flavours and, in a word, *wow*.

Start by separating leaves from stalks. Thinly slice the stalks, but leave the beet leaves whole unless they're enormous, and then maybe tear them in half. In a dry wok or frying pan over high heat, toast a handful of shredded coconut until golden. Remove from the wok and set aside. Now add 1 tbsp mild-flavoured oil and stir-fry the beet stalks until softened. Add a large pinch each of salt and pepper, then add 1 finely chopped garlic clove, about 1 tbsp finely grated fresh ginger and 1 sliced red chilli. When everything is smelling fragrant, add the beetroot leaves and stir-fry until just wilted. Season with a good dash of fish sauce and top with the toasted coconut. Serve on rice, with grilled (broiled) meats or alongside a curry.

Roasted beet leaves

Just like kale chips only *beeter*. Get it?

Preheat the oven to 180°C (350°F). Wash the leaves and dry well. If leaves are small and tender, leave them whole; if they're bigger and tougher, tear them into bite-sized pieces. Place leaves in a large bowl, and add a very light drizzle of sunflower or other vegetable oil, ½ tsp salt and a sprinkling of cayenne pepper. Mix well with your hands, then spread out on a baking tray in a single layer. Roast for 10–15 minutes, until the leaves are crisp and dry.

Gingery beet stem cook-up

Beet stems are crunchy and earthy, have an incredible colour and are packed so full of antioxidants that it seems a shame to throw them away. This beet stem cook-up is somewhere between a relish, a salsa and a sautéed side. It's yummy tossed through a leafy green salad, cooked lentils or grains, or served as a condiment with grilled (broiled) meats or vegetables. It lasts for up to 1 week in the fridge.

In a medium frying pan, heat ¼ cup (60 ml) olive oil. Add 1 thinly sliced onion and your very thinly sliced beet stems, and sauté over medium–low heat for 10–15 minutes. Add 2–3 tbsp grated fresh ginger, a big pinch of chilli flakes, and the zest and juice of 1 orange or lemon. Add plenty of salt and pepper, a generous splash of apple cider vinegar or red wine vinegar and a pinch of sugar. Cook for another 5–10 minutes, until soft and delicious.

Berries

Sometimes we get a bit greedy when we see berries going cheaply and buy all the punnets. One punnet disappears quickly and then the other three sit in the fridge until their mouldy end. Berries have a short shelf life, and if you're asleep at the wheel, by the time you decide to put blueberries on your muesli they may have shrivelled or sprouted hairs. The ideas and recipes here show you how to turn that punnet of disappointment into a triumph.

Go with	Berries mix happily with all the other fruits, but especially stone fruits and rhubarb. Berries love honey, nuts, basil, black pepper, coriander seeds and aniseed, and become the belle of the ball when matched with dairy – milk, cream, ice cream, yoghurt and oozy cheeses.
Storage	Only buy enough berries to eat in a few days – they really don't last long. Store them in the fridge on one of the higher shelves, as they need good air flow. If you accidentally bought a whole tray or are lucky enough to grow berries, freezing is one of the best preservation methods. Spread them out in a single layer and pop them in the freezer. Once completely frozen, transfer to a container and store for up to 3 months.
Substitutes	While each berry type has its own distinct personality, if a recipe calls for a berry, really any berry will do. But you do need to know your berries more intimately for big-batch jam-making, as they have very different pectin levels. If you have no berries, use other soft fruits in their place, like plums, cherries or apricots.

Some ideas for using up tired-looking berries

Berries go from hero to zero while you're thinking about what to do with them. Obviously baking is a great way to use up berries, and there's an encyclopedia of berry muffins, puddings and cakes online. But if you're not a baker or not in the mood, here are some quick ideas to use up a punnet, whether they're in prime condition or on their last legs:

* ***No-cook berry jam*** For quick berry jam to spread on toast or stir into yoghurt, see the No-cook Jam recipe (p 401).

* ***Quick berry compote/sauce*** Cook 125 g (4½ oz) raspberries, blueberries or blackberries; about 180 g (6 oz) mulberries; or 250 g (9 oz) strawberries (i.e. 1 punnet) in a small saucepan over medium–low heat with 1 tbsp each of sugar, honey and water until syrupy. If you're feeling fancy add 1 tbsp balsamic vinegar. Allow to cool, then transfer to an airtight container and store in the fridge for up to 5 days. Pour on yoghurt, ice cream, pancakes.

* ***Macerated berries*** Slice 125 g (4½ oz) raspberries, blueberries or blackberries; about 180 g (6 oz) mulberries; or 250 g (9 oz) strawberries, and pop them in a bowl with 1 tbsp white (granulated) sugar and a splash of booze. Let them sit for 30 minutes, then devour them or store in the fridge for up to 4 days.

* ***Berry booze*** Follow the Cumquat Brandy recipe (p 132) using 125 g (4½ oz) mashed raspberries, blueberries or blackberries; about 180 g (6 oz) mashed mulberries; or 250 g (9 oz) mashed strawberries; ½ cup (110 g) white (granulated) sugar and 2 cups (500 ml) vodka, gin or, for dark berries, rum. Use strained berry booze in a champagne cocktail, drizzle over fresh berries with mint leaves or pour over ice cream.

One-punnet berry vinegar
MAKES 200 ML (7 FL OZ)

If you got sucked into a '2 for 1' berry deal but didn't manage to eat them all before they softened, try making berry vinegar.

Roughly mash 1 punnet of not so perfect berries – 125 g (4½ oz) raspberries, blueberries or blackberries; about 180 g (6 oz) mulberries; or 250 g (9 oz) strawberries – and put them in a jar with 1 cup (250 ml) apple cider vinegar or white wine vinegar. Let sit for a week, then strain into a small saucepan, adding ⅓ cup (75 g) white (granulated) sugar. Simmer for 10–12 minutes or until a little syrupy. Pour into a clean jar and store in the fridge for many moons.

Use in a salad dressing in place of balsamic vinegar, or drizzle over grilled (broiled) meats, soft cheeses or not so sweet desserts.

Slow-roasted oven jam

Ooh la la! Transform your compost-destined berries from rags to riches by roasting them low and slow. Preheat the oven to 160°C (315°F), cut the berries into similar-sized pieces – halves or quarters – and pop them in a small ovenproof dish. Sprinkle generously with sugar of your choice and a squeeze of lemon juice. Roast for 40 minutes or until the berries are starting to collapse. Remove from the oven, mash with a fork and return to the oven for another 10–15 minutes, until the berries are thick, glossy and jammy-looking. Serve with pancakes, French Toast (p 51), scones or ice cream. Add a splash of vinegar and some salt and pepper, and serve with roast meats and oozy cheeses.

Berry berry good lemonade

Pink lemonade! Make your childhood dreams come true, and your adult self happy, by using up 2 punnets of mushy raspberries (250 g/9 oz) or strawberries (500 g/1 lb 2 oz).

Use the Lemonade or Lemon Cordial recipe (p 240) but turn it berry-flavoured by blending the berries, then straining through muslin and adding to the lemon juice. Pour ¼ cup (60 ml) into each serving glass over ice, then top up with sparkling water. You could even add a little vodka if you like.

Bread

We've been making school lunches for more than a decade and still can't get our bread-buying right. There's either no bread in the house or there's way too much and the kids decide they hate sandwiches. We've been boring each other with our stale-bread-saving recipes for long enough, so now it's your turn.

Bread is one of the most wasted foods in households. Aside from morning toast, most of us don't know what to do with a loaf that's a few days old. But bread is precious, and home cooks of the past wouldn't waste a crumb. These recipes are a nod to traditional cooking. They're easy to make, hearty and nutritious, plus they ensure that nothing goes to waste.

Goes with   Everything

Storage   Bread will keep well for 2–3 days wrapped in a beeswax wrap, reusable plastic bag or bread box. Avoid humidity, which tends to make bread go mouldy, and above all don't put your bread in the fridge – it will dry it out and give it the texture of cardboard. If you don't think you'll get through a loaf within 3 days, you can slice and freeze bread for up to 3 months.

Substitutes   Depending on the meal, other grains, pasta, noodles, crackers and so on.

Some ideas to make sure stale bread doesn't get tossed

* Revive stale baguettes by sprinkling with a little water, wrapping in foil and warming in a 160°C (315°F) oven for 5 minutes or so.
* Next time you're roasting a chicken, make a bread base for the chicken to sit on. Cut sourdough bread into big chunks, then coat them with oil, plenty of garlic, salt and dried herbs. Place under the chicken – you don't want the bread sticking out too much or it will burn, but crispy edges are really good. You want the stale bread to soak up all the delicious juices. Roast the chicken as you normally would.
* Make fried cheese sandwiches for breakfast, lunch and dinner.

✶ Stretch out a stew by adding day-old torn bread so it feeds a few more. Try it with the Simple Chickpea Stew (p 110). Cut 250 g (9 oz) stale bread into cubes and leave on the bench to dry a little more. Add the bread cubes to the stew in the last 5 minutes of cooking, along with a little more oil if needed, then simmer until the bread is saucy and tasty.

✶ *French toast* As easy as frying an egg – serve it every morning until all the stale bread is gone. Whisk 2 eggs with 2 tbsp full-cream milk. Working with 1 slice at a time, dip 4 slices of bread in the egg mixture. Melt 1 tbsp butter in a frying pan over medium heat, then fry each slice for 2 minutes on each side or until golden brown. Serve with honey, maple syrup or jam.

Croutons

Store in a jar and make sure Cheat's Caesar Salad (p 4), panzanella, pumpkin soup and lentil stew (p 246) are on the menu this week. Preheat the oven to 180°C (350°F). Heat ¼ cup (60 ml) vegetable oil in a frying pan over medium–high heat. Add 3 finely chopped garlic cloves and stir for a few seconds. Throw in 1–2 cups (50–100 g) stale bread chunks and a good sprinkling of salt, then stir to coat the bread in all the garlicky oil. Transfer to an ovenproof dish and bake for 3–5 minutes, until crisp but not hard. Allow to cool completely, then store in an airtight container for up to 3 days.

Breadcrumbs

Crumb everything in the house.

Preheat the oven to 120°C (235°F). Blitz stale bread into rough breadcrumbs in a food processor, then spread on a baking tray and dry in the oven for 30–60 minutes, depending on how large the breadcrumbs are. Keep checking to ensure they don't burn. Remove from the oven when they look and feel dry and crisp. Store in the freezer for up to 6 months.

To crumb things, set up three plates or shallow bowls. From left to right, put plain (all-purpose) flour in the first bowl, beaten egg in the second and the crumbs in the third. Dip whatever you're crumbing into each bowl, from left to right, turning it over gently with a fork to coat completely, then set aside on a plate until ready to fry. Popping them in the fridge for 30 minutes first can help stop things falling apart.

BREADCRUMB MIX
For extra-tasty crumbed meats and veg, mix 1 cup (about 30 g) of your breadcrumbs with 2 tsp paprika, 1 tsp dried oregano and ½ tsp salt.

Old-school garlic bread

This is how we make amends for all the green food we persuade our teenagers to eat. Cook this when you're trying to win someone over. It works best with left-over baguette or half a loaf of uncut sourdough.

Preheat the oven to 220°C (425°F). Using a bread knife, cut 3 cm (1¼ in) slices into the bread without going all the way through. In a small bowl, mix ½ cup (125 g) softened butter, 1–2 finely chopped garlic cloves, ¼ tsp salt and 1 tsp dried herbs such as oregano or basil. With clean damp hands, give the bread a bit of a rub, then push the garlic butter into each incision and slather the outside too. Sprinkle grated parmesan on top, wrap in foil and bake for 10–15 minutes.

Skordalia – stale-bread and garlic dip

MAKES 1 GENEROUS CUP (ABOUT 250 G)

If all you have is some stale bread and garlic, you can still bring something impressive to the street party. Skordalia is often made using potato, but bread also works well, and the result is pungent, earthy and addictive. Traditionally this is eaten with fish, but bread on bread is a thing – and we encourage it. Spread on crusty bread with fresh tomatoes and sit in the sunshine with your carbs on carbs, or serve with cucumber sticks or lamb koftas and salad.

Sprinkle water over 4 cups (about 200 g) stale white bread torn into pieces. Don't make the bread soggy, but it should definitely be damp all over. Put the bread in a food processor with 6 chopped garlic cloves, ¾ tsp salt and 2–3 tbsp red wine vinegar (depending on how acidic you like things) and give it a quick pulse. Then, with the motor running slowly, pour in ½ cup (125 ml) olive oil and watch your dead old bread turn into a paste. Keep the motor running and add water, 1 tbsp at a time, until the mixture has the consistency of a dip. If your bread is only a little bit stale, you'll only need 1–2 tbsp water; if it's a brick, you may need 4–5 tbsp.

Transfer to a bowl and serve.

Bread and butter pudding

SERVES 4

Bread and butter pudding is not only the best thing since sliced bread, it's a waste warrior's dream, turning stale bread into a comforting dessert so it doesn't end up in the bin. The possibilities for variations are endless – add marmalade to your buttered bread for a bitter edge, or add raisins or whisky-soaked prunes. Make it with raisin bread, brioche, supermarket white or thinly sliced bagels. If you have cream that needs using, replace some of the milk with it.

Preheat the oven to 180°C (350°F). Make a batch of the Baked Custard mix (p 151) but don't bake it. Cut 4 slices of buttered stale bread into quarters and arrange over the base of a buttered ovenproof dish – like you're making a potato gratin. Scatter 2–3 tbsp dried currants, sultanas or chopped dates over the bread if you want. Pour the custard mix over the bread and sprinkle with ground cinnamon or grated nutmeg or add a generous splash of whisky, then bake for 30 minutes or until golden and set.

Kvass
MAKES 2 x 1 LITRE (35 OZ) BOTTLES

Soda made from stale bread? Yes please, I'll have another glass, says everyone in Russia and north-eastern Europe. Kvass is a traditional beverage that Jaimee's Russian grandmother used to make. Because it's fermented it's good for you, but you drink it because it's delicious. It's like a light table beer. The darker the rye bread you use, the better the kvass.

You need 2 cups (about 120 g) torn stale rye bread. If you have rye bread but it's not stale, dry it out in a 120°C (235°F) oven. Into a very clean 2 litre (68 oz) jar pour 1 cup (220 g) raw sugar and cover with 6 cups (1.5 litres) boiling water. Stir to dissolve, then allow to cool. Add rye bread, 1 tbsp caraway seeds and 10 sultanas. Seal and allow to ferment for 4–7 days, opening the jar every few days to release the built-up gases. Once the kvass tastes tart, strain through a sieve lined with muslin or a clean Chux. Bottle the kvass in 2 × 1 litre (35 oz) sterilised (p 501) bottles and seal. Leave at room temperature to carbonate for 2–3 days, then refrigerate and drink within 1 week.

Ribollita

This is an excellent way to turn a small amount of left-over Simplest Minestrone Soup (p 36) into another meal. By adding kale or cavolo nero, a little extra stock and grilled (broiled) stale bread, you can have ribollita on the table in no time.

Put 2 cups thinly sliced greens in a saucepan with 2 cups (500 ml) stock and simmer until tender. While your greens are simmering, rub 2–3 thick slices of stale bread with a little oil and a cut garlic clove. Char lightly under the grill (broiler) or on a barbecue hotplate, then tear into bite-sized pieces.

Add however much minestrone you have left over to the stock and greens, then gently bring back to the boil. Taste and add more salt or pepper if needed. Gently mix the charred bread pieces through the soup. Ladle into bowls, top with grated parmesan and serve.

Left-over rye bread salt

This recipe comes from *Beyond the North Wind* by Darra Goldstein. It's a beautiful example of how resourcefulness is not consolation but innovation. This salt gives a second life to stale bread by turning it into a seasoning. Use it as a finishing salt to give a smoky, salty flavour to meats and vegetables. For the best results you need left-over rye bread or some other really flavoursome bread, such as buckwheat or barley.

Preheat the oven to 240–260°C (475–500°F). Tear stale rye bread into small pieces to make up ⅓ cup (about 20 g) and cover with water. Soak for 30 minutes. Drain the bread but don't squeeze out the excess water. Mix the wet bread with ½ cup (150 g) salt; it will make a mash. Lightly oil a roasting tin, add the mash in a slightly flattened round lump, and bake for 30 minutes.

Carefully remove from the oven and allow the hardened bread and salt to cool. Break it up into smaller pieces then blitz in a spice or coffee grinder or pound to a coarse powder with a mortar and pestle. Keep in an airtight container in the pantry for up to 1 year.

Tasty meatballs – using left-over crappy sandwich bread
SERVES 4

This is for the last bits of sandwich bread in the bag that no one wants to eat.

Preheat the oven to 180°C (350°F). Soak 1 cup (about 45 g) torn-up sandwich bread in a little milk or stock, or even a grated onion. Let it sit for 5 minutes or so. In a medium bowl combine 500 g (1 lb 2 oz) minced (ground) meat of your choice, 3–4 finely chopped garlic cloves, ¼ cup (25 g) grated parmesan (optional), ¾ tsp salt and either a big handful of chopped fresh herbs or 1 tsp dried herbs. If you want to add grated carrot or zucchini (courgette), go wild. Throw in the torn soaked bread and combine gently. Roll tablespoonfuls of the mixture into meatballs and fry them gently in an ovenproof frying pan with a little oil for 4 minutes or until brown all over.

Transfer to the oven and bake for 10 minutes. You could add 500 ml (17 fl oz) tomato passata (puréed tomatoes) before baking if you want a saucy dish. Serve on mashed potato or tomatoey pasta, or with flat breads.

Broccoli

The following recipes are for the times you had good intentions and bought two or three heads of broccoli but then the week got away. While these simple recipes work with lovely fresh broccoli, they're equally good with the slightly yellowing, seven-day-old variety. Feel no shame about your ageing brassicas. Learn how to store broccoli well and follow recipes that use up the whole head.

Goes with	Broccoli is mild, green and grassy. Pair it with any other green vegetable, nuts, seeds, meats and tofu, and intensify its mellow flavours with sharper ingredients like lemons, blue cheese, cheddar cheese, parmesan, mustard, chilli, olives, capers, soy sauce, miso, garlic, ginger or spices. Dress cooked broccoli while it's warm, so it can absorb all the deliciousness.
Storage	To avoid broccoli wilting quickly, wrap the unwashed head in a clean damp cloth, beeswax wrap or reusable plastic bag, leaving the stem free so it can breathe. Wash well before using.
Substitutes	For obvious aesthetic and textural reasons, cauliflower is the best substitute for broccoli. Brussels sprouts roast like broccoli, green beans steam and stir-fry in a similar way, and kale will give you the nutritional powerhouse you're looking for with broccoli.

Some ideas for rescuing broccoli

* Pour Miso Dressing (p 277) over warm blanched, steamed or charred broccoli florets.
* Broccoli doesn't always preserve well, as it can get soft and sulfurous, but the Italian method of cooking in vinegar and preserving in oil is pretty delicious. Follow the recipe for Italian-style Preserved Green Beans (p 40), using a head of broccoli instead of beans.
* Char chopped broccoli in a very hot oiled frying pan and chuck in a handful of olives, some capers, chilli flakes, salt and a squeeze of lemon juice.
* For a yummy green side, make the Japanese-style Sesame Greens (p 40) using broccoli.

Broccoli pesto

Chop up 1 whole head of broccoli including the stems, and blanch in salted water for a few minutes until tender. Drain and set aside to cool and dry. Transfer to a food processor and add a handful of nuts, a handful of grated parmesan, 1–2 garlic cloves, salt, pepper and any stray herbs you have, such as basil, parsley, coriander (cilantro) and/or mint. Blitz to a rough paste then, with the motor running, add the juice of ½ lemon and enough olive oil to make it pesto-y.

Roasted tired broccoli

SERVES 4 AS A SIDE

The tastiest way to revitalise older broccoli (and cauliflower). Serve as a side or add to toasties, omelettes (p 150) and salads.

Preheat the oven to 200°C (400°F). Cut a head of broccoli into florets, leaving the stems on, and put them in a bowl. Add 1 tbsp olive oil, ½ tsp salt and 1 tsp spice – such as ground fennel seeds or ground coriander, paprika, curry powder, chilli flakes. If you have lemon zest, grate that over too. Spread out on a baking tray, giving the florets a little room to breathe, and roast for 20 minutes.

Garlicky green broccoli sauce for pasta

SERVES 4

Make this simple sauce when you're as weary as an old head of broccoli, pile it on pasta and eat it in bed. It's also delicious on toast with eggs. Follow the Whole-head-of-cauliflower Mash recipe (p 83), using 2–3 broccoli heads and cutting the stems, which are tougher, a little smaller.

Broccoli and 'what's left in the crisper' pie filling

Follow the 'What's in the Fridge' Vegie Pie Filling recipe (p 451), using a whole head of broccoli, stems and all, potato and parmesan. It's wholesome and comforting, and you'll pat yourself on the back for cleaning out the fridge.

Grated broccoli salad – tabouleh vibes

SERVES 3–4 AS A SIDE

Alex made this one day when tabouleh was on the menu, she'd forgotten to buy parsley and couldn't face going to the shops again. Grated broccoli became the green and a new recipe was born. This is a simple and adaptable recipe that allows you to mix and match what you have in the fridge. We use the same method with cauliflower, changing the cucumber to dried fruits and toasted nuts, for a pilaf-style grated salad (p 81).

Coarsely grate a small head of broccoli into a large bowl. Add ½ tsp salt and give the broccoli a gentle salty massage. Set aside. Finely dice 1 cucumber and add to the broccoli with the finely grated zest of 1 lemon or 2 tbsp chopped preserved lemon, a big squeeze of lemon juice and ½ tsp sumac or ground allspice, cumin or coriander. Give the salad a good crack of pepper and a drizzle of olive oil, and serve.

If you have any of the following ingredients, add them too – 1 large handful of mint leaves, 1 finely chopped bunch of parsley, finely chopped spring onions (scallions) or ½ thinly sliced red onion, 1 finely diced tomato and 1 thinly sliced chilli. Serve with flat breads, lamb koftas or falafel.

Green eggy fried rice

SERVES 2 HUNGRY TEENAGERS, OR A ROOMFUL OF TODDLERS

We fed this to our toddlers when they were small and now feed it to our giant teenagers when they need some quick comfort food. On more pragmatic days it's an excellent quick meal when all that's in the fridge is left-over rice and a worn-out head of broccoli.

In a wok, heat 1 tbsp neutral oil, then add 1 coarsely grated broccoli head. Add ½ tsp salt, 1 finely chopped garlic clove, a good splash of soy sauce and a pinch of sugar, and stir-fry until the broccoli turns bright green. Add 2 cups (370 g) left-over cooked rice and stir until the rice is hot and the broccoli is just cooked. In a small bowl, whisk 2–3 eggs with a pinch of salt. Push the green rice to the side of the wok and pour the egg into the other side. Mix the egg with a spoon or chopstick until fully cooked then stir it through the rice. Serve in small bowls.

What to do with broccoli stems

Broccoli stems can also be eaten, so don't throw them away. Simply peel off the tough outer layer with a paring knife and cut into smaller pieces than the florets before blanching, roasting or stir-frying – or pickle them (see over the page).

Quick-pickled broccoli stems

Slice broccoli stems into paper-thin rounds using a very sharp knife or a mandoline. Place them in a clean jar, container or even a bowl with spices of your choice – such as a big pinch of chilli flakes, some fennel seeds and a garlic clove.

In a jug, mix ½ cup (125 ml) boiling water, ½ cup (125 ml) apple cider vinegar or white wine vinegar, 3 tbsp sugar and ½ tsp salt. Pour the mixture over the broccoli stems, then cover and refrigerate. Allow to sit for a few days before eating. Add to salads, toasties, falafel rolls, burgers and cheesy crackers. Pickled broccoli stems will last for up to 1 month in the fridge.

See brussels sprouts, cabbage, cauliflower, kale, kohlrabi and wombok for ideas with other brassicas.

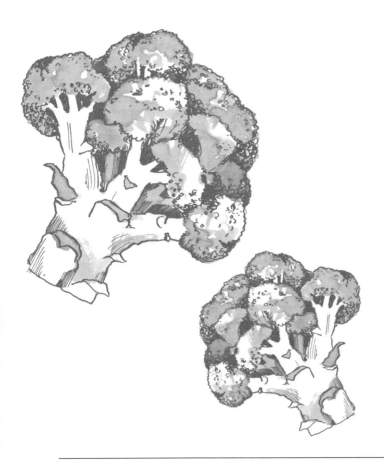

Brussels sprouts

Why would anyone not like brussels sprouts? It's madness, but we do know that there are households across the land where children (even adults) are refusing to eat their brussels sprouts at this very moment. Once Alex served up a plate of brussels sprouts at a dinner party only for one of her guests to tell her she was very brave. Here are some recipes for the brave among us, and to convince the less than brave.

Go with	Apples, pears, grapefruit, celery, cabbage, kale, broccoli, cauliflower, kohlrabi, turnips, eggs, cheeses, anchovies, pork, bacon, beef, mustard, caraway seeds, black pepper, garlic, vinegar, wine
Storage	Don't wash brussels sprouts before storing. Keep them in a reusable plastic bag with a little water in it in the fridge for up to 1 week.
Substitutes	The brassica family members are quite loosey-goosey when it comes to swapping one for another. Substitute with cabbage, kale or even broccoli and you'd hardly know the difference.

Some ideas if you have just a few sprouts rolling around

* Shave them paper-thin and add to salads or pile on top of soup before serving.
* Shred them and add to a spinach pie or the 'What's in the Fridge' Vegie Pie Filling (p 451).
* Slice them thinly and add to batch of Basic Sauerkraut (p 66).
* Cut them in half and chuck them in a roasting tin with other roasting vegetables, such as potatoes, pumpkin (squash) or beets.

Basic brussels slaw

Yes, brussels slaw. It's incredible – at once delicate and robust enough to hold its own with strong flavours and textures. Start with the brussels sprouts and build from there. Use this slaw as a guide for other brassicas – the traditional wedge of cabbage, a bunch of kale or cavolo nero – or non-brassica vegetables like fennel. Serve as a side with a roast chicken or fish, at a barbecue for a twist on a coleslaw, or with poached eggs and bagels.

Slice the brussels sprouts paper-thin using a mandoline or sharp knife. With clean hands, separate the layers until you have a bowl full of ribbons. Season well with salt and pepper. Throw in any torn soft herb leaves (such as parsley, dill or tarragon), thinly sliced crunchy vegetables or fruits (such as apple, celery or fennel), and a bit of feta or shavings of parmesan that are hanging around. Dress with Classic Mustard Vinaigrette (p 283) or Blue Cheese Dressing (p 90).

Roasted brussels sprouts

With their crispy outer leaves and tender insides, roasted brussels sprouts are a perfect side dish in the cold months.

Preheat the oven to 210°C (410°F) and line a roasting tin with baking paper. Whatever your quantity of brussels sprouts, cut them in half, arrange them in the tin and drizzle with enough olive oil to give them a glistening coat. Season with salt and pepper. Roast for 20 minutes. Don't shake the pan, just let them be. Once they're out of the oven, try one of the ideas below.

TO FLAVOUR ROASTED BRUSSELS SPROUTS

- Grate parmesan cheese over them when they're just out of the oven so that it melts, adding a few pinches of chilli flakes or powder and the finely grated zest of 1 lemon.
- Add some chopped crispy bacon, chopped prunes and a splash of sherry vinegar.
- Add pepitas (pumpkin seeds), toasted following the method on p 400, and chopped fresh herbs for a contrast of flavours and textures.

Pickled sprouts for the very brave

We've pickled some very odd things over the years, and pickled brussels sprouts made us laugh out loud, but they're surprisingly delicious, especially with lots of caraway seeds, peppercorns and garlic cloves in the jar. Go on, give them a go. They need a quick blanch in salted boiling water and then can be pickled following the Basic Vegetable Pickling method (p 472).

See broccoli, cabbage, cauliflower, kale, kohlrabi and wombok for ideas with other brassicas.

Buckwheat

Buckwheat is not a true grain – it's related to rhubarb and is gluten-free. It's not a staple in many kitchens, but it might be bought for one dish and then stuffed into the back of the pantry and forgotten about. This is a terrible shame, as buckwheat tastes nutty and is very nutritious. Keep it on hand for when you need to feed a gluten-free friend, because it can be served alongside most dishes, much like rice or couscous. You can pair it with the Simple Chickpea Stew (p 110) or with Mushroom Ragu (p 279).

Goes with	Mushrooms, onions, garlic, leeks, beetroot, peas, cabbage, pumpkin (squash), cucumber, yoghurt, beef, pickled fish, pickled and fermented vegetables, dried fruits, nuts, parsley, dill, tarragon, sage
Storage	Keep buckwheat groats in an airtight container in the pantry for up to 1 year. Store cooked buckwheat in the fridge for up to 2 days or in the freezer for up to 3 months.
Substitutes	Texturally you could swap it with barley, but your recipe won't be gluten-free and of course the cooking method is different (p 29). Rice can also work as a substitute.
How to cook buckwheat	Buy roasted buckwheat for ease. To make enough for 4, preheat the oven to 180°C (350°F). Splash some oil into a small casserole dish, then add 1 cup (185 g) roasted buckwheat groats, sprinkle with a little salt, dot 2 tbsp butter among the groats (if you're dairy-free, just add a little more oil) and cover with 2 cups (500 ml) boiling water. Put the lid on and steam in the oven for 25–30 minutes. Fluff up with a fork when done.

How to make crunchy buckwheat If you only have a tiny amount of raw buckwheat left in the bottom of the bag, you can still make good use of it. Toast it and throw it over a salad. It will add great flavour and texture – think of it like a seed mix. You'll be so impressed you'll want to make a larger quantity. Preheat the oven to 180°C (350°F). Coat whatever amount of uncooked buckwheat you have with a little oil and some salt and pepper. Spread out on a baking tray that has at least a little rim, and toast for 20 minutes or until the groats have darkened; keep a close eye on them so they don't burn. Allow to cool, then store in an airtight container in the pantry for 3 months.

Some ideas for using left-over cooked buckwheat

* Add a little oil to separate the grains, then add to a salad to make it heartier.
* If your cold buckwheat has become solid, cut into slices and fry on each side in some butter. It's absolutely delicious. Drizzle with honey to serve.
* *Left-over-buckwheat porridge* To make a little breakfast for one or two, for every ½ cup (95 g) cooked buckwheat, add ¾ cup (185 ml) milk or nut milk and a little pinch of salt. Cook, stirring often, over very low heat for 5–8 minutes until hot and thick. Serve with dried fruit and honey.

Buckwheat salad

This is the kind of dish that will make you serious about buckwheat. Serve it alongside some meat or have it for dinner on its own. And, get this – you could double it, stir in a bit of sour cream and use it as a pie filling.

Put 2 cups (380 g) cooked buckwheat in a bowl and add ¼ cup sliced pickled mushrooms, sauerkraut (p 66) or any other pickles you have in the fridge, 1 finely chopped boiled egg, the chopped leaves from ½ bunch of dill and plenty of salt and ground pepper. Go ahead and add ¼ cup (30 g) chopped walnuts or even some sultanas if you're feeling frisky. Dress simply with Classic Mustard Vinaigrette (p 283). Serve at room temperature.

Cabbage

Cabbage wins the endurance (and value-for-money) vegetable marathon every time. The fact that it's under-appreciated breaks our brassica-loving, money-saving, versatile-cooking hearts. When raw, it's crisp and a touch peppery; when cooked, it's mild and sweet. Every part of a cabbage is edible, so buy it whole, use it all and, when in doubt, make sauerkraut.

Goes with	Carrots, onions, fennel, potatoes, sweet potato, pumpkin (squash), brussels sprouts, kohlrabi, turnips, radishes, buckwheat, barley, apples, pears, grapefruit, pomegranate, figs, garlic, ginger, chilli, sage, coriander (cilantro), juniper berries, mustard seeds, fennel seeds, black pepper, cloves, tarragon, parsley, dill, horseradish, mustard, pork, bacon, chicken, anchovies, hazelnuts, walnuts, sesame seeds, sunflower seeds, eggs, mayonnaise, cream, blue cheese, butter
Storage	Basically this thing lasts forever. Buy a whole cabbage. If you're intimidated by its size, stick to red cabbage, which tends to be smaller. Store a whole cabbage as is, in the vegetable crisper in the fridge, for up to 1 month. As you cut into the cabbage, just rewrap the unused portion in either a clean damp cloth or a large beeswax wrap. If you have a small amount, slice it up and keep in an airtight container with 1 tbsp water for 5–7 days, remembering to change the water every 2–3 days.
Substitutes	If need be, replace cabbage with kale, brussels sprouts, celery or kohlrabi.

Some ideas for using up a bit of left-over cabbage

* A plain cabbage stir-fry is very satisfying. Follow the steps for the Stir-fried Celery (p 87). Flavour with plenty of ginger and throw in some toasted sesame seeds before serving.
* Add to your Kimchi Pancakes (p 225) and serve with Japanese mayonnaise, pickled ginger and all the sauces. »

* Sneak it into any soup or stew you have on the go. Cabbage takes up the flavour of whatever it's cooked with and can make itself at home in any cuisine. So add that last little bit of cabbage to your bolognese sauce. Why not? If you chop it finely enough, no one will notice.

* Braise wedges of cabbage, adding mustard seeds and bay leaves, and using the Velvety Braised Vegetables recipe (p 159).

* **Cabbage curry** So cheap, easy and nutritious that every student should know how to make it with their eyes closed. Use coconut milk, lots of ground turmeric, cardamom and other spices of your choosing, and serve on plain white rice. Follow the Really Easy Green Bean Curry recipe (p 40), slicing a 300 g (10½ oz) wedge of cabbage to add instead of the beans.

Pickling cabbage

There are many ways to pickle a little cabbage. The two methods we recommend are a mustard pickle, perfect for burgers and hot dogs – see Chow Chow (p 120) – or, even simpler, try Quick-pickling (p 473).

Basic sauerkraut

MAKES 1 x 500 ML (18 OZ) JAR

This really is the most basic sauerkraut, but if you nail this you can ferment anything. You can easily double or triple – or halve – this recipe to suit how much sauerkraut you want in your life.

Cut 500 g (1 lb 2 oz) cabbage into manageable-sized pieces and slice thinly. Don't forget to use the stems and cores – nothing goes to waste. Put the sliced cabbage in a large bowl with a good sprinkle of salt and 1 tbsp caraway seeds, dill seeds, whole black peppercorns or juniper berries.

To break down the cabbage, either squeeze it with clean hands, or pound it using a hefty instrument such as a meat tenderiser or pestle. This might take 5 minutes or more. Break down the cabbage until it's very wet. Take a fist-full of cabbage, and if juice runs out when you squeeze you know it's ready. Pack the cabbage tightly into a clean glass jar, pressing down so the liquid rises above the cabbage and any air bubbles are released. Repeat this process until the jar is filled. Liquid must cover the cabbage by about 1 cm (½ in). Wipe the rim of the jar with a clean cloth and seal.

Now for fermentation: place your jar in a cool dry place for 2 days to 1 week. In this time, your sauerkraut will ferment and you'll notice it starting to bubble and perhaps some juice escaping. Simply wipe the jar down. After 2 days, try your sauerkraut. If you're happy with the flavour, place the jar in the fridge. Sauerkraut may be eaten immediately but will improve with time (we suggest leaving it for at least 1 week).

Massaged cabbage and herb salad

SERVES 4

The beauty of this salad is that the action of massaging the cabbage creates its own dressing, and the rest is simply a matter of a drizzle of this and a handful of that. Do not underestimate the flavour of one-ingredient salads, as they make the most of their hero ingredient and only need a small flourish to bring them to the table in no time. The salting and massaging also makes the salad last well in the fridge for a few days.

You'll need 2–3 cups (150–225 g) thinly sliced red or white cabbage. Pop all the cabbage in a bowl with a generous pinch of salt. With clean hands, gently massage the cabbage until it begins to release its water. You don't want to go as far as you would when making sauerkraut, but there should definitely be a bit of moisture. Add a few big handfuls of chopped dill, tarragon, parsley or coriander (cilantro) leaves, and toss with 1 tbsp oil of your choice. Season with plenty of ground black pepper and a little more salt if you'd like. Feel free to garnish with chopped toasted nuts or seeds. Serve as a side salad to any meats, with tacos or even with a bowl of dumplings.

Sautéed cabbage

Sautéing cabbage in some butter, ghee or good-quality oil is really all you need to make a quick side. Salt and pepper will do the rest, but if you want to go cabbage deluxe, then shred whatever amount of cabbage you have and sauté it in Anchovy Butter (p 3) over medium–low heat for about 15 minutes. Serve alongside sausages, or piled on top of Jacket Sweet Potatoes (p 450) or Fishcakes (p 165).

Colcannon – with yesterday's mashed potatoes

SERVES 4

We're both enormous fans of resourceful cooking, and Irish cooks excel at turning a few everyday ingredients into something deeply comforting and nourishing. We admit to departing significantly from a traditional colcannon here by using left-over mash or even left-over roast carrot, pumpkin (squash) or parsnip, but the spirit is the same.

Begin by blanching 2 cups (150 g) shredded white cabbage in boiling water for 2 minutes until tender. Drain, add a few finely chopped spring onions (scallions) or ½ onion and set aside. Now reheat 2 cups (460 g) left-over mashed potato or mashed-up roast vegetables (or make a fresh batch if you don't have any leftovers). In a small saucepan over low heat, warm ½ cup (125 ml) milk with 1–3 tbsp butter (depending on how buttery the original mash was; if you've made plain mash for this dish, then go for all 3 tbsp butter) until the butter has melted. Put your left-over mash in another saucepan, then slowly add the warm milk until the mash becomes silky again. Add the drained cabbage and onion, and stir everything together in one direction to make a nice whirl. Look the other way and add another 1 tbsp butter, plus salt and pepper to taste. Serve hot alongside sausages and stews.

Cabbage rolls
MAKES ABOUT 12 ROLLS – SERVES 4

Don't be put off just because you've never made these before. They're easy. There are a few steps, but sometimes it's good to make a dinner that takes a little time and a lot of love to prepare. You'll need to make a batch of the Best Barley Side (p 29) for the stuffing, but you could also stuff your cabbage leaves with minced (ground) meat or mushroom fillings.

Carefully detach 12 cabbage leaves from a whole cabbage. Wrap and store the rest of the cabbage for another day (p 65). Bring a large pot of salted water to the boil and plunge the cabbage leaves in, 3–5 at a time. Remove from the boiling water with tongs and allow to cool.

Preheat the oven to 180°C (350°F). Once your cabbage is cool enough to handle, take one leaf and lay it flat on a clean benchtop. About 2 cm (¾ in) away from one edge add 2 tbsp of the barley or other stuffing. Fold the edge of the cabbage leaf over the stuffing, then bring in the sides and roll away from you to make a little parcel. Place this roll in a cast-iron pot and repeat until all the cabbage and stuffing is used. Ideally, the cabbage rolls should sit very snugly in one layer in the pot, but if there are a few sitting on top of each other that's fine. Pour in 400 g (14 oz) tinned tomatoes and 1 cup (250 ml) stock (or even a mixture of water and wine), put the lid on the pot and cook in the oven for 40 minutes. Remove the lid and return to the oven for a further 30 minutes so the liquid reduces. The cabbage leaves will be yielding and the flavours will all have melded together. Top with chopped herbs and serve with sour cream.

See broccoli, brussels sprouts, cauliflower, kale, kohlrabi and wombok for ideas with other brassicas.

Capers

How can something so tiny have so much flavour? Jars of capers are so small that they often get forgotten in the fridge, and so half-used jars can easily accumulate. Let's give these salty, briny, herby, peppery little guys their time in the sun.

Go with
All the other salty good things in life – anchovies, olives, feta, preserved lemon – as well as leafy greens, parsley, dill, tarragon, thyme, oregano, potatoes, broccoli, cauliflower, kale, capsicum (pepper), cucumber, tomatoes, eggplant (aubergine), zucchini (courgettes), asparagus, oranges, eggs, butter, cream cheese, fish and chicken.

Storage
Brined capers will keep well, under their brine, in the fridge for 12 months or more. Salted capers will keep in the fridge for 2 years. So relax.

Substitutes
Your other salty mates in the fridge will do the job – use olives, anchovies or preserved lemon if need be. Even chopped pickles will sort of be okay.

How to fry capers
Fried capers might seem like a step too far, but they're delicious explosions of flavour. They'll stay crisp for a few hours, so you can make them ahead of time. We use them as the star attraction on very simple leaf salads, simple summery pasta dishes, thinly sliced tomatoes with olive oil and grilled (broiled) fish. Drain brined capers, or rinse excess salt off salted capers, and pat dry with paper towel. In a small saucepan, heat ¼ cup (60 ml) neutral oil until very hot – you'll see small bubbles around the edges when it's ready. If you're frying more than 1 tbsp capers, work in batches. Add 1 tbsp capers, being careful of any spitting oil, and fry for about 2 minutes. Using a slotted spoon, remove the capers from the oil and drain on paper towel. Once you've finished with the oil, allow it to cool. Strain it, pour into a jar and use it to fry another batch of capers next week or for salad dressings or frying fish, but don't keep it for more than 1 week.

Some ideas for finishing that jar of capers

✳ Roughly mash hard-boiled eggs then add 1 tbsp chopped capers and 2–3 tbsp mayonnaise for a perfect picnic-sandwich filling.

✳ Make Alex's Tartare Sauce (p 94).

✳ Throw some capers and olives in with roasting chicken legs. Their saltiness will mix with the pan juices for a delicious sauce.

✳ Don't pour that brine down the sink! Add some olive oil to the jar, along with 1 tbsp chopped herbs, and shake it up. You have a salad dressing ready to go.

✳ Chop 1 tbsp capers and mix with about ¼ cup (120 g) cream cheese for a schmear worthy of the best bagels in town.

✳ Add to a potato salad. See the green potato salad or the updated creamy potato salad in the Anything-goes Potato Salad recipe (p 362) for some ideas.

✳ **Caper butter** Replace the anchovies in Anchovy Butter (p 3) with capers and use in the same way. It's amazing for cooking white fish or a chicken breast, sautéing spinach and broccoli, or warming up some tinned white beans.

Caper and lemon dressing
MAKES 100 ML (3½ FL OZ)

Easy and just as good on steamed potatoes or grilled (broiled) fish as it is on a green salad.

Mix 1 tbsp finely chopped capers into ⅓ cup (80 ml) sunflower oil, with 1 tbsp mustard, a pinch of sugar, a big squeeze of lemon juice and a very big pinch each of salt and pepper. Add a little cayenne pepper if you want some warmth.

Puttanesca – or 'I'm staying in my robe today' pasta

SERVES 3-4

We can't resist telling you the story of puttanesca. Roughly it translates to 'lady of the night', because it's the kind of dinner a working gal who didn't make it to the market might throw together from what's in the cupboard. Nigella Lawson affectionately calls it 'Slut's Spaghetti', and we hope we all get days when we can lounge around in our robe, possibly pour a glass of wine before it's officially cocktail hour, make love in the afternoon and not think about dinner until midnight. For those languid days and nights, this is the recipe.

The beauty of puttanesca is that it uses up all the super-flavoursome condiments in the cupboard or fridge, finishing off the capers, olives and anchovies in a one-pot meal.

Bring a large saucepan of salted water to the boil and cook 300 g (10½ oz) spaghetti according to the packet directions. Heat ¼ cup (60 ml) olive oil in a large frying pan over medium heat, then add 5–8 chopped anchovies, mashing them with a wooden spoon as you cook them. Add 3 finely chopped garlic cloves, 3 tbsp drained capers and ¼ cup (40–50 g) chopped black or green olives. Sauté everything together so the flavours really mingle for a minute or so. Add 400 g (14 oz) tinned or fresh chopped tomatoes and simmer over low heat for 10 minutes. You can also throw in a parmesan rind if you have one in the fridge. Drain the pasta and add to the frying pan with a little splash of the pasta water. Mix the sauce into the pasta, then finish with a drizzle of olive oil, salt to taste and grated parmesan. Eat in bed in the nude, if you dare.

Capsicum

The divisive capsicum (pepper). We've been arguing about capsicums for the past decade. Alex adores the red ones roasted, charred, marinated, pickled and raw, while Jaimee swears they taste like acid reflux. Hopefully this section will finally convince Jaimee to pick some up next time they're glowing red and shiny at the markets. They're cheap in late summer at the height of their season.

Goes with	All the other summer crops – zucchini (courgettes), eggplant (aubergine), chilli, tomatoes, corn. Capsicums' natural sweetness is brought out once cooked, so they pair well with bold and intense flavours like capers, olives, feta, anchovies, garlic and preserved lemon. They also go well with beans, lentils, quinoa, mozzarella, basil, parsley, oregano and tahini. Use warm spices like paprika, cumin and coriander seeds to complement them.
Storage	Capsicums are thin-skinned, sensitive and prone to sogginess. They should be stored unwashed in the fridge, in a brown paper bag with a little airflow. Luckily, they're even more delicious slow-cooked than raw, so if they do wrinkle or start to go mushy you can cover it up very successfully.
Substitutes	If you have no capsicums, you can use other peppers or chillies – just remember that some are hotter than others. Texturally, onion and fennel cook like capsicum, so you can slice, sauté or roast them in a similar way. For stews, slow cooking or to stuff, use other summery produce – like zucchini (courgettes), eggplant (aubergine) or seeded tomatoes.

Some ideas for using half a capsicum

✻ Make a little salsa and serve with corn chips and sour cream. Dice the capsicum (pepper) finely and mix with all or some of the following things – diced tomatoes, finely diced onion, fresh corn kernels, a thinly sliced chilli, diced avocado, coriander (cilantro) leaves or finely chopped stems, diced cucumber, salt, lime juice and a finely chopped garlic clove.

✻ Slice and sauté the capsicum (pepper) in a small oiled frying pan, low and slow, with some chopped onion, salt and paprika, then pile on top of fried eggs.

✻ *Capsicum salad for one* Thinly slice ½ capsicum (pepper) and add to green leaves with crumbled feta, a handful of chickpeas and your best dressing vinegar and oil.

Raw capsicum salad with capers and red onion

SERVES 2–3 AS A SIDE

Cut the top off 1 capsicum (pepper) and get rid of the seeds. Cut the capsicum into long, thin strips. Use a sharp knife and don't rush. With your best knife skills, very thinly slice ½ red onion into long strips to match the shape of your capsicum. Put the capsicum and onion in a bowl and add 1 tbsp extra virgin olive oil, 1 tbsp apple cider vinegar, a big pinch each of salt and sugar, and plenty of ground black pepper. If you have a garlic clove, finely chop it and add it too. Add a little paprika and 1 tbsp capers. You can eat it as is, but it's better if you let it sit for a bit, while you cook the rest of your meal, and let the juices flow. Before serving, add plenty of chopped dill or parsley. You can make this same salad with thinly sliced roasted capsicums if you find that raw ones taste too much like a burp.

Roasted capsicum and almond dip

For the best capsicum (pepper) dip in town, see the Most Delicious Almond Dip recipe (p 288). Seriously, make it.

Blistered marinated capsicum for the fridge
MAKES ABOUT 2 CUPS (260 G)

Make a batch of these and your week will be a sweet and smoky dream. They will be the start of many meals – piled on toast with ricotta or avocado, tossed through hot pasta or chickpeas, on a pizza, with cheese and crackers, on burgers or served with grilled (broiled) lamb ...

This is for 1 kg (2 lb 4 oz) capsicums (peppers) but we highly recommend doubling or even tripling it. Blister them following the Easy Oven-blistered Eggplant method (p 143), keeping in mind they won't take nearly as long as the eggplant (aubergine) and there's no need to pierce the skin first.

Pop the blackened capsicums in a bowl and cover them. The heat will make them sweat, and once they're cool the skins will slip right off. Cut the peeled capsicums into thick strips, put them in a large jar or airtight container, and splash over ¼ cup (60 ml) olive oil, ¼ cup (60 ml) red wine vinegar or white wine vinegar, 1 tbsp sugar and 1 tsp salt. Feel free to add some sliced garlic, strips of lemon peel, peppercorns or an oregano or thyme sprig if you have them. Pop the lid on, keep in the fridge for up to 3 weeks, and use them as a starting block for your meals.

If you want to make the capsicums last even longer, cover them with more vinegar, sugar and salt. Remember, all these ingredients are preserving agents and will make food last longer in the fridge.

TO USE MARINATED CAPSICUM
- Toss them through hot pasta with a little butter, chilli flakes, olives, anchovies and whatever cheese you have in the fridge.
- Mix them through warm lentils or chickpeas with finely chopped preserved lemon or lemon juice, plenty of parsley, ground cumin, and more salt and olive oil.
- Purée in a food processor with fresh or dried chillies, salt and mayonnaise, to have on burgers or to serve with fish.
- Put on home-made pizzas or make a pizza toastie with a stretchy cheese such as mozzarella, tomato, olives and salami.

Smooth and silky capsicum

MAKES 400 ML (14 FL OZ)

Braising (p 159) is an excellent cooking method for all neglected nightshades – capsicum (pepper), eggplant (aubergine), zucchini (courgettes) or a combination of all three.

In a frying pan that has a lid, gently heat ½ cup (125 ml) olive oil and add 1 thinly sliced onion, about 500 g (1 lb 2 oz) thinly sliced red capsicums and ½ tsp salt. Sauté for 2–3 minutes or until everything is starting to collapse. Cover and let the capsicum and onion slow-dance over low heat for about 30 minutes. Add 3 sliced garlic cloves, ½ tsp black pepper and a generous thyme sprig. Sauté for another minute or so and cover again. Cook slowly for another 30 minutes, remove the lid, taste and season with more salt if needed.

Serve as a sauce for pasta, with grilled (broiled) meats, fish or omelettes (p 150), or on toast.

Quick capsicum relish

MAKES 1 x 500 ML (18 OZ) JAR

You can turn Smooth and Silky Capsicum (above) into a quick and delicious relish. Add 1 tsp paprika, 1 tsp ground cumin and ½ tsp chilli flakes or powder with the garlic, then pour in ⅓ cup (80 ml) red wine vinegar or white wine vinegar. Add ¼ cup (55 g) white (granulated) sugar and ½ tsp salt, then cook, uncovered, until thick and glossy and relishy, 20–25 minutes. Store in the fridge for a few weeks and eat with fried eggs, steaks or Vegie Burgers (p 111).

Stuffed capsicums

SERVES 2–3

The perfect solution if you're looking for a 1990s dinner-party addition.

Make the Best Barley Side (p 29). Cut 2–3 capsicums (peppers) in half crossways and carefully remove the seeds and membranes so you have red cups. Tightly pack the barley stuffing into each capsicum half and arrange in an ovenproof dish that will hold them snugly enough to keep them upright. Pour in some stock or tomato passata (puréed tomatoes) and bake following the same method as for the Cabbage Rolls (p 68).

Carrots

Affordable, nutritious and versatile – we salute you, humble carrot. Not just for juicing and adding to soups and stews, the carrot can stand proud and be considered a hero. Unfortunately, because they're cheap and common, they're discarded without much thought. Treat a carrot like it's boring and it will give you boring results; respect it for being the Renaissance vegetable it is and say thank you.

Go with	Pumpkin (squash), sweet potato, beetroot, cabbage, sauerkraut, lettuce, kohlrabi, daikon, parsnips, turnips, wombok (Chinese cabbage), snow peas (mange tout), dried beans, lentils, apples, quince, oranges, ginger, onions, spring onions (scallions), celery, chilli, mustard, parsley, honey, maple syrup, butter, cinnamon, nutmeg, cumin, dried fruits, hazelnuts, peanuts, walnuts, poppy seeds, sesame seeds, cream cheese
Storage	Store them wrapped well, unwashed, in the fridge. Beeswax, a reusable plastic bag or an airtight container will help keep them juicy and bright.
Substitutes	Although most substitutes are less sweet than carrots, parsnip, daikon, beetroot or kohlrabi are good replacements for texture. For cooked recipes try pumpkin (squash) and sweet potato.

Some ideas for using the last carrot or two

* If they need cooking right away, make a soup base to use later in the week. Sauté chopped onion and carrot with bay leaves in plenty of oil, low and slow, for about 20 minutes, until soft and sweet. Add 4 finely chopped garlic cloves and sauté until fragrant. Store in the fridge for 5 days or freeze for up to 3 months. You'll high-five yourself next time you're making dinner in a hurry.
* Carrot fritters will help you see in the dark. Use the Parsnip Rosti recipe (p 323) with grated carrot and a big pinch of ground cumin. Serve with Raita (p 491) and chilli sauce.

* ***Pickled carrot*** Follow the Japanese-style Soy-pickled Cucumber recipe (p 128) and you'll turn your almost-compost into gold. Or use the method in the Quick-pickling recipe (p 473) for an excellent half-carrot rescue mission.

Raw carrot salad

Sometimes there are only two carrots in the crisper but you still want to get some vegetables on the table. By peeling the carrots then grating, making ribbons with a vegetable peeler or cutting them into beautiful thin matchsticks, you create the illusion of a bigger, fancier salad.

Transfer the grated carrot, ribbons or matchsticks to a mixing bowl and season well with salt. Add a generous squeeze of lemon or lime juice and a splash of neutral oil, then toss with one or all of the following: a big handful of coriander (cilantro) leaves, a grating of fresh ginger, 1–2 tbsp toasted sesame seeds, toasted dried coconut.

Roasted carrots

We want you to get your head around simple cooking methods for the vegetables that are losing their lustre in the fridge. Roasting is one of our favourites because you can quickly bung your vegies in the oven when you get home from work, and they don't need to be in tiptop shape. In fact, wrinkly vegetables can be rescued by a little oil, spices, salt and heat. Depending on which flavourings you add, you can make roasted vegetables complement whatever else you're serving. Carrots are excellent roasted. They become sweeter, earthier and richer.

Add roasted vegetables to salads; serve them as a side for meats or as a vegetable with curries or in tacos; or toss them thorough rice, couscous or pasta. We recommend always having a container of roasted vegetables in the fridge. Squish leftovers onto sandwiches or in a wrap for lunch the next day, roughly mash them to turn into Fishcakes (p 165), add them to an omelette (p 150) or frittata, or blitz them with chickpeas or nuts to make a delicious dip.

Preheat the oven to 180°C (350°F), or 200°C (400°F) if your oven doesn't get very hot – you want the carrots to caramelise a little. In a baking tray, lay carrots, cut into 4 cm (1½ in) diagonal slices or halved lengthways, or whole baby carrots (all can be unpeeled). Drizzle with oil, then sprinkle generously with salt, pepper and spices of your choice. Roasting times will vary depending on the size of your carrots. Check them after 20 minutes and keep cooking until they are tender, sweet, a little caramelised, and you have to resist eating them straight out of the tray. They'll be good just like this, or try one of the suggestions over the page. **»**

TO DRESS ROASTED CARROTS

- Add 1 tsp ground cumin and a large pinch of cayenne pepper before roasting. Transfer to a serving plate and throw on a big handful of coriander (cilantro) leaves and a squeeze of lime juice. Serve with grilled (broiled) fish or Chilli Con Carne (p 36), in tacos or on the side with a meaty curry.
- Before roasting, add finely grated orange zest, grated fresh ginger and a drizzle of honey. Serve with a roast chicken.
- In the last 5 minutes of roasting, add a handful of cooked or tinned chickpeas. After roasting, transfer to a serving platter, drizzle with the Creamy Tahini Dressing (p 455) and top with chopped parsley. Serve as is or as a side with kebabs, falafel or grilled (broiled) lamb.

Turn tired carrots into velvety braised carrots

Carrots cooked low and slow, with a small amount of liquid in a covered pan, are decadent, rich and velvety, even if they started out as shrivelled witches' fingers. Follow the method in Velvety Braised Vegetables (p 159), cutting the carrots into 3–4 cm (1¼–1½ in) diagonal slices, replacing the oil with butter, adding 1 tbsp honey or brown sugar and some grated fresh ginger, and cooking for 30 minutes.

Fermented carrots

MAKES 1 x 500 ML (18 OZ) JAR

May we suggest that fermented carrots are the best carrots? Use them like a pickle, add them to salads, mix them with roasted vegetables to balance oil or fat, or blend them until smooth and mix with some yoghurt or tahini for a sandwich spread or a dip. Use this recipe for any other vegetables you want to ferment.

Make a brine by boiling 1 cup (250 ml) water with 1 tsp salt in a medium saucepan, then set aside to cool to room temperature. While the brine is cooling, wash and thinly slice 2–3 carrots into whatever shape you like, ensuring first that they will fit into your clean jar. Place ½ tsp whole spices – like coriander, cumin or dill seeds – and 1–2 garlic cloves in the empty jar. Pack the carrots in on top, then fill the jar with the cooled brine, making sure the carrots are completely covered. Wipe the rim of the jar and seal.

Place your jar in a cool dry place for 2 days to 1 week. During this time, you'll notice that the brine begins to bubble and some may escape. Simply wipe the jar down. After 2 days try your carrots, and if you're happy with the flavour, place them in the fridge. If you'd like them a little more sour, or the weather has been cold (low temperatures slow down fermentation), let them sit for longer. Keep tasting until you're happy. Fermented carrots may be eaten immediately but will improve after 1 week in the fridge. Once the jar is open, store in the fridge for up to 6 months.

Carrot and lime jam

Carrot jam is a traditional Persian condiment that's usually served with fish or salty cheese. We make vegetable-based jams out of older vegies that need to be used up. Follow the Celery Jam recipe (p 87), grating in about 450 g (1 lb) carrot and replacing the lemon with 2 limes if you have them.

Carrot breakfast muffins

These can use up daggy old carrots, and are a wholesome way to start the day. They can also go in a lunchbox, or make a lovely afternoon tea. Follow the Seedy Breakfast Muffin recipe (p 371), replacing the pumpkin with grated unpeeled carrots. Use pepitas (pumpkin seeds) or walnuts and feel free to add extra ground ginger. Top with Cream Cheese Icing (p 94).

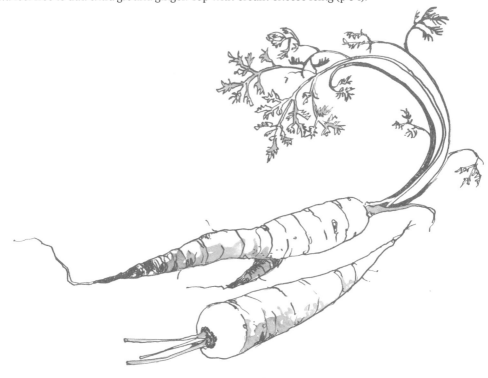

Cauliflower

Some people seem to approach buying a whole head of cauliflower with more trepidation than they do buying property. It's not the commitment so much as the question of what to do with it once you've made that initial recipe you bought it for. Discover how many ways you can eat a cauliflower and what it goes with, and you'll never run out of ideas. And always reach for the one with the leaves – they make a delicious side.

Goes with	Cauliflower is mellow and creamy, so enhance this by adding cheeses, cream, nuts, pasta, potatoes, sweet potato, fish or milk, or give it a flavour punch with capers, anchovies, chilli, cumin, garlic, tahini, nutmeg, mustard seeds, turmeric, fennel seeds, lemon zest or black pepper. Also goes with brussels sprouts, sweet potato and turnips.
Storage	Store whole cauliflower in a reusable plastic bag in the fridge or wrap the head in a big beeswax wrap and leave the stem sticking out at the bottom. A whole cauliflower will stay fresh for 1 week to 10 days. Once you've cut into it, keep the rest in an airtight container in the fridge for 1 week.
Substitutes	Mostly we go with broccoli if cauliflower isn't around, but in a soup or curry you could use cabbage, as the flavour is similar, or potatoes.

Some ideas for using up an abundance of cauliflower

* Make the Odd-knobs Mac 'n' Cheese (p 101). You won't regret it, and whoever you're cooking for will give you a cuddle.
* Bulk out a curry – add to the Really Easy Green Bean Curry (p 40).
* Add to the 'What's in the Fridge' Vegie Pie Filling (p 451).
* Grate and turn into crispy rostis. Follow the Parsnip Rosti recipe (p 323), giving the grated cauliflower a good squeeze with clean hands to remove excess moisture. If the mix needs a little more binding, add an extra 1 tbsp of whatever dairy needs using (cream, yoghurt, cream cheese) to hold everything together.
* ***Cauliflower schnitzels*** We're big fans, and have been trying to convince our families that they're as good as the chicken ones. See p 51 for how to crumb things. After frying, transfer the schnitzels to a 170°C (325°F) oven and cook for 20 minutes or until the cauliflower is tender. Serve with Alex's Tartare Sauce (p 94), hot chips (fries), a salad and a beer. Don't worry if you have odd-sized schnitzels – they'll never look like the ones on Instagram.

Grated cauliflower salad or pilaf

Grating brassicas like cauliflower and broccoli turns them into simple textural salads – they end up being a bit like a grain salad without the grains. Different additions – like herbs, spices, nuts and dried fruits – will mean you can serve this type of salad with so many meals. The Grated Broccoli Salad (p 57) has preserved lemon, cucumber, herbs and cumin, which gives it a tabouleh-like energy.

We follow the same method when using cauliflower, leaving out the cucumber and tomato and instead adding plenty of dried fruits, toasted nuts and dill or parsley, and serving it like a raw kind of pilaf with meatballs, skewers or a stew.

Cauliflower relish

If you've got half a cauliflower left in the fridge at the end of the week and are looking for something delicious to do with it, try the Chow Chow relish recipe (p 120), using about 650 g (1 lb 7 oz) chopped cauliflower instead of corn. Leave out the green capsicum (pepper) and replace with onion, leek or even celery. Tangy and moreish, cauliflower relish will be amazing on toasties, in salad sandwiches and with cheese and crackers in the weeks to come.

Roasted cauliflower

When cauliflower is in season, roasted florets appear on our tables multiple nights a week. Spiced roasted cauliflower can be wrapped up in a burrito with beans, served alongside Dal (p 244), or tossed through pasta with plenty of lemon juice and capers, and some flaked left-over fish if you have it.

Follow the method for roasted carrots (p 77), changing the spices to suit the type of meal you're making. Experiment with adding ½ cup (75 g) lightly oiled pepitas (pumpkin seeds) to the roasting tin for the last 5–7 minutes of cooking.

Some roasted cauliflower flavour ideas: Turmeric, ground coriander or cumin, cayenne pepper and salt / Curry powder and chilli flakes / Lemon zest, finely chopped garlic, chilli flakes, salt and plenty of black pepper.

Crispy spiced cauliflower – deep-frying veg the simple way

Deep-frying isn't as scary as you might imagine. Perhaps don't try it for the first time when everyone is starving and you're stressed, but don't be afraid to give it a go. There are a lot of methods out there, but this is the easiest version for those new to the pleasures of deep-frying at home. And don't forget, it's an excellent method for rescuing vegetables that have been hanging around in the fridge for a while by turning them into crispy delights. Serve simply with rice, pickles or kimchi (p 486) and a flavoursome dipping sauce.

Make a very simple batter in a good-sized mixing bowl by whisking 1 cup (150 g) plain (all-purpose) flour, ½ cup (60 g) cornflour (cornstarch), 1 tsp baking powder, 1 tsp salt and 2–3 tbsp of your favourite ground spices or dried herbs (we like lots of paprika, oregano and mustard powder with a little cayenne pepper). Slowly pour in 1 cup (250 ml) iced water, whisking to a smooth batter and adding a little more water if needed.

Cut ½ head of cauliflower into bite-sized florets, leaving the stem attached when you can.

Pour 2 cups (500 ml) frying oil (rice bran oil, grapeseed oil) into a large heavy-based saucepan or very stable wok and heat over medium heat until the oil reaches 155°C (310°F) or a small piece of bread turns golden brown in 30–40 seconds. Toss the cauliflower florets through the batter then deep-fry in batches until crispy and golden brown. Remove using a slotted spoon and drain on paper towel.

SERVE CRISPY SPICED CAULIFLOWER WITH

- A mixture of mayonnaise and chilli sauce or chilli jam for a creamy spicy hit, topped with chopped spring onions (scallions) and sesame seeds.
- Green Tahini (p 454), pickles and flat breads (p 168).
- The Chimichurri (p 193) for dipping.
- Slaw and Chow Chow (p 120) on the side, to make it American-style.

To reuse the frying oil: Allow to cool completely, then strain carefully through clean muslin into a clean jar. Label it so you remember that this is your frying oil, and store it in the fridge for up to 1 month. When reusing oil, make sure it looks and smells clean and has no foam on the surface.

Whole-head-of-cauliflower mash

SERVES 4

This is an easy, delicious and excellent meal to make when you're on a budget. Buy a whole head of cauliflower, with the leaves still attached, when it's in season and cheap, and turn it into a hearty, nutritious, wintery meal. Serve on pasta with plenty of parmesan, or it's also very yummy served with grilled (broiled) fish. And then you can pile the leftovers on toast and keep yourself well fed for the next few days. Try this recipe with broccoli too, keeping in mind that you'll need 2–3 heads (about 700 g/1 lb 10 oz) and only ¼ cup (60 ml) stock. If your cauliflower didn't come with leaves or you're using broccoli, just omit the leaf sautéing step.

Bring a large saucepan or stockpot of well-salted water to the boil. Separate the leaves from the cauliflower head, wash the leaves well and chop finely. Cut the head into pieces. Once your water comes to the boil, add the cauliflower pieces and simmer for 3 minutes. Drain well.

In a frying pan, heat ⅓ cup (80 ml) olive oil, along with a big pinch of salt, and sauté the chopped leaves for 15 minutes or until tender. Add 3–6 sliced garlic cloves, depending on your penchant for garlic, and sauté until it smells lovely. Add the head pieces with ½ tsp each of salt and pepper and ¾ cup (185 ml) stock or a mix of wine and water. Cover and simmer for 20 minutes. Remove the lid and mash with a fork, then taste and adjust the seasoning, adding the zest and juice of ½ lemon if you have one (it's also delicious without).

CAULIFLOWER STEMS AND LEAVES

Never throw your cauliflower leaves in the bin again. Think of cauliflower as a two-for-one deal – cauliflower and greens.

Some ideas for using cauliflower stems and leaves

* Thinly slice cauliflower leaves and add to a stir-fry. Follow the same method as for the Stir-fried Celery (p 87), adding plenty of grated fresh ginger and chilli flakes.
* Don't forget you can quick-pickle cauliflower stems. Follow the Quick-pickling recipe (p 473).

Sautéed cauliflower leaves

Make a delicious green side by sautéing cauliflower leaves in oil or butter with garlic, lemon and salt. Serve with a roast chicken, add to a frittata or omelette (p 150), use in a vegetable pie or add to a spanakopita.

Heat oil or butter in a frying pan, then add well-washed and finely chopped cauliflower leaves and stems. Add a generous pinch of salt and cook for about 10 minutes. Add some chopped garlic and a squeeze of lemon juice, then continue cooking until the leaves are tender, bright green and delicious.

See broccoli, brussels sprouts, cabbage, kale, kohlrabi and wombok for ideas with other brassicas.

Celery

Go on, be brave ... buy a whole bunch of celery rather than reaching for the plastic-wrapped half-bunch option at the supermarket. All you need to do is commit to storing it well and then learn how to use the entire thing in simple, interesting ways. We promise there's more to celery than bolognese sauce and peanut butter sticks.

Goes with	Apples, crunchy pears, pomegranate, cucumber, carrots, fennel, dried beans, brussels sprouts, potatoes, snow peas (mange tout), nuts and nut butters, barley, lentils, cheeses, mayonnaise, ham, horseradish, mustard, lemons, garlic, chilli, ginger, soy sauce, black pepper, star anise, mint
Storage	Cut the base and leaves off the bunch. Wash the base well and store in a container in either the fridge or the freezer for your next batch of stock. Tightly wrap the unwashed leaves in a clean damp tea towel (dish towel) or beeswax wrap and store in the fridge (you'll find tips and recipes for the leaves on p 88). Wash the stalks and cut them to fit in a large airtight container. Add ¼ cup (60 ml) water to the bottom of the container and store in the fridge for no more than 2 weeks. By changing the water often, you'll get even longer out of your celery.
Substitutes	In salads, apples make a good substitute, or raw white onion works if used sparingly. For cooked recipes go for fennel.

Some ideas for using up a few celery stalks

* Enjoy a small salad of very thinly sliced celery, thinly sliced radishes or fennel, orange or grapefruit segments, a splash each of vinegar and oil, and salt and pepper.
* Make Mirepoix (p 314) – the fancy name for the flavour base of chopped vegetables that starts so many soups, stews and sauces. Usually celery, onion and carrot are cooked slowly in oil or butter until they are soft, sweet and bursting with flavour. If you have some celery that needs using, make a batch of mirepoix and freeze it for another time.
* Have chicken sandwiches for lunch – shredded chicken, mayonnaise, finely chopped celery and plenty of salt and pepper. Add chopped walnuts if you have them.
* Quick-pickle them (p 473).
* **Fermented celery** It's all the good things – salty, crunchy, sour and good for your gut. Follow the same method as for Fermented Carrots (p 78).

Russian-style celery and potato salad

When there's celery in the house or the coolroom at work, Jaimee makes this simple, delicious salad. Start by making Russian Dressing (p 418), then chop 4 celery stalks into 1 cm (½ in) pieces, tearing off a few of the leaves to garnish (keep the rest to make Celery Leaf Syrup or Celery Leaf Pesto, both on p 88) and set aside. Hard-boil 1–2 eggs and dice 1 large potato or 2 carrots (or whatever root vegetable is around). Boil the potato or carrot until tender, then drain and allow to cool. Chop up the boiled eggs and add to a largish bowl with the celery and other vegetables. Season with salt and pepper. Add the dressing, making sure all the ingredients get a good coating. Serve topped with chopped dill leaves (or parsley or tarragon).

Turn limp celery into velvety braised celery

Follow the Velvety Braised Vegetables recipe (p 159), using 4–5 celery stalks cut on an angle into 3–4 cm (1¼–1½ in) pieces and reducing the cooking time to 10 minutes. If you have a tin of white beans or some chickpeas hanging around in the fridge, drain and add them to the pan. Garnish with chopped celery leaves, lemon juice and a chilli condiment.

Stir-fried celery

SERVES 4 AS A SIDE

Kylie Kwong's books taught us the art of one-ingredient stir-fries. Simple and elegant, this light way of cooking turns humble vegetables into stars. Serve as a side with noodles or dumplings, or with spicy tofu, grilled chicken or fish and rice.

Thinly slice 3–4 celery stalks on the diagonal. Heat 2–3 tbsp peanut oil in a wok until it shimmers. Throw in a big pinch of salt and the celery, and stir-fry for 2 minutes. Add 2 sliced garlic cloves, stirring constantly so they don't burn and become bitter. Stir in a pinch of sugar and ¼ cup (60 ml) stock or water, then cook only until the celery is tender. Add a little sesame oil and serve topped with toasted peanuts, slices of fresh chilli and/or coriander (cilantro) leaves.

Celery jam

MAKES 1 x 375 ML (14 OZ) JAR

Vegetable jams are a thing, and are an interesting old-fashioned way to use up limp celery, wrinkly beets, carrots or even parsnips. We add plenty of ground pepper, herbs, lemon zest and/or chilli flakes to make them more savoury. Serve with cheeses, ham sandwiches or grilled (broiled) fish, or add 1 tbsp to a dressing for flavour and sweetness.

If you're following this recipe with root vegetables like carrot or beetroot, grate them coarsely.

Wash ½ bunch (350–500 g/12 oz–1 lb 2 oz) celery stalks well, pulling the strings off the stalks if they're big and tough. Slice very thinly, put in a saucepan and add 2½ cups (625 ml) water and ½ cup (125 ml) apple cider vinegar or white wine vinegar (if you have white wine that needs using, add it in here instead), a thyme or rosemary sprig or a few bay leaves and ½ tsp ground black pepper. Simmer gently for 20–25 minutes until celery is tender. Add the juice and zest of 1 lemon, a pinch of chilli flakes, 1½ cups (330 g) white (granulated) sugar and a generous pinch of salt, then stir until the sugar dissolves. Bring to the boil and simmer again, stirring often, for 30 minutes or until the jam is thick, glossy and at setting point (p 503). Pour into a clean jar or container and store in the fridge for up to 6 months, or pour into a hot sterilised jar (p 501) and store in the pantry for up to 1 year.

CELERY LEAVES

In those weeks when you have celery in the house, don't buy herbs. Use your celery leaves in place of parsley, throwing them liberally into salads, on top of soups, in sandwiches and through grains, or stick them in your pickles and ferments or your gin and tonics.

Celery leaf gremolata with green olives

If a celery bunch was extra bushy, make this gremolata, store it in the fridge in an airtight container and scatter it over all your meals. We particularly like it on scrambled eggs, vegetable soups that need a punch of flavour, and avocado on toast.

Very finely chop 1 large handful of celery leaves and put them in a bowl with the zest of 1 lemon, plenty of ground black pepper, a big pinch of salt and lots of finely chopped green olives. Feel free to add cumin seeds or chilli flakes if you like. Store in the fridge in an airtight container for about 4 days. Once it starts to wilt, stir it through a soup and no one will know.

Celery leaf syrup for gin and tonics
MAKES 1 CUP (250 ML)

You'll never regret having a bottle of this in the fridge. Follow the Ginger Syrup recipe (p 176), replacing the ginger with 1 generous handful of celery leaves and ½ cup (70 g) chopped celery stalks that aren't good enough for eating. Add 1 tsp black peppercorns, the zest of 1 lemon and 1 tsp crushed juniper berries. Use 2 tbsp celery leaf syrup in your next G&T, then try not to drink 10 in one go.

Celery leaf pesto

You'll find this recipe in our book *Use It All*, but it's too good to leave out here. Spread it on toast and top with a fried egg, or add it to a salad wrap, potato salad (p 362) or fish burger.

Put 1–2 cups (20–40 g) celery leaves, a handful of nuts (any kind), 2 garlic cloves, ½ cup (50 g) grated parmesan and a pinch of salt in a food processor, then blitz to a paste. With the motor running, add 100–150 ml (3½–5 fl oz) of a not too intense oil until well combined. Transfer to a clean jar or airtight container and store in the fridge for up to 10 days.

Cheese

Bits of unused cheese are fairly regular guests in the fridge, no? And because cheese is such a luxury ingredient, with a large environmental footprint, wasting it can cause some niggling guilt. But even a scraping of cheese can be put to good use, because it can impart a saltiness and umami flavour to whatever you're cooking. Our tips are based on the bold assumption that you'll be happy to serve a little cheese on nearly every occasion. We know there's a world of amazing ones out there, but we've chosen the most commonly purchased and wasted cheeses to discuss here. Remember, cheese is a rather flexible ingredient. You can substitute most soft cheeses for other soft cheeses and likewise with hard cheese. What's more, you can often swap hard cheese and soft cheese. Ricotta instead of parmesan with pasta is fine, cheddar instead of brie can work too. Just be sensible about it.

BLUE CHEESE

So. Much. Flavour. All at once metallic and floral with a hint of armpit, blue cheese can really divide a household. There's a range of piquancy in blue cheeses, but rarely are they considered mild. Usually blue cheese is bought in smaller amounts, with less chance of waste, but sometimes most of the blue cheese is left on the cheese platter after a dinner party and you might find yourself a bit stuck as to what to do with it.

Goes with	Avocado, cauliflower, brussels sprouts, broccoli, cabbage, asparagus, spinach, pumpkin (squash), celery, apples, pears, apricots, blueberries, cumquats, figs, grapes, peaches, nuts, sage, parsley, ham

---

Storage	Store blue cheese well wrapped in baking paper in the more humid part of your fridge, such as the vegetable crisper, so it doesn't dry out. It will last 3–4 weeks.

Some ideas for using up left-over blue cheese

✳ Crumble it over any cauliflower dish (p 80) – roasted cauliflower straight from the oven or a cauli salad, and it's especially delicious in cauliflower soups.
✳ Make a salad with torn radicchio leaves, sliced pear and crumbled blue cheese.
✳ Crumble it over roasted grapes (p 181) for a flavour sensation like no other.
✳ Make an insane toastie with blue cheese and slices of ripe pear, and eat with a glass of wine.

Blue cheese dressing
MAKES 200 ML (7 FL OZ)

This classic dressing, rich and full of flavour, is the sort you'd use on bitter leaves such as radicchio, endive or rocket (arugula) and not need much else. Drizzle it over Roasted Brussels Sprouts (p 60) and you'll never want to eat anything else. Use it as a salad dressing, or drizzle over steak or baked potatoes. Normally blue cheese dressing is made with buttermilk, but we cheat and add a squeeze of lemon juice to regular milk.

Start by souring ¼ cup (60 ml) milk with a big squeeze of lemon juice and allowing it to stand for a few minutes until you can see the milk forming lumps. Put the milk in a food processor (or use a hand-held blender) with 30–50 g (1–1¾ oz) blue cheese, ½ cup (120 g) mayonnaise, ½ tsp dijon mustard and a pinch each of salt and pepper. Whiz together.

BRIE AND CAMEMBERT

It's quite exciting to have some gooey, buttery brie or camembert in the house, isn't it? We can't imagine how it could get wasted when we've both been known to eat it straight, cracker or no. But let's imagine there was a dinner party and a lovely guest brought a wheel of brie and Alex and Jaimee weren't there to sit next to it and eat it all, so the next day there was some left. Even a tiny sliver can add luxury to a meal.

Go with	Apples, pears, apricots, cumquats, grapes, berries, figs, celery, asparagus, mushrooms, tomatoes, smoked fish, ham, nuts, dried fruit
Storage	Soft cheeses like brie and camembert need to breathe, so don't use plastic. Wrap in baking paper and store in the fridge for no more than 3–4 days.

Some ideas for a little left-over brie or camembert

* Pop on top of halved figs or stone fruits. Put them under the grill (broiler) for 1–2 minutes, drizzle with honey and serve for dessert or breakfast.
* Cut off the rind and throw the creamy part into a salad of soft lettuce leaves and nuts.
* Add it to tonight's omelette (p 150) – you won't be disappointed.
* Use it in a Cheese Sauce (p 274, or see Welsh Rarebit, p 92, or Odd-knobs Mac 'n' Cheese, p 101), but cut off the rind first.

Brie and jam fried sandwich
MAKES 1

Look, this might be almost too wonderful. You're not going to eat it often (that's an order from your doctor, by the way), but when you do it's worth cancelling all other plans and really being in the moment. What more can we say? You're welcome.

Cut 2 slices of sourdough bread and butter on both sides. Spread a generous layer of jam (berry jams are particularly suited to this Liberace of sandwiches) on one side of each slice. Place slices of brie or camembert on one of the jam sides and pop the other slice on top, jam side down. Heat a frying pan over medium heat and melt 1 tbsp butter. Fry the sandwich for about 2–3 minutes each side, until golden, crispy and melty. Hop into your silk dressing gown and enjoy.

CHEDDAR
Probably the most common aged cheese in fridges, cheddar is sharp, a little sweet and a little salty with a sour finish. The more mature it is, the more pronounced are all of these characteristics. For the most part cheddar is a good all-rounder for sandwiches, pizzas, cheese sauces, baking and beyond.

Goes with	Nuts, anchovies, rosemary, thyme, sage, chilli, dried beans, bitter greens, asparagus, mushrooms, broccoli, onions, parsnips, potatoes, tomatoes, bananas, celery, apples, pears, apricots, figs, cured meats and all the condiments – pickles, relishes, kimchi, jam, sauerkraut, marmalade

---

Storage	Store in an airtight container on the top shelf of the fridge for up to 3 weeks.

Some ideas for using up cheddar

* If it's dried up and forgotten in the fridge, use it like a parmesan rind and toss it into a soup or stock as it's cooking. It will give great flavour.
* Grate and mix into mashed potatoes and use to top a cottage or shepherd's pie.
* Make marmalade and cheddar toasties – yes, please.
* Grate into the 'What's in the Fridge' Vegie Pie Filling (p 451).
* Add to Sweet Corn Polenta (p 119).
* Grate the last stump to cover the top of 'There's Nothing Wrong With That Cream!' Potatoes (p 125).
* Make the Odd-knobs Mac 'n' Cheese or Odd-knobs Potted Cheese (both on p 101).

Welsh rarebit
SERVES 1–2

What better way to eat cheddar? If you really want to know, there is a world of controversy surrounding what is essentially cheese on toast. In the UK, the Cheese Society is weighing in on the proper cheese to use, and then there are doubts that the dish is even Welsh, not to mention the fact that there's no such thing as a rarebit. Did they mean rabbit? But there's no rabbit in the recipe. It's a *rarebit* hole to avoid, but you should definitely just make this perfect little meal when dinner can be a relaxed affair and no one needs anything from you.

In a small saucepan over medium heat, mix 1 tbsp mustard powder and 1 tbsp ale or a heavy and flavoursome beer to a paste. Turn the heat to low and add 1 tbsp butter and a good splash of worcestershire sauce. Add another 1 tbsp ale and 1 cup (100 g) grated cheddar. Mix until you have a thick sauce, then remove from the heat. While the cheese sauce is cooling, lightly toast 2 pieces of bread on both sides under the grill (broiler). Whisk 2 egg yolks and a pinch of salt into the cheese sauce and spread the sauce over the toast. Pop back under the grill until the cheese is melted and bubbling. Serve with more worcestershire sauce.

COTTAGE CHEESE
Hello cottage cheese, you've been a little out of fashion since the 1980s but we suspect people are still buying you, because we know we are. As one of the most common fresh cheeses available, cottage cheese is a little tangier than most and has a lumpy texture from the large curds. It's extremely high in protein and low in fat, so it can be added as the creamy element of a dish or meal without being too heavy.

Goes with	Muesli, barley, nuts, honey, berries, apples, apricots, figs, bananas, avocado, soft herbs, all leafy greens, asparagus, tomatoes, sardines, pickles and chilli jam

- -

Storage	Keep cottage cheese in the container it comes in and close the lid properly. If stored like this, opened cottage cheese will keep for about 1 week. You can also freeze unopened cottage cheese for up to 3 months.

Some ideas for using the rest of the cottage cheese tub

✱ Use it as the base of a dip. Blend with herbs of your choice or seeded cucumber or a ripe avocado, and plenty of salt and pepper and a squeeze of lemon juice.

✱ Make a less rich version of Alex's Tartare Sauce (p 94) by replacing the cream cheese with cottage cheese.

✱ Add a little milk to cottage cheese until it has a runny consistency and use in place of buttermilk in baking and pancakes.

✱ Mix it with grated mozzarella to top a pizza or use in a lasagne.

✱ Use as a condiment on baked potatoes.

✱ Spread on rye crackers and top with pickled cucumber.

Whatever-cheese eggy muffins

MAKES 12

These muffins are incredibly easy to make, and are a great quick breakfast or lunchbox snack. You can use whatever cheeses you have on hand, and add ham, chives, chilli or olives, or whatever needs using up.

Preheat the oven to 170°C (325°F). In a medium–large bowl mix 1 cup (265 g) cottage cheese or strained ricotta, 4 eggs, 1 cup (150 g) plain (all-purpose) flour, 1 tsp baking powder, ½ tsp salt, 100 g (3½ oz) of a little something extra you might have – chopped ham, chopped olives, grated and squeezed-out zucchini (courgette), tomato, a little sautéed leek, pickled chillies, it's up to you – and ½ cup (50 g) grated cheddar (or mozzarella or parmesan, or a mix). Butter or oil a 12-hole muffin tin and fill each hole halfway. Bake for 15–20 minutes, until a knife in the centre comes out clean.

CREAM CHEESE

We both have a taste for cream cheese, and find bagels nearly unimaginable without it. Cream cheese most often comes in a block or tub, and its mild flavour means it can be used in sweet or savoury cooking. Even a spoonful can add richness to sauces, and it can also be stirred through cooked grains or polenta.

Goes with   Bagels and pickles, of course. And asparagus, carrots, celery, tomatoes, chilli, capers, chives, dill, raw onions, garlic, sugar, honey, lemons, strawberries, apples, apricots, cumquats, figs, bananas, barley, chocolate.

Storage   Unopened cream cheese will last 1–2 days after its use-by date – take a whiff and decide. If in any doubt, discard. Opened cream cheese will last about 1 week in the fridge if you keep the lid on tight.

Some ideas for using up cream cheese

* Add a generous amount of cream cheese to pork meatballs and you've made a hack Swedish meatball.
* Stuff jalapenos and pop them on a baking tray under the grill (broiler) until charred.
* Add 2–3 tbsp to eggs before scrambling.
* Use in the Odd-knobs Mac 'n' Cheese (p 101).
* Try the Savoury Poppy Seed Spread (p 406), which uses ½ cup (120 g).
* ***Cream cheese icing*** Turn the Seedy Breakfast Muffins (p 371) into afternoon tea with this frosting. With a fork, whisk about 125 g (4½ oz) cream cheese with 2 tbsp icing (confectioners') sugar and a drop of vanilla extract or lots of lemon zest and juice until smooth and creamy.

Alex's tartare sauce
MAKES ABOUT 1 CUP (250 ML)

This is a given for home-made fish and chips and fishcakes (p 165), but it's equally good with roast potatoes or with celery stalks for dipping.

In a food processor, place ½ cup (120 g) cream cheese, 2 tbsp finely chopped dill, 2 tbsp snipped chives, 2 tbsp drained and chopped capers or pickles plus 2 tbsp of the brine, a slug of olive oil, a squeeze of lemon juice and a pinch of pepper or cayenne pepper. Whiz until smooth. You could also do this by hand if you can't be bothered getting the food processor out. Add a little water if it needs loosening.

FETA

Crumbly and as salty as an olive. Pair feta with the mildest of ingredients, like tomatoes, watermelon or cucumber, and it's seasoning enough. Try to buy only a small amount at a time to avoid waste. If you have some extra lying around, consider yourself lucky.

Goes with	Rosemary, basil, coriander (cilantro), dill, mint, oregano, capers, chilli, nutmeg, lemons, olive oil, honey, barley, berries, apples, apricots, figs, melons, pumpkin (squash), potatoes, zucchini (courgettes), green beans, capsicum (pepper), cucumber, tomatoes, eggplant (aubergine), pistachio nuts, lamb, ham

----

Storage	Because of its high salt content, feta has a long shelf life. To make it last even longer, make a brine with 1 cup (250 ml) water and 1 tsp salt, pour the brine into an airtight container and sit the feta in it. The feta should keep fresh for 2 weeks if you change the brine every 3–4 days.

Some ideas for a little left-over feta

* Like ricotta, feta is great in Tasty Meatballs (p 54) and fritters. Crumble it and mix it through.
* Using a fork, mix a little knob of feta with finely chopped olives and a slug of olive oil to make a quick spread for bread. Top with sliced tomato and pepper.
* Scatter a little feta and plenty of ground pepper over roast potatoes in the last 10 minutes of cooking.
* Grill zucchini (courgettes) and crumble the last of the feta on top with lots of torn mint or parsley and a squeeze of lemon juice. Serve as a side dish.
* It will go beautifully in most salads, including lentil and chickpea ones. Try crumbling it into Apricot, Rocket (Arugula) and Pepita Salad (p 11).

Whipped feta

MAKES ABOUT 1⅓ CUPS (330 ML)

Got a lump of feta and want to do something to make the very most of it? Try this whipped feta. Serve it with grilled (broiled) meat or vegetable skewers, warmed flat breads and chopped cucumbers, or spread it on pizza with Grilled Zucchini (p 497) and chilli flakes.

In a blender or food processor, combine about 125 g (4½ oz) feta, 1 tbsp sour cream or cottage cheese or even cream cheese, 1 tsp lemon juice, 1 tsp honey, a pinch each of salt and pepper and ¼ cup (60 ml) water. Blend until the texture is like soft cream cheese. Keep any leftovers in an airtight container in the fridge for a week.

MOZZARELLA

Mozzarella is a classic family favourite. A semi-hard cheese that's rindless and milky, it can come in a pale yellow ball, grated in a plastic bag, or fresh and swimming in brine. It's the stretchy cheese most of us use for home-made pizzas, but melty mozzarella has more to give.

Goes with	Tomatoes, eggplant (aubergine), roasted capsicum (pepper), zucchini (courgettes), spinach, red onions, mushrooms, basil, rosemary, thyme, cured meats, apples, apricots, figs, peaches, melons, citrus fruits, berries, black grapes, olives, olive oil, vinegar

------

Storage	Firmer-style mozzarella cheeses can be stored in an airtight container in the fridge for 1 week. The fresh stuff in brine will be good for up to 4 days if you change the water, adding a pinch of salt, every day.

Some ideas for using forgotten lumps of mozzarella

* Stuff the Old-school Garlic Bread (p 52) with grated mozzarella.
* Scatter grated mozzarella over roast vegetables, such as eggplant (aubergine), tomato or zucchini (courgettes), towards the end of cooking, so that when the roasting tin comes out of the oven the cheese is melting over the rich roasted veg.
* Mozzarella makes a gooey molten mess of a quesadilla, and that's exactly how it's meant to be. Grate whatever mozzarella you have and scatter a small handful over a tortilla. Sprinkle

a pinch each of paprika and dried oregano over the cheese and place another tortilla on top. Place the tortillas in a dry frying pan over medium heat and cook for 1½ minutes each side. The tortillas will crisp up and the mozzarella will be oozing. Cut into wedges and serve.

Fried mozzarella sticks
SERVES 3–4 AS A SIDE

Another crumb-a-thon.

Cut 250 g (4½ oz) mozzarella into batons. If you have a ball of mozzarella, cut it in half, and then into thick slices, then cut these into batons. If you have a block of mozzarella, this will be easier. Crumb each mozzarella stick, using the Breadcrumb Mix on p 51 and the crumbing how-to on the same page, then chill in the fridge for at least 20 minutes.

When ready to get dinner on the table, heat 1 cup (250 ml) of a frying oil, such as rice bran or peanut, in a deep-sided, heavy-based saucepan. When the oil is hot, use tongs to carefully lower in a few mozzarella sticks. Fry for 1 minute, turning often, until golden all over. Remove and drain on paper towel.

Serve warm with tomato sauce, pesto or chilli sauce. See p 83 for tips on reusing the frying oil.

'Clear out the fridge' pizza

When there's just a little bit of this and a scraping of that left in the fridge, making pizza is a great way to use it all up. If we're going to get all authentic and historical here, a true Neapolitan margarita pizza is *not* loaded with mozzarella. It's topped, in fact, with a sprinkling of the tastiest tomatoes, fresh basil and a baby's breath of mozzarella. Somewhere along the way, when pizza left Italy, it turned into some kind of open sandwich, heavy with toppings and oozing cheese.

Have a light touch with your pizza and use up really flavoursome ingredients that can be applied sparingly. This means that if you only have a little bit of mozzarella (or any cheese really) it will be enough for pizza.

To begin, choose your pizza base. Feel free to make your own, but there are plenty of good store-bought options, and pitta bread also works well. Drizzle the base with olive oil, then spread lightly with some tomato paste or left-over pesto or harissa paste.

Now poke around the fridge for toppings: the last anchovies, a few olives (dice them finely if there are only three left), Blistered Marinated Capsicum (p 74), Garlicky Marinated Eggplant (p 144), Home-made Bacon Bits (p 23), Sautéed Leek Tops (p 237) – you get the idea.

Finally, assess the cheese situation. Grate or slice what you have and spread it around. Finish with another drizzle of olive oil, and salt and pepper, some chilli flakes or dried or fresh herbs. **»**

Heat the oven to hot, hot, hot (230°C/450°F or more), then pop in the pizza. The time it takes to cook will depend on the thickness of the base and whether it's uncooked dough or, say, pitta bread. The pizza is done when the cheese has melted and the base is cooked through.

PARMESAN

Parmesan is so sharp and flavoursome that we often use it like a seasoning. A little goes a long way. Italian cooks add the rind or dried-out chunks to soups and stews, fish it out when the cooking is done, dry it off and keep it for another day. Take your cue from their resourcefulness and use every last bit of parmesan, even if it's a dry old piece of leather hiding in the depths of the fridge.

Goes with	Tomatoes, mushrooms, broccoli, kale, spinach, zucchini (courgettes), eggplant (aubergine), fennel, green beans, dried beans, rocket (arugula), basil, rosemary, parsley, chilli, blueberries, figs, grapes, apples, pears, apricots, peaches, nuts, olive oil, garlic, bread, potatoes, pasta

----

Storage	Wrap parmesan in a beeswax wrap or baking paper and keep in an airtight container in the fridge for 1–2 months. If it does dry out, wrap it in a clean damp muslin cloth or clean Chux, then pop in an airtight container in the fridge. Leave overnight and the next day it should be looking alive again.

Some ideas for using up every last bit of parmesan

* Treat a hardened bit of parmesan as you would the rind and add to slow-cooked dishes for extra flavour, particularly tomatoey soups, lentil stews (p 246) or Mushroom Ragu (p 279).
* Grate and add to Breadcrumbs (p 51), then use to crumb meat or vegetables. Cheesy breadcrumbs freeze well, and are good to have on hand for quick crumbing.
* If you have a tiny bit left over, make a very quick cheesy garlic bread to serve with soup. Cut 1–2 slices of bread and rub a cut garlic clove all over the surface. Grate the small bit of parmesan you have evenly over the bread and drizzle with olive oil. Toast under the grill (broiler) for a few minutes, until the parmesan is golden and the bread nicely done. Or add to the Old-school Garlic Bread recipe (p 52).
* Thinly slice and add to salads for bite.

----

* Shave over hot vegetables and let the flavour seep in. See Garlicky, Cheesy Roasted Green Beans (p 39).
* Grate into soups for added umami.

Parmesan rind stock
MAKES ABOUT 4 CUPS (1 LITRE)

If you've saved a few parmesan rinds, and honestly, what are you doing with your life if you haven't, then make this super-flavoured stock. Use it for risotto, minestrone (p 36) or to braise vegetables (p 159).

Preheat the oven to 200 (400°F). In a small roasting tin, place 2 halved unpeeled brown onions, a few unpeeled garlic cloves and 2 halved tomatoes, then sprinkle with salt and add a good slug of olive oil. Roast for 30–40 minutes, until everything is collapsing. Make sure the garlic doesn't burn – if it does you'll have to discard it, as burnt garlic has a habit of ruining everything. Transfer all the vegetables to a medium–large saucepan and add 3–4 parmesan rinds, some bay leaves and peppercorns. Cover with 4 cups (1 litre) water and bring to a simmer over medium heat. Reduce the heat to low and simmer for 30 minutes. Strain and add ¾–1 tsp salt. Use the stock straight away or store in the fridge for 1 week or the freezer for up to 3 months.

RICOTTA
Fresh and creamy ricotta brings richness without being heavy. It's easy to buy too much (or you can only find it in 2 kg/4 lb 8 oz baskets). As it has a short lifespan, we sneak it into everything.

Goes with	Soft herbs (like parsley, dill, mint) and buttery leaves (like lettuce), beetroot, zucchini (courgettes), tomatoes, eggplant (aubergine), nuts, eggs, apples, cumquats, figs, berries, stone fruits, rhubarb, barley, honey, jam, nutmeg, olives, olive oil

---

Storage	Store ricotta in an airtight container in the fridge for 2–4 days. If it's just starting to turn, cook it.

Some ideas for using up ricotta

* Add to cakes and muffins, or any baking. A few tbsp won't disrupt the recipe. Use ricotta in Jaimee's Apple Bake (p 7) instead of sour cream.
* Add a little to Tasty Meatballs (p 54). You'll use less meat and they'll stay moist.
* If asparagus is around, make an elegant salad of steamed asparagus with little ricotta dollops on top. Add a drizzle of your best olive oil and season with plenty of ground pepper and salt.
* Make a toastie that's lighter on the digestion. Or make a two-cheese toastie with ricotta, cheddar and plenty of pickles.
* Thin it with a little water, whisk in a pinch of sugar and use it a bit like single (pure) cream, pouring it over fruit or crepes.
* Fold olives, herbs, salt and finely chopped garlic through 1–2 cups (230–460 g) ricotta. Pour into a small ovenproof dish or ramekin and bake at 200°C (400°F) until golden. The cooking will make it last for a few more days in the fridge. Serve on toast with tomatoes, add to a cheese board, or put dollops through a salad or on top of home-made pizza.
* Make donuts using the Yoghurt Donuts recipe (p 492), replacing the yoghurt with ricotta.

Ricotta salata
MAKES 1 SMALL BALL OF CHEESE

Ricotta salata is salted and dried ricotta cheese that you can use much like parmesan. Making your own ricotta salata turns a little left-over ricotta into an intensely flavoured seasoning to grate over all your pasta needs.

Take ½ cup (115 g) ricotta, place it in a fine mesh sieve and leave for 20 minutes to drain off any excess moisture. Spread ¼ cup (75 g) pure salt (i.e. with no additives) on a plate. Form the ricotta into a ball and roll in the salt to cover all over in a thin layer. Spread a clean square of muslin or a clean Chux on the benchtop and place the ricotta in the centre. Wrap well, place in an airtight container and leave at room temperature for 3–4 days.

Re-salt and rewrap the ricotta every 3–4 days, doing this about 4 times, until it has hardened. Brush off the excess salt, wrap in clean muslin or a clean Chux and store in the fridge for up to 1 month. Grate over pasta or soups as you would parmesan.

ALL THE ODD KNOBS
So you've got a bit of this cheese and a bit of that cheese and it's all quite annoying. Gather them together and make a cheese medley.

Odd-knobs mac 'n' cheese
SERVES 4

This recipe is very forgiving. Make the sauce using whatever cheese is around, and use up all the nearly finished packets of pasta and even replace some of it with cauliflower or broccoli.

You'll need about 1½ cups of cheese for the cheese sauce, plus more for grating on top. You can use up whatever is around: brie and blue, cheddar and mozzarella, a bit of ricotta, parmesan and feta – seriously, whatever. Grate it, crumble it, tear it.

Preheat the oven to 180°C (350°F). Boil 250 g (9 oz) of any short pasta in salted water and drain. In a small saucepan, heat 2 cups (500 ml) milk to just below boiling point. In another saucepan, melt 60 g (2 oz) butter over low heat and stir in 2 tbsp plain (all-purpose) flour until combined and bubbling. This is a roux. When it's bubbling, slowly add the warmed milk, ½ cup (125 ml) at a time, stirring constantly with a wooden spoon or whisk until you have a thick sauce. Add your odds and ends of cheese, salt and pepper, and stir until melted and smooth.

Put your drained pasta in a mixing bowl with an optional ½–1 cup cooked vegetables, such as cauliflower, broccoli or peas and/or pieces of bacon. Pour the sauce over and stir to coat everything. Transfer to an ovenproof dish, grate more cheese on top and bake for 15–20 minutes.

Odd-knobs potted cheese
MAKES 300 G (10½ OZ)

This very British recipe is the most brilliant way to use up the odd knobs of cheese. Serve it with crackers or crusty bread, or with raisin toast for breakfast.

In a food processor, combine 250 g (9 oz) grated or chopped cheese with 90 g (3¼ oz) butter, and blitz to a paste. Add 2 tbsp sherry, port, marsala or even whisky, 1 tsp hot English or dijon mustard and ¼ tsp cayenne pepper. Blitz again until well combined and smooth.

Press the mixture into a ramekin or wide-mouthed jar. Over very low heat, melt 2 tbsp butter in a saucepan. Allow the butter to separate. With a spoon, carefully remove and discard the little white clumps that float to the surface. Pour the golden clarified butter on top of the potted cheese, leaving the milk solids in the bottom of the pan. Cover the ramekin with a beeswax wrap or baking paper and refrigerate for 2 days before eating the potted cheese. It will then last for 2 weeks in the fridge.

See cream, milk, sour cream, whey and yoghurt for ideas with other dairy products.

Cherries

Cherries are the fanciest fruit on the table. They are special and short-lived, so we should be eating them by the fistful when they're in season. For Australians like us, cherries taste like Christmas. Sweet and tart, a bit peppery, a little boozy, cherries lend themselves to being roasted, pickled and stewed for crumbles and pies. And did you know that the stems can even be made into a wholesome tea?

Go with   Chocolate, coffee, honey, coconut, almonds, pistachios, peaches, bananas, rhubarb, watermelon, tomatoes, cinnamon, cloves, poppy seeds, chilli, ham, pork, dark spirits (e.g. rum, whisky, brandy)

Storage   Cherries are best stored unwashed, uncovered and dry, in the coldest part of the fridge. Wash them well just before serving. If you see a damaged one in the bag, remove it straight away to avoid the decay spreading to the other fruits. Cherries will last less than 1 week in the fridge, so buy smaller amounts to eat fresh or buy a box when they're at the height of the season, then pit them and freeze or bottle them, or turn them into jam, to enjoy all year round.

Substitutes   Cherries are stone fruit, so can be swapped with plums, peaches, nectarines and apricots in most recipes. For colour you could use red grapes or raspberries, and for savoury dishes try pomegranate seeds or dried cranberries.

Some ideas for getting to the bottom of the cherry bag

If you have a cup or two of left-over cherries, or a few handfuls of rejected browning squishy ones at the bottom of the bag, then give these ideas a go:

* ***Cherry jam*** Home-made cherry jam is a real treat. Alex makes a jar or two each season and hides them at the back of the fridge so no one else can eat them. Use the Foolproof Jam recipe (p 389).

* ***Quick cherry sauce made with squishy cherries*** Warm a small frying pan over low heat and throw in a few handfuls of mushy pitted cherries, a knob of butter, a little honey or sugar and a splash of water or orange juice. Simmer until the cherries form a chunky sauce. Taste, adding a little more sweetness if needed. Allow to cool, then serve on Greek-style yoghurt, muesli or ice cream.
* ***Cherry rum*** Cherries and rum are like naughty peaches and cream. Infuse dark spirits with any overripe cherries, a few peppercorns and a vanilla bean or 1 tbsp coffee beans. Follow the method for Cumquat Brandy (p 132) and then enjoy during the depths of winter when you need a little reminder of summer. Add to champagne cocktails or drizzle over ice cream.

Roasted cherries

Make roasted fruits part of your weekly repertoire. It's one of our most popular techniques to revive average-tasting fruit in the fruit bowl, withering grapes at the back of the fridge or wrinkly apricots you forgot to eat. Roasting fruit hides all its imperfections and intensifies its flavour; we like to add a splash of vinegar and some spices to make it tangy, sweet and salty. Roasted fruits can be added to salads, tossed through grains like rice, barley and couscous, served with grilled (broiled) meats or on a cheese board, or added to a cheese toastie when you're showing off.

Preheat the oven to 180°C (350°F). Throw pitted cherries into a small baking tray and add a drizzle of olive oil, a generous pinch each of salt and pepper and a splash of red wine vinegar. Sprinkle with sugar and add a scattering of fennel seeds or chilli flakes if you have them. Roast for 15–20 minutes, until the cherries are oozy, saucy and delicious. Allow to cool and eat right away, or store in an airtight container in the fridge for up to 1 week.

Cherry filling for pies, crumbles and crepes

If you bought a box of cherries at the height of the season and didn't get through them, make this moreish pie filling. If you don't have 2 kg (4 lb 8 oz) cherries, make up the shortfall with chopped apples, peaches or berries. This filling freezes very well; just remember to strain it before adding it to a pie so your pastry doesn't get soggy. You can also bottle and heat-process it (p 502) so you can have cherry pie all year round. Follow the method for Apple Pie Filling (p 8), cutting the cherries in half and removing the stones. Save the stones for Cherry Stone Vinegar, over the page.

CHERRY STEMS AND STONES

Cherry stem tea

Cherry stems are full of flavour and are said to have detoxifying properties. Steep dried cherry stems in boiling water for a gentle anti-inflammatory tea. Be aware that some sources recommend that pregnant women avoid this tea.

Spread cherry stems on a baking tray and dry for a few days in a sunny, airy place in the kitchen or pop into a 120–140°C (235–275°F) oven for 20 minutes or until completely dry. Store in a jar or airtight container. To make tea, add 2–3 tbsp cherry stems to a small pot of boiling water and simmer for 5 minutes, then remove from the heat and leave to infuse for 5 minutes. Strain and add a little honey or sugar and a squeeze of lemon juice.

Cherry stone vinegar

Place the stones in a clean jar and cover with red wine vinegar or apple cider vinegar. Seal and leave to sit on the bench for 1–2 weeks. Taste for cherry flavour and strain when the vinegar is nicely infused with it. Store in the fridge and use as a dressing for tomato or beetroot salads. It will keep for ages.

See apricots, peaches and plums for ideas with other stone fruit.

Chicken

You know it's going to be a good day when you wake up and there's left-over chicken in the fridge. Lunches can be made in a jiffy, and dinner has basically cooked itself. The following ideas come from ten years' worth of text messages between us, each one showing off yet another meal that can be made from a handful of shredded chicken.

Storage   Shred left-over cooked chicken and store in a sealed container in the fridge for 3–4 days. Treat it like gold – do not let a single bit go to waste.

Some ideas for enjoying precious left-over chicken

* Fried rice is often on our menu the day after a roast chicken. Add it with the rice in the Green Eggy Fried Rice (p 57).
* Add shredded chicken to Congee (p 394). Heat a little oil in a frying pan, flash-fry the chicken with a pinch of salt, and pile it onto a warm bowl of congee.
* Mix shredded chicken with something creamy, like mayonnaise or a soft cheese, lots of chopped herbs and something salty like chopped capers, pickles or olives. Season with salt (if needed) and pepper, then spread on bread for lunch.
* ***Tasty two-minute soup*** Heat 1 cup (250 ml) broth or stock, then throw in a handful of shredded chicken and the kernels from 1 corn cob. It's two-minute soup without all the bullshit.

Some ideas for shredded chicken in salads

* The Cold Noodle and Wombok Salad With Pickles (p 487) can be made with left-over shredded chicken. Heat the chicken through in a hot wok before adding to the noodles.
* Left-over chicken in the fridge and stale bread on the counter mean caesar salad is on the menu. Crunchy lettuce, shredded chicken, Croutons (p 51) and soft-boiled eggs with Cheat's Caesar Salad Dressing (p 4) make for a simple dinner with no waste.
* Toss left-over shredded chicken through a grain salad for some added protein. Try the Big Grain Salad (p 379) or the Best Barley Side (p 29).

Spiced chicken

Shred any left-over chicken and pan-fry it with a little oil over medium heat. Add some salt, 1–2 finely chopped garlic cloves and plenty of spices. We especially recommend our spice mix 4 (p 420). Once hot, crispy and well seasoned, transfer to a bowl and serve in tacos with beans, in a wrap with salad, on jacket potatoes, or with Cheat's Paella (p 395). Or change the flavour by adding chilli flakes and some finely grated fresh ginger, then serve in rice paper rolls or San Choy Bow (p 250).

Left-over-chicken soup

SERVES 3–4

A roast chicken truly is a great meal. We love making it for our family and pals, but while everyone is enjoying their drumsticks and roast potatoes, we're already scheming about tomorrow night's dinner, which we secretly love even more than the main event. This soup uses the carcass to make a small pot of stock, and any left-over meat can go in with whatever veg is in the fridge. (And don't forget to check out the Chicken and Avocado Soup recipe on p 19.)

After your roast dinner, strip all the left-over meat off the carcass and store in a container in the fridge. In a separate container put the carcass, all the bones and the scraps from everyone's plates. Seriously, relax about this, there's going to be a lot of boiling water and cooking going on. You can store these for up to 3 days in the fridge, so plan this meal for that window.

Pop all the scraps and bones and carcass snugly into a small stockpot, then look in the fridge to see what else needs using up. Now would be a good time to put in any or all of the following: the wrinkled half-tomato that's been hanging around, a few dry old mushrooms, the celery heart you've been saving for this very moment, a bendy carrot, and some parsley stems or the tops of a leek. If there are no vegetables in the fridge, please include a brown onion chopped in half with the skin on, as it gives the stock a lovely colour, a few bay leaves and a sprinkling of peppercorns. Add water to just cover; don't drown out the flavour. Bring to a simmer over medium heat, then reduce the heat to low (never boiling, just a gentle bubbling below the surface) and cook for at least 1 hour. The longer you cook it, the more intense the flavour.

Strain, saving the vegetables and any meaty chicken scraps to feed to your dog. Add ½–1 tsp salt to the stock and use right away or store in the fridge for up to 1 week.

Once your pot is wiped clean, heat 1 tbsp olive oil and sauté 1 small finely diced onion until translucent. Add 3 chopped garlic cloves and sauté for about 30 seconds. Add 2 cups diced vegetables – celery, carrot, potato, cauliflower, zucchini (courgettes), peas, corn, really whatever you have. You'll need to think about how long each vegetable takes to cook, so potatoes now and peas later. Sauté any root vegetables with the onion and garlic for a few minutes, then add your stock. Simmer until everything is tender, adding any softer vegies closer to the end. Add your left-over shredded chicken to warm through, and cooked noodles or rice if you'd like. Taste and then decide on which umami hit you want.

Some chicken soup flavour ideas: Soy sauce and a little fish sauce / Lemon juice and a little tomato paste / 1 tbsp miso paste.

Chickpeas

Chickpeas have a mealy, hearty flavour that suits so many different styles of cooking. As with beans, buying dried is best, as there is less packaging and they'll always taste better. Having said that, a tin of chickpeas in the cupboard is a lifesaver at the best and worst of times, so make sure there's always an emergency tin or two on hand.

Go with	All the herbs (especially coriander/cilantro, mint, parsley, bay leaves, rosemary and thyme), nuts, fennel, silverbeet (Swiss chard), spinach, sweet potato, tomatoes, eggplant (aubergine), chilli, garlic, preserved lemon, tahini, eggs, yoghurt, pasta, coconut milk, coriander seeds, cumin, fennel seeds, paprika, curry powder, ginger, cayenne pepper
Storage	Store unopened tins of chickpeas forever; dried chickpeas in an airtight container will also keep indefinitely if kept free from moisture. Drain left-over tinned chickpeas and store in an airtight container for 3–4 days. Store soaked and cooked chickpeas the same way.
Substitutes	White beans and green peas have a similar texture and flavour to chickpeas. Brown lentils will work for most recipes.
How to soak and cook dried chickpeas	Dried chickpeas will generally more than double in volume once soaked and cooked, so 1 cup (200 g) dried chickpeas will become a generous 2 cups (430 g) cooked. Cover dried chickpeas generously with water and leave to soak overnight. Drain off the soaking water and transfer to a saucepan, cover with water, bring to the boil, then reduce the heat and simmer for 45 minutes to 1 hour, until tender.

Some ideas for using that half-cup or tin of chickpeas

* Add to roast vegetables. Put in a bowl with a drizzle of oil, finely chopped garlic, salt and spices, then add them to the roasting tin for the last 10 minutes of cooking.
* Add to minestrone (p 36) instead of pasta.
* Toss with a green sauce like Chimichurri (p 193) or pesto (p 191) and squash onto a salad roll, or serve them on top of Jacket Sweet Potatoes (p 450) with crumbled feta.
* Add a handful to 1 diced tomato and 1 diced cucumber, then dress with vinegar, salt, olive oil and a little finely chopped garlic.
* Add a small amount to a blended soup for dairy-free creaminess. Try Green Soup (p 440) or a tomato soup (p 463).
* Make a quick and affordable curry with 400–800 g (14 oz – 1 lb 12 oz) tinned chickpeas by using the Really Easy Green Bean Curry recipe (p 40).

'No food processor? No worries' mashed hummus

MAKES ABOUT 1 CUP (165 G)

This hummus makes the most of a small amount of chickpeas.

Tip ½ cup (80 g) tinned or cooked chickpeas into a small bowl, add 1 tbsp boiling water and a drizzle of olive oil, then mash with a fork until the chickpeas are broken down and the water has been absorbed. Cooked chickpeas may need a little more water than tinned. Add 1½ tbsp tahini, a really big squeeze of lemon juice, 1 small finely chopped garlic clove and a four-finger pinch of salt. Mash it all together – don't worry, it will be a bit chunky. Season with more lemon and salt if it needs it. Pop into a small airtight container, pack some carrot sticks and head off to work.

Oven-roasted chickpeas

You forgot to buy a little snack to have with wine? Worry not. If you have a tin of chickpeas, even half a tin, make these to serve with a drink. They also add great texture to salads, so scatter them liberally. Try this recipe with white beans too.

Preheat the oven to 220°C (425°F). Thoroughly dry chickpeas by spreading them on paper towel or a clean tea towel (dish towel) and patting dry. If they're damp they won't crisp up, so walk away for 10 minutes if you're not sure they're super-dry enough. Then spread them in an ovenproof dish and give them a good drizzle of olive oil, making sure each chickpea is nicely coated, and a very generous pinch of salt. We like adding smoked paprika, but chilli, lemon zest and rosemary all work too. Roast for 20 minutes, shaking the pan often, until crispy.

Simple chickpea stew

SERVES 4-6

This is a staple meal in both our households when we can't think of what to cook. It's nutritious, hearty and simple, and we'll be teaching it to the children before they move out. Serve with other dishes like grilled (broiled) meats, or on its own with rice, couscous or polenta. Like most stews, this gets better the next day or the day after that, so make it on a good day so it's there to eat when you're too tired to cook.

Heat ¼ cup (60 ml) olive oil in a frying pan over medium–low heat and sauté 1 thinly sliced onion and 1 thinly sliced capsicum (pepper) or small fennel bulb with a big pinch of salt until soft and sweet, at least 15 minutes. Add 4 sliced garlic cloves and sauté gently for another 10–12 minutes. Add 1 tsp each of ground cumin and paprika, mixing well, then add 2 cups (500 g) drained tinned chickpeas or a scant 1 cup (200 g) dried chickpeas, soaked and cooked to make a generous 2 cups (500 g) cooked chickpeas. Stir in 400 g (14 oz) tinned chopped tomatoes or 2–3 chopped fresh tomatoes, chilli flakes and plenty of black pepper. Add 1 cup (250 ml) stock or water, cover and cook over low heat for 30 minutes, then remove the lid and continue cooking until thick and glossy. If you want to turn it into a one-pot meal, add a big handful of sliced green beans or English spinach to the pot for the last 5 minutes of cooking.

To bulk it out, add torn pieces of stale bread or Tasty Meatballs (p 54), or plenty of spinach or kale and a big squeeze of lemon juice.

Nothing's in the cupboard but chickpeas and pasta

SERVES 4

You only have a tin of chickpeas and half a packet of pasta? Don't stress – you almost have dinner sorted. Essentially, this sauce is made by braising the chickpeas until they become a comforting broth-like creation that coats every strand of pasta. Its genius is its simplicity. If you want to add something more, throw in a big handful of baby spinach or some charred broccoli or Home-made Bacon Bits (p 23) for the last few minutes of cooking.

Bring a large pot of salted water to the boil and cook 300 g (10½ oz) pasta according to the packet directions. Drain and rinse 400 g (14 oz) tinned chickpeas, or rinse 1¼ cups (270 g) soaked and cooked dried chickpeas. Melt 3 tbsp butter with a splash of olive oil in another large saucepan over medium–low heat, add 3 finely chopped garlic cloves and cook until fragrant. If you have it, 2–3 tsp chopped rosemary would be nice in here too. Add the finely grated zest of 1 lemon, lots of pepper, ½ tsp salt, the chickpeas and about 1 cup (250 ml) stock or pasta water, along with a good splash or 1 tbsp of something savoury – miso paste, white wine and lemon juice, stock paste (p 447), or even a little Vegemite. Simmer for about 10 minutes. Grate some parmesan into the broth for more flavour. Taste to make sure it's delicious.

Drain the pasta, reserving a little pasta water, add to chickpeas and stir well to combine. Add plenty more parmesan and cook for another 1–2 minutes. Season with salt and pepper, another drizzle of olive oil and a squeeze of lemon juice.

Vegie burgers

MAKES 4

A go-to vegie burger recipe is essential, whether you're vegetarian or not, because *someone* is always vegetarian, we all need to reduce our meat consumption, *and* burgers are one of the best meals ever invented.

In a food processor, place 400 g (14 oz) drained tinned chickpeas (or beans) or 1¼ cups (270 g) cooked chickpeas, ½ large or 1 small brown onion, ½ cup (60 g) fresh Breadcrumbs (p 51), 1 egg, 2 finely chopped garlic cloves, ½ tsp each of salt and pepper and 1 tbsp worcestershire sauce. Pulse briefly to combine, but don't let it turn into a paste. At this stage we usually pull the mixture out and do the rest by hand so as not to over-process it, but take it slow and you can do the whole thing in the food processor if you like. Add 1 bunch of parsley, coriander (cilantro), dill or even rocket (arugula) leaves. Mix so everything is evenly combined. Divide the mixture into 4, shape into patties and lay them on a plate. Chill in the fridge for at least 30 minutes to make them easier to cook. Heat 1 tbsp neutral oil in a frying pan and fry the patties for 4 minutes on each side. Serve as you would any burger, on buns with all the salad veg, sauces and pickles, and hot chips (fries) on the side.

Aquafaba

Aquafaba is the liquid in a tin of chickpeas (it's important to note that the liquid in a tin of red kidney beans, for example, is *not* aquafaba). This really is an incredible product, but until recently was seen as waste. It can be used as an egg replacement – generally 3 tbsp aquafaba for 1 egg. Many plant-based cooks are using aquafaba to make mayonnaise, 'butter', meringue and much more. There is a world of recipes online and we suggest you start there. Aquafaba lasts about 3 days in the fridge, or you can freeze it in ice-cube trays, transfer the cubes to an airtight bag or container, and freeze for up to 3 months.

Chillies

Too many chillies? Not enough chillies? Luckily there are so many ways to eat and preserve chillies that both dilemmas can be easily addressed. Jaimee is one of those people who think eating should involve chilli-induced sweating, but she's also a firm believer that even if you think you don't like chilli, it can enhance the plainest of dishes and should therefore be taken seriously as a seasoning. Even a poached egg can be given a touch of attitude with a tiny sprinkle of chilli.

Go with

Chillies add a pinch and a punch to everything you cook. They complement all vegetables, tropical fruits, meats, seafood, tofu and tempeh. Most styles of cooking can handle some heat – it's up to you if you want a little warmth or a fire in your belly.

Storage

Chillies will keep in an airtight container in the fridge for 2–3 weeks. We recommend drying your own chillies in the oven (use the Drying Fruits method (p 357) or stringing them up and sun-drying by a window, to make the most of their short season.

Substitutes

Alex came up with a genius substitute for chillies. Finely dice a capsicum (pepper) and sprinkle it with cayenne pepper. Voilà, improvised chilli. Failing that, try to have some chilli flakes or powder on hand at all times.

Some ideas for a few chillies that need a home

✱ **Quick-pickled chillies** Always have a jar in the fridge. It'll get you through winter, when chilli prices skyrocket. Use the method in Quick-pickling (p 473), leaving out the spices – the chilli is flavourful enough. Use as you would fresh chillies.

✱ **Chilli vinegar** Bruise a few chillies, pop them in a jar and cover with 300 ml (10½ fl oz) vinegar of your choice. Leave at room temperature to infuse for a few weeks. Strain into a clean and dry airtight bottle and it will basically keep forever. Splash into stir-fries, use as the base of a salad dressing with a kick, or drizzle on sliced tomatoes. Add 5–10 drops to lemon honey tea for winter colds and chills.

✱ **Quick chilli dressing/dipping sauce** Add to instant noodles for hungry teenagers, or for when you're coming home late. It's also great on a fried egg. Slice ½ chilli (or even that chilli in the fridge that's practically dried). In a small bowl, pour 2 tbsp soy sauce, 1 tbsp sesame oil and a pinch of sugar. Add ½ crushed garlic clove and the chilli. Use immediately.

Green chilli and lime sauce
MAKES 1 CUP (250 ML)

This sauce is so vibrant and alive that it turns even plain rice into a flavour sensation. It's a must for curries, fish tacos, noodle salads or chicken skewers.

Chop 6 fresh green chillies, 3 finely chopped garlic cloves, 1 tsp salt, 1 tbsp sugar, the juice of 2 limes and 2 tbsp fish sauce (optional; if not using, you might want to add more salt). Put it all in a food processor and blend to a rough paste. Chop 1 bunch of coriander (cilantro), roots and all, add to the food processor and give one last short pulse to combine.

Chilli oil using fresh chillies
MAKES ABOUT 1 x 350 ML (12 OZ) JAR

When she's at a Chinese restaurant, Jaimee always sits next to the chilli oil, as it's by far her favourite dining companion. Motivated to know how to make her own using the abundance of chillies she grows, she applied the method used to make chilli oil from dried chillies to her fresh ones. The experiment worked, and this fiery oil can be used as a base for a dipping sauce or to cook with as you would any oil.

In a medium saucepan, pour 1½ cups (375 ml) neutral oil of your choice, such as peanut or grapeseed. Add 3 tbsp sichuan peppercorns, 4 star anise and 1 cinnamon stick. Very slowly heat the oil over low heat for 30 minutes. You want to pay close attention to the spices to ensure they're becoming gently aromatic and not burnt – you can soon smell the difference.

Place 10 chopped fresh chillies in a heatproof bowl or another saucepan and *very* carefully (we mean *super-carefully*) pour the hot oil over the sliced chilli. Allow to infuse and cool for 1–2 hours before straining into a clean and dry airtight 350 ml (12 oz) jar. Keep for 6 months in the pantry.

Fermented chilli
MAKES 1 x 200 ML (7 OZ) JAR

In a food processor or mortar, combine 1 cup (120 g) chopped red chillies, 2 chopped garlic cloves, a few slices of peeled fresh ginger, ¼ tsp each of salt and sugar, and ¼ cup (60 ml) water. Blend or pound together. Once smooth, pour into a clean, dry jar. Leave at room temperature for 3–7 days, burping your jar every second day. Once your fermented chilli tastes spicy and sour, keep it refrigerated for up to 6 months. See p 504 for more fermenting tips.

Chilli top vinegar

If you've made a dish that's a bit of a chilli blow-out and have a good handful of chilli tops left, pop them in a jar, cover with vinegar, and add a little sugar and salt. Let it sit for a few weeks, then strain. You've now made a spicy dressing vinegar from what you would otherwise have discarded.

Coconut, dried

We don't know about you, but there always seem to be a couple of bags or containers in our pantries with small amounts of desiccated or shredded coconut or coconut flakes in them. While dried coconut doesn't really go off but just gets drier, the flavour does deteriorate over time. So start using it up. If your coconut ever turns yellow and rock hard, it's probably time for the compost. If you buy coconut, make a batch of Anzac biscuits and plan a curry with a Coconut Sambol (over the page) for later in the week. Or at the same time as you're baking, make a quick batch of coconut milk. This will stop the pantry getting overloaded and ensure you're not letting good ingredients go to waste.

Goes with	Fresh and dried fruits (especially pineapple, passionfruit, melon, kiwi fruit, apricots, mango, limes, dates, bananas, cherries with chocolate), honey, nuts, oats, sesame seeds, sunflower seeds, coriander seeds, turmeric, lemongrass, chilli, curries, seafood, chicken, daikon, spinach, sweet potato, chickpeas
Storage	Dried ingredients are best stored in airtight containers or jars to keep them moisture-free, bug-free and full of flavour.
Substitutes	Nothing else tastes like coconut. Desiccated or shredded coconut works as a binding agent in baked goods, so instead use chopped or crushed nuts like almonds, Brazil nuts or pistachios. They are similarly creamy and nutty.

Some ideas for using that last bit of dried coconut

* Add to home-made muesli and granola (pp 153, 303).
* Add 1–2 tbsp to your next batch of porridge, or soak with oats for coconut bircher muesli (p 300).
* Replace the seeds in the Seedy Breakfast Muffins (p 371) with coconut.
* Add ½ cup (45 g) to your next pancake batter or to the Simple Oat Cookies on p 303.
* Next time you're crumbing something, add ½ cup (45 g) dried coconut to your Breadcrumbs (p 51). Coconut fish and coconut chicken schnitzels are amazing.

Coconut date balls

MAKES 12 CHERRY-TOMATO-SIZED SNACKS

Combine ¾ cup (65 g) desiccated coconut and ½ cup chopped dried fruit (dates, apricots, figs, sultanas) in a food processor. If you want more flavour, add ½ tsp ground cinnamon. Blitz for longer than you'd think. Tip into a bowl, then roll tablespoonfuls into logs or small balls, coating them with a little more coconut if you have it (they're also fine without). Store in an airtight container in the fridge for 2–3 weeks.

Spiced toasted coconut

Use this to top curries, grilled (broiled) vegetables and fish, or stir it through cooked rice.

Pour whatever desiccated coconut needs using up into a bowl. Drizzle with a tiny amount of oil – just enough to help the spices stick. Add a very generous pinch each of salt and cayenne pepper or chilli flakes, and a big pinch of ground cumin, coriander or paprika. Either toast over low heat in a dry frying pan on the stovetop until golden brown, stirring the whole time, or spread on a baking tray and roast in a 160°C (315°F) oven (fan off) for 5–10 minutes. Make sure you give the pan or tray a good shake halfway through cooking to ensure even browning. Allow to cool, then use right away or store in an airtight container for up to 1 week.

For a sweet version to use on desserts, muesli or porridge, replace the salt with sugar and use ground cinnamon as the only spice.

Coconut sambol

MAKES ABOUT 1½ CUPS (215 G)

Traditionally sambols are made with fresh grated coconut, but this is a simple version for using up dried coconut from the pantry. Serve with rice, curries and fried eggs.

Put up to 100 g (3½ oz) dried coconut (or whatever's left in the bag, adjusting the other ingredients if you have substantially more or less) in a bowl and add 2–3 tbsp boiling water. Mix well and leave to sit for the coconut to rehydrate (it will absorb all the water). Meanwhile, in a food processor, roughly blitz 2 chopped spring onions (scallions), discarding the little roots but using the rest (or ½ roughly chopped onion), with 1 chopped fresh green chilli or 1 tsp chilli flakes. Add the juice of 1 lime or lemon, the rehydrated coconut, a generous pinch of curry powder or spice mix 2 (p 420), and a pinch each of sugar and salt. Pulse to combine.

Store leftovers in the fridge for 3–4 days.

Coconut pantry-strays slice

This delicious slice is made even more delicious because it cleans out your pantry. A snack and a spring clean in one fell swoop. Follow the recipe on p 302, making sure to include the irritating bit of coconut that's been hiding on your top shelf.

Home-made coconut milk
MAKES 400 ML (14 FL OZ)

Home-made coconut milk is easy to make and we often whip up a batch with the last cup of dried coconut. It's a good thing to know what to do if a recipe calls for coconut milk and there's none in the house.

Put 1 cup (90 g) dried coconut in a blender, add 2 cups (500 ml) warm water and a pinch of salt, and blend on high for 1–2 minutes, until thick and creamy. Strain through muslin or a clean Chux to remove any solids. The milk can be stored in a bottle in the fridge for 3–4 days and the left-over pulp can be used for baking, to add to porridge with honey or to thicken curries.

Corn

In summer sweet corn is cheap and you can buy it by the armful. You'll get through quite a few cobs at a neighbourhood barbecue, but then there might be some leftovers. Or maybe you're just really into corn and you need some ideas on what else to do with it other than slather on the butter or make fritters. A single corn cob may look lonely, but it can actually kick off dinner.

Goes with   Butter, milk, mayonnaise, cheeses, chilli, coriander (cilantro), parsley, mint, oregano, garlic, ginger, chicken, bacon, dried beans, pepitas (pumpkin seeds), tomatoes, capsicum (pepper), avocado, zucchini (courgettes), sweet potato

Storage   Keep fresh corn cobs in their husks until ready to eat. They will keep well for a few days, but any longer and the sugar converts to starch and the cob loses flavour. A whole cooked cob will keep in an airtight container in the fridge for about 4 days. You can also remove cooked kernels from the cob and freeze in an airtight container for up to 6 months. Don't throw the cobs away though. Read on.

Substitutes   This is tricky. If you want something starchy like corn, replace it with potato, but if you're thinking of a fresher flavour or a hit of colour, try defrosted frozen peas. And of course we're not opposed to the odd bag of frozen corn.

Some ideas for using up a corn cob or two

Or 1–2 cups left-over grilled (broiled) corn or defrosted kernels – and get dinner started, for real.
* Try the Sunflower Seed and Corn Salad (p 409).
* ***Quick-pickled corn*** Pickle corn using the method on p 473, and add to cabbage and coriander (cilantro) slaw, serve with tacos, or put it on top of the Chilli Con Carne (p 36). It's also delicious on a fish burger.

* **Quick corn salsa** Cut the kernels off 1–2 cobs (or use left-over kernels) and put them in a bowl with some thinly sliced red onion, 1 finely chopped garlic clove and some chilli flakes. Sprinkle with salt, sugar, a little lime juice and a splash of rice wine vinegar. Let sit for 10 minutes to lightly pickle the corn and onion. Make the rest of your nachos and serve.
* **Quick trick for tired corn** If you didn't use up that corn in a few days and it's a bit dry and starchy, it can still come good. Remove the kernels from the cob and heat 1 tbsp butter or oil in a pan. Add the corn kernels and a good pinch each of salt and cayenne pepper, and sauté until the kernels are tender. Top with Home-made Bacon Bits (p 23). Serve on top of baked potatoes or Jacket Sweet Potatoes (p 450) with sour cream.
* **Quick corn soup** Serves 2. Pull the husks and leaves off 3 corn cobs, remove the kernels and set them aside while you make Corn Cob Stock (p 120). Meanwhile prepare the corn kernels as in the Quick Trick for Tired Corn recipe above. Once the stock is ready, strain it, return it to the pot, then add the sautéed corn kernels. You could add some left-over chicken, diced avocado or cooked noodles if you have them, and adjust the seasoning with salt and pepper.

Sweet corn polenta

SERVES 2–3

This is not really polenta at all, but you can serve it like polenta – under some sausages, or with a ragu or ratatouille. Because it has a porridge-like consistency, it's comforting and the kind of thing we serve when we eat dinner on our laps for movie night. If you're serving more people, this recipe doubles very easily.

In a medium saucepan over medium heat, melt 1 tbsp butter. Add the kernels from 3 corn cobs and stir to coat them in butter. Add ½ cup (125 ml) water, ½ cup (125 ml) milk, ½ tsp salt, and black pepper to taste. Reduce the heat to low, then cook, covered, for 20 minutes. Allow to cool slightly, then using a hand-held blender, or transferring to a food processor, blend until the corn has a porridge-like consistency. Stir in ½ cup (50 g) grated cheddar or parmesan or even crumbled feta, and serve.

Corn fritters

Just when we're saying to ourselves 'no more with the fritters', there's a bit of corn hanging around and, lo and behold, it's fritters for dinner. The thing is, everyone loves them and you can drag out all the fridge condiments and use them up too. Use the Green Things Fritters recipe (p 439), replacing the greens with 2 cups (400 g) corn kernels.

Chow chow

MAKES 3–4 x 300 ML (10 OZ) JARS

Chow chow is a Southern US–style relish. We like it because it's really tasty, obviously, but it's also one of those recipes where you can swap ingredients here and there. We've taken quite a few liberties with the method, but it's all been in the name of making the process easier and more delicious. Chow chow is served with barbecued meats, hot dogs, burgers, Fishcakes (p 165), ham and cheese sandwiches and even mashed potatoes.

Heat 2 tbsp neutral oil in a large saucepan or stockpot over medium heat, and sauté 1 diced onion and 3 diced garlic cloves until the onion is translucent. Add 1 diced green or red capsicum (pepper), 3 tsp mustard seeds, 2 tbsp mustard powder, a good pinch of turmeric, ¼ tsp cayenne pepper, 1 tsp of your favourite ground spice (cumin, allspice, ginger) and 2 tsp salt. Cook for about 3 minutes. Add 1 cup (75 g) shredded cabbage, and the kernels from 4 corn cobs, about 650 g (1 lb 7 oz). Give everything a good stir to get the flavours to mingle. Now add 1½ cups (375 ml) white wine vinegar, ½ cup (110 g) white (granulated) sugar and ½ cup (125 ml) water. Cook, uncovered, for about 20 minutes. Take out a quarter of the hot mixture, allow to cool a little, and, taking care not to scald yourself, blend it roughly, either in a food processor or using a hand-held blender. Return the blended portion to the pot and continue to cook for another 10 minutes, until the relish thickens. Keep in an airtight container or clean jar in the fridge for 1–2 months.

If you want to preserve it to store in the pantry, pack into warm sterilised jars (p 501) and heat-process (p 502) for 15 minutes. Store in the pantry for up to 12 months.

CORN COBS AND SILKS

Corn cob stock

MAKES ABOUT 4 CUPS (1 LITRE)

Once you've cut the kernels off the cobs for another recipe, turn the cobs into a simple stock, extracting as much flavour as you can before they end up in the compost.

Lightly blacken 3–4 corn cobs over a gas hob, on the barbecue or in a hot chargrill pan. Transfer the charred cobs to a large saucepan or stockpot and add 2 crushed garlic cloves, 2–3 bay leaves, some peppercorns and ½ brown onion with the skin on. Cover with 4 cups (1 litre) water and add ½ tsp salt. Bring to the boil over medium heat, then reduce the heat to low and simmer, covered, for 20 minutes. Remove from the heat and allow the flavours to develop in the pot as the stock cools. Once cool, strain and adjust the seasoning with salt and pepper. Store in the fridge for up to 5 days or in the freezer for up to 3 months.

Corn silk tea

SERVES 1

This recipe comes from our book *Use It All*, but is well worth repeating here because it's a wonderful way to use corn silks. This tea is used for bladder infections in traditional Chinese medicine. Simmer the silks from 1–2 sweetcorn cobs in 1 cup (250 ml) water for 10 minutes. Remove from the heat and strain. Add a little honey if you like and drink straight away.

Crackers

Grrr to three half-eaten packets of crackers in the cupboard. No use blaming anyone – you're stuck with them now. We found ourselves in this situation for years, which drove us to come up with some solutions. Actually, making everyone finish one packet of crackers at a time is the answer, but since that never seems to happen, these tips will come in very handy. Frustration is the mother of invention.

Go with	Just about everything
Storage	Once you've opened a packet of crackers there's only one way to keep them fresh – in a jar or plastic container with a good-fitting lid.
Substitutes	Bread

Some helpful ideas for annoying half-packets of crackers

* In a small bowl, combine crushed crackers, grated parmesan, dried oregano, ground pepper, a pinch of cayenne pepper and a few knobs of butter. Rub together with clean fingers, then scatter over potato gratins, pasta bakes or mac 'n' cheese (p 101) before putting in the oven.
* Blitz crackers to crumbs in a food processor with grated parmesan, salt and ground pepper. Use instead of breadcrumbs for schnitzels and fish fingers, or to top baked mushrooms.
* Crush or blitz them and add to meatballs, burgers or fritters instead of breadcrumbs.

Resuscitated stale crackers

Before you rush out and buy more crackers for impromptu drinks, check the pantry and see if there's any old half-packets shoved in there. We have a resuscitation technique that will make you pray for stale crackers. This works well with wafer crackers, Saladas (Saltines) and water biscuits, and Alex has even been known to fancy up an old Jatz (Ritz) when no one was looking.

This mix makes enough to resuscitate 15 or more crackers – as many as you have.

Preheat the oven to 180°C (350°F). Melt 3 tbsp butter in a small saucepan with 1 tbsp brown sugar and ½ tsp of any or all of the following – paprika, chilli flakes, dried oregano, ground cumin, garlic powder. Add lots of salt and pepper and mix well. Lay stale crackers flat on a baking tray lined with baking paper and brush the spiced butter on top. Bake for up to 10 minutes, depending on your oven. You want them to be really crisp but not burnt. Remove from the oven, allow to cool, then gobble them with a drink. You could also crunch them onto Jacket Sweet Potatoes (p 450) or a gratin.

Cream

Full dairy flavour here. Cream is very useful in the kitchen, as it gives smoothness and a rich taste to anything it's added to. Fresh cream can be splashed around willy-nilly, but cream that's smelling a bit … well, whiffy is only fit for cooking. By whiffy we mean it's just started to smell slightly sour. Luckily, cooking with verging-on-sour cream is one of our specialties.

Goes with   Potatoes, pumpkin (squash), parsnips, onions, leeks, asparagus, cabbage, cauliflower, kohlrabi, peas, spinach, silverbeet (Swiss chard), mushrooms, thyme, sage, mint, mustard, stone fruits, bananas, passionfruit, quince, berries, cinnamon, nutmeg, wattleseed, barley, oats, chocolate, coffee

Storage   Keep cream refrigerated in the container it came in. Use your nose, not just the use-by date to see if it's no good. If it's 1–2 days past the use-by date and smells okay, there's no need for panic.

Substitutes   Out of cream? Improvise by melting a little butter in a little milk and using that. Or thin out cream cheese or yoghurt with some milk and use that. There are nut 'creams' around that can easily take the place of cream in recipes, or you can blend silken tofu with water to a cream-like consistency.

Some ideas for using cream that's just past its use-by date

Any consistency of cream will work here.

* Add it to your scrambled eggs for a much more velvety texture.
* Use it in your French Toast mix (p 51) instead of milk.
* Add a splash to make any pasta sauce a little richer, especially the Mushroom Ragu (p 279).
* Drizzle into a soup for creaminess – especially Green Soup (p 440).

* ***Simple brown sugar caramel*** Over low heat, melt 2 tbsp butter and stir in ⅓ cup (60 g) brown sugar, mixing well until smooth. Once all the sugar has dissolved into the butter, incorporate 2 tbsp cream, mixing until a thick caramel forms. Add a pinch of salt and serve over puddings, ice cream or grilled (broiled) bananas.

Chocolate ganache

Use this ganache to ice cakes, pour over ice cream, dip strawberries in, or pipe onto cupcakes.

Work with a ratio of 1 part single (pure) cream to 1 part dark chocolate. Half-fill a small saucepan with water and bring to a gentle boil. Place a bowl on top (it must sit on the pan without touching the water) and add some chocolate (whatever you have in the house is fine). Melt the chocolate very slowly until glossy-looking, then take the bowl off the heat and allow to cool for a minute. Slowly add the cream, stirring vigorously until the mixture is smooth and even in colour.

It will keep for about 5 days in the fridge; return it to room temperature before using.

'There's nothing wrong with that cream!' potatoes

This recipe is usually made with fresh cream, but we've made it more times with cream that's just past its use-by date and smelling a little whiffy or sour. It's totally delicious and well worth buying potatoes for if you don't have them on hand.

Preheat the oven to 180°C (350°F). Slice 3–4 large potatoes into rounds about 5 mm (¼ in) thick and thinly slice 1 small brown or white onion. In an ovenproof dish, layer the potato and onion slices. Sprinkle with ¾ tsp salt and pour 1 cup (250 ml) cream over everything, giving the surface a good crack of black pepper. Cover with foil and bake for 30–40 minutes. Remove the foil to check if the potatoes are tender – and if so bake, uncovered, for a further 15–20 minutes.

See cheese, milk, sour cream, whey and yoghurt for ideas with other dairy products.

Cucumber

Kids are into cucumbers. We don't know why, but it's true, and so for the last fifteen years, cucumbers have been the main green thing in both our fridges. Which means we always have either not enough cucumbers or too many, in varying states of freshness. We're done now with the cucumber years, but if you're still there, here's our gift to you. These are recipes for you, not your children – just hand them a whole one with their dinner and they'll be happy.

Goes with	Mint, coriander (cilantro), dill, parsley, lemons, melons, vinegar, feta, capers, olives, olive oil, raw onions, celery, tomatoes, lettuce, garlic, chilli, ginger, cinnamon, mustard seeds, peanuts, soy sauce, sesame seeds and tahini, buckwheat
Storage	Make sure cucumbers are completely dry before storing. Wrap loosely in a clean tea towel (dish towel) and put them in a reusable plastic bag in the crisper for 7–10 days.
Substitutes	Celery is cool and fresh like cucumber and so makes a good substitute in salads and pickles. You could also consider fennel or zucchini (courgettes) or green tomatoes.

Some ideas for using a lonely half-cucumber

* **Cucumber gin** Smash rejected cucumber sticks with basil leaves into a glass. Cover with ice, gin and a splash of tonic, and go and sit outside.
* **Cucumber water** Slice ½ cucumber into rounds and put in a jug of water with lots of fresh mint. Keep in the fridge and enjoy over the next day or two. If you're planning on storing the cucumber water for a few days, remove the cucumber slices and herbs.
* **Raita or tzatziki** Cucumber and yoghurt are a perfect match, bringing cool and tang to the table. Learn how to make excellent yoghurt sauces like Raita and Tzatziki, both on p 491.

Thinly sliced cucumber salad with black pepper and basil

Cut paper-thin slices of cucumber using a mandoline or sharp knife and lay them flat on your nicest little platter. Lightly splash with some vinegar and sprinkle on some salt and a little sugar, then let it sit for 10 minutes. A little pickling brine will form and become the dressing. Crack black pepper over the top, drizzle with a little oil and scatter some basil leaves on top if you have them.

Salting cucumbers

Cucumbers have a very high water content, which makes them cooling and fresh but means they can turn to a soggy mess very quickly (although if you need to skip the salting step we promise nothing terrible will happen). Salting cucumbers is vital for pickling, but is also an excellent way to keep cucumber dishes crisp and crunchy, and revive the tired old cucumbers at the back of the fridge.

Peel or don't peel, depending on how much energy you have, the state of the peel and how fancy you are. If your cucumbers are big and old, cut them in half lengthways and scoop out the seeds. Slice into rounds, cubes or wedges. Put the cucumber in a colander, sprinkle generously with salt and let sit for 15 minutes to 1 hour to release excess liquid. Shake off any remaining liquid, pat dry with a clean tea towel (dish towel) or paper towel, and carry on adding delicious sauces, dressings or vinegar mixes.

TO TURN SALTED CUCUMBERS INTO A SALAD

- Make Russian Dressing (p 418), then toss it through your salted cucumbers with extra black pepper and lots and lots of chopped fresh dill.
- Toss salted cucumbers with chilli paste and toasted sesame seeds as a side for rice or grilled (broiled) fish.
- Make a dressing in a small jar with 1½ tbsp rice vinegar, 2 tsp soy sauce, 2 tsp sesame oil, a big pinch of sugar and some grated fresh ginger. Mix well, pour over your salted drained cucumbers and serve.
- *Simple Greek salad* Salt diced tomato and cucumber together. Drain off any excess liquid, then dress with olive oil, pepper and a splash of vinegar or lemon juice. Top with crumbled feta and chopped olives.

Cucumber pickles

After you've salted cucumber slices (see previous page), pickle them using the Basic Vegetable Pickling recipe (p 472), adding dill seeds, mustard seeds and chilli flakes to the jar or container. Store in the fridge for up to 3 months. Or to preserve, pack into sterilised jars (p 501), cover with pickling liquid, seal and heat-process (p 502) for 15 minutes. Store in the pantry for up to 2 years.

Japanese-style soy-pickled cucumber

MAKES 1 x 300–400 ML (10–14 OZ) JAR

These pickles will be delicious in a few hours and will then last for 2–3 weeks in the fridge. Try this recipe with daikon, chopped iceberg lettuce, celery or radish. Eat your pickles with rice and noodle dishes, dumplings or San Choy Bow (p 250).

Slice and salt 1–2 cucumbers (previous page) and set aside for 15 minutes or so. In a small saucepan, gently heat ¼ cup (60 ml) soy sauce or tamari, 2 tbsp rice vinegar and 1 tbsp caster (superfine) sugar. Stir to dissolve the sugar, then remove from the heat and set aside. Pat the cucumber slices dry with paper towel or a clean tea towel (dish towel) and transfer to a clean jar or container. For extra flavour you can add a few slices of fresh ginger, 1 small chopped chilli, 1 sliced garlic clove or a splash of sesame oil. Cover with the soy mixture, pushing the cucumber down under the liquid. Seal, then swish the jar around to make sure all the cucumber is lightly coated – more liquid will form over time, so don't worry if they're not all completely covered at first. Store in the fridge.

Cucumber shrub

MAKES 2 CUPS (500 ML)

A shrub is an old-fashioned soda made with fruit juice and a little vinegar. It makes a refreshing drink that's a bit more grown up than cordial. Cucumbers aren't traditional, but they're so thirst-quenching that we use them in beverage recipes all the time.

Whiz 500 g (1 lb 2 oz) chopped cucumber and 1 medium handful of mint leaves in a blender, then pass through a sieve into a small saucepan. Press the cucumber mix down to get as much liquid as possible. (You'll end up with about 1 cup/250 ml cucumber and mint pulp; set this aside to make hot sauce later; see below.) Now add ½ cup (125 ml) water and ¾ cup (165 g) caster (superfine) sugar to the saucepan. Stir over low heat until the sugar dissolves, then add 1¼ cups (310 ml) apple cider vinegar. Pour into a clean 600 ml (21 oz) bottle and store in the fridge for 1 week. To serve, pour 1½ tbsp shrub over ice and top with 200 ml (7 fl oz) sparkling water, adding a splash of gin if you'd like a cocktail.

BONUS HOT SAUCE

Never throw your cucumber and mint pulp away. In 10 minutes you can have hot sauce. Put your pulp (about 1 cup) into a small saucepan with 150 ml (5 fl oz) white wine vinegar or apple cider vinegar, 2½ tbsp sugar, ¼ tsp salt, 1 finely chopped garlic clove, 1 tsp grated fresh ginger, the zest and juice of ½ lemon or lime, and ½–1 tbsp chilli flakes. Simmer over low heat for 5 minutes. Serve with grilled (broiled) fish, rice or noodle dishes. Store in an airtight container or a jar in the fridge for 3–4 weeks.

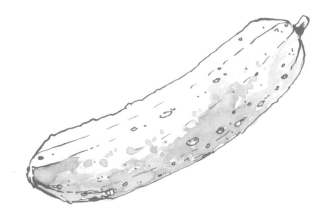

Cumquats

We're obsessed with cumquats and talk about them way too often. Cumquats are citrusy, bitter and fragrant. They're a little different from other citrus fruits – spicier and more acidic. This is because of the extremely high levels of essential oils in the skin, making them perfect for slow cooking, roasting and all types of preserving. These same essential oils are said to make them medicinal powerhouses, so if you're kitchen witches like us, get to know the cumquat and start tinkering.

Cumquat trees are often planted in gardens for ornamental purposes and then cause alarm when kilos of fruit start dropping from the branches. If you're overwhelmed by them this winter, this section will relieve your cumquat panic and hopefully encourage you to put a tree in your backyard or pick up a kilo next time you see them at the markets.

Go with
Anything that needs a sweet, acidic, bitter edge – rich meats like pork or duck, cured meats or rich oozy cheeses. They also go with other fruits (especially other citrus fruits, pineapple and berries), avocado, chocolate, tahini, warm spices (cinnamon, cloves, star anise, peppercorns, coriander seeds, cumin, allspice, juniper berries), earthy grains such as brown rice, barley and couscous, and spirits like whisky and gin.

Storage
Cumquats keep best at room temperature and will last for 1 week or more. If you need to keep them for longer, store them in the fridge in a paper bag, in a spot with a little airflow (i.e. not the crisper).

Substitutes
All citrus fruits can be swapped successfully with each other. Mandarins make a very good replacement for cumquats. Try seville oranges or grapefruits to match the bitterness.

Some ideas for using a couple of cumquats

* Score them and roast them whole in a roasting tin with wedges of onion and fennel, coating everything with plenty of olive oil, salt and pepper.

* Slice them thinly and toss them raw through winter salad greens, like spinach, rocket (arugula), endive or witlof (chicory), with parmesan and walnuts.

* Toss thinly sliced cumquats with sliced radish, then sprinkle with salt and pepper, add a splash of vinegar and serve with fatty meats, fish or cheeses.

* Slice thinly and add to a cheese board. Blue cheese and cumquat is a handsome combination.

* Squish one into your next G&T instead of a slice of lemon.

* **Cumquat bitters** Try our Grapefruit Skin Bitters recipe (p 180) with up to 2 cups (300 g) cumquats instead of grapefruit. Add to cocktails or soda water.

Dried cumquats

Slice cumquats thinly and dehydrate in the oven, following the method for Drying Mandarin Peel (p 259). They'll become crunchy and tart. Toss dried cumquat slices through salads, your next batch of muesli, cake batters or pickle jars, or add to slow-cooked meaty stews for a hit of citrusy flavour.

Sweet and sour cumquats

MAKES 1 x 400–500 ML (14–18 OZ) JAR

This is somewhere between pickling and candying, and turns cumquats into glossy jewels bursting with flavour. Thinly slice sweet and sour cumquats and toss through grain salads or pilafs; serve with any type of cheese; use in stuffings, salads or stews; add to not so sweet desserts; or pop one in a negroni.

Pour ½ cup (125 ml) vinegar into a saucepan and add ½ cup (110 g) white (granulated) sugar and ½ cup (125 ml) water with 1 tsp black peppercorns and a few star anise or cinnamon sticks. Dissolve the sugar over low heat, then bring to a simmer, add up to 2 cups (300 g) cumquats and simmer gently for about 10 minutes, until the cumquats are glossy, shiny and tender. Pack the cumquats into a clean jar or container with the spices, cover with the sweet and sour syrup, and store in the fridge for a really long time. They'll get better and better as they age. Never throw the sweet and sour syrup away – it's liquid gold. Drizzle it over meats, add to cocktails, splash over salad leaves or have a bath in it.

Cumquat brandy

MAKES ABOUT 2 CUPS (500 ML)

Add 1–2 cups split or overripe cumquats to a large jar, cover with 1½–2 cups (375–500 ml) brandy, add ⅓ cup (75 g) caster (superfine) sugar and 1 tbsp either coffee beans or black peppercorns, or a vanilla bean. Put the lid on the jar and leave at room temperature for at least 4 weeks. Swirl around once or twice during that time to dissolve the sugar. Once you're happy with the flavour, strain into a clean bottle and store in the pantry for years. Save the boozy cumquats for fruit cakes and slow-cooked meat dishes. Use the cumquat brandy to deglaze pans, or drizzle it over cakes, ice cream or sliced oranges.

Salt and sugar cumquats

MAKES 1 x 300 ML (10 OZ) JAR

You can preserve cumquats by burying them in salt or sugar, or a combination of both. Salted cumquats can be used like preserved lemons; sugared cumquats can be used in desserts, baking and cocktails. We like to do a combination of sugar and salt for the perfect balance of sweet, salty and bitter, and we use them everywhere. The next time you need to soothe a sore throat, try this traditional Chinese remedy: slice 1–2 preserved cumquats and add to 1 cup (250 ml) boiling water with 1 tsp honey.

Make incisions in the rind of 1 cup (150 g) cumquats, then put them in a small bowl. Add ½ cup (150 g) salt or sugar, or a mixture of both. Give them a sweet and salty massage to release some of the essential oils. Then pack the cumquats into a sterilised (p 501) jar, covering them with the sweet and/or salty mix. Leave at room temperature until the sugar and/or salt have dissolved. This will preserve the cumquats and they will last for years. Store in the pantry or the fridge and use as needed.

Cumquat syrup

Follow the Ginger Syrup recipe (p 176), replacing the ginger with 1 cup (150 g) chopped cumquats. Cumquat syrup can be kept for many moons and is delicious splashed into soda water and boozy drinks, over any dessert, or in sticky marinades for meats, tofu or eggplant (aubergine).

See grapefruit, lemons, limes, mandarins and oranges for ideas with other citrus. *See also* preserved lemon.

Daikon p 134 Dried fruits p 137

Daikon

Did you buy a whole daikon? Good for you, that thing is enormous. Our advice is to pickle half (see opposite) and make salads with the rest. Daikon has a mild heat and a crunch that's hard for it to lose no matter how old it gets. Start buying it for this reason alone – it lasts so well, giving you real bang for your buck.

Goes with   Carrots, wombok (Chinese cabbage), green beans, bean sprouts, coriander (cilantro), onions, apples, pears, nashi pears, lemons, soy sauce, chilli, ginger, fish sauce, vinegar, coconut, pork, chicken, sesame seeds, peanuts

Storage   If the leaves are still attached, cut them off and store them in an airtight container or wrapped in a clean damp cloth in the fridge. The daikon root will keep for up to 2 weeks wrapped in a clean damp tea towel (dish towel) and then in a reusable plastic bag and kept in the fridge. To freeze daikon, cut it to the desired size and blanch in boiling water for 3 minutes. Plunge into cold water and leave for 2 minutes, then drain for about 5 minutes. Pack into an airtight container and keep in the freezer for up to 3 months.

Substitutes   As daikon is a member of the radish family, you can pretty much swap it with little radishes, although you'll need many bunches to make up the volume. In uncooked recipes you can use cucumber in much the same way.

Some ideas for using up the rest of that huge daikon

✻ Thinly slice and use like regular radishes for a radish and butter sandwich.
✻ Dice and add to miso soup.
✻ Add to simple stir-fries.
✻ Grate finely and use to top cooked tofu dishes. Agedashi Tofu (p 458) is extra good when topped with grated daikon.
✻ Don't forget thinly sliced daikon in rice paper rolls.
✻ Grate and add to your next batch of kimchi (p 486).

Daikon salad

SERVES 4 AS A SIDE

The crunchiness and high water content of daikon make it a really refreshing salad ingredient.
Serve this salad alongside fiery Korean food or noodles, or use it as a filling for rice paper rolls as
we do. It's also a light side for any of the dishes in the tofu (p 456) section. Also use this recipe
for cucumbers.

Scrub 500 g (1 lb 2 oz) daikon and cut into thick batons. Place in a large metal or plastic bowl
and give the daikon a good smash using something heavy like a pestle or meat hammer. You
don't want to pulverise it, just break it up a bit. In a small bowl, combine 1 tbsp mild-flavoured
oil of your choice, 1 tbsp rice wine vinegar, 1 tbsp soy sauce, 1 tsp sesame oil, 1 tsp chilli flakes,
and a pinch each of sugar and salt. Whisk and pour over the smashed daikon. Let it sit for
5 minutes before serving.

Delicate fermented daikon

Daikon was one of the first vegetables to be fermented. As it is native to Korea, the first kimchis
were made with it. This recipe uses the same technique as for Fermented Carrots (p 78).

Cut daikon into thin matchsticks or thicker batons, depending on how you like to eat it.
Add a whole chilli and a slice of ginger to the jar for a subtle heat. Eat fermented daikon just as
you would pickled daikon – in stir-fries, in rice paper rolls or San Choy Bow (p 250), or in salads.

Vietnamese-style daikon pickles

MAKES 1 x 500 ML (18 OZ) JAR

The area where we live in Sydney is home to a thriving Vietnamese community. We eat banh mi
baguettes as often as we do cheese and pickle toasties. We owe a debt to this community for
teaching us how pickles can and should accompany almost anything. The local flavour profile is
sweet and sour, and a good Vietnamese pickle must strike this balance. This is the classic pickle
you'll see accompanying an array of Vietnamese dishes. We're making this version with daikon
only, but the classic recipe also has carrot in it. Feel free to mix them together, and to double
the recipe if you've been brave and bought a giant daikon. Make your own banh mi and top
generously with these pickles, or use them in rice paper rolls or a cold noodle salad.

Cut 250 g (9 oz) daikon into matchsticks. You want them the same shape and size, so they
pickle evenly. In a medium saucepan, combine 1 cup (250 ml) water, ½ cup (125 ml) rice
wine vinegar, 1 tbsp sugar and 2 tsp salt. Stir over medium heat to dissolve the salt and sugar

completely, then allow the pickling liquid to come to the boil. Remove from the heat and cool slightly. Pack the daikon into a clean and dry 500 ml (18 oz) jar, then cover with the warm vinegar mixture. Seal and allow the jar to cool before transferring to the fridge. The pickles will take 3 days to be ready and will then last for 1 month in the fridge.

Turn older daikon into a velvety braise

Daikon is not just for eating raw. Braise it and serve it alongside tofu dishes, whole baked fish or sticky chicken dishes. Follow the recipe for the Velvety Braised Vegetables (p 159), using a mix of stock and Chinese cooking wine, and flavouring it with chilli and grated fresh ginger. The cooking time will be 20–30 minutes.

Some ideas for using daikon leaves

Daikon leaves have a strong mustardy flavour. Use them fresh as you would any leafy green, or:
* Slice and add them when making kimchi (p 486).
* Follow the Stir-fried Beet Leaves recipe (p 46).
* Dry them and use as a seasoning, as they do in Korea. Use the Home-drying Techniques for Herbs oven-dried method (p 207). Once they're dry, blitz using a food processor or coffee grinder. Mix with toasted sesame seeds, a little salt, even some blitzed dried mushrooms. Sprinkle over rice, vegetables, tofu and seafood for an extra mustardy kick.

Dried fruits

Because dried fruits store so well, we always have some in our pantries. We're big believers in taking inspiration from what you have rather than automatically flicking through cookbooks. Do a quick pantry audit, discover what you want to use up, then make it a part of your next meal or baking project. For us, dried fruits mean that a Middle Eastern-style meal could make an appearance, or we might bake a loaf or some cookies, or they will remind us to buy a chicken for roasting, and stuff it with the last few dried figs and the stale bread on the counter.

Go with

Dried fruits have a very concentrated flavour that works well with sweet and savoury cooking. All the warm winter flavours work with dried fruits – cinnamon, allspice, vanilla, nutmeg and cloves – as do Middle Eastern spices like cumin, cardamom and coriander seeds. Cook dried fruits with pears, apples, quince, rhubarb, bananas, carrots, pumpkin (squash), sweet potato, onions, buckwheat, coconut, nuts and seeds. Butter, washed-rind cheeses, dark spirits, chocolate and rich meats are dried fruits' indulgent friends.

Storage

Dried fruit is preserved, so it doesn't really go off, it will just get drier over time. Store dried fruits in an airtight container in a dark place, like the pantry, for up to 1 year. If you're buying in bulk, you can store dried fruits in the fridge or even the freezer if you have room. Really ancient dried fruits that have been in the pantry since you moved in should be soaked in water for a few hours or overnight before you use them in baking or slow cooking.

Substitutes

Dried fruits can all be replaced with each other, so if a recipe calls for dates, use figs or sultanas if that's what you have. Yes, the flavour will be slightly different, but they're all sticky, sweet and a little sour. In savoury dishes you could use roasted fruits instead of dried fruits, but there will be more moisture, so adjust accordingly.

Some ideas for using an old bag or box of dried fruits

* Cover a small amount of sultanas, currants or chopped dried fruits with a little boiling water and a dressing vinegar like sherry vinegar, balsamic vinegar or good-quality apple cider vinegar, a pinch of salt and a good grind of pepper. Leave to sit for at least 15 minutes, then add to a grain salad (p 379), a red cabbage salad, or a rocket (arugula), walnut and sharp cheese salad. Use the left-over liquid as part of the dressing.

* Steep dried apples or berries and a thyme or rosemary sprig in hot water for a herbal tea. See Lemongrass Tea (p 205) for tea-making tips.

* In a saucepan over medium heat, sauté onion and garlic until soft and sweet, then add 1 tsp ground Middle Eastern spices like cinnamon, cardamom, allspice. Add dried fruits, a little splash of vinegar and a big pinch of salt, and cook gently for 2–3 minutes. Add rice or couscous, then water or stock, and follow the packet directions for the absorption method. Fluff up the grains with a fork to serve.

* Stuff a chicken. A little dried fruit, a few herbs, a knob of butter and some left-over cooked grains or torn stale bread, with plenty of salt and pepper, make a simple delicious stuffing for a roast chicken.

* Make an old-fashioned apple or pumpkin (squash) chutney and add a handful of currants or sultanas. See 'What's in the Fruit Bowl' Relish (p 333).

* Add to savoury grain salads, such as the Best Barley Side (p 29), Buckwheat Salad (p 63) or Big Grain Salad (p 379).

* Make a batch of Simple Oat Cookies (p 303) for a chewy treat.

* **Dried fruit log** In a food processor, place 1 cup dried fruits – figs, dates, prunes, apricot – with ¼ cup nuts and ⅓ cup (40 g) grated dark chocolate, and blend to a thick paste. With a little olive oil on your hands, roll the mixture into a log, then wrap in baking paper and store in the fridge for up to 1 month. Cut thin slices off as a little treat or to serve after dinner with a glass of wine. See also the Coconut Date Balls on p 116.

Chai-spiced dried fruit compote

MAKES 2 CUPS (ABOUT 600 G)

In a small saucepan, bring 300 ml (10½ fl oz) water to the boil and add 2 black teabags
(English breakfast or earl grey). Remove from the heat and allow the tea to brew for 15 minutes.
Remove the teabags, return to low heat and add 200 ml (7 fl oz) orange juice (and some finely
grated zest if you're using fresh oranges), 1 tbsp sugar and 1 tbsp honey, stirring to dissolve. Add
up to 400 g (14 oz) dried fruits – we particularly like prunes, but figs and apricots work well, or
a mix of sultanas and currants. Add chai spices: 1 tsp ground cinnamon, ½ tsp ground nutmeg,
½ tsp ground cloves, ½ tsp ground cardamom and a good pinch of black pepper. Simmer for
5 minutes, until the liquid is a little syrupy.

Remove from the heat and leave to cool for 10 minutes. Keep chai-spiced fruit compote in
an airtight container in the fridge for a few weeks. If you want to do a double batch and preserve
your compote, pack it into sterilised (p 501) jars and heat-process (p 502) for 30 minutes. Serve
on porridge, muesli, yoghurt and desserts.

Spiced savoury dried fruit relish

MAKES 1 x 300–400 ML (10–14 OZ) JAR

In a medium saucepan, warm ½ cup (125 ml) apple cider vinegar, 1 cup (250 ml) water, ¼ cup
(55 g) raw sugar, ¼ tsp each of salt and pepper, 1 tsp mustard, a pinch of cayenne pepper and
either 1 tbsp grated fresh ginger or 1 tsp ground ginger. Add 1 cup chopped dried fruits, then
remove from the heat and leave to sit for 15 minutes to 1 hour to soften the fruit. Return to low
heat and simmer, stirring often, until the liquid starts to thicken. If it gets too dry before the dried
fruits have softened, add a little more water. Once glossy, allow to cool and store in an airtight
container or a jar in the fridge for about 1 month. Serve with grilled (broiled) meats, cheeses or
ham, or stir through hot buttered brown rice or couscous for a quick Moroccan-style side dish.

Dried fruit tea loaf – seriously, only four ingredients

MAKES ONE 23 x 13 CM (9 x 5 IN) LOAF

This recipe came from the back of a packet somewhere and is so stupidly basic that we've both been making different versions of it for years. All you need is some scrappy dried fruit, flour, tea or juice and sugar. Don't expect this to be a rich and complex loaf – its beauty is that it's simple and old-fashioned. Like the Simplest Banana Bread (p 27), this loaf is more bread-like than cake-like. Slice it thick, toast it in the toaster, slather it with butter and serve it with a strong cup of tea. It holds up well in lunchboxes too.

If you're not using sultanas or currants, chop your dried fruit into small pieces. Soak 1 cup dried fruits with ¼ cup (55 g) white (granulated) sugar in 1 cup (250 ml) strong hot black tea for a couple of hours or overnight. You could use orange juice if you don't like tea. Preheat the oven to 180°C (350°F) and line a 23 × 13 × 7 cm (9 × 5 × 2¾ in) loaf (bar) tin with baking paper. In a bowl, put 2 cups (300 g) self-raising flour (we like wholemeal, but use what you have), and if you're feeling wild add 1 tsp ground cinnamon. Stir the dried fruit mix through – the batter will be very thick. Pour into the tin and bake for 30 minutes, or until a skewer inserted in the centre comes out clean. Cool in the tin for 15 minutes, then turn out onto a wire rack to cool completely.

Fruity pantry-strays slice

Use the easy and adaptable recipe on p 302 to take care of all the stray bits and pieces that are annoying you. Dried fruits, bits of coconut, oats, seeds, finely grated orange zest, chocolate buttons. It's like a choose-your-own-adventure recipe.

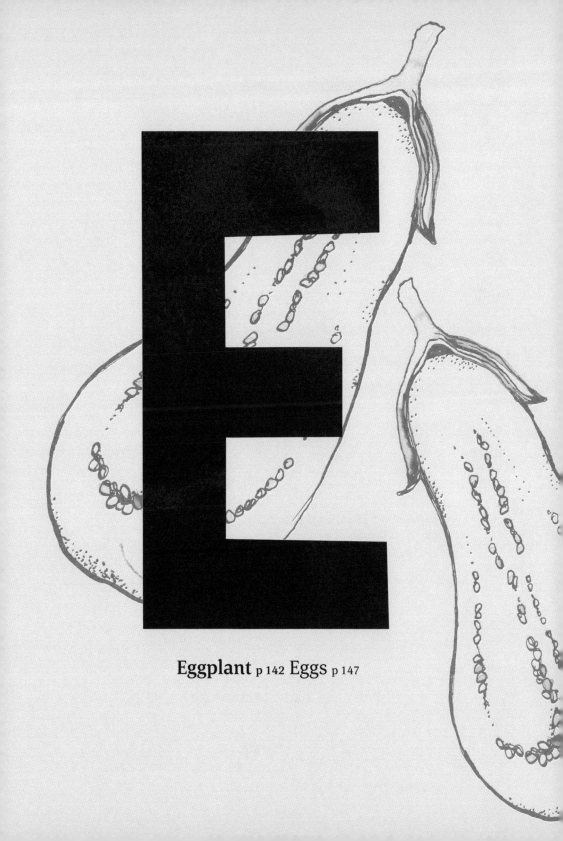

Eggplant p 142 **Eggs** p 147

Eggplant

It's reasonable to say that eggplant (aubergine) is the steak of the vegetable kingdom. It brings substance to meals and can pull off crisp or creamy, depending on how you cook it. Eggplant's reputation for being bitter, and therefore needing to be salted before cooking, is largely unwarranted these days. The bitter flavour, for good or for ill, has been bred out of them. We skip the salting process unless cooking with home-grown larger eggplant varieties. Remember, even when a forgotten eggplant is looking a bit like a deflated balloon in the fridge, it will still come good once cooked.

Goes with Most herbs (basil, chives, parsley, oregano, thyme, bay leaves, coriander/cilantro, rosemary), garlic, miso, tahini, ginger, lemons, chilli, coriander seeds, fennel seeds, paprika, star anise, cheeses, capers, cumin, tomatoes, capsicum (pepper), zucchini (courgettes), okra, dried beans, chickpeas, lentils, walnuts, sesame seeds, anchovies, lamb

---

Storage Don't wash your eggplants before storing them. Keep them dry, pop them in a paper bag in the crisper section of the fridge, and they will stay fresh for about 10 days. Wash before cooking.

Substitutes Eggplant really is its own beast. If you're looking for a substitute, cast your eyes over capsicums (peppers) or okra, which slow-cook in a similar way. Mushrooms and zucchini (courgettes) could also be used for grilling and frying.

Easy oven-blistered eggplant

Blistering your eggplants (aubergines) will give them a deep, smoky flavour that will turn any dish into something impressive. Oven-blistering is the easy, hands-off method, and our go-to for reviving any spotted old eggplants in the fridge that we've been ignoring. It's worth blistering even one old eggplant, but with a kilo (or a couple of pounds) of blistered eggplants in the fridge you'll have a standby you can serve as a dip or make into a pasta sauce without even trying.

Preheat the oven to 220°C (425°F). Stab the eggplant all over with a fork and rub with a little oil. Roast on a baking tray for 50–60 minutes, turning every 20 minutes or so, until black all over and collapsing. Remove from the oven, allow to cool, then cut in half lengthways, scoop out the pulpy flesh and compost the skin. Store in an airtight container in the fridge for up to 5 days and use in any of the following ways, or marinate using the Garlicky Marinated Eggplant recipe over the page and store in the fridge for 2–3 weeks.

THREE WAYS WITH BLISTERED EGGPLANT

* ***Quick baba ghanoush*** Much better than store-bought. Mash the flesh of 1 large blistered eggplant with a fork, add 1–2 tbsp tahini, 1 tbsp lemon juice, ¼ tsp salt and 1 finely chopped or crushed garlic clove. Give all the ingredients a good whisk with the fork to combine.
* ***Eggplant feta mash*** Serve with grilled (broiled) meats, mezze plates or eggs, or just salad and bread. In a medium bowl, mash about ¼ cup (35 g) crumbled feta with 1 tbsp toasted and roughly chopped nuts, 1 handful each of mint leaves and tarragon or parsley leaves, 1 tbsp olive oil and a squeeze of lemon juice. Stir until everything comes together loosely, then stir in the flesh of 1 blistered eggplant. Add salt to taste.
* ***Eggplant pasta sauce*** Conjured from not much. Heat 2 tbsp olive oil in a frying pan over medium heat. Roughly chop 1–2 tomatoes and throw them in the pan. Finely chop 2 garlic cloves and add those too, stirring for 2–3 minutes until the tomatoes collapse and release their juice. Sprinkle in ½ tsp salt, add the flesh of 1–2 blistered eggplants and stir. Add some black olives if you have them, or just a big handful of fresh chopped herbs. Stir through cooked pasta and serve. Dollops of ricotta would be nice if you want some extra creaminess.

Garlicky marinated eggplant

To make your blistered eggplant (previous page) taste great and last well, cover it with this delicious marinade. Then eat it on toast with fresh tomatoes, add to home-made pizzas or serve with grilled (broiled) fish.

Put the flesh of 1 large blistered eggplant (aubergine) in a jar or container and cover with ¼ cup (60 ml) olive oil, ¼ cup (60 ml) apple cider vinegar or white wine vinegar, 1 tbsp sugar and 1 tsp salt. Add some sliced garlic, peppercorns and rosemary leaves or chilli flakes if you have them, then seal and store in the fridge for 2–3 weeks.

Roasted eggplant

Roasting eggplant (aubergine) in the oven makes for a very adaptable side dish that can go with nearly any style of cooking. It's the seasoning that will make it at home with the rest of the meal. So whether you're cooking Italian, Middle Eastern or Japanese, use up that eggplant in the fridge.

Preheat the oven to 200°C (400°F). Cut eggplants into thick wedges or largish cubes (don't cut them too small or they will burn), drizzle liberally with oil, sprinkle with salt and roast for 20–30 minutes, until a little crisp at the edges and soft in the middle. Toss into a salad, or try one of the flavours below.

FLAVOUR IDEAS FOR ROASTED EGGPLANT

- Freshly chopped parsley, lots of pepper and chilli flakes, and a splash of red wine vinegar.
- Drizzled Creamy Tahini Dressing (p 455) and a garnish of pomegranate seeds or dried currants and toasted almonds or pistachios.
- Drizzled Miso Dressing (p 277) and a garnish of toasted sesame seeds.
- Check out the delicious spicy Harissa-roasted Eggplant recipe on p 188 before roasting.

Smooth and silky eggplant with fennel, rosemary and chilli

Neglected nightshades can be transformed with low, slow cooking. This braise makes a shimmering flavoursome eggplant (aubergine) dish to toss through pasta with plenty of parmesan, or to serve with chickpeas or brown rice, with grilled (broiled) meats or on toast.

Use the recipe for Smooth and Silky Capsicum (p 75) and change the flavours to 1 tsp chopped fresh rosemary, ½ tsp fennel seeds and ½ tsp chilli flakes, with a big squeeze of lemon juice at the end.

Deep-fried spiced eggplant – almost too good to be true

Can you turn a wrinkly old eggplant (aubergine) into something totally indulgent? Yes, you can. Follow the same steps as for Crispy Spiced Cauliflower (p 82) and turn 2 eggplants into something at once crisp and creamy. Serve with rice and Japanese-style Sesame Greens (p 40).

Oven-baked ratatouille for summer vegetables

The ratatouille recipe on p 498 is an excellent way to use up eggplant (aubergine). It calls for 1 kg (2 lb 4 oz) mixed summer vegetables, but can be made entirely with eggplant if that's what you're overloaded with.

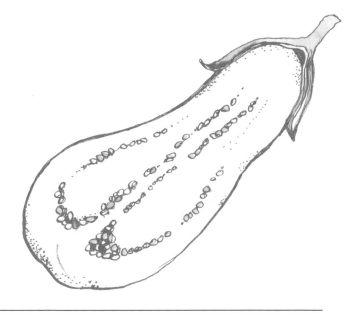

Crumbed eggplant for president

2 MEDIUM EGGPLANTS SERVE 4

It seems that if you crumb it, they will come. Crumbed eggplant (aubergine) has risen to a very legitimate status on pub menus, and it makes a good vegetarian midweek dinner. This is also the starting point for parmigiana (see below) if you want to take things further. This crumbing method can be used for many other vegetables too – cauliflower, zucchini (courgettes) and pumpkin (squash) – but keep in mind that they may have different cooking times.

To make sure the eggplant cooks through yet doesn't burn, it's essential to cut it into slices no more than 1 cm (½ in) thick. Cut lengthways for a prettier presentation or into rounds if your knife isn't very sharp. In one shallow bowl, put ½ cup (75 g) salted plain (all-purpose) flour; in another shallow bowl, whisk 2 eggs; and in a third shallow bowl, put 1 cup Breadcrumb Mix (p 51). Add ¼ cup (25 g) grated parmesan to the breadcrumb mix if you'd like. Dip the eggplant slices in the flour, then the egg, and finally the breadcrumbs to coat, and set aside on a plate. Refrigerate for 15–30 minutes before frying.

Cover the base of a frying pan with 2 cm (¾ in) neutral oil and heat over medium–high heat. Once the oil is hot, fry the schnitzels in batches, cooking on each side for 3–4 minutes until golden and crispy.

Give the schnitties a quick squeeze of lemon juice and serve with onion jam, or Oven-roasted Onion Relish (p 312), mayonnaise and a beer.

TO MAKE EGGPLANT PARMIGIANA

Preheat the oven to 180°C (350°F). Lay the fried crumbed eggplant (aubergine) in a baking tray, add a layer of tomato passata (puréed tomatoes) and 1 cup (100 g) grated parmesan, mozzarella or cheddar, or a combo of what's in the fridge. Bake for 30 minutes. When the tray comes out of the oven, everything will be yielding and melty.

Eggs

Is there another food so complete, so practical, so uncomplicated and so relentlessly adaptable? It's almost embarrassing how much eggs can do for us, so we're obliged to never waste them. The first rule is that fresh is not only best, but non-negotiable, as a non-fresh egg can make you quite sick. Fresh eggs last a long time, so there's really no excuse. What can get tricky as their numbers dwindle in the carton is how to use those last few eggs, or what to do when you find yourself with only yolks or whites. Again, an egg's versatility knows no bounds – there's *always* something you can do with any part of an egg.

Go with   Everything ... flour, butter and dairy to make baked goods; all meats, tofu, dried beans, chickpeas, lentils and nuts; leafy greens and asparagus; grains and pasta; herbs and spices. It all depends how the egg is used. An egg and an apple can go together, for instance, if the egg is boiled, the apple thinly sliced and they're both in a salad. Context is key.

Storage   Temperature fluctuations are the issue for eggs. Store them at a similar temperature to where you bought them: eggs from the fridge should stay in the fridge, eggs from the shelves should stay on the shelves. Keep eggs in their cardboard container on the bench or in the fridge. Eggs will stay fresh for up to 6 weeks after laying, so check the use-by date on the carton.

Substitutes   It depends on the application, but you can use aquafaba (p 111) in place of egg whites as it whips up in a similar way. Silken tofu can replace eggs in baked recipes. Yoghurt can act as a binding agent too, as can mashed banana and avocado. There are also commercial egg replacers available. Check out options and recommendations online before you start substituting.

Some ideas for using an egg or two, or more

* Add to Left-over-fish Kedgeree (p 166). Boil the last few eggs and chop them up to mix into this comfort rice meal.
* Make Kimchi Pancakes (p 225) or fritters. You only need 1 egg for a batch of the pancakes.
* Stir an egg or two through fried rice. Have a look at the Green Eggy Fried Rice (p 57). They really make the meal into a proper dinner.
* Eggs for dinner. It's easy, cheap, quick and nutritious.
* The Braised Leeks (p 236) make very good use of 2 boiled eggs, or boil 3 eggs and make the Turnip Leaf and Dandelion Leaf Salad (p 469).
* If you have a lot of eggs, the Whole-lemon and Chocolate Cake on p 241 uses 8.
* **Baked eggs** Crack 1–2 eggs into a layer of Baked Beans (p 37), sautéed capsicum, Oven-baked Ratatouille (p 498), Mushroom Ragu (p 279) or sautéed mixed greens and pop into a 170°C (325°F) oven until just set, about 12 minutes.

Egg drop soup
SERVES 1

The name 'egg drop' comes from how the soup is made, by dropping raw egg into hot soup to form clouds or ribbons. It's incredibly simple, made with just flavoursome broth and an egg or two. You can fill it out by adding torn spinach leaves, left-over shredded chicken or diced tofu after the egg.

Heat 1 cup (250 ml) chicken stock (see Left-over-chicken Soup, p 106), dashi or miso soup in a small saucepan. In a small bowl, whisk 1 egg. When the soup is hot, swirl it in one direction, then slowly pour in the egg. Remove the saucepan from the heat so the eggs don't overcook. It will only take a minute for the egg clouds to form. Add a dash of soy sauce and mirin, some sesame oil and either coriander (cilantro) leaves or bean sprouts, and enjoy.

Egg and milk pasta sauce
SERVES 1

This may seem a little strange – how can milk and egg make a delicious sauce? Well, they do. It's simple, creamy and comforting, and doubles easily.

In a small bowl, lightly whisk 1 egg with ¼ cup (60 ml) milk, ¼ tsp salt and lots of ground black pepper. Cook 75 g (2¾ oz) pasta according to the packet directions, then drain and return to the pot over low heat. Add the egg and milk mix, and stir until you see it cling to the pasta. Add ½ cup (50 g) grated hard cheese, stir and gobble it up.

Curried-egg sandwich
SERVES 2

Our kids hate these, but when we get together to write and discuss the finer points of how to cook a perfect omelette (you'll find the answer over the page), we enjoy eating nothing more than curried-egg sandwiches.

Rinse 3 whole eggs under lukewarm tap water, then place in a small saucepan of water. Place over medium heat, bring to a simmer and cook for 6 minutes, then drain and cool. Peel the eggs and place them in a bowl. Smash roughly with a fork, then stir in 2 tbsp mayonnaise or a dash of cream, at least 1 tsp curry powder and a good pinch of salt. Add snipped chives if you have them. Spread over fresh bread and make sandwiches.

Prairie oysters
SERVES 1

A prairie oyster is an old-fashioned and gutsy cure-all. In the film *Cabaret*, Sally Bowles seems to survive on prairie oysters alone, claiming they work instantly on even the 'most sinister of hangovers'. On the other hand, the American food writer M.F.K. Fisher always had them before going to the dentist, possibly because they also bestow fortitude.

Mix 1 raw egg with a good dash of worcestershire sauce, a generous nip of brandy or whisky, and a little splash of Tabasco if you want. 'Swoosh' it around as Sally Bowles would say, and knock it back. There, you feel better already, don't you?

Two-egg omelette
SERVES 1 OR MORE

Look, making an omelette is quite individual, so if you have your own method, stick to it. But if you don't and you're looking for tips, this is how we like to make them. A good omelette can truly be the best dinner imaginable.

Per omelette, per person, whisk 2 eggs in a shallow bowl with a pinch of salt until just combined. Place a small frying pan over medium heat, and when hot add 1 tbsp butter. Swoosh the butter around until melted and quickly add the eggs before the butter turns brown. Tilt the pan this way and that, so the eggs cover the surface of the pan. Reduce the heat to low, cook for 2 minutes, then add whatever you fancy – ¼ cup grated cheese and a good crack of pepper will do, as will charred asparagus, 2–3 tbsp kimchi (p 486), or Blistered Marinated Capsicum (p 74). Flip over half the omelette to enclose and cook for a few more minutes, or until the cheese melts or the other fillings meld into the omelette. Slide onto a plate and tuck in.

Spanish potato omelette
SERVES 3–4 WITH LEFTOVERS FOR SANDWICHES

Two potatoes, 10 eggs. Dinner is served.

Preheat the oven to 180°C (350°F). Boil 2 good-sized potatoes until just tender. Drain, allow to cool a little, then thinly slice into rounds. In an ovenproof non-stick frying pan, heat ⅓ cup (80 ml) extra virgin olive oil over medium–low heat. Add 4 sliced garlic cloves and cook gently until fragrant but not burnt. Add the sliced potatoes with ¼ tsp each of salt and pepper, and mix well. Reduce the heat to low and cook, covered, for 10 minutes, or until the potatoes are soft and very tasty, shaking the pan often to avoid burning.

In a medium bowl, whisk 10 eggs with ½ tsp each of salt and pepper and ⅓ cup (35 g) finely grated parmesan. Once the potatoes are delicious, remove the lid and spread out the potato slices to cover the base of the frying pan evenly. Turn up the heat to medium and pour in your eggy mix. When the edges frill up a little, reduce the heat again and cook for 10 minutes, until the egg mixture is almost set – it will still be liquidy on top. Transfer to the oven and let the top cook through. Once it's ready, carefully slide the omelette upside down onto a plate. It will be puffed up and the potato slices will make a very handsome glossy top. Serve with a green salad and an onion relish (p 312).

Baked custard

SERVES 4–6

Alex has been making this baked custard for her son Max since he was small. Now that he's a teenager, he requests it without even realising how happy and sentimental this makes her. Alex learnt this technique from Matthew Evans' beautiful book *Real Food* and it cannot be improved upon. It's perfect – just ask Max. It uses half a dozen eggs to make a simple and special dessert.

Preheat the oven to 150°C (300°F). In a saucepan over medium heat, warm 2½ cups (625 ml) full-cream milk and bring to a low simmer. Remove from the heat. In a large bowl, whisk 6 eggs with 140 g (5 oz) caster (superfine) sugar, then slowly beat in the milk until everything is combined. Strain into an 8-cup (2-litre) ovenproof dish and grate some nutmeg on top or sprinkle with a little ground cinnamon.

Place the ovenproof dish in a deeper roasting tin and pour enough water into the tin to come a third of the way up the side of the dish. Bake for 30–40 minutes, until set. The cooked custard will look a little wobbly but should be springy to the touch, and that's exactly what you want.

Pickled eggs

MAKES 1 x 500 ML (18 OZ) JAR

An English classic. Pickled eggs in the fridge can be added to a quick ploughman's-style lunch, make a great picnic food, or be chopped and added to leafy salads.

Place 5 eggs in a medium saucepan, cover with cold water, bring to the boil and simmer for 9 minutes. Drain and allow them to cool in their shells.

While the eggs are cooling, make a pickling liquid. In a saucepan, combine ½ cup (125 ml) red wine vinegar, white vinegar or apple cider vinegar, 140 g (5 oz) caster (superfine) sugar (or ⅔ cup/140 g raw sugar), ¼ cup (60 ml) water, 2 tsp honey, 4 allspice berries, 4 peppercorns and a few bay leaves if you have them. Bring to a simmer and stir to dissolve the sugar and honey. Remove from the heat and set aside until cool.

Meanwhile, carefully peel the cooled eggs and pack them into a clean 500 ml (18 oz) jar. Once the liquid has cooled completely, pour it over the eggs, making sure they're completely covered. Remove any air bubbles by gently tapping the jar on the bench. Seal the jar, pop in the fridge and allow the eggs to pickle for 1 week. They will then last in the fridge for 3 weeks.

EGG WHITES

Egg whites are about 10 per cent protein, with traces of minerals and vitamins. In dishes, they bring lightness and froth in defiance of heavier ingredients, such as in cakes and pavlovas. The foaminess of an egg white can make wonderful things happen. And don't forget, one left-over egg white means whisky sours tonight.

Storage   Store separated egg whites in an airtight container in the fridge for 4 days. For longer storage, freeze them in an airtight container for up to 3 months.

Meringue

Knowing how to make a simple meringue is very useful for creating all kinds of desserts. As for tips, always use room-temperature eggs because they're easier to beat than cold eggs, and always use caster (superfine) sugar – if you don't, you'll have a gritty meringue. Your bowl needs to be very clean and dry – a simple drop of water can wreck the whole thing. If you're separating egg whites from yolks, you need to be really meticulous about ensuring there's not a speck of yolk in them, or they'll never stiffen.

We use a 1:1 ratio of egg whites to sugar. This means you'll have to weigh your egg whites as well as your sugar. Beat the egg whites using an electric mixer, or with brute strength and a whisk, until the eggs are foamy. Very slowly whisk in the sugar a little at a time, allowing it to dissolve and air to get into the whites to puff everything up. Keep going until stiff peaks form and the meringue has a glossy appearance. From here you can go in a few different directions.

CHOCOLATE MOUSSE
Fold Chocolate Ganache (p 125) into the meringue and set in the fridge for at least 1 hour. Eat within 2 days.

LITTLE MACAROONS
Set the oven to 140°C (275°F) before beating the egg whites. Add a little vanilla extract after all the sugar is in and beat for 2–3 seconds, ensuring it's completely incorporated. Place tablespoonfuls of meringue on a lined baking tray and bake for 1 hour. Allow to cool before eating.

COCONUT MACAROONS
Fold ½ cup (45 g) desiccated coconut (or less if you don't want them too coconutty) per egg white through the meringue with a spatula, then bake as above, increasing the oven temperature slightly if you prefer golden macaroons.

Amigthalota biscuits

MAKES ABOUT 12

These Greek biscuits are perfect with coffee. They're gluten-free and fuss-free.

Preheat the oven to 180°C (350°F). In a medium bowl, stir together 1½ cups (150 g) almond meal and ½ cup (110 g) caster (superfine) sugar, then add 2 lightly whisked egg whites. Mix together to form a paste. Spread ½ cup (50 g) flaked almonds on a plate. Split the almond mixture into 12 even pieces, roll each piece into a log, and roll it in the flaked almonds, then form into a crescent-moon shape. When all the biscuits are shaped, lay them on a lined baking tray and bake for 15–20 minutes, until slightly golden.

Store in an airtight container for up to 1 week.

Tempura-style egg white batter

MAKES ABOUT 2 CUPS (500 ML)

This light crunchy batter is a real treat for using up egg whites that are a few days old. Use it for frying vegetables and tofu. Serve with a little dish each of soy sauce and Fermented Chilli (p 114).

In a small bowl, mix ¾ cup (110 g) plain (all-purpose) flour and ⅔ cup (170 ml) cold water to form a very smooth paste. Whisk 2 egg whites until fluffy, then combine with the flour and water to make a smooth batter. Follow the deep-frying method in Crispy Spiced Cauliflower (p 82).

Spiced nuts or granola

For extra-crunchy flavoursome spiced nuts or granola, coat them in egg white. Start by whisking 1 egg white until light and foamy.

SPICED NUTS
Add 1½ tsp salt, 1 tbsp sugar and 2–3 tsp spices or dried herbs of your choice (try paprika, dried oregano or rosemary, and cayenne pepper) to the whisked egg white. Coat 1 cup (140 g) nuts in the egg mixture, spread on a lined baking tray and toast in a 160°C (315°F) oven for 15–20 minutes.

HOME-MADE GRANOLA
Add 2–3 tsp each of ground cinnamon and finely grated orange zest to the whisked egg white. Coat 1 cup (about 125 g) raw muesli well. Spread on a baking tray lined with baking paper and toast in a 160°C (315°F) oven for 10 minutes or so, then shake and toast for another 10 minutes or until golden. Cool and store in an airtight container.

EGG YOLKS

All the good stuff is in the yolk. Here in the plump yellow centre is where you find the fats and most of the minerals and vitamins, not to mention flavour. Yolks can thicken and emulsify sauces and even become a sauce in their own right when you're in want of something rich and creamy and only have a few eggs on hand. The yolk is gold – treat it as such.

Storage Store separated egg yolks in the fridge for up to 4 days with 1 tsp water over the yolks to prevent them drying out. Egg yolks on their own don't freeze well, becoming jelly-like and impossible to use. First whisk with ⅛ tsp salt or 1½ tsp sugar for every 4 egg yolks, then freeze in an airtight container for up to 6 months. Thaw in the fridge overnight before using.

Egg yolk dressing
MAKES ABOUT ½ CUP (125 ML)

The yolk makes this dressing cling to salad leaves so every inch is wrapped in its silky embrace.

In a small bowl, whisk 1 egg yolk with 2 tbsp red wine vinegar (or sherry vinegar if you have it), a good pinch each of salt and cayenne pepper, 1 tsp mustard powder and 1 tsp marmalade or honey. Once everything is combined, continue whisking while slowly pouring in ¼ cup (60 ml) olive oil until emulsified. Pour in enough to coat your salad and serve right away. The rest of the dressing will keep, refrigerated, for 2 days.

Mayonnaise
MAKES ABOUT 1¼ CUPS (310 ML)

Place 2 room-temperature egg yolks, 1½ tsp white wine vinegar, ½ tsp dijon mustard and a good pinch of salt in a food processor. With the motor running, gradually pour in 1 cup (250 ml) vegetable oil in a thin, steady stream until you have a thick mayonnaise. Make sure you do this slowly, or your mayonnaise will split – if so, you can rescue it by starting again with 2 more yolks, then slowly incorporating the split mayo.

Add 1 chopped garlic clove to make aioli, or flavour your mayonnaise with 1 tbsp chopped preserved lemon or herbs – just add to the food processor with the egg yolks. Store the mayonnaise in a clean jar or airtight container in the fridge for up to 5 days.

Cured egg yolks
MAKES 4

There's no better way to preserve an egg yolk, and the result is unlike anything you've ever tasted – it's almost like really nutty parmesan. Grate the hard, cured yolk over pasta or risotto, or onto salads or tomato on toast for an umami hit. Use pure salt, without any additives.

Combine 2 cups (600 g) pure salt and 2 cups (440 g) caster (superfine) sugar in a bowl and whisk well. Pour half the salt and sugar into a shallow dish. Make 4 egg-yolk-sized dents in the sugar and salt, then carefully place a yolk in each one (if they break, it will still work). Cover with the remaining salt and sugar, then seal the dish with plastic wrap and refrigerate for 1 week.

Preheat the oven to 70°C (150°F). Remove the yolks from the salt and sugar, rinse and pat dry with paper towel, then transfer to a wire rack sitting in a baking tray. Pop in the oven for 30 minutes or until the yolks are dry to the touch – you want them firm but not rock hard. Allow to cool, then store in an airtight container in the fridge for up to 1 month. Grate as needed.

Just-about-anything curd
MAKES 1 x 300 ML (10 OZ) JAR

Curd is a very rich, fruity spread that can be used on or between layers of cake, in crepes, on scones or toast, on ice cream, or in a tart. This base recipe can be altered to accommodate most fruit pulps and citrus juices.

You'll need ½ cup (125 ml) fruit pulp or citrus juice (plus the zest) for this recipe. Prepare the fruit by blending berries; cooking rhubarb and allowing to cool; just scooping out passionfruit pulp; finely grating citrus zest, then juicing and straining. Whisk the fruit pulp or juice and zest with 3 egg yolks. Transfer to a saucepan and place over low heat, then stir while adding ⅔ cup (150 g) caster (superfine) sugar. Whisk for 4 minutes, until the sugar is dissolved and the curd is thickening. Keep the heat low and don't try to go too fast or the egg may curdle. Remove from the heat and add 90 g (3¼ oz) unsalted butter, whisking until well combined and glossy. Pour into a clean jar, then seal and allow to set overnight in the fridge. The next morning, make thick toast, spread generously with curd and get back in bed. This curd will last in the fridge for 2 weeks.

Welsh rarebit

It's the egg yolk that brings everything together for this extra-special treat. If you have some egg yolks, do yourself a favour and make this for lunch. You'll find the recipe on p 92.

Fennel p 157 **Figs** p 162
Fish p 165 **Flour** p 167

Fennel

Fennel is magic – it's a vegetable, a herb and a seed. Store-bought fennel has three parts, each full of flavour and very much edible. The bulb is the round white part we see at the supermarket; the stems, which stand tall from the bulb; and the pretty feathery fronds at the top. Then there are the impressive seeds, used for an aniseed flavour in cooking and for medicinal purposes. Read more about fennel seeds on p 430.

Today is the day you stop throwing fennel stems and fronds in the bin and start using the whole vegetable.

Goes with	Most herbs (basil, chives, parsley, oregano, thyme, bay leaves, coriander/cilantro, rosemary), garlic, miso, tahini, ginger, citrus fruits, chilli, coriander seeds, fennel seeds, paprika, star anise, cheeses, capers, cumin, tomatoes, capsicum (pepper), zucchini (courgettes), okra, dried beans, chickpeas, lentils, walnuts, sesame seeds, anchovies, chicken, fish, lamb

---

Storage	Start by cutting the stems from the bulb, then the fronds from the stems. Store the bulb in a reusable plastic or clean cloth bag in the fridge. The stems like to be tightly swaddled in a beeswax wrap or clean damp tea towel (dish towel). You can use the stems in lots of dishes, but they're more fibrous, so they need to be treated differently (p 161) from the sweet white bulb. Either use the fronds in a dish right away, or store them like dill (p 194) and use them throughout the week as you would parsley or dill – in salads, sandwiches, green sauces like pesto or salsa verde, and soups.

Substitutes	If the bulb is to be used raw, try replacing it with something else crunchy and sweet–savoury, like cabbage or apples. For roasting or baking, replace it with onion, and if you don't have fennel fronds use parsley or dill and add some fennel seeds.

Some ideas for using up fennel

* ❋ Pickle it. Follow the Basic Vegetable Pickling method (p 472).
* ❋ Nestle a chicken on a bed of well-seasoned and oiled fennel wedges before roasting. Yum!
* ❋ Make a slaw. Follow the Basic Brussels Slaw recipe (p 60), replacing the brussels sprouts with paper-thin fennel, apple matchsticks and shaved cabbage.
* ❋ Add sliced or grated fennel to your next batch of sauerkraut (p 66) or kimchi (p 486).
* ❋ Add paper-thin slices of fennel to the Left-over-chicken Soup (p 106), or make a lighter-style minestrone (p 36) with fennel, peas and plenty of finely grated lemon zest.
* ❋ Add thinly sliced fennel wedges to a cheese board or mix with celery stalks and a creamy dressing – like the Blue Cheese Dressing (p 90) or the 'What Needs Using Up' Guacamole (p 18) – for a snack with a drink.

Whole fennel salad

SERVES 4 AS A SIDE

Cut a whole or half fennel bulb (depending on its size) into paper-thin slices – it's best to use a mandoline or a very sharp knife. Cut some of the stems into paper-thin rounds and add to the sliced fennel. Add a slug of your best-quality olive oil, the zest and juice of ½ lemon or orange, a big pinch of salt and plenty of ground pepper, then mix gently using clean hands. Spread over a plate and scatter roughly chopped fennel fronds over the top, along with any or all of the additions below.

Flavour ideas for fennel salad: Chopped olives / Quick-pickled Red Onion (p 312) / Crumbled feta / Orange segments / Chopped toasted almonds or walnuts / Seedy Salad Mix (p 409).

Spicy Korean-style pickle

MAKES 1 x 500 ML (18 OZ) JAR OR CONTAINER

This is Alex's go-to quick pickle when she has half a fennel that's been hanging around too long. It will only last for a week or so in the fridge, so make small batches as you need it. Serve with rice and a fried egg for breakfast, lunch or dinner.

In a medium–large bowl, mix 1 tbsp chilli paste (store-bought, or try Fermented Chilli, p 114), 2 tbsp rice wine vinegar, 1 finely chopped garlic clove, 1 tsp each of honey and sesame oil, ¼ tsp salt and 1 tbsp toasted sesame seeds.

Cut a fennel bulb of up to 300 g (10½ oz) into elegant 2 cm (¾ in) long strips, removing the core. If you don't have enough fennel, add a little onion. In a pot of boiling well-salted water, blanch the fennel for 1–2 minutes, then drain and run under cold water. Allow it to air dry or pat it dry. Stir the still slightly warm fennel slices into the spicy pickle mixture. Transfer to an airtight container or a jar, leave for 24 hours before eating, then store in the fridge for up to 1 week.

Roasted fennel

Roasted fennel is the bomb. Make it weekly in fennel season and serve it as a side dish.

Preheat the oven to 180°C (350°F). Cut the bulbs lengthways into wedges and place in a roasting tin. Drizzle generously with extra virgin olive oil, then add plenty of salt and pepper and the juice and zest of 1 lemon or orange. Roast for 30 minutes, shaking the tin now and then.

Velvety braised vegetables

It's very helpful in a low-waste kitchen to understand the merits of braising vegetables. Braising is a classic technique that uses small amounts of liquid, low heat and a covered heavy-based pan to intensify the flavour of ingredients, turning vegetables into tender beauties, even if they happen to be ten days old. Obviously, this method works with produce straight from the market, but it's equally delicious with our battered old pals that we can't bear to throw away. Braised vegetables can be eaten as a side dish, mixed through pasta or grains, piled onto toast with eggs, used as a topping for a pizza or just eaten straight out of the pan.

You don't need a recipe to braise vegetables – you just need to understand the concept and then you're free to choose your own adventure. Use whatever quantity of vegetables is in your fridge or garden, choosing flavours that suit your meal or mood, and a cooking liquid that suits them. Fennel, cabbage, carrots, capsicum (pepper), daikon, eggplant (aubergine), green beans, okra, potatoes and zucchini (courgettes) all give delicious results.

Choose your vegetables and cut into slices or wedges or halves. The smaller you cut your vegetables, the shorter the cooking time. Over medium heat, very generously cover the bottom of a heavy-based casserole dish or frying pan with a fat of your choice – olive oil, other oils, butter, ghee, lard. Whatever floats your boat.

If you'd like to include an aromatic (absolutely not a deal-breaker if you don't), add thinly sliced onion, leek or spring onions (scallions) and sauté until soft and sweet, but not brown. Add sliced garlic if you'd like, then cook for another 1–2 minutes.

Add the vegetables and decide whether you want to brown them first for depth of colour and extra caramelisation or to keep things clean and light. To brown vegetables, keep the heat at medium, cook until lightly caramelised, then turn and cook again on the other side, before adding the liquid. Whatever you decide, try to keep your vegetables in a more or less single layer – not too much piled in at once.

Now it's time to add your liquid. And you get to decide – look in the fridge and pantry and see what needs using: stock, wine, tinned tomatoes, water with a little added lemon juice, cider, shaoxing wine or cooking sake, even milk, or a combination of whatever you have. Add enough liquid to come about a third of the way up the vegetables, keeping in mind that a slice of zucchini won't need as much liquid as a slice of potato.

Add any spices or herbs you'd like to use up – a thyme sprig, a few bay leaves, finely grated lemon zest or a few strips of orange peel, chilli flakes, 1 tsp fennel seeds, a pinch of paprika, some grated fresh ginger – and season well with pepper and salt.

Bring the liquid to a simmer, then reduce the heat to very low and cover. If you don't have a lid, try a baking tray or pizza tray with something heavy on top. Cook gently, undisturbed, for at least 15 minutes for softer, smaller vegetables and up to 1 hour for tougher vegetables. You want everything to be tender and collapsed. Keep a little texture if you like, or go the whole way, cooking until everything is a melty pot of glossy dreams.

Remove the lid and either keep the dish saucy or turn the heat up and simmer to reduce any excess liquid. Taste, season as needed with salt, pepper or lemon juice and transfer to a serving plate. Top with chopped fresh herbs.

Finest braised fennel

SERVES 4

Put your braising technique (above) to good use with this tasty treat.

Cut 2–3 small–medium fennel bulbs into quarters, and then into wedges. In a heavy-based casserole dish or frying pan over medium heat, pour ½ cup (125 ml) extra virgin olive oil, then arrange the fennel wedges in the bottom of the pan in one even, well-packed layer. When the wedges are golden brown, turn them over with tongs to brown the other side. Add 3 chopped garlic cloves, ¾ tsp salt, ½ tsp cracked pepper, a pinch of chilli flakes, and the zest and juice of 1 orange or lemon. Give everything a good mix, and add either ½ cup (125 ml) stock – or wine, if you have some open in the fridge – or the half-punnet of wrinkled cherry tomatoes no one wants to eat. Add some herbs, such as thyme, bay leaves, mint, rosemary or parsley. Reduce the heat to very low and cover. Simmer, undisturbed, for 20–30 minutes. Remove the lid, taste, season as needed, then either serve as is with crusty bread or add to hot cooked pasta.

Fennel gratin

So grown-up – and something we look forward to eating often when the children move out of home. Follow the directions for the 'There's Nothing Wrong With That Cream!' Potatoes (p 125), using thinly sliced fennel and a good-quality hard cheese.

FENNEL STEMS AND FRONDS

Some ideas for using fennel stems

* Crunchy and bitey, fennel stems will add texture and flavour to so many salads. Lightly pickle them by putting them in a bowl with a splash each of boiling water and apple cider vinegar, and a pinch each of sugar, salt and chilli flakes. Leave to sit for 10 minutes, then add to salads.
* Add thinly sliced stems to any vinegar-based pickles – cucumber, zucchini (courgette), green bean, beetroot, celery or carrot – for a little aniseed flavour.
* Slice thinly and sauté with onions and carrot or celery for the base of your next soup or stew. See p 314 for Mirepoix tips.
* Save and add to your next batch of stock. See p 446 for more stock-making tips.

Some ideas for using fennel fronds

As we mentioned earlier, you can use fennel fronds like herbs, so if you have plenty of them, don't buy any other herbs this week. Chop them finely and add to salads, eggs and potato dishes. You could also:

* Try the Salsa Verde (p 194).
* Use them instead of celery in the Celery Leaf Gremolata With Green Olives recipe (p 88).
* Give Chimichurri (p 193) a go.
* Chop and add to your next batch of pickles (p 472), sauerkraut (p 66) or kimchi (p 486).

Figs

The bliss of the fig season is brief, lasting from late summer to early autumn, when these fragile beauties are lying around being warmed by the sun. They mark the lazy days of summer and the last nights of eating outdoors. They're best eaten fresh, at room temperature and unadorned. But if you have a tree or you've bought figs by the tray, you may find yourself needing a few ideas for making the most of your bounty. An excess of figs is almost too good to be true. Stay home all weekend if you have to, but waste not a single one.

Go with	Nuts, couscous, rice, flat breads, cheeses, leafy greens, cured meats, rosemary, thyme, mint, oranges, grapes, raspberries, tomatoes, honey, tea, chocolate, ice cream, yoghurt
Storage	Figs don't hang around, so act quickly once you get them home. Store them in a dry reusable plastic bag in the fridge for up to 2 days. Remember to take them out well before you want them, as they're best eaten at room temperature. If your figs are getting a little mouldy, cut off the mould and make jam.
Substitutes	Dried figs work for flavour; strawberries and ripe apricots work for texture.

Some ideas for using up a few figs

* Make a simple fig salad. We really love a one-ingredient salad, especially when that one ingredient is figs. Follow the Grape Salad recipe (p 182). If you'd like to go the extra mile, add a few toasted nuts and a tiny bit of crumbled blue cheese or a dollop of ricotta.
* Figs with yoghurt and toasted pistachios make a beautiful breakfast or not so sweet dessert.
* Have figs on toast. Overripe figs are practically jam. Squash onto toast with some creamy cheese, or with a drizzle of olive oil, some honey and salt and pepper.

✳ Grill them. This is a good bruised-fig rescue. Cut figs in half and pop them under a grill (broiler) for a few minutes – you can sprinkle them with a little sugar if they're going on ice cream. See Apricots Can Be Rescued by Grilling (p 11) for more details.

Roasted figs

Try this for a sweet–savoury sensation. Roast figs following the Roasted Cherries recipe (p 103). Figs won't take long to cook, so check them after about 7 minutes. Add to bitter leafy greens with toasted nuts, or to a grainy salad.

Poached figs for a quick and elegant dessert
SERVES 3-4

Make the Tea and Honey Poaching Syrup on p 337, then lower 4–6 figs into the saucepan and poach for 5–10 minutes. Lift the figs out and set aside. Increase the heat and simmer to reduce the syrup for 4–8 minutes. Taste, adding 1–2 tbsp brown sugar if you'd like a sweeter syrup, stirring to dissolve. Pour over the figs to serve.

Fig jam

If you have an abundance of figs, go straight to the Foolproof Jam recipe (p 389) and make fig jam. Add a muslin bag of earl grey tea leaves to the cooking fruit.

Fig crostata
MAKES 1 x 30 CM (12 IN) PIE

This rustic style of sweet pie is so easy and forgiving it's almost like not cooking at all. The beauty of it is that you can use up pantry strays, a little jam, some nut meal, even breadcrumbs, a bit of ricotta … and any fruit you have on hand.

Start by making a very rough frangipane. In a small bowl, combine 50 g (1¾ oz) softened butter, ½ cup (50 g) nut meal and 50 g (1¾ oz) sugar (icing/confectioners' is best, but if you only have caster/superfine or even brown, that's okay too), then mix with a fork and set aside. If you don't want to make a frangipane, read on for alternatives. »

Roll out store-bought sweet shortcrust pastry or Sour Cream Pastry (p 418) with a little sugar in the mix, to make a 30 cm (12 in) circle. Place the pastry on a baking tray wide enough for it to fit comfortably.

Preheat the oven to 170°C (325°F). Spread the frangipane or 2–3 tbsp jam on the pastry, leaving a 5 cm (2 in) border, or scatter 2–3 tbsp breadcrumbs then 1 tbsp sugar over it. Cut 8–12 figs in half, place cut side up on the frangipane and fold the border over. Sprinkle 2 tbsp sugar and a few thyme leaves on top.

Bake for 45 minutes, or until the pastry is golden and the figs are soft and jammy. Allow to cool a little before serving. This is best with vanilla ice cream or fresh cream.

FIG LEAVES

Some ideas for using fig leaves

If you're lucky enough to have a fig tree, you'll have lots of broad and beautiful fig leaves. We're coming to your house. Fig leaves taste of fig, with coconut for company. You can use them for sweet or savoury cooking. Try these ideas:

* Make fig leaf syrup. Follow the Ginger Syrup recipe (p 176), using 5–10 fig leaves instead of ginger. Pour it over ice cream or cakes, or use in cocktails.
* Make fig leaf tea. Fig leaves contain properties that may help move food through the intestine, reducing cholesterol. Whether this works or not, fig leaf tea tastes great. Follow the tea recipe on p 205, using 3–4 leaves in a small saucepan.
* Wrap them around meat, fish, vegetables and fruit before roasting, keeping the cooking time the same. The leaves will impart their lovely flavour.

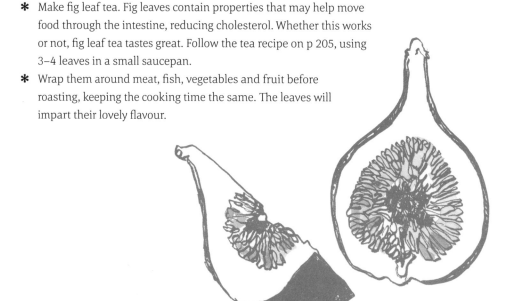

Fish

Stop being afraid of left-over cooked fish. It's a welcome sight in the fridge, and the start of tomorrow's meal, together with whatever's already on hand in the fridge and pantry. That might be nothing more than half a packet of pasta and half a jar of capers, or some left-over mash and a lonely spring onion. Think of it as a whole new meal rather than boring leftovers.

Storage   Flake left-over cooked fish and store it in a sealed container in the coldest part of the fridge for 2–3 days.

Some ideas for left-over fish

* Flaked fish is delicious through fried rice. Add it with the rice to the Green Eggy Fried Rice on p 57.
* Warm up a light tomato broth with equal parts stock and puréed fresh tomatoes or tomato passata (puréed tomatoes), then add thinly sliced fennel or zucchini (courgettes), flaked fish, lemon juice and plenty of fresh herbs.
* Heat oil or butter in a frying pan, add flaked fish, salt, pepper and capers, and warm through. Toss through hot pasta with plenty of lemon juice, basil leaves and chilli oil if you have them.
* Make fish tacos. Follow the same method as for Spiced Chicken (p 106), remembering to cook the fish for slightly less time than the chicken so it doesn't go dry.
* Don't freak out, but a curried fish sandwich is a truly beautiful thing. Follow the Curried-egg Sandwich recipe (p 149), replacing the egg with cooked left-over fish.
* Heat fish in a hot frying pan with a little soy sauce and salt, and use as the protein in San Choy Bow (p 250).
* Add any left-over fish to the top of the Cheat's Paella (p 395) and cover for the last 5 minutes of cooking. Make sure the fish has enough time to heat through but not dry out.
* **Fishcakes** See Herb, Potato and Vegetable Fritters (p 364), adding up to 1 cup (300 g) flaked cooked fish and gently mixing through.

Left-over-fish kedgeree

SERVES 4

Boiled eggs, fish, rice and curry powder: kedgeree is hearty, easy to pull together and makes everyone very happy.

Hard-boil 4 eggs and set aside. In a medium–large saucepan with a lid, heat 1 tbsp each of olive oil and butter, add 2 finely chopped garlic cloves, 2 tsp curry powder and a big pinch of salt, and sauté for 30 seconds. Add 1¼ cups (250 g) white rice and 2 bay leaves. Mix well, coating the rice in the spices. Add 2 cups (500 ml) stock and bring to the boil, then cover and cook over the lowest heat for 15 minutes. Remove from the heat, fluff up the rice with a fork, add 1 cup (300 g) flaked left-over cooked fish and mix gently. Replace the lid for 5 minutes or more, to heat the fish through and to finish cooking the rice. Remove the lid, add the diced hard-boiled eggs, and plenty of chopped herbs (chives, parsley or dill), ground pepper and more salt if it needs it. Replace the lid and let sit for another 5–10 minutes before serving.

FISHBONES AND THE HEADS

If you've been a legend and roasted or baked a whole fish, then no doubt you'll be wondering what to do with the scraps.

Fish stock

Fish stock is a good way to use up not only all those fish scraps, but also corn cobs, parsley stems, half a tomato, an old carrot or the fennel stalks we told you to save. Use this stock later in the week as the base for corn soup, tomato and fish soup, risotto, stew or Cheat's Paella (p 395). You could also replace the wine in the White Wine Mussels (p 482) with fish stock.

In a heavy-bottomed stockpot, heat 2½ tbsp olive oil and gently sauté 1 roughly chopped onion plus 2 cups other chopped vegetables for 10 minutes. Use whatever veg you need to use up – celery leaves and tops, fennel and carrots all work well, as do parsley stems, spring onions (scallions) and leeks. Add a few chopped garlic cloves and cook gently for another few minutes. Add the fishbones and head, along with 1 tsp peppercorns and 1 thyme sprig or 2–3 bay leaves, then put the lid on. Reduce the heat to low and let the fish scraps steam for 5 minutes, shaking the pan every now and then. Take the lid off and add 1 cup (250 ml) white wine if you have it. Bring to a simmer and add up to 4 cups (1 litre) water, depending on the size of your fish skeleton – you want it to be just covered. Continue to simmer very gently for 20 minutes. Taste, add ¼ tsp salt, then taste and add more if needed. Strain, cool and refrigerate for up to 4 days or freeze for up to 2 months.

Flour

A tiny amount of flour at the bottom of the bag is really annoying. Throwing it out is wasteful. Keeping it seems useless. What are you supposed to do with it? We feel you. Our tip is this: keep a paper bag in the freezer, tip in the last bits of a flour packet whenever it's nearly finished, and let this collection of flour build up. We mix plain (all-purpose) and wholemeal (whole-wheat) flour together, and even a little bit of rye or chickpea flour (besan) here and there. To ensure this mixture stays versatile, though, keep it predominantly wheat flour. You can then use this mix of flours to make flat breads, pastry or cookies, and for crumbing. Otherwise, when you have a near-empty bag, let its meagre contents direct you towards making the few things that need only a tiny amount of flour.

Storage	All flours are best kept in cool and dry places. The very best storage is in the fridge or freezer. Remove the flour from the paper bag it came in and keep in an airtight container. In the fridge, flour will last for 6 months, in the freezer it will last for 12 months. Whole-wheat flours, however, are high in oils that quickly go rancid and should therefore be used within 3 months.

Some ideas for using up a scant amount of flour

* You guessed it, crumb something. A little flour, a little egg and a little breadcrumbs. Use up the last of the flour and make your household happy at the same time. See p 51 for crumbing tips, and p 146 for crumbed eggplant.
* Use it to thicken sauces. This is good when making a pie filling, as you want the sauce to be quite thick so it doesn't seep out of the pie or make the pastry soggy.
* Dust meat or fish in a little salted flour before stir-frying to help keep the moisture in the flesh.
* Make potato gnocchi, as you need more potato than flour.
* Roast some meat and make old-fashioned gravy. The Pan-juice Gravy recipe (p 233) will give you some pointers.
* Make Bechamel Sauce (p 274) as the base for a lasagne, or the Odd-knobs Mac 'n' Cheese on p 101. »

* Make your stainless-steel sink look new. Sprinkle the last bit of flour around the sink and use a sponge or scourer to give it a good clean. The flour is mildly abrasive and will slough away all the dirt you didn't even know was there.
* We've said many times that we're not natural bakers. But with children to get through school, and in an effort to avoid buying too many packaged snacks, we've ended up with a few recipes up our sleeves. When there's a bag of flour hanging about, we let it lead us to a baking recipe that will also help us to clear out what is in our pantries and fruit bowls: Sour Cream Pastry (p 418) for fruit tarts, Simplest Banana Bread (p 27), 'Use Up That Jar' Cookies (p 455), Dried Fruit Tea Loaf (p 140) and Seedy Breakfast Muffins (p 371).

A simple flat bread for one or two

MAKES 2

This is the easiest flat bread ever. There's no yeast, no resting time, just flour and water (and salt if you want). Serve it with any style of cooking. It's perfect for one or two for lunch. Make this using self-raising flour and you'll get a fluffy flat bread, which is also a wonderful thing.

In a small bowl put ⅔ cup (100 g) plain (all-purpose) flour and a pinch of salt. Mix together and add ¼ cup (60 ml) warm water. You may need a little more water, depending on the flour. Start with this, then add more a few drops at a time if needed until the flour and water come together in a dough. Knead until smooth. Heat a dry frying pan over high heat until very hot. Divide the dough into 2 equal portions and roll out. We like an oval for this bread, about 20 cm (8 in) long and 10 cm (4 in) wide. One at a time, cook the flat breads for about 2 minutes each side. You should get some nice charred spots. Eat right away.

Flotsam and jetsam flat breads

MAKES 6–8

It's easier to make these flat breads than it is to go to the shops and buy some. This recipe will literally help use up the flotsam and jetsam of the fridge and pantry: milk, cream, yoghurt, nut milk, buttermilk or a mix. The flour should be wheat, but it can be white or wholemeal plain (all-purpose) or self-raising. When cooking in this way, you do need to be prepared to make adjustments. Not all flours are created equal: what you buy in the supermarket is different from what you buy at the health-food shop, so our instructions are a good solid starting point, but you may need to experiment and add a little more of this and that to get these flat breads perfect. Remember that the dough needs to come together in a ball with a slightly sticky but not at all wet surface. Dust the ball with some extra flour if it seems too wet. If too dry, dampen your hands and knead the dough. Use these flat breads to make burritos, or serve them with curries, falafel, koftas or Ful Medames (p 32).

In a medium bowl, mix 2 cups plain (all-purpose) flour or self-raising flour, 1 tsp salt and, if you like, 1–2 tbsp seeds such as poppy, nigella, sesame or fennel. In a small bowl, mix ¾ cup (185 ml) liquid (milk, cream, yoghurt, nut milk, buttermilk or a mix, or just plain old water) with 2 tbsp oil of your choice. If you're using wholemeal flour, you'll need a little more liquid – start with an extra ¼ cup (60 ml).

Mix the wet ingredients into the dry and knead the dough for about 2 minutes, until smooth. Wrap in a clean tea towel (dish towel) or beeswax wrap and set aside to rest for 30 minutes. Don't skip this step. Resting times are important to let gluten relax, otherwise your flat breads will be like leather.

Divide the dough into 6–8 equal pieces. Roll each one into a ball, flatten it, then roll out to about 12 cm (4½ in) in diameter.

Heat a medium dry frying pan over medium–high heat and, one at a time, cook the flat breads for about 2–3 minutes on each side. Keep warm under a clean tea towel (dish towel) until you've cooked all the flat breads. Serve warm.

G

Garlic

Unless you're a farmer you probably won't find yourself inundated with garlic. It is, however, a commonly wasted ingredient because most of us buy it cheaply and thoughtlessly, then scoop up a handful of garlic litter – the loose papery cloves – and just chuck it before buying more plump bulbs. But if we can learn to fully appreciate not only the flavour of each and every clove, but also the potential each one has to grow into another whole bulb, then we might see this everyday ingredient in a new light.

Goes with	What doesn't it go with? All vegetables, fresh herbs, mango, lemons, limes, dried beans, dried beans, chickpeas, lentils, nuts and seeds, buckwheat, quinoa, ginger, chilli, spices, miso, bread, olives, all meats and seafood, eggs, cheeses, yoghurt

----

Storage	Moisture will make garlic go mouldy, so keep bulbs and cloves cool and dry. Store them on the benchtop in a little bowl or paper bag. Whole heads will keep for many months if unbroken, and cloves will keep for about 10 days.

Substitutes	Sneaky garlic powder is a bit weird, but it makes a very reliable substitute for the real thing.

Some ideas for using up garlic

* Grow your own. One sprouted clove can be planted to grow into a whole bulb. Plant a sprouted clove, sprout side up, in a sunny position and give it a light water and mulch. Your garlic should be ready to harvest in about 7 months.
* Make the stock paste on p 447 using up all your random left-over cloves.
* Add a few cloves to the Odd-knobs Ginger Paste (p 175).
* If you have some old bread that needs using and there's half a head of garlic in the kitchen, try the Skordalia recipe (p 52). It's a most flavoursome dip to serve at a party.
* Whip up some Old-school Garlic Bread (p 52) and make everyone happy. »

* ***Cheat's garlic bread*** Rub a cut garlic clove on toast, drizzle with oil and season with salt and pepper. Serve with eggs, a tomato salad or soups, or for breakfast when you have a cold.
* ***Roasted head of garlic*** Preheat the oven to 180°C (350°F). Lightly oil a bulb of garlic and wrap tightly in baking paper by gathering the edges together and twisting to seal. Put on a baking tray and roast for 30–40 minutes. Remove from the oven, allow to cool, then pop the cloves from their skins. Spread on toast or use in cooking as you would raw garlic.

Garlic butter

Follow the method for Anchovy Butter (p 3), using either finely chopped raw garlic or roasted garlic (see above) and ditching the cinnamon. Use about 6 cloves to 125 g (4½ oz) butter. Sauté everything in it – it's really good – or spread it on toast and serve it with soup. Stuff the Old-school Garlic Bread (p 52) with knobs of this. Garlic butter is amazing to have in the fridge. It'll turn a boring meal into something much better.

Pickled garlic

This is an excellent way to preserve garlic if you have too much, or to make the most of the garlic season. Don't be scared to use pickled garlic in your everyday cooking – the extra acid suits most recipes. And never throw away the liquid once you've eaten all your pickles. Garlic vinegar is incredible in salad dressings, for seasoning in a tomato salad, or even drizzled over oysters.

Follow the Basic Vegetable Pickling method (p 472), leaving out the spices. Note that garlic can go blue as it sits in vinegar. This isn't harmful, but to avoid radioactive-looking pickles, blanch the cloves (with the skin on) in boiling water for 60 seconds. Remove from the pot, allow to cool, then peel and pickle as normal.

Garlic confit

MAKES 1 x 400 ML (14 OZ) JAR

Ooh confit, fancy. To confit anything is to cook it low and slow in fat. It's a very old preserving technique that also coaxes the most intense flavours from ingredients. For modern preservers there's some iffiness about preserving garlic in oil, but this confit recipe is a short-term preserve that can only be kept for 2 weeks. The other important point here is that you must keep your confit in the fridge. There can be serious safety concerns when preserving garlic in oil then keeping it at room temperature, so make your confit, seal it, pop it in the fridge, and use those mellow, nutty garlic cloves in all your pastas, risottos, roasts, cooked vegetables, salad dressings, dips – you get the picture – for the next fortnight.

Preheat the oven to 130°C (250°F). In a small ovenproof dish, place the separated and peeled cloves of 4 garlic bulbs, 1 tsp black peppercorns and 2 bay leaves (or other woody herbs). Pour 1 cup (250 ml) olive oil over everything and cover with foil. Slow-cook in the oven for 60–75 minutes, checking after 45 minutes to make sure all the garlic is still covered with oil, topping it up if necessary. Remove from the oven and allow to cool. Pour the entire contents of the dish into a dry sterilised (p 501) jar and refrigerate. To use, remove cloves from the oil using a clean spoon, then use as you would a normal clove. We repeat: this confit garlic will keep in the fridge for no more than 2 weeks.

Garlic oxymel

Oxymels are a combination of vinegar and honey, together with an ingredient that has medicinal properties. Traditionally, it was a way of making medicine easier to take and frankly it still is. Garlic has been valued for its health benefits for thousands of years. It has anti-inflammatory, antibiotic and antihistamine properties, can help lower cholesterol and blood pressure, and can also support the liver in detoxifying the body. But chomping on cloves of raw garlic is pretty rough, so make this concoction and take your daily dose pleasantly.

In a clean and dry jar, mix ¼ cup (60 ml) apple cider vinegar with 3 tbsp raw honey, then add 4–5 chopped garlic cloves. Set aside on the benchtop to infuse for 1–2 weeks, then keep in the fridge for up to 6 months. Add 1 tbsp to hot water for a morning tea, or take a spoonful to help fight off cold symptoms or when feeling run down.

See leeks, onions and spring onions for ideas with other alliums.

Ginger

Ginger's warmth and deep earthy notes, punctuated by lemon and camphor, add richness and spice to both savoury and sweet cooking. Or not even cooking: add a knob of fresh ginger to hot water and you have a sinus-clearing, stomach-settling tea in seconds. Ginger is another ingredient that seems to linger in small knobs, getting dry and wrinkly with neglect. But even these small pieces pack a punch of flavour, so don't overlook them. Gather them up and make use of their surprising strength.

Goes with	Garlic, chilli, warm spices (like cinnamon, cloves, allspice, coriander seeds, mustard seeds, cumin, turmeric, curry leaves, star anise), lemongrass, most vegetables, citrus fruits, rhubarb, apples, pears, quince, stone fruits, bananas, mango, passionfruit, pineapple, honey, nuts and seeds, lentils, coriander (cilantro), mint, quinoa, miso, tofu, chickpeas, chicken, beef, pork, chocolate
Storage	Store ginger in the fridge in a paper bag. Keep the skin on and it will be fine for a few weeks. For longer storage, freeze ginger in a small airtight container, then use a Microplane to shave it straight into your dishes from frozen.
Substitutes	Depending on what you're using ginger for, you have a few options if you need a substitute. Ground ginger is handy stuff and can be used for sweet or savoury cooking. Watch out though: it's more potent than fresh ginger, so use less of it. If you're using ginger as a warm spice in cooking, then consider cinnamon, nutmeg or star anise as a replacement.

Some ideas for using odd ends of ginger

* Whip up a sticky, spicy dipping sauce for dumplings, stir-fries or fish fingers. Grate at least 1 stray cm (½ in) of ginger into a small bowl. Add 1 tbsp each of soy sauce and honey, and 1 tsp sesame oil or chilli oil. Double or triple the quantities if you have more of everything.
* Make Mapo Tofu, of Sorts (p 459) – it's ginger city.

* Grate ginger into your next batch of compote, marmalade or fruity jam.
* Add slices of ginger to jars of pickled chillies, okra, beetroot or grapes.
* Include plenty of ginger in your home-made kimchi (p 486).
* **Ginger oxymel** Follow the same steps for the Garlic Oxymel (p 173), adding the odd ends of ginger instead of the garlic. Take this oxymel to soothe sore throats and help relieve nausea.
* **Ginger tea** Follow the Lemongrass Tea recipe (p 205), using 4 tbsp sliced ginger instead of the lemongrass.
* **Ginger vinegar** Grate ginger into a small jar and cover with white wine vinegar or rice wine vinegar. Seal and let it sit for a few weeks on the counter. Strain and use as the dressing base for slaws, noodles or carrot salads, or toss it through stir-fries.

Pickled ginger

Make your own pickled ginger, take it with you to the sushi train (conveyor-belt sushi) and pay no mind to those who might think you a little eccentric. Only do this, of course, if the restaurant's ginger is free.

Thinly slice a small knob of fresh ginger, sprinkle generously with salt and let it sit for at least 30 minutes. Pat dry with paper towel or a clean tea towel (dish towel) and pop into a container or clean jar. In a small saucepan, heat ½ cup (125 ml) rice wine vinegar and 2 tbsp caster (superfine) or white (granulated) sugar. Once the syrup is hot and the sugar has dissolved, pour it over the ginger slices. Seal tightly, allow to cool, then store in the fridge for up to 1 year.

Odd-knobs ginger paste
MAKES ABOUT 1 CUP (200 G)

This little recipe is indispensable for using up kitchen scraps. It packs a punch and can be used as the base for a curry or laksa, stirred into yoghurt for a quick marinade, or added to a noodle dish or fried rice.

Gather up all those old knobs of ginger, wash them (don't bother peeling unless they're really old and gnarly) and throw them into a food processor with a bit of garlic, onion, chilli, carrot, celery and herb stems. You want about 200 g (7 oz) of ingredients all up, so make up this amount with whatever you have. Give it a good blitz then add 2 tsp salt and blitz again to make a paste. Transfer to a clean and dry container and keep refrigerated for up to 1 month. You could add a layer of neutral oil on the surface to help the ginger paste last even longer, about 2 months in the fridge.

Next time you sauté onions, add 1–2 tbsp ginger paste and let your tastebuds sing.

Ginger syrup

MAKES ABOUT 200 ML (7 FL OZ)

This simple syrup is luscious and spicy. Pour it over ice cream or fruit salads, add it to hot water for a tea, drizzle it over cakes, make it the base of a rum cocktail, or use it as a replacement for honey or molasses in baking or as part of a marinade for ribs or chicken wings. Syrups are a common waste hack in our own kitchens, as a way to use up herb stems (p 191), old citrus (p 132) or even pineapple skins (p 353).

In a small saucepan, combine 1 cup (250 ml) water, ½ cup (110 g) caster (superfine) sugar and 30–60 g (1–2¼ oz) sliced ginger, depending on what needs using. You can leave the skin on – just give it a good wash. Bring to the boil over low–medium heat, then reduce the heat and simmer gently for about 15 minutes. The syrup will turn a light golden colour. Remove from the heat and let it cool. Strain the syrup into a clean and dry jar and keep in the fridge for up to 3 months.

The left-over semi-candied ginger will keep in the fridge for 1–2 weeks and makes a delicious snack. Or chop it finely and use in baking or to garnish a cocktail.

Quick ginger beer

If you have Ginger Syrup (above) in the house there's no need to buy ginger beer from the shops. To make a delicious home-made soda without additives, fill a glass with ice and, for every 1 cup (250 ml) sparkling water, add 2 tbsp ginger syrup. A squeeze of lime juice to finish is extra nice.

Grapefruit

Grapefruit used to be puckeringly sour and bitter. Once upon a time, if you saw a pink grapefruit, blood may have been drawn in the fight to claim it, so rare was its appearance in the supermarket. Now growers are actively breeding out sour and bitter flavours, and grapefruits almost always seem to be pink. It's a shame, because bitter is an important flavour. Bitterness can sometimes indicate toxicity, but many bitter foods that we know to be safe to eat can help stimulate digestion. Seek out bitter grapefruit, ask the supermarket for them and acquire a taste for their tart flesh. As with all citrus fruits, every part of the fruit is useful: the skin holds all the volatile oils and the pith is powerfully bitter, so put the whole thing to good use.

Goes with	Tofu, olives, bitter green leaves, brussels sprouts, raw cabbage, fennel, onions, avocado, ginger, other citrus fruits, coriander seeds, fennel seeds, juniper berries, peppercorns, cloves, cinnamon, star anise, vanilla, honey, brown sugar, yoghurt, woody herbs (like thyme, rosemary, bay leaves), most spirits
Storage	Store whole grapefruits in the crisper of the fridge for up to 2 weeks. Cover cut grapefruit with a beeswax wrap or pop into an airtight container and eat within the week.
Substitutes	All citrus fruits swap nicely with each other. Grapefruits are bigger and often more bitter, so replace 1 grapefruit with 2 oranges or, better yet, 1 orange and 1 lemon.

Some ideas for using half a grapefruit

* Squeeze it into a glass and enjoy a fresh wake-up juice or add a splash of tequila for a night-time juice.
* Check out the recipes in <u>cumquats</u> (p 130), <u>lemons</u> (p 238), <u>limes</u> (p 252), <u>mandarins</u> (p 257) and <u>oranges</u> (p 315). Most citrus recipes work with other citrus.
* ***Simple grapefruit salad*** Peel and slice grapefruits, black olives and mint. Drizzle with olive oil and season with salt and pepper.
* ***Grapefruit marinade*** Let the acidity of grapefruit juice tenderise the meat and the zest give it flavour. In a small bowl, mix the zest and juice of ½ grapefruit with 1 tbsp soy sauce or shaoxing wine, and 1 finely chopped garlic clove. Pour over beef or pork strips and marinate in the fridge for at least 4 hours before cooking.

Grapefruit and avocado breakfast salad
SERVES 2

This seems a bit kooky Californian, but we're into it. Tart grapefruit and buttery avocado make for a combination that is both bright and creamy. Obviously this salad can be eaten at any time of the day, and alongside some chicken, or fish or with some grilled (broiled) tempeh, it would be a complete meal. The addition of a poached egg or two makes it even more breakfasty. Use pink grapefruit if you want to eat with your eyes.

Mix 2 tbsp yoghurt, 1 tbsp oil of your choice, a big squeeze of lime juice and a pinch each of salt and pepper, then set aside. Put 1 cup torn salad leaves in a bowl. Peel 1 grapefruit, remove the pith and seeds, and slice into bite-sized pieces. Peel and slice 1 avocado and layer the grapefruit and avocado among the salad leaves. Drizzle the yoghurt dressing over the top and finish with toasted flaked coconut, or seeds and torn herb leaves.

Grapefruit chocolate cake

If you have a bitter–sweet tooth, try the Whole-lemon and Chocolate Cake (p 241), using 1 small grapefruit instead of the lemons. It tastes like a chocolate cake and a jar of marmalade made love.

Grapefruit curd and grapefruit cordial

You'll find the recipes you need for these grown-up sweet treats on pp 155 and 240. Follow the same methods, using grapefruit juice and zest.

Grapefruit marmalade

MAKES 4–5 x 300 ML (10 OZ) JARS

This is our favourite marmalade recipe. You can use any citrus you like, but grapefruit marmalade is a true classic. All grapefruit wants is some sugar and it's ready to be its best self.

Halve and juice 1 kg (2 lb 4 oz) grapefruit. Flatten each juiced half with the palm of your hand and thinly slice the peel into matchsticks. Combine the peel and juice in a good-sized wide saucepan or jam pan, then add 12 cups (3 litres) water and spices or herbs if using (a few thyme or rosemary sprigs, or 1 tbsp juniper berries or black peppercorns). Simmer over low heat until the peel is soft and translucent, 1–1½ hours. Remove from the heat and slowly stir in 1 kg (2 lb 4 oz) white (granulated) sugar until dissolved. Return to medium heat and bring to the boil. Boil steadily, stirring every now and then, until the marmalade has reached setting point (p 503).

While the marmalade is cooking, sterilise your jars (p 501). When the marmalade is ready, carefully remove the jars from the oven and place on the bench. Let them cool for a minute or two, then carefully spoon the marmalade into the jars, wipe the rims with clean paper towel and seal immediately. Leave to cool. Check the lids for the correct seal (p 503), then store in a cool, dark place for up to 12 months. To extend the shelf life to 2 years, heat-process (p 502) the jars for 10 minutes.

Skins and pith

Dry grapefruit peel following the method in Drying Mandarin Peel (p 259). Use dried grapefruit peel for gin and tonics, to make syrups (p 258) or to add a bitter edge to slow-cooked dishes.

Grapefruit skin bitters

MAKES 2 CUPS (500 ML)

There's one place where bitter flavours are still much appreciated, and that's in beverages. Aperitifs and digestives are made with bitter ingredients considered to be good for digestion. You might have tonic water in your fridge for gin and tonics, or to mix with juice or cordial. This recipe is a cheat's version of tonic water that also utilises the bitterness of grapefruit scraps.

Use the peel and pith of 2 large grapefruits (300–400 g). Put these scraps in a saucepan with ¾ cups (165 g) caster (superfine) sugar, 5 allspice berries, 2 star anise, 1 roughly chopped lemongrass stem (white and green bits), 1 tbsp juniper berries, ½ tsp salt, ¼ tsp black peppercorns and 2 cups (500 ml) water.

Bring this all to the boil over medium heat, then reduce the heat to low and gently simmer, covered, for 20 minutes. Remove from the heat and leave at room temperature to steep overnight. Strain into a clean and dry bottle or jar and store in the fridge for up to 2 weeks. Start with 2 tbsp bitters to 30 ml (1 fl oz) gin and top with sparkling water for a classic gin and tonic, then add more bitters to taste. Add a preserved cumquat (p 132) to make it fancy.

See cumquats, limes, mandarins and oranges for ideas with other citrus. *See also* preserved lemon.

Grapes

Where did all the good grapes go? Most of the grapes sold in the supermarket have a mild 'nothing' sweetness. If you can find more interesting varieties such as muscat, you're in for a treat, because they can be musty and jammy and, of course, like wine. The white seedless variety is the one that seems to get wasted the most, as it comes back from school half eaten or sits in the fruit bowl waiting for someone to notice it. Luckily, it doesn't take much to turn a compost-bound grape into the ingredient that saved dinner.

Go with   Nuts, cheeses, berries, peaches, figs, melons, pomegranate, cured meats, chicken, pork, warm spices, grains such as couscous, brown rice, vinegar, sugar, olive oil, woody herbs (like rosemary, thyme)

Storage   Don't wash grapes until you're ready to eat them. Their natural bloom, most visible on darker varieties, protects them and makes them last longer. Keep grapes on their stems and refrigerate in an airtight container for 2–3 weeks.

Substitutes   Nashi pear has a light flavour quite like white grapes, and you can cook blueberries with similar results to red grapes. Currants, cherries and pomegranate seeds could also work.

Some ideas for using a handful of grapes

* Save a few wrinkly grapes by roasting them. Follow the Roasted Cherries recipe (p 103), then add them to a very simple radicchio and parsley salad. Use the pan juices as the dressing. Roasted grapes are also a nice addition to roasted meats or creamy cheeses.
* Add sliced grapes to the Best Barley Side (p 29) or the Big Grain Salad (p 379).
* If you're making focaccia, use halved grapes and rosemary as the topping.
* Freeze grapes and use them like ice cubes in cordials or cocktails.
* Make a fresh version of sultana cake by replacing the apples in Jaimee's Apple Bake (p 7) with grapes. Black grapes make a particularly striking cake.

Grape salad

SERVES 3–4 AS A SMALL SIDE

Grapes make a sophisticated 1970s-vibe savoury salad. Serve with grilled (broiled) fish or lamb, with falafel or haloumi cheese, or as part of a Mediterranean-style shared spread.

Wash and dry about 250 g (9 oz) white grapes and put them in a serving bowl. Wash, dry and halve 250 g (9 oz) black grapes, carefully remove the seeds, then add to the bowl. Sprinkle 2 tsp caster (superfine) sugar over the grapes and add the finely grated zest of 1 orange. Cover with a beeswax wrap and leave at room temperature for 1–2 hours. The grapes should release some of their juice. Sprinkle with salt and pepper. Squeeze in the juice of the orange and mix in 1 tbsp olive oil and 1 tsp fennel seeds.

Dried grapes

Amaze your small children by putting the grapes no one wants to eat in a low oven and opening it up at the end of the day to find sultanas. Follow the Drying Fruits method on p 357.

Quick grape relish from lunchbox-reject grapes

MAKES 1 CUP (250 ML)

Heat 2 tbsp olive oil in a frying pan over medium heat and sauté ½–1 red onion until soft and sweet. Add 3 chopped garlic cloves, 2–3 tsp chopped rosemary or thyme, some lemon or orange zest and juice, and lots of ground black pepper. Sauté for 1–2 minutes, then add up to 2 cups (360 g) chopped rejected grapes. Sauté for 5 minutes, until the grapes start to soften, then add 2–3 tbsp vinegar of your choice, 2 tsp sugar and ½ tsp salt. Sauté for another 5–7 minutes, or until the grapes start to collapse and caramelise a little. Serve with sausages or roasted pumpkin (squash) and a brown rice salad. Refrigerate in a clean jar or airtight container for up to 2 weeks.

Preserved sweet and sour grapes

Sticky, sour and spiced preserved grapes are excellent to have in the fridge. By cooking them in a combination of vinegar, sugar and spices you end up with glossy orbs of flavour that will add a punch to cheese plates, or can be sliced and added to salads like the Basic Brussels Slaw (p 60), roasted meats or a grainy salad like the Best Barley Side (p 29). We also add them to drinks or serve them with not so sweet desserts.

Follow the Sweet and Sour Cumquats recipe (p 131), replacing the cumquats with 1–2 cups (180–360 g) of whatever grapes you have on hand. You'll only need to simmer them for 3–5 minutes; grapes aren't as dense as cumquats, so they need less cooking time.

VINE LEAVES

If you grow your own grapes, you'll have vine leaves. Their flavour is grassy and lemony, and the tendrils are particularly sour in the best way.

Some ideas for using vine leaves

* Add them to salads. When young and tender they can be torn and used like any salad leaf. When they're larger they can be more leathery. That's the time to sauté them or use them in the Greens Pie Filling (p 412).
* Make dolmades. Use fresh or preserved vine leaves to make this Greek favourite – your own preserved vine leaves will make it extra special.
* Wrap fish. If you're using fresh leaves, give them a quick blanch in boiling water first, or if you're using preserved leaves, rinse them well. Wrap the fish in the vine leaves and tie with kitchen string. Brush with olive oil and season with salt and pepper. Cook on the barbecue for 15 minutes, turning every 5 minutes or so, or cook in a 230°C (450°F) oven for 20 minutes. Allow the fish to steam in the leaves for 5 minutes before serving. Unwrap to serve.

Preserved vine leaves

MAKES 1 × 500 ML (18 OZ) JAR

Depending on the size of your vine leaves, you'll need about 25 for a 500 ml (18 oz) jar. Bring a large pot of water to the boil and have a bowl of iced water ready. Working in batches of 5–6 leaves, plunge vine leaves into boiling water, then fish out with a slotted spoon or spider and refresh in iced water. Pat dry and allow to cool. Bring 1 cup (250 ml) water to the boil with ¼ cup (60 ml) lemon juice, 2 tbsp white wine vinegar and ¼ tsp salt. Boil to dissolve the salt, then remove the pickling liquid from the heat. Make stacks of about 6 vine leaves, roll them up as if you were rolling a cigar (pretend, okay?), and fit the rolls into a 500 ml (18 oz) jar. Cover with the pickling liquid and seal securely. Heat-process (p 502) for 20 minutes. Store in the pantry for up to 6 months, then refrigerate once opened and use within 3 months.

H

Ham

A little ham sliced off the bone or bought from the deli is handy for lunches, but can also find a few more uses than just sandwiches. Ham has plenty of salty flavour that can be used as a seasoning in your cooking.

Goes with   Lentils, eggs, cheeses, peas, leafy greens, asparagus, broad beans, tomatoes, okra, celery, olives, cumquats, oranges, cherries, grapes, figs, melons, pears, apples, pineapple, avocado, herbs, honey, macadamias

Storage   Thinly sliced ham from the deli or supermarket will keep in an airtight container for 4–5 days. Slices of ham can also be frozen. Wipe any moisture off the surface and wrap tightly in foil, making sure to press out all the air, then place in an airtight container. It will keep this way for up to 2 months. Defrost ham in the fridge overnight. If you need to store a whole leg of ham, on or off the bone, the best way is to submerge a ham bag or clean tea towel (dish towel) in 2 cups (500 ml) water and 1 tbsp vinegar. Wring it out and keep the ham in it, in the fridge, for up to 2 weeks. Re-soak the bag when it dries out.

Substitutes   Bacon, obviously, and prosciutto. If you're looking for a meat-free salty flavour punch to add to stocks and stews, then parmesan rinds or sun-dried tomatoes will do nicely instead of a ham bone.

Some ideas for finishing off a bit of ham

* If you have the ham bone, please make stock or soup.
* Make the Brie and Jam Fried Sandwich (p 91) with ham and cheese instead of jam and cheese.
* Chop it up and make a ham and pineapple pizza. Go on, we won't tell anyone.
* Make the Whatever-cheese Eggy Muffins (p 93) and add some chopped ham.
* Thrill the kids with green eggs and ham. Blitz basil or parsley to a paste and whisk into eggs before scrambling. Fry left-over ham to serve alongside.
* Dice up the ham and throw it into pasta with green olives, parsley and plenty of olive oil. Toast Breadcrumbs (p 51) to scatter on top.
* Use it in a potato salad (p 362) instead of bacon.
* Add a small handful of chopped ham to Mirepoix (p 314). While it's not traditional, it will add salty smokiness when sautéing onions and celery for soups and stews.
* Add it to Odd-knobs Mac 'n' Cheese (p 101).

Crispy hammy bits

Crisping up ham in the oven is like making cheat's bacon, and a great way of transforming a few left-over ham slices into a useful punch of flavour and texture to add to a caesar salad (p 4), potato salads (p 362), lentil dishes, pasta dishes, soups and stews. The salty flavour of ham does intensify when crisped, so don't add extra salt, just a good crack of black pepper. Follow the oven method for Home-made Bacon Bits (p 23), cooking for a little less time than for bacon, then chopping roughly.

Ham in greens

This dish is a variation on a Southern US classic that customarily uses collard greens to go with ham. We suggest the Tastiest Bunch of Kale (p 221), and either adding roughly chopped pieces of left-over ham for the last 10 minutes of cooking or seasoning with the Crispy Hammy Bits above. Serve with mashed potato, grilled (broiled) meats, Sweet Corn Polenta (p 119), corn bread, and other picnic- and barbecue-style dishes.

Harissa paste

Harissa paste is a fiery condiment used in North African and Middle Eastern cooking. It's often bought for a specific recipe and then the half-filled jar gets lost at the back of the fridge because no one quite knows how to finish it. Use it to add kapow to soups and stews, add a kick to salad dressings or to make burgers for grown-ups.

Goes with Fish (especially sardines), lamb, chicken, chickpeas, couscous, lentils, potatoes, eggplant (aubergine), capsicum (pepper), zucchini (courgettes), okra, carrots, fennel, onions, garlic, hummus, yoghurt, lemon, eggs, coriander (cilantro), parsley

---

Storage Once opened, harissa paste should be stored in the fridge for 4–6 weeks. Keep in mind that the more acid (lemon or vinegar), salt and oil it contains, the longer it will keep, as these ingredients preserve foods.

Substitutes If a recipe calls for harissa paste, it probably needs some heat. Try another chilli paste or hot sauce and add plenty of warm spices (ground cumin, coriander seeds, paprika or caraway seeds).

Some ideas for finishing up that jar of harissa paste

* Dollop on pizza with Garlicky Marinated Eggplant (p 144) and goat's cheese. See 'Clear Out the Fridge' Pizza (p 97) for more.
* Stretch out the last scrapings by adding some olive oil and a splash of vinegar, giving the jar a good shake and pouring over roasted pumpkin (squash) or a lentil salad.
* Slow-cook lamb shanks with a big dollop of harissa paste and a tin of tomatoes.
* Stir a spoonful into hummus.
* Stir a little into yoghurt to use as either a dip or a marinade for chicken or fish.
* Mix oil and harissa paste with something sweet like honey or maple syrup, then coat carrots, wedges of pumpkin (squash) or chickpeas in this mixture before roasting. »

* Add 1–2 tbsp to the Simple Chickpea Stew (p 110) or Green Beans and Grains (p 41).
* *Spicy burger sauce* Mix 3 tbsp harissa paste with ⅓ cup (85 g) mayonnaise (p 154).
* *Harissa rice* This is such a simple way to make a flavoursome rice dish to eat with meat or roasted vegetables. Follow the Anything-goes Rice recipe (p 394), adding 2–3 tbsp harissa paste with the garlic.
* *Harissa roast potatoes* Follow the Pesto Roast Potatoes recipe (p 346), using 2–3 tbsp harissa paste instead of pesto.

Harissa-roasted eggplant

SERVES 4 AS A SIDE

Preheat the oven to 180°C (350°F). Cut 2 eggplants (aubergines) lengthways into 6 wedges or slices. In a large bowl mix 3 tbsp harissa paste and ¼ cup (60 ml) oil of your choice, then add the eggplant and coat every piece well. Spread the eggplant on a baking tray and bake for 30 minutes or until soft inside. Allow to cool.

Meanwhile, make a dressing with ⅓ cup (95 g) plain yoghurt, the juice and zest of 1 lemon, 1 finely chopped garlic clove and ¼ tsp sumac if you have it. Arrange the cooled eggplant on a serving plate and drizzle with the yoghurt dressing. Garnish with herbs and serve with hummus and flat breads, the Pine Nut Sort of Hashweh (p 295), koftas and tabouleh.

Harissa simmer sauce

Make this when you're sick of looking at the jar of harissa paste in the fridge. Use it to simmer browned meatballs, chicken, cooked or tinned chickpeas, or vegetables like cauliflower, green beans and potatoes.

Heat oil or butter in a saucepan over medium heat and sauté 1 small diced onion until soft and sweet. Add 3–4 tbsp harissa paste and 400 g (14 oz) tinned chopped tomatoes. Add ½ cup (125 ml) stock or wine and a big squeeze of lemon juice, then simmer for 5 minutes or so. Taste, then add salt and pepper and another squeeze of lemon juice as needed. Add about 500 g (1 lb 2 oz) browned meatballs or chicken thighs, 1–2 cups cooked chickpeas or parboiled potato or cauliflower, or a big handful of green beans. Simmer until the meat or vegetables are cooked through and the sauce is glossy. Top with chopped fresh herbs, such as coriander (cilantro), parsley or mint, and serve with couscous.

Herbs, soft

Fresh herbs – parsley, mint, dill, coriander (cilantro), chives, basil – are like soft lettuce leaves, and one of the most perishable items at the supermarket, meaning they end up being bought, neglected and thrown away within a matter of days. Plus, they're generally wrapped in plastic, so from a sustainability viewpoint, store-bought herbs set off alarm bells. If you're not a herb-grower, we're here to help you make better buying, storing and cooking decisions and stop sentencing your herbs to a slimy end at the back of the fridge.

First, get to know your green friends. The more you understand an ingredient, know its place in the kitchen, value it and basically fall in love with it, the less likely you are to throw it away. Soft herbs have soft leaves, with stems you can eat, or at least extract flavour from. Yes, they have their own taste, but really, you can swap them with each other without too much thought. The confidence to use what you have, rather than what a recipe calls for, should stop you buying multiple bunches you don't really need.

You can also use celery leaves, fennel fronds or carrot tops in place of soft herbs. So if those vegetables are already in your basket, maybe skip buying herbs this week, and embrace root-to-tip cooking. And a little reminder that soft herbs should generally be added at the end of the cooking process, just before serving, to brighten and lighten a dish.

In the following herb recipes, ideas and waste hacks, any soft herb can be used, or a combination of what you have. We'll make a note if there's anything that's truly awful and shouldn't be done, but otherwise we advise experimenting. Some of our best recipes have come from an intense desire to use something up and get dinner on the table.

BASIL

Never buy basil in winter. It's a summer herb and should appear in the kitchen once the tomato season starts. As basil is difficult to store well, don't buy too much, unless you're making batches of pesto.

Goes with   Green beans, broad beans, peas, fennel, tomatoes, eggplant (aubergine), zucchini (courgettes), capsicum (pepper), spinach, wombok (Chinese cabbage), chilli, summer fruits (peaches, berries, mango, pineapple, persimmons), nuts, cheeses, black pepper, paprika, garlic, lemons, limes, bacon, chicken, fish, eggs

---

Storage   Basil hates cool, damp environments, so the fridge is a torture chamber for a bunch of basil. It's best kept, like a bunch of flowers, in a jar on the bench. Make sure there are no leaves under the water level. Pick leaves as you need them, then quickly make one of the green sauces in the following pages.

Substitutes   Basil tastes like pepper, cloves and star anise – Italian cooks add a clove to their stews if their basil isn't intense enough. For salads, tarragon, mint, dill or parsley would be a fine option, or for Italian meals, use fresh or dried oregano.

Some ideas for using up basil

* Make any of the green sauces in this section – Classic Basil Pesto (opposite), Bright Green Sauce (p 193), Minty Green Goddess Sauce (p 197), Salsa Verde (p 194) or Chimichurri (p 193).
* Pile basil leaves on top of takeaway pizza. It saves you making a salad.
* Make green eggs by blitzing basil with salt and oil and stirring it through whisked eggs before scrambling.
* Basil goes beautifully with strawberries. Chop strawberries, sprinkle with sugar, add lots of torn basil leaves and a drizzle of balsamic vinegar. Let sit for 15 minutes, then serve.
* Preserving basil is tricky because it loses its flavour and colour and goes slimy. You can dry basil following the method on p 207, although it won't be as intense in flavour. Or you can make a basil butter, as the fat in the butter will preserve the colour and flavour – see Herby Compound Butter on p 192. Or you can freeze basil by following the directions on p 195.

Classic basil pesto – or 'What's in the fridge' green sauce

MAKES ABOUT ¾ CUP (185 ML)

You can replace the basil with any soft green herbs, including celery leaves, carrot tops and fennel fronds, and don't be afraid to mix and match if you have a little of this and a little of that to use up. You can also replace the pine nuts with whatever nuts or seeds you have on hand. This is an excellent method for using up *very* tired herbs. Once they're blitzed, no one will know.

In a food processor, put 1–2 large handfuls of basil leaves, 1 garlic clove, an optional ⅓ cup each of pine nuts and grated parmesan, and a big pinch of salt. Blitz to a paste and then, with the motor running, drizzle in 100–150 ml (3½–5 fl oz) oil of your choice, until well combined and of a good consistency. Taste, season as needed, then store in a clean jar with a layer of oil on the surface to prevent discolouration. Keep in the fridge for up to 10 days.

Some ideas for using basil stems

* Add basil stems to a jug of water and keep in the fridge for a few days.
* *Basil stem syrup* Pour over ice cream or fruit salads or into drinks. Use the Ginger Syrup recipe (p 176), replacing the ginger with the stems from 1 bunch of basil. Add 1 tsp black peppercorns for a savoury edge.
* *Basil-infused vodka* Follow the Cumquat Brandy infusion method (p 132), using vodka, the stems from 1–2 bunches of basil, strips of peel from 1 lemon and a little pinch of chilli powder. You can also use the leaves here if you want extra-aniseedy vodka.

CHIVES

What else are chives for except snipping onto a baked potato with sour cream? If you grow them, you'll be well versed in throwing them into everything, but if you've just bought a bunch and are looking for ways to use the rest up, then read on.

Go with   Chives are an entirely edible member of the allium family (onions, leeks, garlic), adding a mild, fresh oniony flavour to dips and sauces, salads, sandwiches and egg dishes. Use them with potatoes, tofu, fish or chicken. Add to creamy things like mayonnaise, cottage or cream cheese, sour cream or butter. They also suit tomatoes, zucchini (courgettes), eggplant (aubergine), pumpkin (squash), fennel, sweet potato, asparagus, broad beans, green beans, snow peas (mange tout), turnips, wombok (Chinese cabbage), avocado, garlic and horseradish.

Storage	For quick and easy use, and so you don't forget you bought them, keep chives in a jar, with a little water, on the bench. A reusable plastic bag over the top will keep them fresher for longer. To store for more than a few days, wrap in paper towel or a clean tea towel (dish towel) or clean Chux and store in a bag or airtight container in the fridge. You can freeze chives in a snaplock bag and snip off bits as you need them, no need to defrost.
Substitutes	Thinly sliced leeks, spring onions (scallions) or wild garlic (ramsons), but remember they're not as mild as chives, so use less. Parsley, coriander (cilantro) or celery leaves will bring a similar freshness when used as a garnish.

Some ideas for using up chives

* Add snipped chives to any salad – green, lentil, tomato or caesar (p 4). Just use them up.
* If you've got chives in the house, plan on having baked potatoes or Jacket Sweet Potatoes (p 450) for dinner. Even the smallest ingredient can be the inspiration for a meal.
* Smash avocado with chives, lemon juice and salt, then spread on toast.
* Make Alex's Tartare Sauce (p 94) or add snipped chives to Tzatziki (p 491).
* Snip chives into any of the mayonnaise sauces under Cheat's Aioli (p 269).
* Try the Savoury Poppy Seed Spread (p 406). You only need 2 tbsp finely chopped chives.
* Add chives to scrambled eggs, omelettes (p 150) or Whatever-cheese Eggy Muffins (p 93).

Herby compound butter

Herby compound butters not only taste amazing, but are an excellent way to preserve excess herbs – the fat in the butter will keep your herbs from deteriorating in colour and flavour. They can be wrapped in baking paper and stored in the fridge for 3–4 weeks or the freezer for months. Chive butter is a favourite of ours for cooking potatoes and omelettes (p 150), sautéing snow peas (mange tout) or asparagus, or sneaking on top of a steak, but basil or dill butters are also delicious. Follow the Anchovy Butter recipe (p 3), using 3–4 tbsp finely chopped herbs, with plenty of salt and a little pepper (omit the cinnamon and cayenne pepper), for each 125 g (4½ oz) butter.

CORIANDER (CILANTRO)

Coriander is worth buying as more than just a garnish for tacos. It's a clever herb, giving us something helpful in the kitchen, from the roots to the leaves. Use the leaves for garnishes; thinly slice the soft stems for salsas or blitz them into sauces; and wash and finely chop the roots to add to sautéed onions or throw them unchopped into the pot when making stock.

Goes with	Coriander is used in different cuisines all around the world, and goes with too many ingredients to list. You'll find it in or on top of Indian curries; in Spanish dishes and Mexican salsas; and in Chinese, Thai and Middle Eastern dishes. It isn't traditionally used in Italian cooking, so keep it out of your bolognese sauce, but otherwise experiment. It's lemony, warm and super fresh. Use it with other intense flavours, like fresh ginger, chilli and lots of garlic.
Storage	Wrap gently in a clean damp cloth, then place in a reusable plastic bag or an airtight container in the fridge for 5 days, or more if it still looks okay. Wash it before you use it, not before you store it.
Substitutes	Parsley and a little lemon juice would be the best replacement for coriander. We also use celery leaves if there's no coriander in the house.

Bright green sauce – dressings for the week ahead

In a food processor, put 2–3 cups soft green herbs and chopped herb stems (basil and mint stems are best turned into syrups; they don't pulverise well), add 2 garlic cloves, the finely grated zest and juice of ½ lemon, and ¼ tsp each of salt, pepper and sugar. Blitz to a paste then, with the motor running, pour in ½ cup (125 ml) neutral oil like grapeseed, sunflower or a good-quality vegetable oil. Taste, season as needed, then store in a sealed jar in the fridge for up to 1 week, and drizzle over everything in that time.

CHIMICHURRI

Use this on tacos, steamed green beans, boiled eggs, grilled fish or lamb. Replace the lemon with 1–2 tbsp red wine vinegar and add ½ tsp each of ground cumin and chilli flakes. »

SALSA VERDE

Follow the directions for the Bright Green Sauce, then add ¼ cup (about 50 g) chopped pickles or capers and 1 finely chopped fresh green chilli, and pulse gently. Serve with grilled vegetables and meats.

Some ideas for using coriander (cilantro) stems and roots

* Wash the roots really well in a small bowl of water to remove any gritty bits. Then add to Odd-knobs Ginger Paste (p 175) or End-of-the-week Vegie Stock Paste (p 447).
* Finely chop coriander stems and roots, then either pound with a mortar and pestle or crush with the back of a spoon, along with chopped fresh chillies, finely chopped garlic and salt. Store in the fridge for up to 1 week, and add to stir-fries, curries and marinades.

DILL

Dill has our hearts. It's for all our favourite things: pickles, sauerkraut, Jaimee's Russian dumplings, sour cream and home remedies.

Goes with	Potatoes, eggs, asparagus, cucumber, cabbage, sauerkraut, beetroot, tomatoes, zucchini (courgettes), green beans, broad beans, peas, fennel, mushrooms, capers, horseradish, nuts, sour cream, soft cheeses, yoghurt, mayonnaise, lemons, pomegranate, black pepper, vinegar, garlic, rice, buckwheat
Storage	Wrap dill gently in a clean damp cloth, then place in a reusable plastic bag or an airtight container in the fridge for about 5 days. Wash it before you use it, not before you store it.
Substitutes	Dill is from the celery family and tastes like chilled-out caraway seeds, making it easy to substitute. A small amount of caraway seeds in a dish will taste remarkably like dill, and for colour use finely chopped celery leaves.

How to freeze dill (and other herbs) If you're left with too much dill, finely chop dill leaves or blitz them in a food processor and mix with olive oil. Pack into ice-cube trays and top with more oil. The frozen herbs will stay green and fresh-tasting for 3 months. On winter's darkest days you can just pop them out and throw them into a soup or stew, or heat them in a pan to cook a piece of fish.

Some ideas for using up dill

* Make Basic Sauerkraut (p 66), using up the last bits of cabbage and dill. Add a grated ½ apple too if you have one hanging around.
* Whip up the Massaged Cabbage and Herb Salad (p 67) and add the rest of the dill.
* Make a cucumber salad (p 127) and toss in a generous amount of chopped dill.
* Finely chop and add to sour cream, cream cheese or labneh with a little lemon and finely chopped garlic, and have fish burgers for dinner.
* Make the Bright Green Sauce (p 193) with dill and drizzle it over warm potatoes, baked fish, roasted beetroot or meatballs.
* A very simple salad with diced and well-seasoned tomatoes, a finely chopped garlic clove, a splash of red wine vinegar and lots of chopped dill is a welcome addition at breakfast, lunch or dinner.
* Make a gut-soothing tea with a big handful of dill and a little honey. See p 205 for tips on tea-making.

Green rice
SERVES 4–6

We love rice dishes that use up a bit of this and a bit of that. This green rice dish is based on a Cuban recipe that uses coriander (cilantro), but our version uses any tired herbs – like dill or parsley – and either a green capsicum (pepper), some shredded white cabbage or half a fennel bulb. Green rice can be served with fish, egg dishes, meatballs, falafel or barbecued zucchini (courgettes) and capsicums (peppers). Follow the Anything-goes Rice recipe (p 394), using fennel, shredded cabbage or green capsicum as the vegetables and the leaves from 1 bunch of soft herbs, even if they're very tired-looking.

Some ideas for using dill stems

∗ If there are dill stems in the house, it means it's time to make pickles. Follow the Basic Vegetable Pickling recipe (p 472), adding dill stems and black peppercorns to each jar.

∗ Make a stem version of Salsa Verde (p 194). Chop the stems up a little before blitzing them.

∗ Very thinly slice dill stems and sauté with onions and garlic as the base of a warm lentil salad.

∗ Make a very elegant Two-egg Omelette (p 150) by adding a handful of very finely chopped dill stems and lots of black pepper.

MINT

Mint is a good-times summer herb for cool drinks, green salads and yoghurty dips – and to relieve the gut after too much fun has been had. There are lots of mint varieties, but here we're focusing on the most common mints, spearmint and peppermint.

Goes with	All the cool things – cucumber, zucchini (courgettes), tomatoes, celery, fennel, ginger, lemongrass, lime juice, gin, lemons, coriander (cilantro) and yoghurt. It also pairs well with figs, mango, melon, passionfruit, pineapple, kiwi fruit, persimmons, pomegranate, avocado, corn, turnips, wombok (Chinese cabbage), chilli, cinnamon, star anise, nuts, sesame seeds, tofu, seafood, feta, ricotta, cream, garlic, lamb, potatoes, peas, snow peas (mange tout), dried beans, chickpeas, lentils, broad beans and green beans.
Storage	Mint, like basil, hates the cold and damp and is best stored in a jar of water on the bench. Having said that, mint isn't quite as sensitive as its pal basil, so it can be wrapped in a clean cloth and popped in a reusable plastic bag or an airtight container, then stored in the fridge for about 5 days.
Substitutes	If you're out of mint, use parsley or coriander (cilantro) for savoury dishes and basil for sweet dishes. We know it's not the same, but it'll get a meal on the table without you having to go to the shops.

Some *encourage-mint* for using up a bunch or a few sprigs

✱ Mint means it's curry night, or time to serve up koftas and flat breads. Head to Basic Yoghurt Condiments (p 491) for Raita and Tzatziki.

✱ Mint also means it's time for a round of mint juleps. Muddle mint in a simple sugar syrup, then add bourbon and lots of ice.

✱ Make a mint jelly using the Rosemary and Apple Jelly recipe (p 209).

✱ Add handfuls to Maddie's Grandma's Tabouleh (p 199).

✱ Finely chop mint and stir it through buttered warm peas with plenty of salt and pepper.

✱ *Mint syrup* Follow the Ginger Syrup recipe (p 176), replacing the ginger with 1 bunch of mint. Drizzle the syrup over fresh pineapple or mango, or on ice cream, or add to drinks. If you've grown lots of mint, make a big batch of syrup, heat-process it (p 502) for 20 minutes and store in the pantry.

✱ *Fresh mint tea* Add a bundle of mint to hot water or hot black tea with a slice of lemon and a cinnamon stick. See Lemongrass Tea (p 205) for more details.

Minty green goddess sauce

MAKES ABOUT 2 CUPS (500 ML)

Green goddess sauces are so good they're worth building a meal around. This version is for tuna or chicken sandwiches, Fishcakes (p 165), burgers or potato wedges, or for drizzling over avocado on toast. It also makes a pretty luxe salad dressing.

In a blender or food processor, place 1 bunch of mint leaves, ½ cup other herbs or soft green leaves (rocket/arugula, celery leaves, tarragon, dill or parsley), 2 tbsp lemon juice, 1 tsp finely grated lemon zest and ½ tsp salt. Blitz, add ¼ cup (60 g) mayonnaise and ¼ cup (65 g) sour cream (or a combo of whatever other creamy things you have), then blitz again. Store in an airtight container in the fridge for up to 5 days. If you want to use this sauce as a salad dressing, you can thin it out by whisking in a little water.

PARSLEY

Parsley is the king of herbs when it comes to health – full of antioxidants and vitamins. It's the kind of herb we could be eating daily by the handful, especially as it's mild and can be liberally thrown around without offending anyone. Unlike other soft herbs that need a gentle touch, parsley is quite hardy. It can handle being very finely chopped for salads and dressings without bruising, it can be cooked for a little longer than its fragile friends, and it can even withstand deep-frying. It's a good herb to buy if you don't use herbs often, because it lasts for a long time if stored correctly.

Goes with	Lentils, broad beans, dried beans, green beans, tofu, fish, eggs, mayonnaise, nuts, capers, soft and tangy cheeses, yoghurt, bay leaves, cumin, juniper berries, pomegranate, buckwheat, barley, most vegetables – avocado, cucumber, asparagus, beetroot, corn, fennel, tomatoes, eggplant (aubergine), capsicum (pepper), zucchini (courgettes), cabbage, sauerkraut, parsnips, turnips, potatoes, pumpkin (squash), carrots, mushrooms
Storage	Wrap parsley gently in a clean damp cloth, then store in a reusable plastic bag or an airtight container in the fridge for about 1 week. Wash it before you use it, not before you store it.
Substitutes	Carrots and parsley are both in the celery family, so if you don't have parsley use carrot tops instead, or celery leaves. Mint, basil and dill would also work without too much drama.

Some ideas for getting rid of parsley

* Throw parsley into every salad, omelette (p 150), sandwich and juice you make this week.
* Chop it and freeze it. It's quite robust, so it freezes okay just in an airtight container. Or follow the How to Freeze Dill method on p 195.
* Make a simple salad with parsley leaves, celery leaves and Quick-pickled Red Onion (p 312), then dress with lemon juice, salt, pepper, extra virgin olive oil and a little pickling liquid.
* Make Green Tahini (p 454) and drizzle it over roasted vegetables, or use it as a spread on wraps with falafel or as a dip with celery and carrot sticks.

* The Celery Leaf Gremolata With Green Olives (p 88) is delicious. Replace the celery leaves with parsley leaves and use it to garnish soups, lentil stews (p 246) or grilled (broiled) meats.
* ***Parsley pesto*** Use walnuts or almonds and follow the Classic Basil Pesto recipe (p 191).
* ***Herby meatballs*** Follow the Tasty Meatballs recipe (p 54), adding 1 cup (about 60 g) finely chopped parsley leaves. Serve with any of the green sauces listed on pp 190–194.

Parsley pasta sauce

On your chopping board, roughly chop 4 anchovies and 2 garlic cloves, then use the flat of your knife to mash them together. Combine in a bowl with 1–2 large handfuls of very finely chopped parsley (or basil or dill, or a mix of all the green things), add ½ cup (110 g) chopped green olives or 2–3 tbsp chopped capers or preserved lemon, or both. Mix through ½ cup (125 ml) extra virgin olive oil and season with salt and pepper.

This sauce will keep in the fridge for 3–4 days. Mix it through hot pasta with a big squeeze of lemon juice, heaps of grated parmesan and toasted breadcrumbs.

Maddie's grandma's tabouleh
SERVES 4–6

Maddie is Alex's daughter Maeve's' good mate who shares excellent food tips from her grandparents when she comes over.

Soak ½ cup (90 g) burghul (bulgur) according to the packet directions, then fluff up with a fork. Finely dice 4 tomatoes, then place in a colander with a little salt to drain. Add a finely diced onion if you'd like. Combine 4 big handfuls of finely chopped parsley with the burghul, tomatoes, onion if using, and plenty of chopped mint. Dress with *lots* of extra virgin olive oil, lemon juice, salt, pepper and either ½ tsp spice mix 5 (p 420) or a little ground allspice and ground cinnamon.

Some ideas for using parsley stems

* Parsley stems are full of flavour and are much needed for stocks (p 446), and for cooking dried beans, chickpeas and lentils. Just toss a handful into the cooking water.
* Chop them very finely and sauté them with onion, leek, celery and carrot as the base of any soup, stew or pie, a mixture the French call Mirepoix (p 314).
* Gently sauté them with garlic in plenty of oil and butter, then fry a piece of fish.
* Chop and add to Bright Green Sauce (p 193), Chimichurri (p 193) or Salsa Verde (p 194).

Herbs, woody

Woody herbs are more like leaves from a tree. They have stick-like stems and are intense in flavour because of their high levels of aromatic oils. Rosemary, thyme, bay leaves, curry leaves, oregano and sage fall into this category. They are usually added during the cooking process to enhance slow-cooked dishes. They are also vital in preserving and home remedies. Don't worry about using fresh woody herbs if a recipe calls for dried and vice versa – just remember that home-dried herbs lose some of their intensity, so amp up the quantity the recipe calls for.

Storage
If you buy woody herbs they generally come in a small bunch, and you use a sprig or two then wonder what to do with the rest of it. You have two options for storage: wrap them in a slightly damp clean cloth and store them in a reusable plastic bag in the fridge for 2 weeks or more; or hang the bunch upside down in a well-ventilated area – such as near a window – to dry. As they dry, use a sprig here and there in cooking or to make herbal tea. Once completely dry, strip off the leaves and store them in an airtight jar for 3–6 months. If you have excess woody herbs you'd like to use, try some of our super-simple preservation methods – see Herby Vinegar (p 202), Oregano Salt (p 207) or Sage Elixir (p 211) – and turn them into something even more delicious to use down the track.

BAY LEAVES

In almost every cooking class we teach, someone asks, 'What do bay leaves even do?' Jaimee can't resist replying, 'What don't they do?' We are bay leaf lovers. We believe in their flavours and their powers. Bay leaves taste like the woods – eucalyptus, nutmeg and earth. They are for dishes that need lengthy simmering, as the heat and the slow cooking release the bay's oils and deepen the flavour of your dish. And legend even has it that bay can foster telepathic powers and protect us from thunder and lightning. As we said, what don't bay leaves do? The only thing you can't do is eat them – they need to be fished out of whatever dish you've used them in.

Go with   Other herbs like thyme, parsley, sage and rosemary, as well as spices like cumin, coriander seeds, fennel seeds, allspice, cinnamon, nutmeg, cloves, juniper berries, paprika and peppercorns. Bay will add flavour to meaty stews, tomato-based sauces, eggplant (aubergine), fennel, chickpeas, lentils, dried beans, pickles, grapefruit, marmalade, milk, custard and ice cream.

Storage   Store fresh bay leaves wrapped in a slightly damp clean cloth, then inside a reusable plastic bag or an airtight container in the fridge for many weeks, or for many months in the freezer. Stored in an airtight container, dried bay leaves keep their flavour well for 3–6 months; after this they lose their intensity, but don't throw them away – just add extra to your dish.

Substitutes   Fresh bay leaves smell stronger and can be a little bitter; dried are more intensely herbal in flavour and will add more punch to your dish. One dried bay leaf is equivalent to two fresh. If there's no bay in the house, add some black peppercorns and a juniper berry or two. Or replace with a thyme sprig, a few parsley stems and a whole clove.

Some ideas for using bay leaves in more than just spag bol

✱ Put a few of them in your rice or flour jars to deter insects.

✱ Make dried bouquet garni, the classic herb mix used for making stocks, soups and casseroles. In a jar or airtight container, put 8 bay leaves, 4 tbsp each of dried parsley and dried thyme, and 2 tbsp dried marjoram or dried rosemary. Store in the pantry for 3–6 months. Add 2 of the bay leaves and 2–3 tsp of the rest to your next stock, stew or casserole.

✱ Add a few to the water when boiling potatoes, blanching carrots or cooking lentils.

✱ When making a Bechamel Sauce (p 274) or Pouring Custard (p 274), add a few bay leaves to the milk.

✱ If you're using store-bought tomato passata (puréed tomatoes), add a few bay leaves and a thyme sprig when heating for a home-made vibe.

✱ Add 3–4 bay leaves and ½ tsp black peppercorns to your next batch of marmalade. It gives a nice savoury edge to citrusy preserves.

✱ Put a bay leaf in each of your pickle jars.

✱ Make a calming and healing tea with 6–8 bay leaves, strips of peel from 1 orange, and 2 cinnamon sticks. Follow the Lemongrass Tea method (p 205).

Herby vinegar

MAKES 1 x 250 ML (9 OZ) BOTTLE OR JAR

Put the last of the herb sprigs, including bay leaves, thyme, rosemary, oregano, sage, parsley or basil stems, in a 250 ml (9 oz) jar and cover with apple cider vinegar or white wine vinegar. Add ½ tbsp black peppercorns, 2–3 strips of lemon peel and a garlic clove, along with 1 tsp sugar and ½ tsp salt. Leave to infuse on the benchtop for 2–4 weeks, tasting often until you're happy with the flavour. Strain into a clean bottle or jar, then use as the base of a salad dressing, adding oil and a little mustard. It will last for 1 year.

CURRY LEAVES

Curry leaves are nothing like curry powder. They are the leaves from curry trees, which belong to the citrus family. And while we're big fans of Keen's curry powder, it's not the same thing as frying fresh curry leaves in hot oil. Curry leaves add zest, a little like lemongrass does, to curries, soups and stews. They can be used in preserving – chutneys, pickles and oil infusions – and can be added to flat breads and egg dishes. Unlike bay leaves, curry leaves are edible and don't need to be fished out of a dish before serving.

If you have a curry tree, you'll be looking for recipes that use more than three leaves. If you bought a packet of dried leaves and three-quarters of them are still hanging around in the pantry, now is their time to shine. Just remember that the fresh leaves are more powerful, so you'll need a handful of dried ones to match the flavour.

Go with	Mustard seeds, ginger, lemongrass, chilli, star anise, turmeric, cashews, peanuts, curries, vegetables, fish, rice, eggs, pickles, chutneys
Storage	Store dried leaves, like other spices, in an airtight container in the pantry. Keep fresh curry leaves on the stem until needed, then pick off the leaves and add to your dish. Store fresh leaves in a container in the fridge between paper towels or in a clean tea towel (dish towel) or clean Chux for 1–2 weeks. Curry leaves freeze well and there's no need to defrost – you can throw them straight in from the freezer. They may change colour once frozen, but will taste the same.

Substitutes   While curry powder is not a substitute, if you're making Dal (p 244) and you're out of curry leaves, throw in 1 tsp curry powder when no one's looking. If there's no curry powder in the house, lemon zest and cumin, fennel or mustard seeds will do something vaguely similar.

Some ideas for using up curry leaves

* Add a few when cooking a noodle or chicken soup.
* Pop a few in your pickling jars, with mustard seeds, chilli flakes and a garlic clove.
* Dry fresh curry leaves using the herb-drying method on p 207. Or leave them out in a shallow bowl for a few days until completely dry. Store as is, or crush them with your hands first.
* Make a chickpea curry (p 109), or the Really Easy Green Bean Curry (p 40).
* Please try the Tarka (fried spice topping) on p 245. It's amazing and will turn your dal into something very special.

Coconut curry leaf sambol

Give our basic Coconut Sambol recipe (p 116) some extra flavour by adding 1 large handful of fresh curry leaves and a knob of fresh ginger, chopped, to the food processor. Serve with curries and rice.

Curry leaf oil

Curry leaves will release their flavour into hot oil, making a full-flavoured infusion to add to curries before serving, to use as a dressing for hot potatoes, to cook fish or chicken in, or to rub onto flat breads.

Follow the same method as for Chilli Oil (p 113), replacing the star anise, cinnamon and sichuan peppercorns with 3 tbsp mustard seeds, 1 tbsp coriander seeds and 2 tsp cumin seeds. Replace the chillies with 1 large handful of fresh curry leaves. Heat the oil for 15 minutes only, to avoid burning the seeds.

LEMONGRASS

If you're lucky enough to live somewhere warm enough to grow your own lemongrass, you may be desperate to find things to do with it. Even buying a bundle of stems at the supermarket can be overwhelming, let alone a razor-sharp bush taking over your entire backyard. We hope this helps.

Goes with   Mint, lime and lime leaf, coriander (cilantro), curry leaves, cinnamon, cardamom, coriander seeds, turmeric, garlic, ginger, chilli, coconut, mango, bananas, tomatoes, fennel, leafy greens, all meats

Storage   Wrap in a clean damp cloth in the fridge for 2–3 weeks, or chop and freeze in an airtight container for up to 6 months. Sheer neglect will dry lemongrass very well: chop the stalk into small pieces, spread on a tray and leave for 2–3 days. Once dried, it will keep in an airtight container for 2–3 months. Keep in mind that dried lemongrass is not as pungent as fresh.

Substitutes   Lemongrass doesn't just taste of lemon, it has a slightly spicy mintiness to it. So if a recipe calls for lemongrass and you don't have it, use lemon zest with fresh ginger or dried mint.

Some ideas for using lemongrass stems

The tender stems are where all the action is, full of lemony flavour and scent. They can be sliced into salads, stir-fries or slow-cooked dishes that need a lemony lift, or pounded into spice pastes for curries.

* Preserve sliced lemongrass stems in a mix of equal parts lemon juice and vinegar. Keep them in a jar in the fridge forever, to use when there's no fresh lemongrass. You can keep adding to the jar if you need to – just ensure there's enough liquid to cover the lemongrass.
* Add sliced lemongrass stems to sautéed onions, garlic and white wine for steaming mussels in. See p 482 for a quick winey mussel recipe.
* **Lemongrass syrup** This is incredible drizzled over fresh fruit or desserts, in cocktails or for sticky chicken wings. Follow the Ginger Syrup recipe (p 176), using 1–2 sliced lemongrass stems instead of ginger.

Lemongrass tea

SERVES 4

Make lemongrass tea – it's said to calm one's spirit, aid sleep, improve circulation and soothe sore throats. Herbal teas are a big part of our lives. Jaimee 'Tea Master' Edwards makes bespoke blends: if you're feeling blue she adds saffron and rosemary; if you're getting sick she'll add turmeric, ginger and citrus; or if you've overeaten, a mint and coriander (cilantro) tea appears before you. Follow this recipe with whatever bits and bobs need using up – half apples, bits of pear, strips of citrus peel or a few sad cherries have also been known to make their way into Jaimee's pot. For 3–4 cups (750 ml – 1 litre) water, you'll need somewhere between 1 handful and 1 cup aromatics, depending on their flavour potency – i.e. you'll only need a sprig of rosemary, whereas you'll need a cupful of chopped peach.

Put 3 fresh lemongrass stems (and the leaves too, if you need to use them up) in a saucepan with 4 cups (1 litre) water. Bring to a simmer, then remove from the heat. Add 3 tbsp honey or sugar and stir to dissolve. Let it sit for 20 minutes or so, or until the tea tastes lemony and delicious. Strain. For hot tea, return to the boil. For iced tea, pour into a bottle and store in the fridge for up to 5 days.

Some ideas for using lemongrass leaves

You'll only encounter lemongrass leaves if you grow your own, in which case you'll want to find a use for them. While they're not to be eaten, they do give off an incredible lemony aroma, making them great for infusing into all our favourite things – hot baths, cups of tea, hot and sour soups and bottles of spirits.

* Tie the leaves into knots to gently bruise, then add them to a running bath.
* While the bath is running, tie a few more knots and add them to a bottle of vodka or gin. Leave for at least 1 week, then remove from the bottle once you're happy with the flavour.
* Add bruised leaves to the water when steaming fish, potatoes or greens.
* Add a knot of lemongrass leaf to a sweet and sour soup, fish or chicken broth, or noodle soup. Remove before serving, as you would a bay leaf.
* Add scrunched-up leaves to a parcel of fish with a splash of wine, a knob of butter and plenty of pepper. Bake in a 180°C (350°F) oven or on the barbecue for 10 minutes or until just cooked through.

OREGANO

While most herbs lose their flavour when dried, oregano becomes a superhero. So shower your stews and salads with fresh oregano leaves, but tread cautiously with the dried variety. We're fond of both options and find oregano an especially useful herb if you're feeding children, as it makes everything taste like it came from the local pizza shop.

Goes with	Garlic, olive oil, tomatoes, onions, red meats, chicken and fish, eggs, butter, feta, olives, capers, black pepper, cumin, paprika, most other herbs, quinoa, nuts, corn, capsicum (pepper), eggplant (aubergine), zucchini (courgettes), fennel, dried beans (especially black beans or cannellini beans). It can be used in both Mediterranean and Mexican cooking.
Storage	Wrap in a slightly damp clean cloth and store in a reusable plastic bag in the fridge for 2 weeks or more; or dry bunches (opposite), strip off the leaves and store in an airtight jar for 3–6 months.
Substitutes	If there's no oregano in the house, don't sweat it. Any other woody herb will give a similar result, so experiment with marjoram, thyme, a little rosemary, even parsley, or a combination of a few.

Some ideas for using up oregano

* Add to the Old-school Garlic Bread (p 52) or an omelette (p 150).
* Make a marinade for chicken, fish, potatoes or eggplant (aubergine). In a small bowl, mix ¼ cup (60 ml) olive oil, ¼ cup (60 ml) lemon juice, and either 1 small handful of chopped fresh oregano or 2 tsp dried oregano. Add 2 finely chopped garlic cloves, and pepper and salt to taste. Stir in 2–3 tbsp yoghurt if you have some that needs using up.
* Add a sprig to Blistered Marinated Capsicum (p 74) or to the Italian-style Preserved Green Beans (p 40).
* Put ½ bunch of oregano inside a roast chicken before it goes in the oven, with ½ lemon and a few garlic cloves.
* Oregano has antibacterial properties. Steep it in boiling water for 4 minutes when you have a sore throat. Add honey and lemon juice and go to bed.

Home-drying techniques for herbs

- **Simple neglect** Because of their low water content, woody herbs don't go mouldy that easily, so feel free to chuck them on the bench, leave them for a few days and voilà – dried herbs. Having said that, there are proper ways to dry herbs that will give you much better results.
- **Air-dried** Hang small bunches of herbs, tied with a rubber band or piece of string, upside down in the kitchen. It needs to be a well-ventilated place, away from steam and moisture. Leave them hanging until completely dry, but not long enough to get greasy and dusty. For herbs with bigger leaves, like curry, bay or sage, pick them off the stem and leave them in a shallow bowl or sieve for anywhere from a few days to a week and you'll have well-dried leaves to store in jars in the pantry.
- **Oven-dried** To dry herbs quickly in the oven, spread them on a baking tray and place in the oven on its lowest setting until completely dry. The fresher the herbs are, the longer they will take. Check them every 10 minutes. Allow to cool completely before storing.

Once dried, strip the leaves, and either store whole or blitz them into a powder using a spice grinder. Store dried herbs and herb powders in an airtight container in the pantry for 3–6 months.

Oregano salt

MAKES ⅓ CUP (100 G)

Flavoured salts are a handy thing to have next to the stove or on the table. Herby salts can be added to potatoes before roasting or to fish before grilling, sprinkled over corn with lots of butter, or used to season beautiful fresh tomatoes and mozzarella.

In a jar, mix 2 tbsp dried oregano or powdered dried oregano with ⅓ cup (100 g) pure salt (i.e. with no additives). Add 1 tsp chilli flakes or powder, dried citrus powder (p 260) or ground white pepper. Shake well and keep it on the counter, so you remember to sprinkle it on everything. Double or triple the quantities if you want to make more.

Pizza and pasta spice mix

Have a jar of spice mix 1 (p 420) on hand at all times. Add it to tinned tomatoes with salt and a little oil for the simplest pasta sauce, and to pizzas, stews, roast vegetables and meatballs or burgers.

ROSEMARY

Piny, minty and peppery – the invigorating smell of rosemary on your hands or in your kitchen will lift your spirits. Rosemary gives your system a boost – helping to clear your sinuses, your mind and your digestion. It's a staple in the kitchen, and should be used more often in cooking and in home remedies. Rosemary is strong and robust, and so works well in oil preserving, vinegar pickling, and chutney- and jam-making.

Goes with   Roasted meats, bacon, hearty stews, roasting vegetables and starchy things like breads and biscuits (cookies), potatoes, sweet potato and pumpkin (squash); pears, apples, apricots, peaches, grapes, figs, rhubarb, grapefruit, lemons, peas, tomatoes, eggplant (aubergine), fennel, lentils, dried beans, chickpeas, nuts, cheeses, bay leaves, fennel seeds

Storage   Wrap in a slightly damp clean cloth and store in a reusable plastic bag in the fridge for 2 weeks or more; or dry them (p 207), strip off the leaves and store in an airtight jar for 3–6 months.

Substitutes   Rosemary is distinct, but if you don't have any, use thyme instead.

Some ideas for using rosemary in the kitchen

* Rosemary butter is easy to make and can be liberally rubbed over chicken before roasting. Or drop a knob of the rosemary butter onto steamed baby potatoes before serving. Follow the Anchovy Butter recipe (p 3), replacing the anchovies with 2–3 tbsp finely chopped rosemary.
* If you're barbecuing or cooking on coals, add rosemary sprigs to the grill or fire to give off a smoky, piny flavour to whatever you're cooking.
* Finely chop rosemary and add it to one of the flat breads on p 168 or Linseed Crackers (p 403).
* Add chopped dried rosemary to the Breadcrumb Mix (p 51).
* Stick a rosemary sprig in a cocktail or a G&T.
* Make rosemary powder, following the drying herbs method on the previous page, and use it on roast potatoes, barbecued lamb, fresh ricotta or a tomato salad.
* Make a beautiful rosemary sugar by adding a rosemary sprig to a jar of sugar. The rosemary flavour will slowly infuse the sugar, which can then be used to sprinkle over biscuits and cakes, or to roll donuts in.

✱ We use rosemary a lot when preserving. It's fresh and brightening when added to apple or pear chutneys. Add 2–3 tbsp chopped rosemary in the last 5 minutes of cooking. You could also add a rosemary sprig to a lemon marmalade, chopped rosemary to rhubarb jam (in the Foolproof Jam recipe, p 389), or a few rosemary sprigs to your next jar of Salt-preserved Lemons (p 241).

Rosemary and honey baste

MAKES ABOUT ⅔ CUP (170 ML)

Make a honey and rosemary baste for sticky lamb or chicken or caramelised sweet potatoes. In a small saucepan, warm 3 tbsp honey with ¼ cup (60 ml) wine (whatever you have), then add 3 finely chopped garlic cloves, 2 tbsp chopped rosemary and a pinch each of salt, pepper and chilli flakes. Brush over lamb or chicken while barbecuing or sweet potatoes while they are roasting.

Rosemary and apple jelly

MAKES 2 x 250 ML (9 OZ) JARS

Home-made herbed jellies make you feel wholesome and old-fashioned, like you just stepped in from the orchard in your gumboots. This is a more rustic, savoury-ish version with added vinegar and salt. Rosemary is lovely, but experiment with mint, thyme, basil or lavender. Serve with roast meats, roasted carrots and buttery peas, or hard cheeses on rye bread.

Peel, core and roughly chop 600 g (1 lb 5 oz) apples and place the scraps in a clean muslin bag or tie up in a clean Chux. Put the chopped apples in a saucepan and add 1 cup (250 ml) apple cider vinegar, 1 cup (250 ml) water and the scrap bag (the pectin in the scraps will help the jelly set). Cook gently for about 30 minutes, until the apples are very soft. Press the mixture through a sieve, or if you have a food mill, run it through the finest setting and capture the pulp. Transfer the strained apple liquid to a wide saucepan or jam pan and add the finely grated zest and juice of 1 lemon, 400 g (14 oz) white (granulated) sugar and a generous pinch of salt. Boil over medium heat for 20–25 minutes, stirring often. Remove from the heat and add 3–4 tbsp chopped rosemary (or other fresh herbs of your choice). Test for setting point (p 503) and pour into warm sterilised jars (p 501). Store in the pantry for 6 months or heat-process (p 502) for 10 minutes for longer storage.

SAGE

It's very hard for us not to write an entire essay on the healing properties of sage, but as this is a cookbook, just know that sage was used medicinally for a very long time before there was any interest in it for cooking. Herbal, warm and earthy, sage is part of the mint family. It's piny and a little bit citrusy, and excels all through autumn and winter in soups, stews, pasta dishes, stuffings and apple pies. And if you do have a little bit left over, make a herbal tea that's said to soothe sore throats and menopausal symptoms, and to enhance memory. See Lemongrass Tea (p 205) for more herbal tea tips.

Goes with   Sage is intense in flavour, so it suits hearty dishes. It's used to cut through the richness of sausages, cured meats, anchovies, cheeses, cream, butter and nuts, and suits winter fruits and vegetables like pumpkin (squash), onions, sweet potato, cabbage, fennel, dried beans, lentils, apples and pears, juniper berries, and other woody herbs such as bay leaves, thyme and oregano. Also good with tomatoes and buckwheat.

Storage   Sage is best stored in a jar of water on the bench and used lightly and often over a week or so. If you'd like to store sage for longer, wrap the bunch in a slightly damp clean cloth, then pop in a reusable plastic bag in the fridge.

Substitutes   Dried sage is stronger than fresh leaves, so go easy on the store-bought dried variety. If you don't have sage, try rosemary, marjoram, thyme or tarragon.

Some *sage* advice for using up that bunch

* Freeze in ice-cube trays, following the method on p 195.
* Add leaves to the Odd-knobs Mac 'n' Cheese (p 101) or the Whatever-cheese Eggy Muffins (p 93).
* Chop the last sprig from the bunch and add to a meatloaf or meatballs.
* Make a batch of the Rosemary and Apple Jelly (p 209), replacing the rosemary with thinly sliced sage leaves.
* Head to the Roast Apple and Sage Stuffing (p 6), Simple Stewed Apples (p 7) and Apple Pie Filling (p 8) recipes and add sage liberally.

* Make sage butter for ra_____ r gnocchi. In a small saucepan over medium–low heat, melt 125 g (4½ oz) butter, s_____ often. Once the butter starts to foam, add 2 chopped garlic cloves, stirring often f_____ minutes, until the butter starts to brown. DO NOT STEP AWAY FROM THE PAN. Add _____ handful of sage leaves and stir until crispy and dark. Remove from the heat and pou_____ avioli or other pasta. Top with Breadcrumbs (p 51), grated parmesan or toasted c_____ walnuts.
* If sage is going wild in _____ den, make smudge sticks and burn away the bad vibes.

Crispy sage leave_

Learn how to crisp-fry sage _____ It's one of the most delicious ways to eat sage, adding a little bit of fancy to potato gnocc_____ a, pumpkin (squash) soup or roasted vegetables – or just pop them straight in your mout_____

In a frying pan, heat a g_____ s layer of oil of your choice over medium–high heat. Once the oil starts to shimmer, add p_____ age leaves, being mindful not to crowd them. They'll only take 15–30 seconds to turn crisp____ O NOT STEP AWAY FROM THE PAN. Remove with a slotted spoon and drain on paper t_____ nce cool, sprinkle generously with salt. Enjoy.

Sage elixir

One of the ways to extract _____ ealing properties is to soak it in alcohol to make a tincture or elixir. Pam Corbin ('Pam th_____ f River Cottage fame), says she has a capful of sage elixir every morning for good health a_____ evity. Follow the Cumquat Brandy recipe (p 132), replacing the cumquats with 2 cups (40_____ leaves and leaving out the spices. Use vodka or a fruit brandy. Leave on the bench for ab_____ onth (a moon cycle, if you're a true kitchen witch or wizard), shaking the jar when you_____ ber. Strain and store in a clean bottle, having 1 tbsp here and there when you n_____ pi_____ up or have a sore throat. You could also use this tincture in cocktails as a rep_____ tters.

Honey

First up, make sure that what you're buying is actually honey. Controversially, many commercial honey brands have been found to cut honey with sugar syrup to make a cheaper product. Read the label to make sure the ingredients just say honey. Second, buy raw honey – that is, not heat-treated (pasteurised) honey. Raw honey contains a plethora of minerals and has antibacterial and other medicinal properties that make it a good ingredient for home remedies. If you can, buy honey from the health-food aisle, a health-food shop, farmers' markets or a beekeeper if you're lucky enough to know one – or *bee* one.

Honey never goes off, so it's pretty hard to waste. It may crystallise or candy (form sugar crystals and turn whitish), but you can either eat it like that or reliquefy it by standing the jar in a bowl of hot water until the sugar crystals dissolve again.

Goes with	Cheeses, yoghurt, nuts, sesame seeds, oats, berries, tropical fruits, rhubarb, apples, stone fruits, figs, citrus fruits, tahini, ham, bacon, chicken, ginger, nutmeg, cinnamon, thyme, fennel, carrots, pumpkin (squash), sweet potato, beetroot
Storage	Honey can last as long as 3000 years. The archaeologists who discovered Tutankhamen's tomb tasted the jar of honey they found there and, to their astonishment, it was still perfectly good. So it's safe to say that your jar of honey is good for a while. The reason for honey's long shelf life is its low water content. Don't use dirty or wet utensils when serving honey or you'll mess with that water content and your honey might go funny.
Substitutes	For flavour, maple syrup replaces honey nicely. A little molasses or golden syrup in cookie or cake recipes works well too.

Some ideas for the last spoonful or two of honey

✱ Make the Garlic Oxymel (p 173); it's perfect for soothing sore throats.

✱ Make a sticky sauce for chicken wings, tofu or ribs. Use the Sticky Spicy Marmalade Marinade recipe (p 267), replacing the marmalade with honey.

✱ Add 1 tsp honey to a salad dressing to balance the acidity of vinegar or lemon juice.

✱ Use 1 tbsp to sweeten nut milks – see the Macadamia Milk recipe on p 292.

✱ Drizzle it over hard bitey cheese.

✱ Mix it with softened butter and a pinch of salt, then spread on toast.

✱ Drizzle honey over roast pumpkin (squash) or sweet potato for the last 10 minutes of cooking.

✱ Make the Rosemary and Honey Baste (p 209) for lamb, chicken or sweet potatoes.

✱ Add a little honey when jam-making – for flavour, rather than to preserve. It's especially nice with Rhubarb Jam (see the Foolproof Jam recipe, p 389).

✱ Make a batch of nut bars to use up the last of the honey jar. Follow the Pistachio Nut Bars recipe (p 297), using whatever nuts you have in the pantry or fridge.

Infused honey
MAKES 1 CUP (350 G)

Honey takes up the flavour of robust herbs and spices very well, and infused honeys are a lovely way to add complex flavours to sweet and savoury cooking. Drizzle over cakes or roasted vegetables, mix into dressings and marinades, and add to tea or booze.

Choose dried woody herbs that are high in volatile oils, such as rosemary, thyme, lavender or sage. Or use whole spices such as a cinnamon stick, black peppercorns, allspice berries, juniper berries or cloves.

Add 2–3 tbsp woody herb leaves or spices to 1 cup (350 g) honey in a clean jar. Seal and leave for 1 month before using. You can just leave your ingredients in the honey – it will only get better for it. If you're using dried herbs and spices, this will last for years.

Horseradish

Fresh horseradish is so expensive. The plant itself grows like a weed, but it's not grown widely and is difficult to harvest, hence the price. We recommend growing your own if you live in a temperate to cold climate. Horseradish is related to mustard and wasabi, and shares their burning signature. A little horseradish goes a long way. It's often bought for a specific reason or recipe, and then this wonky-looking root hangs about with not much to do. Until now.

Goes with	Potatoes, cabbage, sauerkraut, beetroot, peas, celery, tomatoes, onions, apples, pears, dill, chives, mayonnaise, sour cream, beef, oily fish
Storage	Uncut horseradish will be fine in a bowl on the counter for a week or so. Cut horseradish dries up quickly, so put it in an airtight container and keep in the fridge for a few weeks. Horseradish freezes well: grate it, freeze it in ice-cube trays and defrost as needed.
Substitutes	Mustard and wasabi make good substitutes.

Some ideas for using a little left-over horseradish

* Propagate it, for more horseradish. Pop the root end of the horseradish in enough water to cover the root halfway. Keep on the windowsill and top up with water until you see some green sprouts. Plant in the garden or a large balcony pot, allowing the sprouting green shoots to peek through the soil. The leaves will grow quickly and can be picked and eaten. The roots will take a full year to get big enough for harvesting.
* Make a proper bloody mary. Pop some ice in a highball glass and pour in 30 ml (1 fl oz) vodka. Top with good-quality tomato juice, then add a squeeze of lemon juice, a good dash of worcestershire sauce, a splash of Tabasco sauce and a healthy grating of horseradish. Mix with a long spoon and garnish with a celery stick.
* Boil baby potatoes whole and serve with sour cream and grated horseradish on top.
* Roast some beetroot, then dress with olive oil, black pepper and freshly grated horseradish.

* Add to the Whole-bunch-of-beets Kraut (p 44).
* Add to Pea Soup (p 340) for brightness and zing.
* Grate it over freshly shucked oysters and invite us over.
* If you have too much horseradish, you can preserve it in vinegar. Finely grate horseradish into a jar or bottle and cover with white wine vinegar, apple cider vinegar or malt vinegar. Leave it to sit for a month or so, then strain and store in the pantry for up to 1 year. Use as the base of a dressing with a kick.

Horseradish cream
MAKES ABOUT ⅔ CUPS (170 ML)

You can buy this in the supermarket, but the home-made version is so much better. It goes with roast beef, oily fish and Eastern European–style dumplings. Or thin it with some neutral oil and water to make a dressing for a simple cabbage slaw.

In a small bowl, mix ¼ cup (65 g) sour cream and 1 tbsp mayonnaise. Add 3 tbsp very finely grated horseradish (use a Microplane if you have one) and 1 tsp dijon mustard. Mix very well. Any leftovers can be stored in an airtight container in the fridge for a week or so.

Jam p 217

Jam

If your fridge looks anything like ours, you'll have way too many half-opened condiment jars in there. Once in a while we go into a frenzy and set ourselves a challenge to use things up, rather than throw them away. And if you make jam, you'll definitely have too many jars of it taking up valuable real estate. Here are some tips to help move them out.

Goes with   Toast and lots of butter, of course. But also, tahini, nuts and nut butters, ice cream, yoghurt, cream, all the cheeses, meats, citrus and spirits. Or any meal that needs a hint of sweetness. Don't be afraid to use jams in dressings and marinades.

Storage   Keep unopened jars of jam in a cool, dark place for many years. We argue about whether an opened jar should be kept in the fridge. It comes down to the amount of sugar in there and how hot your kitchen is. Low-sugar jams have a shorter lifespan, so should be stored in the fridge and eaten more quickly. Old-fashioned jams often have a higher sugar content and can last here, there and everywhere. A few jars have been in Alex's fridge since she moved in five years ago, and they're still going strong. If you have room, store jam in the fridge. If you forget to put it back in the fridge for a week, don't freak out. It'll be fine.

Substitutes   No jam in the house? Try marmalade, honey, golden syrup or molasses for sweetness. Or macerate ripe fruits by tossing with lots of sugar then leaving at room temperature for 30 minutes to make an impromptu jam.

Some ideas for using up that jar of jam

✳ Turn jam into a syrup for French Toast (p 51) or pancakes by warming it in a saucepan with a splash of water and a little lemon juice – it's an excellent replacement for maple syrup. »

---

* Use the last scraping of the jam jar to make a salad dressing. All well-balanced dressings need a little sweetness, so pour extra virgin olive oil into an almost empty jam jar with 2–3 tsp mustard, a pinch each of salt and pepper, and a splash of vinegar, then shake hard to emulsify.
* Make a jam and cheese toastie. And check out the insane Brie and Jam Fried Sandwich on p 91.
* Take a tub of vanilla ice cream out of the freezer and let it soften slightly. Fold plenty of jam through it and refreeze – instant ripple ice cream.
* Make jam drop cookies, a sponge cake or a jam tart, or take a little puff pastry, cut it into squares, dollop on jam, then fold over and seal to make jam turnovers.
* Try the Bread and Butter Pudding (p 52), spreading jam on your buttered bread before assembling and baking.
* Make the sweet treat Fig Crostata (p 163), with jam as the base instead of almond meal, and using any fruit you have lying around.
* Head to the marmalade section (p 266) for more use-up-that-jar tips.

Sweet and savoury steak sauce

MAKES ½ CUP (125 ML)

In a small saucepan, sauté 1 chopped onion and 2 chopped garlic cloves in olive oil over medium heat until soft and sweet. Add ½ tsp ground spices such as cumin, coriander or paprika, ½ cup (165 g) jam, 2 tbsp balsamic or red wine vinegar and a big pinch of salt. Cook for a few minutes until sticky and well combined. Serve with steak or sausages.

Peanut butter jam drops

These look like old-fashioned jam drops but taste like a peanut butter and jam sandwich. Follow the 'Use Up That Jar' Cookies recipe (p 455), using ⅓ cup (90 g) peanut butter. After you've cut the dough log into rounds, gently press your thumb into the centre of each one. Fill each shallow indentation with ½ tsp jam and bake the cookies for 15–20 minutes.

K

Kale

When kale is in season, the bunches are as big as a Christmas tree and can be difficult to fit in the shopping basket, let alone the fridge. If you're a green smoothie type, you'll be fine, but for the rest of us who just want a little extra leafy-green goodness in our diets, how on earth do we get through it?

Luckily, we're obsessed with trying to get supergreens into the children, so we have a wealth of knowledge on the subject of kale. Our advice: if you buy a mammoth bunch of kale, don't buy heaps of other greens that week.

Goes with   Lemons, chilli, leeks, garlic, ginger, parmesan, olives, preserved lemon, capers, bacon, brussels sprouts, tomatoes, mushrooms, green beans, sauerkraut, tofu, tahini, lentils, nuts and seeds

---

Storage   Store kale like other leafy greens – roll in a slightly damp clean tea towel (dish towel) with the ends tucked in, as if you were rolling a sandwich wrap. Store the kale baby in a reusable plastic bag in the fridge for up to 10 days. Wash kale as you're using it, rather than before it goes in the fridge.

Substitutes   Silverbeet (Swiss chard), mustard greens, sprouting broccoli, turnip or kohlrabi tops, beetroot tops, white cabbage, Chinese broccoli

Some ideas for using up all that kale

* Use the last few kale leaves for Green Soup (p 440).
* Remove the stems, cut the leaves into very fine ribbons and add to a green salad or slaw.
* If there's left-over mash in the fridge and some less than perfect kale that needs using up, we have the waste warrior's dream recipe for you – Colcannon (p 67).
* If your kale has seen better days, try the Greens Pie Filling (p 412).
* ***Crispy kale*** We know it's old hat, but what better way to use up half a bunch of forgotten kale? Follow the method for Roasted Beet Leaves (p 46), tearing the kale leaves into bite-sized pieces before roasting.

✳ ***Kale pesto*** It sounds too good for you to be delicious, but you'll be pleasantly surprised – it's both good for you *and* delicious. Nutty, green and earthy, it's excellent on pasta, on a sandwich or with avocado on toast. Follow the Classic Basil Pesto recipe (p 191), making sure you remove the stems and tough ribs and give the kale a little massage (see below) before it goes into the blender. Kale pesto may need a splash more oil than herby pesto.

Massaged kale salad
SERVES 4 AS A SIDE

A kale salad can be a beautiful thing, or it can taste like you've shredded a cereal box. The difference lies in knowing how to treat your kale. This very simple raw kale salad can be a staple in winter and is a good match for hearty soups, stews or roasts.

As in the Massaged Cabbage and Herb Salad (p 67), giving shredded or thinly sliced kale a gentle massage with a bit of salt before adding the other ingredients will soften the texture and add a little moisture. Very thinly slice 2–3 cups of kale leaves, stems removed, and pop in a bowl with a generous sprinkling of salt. Give your kale a nice massage, releasing some of its juices.

If you wanted to add more ingredients to this simple salad, you could shave some brussels sprouts or fennel, or thinly slice a crunchy red apple or add some paper-thin slices of celery. Mix well, then squeeze in some lemon juice, and add a generous glug of good-quality extra virgin olive oil and plenty of ground pepper. Top with toasted sunflower seeds or chopped toasted almonds or some sprouts if you have them. You could also dress this salad with the Creamy Tahini Dressing on p 455.

The tastiest bunch of kale – five recipes in one

Some of our best work comes from an intense desire to use up something we wish we'd never bought. Kale is often on that list, so we've devised a way to use the whole thing in one go. Kale changes if it's cooked low and slow, and in our opinion becomes much more delicious. This is a five-in-one, choose-your-own-adventure recipe. It can be a side dish, tossed through pasta or served on toast with eggs. Add white beans and tomatoes to make it a stew or more stock to make it a soup, scattered with garlicky croutons.

Wash your giant bunch of kale. Tear the leaves from the stems and take out any tough ribs. Set the leaves aside, then very thinly slice the stems. In a flameproof casserole dish or large saucepan, heat ⅓ cup (80 ml) olive oil over medium heat, then sauté 1 sliced small onion with the kale stem slices and ¼ tsp salt. Cook until soft, 10–12 minutes. Add 4 sliced garlic cloves, plenty of ground pepper, and chilli flakes if you'd like, then sauté for another few minutes. »

Add 2 cups (500 ml) of a tasty liquid (stock, wine, tinned tomatoes or a combination of what you have), and a herb sprig (thyme, oregano, rosemary) or a few bay leaves. Tear the kale leaves into pieces and add them to the hot liquid. Reduce the heat to low and gently simmer, covered, for about 40 minutes, until the kale has softened. It will no longer be bright green, so don't be alarmed. Remove the lid, add a big squeeze of lemon juice and some finely grated lemon zest and taste for seasoning, adding more salt and pepper as needed and mixing again. Now you get to choose your own adventure.

AS A SIDE
Serve with grilled (broiled) fish or lamb, or with polenta or mashed potatoes, or pile it on toast with avocado.

FOR BAKED EGGS
Make 4–6 indents in the kale and crack an egg into each hole. Cover and pop in a 170°C (325°F) oven until the eggs are set, about 10 minutes. Serve with dollops of goat's cheese or ricotta.

FOR PASTA
Cook your pasta while your kale dish is simmering. Once the pasta is cooked, add it to the kale pan with a little of the cooking water and simmer for a few more minutes until the liquid has thickened a little. Add heaps of shaved parmesan, more olive oil and ground pepper, and serve.

FOR A HEARTIER STEW
Add 400 g (14 oz) drained tinned (or soaked and cooked dried) white beans or chickpeas with the kale, and either 400 g (14 oz) tinned tomatoes or some chopped fresh tomatoes or cherry tomatoes. Simmer, covered, for 10 minutes. Remove the lid and cook gently until the mixture thickens. Stir through 1 tbsp harissa paste or Fermented Chilli (p 114) and serve with crusty bread.

FOR A SOUP
Add 2–4 extra cups (500 ml – 1 litre) stock and another cup of vegetables – thinly sliced zucchini (courgettes), just-tender potato pieces, or fresh or frozen peas. Top the soup with 1 tbsp pesto or lots of chopped herbs, Home-made Bacon Bits (p 23) or Croutons (p 51).

Stir-fried kale and kimchi

SERVES 2–3 AS A SIDE

This quick flavoursome dish can be eaten as is, or with rice and a fried egg. Teach it to your kids before they move out and you won't have to worry about their share-house nutrition.

Strip about 6 kale leaves from their stems and tear them into bite-sized pieces. Very thinly slice the stems. Heat 2 tbsp neutral oil in a wok or frying pan over medium heat, throw in the stems with a pinch of salt, and cook, stirring often, for 2–3 minutes, until the stems are bright green and starting to soften. Add 2 sliced garlic cloves, then throw in the kale leaves and ½ cup (105 g) kimchi. Stir-fry for a few minutes, until the kale leaves are tender. Serve with rice.

See broccoli, brussels sprouts, cabbage, cauliflower, kohlrabi and wombok for ideas with other brassicas.

Kimchi

Kimchi is serious business. It's the national condiment of Korea and the national condiment of our hearts. Whether you make your own kimchi (p 486) or buy it, having it on hand will instantly add complexity and depth to dishes that need it – two-minute noodles, we're looking at you. Don't be afraid to experiment with kimchi in cooking; we've seen some adventurous recipes like kimchi and butter pasta. Why not? Kimchi is the best condiment to have in the fridge for the days when there are no vegetables in the crisper and no energy in your bones.

Goes with	Rice, noodles, eggs, tofu, meat of all kinds, seafood, daikon, carrots, beans, leafy greens, cabbage, mushrooms, even cheddar and bread if you're talking a kimchi toastie.
Storage	Store purchased kimchi, or your home-made kimchi after fermentation, in the fridge in the jar or container it came in. Check the use-by date, but smell it and judge for yourself. We're going to say that kimchi can stick around for a long time, 6–8 months.
Substitutes	Kimchi is its own special ingredient. If you are totally out, you could thinly slice and massage some salted cabbage and add lots of chilli and a squeeze of lemon. You could also use sauerkraut for a similarly fermented alternative. Just add a dash of heat in one form or another to approximate kimchi's kick.

Some ideas for using up that jar of kimchi

* Scrambled eggs or an omelette with kimchi is a really good way to start or end the day. See p 150 for omelette-making tips.
* Our kimchi toastie at Cornersmith isn't a bestseller for nothing. Fill a sandwich with kimchi, draining some of the brine so the toastie doesn't get soggy, and very tasty cheddar, then put in a sandwich toaster, preferably one that seals the bread together into a tasty pocket.

* Enhance a spicy beef or tofu stew (p 458) by adding the salty, spicy, umami kick of kimchi.
* For a comforting simple meal, add kimchi and cooked noodles to hot home-made stock.
* Add kimchi to the Brown Rice, Mushroom and Spinach Soup (p 392).
* On tired nights, pop kimchi on top of rice with a fried egg.
* Make the Stir-fried Kale and Kimchi (p 223).
* Mix roughly chopped kimchi and kimchi juice into something creamy – like mayonnaise, sour cream or cream cheese – and serve with hot chips (fries) and fish fingers.

Thank you for not wasting kimchi brine

* Drink the left-over brine. It's a spicy probiotic drink that makes a great pick-me-up. And people pay a fortune for it in fancy health-food shops.
* Make a basting sauce for grilled (broiled) chicken pieces or a dressing for noodles by mixing a little brine with sesame oil.
* Add a little to a bloody mary – it's very good indeed.
* Splash it into a soup that's lacking something you can't quite put your finger on.
* Thin out mayo with a little kimchi juice and add more salt for a spicy slaw dressing.

Kimchi pancakes
MAKES 4, SERVES 2

Kimchi pancakes are dinner in a flash, or a late Sunday breakfast. We pile even more kimchi on top and eat with soy sauce or our favourite dipping sauce. You can easily double this recipe.

In a medium bowl, mix ¾ cup (185 ml) water and 1 egg. In another large bowl mix 1 cup (150 g) plain (all-purpose) flour and 1 cup (210 g) chopped kimchi, making sure all the kimchi is coated in flour. Now mix the wet ingredients into the dry and combine well. The mixture will be a little like a runny crepe batter. Leave it to sit for about 10 minutes.

Heat a medium frying pan over medium heat and add 1 tsp vegetable oil. Pour in about a quarter of the batter and cook for 4 minutes. Flip carefully and cook the other side for 3 minutes. Repeat until all the batter is used.

Kiwi fruit

We're going to suggest that kiwis are best eaten perfectly ripe, cut in half, with a spoon. They're very good for you, high in all the vitamins and minerals that everyone talks about. Kiwi fruit will add tang to a fruit salad, acid to too-sweet desserts and an old-school look when sliced with banana on top of a pavlova. And if you've got a vine (or freezer) full of kiwis, we've got a jam recipe to help you manage the glut.

Goes with   Other tropical fruits (coconut, passionfruit, papaya, guava, starfruit, pineapple, mango, bananas), mint, limes, lemons, chilli, yoghurt and, strangely, chicken and fish

---

Storage   Unripe kiwis should be stored in the fruit bowl for about 5 days. Once they're ripe, they're best stored in the fridge. If you want to speed up the ripening process, pop them in a paper bag with a banana. If the fruit bowl or vine is full of kiwi fruit, then peel them, cut them into cubes or slices, and store them in an airtight container in the freezer – perfect for Kiwi Fruit Whip (opposite) or jam-making. If you're doing slices, it's best to freeze them in a single layer first. (Although does anyone really do that? We just dig frozen flesh out with a fork and swear we'll do it next time.)

Substitutes   Pineapple has the same tartness, sweetness and acidity as kiwi fruit. Green grapes could be substituted for colour and texture.

Some ideas for using up kiwi fruit

* Use to decorate a pavlova.
* Make a monochromatic fruit salad with kiwi, mint and green melon. Drizzle with the Pineapple Skin Syrup (p 353) or one of the herbal syrups (pp 191, 197, 204), and a splash of white rum.

---

* Follow the quick Pineapple Salsa recipe (p 351), replacing some or all of the pineapple with cubed kiwi fruit. It's tangy and salty and spicy, and great with corn chips or on tacos.
* Make a kiwi hot sauce. Follow the Half-a-melon Hot Sauce recipe (p 271), replacing the melon with an equivalent amount of ripe kiwi fruit.

Kiwi fruit marinade for meat

MAKES ABOUT 1 CUP (200 G)

Did you know that kiwi fruit tenderises meats? The flesh and the skin contain an enzyme called actinidin, which naturally breaks down proteins and connective tissue. So while it might sound like a stretch, a kiwi marinade not only adds a fruity tartness to your meat, but also allows an enzymatic tenderisation process, making your steaks, chicken or pork succulent.

In a bowl, roughly mash 2 peeled kiwi fruit. Mix in 2 tbsp olive oil, 1 tsp apple cider vinegar or soy sauce and plenty of pepper. Experiment with adding crushed garlic cloves, a small knob of grated fresh ginger, a little cayenne pepper or 1 tbsp brown sugar, if you like. Coat chicken thighs, pork or steaks in the marinade and refrigerate for 15 minutes. Pat dry before grilling (broiling).

Kiwi fruit jam

You heard right. Turn all that kiwi fruit into a tangy golden spread for crumpets, cakes or crackers with butter and cheddar. Follow the Foolproof Jam recipe (p 389), using kiwis and lemon. Kiwis are low in pectin but very high in acid, meaning your jam will be bright and clear. If you're making a bigger batch, it would be a good idea to add some green apples to help it set.

Kiwi fruit whip

SERVES 2

Turn incredibly overripe kiwi fruit into cheat's sorbet.

Freeze 3 sliced kiwi fruit (even just 1 hour in the freezer is fine), then pop in a food processor with 1 tbsp honey or sugar, a squeeze of lemon juice and ¼ cup (60 ml) coconut milk or single (pure) cream. Blend until smooth, adjust the sweetness to your taste, then serve as is or pour into a container and return to the freezer. For a smooth sorbet-like texture, remove from the freezer after 1 hour, give it a good whiz with a hand-held blender or electric beaters and pop back in the freezer. Repeat this a few times over the day. Store in the freezer for up to 1 month.

Kohlrabi

Do you walk straight past kohlrabi at the market and try not to make eye contact? Or did you buy it to be adventurous, but don't have that many ideas about how to use it? Fair enough, it's an underutilised vegetable and most of us need a better introduction. First, kohlrabi is a brassica, so that might immediately spark some ideas as to how it can be used. Second, the whole vegetable is edible – root to leaf and all parts in between have a mild cabbage-like flavour. The skin of kohlrabi can be quite tough, so we recommend peeling it if you're sautéing or eating it raw in salads.

Goes with	Cabbage, sauerkraut, brussels sprouts, beetroot, carrots, onions, leeks, turnips, fennel, mushrooms, apples, bacon, butter, cream, mustard, barley, nuts and seeds, dill, parsley, pepper
Storage	Store kohlrabi leaves and bulbs separately. Wrap the leaves and stems in a clean damp tea towel (dish towel), place in a reusable plastic bag or cloth bag in the fridge and keep for 3–5 days. Keep the bulb loosely wrapped in a clean damp tea towel (dish towel) in the crisper for up to 1 week.
Substitutes	Turnips, cauliflower and broccoli stems all have a similar texture to kohlrabi. If you need to replace raw kohlrabi in a salad, cabbage is a good understudy.

Some ideas for using up kohlrabi

Who knew there were so many?

* Make kohlrabi salad, a one-ingredient salad that saves the day. Remove the kohlrabi leaves and stems. Slice them very thinly and set aside. Peel the kohlrabi bulb, then cut into pretty little matchsticks and combine with the leaves and stems in a serving bowl. Dress with Miso Dressing (p 277), sprinkle with toasted sesame seeds and serve.
* Pickle it. Kohlrabi makes a crunchy pickle. Cut the bulb into fine matchsticks or rounds and follow the Basic Vegetable Pickling recipe (p 472).

* Cook up some kohlrabi fritters (don't tell the kids what's in them). Grate the kohlrabi bulb and follow the Parsnip Rosti recipe (p 323).
* Roast it. Cut the peeled kohlrabi bulb into quarters and follow the roasting method on p 77, roasting for 40–60 minutes. In the last 5 minutes of cooking, sprinkle with plenty of grated parmesan cheese.
* Make a quick slaw. Cut 1 kohlrabi bulb and 1 apple into matchsticks. Toss with some neutral oil and lemon juice, salt and pepper, and lots of dill or parsley leaves.

Whole kohlrabi sauté
1 KOHLRABI SERVES 2

This side has plenty of texture and flavour. You can multiply the quantities, depending on how much kohlrabi you have or how many people you need to feed. Serve it wherever you would a cabbage or potato dish – with sausages or meatloaf, oily fish or a lentil dish.

Peel the kohlrabi bulb and cut into 2 cm (¾ in) cubes, then chop the green tops. Heat 2 tbsp butter or oil in a saucepan over medium heat. When just melting, add the bulb pieces and sauté for about 5 minutes, until they begin to brown. Add 1 diced onion and sauté for another 5 minutes. When the onion is translucent, add the kohlrabi tops with 1 tbsp white wine vinegar, salt and pepper, then cook until the greens are wilted and tender.

Mashed kohlrabi

A 'not potato' mash is a really good idea. Not only is it a way to use up the saggy baggy vegetables in the fridge, but it throws a curveball at the weeknight-dinner grind. Kohlrabi mash is much loved in Germany, so you can confidently serve this alongside some sausages or lentils and know that everything will be okay.

Remove the leaves from 1 kg (2 lb 4 oz) kohlrabi and keep them for another use (see over the page). Peel and quarter the bulbs. Fill a large saucepan with water, add a good pinch of salt, and toss in the kohlrabi. Bring to the boil and cook for about 30 minutes, until tender. Drain.

Kohlrabi is fibrous, so purée it using a hand-held blender or in a food processor until it turns to a soft creamy mash. Stir in 2 tbsp softened butter and 2 tbsp cream or milk, then season with salt and pepper, adding some grated nutmeg if you have it.

Some ideas for using kohlrabi leaves

* Make chips (fries) using the Roasted Beet Leaves recipe (p 46). Depending on how large the kohlrabi leaves are, tear them into bite-sized pieces.
* Slice them thinly and add to any kraut you're making.
* Sauté them as you would the Stir-fried Beet Leaves (p 46).

See broccoli, brussels sprouts, cabbage, cauliflower, kale and wombok for ideas with other brassicas.

Lamb

Left-over cooked meat in the fridge is a thing of beauty, meaning that dinner is already well on the way. The trick is having a few ideas up your sleeve to turn a small amount of meat into another simple meal, rather than staring at it for a week and then throwing it away.

Storage   Left-over roast lamb (or beef) will last for about 4 days in the fridge. If it's been slow-cooked and is sealed with a layer of fat on the surface, it will last even longer.

Some ideas for using left-over lamb

* Replace the fish in the Left-over-fish Kedgeree (p 166) with lamb and ½ cup (80 g) peas, and turn it into a spiced lamb rice dish.
* Add chopped left-over lamb to the Simple Chickpea Stew (p 110). Throw it in the pot to warm through in the last 10 minutes of cooking, top with plenty of chopped parsley and serve with flat breads (p 168).
* Shred left-over lamb and sauté in a hot oiled pan with 2–3 tsp spice mix 4 (p 420) to make it full of flavour. Serve as part of a taco meal or with flat breads (p 168) and a slaw.
* Add about ½ cup (75 g) left-over lamb to the Green Things Fritters (p 439).
* Try left-over lamb with Chimichurri (p 193) or any other green sauce, mayonnaise and pickles on a fresh bread roll.
* Shred or chop left-over lamb and add it to Wally Rath's Barley Vegetable Soup (p 30). It will just need to be warmed through, so add it for the last 5 minutes of cooking. You could also add lamb to a lentil soup (p 246) or to Brown Rice, Mushroom and Spinach Soup (p 392).
* Add a few handfuls of chopped left-over lamb to Pumpkin Ratatouille (p 371) for the last 5 minutes of cooking to heat through.

Spiced lamb and chickpea pie filling

We have deliberately included pie filling recipes in this book, rather than complete pie recipes. That means you can buy or make pastry for a family-sized pie, turn the mix into pasties or curry puffs, or top it with mashed potato and turn it into a shepherd's or cottage pie. This pie mix is a very simple clean-out-the-fridge recipe that uses left-over cooked meats like roast lamb, beef or chicken, or any meat from a slow-cooked stew.

Heat ⅓ cup (80 ml) olive oil in a large frying pan over medium heat, then sauté 1 sliced onion until soft and sweet. Add 2 sliced garlic cloves, 1 tbsp grated fresh ginger, 2 tsp ground cumin and 1 tsp paprika. Sauté for another minute or so, then add 1–2 cups (150–300 g) shredded cooked lamb from a roast or stew and 1 cup (160 g) cooked or tinned chickpeas or left-over cooked grains like brown rice or barley. If there are plenty of pan juices, you may want to sprinkle in 1–2 tbsp plain (all-purpose) flour to thicken the filling. If you're using roast lamb that's a bit drier, you may need to add 400 g (14 oz) tinned tomatoes. Cook this down until the mixture thickens, then add 1 tbsp harissa paste or something else spicy, and lots of salt and pepper. Simmer for 2–3 minutes until the flavours come together. Allow to cool, then put on your pieman's hat.

Pan-juice gravy

Never throw away pan juices. Pan juices are where it's at. After roasting a chicken or joint of meat, it is sacrilege to wash the pan juices down the drain. Either make gravy right away or scrape the juices into a jar or airtight container and keep in the fridge for later in the week. Pan juices can also be used for roasting vegetables.

In a saucepan, melt 50 g (1¾ oz) butter and whisk in 2 tbsp plain (all-purpose) flour. Heat until bubbling, to make a roux. Add ¼ cup (60 ml) pan juices and whisk again, then slowly add ½ cup (125 ml) stock, a little at a time, whisking as you go, letting the gravy bubble and cook. You can add up to 1 cup (250 ml) stock, depending on how thick you like your gravy. Add plenty of salt and pepper and serve.

Leeks

Until recently, wasting half a leek was effectively an instruction in most cookbooks. It was very common to see 'use white part only' when describing how to prepare leeks. This is nonsense and has led to so many people thinking that the green tops are inedible. Not only are the green parts of a leek edible, they're also the tastiest. They need to be cooked a little longer to make them succulent, but there's nothing difficult about that. To get the most out of leeks, use all parts.

Go with	Leeks go with other members of the allium family: onions, garlic, chives, spring onions (scallions). Sturdy leafy greens such as kale, cavolo nero, other brassica leaves and silverbeet (Swiss chard). Parsnips, mushrooms, kohlrabi, potato, turnips, fennel seeds, chives, buckwheat and barley. Hard cheeses, eggs, milk, cream, butter, tofu, chicken and bacon.
Storage	Don't wash or trim leeks before storing. Wrap them loosely in a reusable plastic bag or a cloth bag and they will store well in the fridge for up to 2 weeks. If you're not sure how to use the green parts just yet, freeze them. The best way to do this is to slice them and blanch them quickly in a pan of boiling water. Let them cool, put them in an airtight container and they can be frozen for up to 10 months. Next time you're making any kind of stock, get the leek tops out and chuck them in.
Substitutes	If you're out of leeks, 2 small onions will stand in just fine for volume and flavour. For flavour alone, go for spring onions (scallions) and chives, or a combo of all three.

Some ideas for using that lonely leek in the fridge

✱ Modify your Mirepoix (p 314), the traditional French base flavour for soups and stews.
It's usually onion, carrot and celery, but if there's a leek that needs using, chuck it in instead.
Use your mirepoix right away or freeze until you need it.

✱ Sauté the leek low and slow with butter, garlic, salt and pepper, and make yourself the
Two-egg Omelette (p 150).

✱ Use leeks instead of onions in any recipe – see onions (p 311) for more ideas.

✱ **_Leek and herb broth_** Halve 1 large or 2 smaller leeks lengthways and wash thoroughly. Chop
into 3 pieces, put them in a saucepan and cover with 3 cups (750 ml) water. Add 3 smashed
garlic cloves, a good pinch of salt, some parsley or dill stems and 1–2 bay leaves if you have
them. Simmer gently for 20 minutes, then strain and use as you would any stock.

✱ **_Whole leek confit_** Confit is a method of slow-cooking an ingredient in oil. It preserves
the flavour and revives even the most tired of vegetables. Instead of sautéing an onion or
leek, use both the leek and the flavoured oil from the confit as a shortcut when cooking.
Follow the method for Garlic Confit (p 173) and ensure you take note of the food-safety
information there.

Leek as a pasta sauce
SERVES 2

Halve the leek lengthways and wash it well. Thinly slice the white and green parts. Heat 2 tbsp
olive oil and 2 tbsp butter in a frying pan over medium heat. Add the green parts of the leek
first, along with ¼ tsp each of salt and pepper, and sauté for 5 minutes, until they begin to
soften. Add 3 finely chopped garlic cloves, the white parts of the leek and 1 tbsp fresh thyme
leaves, then sauté for another 10 minutes, until the leeks are soft. Add 1 cup (250 ml) white
wine, stock or water. Cook, covered, for 10 minutes. Stir in ½ cup (50 g) grated parmesan and
serve on top of hot pasta.

Leek and potato soup

SERVES 4

As the saying goes, 'If it ain't broke, don't fix it.' Leek and potato soup is a classic that doesn't need any adjustments. What might prove a little scandalous here is the use of leek tops. They will certainly give the soup a pale green tinge as opposed to the creamy white of most versions. Oh well. The flavour here is still subtle and comforting, if more rustic. Serve with crusty bread and butter and a simple green salad.

Halve 4 leeks lengthways, then wash thoroughly and shake dry. Thinly slice both white and green parts, keeping them separate. In a large heavy-based saucepan, melt ⅓ cup (90 g) butter over medium–low heat. Add the green parts of the leek first, along with ½ tsp each of salt and pepper, and sauté for 2–3 minutes. Add the white parts of the leeks and 2 finely chopped garlic cloves. Sauté gently for a few minutes. Dice 2 potatoes (no need to peel, but do wash and scrub clean) and add to the leeks with 1 large thyme sprig and 1–2 bay leaves. Sauté for another 1–2 minutes. Add 4 cups (1 litre) chicken or vegetable stock, reduce the heat to low and simmer for about 20 minutes, until the potato is soft.

Remove the thyme sprig and bay leaves and simmer for another 1–2 minutes. Add 1 cup (250 ml) single (pure) cream and blend using a hand-held blender. Gently reheat if needed.

Braised leeks with parsley and egg

SERVES 4 AS PART OF A SHARED MEAL

The classic flavours of this very simple and extremely elegant side go with poached chicken, pan-fried fish or a light soup such as the Wilted Lettuce Soup (p 248) or the Green Soup (p 440).

Preheat the oven to 180°C (350°F). Line a shallow baking tray with enough foil to leave about 20 cm (8 in) over each edge. Wash 2–3 leeks very well – you may need to tear the green parts open to expose the inner part where the dirt hides. Allow to dry. Cut the leeks on a sharp angle into bite-sized chunks and spread over the baking tray. Drizzle generously with oil of your choice and add a thyme or rosemary sprig. Season with salt, pepper and nutmeg, add 150 ml (5 fl oz) water and seal the foil around the leeks like a parcel. Bake for 45–60 minutes, until the leeks are soft.

Meanwhile, hard-boil 2 eggs. Rinse, peel and roughly chop, then add 2–3 tbsp snipped chives or parsley. Once the leeks are cooked, remove from the oven and let them steam in the parcel for 10 minutes. Open and leave to cool while you make the Classic Mustard Vinaigrette (p 283). Arrange the leeks on a plate, pour the vinaigrette over them and top with the chopped egg. Finish with a few handfuls of chopped parsley. Season with more salt and pepper if needed.

GREEN LEEK TOPS

All right, all right, sometimes you *might* only use the white part of the leek. If that's the case, then please don't put the green part in the compost. Keep it, freeze it (p 234) and use it in End-of-the-week Scrap Stock (p 446), or make this leek top sauté.

Sautéed leek tops

The fibrous green tops are so full of flavour that they must never be ditched. Add these sautéed leek tops to omelettes (p 150) or pasta dishes, or stir them through a grain salad. You could even serve them as a side when there are no other greens in the house.

Make sure the leek tops are very well washed and completely dry. Cut into slices about 2 cm (¾ in) thick. Heat ¼ cup (60 ml) oil of your choice in a frying pan over medium heat and add the leek tops. Stir constantly for a few minutes, until they release some of their juices. Reduce the heat to low, then cover and cook for 10 minutes. Remove the lid, season with a pinch each of salt and pepper, and add 1 finely chopped garlic clove per leek top. Cook for another 10 minutes, stirring frequently, until the leek tops brown a little at the edges.

See garlic, onions and spring onions for ideas with other alliums.

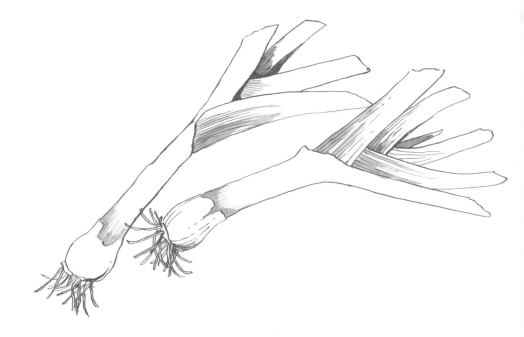

Lemons

Like salt and garlic, lemons are indispensable in the kitchen. The problem is, in summer when you're after their zesty, bright freshness, you might find imported lemons at an exorbitant price. The key to keeping the flavour of lemon in your kitchen all year round is to make the most of the abundance of citrus during the winter months and start squirrelling away the juice, zest and peel, plus filling up a few jars with lemony preserves. You'll find lots of lemon preserve recipes below, but also check out the other citrus sections – cumquats, grapefruit, limes, mandarins and oranges – for more citrus preserving tips.

Go with   What doesn't lemon go with? Fish, mayonnaise, gin, all fruits and vegetables, chickpeas, lentils, dried beans, leafy greens, herbs, garlic, chilli, ginger, cinnamon, cumin, fennel seeds, olives, nuts, poppy seeds, tahini, chicken, lamb, cream cheese, feta, mozzarella, honey and desserts.

Storage   Lemons are fine in the fruit bowl for a week or so, but if you're looking to store whole fruit for longer, pop them in the crisper for a few weeks. They need air, so don't suffocate them in a sealed bag or airtight container.

Substitutes   Lemon is lemon, but if you don't have one in the house, don't run to the shops – try a squeeze of lime juice, or any other citrus you have. If you only have sweeter citrus fruit, such as orange, add a splash of vinegar. Preserved lemon can be used in place of fresh lemon in most savoury dishes, dressings and marinades. Pickling liquid or kimchi brine can replace lemon juice if a dish needs more acid. But in sweet dishes, use a few tablespoons of marmalade if you don't have any fresh lemons.

Some ideas to avoid throwing away half a lemon

Cut lemons will last for about 5 days in an airtight container in the fridge. Squeeze some into a cup of hot water or pour yourself a G&T and take five. But if you're still stumped on how to use up half a lemon, here are a few tips.

* Use it as a weight to hold your fermented vegetables or kraut down under the brine.
* Char it. Heat a frying pan or barbecue, brush a little oil on the cut side of the lemon and place cut side down on the pan or hot plate until blackened, about 3 minutes. Squeeze over fish, chicken or grilled (broiled) asparagus.
* When roasting a chicken or a fish, pop a half-lemon inside the cavity.
* Freeze it for making Fish Stock (p 166) or Pectin Stock (p 9).
* Add brightness to a herbal tea. Turn to p 205 for tea-making tips.

Some ideas for making the most of lemons

* *Lemon juice* If you have an abundance of lemons or score a cheap bag at the supermarket, juice them, pour the juice into ice-cube trays and freeze them. Once frozen, remove from the tray and store your lemon-juice cubes in an airtight container in the freezer for up to 6 months. Use whenever you need lemon juice.
* *Lemon zest* Zest lemons before juicing. Take the extra few minutes and you'll high-five yourself later. Lemon zest can be stored in an airtight container or a jar in the freezer, and you can keep adding to it. Or you can dry lemon zest in the sun or a 100–120°C (200–235°F) oven. Once completely dry and cool, store in a jar in the pantry for up to 6 months.
* *Lemon peel* Peel lemons before juicing. Try to just get strips of the yellow skin, rather than lots of the bitter white pith. Store lemon peel in a jar of sugar, salt or white wine vinegar. You'll end up with preserved lemon peel and lemony flavoured sugar, salt or vinegar. Two birds, one stone. You can also freeze lemon peel strips or dry them in a 100–120°C (200–235°F) oven and store like zest above. See Drying Mandarin Peel (p 259).

Some ideas for preserving lemons

* ***Lemon-flavoured butter*** Butter laced with lemon zest lasts well in the freezer and is perfect for when there are no lemons in the fruit bowl. Follow the Anchovy Butter recipe (p 3), folding through the finely grated zest of 3 lemons instead of anchovy. Mix this zesty butter through hot pasta with capers and parsley, use it to fry a piece of fish, or melt it in a small saucepan with a little oil and mustard and plenty of fresh herbs and pour over hot potatoes.
* ***Lemons preserved in vinegar*** Add the zest and juice of 1–2 lemons to 1 cup (250 ml) white wine vinegar or apple cider vinegar. Allow to sit for a few weeks for the flavour to develop, then store in the fridge basically forever. Use when lemons are scarce – great for salad dressings, or add 1 tbsp to give a little lift to soups and stews.
* ***Lemon curd*** It's like spreading sunshine on your scones and toast. Follow the Just-about-anything Curd (p 155) recipe, using the zest of 2 lemons and ½ cup (125 ml) lemon juice.
* ***Lemon marmalade or lemon jam*** These are pantry staples in our kitchens. Lemon marmalade has the peel and is sour, rather than intensely bitter like grapefruit marmalade. Lemon jam uses just the flesh and could pass as lemon curd if you weren't looking too closely. Follow the Grapefruit Marmalade recipe (p 179), replacing the grapefruit with lemons (throw in a few bay leaves; it's very nice), or the Orange Jam recipe (p 317), replacing the cloves with cardamom pods.

Lemonade or lemon cordial

So easy to make, so easy to drink, and an excellent gift when lemons are everywhere. This is a concentrate, so serve 1 part cordial to 4 parts water or soda water. Use this recipe for all citrus cordials, but if you're not using lemons remember to add the juice of at least 1 lemon to your other citrus fruit to ensure the right acid levels. See also the Berry Berry Good Lemonade variation (p 49).

In a large saucepan over low heat, dissolve 500 g (1 lb 2 oz) white (granulated) sugar in 2 cups (500 ml) water. Add 2 cups (500 ml) lemon juice (from about 8 large lemons) and as much finely grated zest as you like. More zest equals more flavour but also more bite. Most kids hate it when it's too zesty, so go easy if your target audience is under 10. Bring to a simmer then remove from the heat.

If you're going to use the cordial over the next few weeks, store in a clean bottle in the fridge for up to 3 weeks. If you're looking to store it in the pantry, you'll need to pour the hot cordial into hot sterilised bottles (p 501). Seal the bottles, allow to cool, then store in the pantry for up to 3 months. For longer storage, heat-process (p 502) for 15 minutes.

Salt-preserved lemons (or limes)

MAKES 2 x 500 G (1 LB 2 OZ) JARS

This recipe is in our other cookbooks, but you just can't have a pantry without preserved lemons.

You'll need 1 kg (2 lb 4 oz) lemons or limes for this recipe (plus extra for juicing if your lemons are dry). See p 366 for our top tips for using preserved lemon in everyday cooking.

Cut the lemons or limes into quarters (or halves if they're very small). Put 1 tbsp salt in each sterilised jar (p 501) and top with a few layers of lemon or lime, pressing down on them as you go to release the juices. Sprinkle with another layer of salt, then add another layer of fruit. Slide 1 tsp black peppercorns, 1–2 bay leaves and a pinch of chilli flakes down the side of each jar. Repeat layering the fruit and salt until the jar is almost full (leave a 1 cm/½ in gap at the top), remembering to keep pushing down as you go – the fruit needs to be entirely covered in juice. If your fruit hasn't released enough of its own juices, squeeze a few extra lemons or limes and pour the juice over to cover. Wipe the rim of each jar with paper towel to remove excess salt, then seal and let it sit in a cool, dark place for 6 weeks. You know your lemons or limes are preserved when the salt has completely dissolved into a gel-like liquid. Once a jar is opened, store in the fridge for up to 1 year.

Whole-lemon and chocolate cake

MAKES 1 x 22 CM (8½ IN) CAKE

Flourless citrus cake is a classic. Always moist, never too sweet, and a whole lot more interesting than a sponge cake. This one is made more lush with chocolate and whole citrus. We use lemons here but feel free to use other citrus fruit instead.

Place 2 lemons (250–280 g/9–10 oz) in a saucepan and cover with cold water. Bring to a boil and simmer for 30 minutes or until the lemons are completely soft. Drain and allow to cool completely. Break the cooled lemon up a bit, pull out as many seeds as you can, then blend to a pale paste using a hand-held blender or food processor.

Place a heatproof bowl over a saucepan of simmering water, ensuring the bowl isn't touching the water, then add 200 g (7 oz) dark chocolate and 100 g (3½ oz) butter and melt together, stirring to combine. Remove from the heat and allow to cool.

Preheat the oven to 180°C (350°F) and grease a 22 cm (8½ in) cake tin with butter. In a large bowl, beat 8 eggs with 1 cup (220 g) caster (superfine) sugar until frothy. Fold in 3 cups (300 g) almond meal, 1 tsp baking powder, the blended lemons and the chocolate mixture. Stir gently to combine, then pour into the tin. Bake for 1 hour and 20 minutes or until a skewer inserted in the centre comes out clean. Allow to cool completely before serving.

LEMON LEAVES

Some ideas for using lemon leaves

Lemon leaves are aromatic and citrusy. If you have access to a lemon tree, experiment with using the leaves in your cooking – treat them like bay leaves to impart flavour when grilling, simmering or infusing. Try these tricks.

* Make a lemon leaf herbal infusion using the Lemongrass Tea recipe (p 205).
* Squash meatballs between lemon leaves and grill on the barbecue.
* Add lemon leaves to a fish parcel, or stuff them into the cavity of a whole fish or chicken before cooking.
* Add lemon leaves to curries, fish soups, broths or white bean stews.

See cumquats, grapefruit, limes, mandarins and oranges for ideas with other citrus. *See also* preserved lemon.

Lentils

Ah, to leave home and live off lentils is to taste true independence. Almost no other ingredient can lend itself to resourcefulness and thriftiness like lentils. For inspiration we turn to Indian and Italian cooks who use lentils as a main dish, as a vegetable side, in a soup and everything in between. Lentils take up flavour very well; a little can go a long way, and can add bulk to other ingredients.

Go with	Onions, carrots, celery, parsnips, potatoes, pumpkin (squash), tomatoes, green beans, peas, fennel, eggplant (aubergine), zucchini (courgettes), roasted capsicum (pepper), silverbeet (Swiss chard), garlic, mint, parsley, bay leaves, sage, rosemary, black pepper, coriander seeds, curry powder, paprika, turmeric, fennel seeds, mustard seeds, pine nuts, pistachios, lemons, tahini, bacon, ham, sausages, cheeses, eggs
Storage	Store dried lentils in an airtight container in the pantry for up to 1 year. Unopened tinned lentils can be stored for as long as the use-by date on the tin. Cooked lentils or lentils from an opened tin will keep in an airtight container in the fridge for 4–5 days or in the freezer for up to 2 months.
Substitutes	You can swap different lentil varieties with each other, or use dried beans instead in stews and soup recipes. Keep in mind, though, that red split lentils cook very quickly and lose their shape, so if you want to make a salad, for instance, you'll want the more robust texture of green or brown lentils.
How to cook dried lentils	Rinse lentils well and pick out any little stones. You can cook them in just water, but we like to add a peeled bruised garlic clove and maybe a bay leaf or a few parsley stems. You can also cook lentils in stock for extra flavour. Generously cover 1 cup lentils (205 g red, 210 g puy, 215 g green or brown) with liquid. Bring to a simmer, then cook over medium heat until tender. Different lentil types need different cooking times, so keep an eye on them. Drain. Depending on the variety, dried lentils can double in size.

Some ideas for using up left-over cooked lentils

* Season with salt, pepper and paprika, then add to roast carrots, beetroot or brussels sprouts for the last 5 minutes of cooking.
* Make the Chilli Con Carne (p 36), using lentils instead of kidney beans.
* Add a little to the Best Barley Side (p 29).
* Add a handful to the Raw Grated Beet Salad (p 45) to make it a complete meal.
* **Simple lentil salad** Mix 400 g (14 oz) rinsed and well-dried tinned or cooked lentils with ¼ cup (40 g) currants, ½ red onion, very thinly sliced, and the leafy tops of 1 bunch of parsley. Dress with a squeeze of orange juice, a splash of red wine vinegar, 1 tbsp olive oil and a very generous pinch each of salt and pepper.

Quick lentil dip

If you're using dried lentils, cook them first. Place 400 g (14 oz) drained tinned or cooked lentils in a food processor with 2 finely chopped garlic cloves, a good pinch of salt and the finely chopped stems of ½ bunch of well-washed coriander (cilantro). Blitz until smooth. Now add the coriander leaves from the ½ bunch, ½ tsp ground cumin, ¼ cup (60 ml) olive oil and the juice of ½ lemon. Blitz again until very smooth, adding 1–2 tbsp water if needed to loosen.

Serve with crackers or flat breads.

Dal

SERVES 4 AS A MAIN, 6 AS PART OF A SHARED MEAL

Every cook should have a dal recipe up their sleeve. Here's the thing, though – dal really needs to be dressed up with a serious spice mix. Without this, dal kind of moves into the porridge category. Yes, there are dal recipes where the spice is cooked into the lentils, but the technique here gives you more flexibility. In Indian cooking the spice mix that tops a dish is called tarka, a deeply aromatic combination of fried spices that leaves your senses in a state nothing short of rapturous. Plain dal, sensational tarka. Change your life, eat it for breakfast.

Rinse 2 cups yellow split peas (440 g) or red lentils (410 g). Place them in a large saucepan, add 1 tbsp grated fresh ginger and 1 tsp ground turmeric, then cover with 5 cups (1.25 litres) water. Bring to the boil over medium heat. Some foam will rise to the surface of the water, but simply skim this off.

Reduce the heat and cook, covered, until the lentils are very soft and breaking up. They should have a thick, porridge-like consistency. Once cooked, add ½ tsp salt. While the dal is cooking, make the tarka below or the Cheat's Tarka on p 429.

Serve in bowls and spoon tarka evenly over each bowl.

TARKA

Heat ⅓ cup ghee (65 g), butter (60 g) or oil (60 ml) in a frying pan. Add 1 tbsp chilli flakes, 3 very thinly sliced garlic cloves, 2 tsp fennel seeds, 20 fresh or dried curry leaves and 1 tsp salt. Fry for about 1 minute, then add 2 tbsp mustard seeds and fry until they pop, only a few seconds. Remove from the heat, squeeze in the juice of ½ lemon and give the pan a shake.

Simple lentil base four ways

SERVES 4

Here we start with a base recipe that can then be turned into a variety of different dishes. This way of cooking is like building a structure with a really good foundation. From there you can add other ingredients that will turn a simple base such as this into a hearty stew or warming soup.

Drain 800 g (1 lb 12 oz) tinned or 3 cups (600 g) cooked lentils. In a medium saucepan, heat ¼ cup (60 ml) neutral oil, add 1 large diced onion (or 2 small) and 1 tsp each of salt and pepper, and sauté until the onion is translucent. Add 1 finely diced carrot or parsnip, 2 celery stalks and 4 finely chopped garlic cloves, then sauté gently for 15 minutes, stirring often. Once this mix is well cooked, add the finely grated zest of 1 lemon, 2 bay leaves, and a thyme or oregano sprig. Now add the lentils and 1 cup (250 ml) stock of your choice. Reduce the heat to low and cook for 20 minutes. In this time the liquid will be absorbed and the texture of the lentils will become thick. Taste and adjust the seasoning.

Now choose how you'd like to eat your lentils.

AS A SIDE OR CONDIMENT

Use as a topping for baked potatoes, as a side with sausages, or serve on its own with a green salad and a piece of toast. It can also be used as the filling for a pie. Cover in pastry, or mashed potatoes for a vegetarian shepherd's pie. You could stir through some grated cheddar or parmesan for extra richness.

AS A BASE FOR BAKED EGGS

Preheat the oven to 170°C (325°F). Heat the Simple Lentil Base in an ovenproof frying pan until warmed through. Make four indentations in the lentils and crack 4 eggs into them. Bake for 10–15 minutes, until the eggs are set. Top with chopped herbs or crumbled or grated cheese. »

AS A STEW

Place the Simple Lentil Base (p 245) in a large saucepan and add 400 g (14 oz) tinned tomatoes and some cooked bacon or smoked sausage, or left-over meatballs if you have them. You could also add some diced cooked potato, or sautéed mushrooms, or a few big handfuls of spinach. Throw in some parmesan rinds if you have them and cook for another 20 minutes. Serve with polenta, mashed potatoes, Mashed Kohlrabi (p 229) or 'There's Nothing Wrong With That Cream!' Potatoes (p 125).

AS A HEARTY SOUP

Add 4 cups (1 litre) stock to the Simple Lentil Base (p 245) and you have soup that makes a hearty meal. Adjust the seasoning if necessary. Cover the saucepan and heat through for 20 minutes. Serve with crusty bread and butter.

Lettuce

Really ask yourself, what is lettuce? This is the sort of soul-searching question that might reveal culinary limitations that shock you. If lettuce is nothing but salad filler to you then *lettuce* expand your perspective. Sure, lettuces bring freshness to the table like no other vegetable, but why do most of us treat it like a one-trick pony, destined to be doused in vinaigrette for all eternity? We suspect they're one of the most wasted vegetables in households. The first thing to remember is to buy only as much as you intend to eat in a very short period, because a lettuce's lifespan is as short as a butterfly's. But if you do have a lettuce past its salad days or are looking to expand your repertoire, then here you'll find some other ways to eat it.

Here we divide lettuces into 2 categories: soft and crunchy. We treat them a little differently and offer ideas for using up a little or a lot or both.

SOFT LETTUCES

To state the obvious, soft lettuces are really soft. We're talking varieties like butter lettuce, oak-leaf lettuce, the burgundy mignonette, coral lettuce and lamb's lettuce (corn salad), and we're including rocket (arugula) even though it's in the cabbage family. Each of these has a melt-in-the-mouth quality and their leaves are very delicate. When they're fresh they make the loveliest salads, dressed simply, with a little added cheese or a sprinkle of toasted seeds. When they're getting tired, save them by cooking them before they turn to slime.

Go with	Oil, vinegar, mustard, citrus fruits, cucumber, tomatoes, avocado, carrots, spring onions (scallions), olives, capers, cheeses, mayonnaise, nuts, seeds
Storage	Because of their high water content lettuces are very perishable, softer lettuces even more so. Don't wash your lettuce until you need to use it. An intact head will stay fresh for 5–7 days wrapped loosely in a reusable plastic bag in the fridge. Keep unopened bags of lettuce leaves in the fridge for as long as the packet states. Once opened, store in the fridge in the bag they came in for no more than 1–2 days.

Substitutes   You can replace all varieties of soft lettuce with each other. In smaller quantities, parsley or celery leaves can be used as the base of a salad.

Some ideas for using up a bit of soft lettuce

* Whip up a delicate salad for one. Put a handful of soft lettuce leaves or the last leaves of a supermarket bag of lettuce in a small bowl. Add the leaves of some soft herbs and a few drained capers or chopped pickles if you have them. Dress with a drizzle of neutral oil, a squeeze of citrus juice and a pinch of salt.
* Make the Spring Greens Medley (p 341) with lettuce and any other spring greens – asparagus, peas, green beans, snow peas (mange tout) – that need using. Slice the lettuce into fat ribbons and add to the mix. If you have some fresh mint, scatter it liberally on top. Serve with grilled fish, a frittata, or Bean Mash made with white beans (p 36), and bread.
* Relive your childhood with Vegemite and lettuce picnic sandwiches. School-lunch vibes here, but so satisfying. Spread soft white bread with softened butter then a smear of Vegemite, add lots of fresh lettuce leaves and top with another slice of buttered bread. Eat immediately or wrap to go.

Wilted lettuce soup
SERVES 4 AS A MAIN, 6 AS A STARTER

So a whole head of lettuce wilted in the fridge. It's definitely not going to make much of a salad, but it is going to make one hell of a soup. Both Chinese and French cuisines feature lettuce soups. This version has more European flavours and is lovely hot or cold. If you don't have any left-over mashed or cooked potato in the fridge, start by cooking about 200 g (7 oz) potato.

In a large saucepan over medium heat, melt 1 tbsp butter and 1 tbsp oil. Add 1 diced onion and 4 finely chopped garlic cloves, and sauté until the onion is soft and translucent. Next add 1 cup (about 200 g) cooked potato, mashed or diced, 1 head of chopped lettuce leaves, 1 bunch of parsley leaves, ½ bunch of dill leaves and ½ tsp salt (less if using store-bought stock). Stir until all the ingredients are coated, then cook for 2 minutes. Add 4 cups (1 litre) vegetable or chicken stock, cover the saucepan and cook for 15 minutes.

Using a hand-held blender, blend until smooth. If you want to add a dash of cream, go ahead; otherwise serve with the most delicious bread and butter.

CRUNCHY LETTUCES

These are the more robust lettuces in the family. They can take the weight of heavier ingredients, holding their own in a bit of rough-and-tumble. In this category we include varieties such as iceberg lettuce, cos lettuce, endive or radicchio. These are the lettuces for experimenting with cooking and pickling.

Go with   Oils (especially sesame oil), vinegar, olives, garlic, ginger, chilli, anchovies, yoghurt, cheeses, soy sauce, tahini, miso, mustard, parsnips, cucumber, tomatoes, avocado, carrots, radishes, figs, citrus fruits, persimmons, pomegranate, chives, nuts, seeds

---

Storage   Don't wash the lettuce until you use it. A crunchy lettuce variety will last for 4–5 days in the fridge if wrapped in a clean damp tea towel (dish towel), then in a reusable plastic bag or cloth bag.

Substitutes   As with the soft lettuces, crunchy lettuce varieties can be swapped with each other. For salads with a similar robustness, you could use silverbeet (Swiss chard) or rainbow chard leaves.

Some ideas for using up a bit of crunchy lettuce

* Make a caesar salad with torn cos lettuce. See p 4 for a quick recipe.
* *Stir-fried lettuce* Get all your ingredients sorted first: 2 tbsp neutral oil, ½ tsp crushed sichuan pepper or ground black pepper, 3–4 cups (about 250 g) torn crunchy lettuce, 2 finely chopped garlic cloves, 1 tbsp soy sauce and ¼ tsp sugar. Heat a wok or large frying pan over medium–high heat until just smoking. Add the oil, sichuan pepper and a big pinch of salt, then add the lettuce and garlic, stirring frequently for about 1 minute. Add the soy sauce, then the sugar and mix for another 30 seconds or so. Remove from the heat and serve.
* *Charred lettuce* Preheat the barbecue grill plate or a chargrill pan over high heat. Cut a crunchy lettuce – we like radicchio – lengthways and then into thick wedges. Brush all sides with neutral oil, then char each side on the grill plate or pan, turning until all sides are charred. Remove from the heat and drizzle with a garlicky yoghurt dressing (see Harissa-roasted Eggplant, p 188), or Green Chilli and Lime Sauce (p 113). »

* **Baked radicchio** Cooking radicchio mellows out its natural bitterness and is good for when it's not in the freshest condition. Serve it with wintery meals or pasta dishes. Preheat the oven to 200°C (400°F). Slice 2 radicchio lengthways and arrange in an ovenproof dish, cut side down, in a single layer. Season with ½ tsp salt, ½ tsp pepper, 1 tsp fennel seeds and ¼ cup (60 ml) olive oil. Bake for 10 minutes. Turn the radicchio and bake for another 10 minutes, then turn again and bake for a final 10 minutes, or until the base is tender. Allow to cool for a few minutes before serving.

* **Soy-pickled lettuce** Don't be scared – pickled lettuce is so delicious that we eat it straight out of the jar. Use the recipe for the Japanese-style Soy-pickled Cucumber (p 128), using 3–4 cups (about 250 g) sliced crunchy lettuce. You can really be a little rough with the lettuce and scrunch it into a jar or airtight container so it's covered with the soy brine. Eat it with an egg on rice for a quick dinner or lunch, or serve alongside San Choy Bow (below) or with rice paper rolls.

San choy bow

The exact origins of this dish are hard to pin down. It's definitely Chinese, but from which region we can't be sure. What we do know is that it's one of the greatest ways to make a complete meal from a small amount of protein, some vegetables and plenty of condiments.

Use a crunchy lettuce for this dish, as it will add texture as well as freshness. It's a great way to use a whole head of lettuce, and if you're feeding kids they hardly know they're eating their salad. Most often iceberg lettuce is used, but we use whatever is around. If you're using iceberg, the trick to getting those perfect lettuce cups is to hold the whole head core side down and bash it against the benchtop. The core should then pop out. Slice the base of the lettuce off, then peel the leaves apart under running water.

Dry the lettuce before placing it on a serving plate.

Like the 'Clear Out the Fridge' Pizza (p 97) and our taco Tuesdays, we use San Choy Bow as a meal to clean out the fridge. On the table go the lettuce leaves, then any of the following things that we have hanging around. Make it a casual feast and let everyone build their own.

TO FILL YOUR LETTUCE CUPS

- Some left-over chicken or fish reheated in a hot frying pan or wok with a little soy sauce, salt and sesame oil.
- A little sautéed minced (ground) meat mixed with shredded cabbage, garlic and soy sauce.
- Left-over rice heated in a wok with some soy sauce, salt and rice wine vinegar (or the Green Eggy Fried Rice, p 57).
- Any left-over tofu dishes, such as the Mapo Tofu, of Sorts (p 459).
- Some left-over rice noodle salad like the Cold Noodle and Wombok Salad With Pickles (p 487).

Have a little bowl with some simple sliced vegies, such as:
- carrot matchsticks
- thinly sliced radish
- bean sprouts
- thinly sliced snow peas (mange tout).

Then get out the condiments:
- Soy-pickled Lettuce (opposite) or Pickled Ginger (p 175)
- Fermented Chilli (p 114)
- Not So Classic Kimchi (p 486).

Limes

Limes are more savoury, herbal and spicy than lemons or other citrus fruit. They have a sharp and salty flavour that lends complexity to both sweet and savoury dishes and is a perfect addition to drinks. The problem is their season is short and out of season they cost a bomb. Eat all the fresh limes you can when they're cheap, and stock up the freezer and pantry for the rest of the year. If you have a lime tree you're a lucky, lucky duck. Share them with your neighbours and learn how to preserve them.

Go with	Avocado, coconut, greens, fennel, okra, pumpkin (squash), garlic, ginger, chilli, berries, melons, pineapple, mango, bananas, kiwi fruit, coriander (cilantro), basil, cardamom, pepper, lemongrass, nuts, fennel seeds, coriander seeds, juniper berries, star anise, yoghurt, honey, salt, seafood, clear spirits such as vodka and gin
Storage	Lime skin gets very hard and dry if the fruit is left out on the bench for longer than a few days. Whole limes are best kept in the crisper. Store cut limes in an airtight container in the fridge for up to 5 days. They should be zested before being juiced, and the zest saved for a rainy day. See the tips for lemon zest on p 239. If your limes are feeling hard or dry, they may need a little warm massage to get the juices flowing. Roll them back and forth on the benchtop, warming them up with your hand, so they release some of their moisture. You can also pop them in the oven or microwave for a tiny bit, or put them in a heatproof bowl and cover with boiling water for a few minutes. Just don't forget them!
Substitutes	If a savoury recipe calls for lime and you don't have one, use a lemon and add extra lemon zest and a little black pepper for a bit of edge. You could also add a splash of vinegar or a little tamarind. For desserts and preserving, go for lemons or grapefruits. It won't be the same flavour, but one citrus fruit can be easily swapped with another.

Some ideas for using up one lime

* Limes can be interchanged everywhere other citrus is used. Try lime marmalade (use the Grapefruit Marmalade recipe, p 179), lime bitters for G&Ts (see Grapefruit Skin Bitters, p 180) and salt-preserved limes (see Salt-preserved Lemons, p 241).
* Add lime zest and juice to the Odd-knobs Ginger Paste (p 175) and use for quick Thai curries, broths, marinades and noodles.
* *Green chilli and lime sauce* For drizzling over tacos, roasted or grilled vegetables, fries or Chilli Con Carne (p 36). See p 113 for the recipe.
* *Lime dressing* For noodles, Vietnamese-style salads, spicy slaws or blanched green vegetables. In a jar, mix the juice of 1 lime with an equal amount of fish sauce, a splash of rice wine vinegar, 1 tsp caster (superfine) sugar, 1 tsp sesame oil, 1 finely chopped garlic clove and some thinly sliced red chilli. Shake and pour.
* *Sticky spicy lime glaze* In a small saucepan over medium heat, mix 3 tbsp honey, ½ tsp salt, the juice and zest of 1 lime, 1 tbsp neutral oil, 2 finely chopped garlic cloves and ½ tsp chilli flakes or powder, or 1 tbsp chilli sauce or sambol. Cook for 2–3 minutes, then brush over fish before cooking or sweet potato before roasting, or drizzle over grilled (broiled) pineapple.
* *Lime syrup* Follow the Mandarin Syrup recipe (p 258), using limes instead. If you want a little extra flavour, add some lemongrass, ground cardamom or chilli flakes.

Cured fish and quick-pickle onions with lime juice

In a bowl, combine 500 g (1 lb 2 oz) thinly sliced or finely diced uncooked firm white fish fillets with ½ thinly sliced red or brown onion. Cover completely in lime juice – you will probably need 1 cup (250 ml). Cover and refrigerate for 90 minutes. Remove the fish and onion from the bowl, discarding the lime juice, and place on a serving platter. Sprinkle with sugar and salt, then top with any of the following: diced flavoursome tomatoes, diced avocado, lots of coriander (cilantro) or dill or parsley leaves, chopped olives, thinly sliced chillies, finely grated lime zest, capers. Drizzle good-quality olive oil over the top and serve with fancy corn chips.

If you just wanted to pickle onions, follow the same instructions but add some salt and sugar to the lime juice, along with a generous pinch of chilli flakes.

Oven-roasted limes, lemons and oranges

We roast and slow-cook so many things in winter, but citrus fruit doesn't often make it into the oven. Oven-cooking methods are excellent for an abundance of citrus or for a few old wrinkly oranges that everyone is avoiding. Roasting will concentrate the sugars and intensify the flavour. Add chopped roasted citrus to salads, a tray of roasted vegetables, a panful of sautéed greens, pilafs or couscous. You can serve it on a cheese plate or put a slice in the bottom of a glass of fizz.

Preheat the oven to 180°C (350°F). Thinly slice the citrus fruit into rounds (thin-skinned fruits like oranges, Meyer lemons and limes work the best) and spread in a single layer on a baking tray lined with baking paper. Roast them as is, or drizzle a little vinegar over them and sprinkle with a pinch each of sugar and salt.

Place on the middle shelf of the oven and roast for 15–25 minutes, depending on the size and thickness of your slices. They're ready once they're a little tender and the edges are starting to caramelise. Eat straight away, or allow to cool, then store in the fridge for up to 1 week.

Sweet pickled limes: no cooking

This is an easy, no-cooking Indian-style pickle to serve with curries and rice. It takes hardly any effort, but it does need time to sit for the flavours to develop. Make it when limes are cheap or too many arrive in your vegie box.

Finely dice 400 g (14 oz) limes, removing as many seeds as you can and catching any juice that escapes. Put the lime and juice in a bowl and add ¼ cup (75 g) salt and ¼ cup (60 g) brown sugar, 1 tbsp mustard seeds, 1 tsp chilli flakes and ¼ cup (55 g) grated fresh ginger. Pack the mixture tightly into a clean sterilised jar (p 501), pushing it down as you go. Wipe the rim clean and put the lid on. It will need to sit for a month or more before it's ready – if the weather is cool you can keep it on the bench, but if it's hot, put it in the fridge. Give the jar a shake or a stir with a clean implement every now and then. Once the limes have softened and are full of flavour, store in the fridge for up to 6 months.

LIME HALVES AND LIME LEAVES

Some ideas for using spent lime halves

After squeezing every last drop of juice from a lime, don't throw the empty halves in the bin:

* Use them instead of grapefruit in the Grapefruit Skin Bitters (p 180).
* Use them instead of oranges in the Spent-orange-halves Kitchen Cleaner (p 319).
* Dry them using the Mandarin Peel Fire-starters instructions (p 260) and save them for your winter fires.

Lime leaves

Lime leaves add zesty flavour when infused into hot liquids – like water for tea, syrups for cocktails and desserts, or a fish or chicken stock. See Lemon Leaves (p 242) for tips on how to use citrus leaves in the kitchen.

See cumquats, grapefruit, lemons, mandarins and oranges for ideas with other citrus. *See also* preserved lemon.

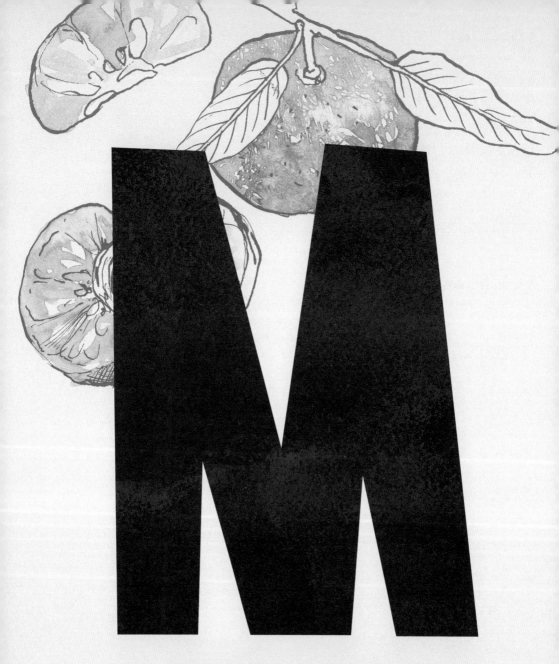

Mandarins

Alex's all-time favourite fruit. When they're in season, there's always a mandarin in her jacket pocket. While mandarins make the perfect snack, there's a superabundance of ways to cook with them and preserve them, whether you have one old boy left in an almost empty fruit bowl or a tree-full to deal with.

And please don't throw away the peel. Aromatic and spicy, it makes a beautiful addition to a low-waste pantry; it's even said to have medicinal properties.

Go with   Chocolate, honey and all the aniseedy things like licorice, fennel and star anise. Other citrus fruits, warm spices (cinnamon, allspice, cloves, star anise), ginger, vanilla, tea, slow-cooked meats.

Storage   Store mandarins in the fruit bowl for up to 5 days. They'll be juicier and have better flavour when kept at room temperature. For longer storage, keep mandarins (and all citrus) loose or in a mesh bag in the crisper in the fridge. They need some airflow.

Substitutes   Oranges, tangelos, pink grapefruits or blood oranges will give you a similar sweet citrusy flavour.

Some ideas for using mandarins

* All the recipes in <u>oranges</u> (p 315) will work well with mandarins.
* ***Mandarin and soy dressing*** Great on noodles, avocado, grilled (broiled) fish or chicken, or a cucumber salad. Using a fork, whisk together the zest and juice of 1 mandarin, 1 tbsp soy sauce, 2 tsp sesame oil, plenty of ground pepper, ¼ tsp each of salt and sugar and a little grated fresh ginger and/or garlic. Mix well and pour over everything.
* ***Quick mandarin drink*** Zest and juice 1 mandarin and mix with a little sugar, then add sparkling wine or soda water and a thyme sprig for a quick but fancy drink. **»**

✳ **Mandarin jam** An absolute winner. Follow the Orange Jam recipe (p 317), replacing the oranges with mandarins and the cloves with star anise.

✳ **Poached mandarins** Poach whole peeled mandarins in a simple spiced tea and honey syrup following the poaching instructions on p 336. Use up to 4 mandarins, making sure to flavour them with slices of fresh ginger and cinnamon sticks. Poach gently for 30 minutes, or until very tender but not falling apart. They'll keep well in the fridge for a few weeks and are delicious served on ice cream, with cakes or with yoghurt and granola.

✳ **Whole-mandarin cake** Use the Whole-lemon and Chocolate Cake recipe (p 241), replacing the lemons with about 300 g (10½ oz) mandarins, skin and all. Enjoy with your feet up and a cup of earl grey tea.

Mandarin syrup

Make a rich, flavoursome syrup for cocktails, desserts and sticky marinades by simply combining mandarin juice and sugar. Make sure you save the peel (see opposite for tips on how to use it). For every 1 cup (250 ml) juice, add ½ cup (110 g) white (granulated) sugar and heat gently until the sugar is dissolved. If you'd like to add spices, try a few slices of fresh ginger, a cinnamon stick and a couple of cloves. Simmer for 10 minutes, until slightly thickened.

Pour into a clean bottle and, once cool, store in the fridge for up to 2 months. For longer-term preserving, pour into hot sterilised bottles (p 501), heat-process (p 502) for 10 minutes and store in the pantry for up to 1 year.

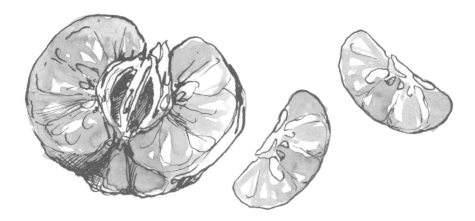

Sweet and sour quick mandarin relish

MAKES ABOUT 1 x 250 ML (9 OZ) JAR

This one is good for those mandarins that tricked you – looking delicious on the outside but tasting like mattress foam on the inside. Serve with chicken, pork sausages and cheese plates, or stir a few tablespoons through couscous, a grain salad or slow-cooked dishes.

In a small saucepan, combine ¼ cup (55 g) sugar, ¼ cup (60 ml) water and ¼ cup (60 ml) apple cider vinegar. Warm gently over low heat to dissolve the sugar, then add ½ tsp each of salt and pepper, 1 tsp of a spice you like (fennel seeds, grated fresh ginger, ground cumin) and a pinch of cayenne pepper or chilli flakes. Turn up the heat and let the syrup simmer for 5 minutes, until a little sticky. Add 3 peeled and roughly chopped mandarins (any seeds removed), then cook, stirring well and often, until glossy and caramelised.

Store in a clean jar or airtight container in the fridge for up to 3 weeks.

MANDARIN PEEL

Mandarin bitters

Perfect for cocktails. Follow the Grapefruit Skin Bitters recipe (p 180), replacing the grapefruit skin with the skin and pith of 5–6 mandarins.

Drying mandarin peel

Dried mandarin peel is used traditionally in Chinese cooking to add flavour to soups, Congee (p 394) and slow-cooked meat dishes. If you have a jar of dried mandarin peel in the pantry you can add a spicy citrus flavour when braising lamb or fennel, or making bone broths and ramen or even a spicy pumpkin (squash) soup.

To remove pesticides, give your mandarins a warm wash with a little detergent, vinegar or bicarbonate of soda (baking soda), dry with a clean tea towel (dish towel), then peel.

If you're having a very sunny winter, you can dry peel in the sunshine – but it will take a few days, so check the weather forecast first.

To oven-dry citrus peel, preheat the oven to 70–110°C (150–225°F), as low it will go. Lay the peel flat on a baking tray in a single layer. If you're using a fan-forced oven, place an upside-down wire rack over the peel to stop it flying around. It will take anywhere from 20 minutes to 1 hour to dry, depending on the oven temperature and the peel thickness and size. »

You want the peel to feel completely dry. Mandarin peel will feel a little spongy – sort of like a prawn cracker – when it's done. Allow to cool completely, then store in an airtight container in the pantry. With no moisture left, the peel will last indefinitely, although the colour and flavour will change over time. Discard if it is exposed to moisture or loses its flavour.

Mandarin peel powder

Mandarin peel powder is full of flavour and has the right amount of bitterness to act as a seasoning. Put a few generous handfuls of dried mandarin (or other citrus) peel in a spice grinder or powerful food processor and blitz to a fine powder.

TO USE MANDARIN PEEL POWDER

- Add 2 tbsp mandarin peel powder (or any citrus peel powder) to 100 g (3½ oz) caster (superfine) sugar to sprinkle on shortbread, donuts and scrolls or fold through whipped cream. Try it on the Bittersweet Cookies (p 266).
- Add 2 tbsp mandarin peel powder and 1 tbsp chilli flakes to ⅓ cup (100 g) salt and use as a seasoning for meats and fish, roasted vegetables, salad dressings, noodles, eggs and Congee (p 394).
- For a dry spice rub, mix 2–3 tbsp mandarin peel powder, 2 tsp paprika, 1 tsp white or black pepper, 2 tsp salt and 1 tbsp dried herbs such as oregano, rosemary or thyme. Use when grilling (broiling) meats or to rub over pumpkin (squash) wedges before roasting, or add a few pinches to a salad dressing.

Mandarin peel fire-starters

Dried citrus peel (previous page) makes an excellent fire-starter – all that citrus oil ensures very efficient ignition. Throw it into the kindling when lighting a campfire or your firepit.

See cumquats, grapefruit, lemons, limes and oranges for ideas with other citrus. *See also* preserved lemon.

Mango

So you excitedly bought a tray of mangoes for summer and now all you can hear yourself saying is 'Does anyone want me to cut them up a mango?' – with no response. Here are some solutions to help you get through the box without having to eat them all yourself.

The beauty of mangoes is that every stage of their ripeness is delicious. Underripe mangoes are great in salads and pickles, perfectly ripe mangoes are for eating fresh, and overripe, bordering on rotten mangoes are perfect for compotes, lassis and chutneys.

Goes with	Coconut, melons, lemongrass, pineapple, kiwi fruit, passionfruit, papaya, lychees, berries, limes, avocado, basil, mint, coriander (cilantro), chilli, salt, ginger, garlic, spring onions (scallions), macadamias, peanuts, honey, vanilla ice cream
Storage	Keep mangoes that you're planning on eating soon on the benchtop – away from bananas, unless you want to ripen them. Mangoes for later should be stored in the fridge, where they'll last for 1–2 weeks.
Substitutes	There's nothing as velvety as a mango, but you can replace it with melon, pineapple or kiwi fruit for uncooked dishes like fruit salads and salsas. For cooked dishes and baking, use stone fruits like peaches or nectarines; bananas will give you similar texture when puréeing.

Some ideas for using up the one mango no one wants

* ***Quick mango salsa*** Make the Pineapple Salsa (p 351), replacing the pineapple with diced mango. Serve with fish tacos, or grilled chicken or haloumi cheese. While it's yummy with ripe mangoes, it's even more delicious with green mango.
* ***Mango porridge*** Make the Banana Porridge recipe (p 25) with overripe mango instead of banana. Top with toasted macadamias and maple syrup. »

* ***Little mango salad*** Switch to savoury, with this sweet and spicy mango salad. Place very thin green or yellow mango slices in a bowl and dress with a little rice wine vinegar, sugar and salt. Top with thinly sliced chilli or chilli flakes, toasted macadamias and mint or coriander (cilantro) leaves.

* ***Mango compote*** Add to milkshakes, muesli, yoghurt or ice cream. This one is for the very overripe, forgotten mangoes. Put roughly chopped mango flesh in a saucepan. For every mango, add 1 tbsp honey, 1 tbsp lemon juice and a splash of water. You might also want to add a splash of vanilla extract, or a star anise or some grated fresh ginger. Simmer over low heat until the mango is soft and falling apart. Mash with a fork or, for a bigger batch of purée, with a hand-held blender or in the food processor. Once cool, store in an airtight container in the fridge for 4–5 days or the freezer for up to 3 months.

* ***Mango lassi*** Blend 1 cup (185 g) chopped ripe mango with 1 cup (260 g) plain yoghurt, 2 tbsp white (granulated) sugar or honey, a little ice and up to ½ cup (125 ml) milk of your choice, depending on how thick you like your drink. Experiment with adding a little splash of rosewater or ground cardamom.

* ***Mango whip*** Follow the Kiwi Fruit Whip instructions (p 227), replacing the kiwi fruit with mango, for quick frozen mango whip, like cheat's ice cream.

* ***Mango upside-down cake*** Follow the Pineapple Upside-down Cake recipe (p 352), using mango instead of pineapple.

* ***Mango iced tea*** For a refreshing and fruity drink, follow the Peach Iced Tea recipe (p 332), using a whole mango, a few slices of fresh ginger and a squeeze of lime juice.

PRESERVING MANGOES

Green mango pickles
MAKES 2 x 400 ML (14 OZ) JARS

One of the most delicious pickles ever – and an excellent way to use up the green mangoes your neighbour keeps giving you. Serve with curries, through noodle salads, in rice paper rolls or on fish burgers. You can also finely dice these pickles, then mix with a small amount of the brine, lots of fresh coriander (cilantro) and thinly sliced chilli to make a quick salsa for seafood or tacos.

Cut the skins off 1 kg (2 lb 4 oz) green mangoes, then slice the cheeks into long strips. Place in a bowl and sprinkle with 1 tbsp salt. Mix with your hands to coat evenly. Set aside at room temperature for at least 1 hour to draw out any excess moisture.

Make a pickling liquid in a saucepan by mixing 1 cup (250 ml) white vinegar or rice wine vinegar, 1 cup (250 ml) water, ⅓ cup (75 g) white (granulated) sugar, ¼ tsp ground turmeric and ½ tsp salt. Place over low heat, stirring to dissolve the sugar, and bring to a simmer. Meanwhile, drain the mangoes and discard the excess liquid. In two clean 400 ml (14 oz) jars put a generous pinch of any or all of the following spices – fennel seeds, cumin seeds, mustard seeds, chilli flakes, fenugreek seeds, black peppercorns. If you have any curry leaves, add a few to each jar. Carefully pack the mango slices in the jars. They will have become quite soft from the salting – you want to get as much as you can into the jar without squashing or breaking up the slices. Cover with the pickling liquid, making sure the slices are completely submerged. Seal.

We prefer to keep these pickles in the fridge, as the texture seems to deteriorate quite quickly. They're best eaten within 3 months. If you prefer to store them in the pantry, use sterilised jars (p 501) and heat-process (p 502) the filled jars for 10 minutes. They will keep for up to 6 months.

Mango hot sauce

This is so good. If you have a glut of mangoes, make a batch, heat-process the jars (p 502) and save for brightening up winter meals. Follow the Half-a-melon Hot Sauce recipe (p 271), replacing the 3 cups melon with 3 cups (555 g) chopped green mangoes or ripe mangoes. Just remember that mango makes a thicker sauce than melon as it has a lower water content and is more fibrous, so loosen the mix with a little extra water and vinegar to give it a sauce-like consistency.

Mango and lime jam

You won't find mango jam in the supermarket aisles, but it's bright, tropical and yummy on pancakes or banana bread, or in the middle of a sponge cake. Follow the Foolproof Jam recipe (p 389), keeping in mind that mangoes are low in acid and pectin, so you'll need to add the zest and juice of 2 extra limes or 1 extra lemon.

Mango chutney

Make this to go with a celebratory ham, or roasted fish, a curry or a cheese sandwich. Follow the 'What's in the Fruit Bowl' Relish recipe (p 333), using peeled and chopped mango as a base. Your spice mix for mango chutney could include any of the following – grated fresh ginger, mustard seeds, chilli flakes, ground cardamom, lime zest.

MANGO SKINS AND STONES

Don't forget just how much flavour is left in the skins and stones of chopped-up mangoes. To extract as much as possible, try one of the following infusion methods.

Mango scrap syrup
MAKES ABOUT 350 ML (12 FL OZ)

Place the skins and seeds from 1–2 mangoes in a saucepan with 2 cups (500 ml) water and 1 cup (220 g) white (granulated) sugar. Add some extra flavours – 1 cinnamon stick, 2 star anise, some black peppercorns, some mint stems, strips of lime peel, a few slices of fresh ginger. Simmer over low heat for 15 minutes, then remove from the heat and allow the flavours to infuse. Once cool, strain and pour into a clean jar or bottle and store in the fridge for up to 2 months.

Mango scrap vinegar

Follow the Apple Scrap Vinegar recipe (p 9) to make a fruity, summery home-made vinegar, using the scraps from 2–3 mangoes.

Spicy fruity dipping sauce

In a jar or airtight container, cover a mango stone and 1–2 red chillies, halved lengthways, with apple cider vinegar. Add ½ tsp each of salt and sugar, then leave to sit at room temperature for a few days to a few weeks. Keep tasting, and when the vinegar is fruity and spicy, strain and store in a clean bottle or jar in the fridge for up to 1 year. Pour into a small serving dish, add a little sesame oil and use as a dipping sauce for dumplings, as the base of a salad dressing, or for drizzling over noodles.

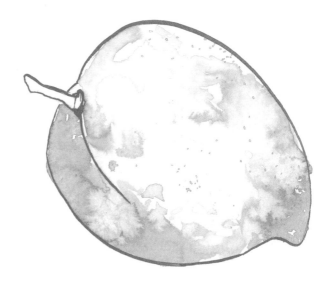

Marmalade

Good toast, excellent butter and heaps of marmalade is the best breakfast, and crackers with cheese and marmalade is the best afternoon tea. If, like us, you're having either of these things on a daily basis, you'll get through a jar of marmalade in no time. We're big on bitter flavours and use marmalade for more than just spreading on carbs every morning and afternoon. Its bittersweet edge adds complexity to savoury dishes, baked goods and sauces. But if you're wondering how to use up the jar of marmalade that has been hanging around in the fridge for the last three years, then this section is for you.

Goes with   Bitey cheddar and rye bread, butter, custard, chocolate, whisky, figs, grapes, nuts, dried fruits, garlic, ginger, soy sauce, fennel, caramelised onions, bitter lettuce, blue cheese, cabbage

---

Storage   See jam on p 217 (in many ways they're the same thing).

Substitutes   Use jam if you have no marmalade, but add grapefruit, lemon or orange zest, or a squeeze of citrus juice, a little pepper and a generous spoonful of sugar.

Some ideas for using up that jar of marmalade

∗ The first step is to check out 'Some Ideas for Using Up That Jar of Jam' (p 217). They'll all work with marmalade, just with a bitter edge.

∗ Shake 1 tbsp marmalade into cocktails for a bittersweet drink. Marmalade whisky sour, anyone?

∗ Add marmalade to baking. Try spreading a layer of marmalade on an apricot crostata (check out the Fig Crostata on p 163), or glaze the Whole-lemon and Chocolate Cake (p 241) by brushing with some warmed marmalade while the cake is cooling.

∗ **Bittersweet cookies** Turn the 'Use Up That Jar' Cookies (p 455) into marmalade cookies by replacing the tahini with the same amount of marmalade and reducing the sugar by half.

---

* **Cheese and marmalade toastie** We can't sing the praises of this toastie enough. Spread your favourite bread with butter then heaps of marmalade, top with melty cheese and another slice of bread. Brush the outside of the bread with olive oil. Then put into a sandwich toaster or sandwich press or, if you're hungover, fry it in butter in a frying pan over medium heat. Eat for breakfast, lunch, dinner or a midnight snack. Or try the crazy Brie and Jam Fried Sandwich (p 91) with marmalade for a decadent night on the couch.
* **Marmalade dressing** This versatile salad dressing works well on cabbage slaws or bitter leaves like rocket (arugula) and radicchio, or poured over hot steamed or Roasted Brussels Sprouts (p 60). In a jar, combine 2 tbsp apple cider vinegar, 1 tsp dijon mustard, ¼ tsp each of salt and pepper and 1–2 tbsp marmalade, depending how bitter it is, then shake well. Add 1½ tbsp extra virgin olive oil and 1 tbsp sunflower or vegetable oil, then shake again.
* **Marmalade syrup** For crepes and French Toast (p 51). Make this when you've run out of maple syrup or want a more grown-up sauce for special breakfasts and desserts. In a small saucepan, warm ¼ cup (85 g) marmalade, 1–2 tbsp water and a knob of butter, whisking with a fork until runny. Add a pinch of salt or, for a boozy version, replace the water with whisky, bourbon or rum.

Sticky spicy marmalade marinade

Sticky marinades are always a hit. Generally they use brown sugar to get that lipsmacking gloss. Here we're using the last of the marmalade jar to achieve the same results. Use for chicken, tofu or ribs.

Scrape out that almost empty jar of marmalade (about 3 tbsp) into a jar or small bowl. Add ⅓ cup (80 ml) soy sauce, ¼ cup (60 ml) orange juice, 2 tbsp worcestershire sauce or kimchi brine, 2 tbsp grated fresh ginger, 1 tbsp sesame oil and ¼ tsp salt, plus a generous splash of hot sauce or 1 tsp chilli flakes if you want it hot. Shake or whisk to combine. Adjust to suit your taste – you're after a nice balance of sweet and savoury.

Mayonnaise

Possibly the greatest sauce ever emulsified. Creamy and tart (surely a compliment to anyone), mayonnaise is one of the most popular condiments in the world. From Australia and Japan to Chile and Russia, almost everyone loves mayonnaise. This means that there are many ways to use up a jar of mayo, as it can adapt itself very well to almost any cooking style. See p 154 for an easy home-made mayonnaise.

Goes with	Mostly everything, but particularly leafy greens, asparagus, avocado, celery, corn, potatoes, tomatoes, cabbage, lemons, parsley, dill, chives, curry powder, horseradish, mustard, pickles, tuna, chicken, eggs
Storage	Unopened store-bought mayonnaise can be kept in the pantry until the use-by date. Once opened, keep mayonnaise in the fridge for up to 2 months. Home-made mayonnaise, on the other hand, will only keep for about 3 days, so eat up.
Substitutes	Out of mayo? Sour cream with a little squeeze of lemon juice or a drop of vinegar will stand in quite nicely. Yoghurt or watered-down cream cheese will work in potato salads (p 362) or as the base for a dip. And if you're just after creaminess, hummus or avocado make good substitutes as a spread.

Some ideas for using up a jar of mayonnaise

* Make like the Dutch and serve mayo with hot chips (fries).
* Whip up Alex's Tartare Sauce (p 94).
* If there's just a scraping of mayo in the jar, add a dash of Tabasco or worcestershire sauce, 1–2 tbsp neutral oil, a little splash of water and a big pinch of salt. Shake it up and voilà. You have a creamy salad dressing with some oomph.
* Make the Curried-egg Sandwich (p 149).
* Whip up some Minty Green Goddess Sauce (p 197) for fish burgers and salad dressings.

* Turn a tomato sandwich into a decadent delight. Slather 2 slices of soft white bread with mayo, and fill with slices of the very best of the season's tomatoes and some salt and pepper. Perfection.
* Add 2–3 tbsp mayonnaise when mashing potatoes for creaminess without heaviness.

'Don't knock it till you've tried it' cake

No butter, no oil, no eggs, but flour, chocolate and mayonnaise? You actually have a cake in the making. Before you shudder in disgust, mayonnaise in cake is a thing. It's an American Depression-era thing, but a thing nevertheless. Remember that mayonnaise is nothing but emulsified oil and egg and these are the main ingredients for a cake anyway. So open your mind and heart to the possibility. We've tested and retested this recipe and it's really great, we promise. Expect more fudgy brownie than fluffy cake.

Preheat the oven to 180°C (350°F) and line a 20 cm (8 in) round cake tin with baking paper. Combine 1 cup (235 ml) mayonnaise, ¾ cup (165 g) caster (superfine) sugar, 2 cups (300 g) self-raising flour, ½ cup (55 g) unsweetened cocoa powder and 1 cup (250 ml) water. Pour into the cake tin and bake for 35 minutes or until a skewer inserted in the centre comes out clean. And don't forget when serving, there's no need to share all your cooking secrets.

Cheat's aioli (and friends)

Have ¼–½ cup mayonnaise left? You can add nearly anything to it to make a spread or dip for sandwiches or burgers, to dip hot chips (fries) into, or to dollop on top of grilled vegies, chicken, fish or tofu. Try any of the following.

TO TRANSFORM MAYONNAISE
* Add 1–2 finely chopped garlic cloves for a quick aioli.
* Stir in 2–3 tbsp chopped pickles and a bit of the pickling liquid.
* Add 2–3 tbsp chopped kimchi (p 486) and kimchi juice.
* Mix in ½ tsp curry powder.
* Add 2–3 tbsp harissa paste.
* Stir in ½ tsp smoked paprika.
* Mix in 3–4 tbsp pesto.
* Add a little sesame oil and 1 tbsp toasted sesame seeds.
* Mix in 2 tbsp tomato paste (concentrated purée) for a make-do ketchup.
* Stir in 1–2 tbsp finely diced Salt-preserved Lemon (p 241) or Sweet Pickled Limes (p 254).

Melon

Rockmelon (cantaloupe) and honeydew melon aren't just for 1970s fruit salads, although we are fond of a melon baller. Please don't buy a half-melon wrapped in plastic. Be brave – buy the whole thing and experiment with adding melon to unexpected dishes. And if all else fails, we've included a Half-a-melon Hot Sauce recipe (opposite) that will make you grateful you bought the whole melon in the first place. See watermelon (p 476) for more recipes.

Goes with   Cucumber, mint, limes, mango, pineapple, watermelon, grapes and berries are all pals of melons, but melons are especially delicious with salty foods like olives, feta cheese and cured meats. They're also strangely good with vinegar, salt and chilli, so try quick-pickling firm melons (p 272). And don't forget creamy things like ice cream, yoghurt, fresh mozzarella, coconut and cashews.

Storage   Melons should be left to ripen at room temperature. A melon is ripe if it gives a little when pressed at the stem end and smells like sweet melon at the other end. Once ripe, melons should be eaten, or stored in the fridge, uncut, for about 4 days. Leave the seeds in half-melons, cover in beeswax wrap and store in the fridge. Skinned, cut melon can be kept in the fridge in an airtight container for 2–3 days.

Substitutes   Melons can all be swapped with each other – just remember that watermelon, as the name suggests, has a very high water content. Also try cucumbers, green grapes or kiwi fruit.

Some ideas for using up melon

* *Savoury melon salad* Cut rockmelon (cantaloupe) or honeydew melon into bite-sized slices and mix with small wedges of cucumber, black olives, Quick-pickled Red Onion (p 312), mint leaves, a squeeze of citrus juice and plenty of salt and pepper.
* *Melon salsa* If you have a quarter of a melon left, make a quick spicy salsa following the Pineapple Salsa recipe (p 351). This would be delicious with seafood and grilled corn or fresh cheeses.
* *Melon and syrup* Thinly slice ripe melon and drizzle with a home-made herbal syrup and a pinch of salt. Try Lemongrass Syrup (p 204) or Ginger Syrup (p 176). Top with mint leaves and serve as a simple end to a meal.
* *Ripe melon and ice cream* If you have a melon baller it'll be funnier. Serve with vanilla ice cream, toasted coconut, a drizzle of honey and a pinch of salt.

Half-a-melon hot sauce
MAKES 3–4 CUPS (750 ML – 1 LITRE)

So you bought a whole melon, only ate half of it and the rest has been staring you down for the past week? It's time to admit defeat and make this simple hot sauce that will use the rest up in one fruit-ninja move. This recipe works with rockmelon (cantaloupe), honeydew, watermelon and pineapple.

Cut your melon in half, scoop out the seeds and cut the skin off. Sometimes things do have to go in the compost – that time is now. Roughly chop the melon and place it in a food processor. You'll need 3–4 cups (about 500–700 g) fruit, but if you have less, reduce the other ingredients. If you have more, then increase them. Taste as you go – it's hard to go wrong with this recipe.

Add to the food processor 3 chopped garlic cloves, and as many fresh chopped chillies as you like/have. Start small and add more if you want it fiery. Add something from the allium family, like a few sliced spring onions (scallions), ½ brown onion or a little bit of white leek. A small knob of ginger is delicious, but not essential. Add the zest and juice of 1 lime or lemon, 1 tsp salt, 1 cup (250 ml) apple cider vinegar and ¼ cup (55 g) caster (superfine) sugar. Blitz until very smooth. Taste and adjust if needed. You can leave the sauce light and fresh and store it in clean jars or bottles in the fridge for up to 3 months, or transfer it to a saucepan and simmer for 20 minutes for a richer and thicker sauce.

To preserve, pour hot sauce into hot sterilised jars or bottles (p 501) and heat-process (p 502) for 15 minutes. It can then be stored in the pantry for up to 1 year.

Quick-pickled melon

For firm melons only.

In a small saucepan, pour ½ cup (125 ml) apple cider vinegar and ½ cup (125 ml) water. Add ¼ cup (55 g) white (granulated) sugar, ½ tsp salt, 1 cinnamon stick or star anise or 1 tsp allspice berries, and a generous pinch of chilli flakes or sliced fresh chilli. Bring to the boil over medium heat, stirring to dissolve the sugar. Remove from the heat and cool to room temperature. Cut honeydew or slightly unripe rockmelon (cantaloupe) into batons and put in a bowl. Once the vinegar mixture is cool, pour over the melon and leave to sit for 10 minutes.

Serve quick-pickled melons with mozzarella, cured meats and a baguette.

Keep any left-over pickles in their brine in the fridge for up to 1 week. Don't throw the used liquid away – use it to quick-pickle something else or as a salad dressing base.

Milk

Milk is one of the most wasted household staples. Cartons are often bought and opened before the old one is finished, or left undrunk in the first place. Fresh milk is good for drinking and pouring on cereal, but once it starts getting a tiny bit whiffy or sour-smelling it's often thought to be unusable. In our book, this is simply when you start cooking with milk. If you have milk close to its use-by date, or even a day or two after, and it smells fine or is just on the edge, don't pour it down the sink – think about how you can use it for the start of a meal. Some sources say it's perfect for making yoghurt.

Goes with	Eggs, bread, butter, bananas, berries, leeks, cauliflower, corn, nuts, bay leaves, nutmeg, tea, coffee, chocolate, barley, oats, rice, honey, maple syrup, peanut butter, cookies, apple pie
Storage	Store milk in the fridge until its use-by date. Try not to forget to put it back in the fridge straight after using, as temperature fluctuations can encourage bacterial growth. Milk that's just past its use-by date is fine if cooked.
Substitutes	Thin out cream with a little water as a substitute for milk. Nut milks and soy, rice, coconut or oat milk can all be used in place of milk.

Some ideas for using up milk

* ***Milkshakes*** Blend milk, fruit or compote, honey and a little vanilla or cinnamon. Add ice cream if you're feeling indulgent.
* ***Baked custard*** See p 151. It uses up plenty of milk. Or if you have milk and bread that need using, turn them into Bread and Butter Pudding (p 52).
* ***Cheat's buttermilk*** Real buttermilk can be hard to find and is often hard to use up anyway. When a recipe (such as scones) calls for buttermilk, we either use slightly overdue milk or we make the cheat's version by adding a big squeeze of lemon juice or 1 tsp apple cider vinegar to full-fat milk and letting the milk curdle.

Make your own yoghurt

MAKES 3–4 CUPS (780 G – 1 KG)

You'll need a sugar thermometer and a smidgin of live plain yoghurt, but that really is all.

In a saucepan, warm 4 cups (1 litre) milk to 180°C (350°F). Remove from the heat and allow to cool to lukewarm. Thoroughly stir in 1 tsp natural unflavoured yoghurt. Transfer the milk to a spotlessly clean jar, seal well and wrap in a towel. Keep covered in a dark place for 6–8 hours. It will have thickened to a creamy yoghurt. Store in the fridge for 2–3 weeks.

Bechamel sauce

MAKES ABOUT 2 CUPS (500 ML)

Warm 2 cups (500 ml) milk in a small saucepan. In another saucepan, melt 60 g (2¼ oz) butter over low heat. Slowly add 2 tbsp plain (all-purpose) flour, stirring constantly, until the butter and flour are combined and bubbling. This mixture is the roux. Very slowly stir in the warm milk, ½ cup (125 ml) at a time, then stir over low heat until thickened.

Season with salt and pepper, and from here the world is yours. Make cauliflower cheese or a fish pie, or use it as a base for a pasta bake, such as Odd-knobs Mac 'n' Cheese (p 101).

FOR CHEESE SAUCE

Add 1½ cups (150 g) grated cheese once the bechamel sauce has begun to thicken.

Milk tea ice blocks

MAKES 4–6

The perfect way to have an afternoon cuppa when it's sweltering outside.

In a small saucepan, warm 2 cups (500 ml) milk with 4 teabags. Remove from the heat before it boils, then stir in 2 tbsp honey and 2 tbsp sugar. Steep for 10 minutes, then remove the teabags and allow to cool completely before pouring into 4–6 ice-block (popsicle) moulds. Freeze.

Pouring custard

MAKES ABOUT 3 CUPS (750 ML)

Gently warm 600 ml (21 fl oz) whole milk in a saucepan over low heat. In a bowl, whisk 4 egg yolks with 2 tbsp caster (superfine) sugar. (Save the egg whites for another recipe, see p 152.)

Once the milk begins to simmer, remove from the heat. Slowly pour the milk into the egg and sugar mix, whisking constantly. Once combined, return the custard to the saucepan, and cook over very low heat for 15 minutes, stirring often, until thickened.

Milk pudding
SERVES 4

This simple, delicate cold pudding can be topped with shavings of chocolate, fresh berries or thinly sliced melon. It's a perfect dessert on a hot day or when there's milk that needs using up quickly.

In a small saucepan over low heat, warm 2 cups (500 ml) milk, ½ tsp vanilla extract and ⅓ cup (75 g) caster (superfine) sugar, stirring until the sugar has dissolved. In a bowl, mix ⅓ cup (40 g) cornflour (cornstarch) with 2 tbsp cold water to make a strange slippery paste that feels like a school science experiment. Just before the milk starts simmering, add the cornflour mix, stirring constantly, and cook until the mixture becomes very thick. Pour into 1 medium or 4 small ramekins, sprinkle with grated nutmeg or ground cinnamon and refrigerate until set.

See cheese, cream, sour cream, whey and yoghurt for ideas with other dairy products.

Miso paste

When Jaimee's kids were little, she would spread miso paste on toast and tell them it was Vegemite. Inevitably, the day came when they discovered real Vegemite and, on principle, made a fuss about how dreadfully deprived they had been. Jaimee still maintains that miso on buttery toast is the superior option. The lesson here is that miso should not be restricted to soup. Having miso paste in the fridge means you can add a depth of flavour that only comes from something that has been fermented over a long time and has a tradition more than 2000 years old. Respect.

Miso pastes come in huge variety and complexity. The most readily available varieties are white (sweet), brown and red. The darker the miso paste, the more intense the flavour, so you may want to adjust your quantities with this in mind.

Goes with	Depending on how you're using it, miso can go with anything, including crunchy lettuces, broccoli and green beans. Leafy greens are perfect when wilted in miso soup. Miso marinades and glazes go well with chicken, fish, red meat, tofu, tempeh, eggplant (aubergine), pumpkin (squash), sweet potato, onions, garlic, ginger, tahini, soy sauce and mirin. And don't forget miso in sweets and baking.
Storage	Store miso paste in the fridge. To protect against oxidation, place some baking paper on the surface of the miso if it's in a jar or airtight container. Miso paste will get darker and denser as it ages, but if stored well it should keep indefinitely.
Substitutes	In recipes where miso is contributing its unique umami flavour, you can replace it with soy sauce or fish sauce. You can even mix a little of either of these sauces with tahini to make a hack stand-in for miso dressings or glazes.

Some ideas for using miso paste

* Add a big spoonful of miso paste to stews, ragus and soups that are lacking in umami flavour. We use it in our Mushroom Ragu (p 279).

* **Miso caramel** This is salted caramel at its sweet and savoury best. Pour it over French Toast (p 51), waffles, cakes, crepes or banana splits. Makes 300 ml (10½ fl oz). In a small saucepan, heat ¾ cup (165 g) caster (superfine) sugar and ¼ cup (60 ml) water. Do not stir; allow the sugar to dissolve, then come to the boil. Watch it very carefully. As soon as the sugar turns a deep golden colour, remove from the heat and allow to cool for a few seconds. Stirring constantly, add ½ cup (125 ml) cream and 2 tbsp miso paste. Keep stirring until smooth and combined. Use immediately or store in the fridge for up to 4 days.

* **Miso dressing** For salads, or for drizzling over lightly cooked vegetables (wilted spinach, steamed broccoli, Charred Green Beans, p 39, or Roasted Eggplant, p 144) and even tofu, chicken or fish. In a small bowl, combine 3 tbsp miso paste, 2 tbsp mirin, 1 tbsp rice wine vinegar and 1 tsp sugar. Store in an airtight container in the fridge for 2 weeks.

* **Miso butter** We put a dollop of this on the Kimchi Pancakes (p 225). It's also excellent for melting onto roast pumpkin (squash) or boiled potatoes. Mix 3 tbsp softened butter with 2 tbsp miso paste and 2 tsp toasted sesame seeds.

* **Miso mayonnaise** Use this on sandwiches, with hot chips (fries) or fish burgers. Mix 3 tbsp mayonnaise with 3 tsp miso paste.

* **Miso cookies** For sweet and salty treats, follow the 'Use Up That Jar Cookies' recipe on page 455, but only add 2 tbsp miso in place of the tahini.

Miso glaze

For the best results, use a smooth miso for this recipe. Use to baste barbecuing or roasting meats, pumpkin (squash), sweet potato, eggplant (aubergine) or tofu, but only towards the end of cooking, as the sugar may burn. The consistency is thick and sticky and begging for a barbecue. If you want to loosen it a little, add a splash of water.

In a small bowl, mix ½ cup miso paste (about 140 g), 3 tbsp mirin, 2 tbsp brown sugar and a very generous grind of black pepper. Whisk with a fork until everything is combined.

Mushrooms

These earthy delights are to be cherished. Eaten raw their flavour is lighter, faintly floral and of the soil. Once cooked, mushrooms become more robust, with notes of nuts and meat. They have long been called 'meat for vegetarians' and we stand by this claim, not so much because mushrooms are high in protein (they have about 3 g/⅛ oz protein per 100 g/3½ oz) but because their texture and flavour means they can replace meat in many dishes. If you can, seek out the enormous variety of mushrooms now available and experiment with their subtly different textures and flavours, but if you can only get your hands on the old button mushroom, don't sweat it – they're dependable and delicious.

Go with	Onions, leeks, garlic, potatoes, pumpkin (squash), parsnips, spinach, silverbeet (Swiss chard), kale, kohlrabi, wombok (Chinese cabbage), sauerkraut, oranges, oily fish, bacon, chicken, firm tofu, woody herbs, parsley, dill, strong cheeses, mozzarella, cream, nuts, cloves, star anise, cinnamon, nutmeg, coriander seeds, fennel seeds, juniper berries, buckwheat, barley, wine, ginger, chilli, soy sauce
Storage	Mushrooms are quite perishable. Never store them in plastic. If they came in a plastic-wrapped tray, remove them and store in a paper bag in the fridge, but avoid the crisper section as it's too humid. Mushrooms will keep for a week.
Substitutes	Mushrooms are really their own beast. No other vegetable makes an easy substitute. Meats and tofu do a good job for dishes like ragu and dumpling fillings. If you need their rich umami flavour in soups, broths and stews, use dried mushrooms, a parmesan rind or sun-dried tomatoes.

Some ideas for using up a couple of dry old mushies

✱ Add them to your next batch of stock. They will add a deep, bold flavour and colour. Check out the End-of-the-week Scrap Stock (p 446).

✱ Any mushrooms that have already started drying can be finished off in a 70°C (150°F) oven. Place whole or sliced mushrooms on a baking tray and leave in the oven until completely dried, turning once. It should take 1–2 hours, depending on the size of your pieces and how dry they were to start with. Add dried mushrooms to stocks, soups, stews and ragus for a hit of extra flavour. Or grind to a powder and mix with salt for an earthy seasoning.

✱ Give them a quick pulse in a food processor and add to bolognese sauce, lentil dishes, the Best Barley Side (p 29) or Tasty Meatballs (p 54).

✱ Sauté mushrooms in a frying pan over medium heat with plenty of butter or oil, 1–2 finely chopped garlic cloves, a squeeze of lemon juice, a generous pinch each of salt and ground black pepper and lots of chopped parsley. Eat on toast, or add to a cheese toastie or an omelette. See p 150 for the best way to make an omelette.

✱ Add ole mushies to the 'Clear Out the Fridge' Pizza (p 97).

✱ Make the wholesome Brown Rice, Mushroom and Spinach Soup on p 392.

Mushroom ragu
SERVES 4

A mushroom ragu is going to take you places. Make a batch and let it be the base for lasagne, toasties or baked eggs, or a topping for polenta or pasta. If you'd like, you could add ½ cup (125 ml) cream during the simmering stage.

Slice 800 g (1 lb 14 oz) field mushrooms. Heat ¼ cup (60 ml) olive oil in a large frying pan over medium heat. Add 1 sliced onion and sauté for 5–7 minutes, until translucent. Add 3–4 sliced garlic cloves, ¼ tsp each of salt and pepper, 5–6 fresh sage leaves and 1 tbsp chopped fresh rosemary or thyme. Sauté for a further 2–3 minutes, then add the mushrooms a handful at a time – take your time with this. Once all the mushrooms are in and looking dark, delicious and cooked through, add ¼ cup (60 ml) red or white wine and 2 cups (500 ml) stock of your choice. Simmer over low heat, stirring occasionally, for a further 25–30 minutes or until the ragu is thick, add 2–3 tsp of something full of flavour (dijon mustard, tomato paste/concentrated purée, worcestershire sauce or miso paste) and another ¼ tsp each of salt and pepper if needed. Simmer for another 5 minutes or so.

This mushroom ragu will last for 1 week in the fridge, or freeze it in smaller portions for up to 2 months.

Raw mushroom salad

SERVES 1–2

This is a very simple and elegant little salad. Honestly, you can eat it as is, with a boiled egg on the side, or with a steak if it's date night.

With a very sharp knife or mandoline, slice 200 g (7 oz) mushrooms. Place them in a bowl and season with salt and pepper and 2 tbsp mixed herbs of your choice – chives, dill, parsley, thyme leaves, tarragon. Arrange the mushrooms prettily on a serving plate, drizzle with the Classic Mustard Vinaigrette (p 283) and top with shavings of parmesan. Allow the mushrooms to soak up the dressing for about 10 minutes before serving.

Mushroom pâté

MAKES 1½ CUPS (375 ML)

Pâté spread on fresh crusty bread and a simple leaf salad is picnic food at its best. It's also dinner, if you ask us. This mushroom pâté is as decadent as a version made from livers, but vegetarian-friendly. Because there's a decent quantity of butter involved, you can even make this with mushrooms that are looking a little shrivelled.

In a frying pan over low heat, melt 50 g (1¾ oz) butter with 1 tbsp olive oil. Gently sauté 2 thinly sliced spring onions (scallions), 2 finely chopped garlic cloves, 1 thyme sprig and a few bay leaves until fragrant. Dice 500 g (1 lb 2 oz) mushrooms and add to the pan a handful at a time, letting the mushrooms cook a little before adding more. When all the mushrooms are in, increase the heat to medium–low and cook for about 8 minutes, until the liquid released by the mushrooms has almost evaporated. Add ¼ cup (60 ml) sherry, port or marsala, ½ tsp each of salt, ground pepper and freshly grated nutmeg, and 2–3 tsp red wine vinegar. Cook for another 10 minutes, stirring often. Remove from the heat and allow to cool a little.

Discard the thyme sprig and bay leaves, then transfer the mushrooms and all the pan juices to a food processor. Blend, add 25 g (1 oz) cold butter, then blend again until very smooth. Transfer to a small ramekin, bowl or jar, and refrigerate for at least 1 hour until set.

This lasts well in the fridge for up to 1 week.

Roasted mushroom broth and mushroom dumplings

SERVES 4, MAKES 24 DUMPLINGS

This recipe demonstrates what zero-waste cooking is all about. Roasting the mushrooms first intensifies their earthy flavour to create a rich broth, and incredibly the mushrooms themselves retain their flavour for the dumpling filling. You'll need about 24 dumpling wrappers.

TO MAKE THE BROTH

Preheat the oven to 180°C (350°F). Lay 500 g (1 lb 2 oz) mushrooms, stems up, in a roasting tin and sprinkle with 1 tsp each of salt and pepper. Cut 1 unpeeled onion into 6 wedges, and add to the tin, along with ½ unpeeled garlic bulb. Drizzle with oil, then roast for 30 minutes.

Remove from the oven and discard any burnt garlic cloves, as they will make the broth very bitter. Transfer to a saucepan and add 5 cups (1.25 litres) water. Add a few slices of fresh ginger, 2 bay leaves, a pinch of chilli flakes and 1 star anise. Bring to the boil and simmer over low heat for 20 minutes, or until rich, dark and delicious. Taste and add more salt and/or pepper if needed. Strain the broth, retaining the roast mushroom mixture, and set aside.

TO MAKE THE DUMPLINGS

Using tongs, squeeze any excess liquid from the mushroom mixture. Transfer to a food processor, removing the onion and garlic skins and discarding the bay leaves and star anise. Add a pinch each of salt and pepper and blitz to form a rough paste. Taste and adjust the seasoning.

Lay a dumpling wrapper on a clean benchtop, place 1 generous teaspoonful of the mushroom mixture in the middle, dampen the edges of the wrapper with a little water, and form into a dumpling, ensuring it is well sealed. Repeat with the remaining mixture. Lay the dumplings on a plate in a single layer.

Bring a big pot of salted water to the boil, then cook the dumplings in batches of eight for a few minutes, until they rise to the surface. Using a slotted spoon, remove the dumplings from the water and divide among four bowls.

Return the mushroom broth to the boil and ladle it over the dumplings. Top with kimchi (p 486) and sesame oil. Feel free to add green vegetables or noodles.

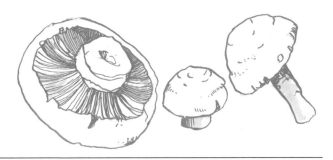

Mustard

Mustard is one of the most pungent condiments found in pantries the world over. It's a paste made from ground mustard seeds (themselves bitter and spicy), vinegar, sugar and spices. There's a lot going on in mustard, and for that reason a little goes a long way. Mustard is used as a spread, and in sauces, glazes, dressings, soups and marinades. It is, in fact, something of a seasoning. When you're down on spices, add mustard for flavour – it has more to offer than just being pulled out on hamburger night. See also *Mustard Seeds and Mustard Powder* on p 432.

Goes with	Mustard and cold meats are meant to be. Mustard is also very good with oily fish such as sardines. And sausages, potatoes, carrots, asparagus, broccoli, beetroot, pumpkin (squash), kohlrabi, celery, fennel, cabbage, sauerkraut, brussels sprouts, turnips, spinach, lettuces, oranges, pineapple, cream, mayonnaise and eggs.
Storage	Because mustard seeds are antimicrobial, mustard can be stored for a very long time. Unopened mustard can be kept indefinitely. Once opened, mustard is safe to keep in the pantry for 1 month and in the fridge for 1 year, perhaps more.
Substitutes	Try to always have mustard powder on hand. It's handy in itself and can be invaluable when you're out of prepared mustard. There's a recipe for making a quick mustard from powder on p 433. Prepared horseradish or wasabi can take mustard's place if need be.

Some ideas for using up that mustard jar

* Just a scraping of mustard left in the jar? Add 1 tbsp oil, 2 tsp vinegar and a pinch each of sugar and salt, then shake the jar for an easy salad dressing.
* Try making apple, cheese and mustard toasties.
* Rub mustard all over beef or chicken before roasting.

* Stir mustard through chopped boiled eggs with mayonnaise, plenty of chives and salt and pepper for the best egg sandwiches.
* Put a little mustard in the 'There's Nothing Wrong With That Cream!' Potatoes (p 125).
* Add 1 tsp mustard to compound butters, such as the Herby Compound Butter (p 192) or the Lemon-flavoured Butter (p 240), to give them even more oomph.
* If there are 2–3 tsp mustard left in the jar, pour in some left-over white wine or even sparkling wine and shake. Use this to baste a roast chicken or chicken pieces.
* Stir 1 tbsp mustard through a warm braised vegetable dish, such as the Finest Braised Fennel (p 160) or Braised Leeks (p 236), just before serving. Don't let the mustard boil.
* If you don't have mustard seeds, add 2–3 tbsp mustard to chutneys or relishes.

Classic mustard vinaigrette

Learn this dressing by heart. It goes with everything. In fact, feel free to double it and use it all week.

Whisk 2 tsp mustard, 2 tbsp red wine vinegar and ⅓ cup (80 ml) olive oil until well combined. Add 1 finely chopped garlic clove and season with a pinch each of salt, pepper and sugar. Keep in a jar in the fridge for up to 1 week.

Nuts p 285

Nuts

Half a packet, a quarter of a packet, some escaped and loose in the pantry ... nuts can go stale before you even think about what to do with them. But there are so many options. Nut-bearing trees are some of the oldest flowering plants on earth – so old, in fact, that they were around before the land masses began to divide into continents. Their longevity means that they span many cultures and thus there is no lack of culinary inspiration when it comes to nuts. Look near and far for ideas and never think that there's nothing to do with even a thimbleful of nuts.

Don't be nervous about swapping one nut with another. We're not suggesting that all nuts taste the same, but if you use the pistachios in your pantry instead of going out to buy pine nuts, everything will be fine. It might even be better.

Storage	Nuts are high in fat and are therefore susceptible to rancidity if kept for too long. To keep nuts fresh, store them in an airtight container in the fridge for up to 6 months. Pine nuts and macadamias should be stored in the freezer for up to 6 months, as their oil content is even higher and they can therefore go rancid quickly. If you have no option but to store nuts in the pantry, buy small amounts and eat them quickly.

How to toast nuts

Toast nuts before crushing them or adding them whole to dishes. It brings out their flavour and ensures they stay crunchy.

- *Oven method* Preheat the oven to 150°C (300°F). If you want to season the nuts, use 1 tsp oil and 1 tsp seasoning (e.g. salt, cumin, paprika) for each 100 g (3½ oz) nuts. Spread out the nuts on a baking tray in a single layer and pop them in the oven. The smaller the nut the shorter the toasting time, so pine nuts will take about 10 minutes and macadamias about 30 minutes. If you're doing a mix of nuts, add the smaller nuts in the last 10 minutes of cooking. Check them regularly to avoid them burning – set a timer and move the nuts around every 3–5 minutes to ensure they toast evenly. Allow the nuts to cool completely before you store them in an airtight container in the pantry for up to 2 weeks. You can refresh them in the oven for 5–10 minutes if they go a little soft. »

- *Dry frying pan method* If you're short on time you can toast nuts in a dry frying pan over low heat. You don't get the same crispness all the way through as with the oven method, but it still brings out the flavours. Because of the direct heat this method works quickly, but you do have to watch the nuts carefully – DO NOT WALK AWAY – and constantly move them around to prevent them burning. Whatever nut you're toasting, they'll be ready when they're golden and smell toasty. Allow the nuts to cool completely before you store them in an airtight container in the pantry for up to 2 weeks.

ALMONDS

Actually a seed, not a nut at all, and a relative of the peach and apricot, almonds are the most popular 'nut' on the market. But try not to take them for granted, as they do have a rather hefty environmental footprint. We love almonds for their distinctive slightly milky, slightly bitter flavour, which makes them adaptable to both sweet and savoury cooking.

Go with	Apples, pears, stone fruits, berries, quince, figs, lemons, oranges, persimmons, rosemary, parsley, basil, bitter green leaves, green beans, broad beans, broccoli, cauliflower, asparagus, silverbeet (Swiss chard), paprika, chilli, cinnamon, ginger, pumpkin (squash), beetroot, chocolate, chicken, pork, cheeses, yoghurt, rice, seeds, grains, oats, cakes and so much more. Really, it's hard to find things almonds don't go with.
Substitutes	The milky texture of almonds is best replaced by other nuts with a similar texture, such as Brazil nuts, macadamias or cashews. If you're just after the flavour of almonds, you could use amaretto liqueur or almond extract.

Some ideas for using up the rest of the almond packet

∗ Almonds add texture, flavour and nutrients to salads. Add a handful of chopped toasted almonds to the Big Grain Salad (p 379), Buckwheat Salad (p 63), Basic Brussels Slaw (p 60), Simple Lentil Salad (p 244), beetroot salads and leafy green salads.

∗ Add almonds to the Meringue recipe (p 152). Fold about 100 g (3½ oz) chopped toasted and cooled almonds through the meringue just before baking. An added 1 tsp ground allspice or wattleseed would be extra delicious. Save a few of the almonds for scattering on top before baking.

∗ **Grind your own almond meal** Put what almonds you have left in a food processor or spice grinder and blitz to a fine powder. Use this to replace a small amount of the flour in a cake or cookie recipe to create a denser texture.

∗ **Almond cream** In a food processor, blitz 200 g (7 oz) blanched almonds to a fine powder, then add 100 g (3½ oz) caster (superfine) sugar and blitz again. With the motor running, very slowly pour 450 ml (15½ fl oz) water into the almonds to make a cream. Transfer to a bowl, cover and refrigerate for at least 30 minutes. You will have enough pouring cream for four servings of dessert.

∗ **Home-made almond milk** It's easy to make. Follow the steps for Macadamia Milk (p 292), replacing the macadamias with almonds.

∗ **Almond biscuits (cookies)** The Macadamia Biscuits (p 292) are equally good made with almonds; they're not quite as buttery but they have a lovely crisp texture. Serve with tea.

∗ **Home-made almond butter** So easy. Follow the Macadamia Nut Butter instructions (p 292).

Almond crust

Use this for crumbing meats or vegetables. Yes, we know. Crumbing meat and vegetables can seem like a pain – three bowls of ingredients and a mess. In the middle of crumbing whatever it is, you swear you'll never do it again, but then you serve dinner and everyone thinks you're the best cook in the world, so you do it again. And this version is really worth it.

Roughly blitz ½ cup (80 g) almonds with 1 tbsp dried herbs, such as rosemary, thyme, sage or a mix, and 1 tsp salt. Make sure you don't blitz them too finely. Set up three bowls: one with ¼ cup (35 g) plain (all-purpose) flour, one with a beaten egg and one with the almonds. Dip a chicken thigh or thickly sliced eggplant (aubergine) or other vegetable first in the flour, then the egg, then the blitzed almonds. Fry in oil or butter over medium heat until browned on each side. Finish in a 180°C (350°F) oven until cooked through.

The most delicious almond dip

MAKES 2 CUPS (ABOUT 480 G)

When you're sick of hummus, make this dip. It's rich, full of spicy flavour, and creamy without any dairy. What's more, it finishes up the last of the almonds in the packet and you can use whatever roasted vegies you like. We've made it with grilled or blistered capsicums (peppers), roasted carrots, roasted tomatoes, beets or left-over roast pumpkin (squash). Serve with vegie sticks or crackers, on sandwiches, or with grilled (broiled) meats.

In a food processor, blitz 1 cup (160 g) almonds, 1–2 cups roasted sweetish vegetables, 2–3 garlic cloves, the juice of ½ lemon, ¾ tsp salt and 1 tsp ground spice of your choice (cumin, coriander, paprika, fennel) – add a little cayenne pepper or chilli flakes if you'd like your dip to have a kick. Blend to a rough paste then, with the motor running slowly, add ½ cup (125 ml) olive oil, and a splash of water, blending until smooth. Taste, add a little more lemon juice or salt if needed, and blend again.

CASHEWS

A nut mild in flavour, buttery and a little sweet. When cooked, cashews become very tender and have an almost meaty texture, and when blended they're very creamy. Their mild-mannered ways mean they can be quite adaptable to many different styles of cooking, and their large size can be useful for bulking up curries and stir-fries. Cashews are people-pleasers – there's not much you can't ask them to do.

Go with   Mint, coriander (cilantro), curry leaves, Thai basil, coconut milk, dairy products, tofu, chicken, beef, onions, celery, kale, asparagus, snow peas (mange tout), green beans, broccoli, cauliflower, tomatoes, avocado, melons, lemons, limes, persimmons, turmeric, cinnamon, cardamom, ginger, sesame seeds, chocolate

---

Substitutes   Replace cashews with peanuts in similar recipes, or try pistachios, as the two are cousins. Even pine nuts would work if you're feeling flush.

Some ideas for using up the rest of the cashew packet

* Cashews are great in stir-fries. Add them to the Stir-fried Celery (p 87) after the celery.
* Blitz salted cashews to a fine powder and use instead of parmesan over pasta. You can mix in some dried oregano for extra flavour if you like.
* Try the Peanutty Koftas recipe on p 293, replacing the peanuts with cashews.
* *Cashew and honey nut bars* Follow the Pistachio Nut Bars recipe (p 297), replacing the pistachios with cashews, and the orange zest with 1 tbsp desiccated coconut.
* *Cashew tarka* Tarka is a fried spice mix that's often spooned on top of Dal (p 244) just before serving, and adding nuts makes it exceptionally delicious. Roughly chop 1 cup (155 g) cashews and toast in a dry frying pan over medium heat until golden. Add 2 tbsp ghee, butter or oil, 3 sliced garlic cloves, 20 curry leaves and 1 tsp cumin seeds. Stir constantly. Once the curry leaves are crisp, add 1 heaped tbsp mustard seeds and stir until they begin to pop.
* *Cashew salsa* Toast 100–150 g (3½–5½ oz) cashews (pp 285–86) and allow to cool. Very finely dice ½ large tomato and mix it in a bowl with 1–2 thinly sliced long red chillies, the zest and juice of ½ lime and plenty of salt and pepper. Roughly chop the cashews and stir into the tomato mixture. Drizzle a good slug of olive oil over the salsa. Season well with salt and pepper and top with torn mint leaves. Serve with other Mexican dishes or with curries.

Cashew curry
SERVES 4 WITH RICE

A cashew curry is a classic Sri Lankan dish. Jaimee is mad about Indian and Sri Lankan food, and this not so authentic version pays homage to the food she loves so much. What Jaimee has learnt from Indian and Sri Lankan cooking is to not skimp on the spices. Be heavy-handed, generous and bold. Make your curries dance across the room with flavour. This one has its dancing shoes on, while also being creamy and nourishing.

Boil 250 g (9 oz) raw cashews for 10 minutes, then drain. Heat 2 tbsp oil of your choice or ghee in a large saucepan. Add 1 diced large brown onion and 1 tbsp grated fresh ginger, then sauté until the onion is translucent and fragrant. Add 3 finely chopped garlic cloves, 10 curry leaves, 1–2 sliced green chillies, 2 tsp ground turmeric, 2 tsp ground cumin, 1 tsp ground cardamom, ½ tsp salt and lots of ground pepper. Stir for a few more seconds, then add the drained cashews and 400 ml (14 fl oz) coconut milk. Reduce the heat to low and cook, uncovered, for 30 minutes. Serve over rice.

HAZELNUTS

Hazelnuts are a true nut, meaning they're a seeded fruit with a hard dry shell that needs to be cracked. They have a natural richness and a chocolatey flavour that whispers 'Nutella' in our ears. Having said that, hazelnuts are wonderful in savoury dishes, particularly Italian cooking. Use them wisely to make the most of their flavour, and if you can't go past Nutella, we have a recipe for that too.

Go with Chocolate, all dairy products, coffee, rosemary, oregano, sage, fennel, cabbage, kale, kohlrabi, silverbeet (Swiss chard), crunchy lettuces, carrots, beetroot, pumpkin (squash), parsnips, strawberries, raspberries, bananas, pears, apples, peaches, quince, figs, persimmons, poppy seeds, sunflower seeds, oats, warm spices (cinnamon, allspice, cloves, star anise), pork, white fish, honey, brown sugar, cinnamon, nutmeg

---

Substitutes You don't want to mess around too much when replacing hazelnuts, but almonds and walnuts will do the trick.

How to skin hazelnuts Whether you have oven-toasted or dry-pan-toasted (pp 285–86) hazelnuts, you can remove the papery skins by wrapping the hot nuts in a clean tea towel (dish towel) and rubbing them all together for a few minutes. Unwrap and the papery skins should have rubbed off.

Some ideas for using up the rest of the hazelnut packet

* Parsnips and hazelnuts are a good match. Try the Winter Parsnip and Hazelnut Salad (p 322).
* Add chopped hazelnuts to the Seedy Breakfast Muffins (p 371) or the Simplest Banana Bread (p 27).
* ***Hazelnut parsley pesto*** Follow the Classic Basil Pesto recipe (p 191), using parsley instead of basil and ⅓ cup (40 g) toasted and chopped hazelnuts instead of the pine nuts.
* ***Home-made Nutella*** In a food processor, blitz 250 g (9 oz) toasted and skinned (above) hazelnuts until they turn to a paste; this might take a few minutes. Add ¼ cup (30 g) unsweetened cocoa powder, ½ cup (60 g) icing (confectioners') sugar and ½ tsp vanilla extract. Blitz again. Finally, add 2 tbsp neutral oil of your choice. Blend until combined into a smooth spreadable paste. Keep in an airtight container in the fridge for up to 4 weeks.

Simple sweet hazelnut crust for tarts and pies

This gluten-free pie crust has a crumbly biscuit-like texture and a wholesome nutty flavour. Use it for the sorts of pies and tarts that have a final setting stage in the fridge, such as lemon tarts, non-baked cheesecakes and pumpkin pies, or our Sweet Potato Pie (p 451). Almonds will also work here, as would pecans.

Preheat the oven to 180°C (350°F). Start by blitzing 1½ cups (210 g) skinned (p 290) hazelnuts to a medium–fine meal. Tip the hazelnut meal into a bowl and add 2 tbsp caster (superfine) sugar, some lemon zest or ½ tsp ground cinnamon or grated nutmeg and ¼ tsp bicarbonate of soda (baking soda). Mix well. To this dry mix, add ¼ cup (60 g) melted butter and 1 tbsp ice-cold water. Knead until well combined. Press into a greased pie dish, covering the base and sides. Bake for 10–15 minutes, until just turning golden. Allow to cool completely before filling.

MACADAMIAS

Australia's very own nut shines on the world stage – the Cate Blanchett of the nut world, if you will. The macadamia is native to northern New South Wales and southern Queensland, giving it an air of the tropics. Macadamias are creamy with a slight lemon flavour. They're higher in healthy fats than most nuts and so even a small amount can turn a fruit salad into a substantive meal.

Go with   Mango, bananas, pineapple, papaya, limes, lemons, figs, persimmons, chilli, coriander (cilantro), mint, coconut, cinnamon, nutmeg, soft cheeses, yoghurt, honey, ice cream, seafood, granola

------

Substitutes   Stick with other creamy nuts for substitutions: cashews, pine nuts and peanuts all work well.

Some ideas for using up the rest of the macadamia packet

* Fold ½ cup (60 g) chopped macadamias through the batter for the Pineapple Upside-down Cake (p 352) or the Seedy Breakfast Muffins (p 371).
* Add macadamias to the Oaty Crumble Topping (p 302) or Maple Granola (p 303).
* Mango and macadamia are a good pairing in sweet or savoury dishes. Try adding chopped macadamias to the Quick Mango Salsa (p 261) or the Mango Salad (p 262). »

* Make an easy dessert with grilled banana (p 25), vanilla ice cream and chopped macadamias.
* *Macadamia nut butter* All it takes is patience and a food processor. Put whatever amount of macadamias you have in the food processor – 250 g (9 oz) is a good starting point – and blitz. Blitz past the crumbled stage, and past the sticking stage, scraping down the sides as needed, and keep going until you get a smooth creamy paste. This could take at least 5 minutes. You can add a little pinch of salt or sugar if you so desire.

Macadamia milk

MAKES 2 CUPS (500 ML)

Making your own macadamia milk is a good way of using up that last half-packet of nuts.

Soak ½ cup (75 g) macadamias in a bowl of water overnight. Transfer the drained macadamias to a high-powered blender and add a tiny pinch of salt and 2 cups (500 ml) water. Blend until very smooth. Strain the nut milk through a nut bag, muslin or a clean Chux, retaining the pulp. Keep the macadamia milk in the fridge for up to 5 days.

You can turn the pulp into nut meal to use in baking as you would store-bought almond meal or hazelnut meal. You'll need to dry it out in the oven first. Preheat the oven to 150°C (300°F). Spread the nut pulp out in an ovenproof dish and dry for about 30 minutes. Gently shake the dish every 15 minutes to ensure even drying. Once completely dry, allow to cool, then store in an airtight container in the fridge for up to 3 months.

Macadamia biscuits

MAKES 12

Macadamias lend their butteriness to these biscuits (cookies), which are like shortbread but without the flour and butter. They are very good indeed with a cup of tea or coffee.

Preheat the oven to 150°C (300°F). In a food processor, blitz 2 cups (310 g) macadamias to a coarse flour. Tip into a bowl and add 1 egg, 2 tbsp water, 2 tbsp caster (superfine) sugar and ½ tsp herb or spice of your choice – thyme is lovely, ground cinnamon is a crowd-pleaser, ground coriander is fragrant – it's up to you. Mix well to make a smoothish dough.

Tip the dough onto a large sheet of baking paper and place another sheet on top. Using a rolling pin, roll out the dough between the paper until it's about 5 mm (¼ in) thick. Slide onto a baking tray, then remove the top sheet of baking paper. Sprinkle the dough with a little caster (superfine) sugar if you like. Use a sharp knife to score the dough about three-quarters of the way through into squares, then bake for 20 minutes.

Cool on the tray and cut into squares, then keep in an airtight container for 3–4 days.

PEANUTS

Not strictly speaking a nut, but a legume that grows underground. More than half the peanuts grown are made into peanut butter, which is quite easy to make yourself (see the Macadamia Nut Butter, opposite, for the method). Raw peanuts have a distinctive bean-like flavour, but when roasted they become darker, more roasty and caramelly. Use peanuts in savoury and sweet dishes; from Mexican mole and Indonesian gado gado to ice-cream sundaes, they're at home anywhere. Luckily they're the most affordable nut on the market.

Go with   Apples, grapes, bananas, lemons, limes, mango, figs, persimmons, carrots, daikon, potatoes, broccoli, celery, cucumber, snow peas (mange tout), tomatoes, chilli, ginger, coriander (cilantro), curry leaves, curry powder, cinnamon, nutmeg, coriander seeds, turmeric, coconut, chocolate, all meats including seafood

---

Substitutes   Cashews and macadamias are a good alternative.

Some ideas for using up the rest of the peanut packet

✳ Add them to salads. We toast peanuts (pp 285–86) then chop and add them to salsas, noodle salads, stir-fries and tropical fruit salads. Also try adding toasted and chopped peanuts to any of these dishes: Roasted Tired Broccoli (p 56), Really Easy Green Bean Curry (p 40), Daikon Salad (p 135), Grapefruit and Avocado Breakfast Salad (p 178).

✳ *Peanutty koftas* In a food processor, blitz 1 cup (140 g) peanuts with ½ onion until roughly chopped. Transfer to a bowl and mix with 400 g (14 oz) minced (ground) lamb, 1 egg, ½ tsp each of salt and pepper, 1 tsp chilli flakes or powder, ½ tsp ground allspice and 1 tbsp tomato paste (concentrated purée). Form the mixture into football-shaped balls around skewers or roll into walnut-sized balls. Cook on the barbecue or under the grill (broiler).

✳ *DIY peanut butter* So easy. Follow the steps for Macadamia Nut Butter opposite, using peanuts instead.

✳ *Cheat's salted peanut ice cream* For cheat's home-made ice cream, soften a tub of vanilla ice cream and fold into it either home-made peanut butter (above), or chopped toasted peanuts with choc chips or Chocolate Ganache (p 125) and a big pinch of salt. Refreeze and serve.

Satay sauce
MAKES ABOUT 2 CUPS (500 ML)

Most satay sauces need peanut butter, but this one is super easy and just uses whole peanuts. Serve with chicken skewers, grilled (broiled) tofu or rice paper rolls.

Heat a dry frying pan over low heat and toast 1 cup (140 g) peanuts until very fragrant. Add 1 tbsp oil of your choice, 2 finely chopped garlic cloves and 1 chopped fresh chilli. Stir-fry for a few minutes to cook the garlic. Transfer to a food processor and blitz. Now add 2 tbsp brown sugar, 1 tbsp fish sauce, 2 tsp sesame oil, ½ tsp soy sauce, the juice of ½ lime, ⅓ cup (80 ml) coconut milk and ⅓ cup (80 ml) water. Blitz well until you have a smooth paste. Add a little more water if it's too thick for your liking.

Peanut brittle – or 'the ends of all the nut packets' brittle
MAKES ABOUT 750 G (1 LB 2 OZ)

Brittle is a real treat. Sweet, nutty and with a touch of salt. Enjoy a big shard, decorate a cake with it, or crush it up and scatter it over ice cream or banana splits. This recipe is for a classic peanut brittle, but you can use any nut and it's a great way to use up ends of packets.

Line a small heatproof dish with baking paper, then lightly butter or oil it. In a saucepan, mix 2 cups (440 g) caster (superfine) sugar with ½ cup (125 ml) water and a pinch of salt. Place over high heat and allow the sugar to melt, without stirring, until it turns light golden. Lower the heat to medium and continue to cook for 5–10 minutes, stirring occasionally, until it turns golden amber. Remove from the heat, stir in 1½ cups (210 g) roasted peanuts, then pour immediately onto the lined dish. Spread out with a spatula to about 1 cm (½ in) thick. Allow to cool and harden completely. Break up into pieces and store in an airtight container for up to 2 weeks.

PINE NUTS
Boy, are these things pricey! We'll tell you why: the pine trees these nuts come from take up to 75 years to mature, and harvesting is done by hand, so there is *a lot* of work going into that tiny packet of pine nuts. Use pine nuts respectfully; once you're aware of the way they're grown, you'll never waste a single kernel. Their diminutive size belies their distinctive flavour – buttery, sweet and a little resiny. Even a few lightly toasted pine nuts on top of some hummus or in a salad is like a little sprinkling of gold dust.

Go with	Dried beans, chickpeas, lentils, rice, meats (especially minced/ground meat), broad beans, silverbeet (Swiss chard), pomegranate, dried fruits, figs, honey, dairy products, sunflower seeds, tahini, basil, sage, rosemary, parsley, dill

----

Substitutes	Go for chopped almonds, pistachios or hazelnuts.

Some ideas for using up the rest of the pine nut packet

* Make the Yoghurt Pasta on p 490. Sautéing the pine nuts in butter is the making of this dish.
* Make Classic Basil Pesto (p 191).
* The Most Delicious Almond Dip (p 288) works well with pine nuts or a combination of both pine nuts and almonds. Try making it with roasted carrots.
* Zucchini (courgettes) and pine nuts work well together. Top Garlicky Parsley Zucchini or Grilled Zucchini Pasta (both on p 497) with pine nuts. Or scatter them on top of any of the Easy Oven-blistered Eggplant options (p 143) or Braised Leeks (p 236).
* In a small frying pan, toast pine nuts with a drop of oil and 1–2 tsp ground cumin, paprika, sumac or fennel seeds and a pinch of salt. Add to the top of dishes like the Braised Tomatoey Okra (p 306), Grains and Olive Salad (p 309) or tomatoes on toast.
* Add them to the Pistachio Nut Bars (p 297).
* Make a 'Clear Out the Fridge' Pizza (p 97) with pesto, pine nuts, potato and parmesan.

Pine nut sort of hashweh
SERVES 4 AS PART OF A SHARED MEAL

Hashweh is a Levantine staple that translates to 'stuffing'. It's usually made with minced (ground) meat and loaded with nuts and spices. Here we make it all about the nuts, spices and dried fruit, but if you have a little minced meat, please do add it. Use this mix on top of rice or hummus, or serve over Roasted Eggplant (p 144), or with flat breads (p 168) and salad.

In a medium–large frying pan, heat 2 tbsp oil of your choice, then sauté 1 diced large onion and 2 finely chopped garlic cloves until the onion is translucent. Add 1½ tsp ground cumin, 1 tsp paprika, ½ tsp ground cinnamon, ½ tsp ground black pepper and ¼ tsp salt. Sauté for a few seconds. To this spice mix add ¾ cup (115 g) pine nuts and ½ cup (75 g) currants or other dried fruit (chop into very small pieces if using dried apricots, dates or figs) and continue to cook until the pine nuts are golden. If using minced (ground) meat, add up to 200 g (7 oz) and fry until browned. Before serving, give it a big squeeze of lemon juice and/or a sprinkle of sumac.

PISTACHIOS

Another nut that's not a nut but a seed, pistachios are often associated with Middle Eastern cooking. Buy them in their shells, as they will stay fresher for longer. Their flavour is grassy and floral, so they're widely used in desserts and savoury dishes. Their striking greenness with a blush of pink is half their pleasure. Even a few crushed pistachios on yoghurt in the morning is a pretty start to the day.

Go with   Dried fruits, stone fruits, pomegranate, lemons, limes, grapes, figs, plums, lettuces, parsley, coriander (cilantro), dill, mint, pulses, rice, buckwheat, oats, barley, lamb, fish, feta, goat's cheese, yoghurt, honey, cinnamon, nutmeg, allspice, saffron, vanilla

---

Substitutes   Pistachios are related to cashews, so swap them freely. Almonds and pine nuts would also work.

Some ideas for using up the rest of the pistachio packet

✳ Add a handful of pistachios to a platter of roasted kohlrabi, beetroot or carrots. Drizzle with the Creamy Tahini Dressing (p 455) and top with plenty of chopped herbs.

✳ The Pumpkin Ratatouille on p 371 is topped with a generous handful of toasted pistachios.

✳ Fold chopped pistachios through the Anything-goes Rice (p 394) before serving.

✳ Add pistachios to the Peanut Brittle (p 294).

✳ Switch pistachios for the peanuts in the Cheat's Salted Peanut Ice Cream (p 293), adding a splash of rosewater and chopped cranberries instead of chocolate and omitting the salt.

✳ ***Pistachio and yoghurt dip***   In a food processor, blitz ½ cup (70 g) toasted pistachios (pp 285–86) with a generous pinch each of salt and pepper until fine, then slowly add 2 tbsp neutral oil until you have a smooth paste. In a serving bowl, mix ¾ cup (200 g) plain yoghurt with a little pinch of salt and a squeeze of lemon juice, then spoon in the pistachio paste and make a pretty swirl. Sprinkle with a little sumac or paprika. Serve with falafel or meatballs.

Pistachio nut bars

MAKES 8–10 SMALL BARS

Let's say you know someone who can boil an egg and make toast, but otherwise they use their oven for shoe storage. We promise that even they could still add these chewy nut bars to their repertoire. They'll need to take their shoes out of the oven, though. The beauty of these bars is that they can be made with any nut combination, so feel free to use whatever you have. Here we've added a little orange zest, but you could skip it, or add more ground cinnamon, or some unsweetened cocoa powder instead.

Line a 20 cm (8 in) square baking tray with baking paper and preheat the oven to 160°C (315°F). In a small saucepan, warm ½ cup (175 g) honey with the finely grated zest of 1 orange, a pinch of salt and a pinch of ground cinnamon until the honey is runny. In a heatproof bowl, mix 1½ cups (210 g) pistachios and ½ cup (75 g) sesame seeds. Pour the honey mixture over the pistachios and mix until well combined. Pour the mixture into the baking tray and press down firmly. Bake for 25 minutes or until golden.

Allow to cool in the tray for 20 minutes, then slice into whatever size bars you'd like and leave to cool for an hour longer. Store in an airtight container in the fridge for up to 3 weeks.

WALNUTS

This wobbly brain-shaped nut is second only to almonds in popularity. Walnuts are native to Europe, America and Asia, so you'll see them being used in all kinds of cooking. Raw walnuts quickly lose their fresh flavour, but toast them (pp 285–86) and it becomes sharper and deeper, with a pleasant bitterness.

Go with   Eggplant (aubergine), beetroot, cabbage, kale, kohlrabi, celery, broccoli, broad beans, bitter leaves, carrots, parsnips, mushrooms, garlic, oranges, apples, pears, stone fruits, bananas, grapes, quince, figs, pomegranate, persimmons, parsley, oregano, rosemary, sage, warm spices (cinnamon, allspice, cloves, star anise), oats, hard cheeses, blue cheese, yoghurt, pepitas (pumpkin seeds), sunflower seeds, tahini

------

Substitutes   Almonds, hazelnuts and pine nuts are all good options.

Some ideas for using up the rest of the walnut packet

* Add walnuts to the Simplest Banana Bread (p 27) or Simple Oat Cookies (p 303).
* Turn the Seedy Breakfast Muffins (p 371) into apple and walnut muffins, replacing the pumpkin (squash) with 2 cups (400 g) grated apple and the seeds with 1 cup (125 g) chopped toasted walnuts.
* Make the Walnut and Pomegranate Side on p 359.
* *Walnut and crunchy lettuce salad* Toast and roughly chop a handful of walnuts. Toss them with bite-sized pieces of crunchy lettuce and dress with the Blue Cheese Dressing (p 90).
* *Apples stuffed with walnut paste* Preheat the oven to 180°C (350°F). In a food processor, blitz ½ cup (115 g) walnuts with ¼ tsp ground cinnamon, ¼ cup (60 g) brown sugar and 2 tbsp butter to a rough paste. Core 4 small apples, leaving their bases intact. Stuff the apples with the walnut paste, pack snugly into a small ovenproof dish, then cover and bake for 30–40 minutes, until the apples are well cooked.

Walnut pasta sauce

SERVES 4

This rich and satisfying sauce is almost like a pesto, but without the green, which might please some people. Serve a salad on the side to assuage fears of scurvy, or just relax and lean in to the brown.

Start by toasting 1 cup (115 g) walnuts in a dry frying pan with the chopped leaves of 1 rosemary sprig until golden. Using a mortar and pestle, crush the warm nuts and rosemary with a roughly chopped garlic clove, or blitz roughly in a food processor. Be careful not to turn it into a smooth paste. Season with ¼ tsp salt and ½ tsp ground black pepper. With the food processor running, add ½ cup (50 g) grated parmesan and slowly drizzle in ¼ cup (60 ml) olive oil. Taste and season again if needed.

Bring a pot of salted water to the boil and cook 300 g (10½ oz) pasta as per the packet directions. Drain and reserve about ½ cup (125 ml) of the cooking water. Warm the walnut sauce in a frying pan and loosen with a little of the pasta water. Stir through the cooked pasta, and serve with more grated parmesan.

O

Oats

While Jaimee worries if there isn't a cabbage in the house, Alex gets edgy if she's out of oats. Oats provide easy, affordable breakfast options and are the basis for baked goods that make us feel like wholesome parents, even when we know the kids are buying Slurpees on the way home from school. Here are our top tips if you've only known the oat as porridge.

Go with   Milk, butter, yoghurt, cream, nuts and seeds, dried fruits, warm spices, sugar, honey, syrups, salt, all the fruits, coconut, chocolate

---

Storage   Oats are fine stored in an airtight container in the pantry, but if you have a big fridge, store them in there. The cool environment stops the oil in the oats from going rancid and keeps them safe from pesky pantry moths.

Substitutes   If there are no oats for your morning porridge, try making it with cooked rice, or other cooked grains such as quinoa, buckwheat or barley. For baking, try any flaked or puffed grain, bran or coconut.

Some ideas for using the last of the oats

* Use them in baking. Add a handful of rolled oats to bread doughs, flat breads (p 168) or muffins, or stir through cookie dough for a little added texture. Try adding a handful to the Seedy Breakfast Muffins (p 371) or, for a savoury option, add a handful of oats and seeds to the Flotsam and Jetsam Flat Breads (p 168). You may need to add a little extra liquid too.
* ***Bircher muesli*** Put the last of the rolled oats in a bowl and add enough apple or orange juice to just cover, then leave, covered, in the fridge overnight. When you wake up in the morning, stir through some yoghurt and grated apple. Eat as is or top with toasted coconut, granola, nuts or fresh fruits.

* *Overnight yoghurt oats* Mix 1 cup (95 g) rolled oats with 1 cup (250 ml) milk of your choice and 1 cup (260 g) plain yoghurt, add honey or maple syrup to taste, and pop in the fridge overnight. Serve with fresh fruit for a good breakfast when you're in a hurry.

* *Fruity porridge* If you've got an overripe banana in the fruit bowl and ½ cup (50 g) rolled oats in the pantry, you can turn it into a wholesome warming breakfast using the Banana Porridge recipe (p 25). If it's summertime, try it with ripe mango. For porridge with no leftovers, use ½ cup (50 g) rolled oats and about 350 ml (12 fl oz) liquid per person.

* *Oat milk* Non-dairy milks are easy to make at home. Oat milk made from rolled oats is creamy and delicious, although it's best used cool, not heated. Follow the Home-made Coconut Milk recipe (p 117), using 1 cup (95 g) rolled oats, 4 cups (1 litre) cold water and 2 tsp something sweet like brown sugar or maple syrup. Makes 800 ml (28 fl oz), so halve the recipe if you don't think you'll get through that much in 5 days.

* *Oat flour* Whiz rolled oats in a high-powered blender or food processor to make oat flour. You're looking for a soft powdered consistency rather than sand. Oat flour can be used in baking, pancakes and waffles, or to help bind meatballs and burger patties.

* *Oats in soups and stews* Add ¼ cup (25 g) rolled oats to vegetable soups and stews for nuttiness, extra nutrition and thickening. The oats don't take long to cook, so add them in the last 10–15 minutes, with any leafy greens. Try adding oats to Wally Rath's Barley Vegetable Soup (p 30), Green Soup (p 440) or Leek and Potato Soup (p 236).

Oat and apple pikelets

MAKES 12

We made these for the children when they were small. The idea came from running out of flour, but they're also good if you're looking for low-gluten recipes.

In a high-powered blender or food processor, blitz 2 cups (190 g) rolled oats to a fine powder. Add 1 tsp baking powder, ½ tsp ground cinnamon, 1 tbsp brown sugar and a pinch of salt, then blitz again to combine. Tip into a mixing bowl and set aside. Now blitz 1 cup (250 ml) milk, 1 egg, 1–2 tbsp maple syrup and 1 tbsp oil of your choice in the blender or food processor. Stir into the dry ingredients, then grate in 1–2 peeled apples and combine gently. Melt a little butter in a frying pan. Working in batches, fry ¼ cupfuls of the mixture, a few at a time. Cook just like pancakes or pikelets, and serve with honey, maple syrup or jam.

Oaty crumble topping – or yummy snack

MAKES ABOUT 3 CUPS (460 G)

This topping makes enough for one crumble or six deconstructed desserts. It can be baked on its own in the oven and added to poached or stewed fruits and ice cream or custard and grilled banana (p 25). Or it can be added raw to the top of a dish of stewed fruit for a crumble.

In a bowl, mix 1 cup (150 g) plain (all-purpose) flour with ½ cup (110 g) brown sugar, ½ tsp baking powder and 1 tsp ground ginger. With clean fingers, work in 100 g (3½ oz) diced butter until the mixture has a lumpy, sandy texture. Toss 1 cup (95 g) rolled oats through the mixture, then spread out on a baking tray lined with baking paper. Pop in the fridge for 10–15 minutes while preheating the oven to 170°C (325°F). Bake for 20–25 minutes, stirring a few times during cooking. Allow to cool and get crunchy.

Store any leftovers in the fridge for up to 10 days. Refresh in a 150°C (300°F) oven to make it crunchy again. You can freeze this mixture unbaked and add it to stewed fruits for a quick crumble.

Pantry-strays slice

MAKES ABOUT 16

This healthy slice makes a great alternative to commercial muesli bars and can be made with whatever bits and pieces you have in the pantry, including stale cereal.

Preheat the oven to 160°C (315°F). In a bowl, make a mix of rolled oats, left-over cereals (flakes, puffs, crumbled Weetbix, whatever) and pantry strays (bran, dried coconut, chopped dried fruits, sultanas, sunflower or other seeds, choc chips, chopped nuts). You'll need 3 cups altogether, so feel free to make this up with whatever needs using, but use at least 1 cup (95 g) rolled oats and 1 tbsp LSA (ground linseed, sunflower seeds and almonds), bran or similar to bind everything together.

In a small saucepan, combine ½ cup white (granulated) sugar (110 g) or honey (175 g), ½ cup (140 g) nut butter or tahini (135 g) and ⅓ cup (90 g) butter or coconut oil. Warm, stirring often, until the fat element has melted and the sweet element is dissolved.

Mix wet and dry ingredients together. Line a 20 cm (8 in) square baking tin with baking paper then, with clean hands, firmly press the mixture into the tin. Cover another sheet of baking paper and push down again with your hands. Remove the top sheet of baking paper and bake for 20 minutes or until golden. Allow to cool, then set in the fridge overnight. Cut into squares and store in an airtight container in the fridge for up to 2 weeks.

Simple oat cookies – add what you have
MAKES 12

Somewhere between an Anzac biscuit and an oatmeal cookie. You can whip these up easily without making too much washing up, and use up the bits and pieces you have on hand.

Preheat the oven to 170°C (325°F) and line a baking tray with baking paper. In a large bowl, mix 1 cup (95 g) rolled oats, ½ cup (75 g) flour of your choice, ½ cup random bits (seeds, nuts, dried coconut, raisins), ⅓ cup (75 g) sugar of your choice and a pinch of salt. In a small saucepan, melt 80 g (2¾ oz) butter with 1 tbsp something syrupy like honey, golden syrup, agave syrup or molasses, then use a fork to whisk in ½ tsp bicarbonate of soda (baking soda). Mix the wet and dry ingredients together, roll into balls and arrange on the baking tray. Flatten each ball lightly with a fork and bake for 10–12 minutes. Cool on the tray for 5–10 minutes, then transfer to a wire rack to cool completely. Store in an airtight container in the pantry for up to 1 week.

Maple granola

This simple, not so sweet granola uses oats and the stragglers from the pantry. If you like your toasted muesli a little sweeter, add another 1 tbsp maple syrup or brown sugar.

Preheat the oven to 160°C (315°F). In a large bowl, mix 2½ cups (240 g) rolled oats, 1½ cups of a mix of nuts, seeds, dried coconut or rice puffs, a big pinch of salt and 1 tsp of your favourite ground spice, such as cinnamon or ginger. In a small saucepan, melt ⅓ cup (80 ml) coconut oil or oil of your choice with ⅓ cup (90 g) maple syrup or sweetener of your choice. Pour the sweetened oil over the muesli mix and stir to combine, ensuring everything is lightly coated. Spread out on a baking tray lined with baking paper and toast in the oven for 10 minutes. Remove and give everything a quick shake or stir, then bake for another 10–15 minutes, until golden.

Allow to cool completely before transferring to a jar or airtight container. If you're feeling it, add some chopped dehydrated citrus pieces or chopped dried fruits. Store in the pantry for up to 2 weeks. If your granola loses its crunch, refresh it in a 160°C (315°F) oven until crisp again.

Okra

Don't be afraid of okra. Next time you see it at the market, be brave and buy a few handfuls, choosing the smallest fingers for tenderness. Okra is predominantly used in Indian, Middle Eastern and Southern US cooking. It gets a bad reputation for being slimy, but there are ways of minimising that texture – and bear in mind that the mucilage in okra is said to have healing benefits for the digestive tract. The gooiness is celebrated in West African, Creole and Cajun cooking, where it's used as a thickener for soups and stews.

If you'd like to keep some crunch, cook okra quickly, in a wok, hot pan or very hot oven. Or if you're fond of richer dishes (or took too long thinking about what to do with the okra you bought and it lost its crunch) turn to the Turkish and Greek low-and-slow tomatoey cooking styles. The acid in the tomatoes will prevent too much sliminess.

And if you're a pickler, put Alex's Chilli Pickled Okra (p 307) on your to-do list this summer.

Goes with	Flavour-wise, treat okra like eggplant (aubergine) and tomatoes. Okra matches well with garlic, ginger, onions, tomatoes, chilli, lemons, limes, most herbs, tahini, lamb, ham, fish, eggs, lots of olive oil, fennel seeds, coriander seeds, cumin and black pepper.
Storage	Fresh okra is very perishable. It lasts best, unwashed, in a paper bag in the crisper compartment of the fridge, but only for a few days. Any moisture will encourage sliminess.
Substitutes	Texturally, you could slow-cook eggplant (aubergine), zucchini (courgettes), green beans or mushrooms as you would okra. For fast cooking, try green beans, celery or, at a stretch, broccoli.

How to prepare okra	If it's the slime factor that's putting you off welcoming okra into your home, try this clever tip for helping it maintain its crunch. Wash okra well, keeping the cap intact. Place in a bowl, sprinkle generously with salt, splash some white wine vinegar over it, and let it sit for at least 30 minutes. Rinse and dry, then carry on cooking. The acid in the vinegar helps reduce the gumminess, which is why okra is often cooked with tomatoes and lemon juice and why it makes such a delicious pickle.

Some ideas if you bought okra and now you're confused

* Turn the Green Beans and Grains (p 41) into okra and grains.
* Batter and deep-fry it. It's so good. Try the Tempura-style Egg White Batter (p 153), coating the okra whole, then deep-frying (p 82). Serve with one of the spicy versions of Cheat's Aioli (p 269).
* *Braised okra* Cook low and slow, following the Velvety Braised Vegetables recipe (p 159). Be sure to add some tomatoes. Or use the Braised Tomatoey Okra recipe over the page.
* *Stir-fried okra* Hot and fast cooking will keep okra crunchy and green. Follow the Stir-fried Celery method (p 87), adding grated fresh ginger and sliced chilli.

Roasted okra

If you're really opposed to the oozy texture of okra, try roasting it.

Pop washed but very dry okra in a bowl and drizzle with a little oil (peanut or sunflower is good), plenty of salt and pepper and 1–2 finely chopped garlic cloves. Mix well, then spread out in a roasting tin, being mindful not to overcrowd it. Roast in a 220°C (425°F) oven for about 10–15 minutes, until just tender. Larger okra may take a little longer. Allow to cool slightly, then transfer to a serving plate, dress with any of the dressings below and top with toasted sesame seeds.

To dress roasted okra: Chilli sauce, lemon juice, oil and salt / Green Chilli and Lime Sauce (p 113) / Mandarin and Soy Dressing (p 257) / Garlic Yoghurt Sauce (p 491).

Spiced pan-fried okra

SERVES 4 AS A SIDE

This dry-fried okra is based on an Indian cooking style that uses high heat and plenty of spices to make a flavoursome okra side dish with minimal gumminess. Choose 200–300 g (7–10½ oz) small firm okra. Wash and dry well, cut off the caps, then cut each finger into 2 cm (¾ in) rounds. Heat 1–2 tsp neutral oil in a large frying pan over medium heat, then add the okra, letting it cook undisturbed for 1–2 minutes. Shake the pan and leave undisturbed again. Keep cooking for about 6–8 minutes, until the okra is golden, only shaking the pan and reducing the heat if it looks like the okra is burning. Once the okra is tender but crisp, add 1–2 tsp spice of your choice, or a mix of ground cumin, ground coriander, chilli flakes, mustard seeds, fennel seeds – and a big pinch of salt. Fry for another 1–2 minutes then serve immediately with rice and a curry.

Braised tomatoey okra

SERVES 4-6

This is by far the most delicious way to eat okra. Make this as part of a meal with flat breads (p 168), hummus, boiled eggs, haloumi or Peanutty Koftas (p 293). It's good on toast the next day as well.

In a large frying pan, heat ¼–⅓ cup (60–80 ml) extra virgin olive oil, and sauté 1 sliced small onion for 5 minutes or so. Add 6 sliced garlic cloves, 1 tsp salt and lots of ground pepper, then sauté for a few more minutes. Add 350–500 g (12 oz – 1 lb 2 oz) okra, 400 g (14 oz) tinned crushed tomatoes, ¼ cup (60 ml) lemon juice and a woody herb sprig (oregano, thyme, rosemary, bay leaf). Mix gently, but not too often, bring to a simmer, then reduce the heat to low and cook gently, covered, for 30–40 minutes. Remove the lid, taste and adjust the seasoning if needed. Allow to sit off the heat for 10 minutes before serving.

Chilli pickled okra

MAKES 2 x 500 ML (18 OZ) JARS

This hot pickled okra is delicious – a real punch of flavour to serve with tortillas and beans, or thinly sliced through slaws, or as part of a Mediterranean-style feast. Keep the okra whole in the jar and be careful not to pierce or break the skin, to avoid any sliminess leaching out.

Sterilise your jars (p 501). Once they are cool, add to each jar 1 peeled garlic clove, 1 slice of fresh ginger, 1 tsp chilli flakes or a whole chilli, and either some black peppercorns or coriander seeds. Pack 350–450 g (12 oz – 1 lb) okra vertically to firmly fill the jars. Make a pickling liquid by combining 1½ cups (375 ml) white wine vinegar, 200 ml (7 fl oz) water, ¼ cup (55 g) white (granulated) sugar and 1½ tsp salt in a saucepan. Bring to the boil, stirring to dissolve the sugar, then remove from the heat. Pour the hot liquid into the jars, ensuring the okra is completely submerged, then seal. Once cool, store in the fridge for 1–2 months, or heat-process (p 502) for 10 minutes and store in a cool, dark place for up to 1 year. Allow to sit for at least 2 weeks before using.

Olives

It's quite difficult to have olives go off. The combination of salt-curing, vinegar and olive oil ensures they will last for longer than the motor of the average fridge. This generally means you'll find a few half-used jars and containers lurking at the back of the top shelf. We're big fans of the fridge-audit dinner. The satisfaction of finishing off a few jars is second to none. So go on, take up the challenge: gather all the decade-old olives and turn them into a meal.

Go with	Olives go with other salty things, such as preserved lemon, capers, ham and anchovies. They also go with creamy cheeses, such as ricotta, feta cheese, goat's cheese and mozzarella; starchy foods, such as bread, potatoes and pasta; and all the deliciously intense flavours of citrus fruits, olive oil, garlic, pepper, chilli, juniper berries and green herbs. Olives add saltiness to green beans, broccoli, kale, capsicum (pepper), tomatoes, melons, persimmons, pomegranate, cucumber, fennel, lettuces.
Storage	Olives in salt or vinegar will last the longest. Olives marinated in oil will also last a very long time, as they have been salt-cured before they go under the oil. Keep all varieties of olives submerged under the liquid they came in, or if they came from the deli without a liquid and you're not going to get through them all in a week or so, marinate them following the instructions over the page for longer-lasting olives.
Substitutes	Nothing else really tastes like an olive, but instead of running to the shops, use capers or finely diced preserved lemon. And definitely don't be afraid to switch green and black olives.

How to marinate olives

Fancy up average jarred olives by marinating them. This is also a good tip for olives not in a liquid that you'd like to make last a little longer. For the marinade, mix ¼ cup (60 ml) olive oil, 2–3 tbsp red wine vinegar or apple cider vinegar, 2 tsp sugar and 1 tsp salt. Add some sliced garlic, lemon peel, peppercorns and/or an oregano or thyme sprig if you have them. Chilli flakes, rosemary, fennel seeds, coriander seeds and strips of orange peel would also be nice. Put the olives in a clean jar or airtight container, cover with the marinade and store in the fridge for up to 2 months. Bring to room temperature before serving. Once you've eaten all the olives, use the left-over liquid for salad dressings.

Some ideas for using up that jar of olives

* If olives need using, our first recommendation is to make Puttanesca (p 71) and a martini.
* Add a few spoonfuls of olives to a salad. Try the Simple Greek Salad (p 127), Simple Grapefruit Salad (p 178) or Niçoise Salad of Sorts (p 39).
* The Celery Leaf Gremolata With Green Olives (p 88) adds flavour to soups, egg dishes and avocado on toast. If you don't have celery leaves, make it with parsley instead.
* If you only have a few olives left in the fridge, make a batch of the Whatever-cheese Eggy Muffins (p 93).
* Coat hot pasta in olive oil or butter, lemon juice and zest, lots of pepper and salt, and as many chopped olives as you have in the fridge. Pile on cheese of your choice and herbs of your choice. While your pasta is cooking, make a martini and pop an olive in it.
* Half a jar of olives and some cheese in the fridge means pizza for dinner. Check out the 'Clear Out the Fridge' Pizza (p 97).
* *Grains and olive salad* Gently mix 1–2 cups cooked grains (barley, farro, couscous, brown rice) with ½–1 cup chopped olives and 1 large handful of chopped herbs like parsley, dill or basil. Dress liberally with lemon juice, olive oil, salt, a finely chopped garlic clove and plenty of ground pepper. Add a little sumac if you have it on hand.
* *Olive and white bean side* Preheat the oven to 180°C (350°F). In a small ovenproof dish, combine 400 g (14 oz) drained tinned white beans and your excess olives, whole, with a generous splash of the liquid, plus something else wet (olive oil, stock or wine), a knob of butter, a few sliced garlic cloves, lots of salt and pepper and a woody herb sprig (oregano, rosemary, bay leaf, thyme). Bake for 20 minutes or so, until hot and bubbling. Serve with fish, roasted vegetables or flat breads (p 168).

Tapenade

Tapenade is all the tastiest things pounded or blitzed together to make an intensely flavoured spread for bread, to serve with tomatoes or white fish, or to use as a pizza base or in a toasted sandwich. It consists of green or black olives, capers, garlic, olive oil and anchovies. Use what you have and what you like, gently pulsing the ingredients in a food processor, pounding them with a mortar and pestle or chopping them finely to form a rough paste.

Start with up to 1 cup pitted olives, 1 tbsp capers, 1–2 anchovies if you like them and 1 chopped garlic clove. Add a pinch of dried thyme or oregano and 2–3 tbsp of your best extra virgin olive oil. Blitz, pound or chop to a rough paste, making it looser with more olive oil if you'd like. Use right away or store in the fridge – in a clean jar and covered with a layer of oil – for a very long time.

Onions

Running out of onions is probably a more common problem than being overloaded with them. But if you're wondering how to deal with a few too many onions, we've got some braising, sautéing and relish-making ideas for you. The main onion question we're asked is what to do with half an onion. We've included some tips for you, although our best recommendation is to use the whole onion rather than half an onion if it won't upset the balance of the recipe you're making.

Go with   Some ingredients don't need a 'go with' list, and onions are one of them. Onions go with all savoury vegetables – actually all savoury foods – and in the right context they go with fruits as well. Think pineapple salsa, apple chutney or pickled plums.

Storage   Store onions in a cool, dry and dark place. They're best kept in a well-ventilated basket in the pantry. Peeled, cut or sliced onions can be kept in the fridge for up to 1 week, but need to be stored in a sealed container or bag.

Substitutes   No onions? Opt for leeks or leek tops, spring onions (scallions), shallots, celery, fennel or even a green capsicum (pepper).

Some ideas for using half an onion

* Slice and add it to a small batch of Not So Classic Kimchi (p 486) or Kraut (pp 44, 66).
* Clean your barbecue grill with it – no need for steel wool.
* Make stock. Don't feel like you have to labour over a huge pot all afternoon in order to make home-made stock. We're big believers in making small batches of quick and simple stock every few days, using up scraps from the fridge. Check out the Corn Cob Stock (p 120), the End-of-the-week Scrap Stock (p 446) or the Parmesan Rind Stock (p 99). Half an onion, with the skin on, will give good flavour and colour to stocks that only need 20 minutes' cooking time. See p 445 for more on stock. »

* Grate ½ onion, and soak torn bread in the onion juices. Add oniony bread to meatballs (p 54) or burger mince. There's half an onion in the Peanutty Koftas on p 293.
* **Quick-pickled red onion** Thinly slice ½ red onion (or brown or white) and cover with the Quick-pickling liquid on p 473. Add some chilli flakes, peppercorns and a few allspice berries or cloves. Allow to sit for 20 minutes, then use the pickled onion on tacos or burgers, or in green salads, potato salads (p 362) or toasties.
* **Little red onion salad** Paper-thin slices of red onion sprinkled with salt and a little sugar, a little lemon juice, lots of chopped parsley and a generous sprinkle of sumac.
* **Little brown onion salad** Mix very finely diced ½ brown onion with chopped green olives, chopped walnuts and chopped parsley. Dress with salt, pepper, olive oil and lemon juice.
* **Fire tonic** Place ½ onion, 3 bruised garlic cloves and 2 whole chillies in a jar and cover with apple cider vinegar. Leave to infuse for 4 weeks, then strain and add 2–3 tbsp to a cup of hot water and drink to help soothe coughs and colds.

Oven-roasted onion relish
MAKES 1½ CUPS (200 G), SERVES 4–6 AS A CONDIMENT

This is for when you want onion relish at your barbecue but you don't want to stand around stirring a pot all afternoon. The onions are roasted in vinegar and sugar, and you can add spices and flavours to suit your meal. We've kept it simple with just herbs, salt and pepper here, but feel free to add ground cumin, cloves and cayenne pepper for more intensity.

Preheat the oven to 180°C (350°F). Slice 3 onions in half, then into 1 cm (½ in) strips. Pop them in a casserole dish or other ovenproof dish and add ¼ cup (60 ml) apple cider vinegar, ¼ cup (60 g) brown sugar, 1 tbsp chopped herbs (such as rosemary or thyme), ½ tsp each of salt and pepper, and ¼ cup (60 ml) olive oil. Mix well, cover with the lid or foil and cook in the oven for 60 minutes. Remove the lid or foil and cook for another 15 minutes, until the liquid has evaporated a little and the onions are browning at the edges. Add a little more salt and pepper and serve either hot or at room temperature. Store in a clean jar or airtight container in the fridge for up to 2 weeks.

Beautiful braised onions

SERVES 4

Once you know how to cook, you start to realise that everything is a variation of something else. We've dotted a few of these foundation recipes throughout the book to show you that a sautéed side can become a stew, can become a pasta dish, can become a soup. These beautiful braised onions are a good example of this kind of cooking: you can use them in many different meals. This recipe uses three onions, but we often double or even triple it and have a batch of braised onions in the fridge to use over the next week, whether it's as a side for sausages and steaks, to have on burgers, to pile on top of pasta or to turn into a soup.

In a cast-iron casserole dish with a lid, or a good-sized frying pan with a lid, melt 50 g (1¾ oz) butter with ¼ cup (60 ml) olive oil over medium heat. Add 3 sliced onions, ½ tsp salt and a thyme sprig, then sauté for about 5 minutes. Add ¼ cup (60 ml) fortified wine (vermouth, muscat, sherry, port if you like), put on the lid, reduce the heat to low, and cook gently for at least 1 hour, or until the onions are soft, sweet and falling-apart delicious. Remove the lid and simmer to reduce some of the excess liquid.

Taste, season as needed and transfer to a pretty bowl to serve with grilled meats or roasted vegetables. Store left-overs in the fridge for up to 1 week.

TO TURN INTO A PASTA DISH

While the onions are braising, cook 300 g (10½ oz) pasta. Add the hot pasta to the casserole or frying pan with a little of the pasta water. Pile grated parmesan on top, add plenty of ground black pepper and serve.

TO TURN INTO ONION SOUP

When the onions are rich and delicious-looking, add ½ cup (125 ml) white wine and allow it to bubble for a few minutes. Stir in 2 tbsp plain (all-purpose) flour to thicken, then add 4–6 cups (1–1.5 litres) beef stock (home-made or the best quality you can buy). Simmer for 20 minutes or so, season with salt and pepper, and serve with cheese toasties.

Mirepoix – the base for better-tasting meals

The best thing Alex learnt at cooking school was the importance of a well-cooked mirepoix, the classic French base of chopped onion, carrot and celery sautéed gently and slowly in butter or oil. These vegetables release their aromatics and sweetness and become the base flavour for stews, soups and sauces. Taking your time with this step will seriously amplify the flavour in your meals. We often make a big batch of ad hoc mirepoix at the end of the week as a way to use up the last few tired celery stalks or the browning half fennel bulb, then store it in the fridge or freezer to use at a later stage.

Start by looking in your fridge for any of the following vegetables that can be 'sweated' in oil or butter: onions, leeks, spring onions (scallions), celery, fennel, carrot, parsnip, garlic, capsicum (pepper), shallots, a little cabbage. If you have some bacon or ham that needs using, slice it up and chuck it in too. Try to match compatible flavours – please don't put parsnip and capsicum in the same pot.

It's important to cut everything to a similar size and shape for uniform cooking. If your final dish has a relatively short cooking time, cut everything very small; if it's a long, slow cook, the pieces can be bigger.

Heat a generous amount of oil or butter in a medium–large saucepan over medium heat, add the onions and leeks, if using, and sauté. Once they're starting to soften, add the garlic and other vegetables, then reduce the heat to low and sweat the vegetables gently – you're not looking for any browning, just sweet, flavoursome and juicy veg. Really take your time with this step – the longer the cooking, the more flavour will be released into the rest of the meal.

You can also add herbs and finely chopped herb stems. Add thinly sliced dill and parsley stems with the onions, and any other soft herbs closer to the end of cooking. Woody herbs like thyme, rosemary or bay leaf can be added with the garlic.

See garlic, leeks and spring onions for ideas with other alliums.

Oranges

During the winter months our fruit bowls are full of oranges. They give us our daily dose of vitamin C and appear in juice form for breakfast, on our toast as marmalade, and in fruit salads, green salads and desserts. Oranges are a clever two-in-one fruit, as their flesh is juicy and sweet and their peel is bitter, spicy and herbal, making them a very useful ingredient in the kitchen.

Go with   Almonds, walnuts, carrots, fennel, beetroot, onions, olives, capers, other citrus fruits, figs, rhubarb, berries, stone fruits, pomegranate, avocado, bitter green leaves, mushrooms, all the herbs, tahini, dark chocolate, vanilla, honey, poppy seeds, warm spices (cinnamon, allspice, cloves, star anise), fennel seeds, mustard, pepper, chilli, mozzarella, cured meats

---

Storage   Oranges can be kept in a fruit bowl on the counter for a week or so, but if you've bought a huge bag, pop half the oranges in the crisper compartment of the fridge for a few weeks – they need air, though, so don't wrap them tight.

Substitutes   If you don't have oranges, start with the orange-coloured citrus like mandarins or cumquats. Next you could reach for a lemon or a grapefruit, but you'll need to adjust the recipe's sweetness accordingly.

Some ideas for using the last orange in the fruit bowl

* When you're out of maple syrup and pancakes or French Toast (p 51) are almost on the table, make this quick sauce. Put the juice of 1 orange in a small saucepan with 1 very generous tbsp honey and a big knob of butter. Gently warm to melt the butter. Whisk with a fork and serve.
* Zest and juice 1 orange and add to a tray of roast vegetables like fennel wedges, beetroots, pumpkin (squash), carrots (p 77) or sweet potatoes, with salt, pepper and oil.
* Add orange juice and zest to Simple Brown Sugar Caramel (p 125). Pour over pancakes, ice cream and cakes. »

* Oranges are high in pectin, so add your last orange to a batch of jam. Rhubarb and orange jam is an excellent winter jam for toast and baked goods. Follow the Foolproof Jam recipe on p 389.
* Roast orange slices in a 220°C (425°F) oven for 10–15 minutes, or until caramelised, then tear them up and toss through salads and grainy dishes for a zesty bite.
* Clean the sink. Sprinkle half an orange with salt and rub all over your sink. Rinse well and voilà. See also p 319.
* *Orange vinaigrette* Make this when there are no lemons in the house and you have a salad that needs dressing. In a jar, combine the juice and zest of 1 orange, 2 tbsp olive oil, 1 tsp dijon mustard, 1 tbsp apple cider vinegar, and a pinch each of salt and pepper, and a pinch of sugar or 1 tsp marmalade. Shake well.
* *Orange and rosemary tea* Peel 1 orange with a vegetable peeler, then squeeze it for juice. Pour the juice into a small saucepan with 2 cups (500 ml) water and add the peel pieces. Pop in a big rosemary sprig and a cinnamon stick, and bring to the boil. Remove from the heat, add 1–2 tbsp honey, and leave to steep for 15–30 minutes. Strain, reheat and enjoy.

Sweet oranges to end a meal

SERVES 3–4

Cut the skin and pith off 3 oranges, then thinly slice the flesh into rounds. Lay the orange slices on a platter so they look beautiful, and sprinkle with a little sugar, ground cinnamon and rosewater or Cointreau. Or drizzle with any of the home-made syrups in the book – basil stem (p 191), mint (p 197), lemongrass (p 204), ginger (p 176), pineapple skin (p 353) or mandarin (p 258).

Savoury orange salad

SERVES 3–4 AS A SIDE

Cut the skin and pith off 3 oranges, then thinly slice the flesh into rounds. Arrange the orange slices on a flat platter, drizzle with good-quality extra virgin olive oil, and sprinkle with salt and plenty of pepper. Scatter pretty Quick-pickled Red Onion (p 312) on top, adding 2–3 spoonfuls of pickling liquid, then finish with chopped dill or parsley and/or crumbled feta and ½ tsp fennel seeds. Serve this with a whole roast fish for a very impressive meal. Or with rich cheeses and good bread, a chickpea dish or grilled (broiled) lamb.

Orange and chocolate cake

Follow the Whole-lemon and Chocolate Cake recipe (p 241), using 300 g (10½ oz) oranges instead of lemons.

Some ideas for preserving oranges

* **Spiced orange marmalade** For your toast in winter. Follow the Grapefruit Marmalade recipe (p 179), using oranges instead of grapefruit, and adding a muslin spice bag with 1 knob of fresh ginger bruised with the flat of a knife, 2 cinnamon sticks, 1 tbsp black peppercorns and a few star anise or cloves. Or make the Orange Jam below.
* **Ginger and orange syrup** For cocktails and cakes. Follow the Mandarin Syrup recipe (p 258), adding 1 tbsp grated fresh ginger.
* **Sweet and sour orange relish** Use the Sweet and Sour Quick Mandarin Relish recipe (p 259), replacing the mandarins with oranges.
* **Orange-flavoured butter** Follow the method in Some Ideas for Preserving Lemons (p 240). It's delicious on waffles, for frying French Toast (p 51), or for sautéing fennel.

Orange jam

MAKES 4 x 250 ML (9 OZ) JARS

This is a sweet and savoury orange jam, rather than a marmalade, spiked with cloves and peppercorns, plus a little salt and a splash of vinegar to cut through the sweetness and give it a bitier edge. Eat this jam on crepes, French Toast (p 51), toast with ricotta, and even a chicken and mayonnaise sandwich. Use it as a base for meat marinades, or add 1–2 tbsp when deglazing a pan with white wine. And give the recipe a go with any other citrus. Lemon and bay leaf jam is a favourite with us.

For this jam, you only need the inside of the fruit, but there's a lot of flavour in the peel, so make sure you keep it and read about all the delicious things you can do with it on the following pages.

Cut the peel and pith off about 2 kg (4 lb 8 oz) oranges and weigh the flesh. You'll need about 1 kg (2 lb 4 oz) orange flesh. Remove any seeds and cut the flesh into 2 cm (¾ in) pieces. In a wide saucepan or jam pan, combine the fruit pieces, 1 cup (250 ml) water, 4 bay leaves, ½ tsp black peppercorns and 4 whole cloves. Place over low heat and gently soften the orange until the pieces are starting to break down, about 20 minutes. You may need to add a little more water as they start to soften. »

Add 600 g (1 lb 5 oz) white (granulated) sugar, ½ tsp salt and ¼ cup (60 ml) apple cider vinegar (optional), stirring to dissolve the sugar and salt. Increase the heat to medium and bring the jam to a rolling boil. Because the pectin is so high in this jam, it should only take 15–20 minutes to reach setting point (p 503).

Sterilise 4 × 250 ml (9 oz) jars (p 501). When the jam is ready, carefully remove the jars from the oven and place on the bench. Allow to cool for 1–2 minutes, then carefully spoon the jam into hot jars, making sure to distribute the bay leaves and peppercorns evenly between all four. Wipe the rims clean with paper towel and seal immediately. Leave to cool, then check the lid for the correct seal (p 503). Store in a cool, dark place for up to 1 year. Once opened, store in the fridge for up to 6 months.

ORANGE PEEL

Before you juice or eat an orange, zest it or carefully remove the outer orange skin with a vegetable peeler, avoiding as much pith as possible. There's so much flavour in the peel, and it adds spicy, citrusy kapow to slow cooking and baking. See p 239 for how to store grated zest or p 259 for how to make your orange peel last by dehydrating it.

Some ideas for using orange peel

* ***Orange pepper*** Grind dried orange peel to a powder in a food processor or spice grinder, or with a mortar and pestle. Make orange sugar or orange salt by adding the powder to a jar of salt or sugar, but our favourite trick is to add it to ground pepper, making an intense seasoning for grilled meats, roasted vegetables, salad dressings or noodle dishes, or to sprinkle on ricotta on toast. For every 50 g (1¾ oz) ground black or white pepper, add 1 tbsp dried orange powder. Shake well and store in an airtight jar or container in the pantry. Black pepper will give an instant bite; white pepper will create a warmth that creeps up on you. Or try a mix of both. Experiment with adding other ingredients to your orange pepper, like fennel seeds, chilli flakes or sesame seeds.
* ***Orange peel bitters*** Experiment with making orange peel bitters for G&Ts. Use the Grapefruit Skin Bitters recipe (p 180).

Spent-orange-halves kitchen cleaner

Pop your discarded orange peel or halves into a big old jar, cover with white vinegar and seal. Let it sit for a few weeks, or up to a few months. Strain, discard the peel and return the liquid to the jar. To make a quick kitchen cleaner, combine equal parts water, orange-infused vinegar and a little washing-up liquid in a spray bottle.

See cumquats, grapefruit, lemons, limes and mandarins for ideas with other citrus. *See also* preserved lemon.

Parsnips

Sure a parsnip looks like a carrot dressed as a ghost for Halloween, but its flavour puts it in a league of its own. It has a nutty, spicy earthiness that's very welcome in winter when it's seen haunting the markets. As parsnips have fallen out of fashion in Australia, knowledge about what to do with them seems to have all but vanished. Hence the odd parsnip gets bought and then goes rubbery in the fridge, never standing a chance. But parsnips are really very versatile. They love to be mashed, roasted, fried, grated – you name it, parsnips will deliver.

Go with Peas, carrots, pumpkin (squash), onions, leeks, potatoes, fennel, beetroot, mushrooms, bitter leaves, apples, pears, cinnamon, cloves, nutmeg, parsley, hard cheeses, cream, lentils, pork, chicken, white fish, bacon, walnuts, hazelnuts, thyme

---

Storage Store unwashed parsnips wrapped in a clean damp tea towel (dish towel) in the crisper section of the fridge for 2–3 weeks. Re-dampen every few days. Cooked parsnip can be stored in an airtight container in the fridge for up to 3 days.

Substitutes Go for a carrot for texture, but fennel for strong flavour. A potato could also work.

Some ideas for using up a parsnip or two

* Don't be afraid to add parsnips to sweet baked goods. Use parsnips in the Seedy Breakfast Muffins (p 371). Be generous with the nutmeg.
* Include diced parsnip in Wally Rath's Barley Vegetable Soup (p 30) for some old-fashioned comfort.
* ***Mashed parsnips*** They're absolutely delicious. Slice parsnips, place in cold water and boil until soft. Add milk or buttermilk and butter, then mash. Season with salt and pepper. »

* **_Parsnip and leek soup_** Replace potato with parsnips in the Leek and Potato Soup (p 236) for a spin on a classic.
* **_Savoury parsnip muffins_** These are really good. Make the Whatever-cheese Eggy Muffins (p 93) with grated parsnip, nutmeg and black pepper.

Parsnip fries

Are you going to trick the children with these more nutritious fries? No. Is this a very simple way to be restaurant-level fancy? Yes. Serve parsnip fries with some grilled white fish and everyone will think you've changed careers.

Begin by julienning 4–5 parsnips: halve each parsnip lengthways, then lay cut side down and slice into long thin strips. In a deep-fryer or large heavy-based saucepan, heat 2 cups (500 ml) frying oil (such as vegetable oil or rice bran oil) until very hot. A good test is to pop a little piece of bread in and if it turns golden brown in about 20 seconds, you're really to roll. In small batches, fry the parsnips for 10–15 minutes, depending on how thick you cut them, or until golden. Carefully remove with a slotted spoon or tongs and drain on paper towel. Continue until all the parsnip is fried. Sprinkle with salt and pepper and serve with a little bowl of mayonnaise flavoured with mustard.

Winter parsnip and hazelnut salad

In winter, roasted vegetable salads can be meals in themselves or make for hearty sides. Preheat the oven to 180°C (350°F). Halve 3–4 parsnips lengthways, then slice into long strips, but not too thin or they will burn. Place them in a roasting tin, drizzle oil of your choice over them, and sprinkle with a good pinch of salt and pepper. Roast for 25–30 minutes, until soft and golden. Meanwhile, toast ½ cup (75 g) hazelnuts using either the oven or dry frying pan method (pp 285–86). Allow to cool, then chop roughly. Transfer the cooked parsnips to a serving dish, then scatter the hazelnuts and some chopped parsley over the top. Dress with Classic Mustard Vinaigrette (p 283). You could also add a sprinkling of Home-made Bacon Bits (p 23) for even more flavour.

Parsnip rosti

MAKES ABOUT 8

Rostis make a good meal when you're at the end of the weekly vegetable shop. These are easily adaptable with other vegetables of a similar texture, such as potato, kohlrabi or carrot, or a combination of what you have. Serve with a leafy salad and some buttered crusty bread.

Coarsely grate 2 parsnips (300–350 g/10½–12 oz) into a bowl. (If using potato, squeeze out the excess moisture.) Add 1 small diced onion, 1 beaten egg, 1 tbsp cream, buttermilk or yoghurt, 2 tbsp plain (all-purpose) flour, ½ tsp salt and ¼ tsp grated nutmeg. Mix everything gently to combine. Heat ¼ cup (60 ml) frying oil, such as rice bran oil, in a large frying pan over medium–low heat. Working in batches, fry ¼ cupfuls of the parsnip mixture a few at a time. Fry for about 7 minutes on each side or until golden. Drain on paper towel and enjoy.

Passionfruit

Fruity sweet, but with the acidity of lemon, passionfruit are old-school backyard fare, perfect for summer breakfasts, afternoon-tea baking and home-made ice cream. If you're lucky enough to have a vine, you'll be desperate for ways to get through them, or if you've bought quite a few and have no idea how to use them, we've got you.

Goes with	Passionfruit is a key ingredient in the old-favourite fruit salad mix – kiwi fruit, banana and strawberry. Or head to the tropics and combine passionfruit with papaya, coconut, mango, custard apples, pineapple and mint, honey, white rum and ginger. And don't forget the creamy classics – vanilla ice cream, whipped cream and yoghurt.
Storage	If the weather isn't too hot, store passionfruit at room temperature; if it's sweltering, pop them in the fridge. If you're not going to get through them in a week or so, you can freeze the pulp in small containers or in ice-cube trays, adding a little sugar to each cube to help preserve the colour and texture.
Substitutes	Try mango, pineapple or nectarine with a little lemon juice to match the acidity and sweetness of passionfruit.

Some ideas for using up passionfruit

* Stir passionfruit pulp, a little caster (superfine) sugar and runny honey through creamy yoghurt. Top with sliced banana and toasted nuts or toasted coconut.
* Pile passionfruit and sliced banana on Meringue (p 152), with lots of fresh cream.
* **Passionfruit icing** In a heatproof bowl, put 1½ cups (185 g) icing (confectioners') sugar, 2 tbsp butter and the pulp of 2–3 passionfruit. Place the bowl over a saucepan of simmering water, ensuring the bowl doesn't touch the water, and mix until soft and spreadable. Use passionfruit icing for vanilla cakes, banana cakes or hummingbird cakes, or sandwich between two sweet biscuits.

* ***Fruity iced tea*** Follow the Peach Iced Tea recipe (p 332), using the pulp from 4–6 passionfruit, replacing the black tea with green tea, and adding some mint leaves.

Passionfruit syrup for desserts and cordial

MAKES ABOUT 1½ CUPS (375 G)

Put 1 cup (250 g) passionfruit pulp and ½ cup (110 g) white (granulated) sugar in a small saucepan. Place over low heat, stirring until the sugar dissolves. Remove from the heat just before it reaches a simmer, then allow to cool. Pour into a clean jar as is, or strain if you want to remove the seeds. Store in the fridge for about 1 month.

Passionfruit curd

Turn passionfruit into a spread for summer afternoon teas. Perfect in sponges or on scones or pikelets. Follow the Just-about-anything Curd recipe (p 155), using ½ cup (125 g) passionfruit pulp – from 3–5 passionfruit, depending on their size.

Passionfruit gelato

MAKES 2 CUPS (500 ML)

Making your own gelato really isn't such a big deal, but the results certainly are. Passionfruit makes a sweet and tart gelato that's perfect for dinner when it's 1000 degrees outside. Or have it for dessert if you're being more sensible.

You need 1 cup (250 g) passionfruit pulp (from 6–8 passionfruit). Halve each passionfruit, scoop out the pulp and set aside. In a saucepan combine a little under 1 cup (220 g) white (granulated) sugar and 100 ml (3½ fl oz) water over low heat, stirring until the sugar has completely dissolved. Remove from the heat, mix in the passionfruit pulp and let it cool completely. Whip ½ cup (125 ml) thick (double) cream to soft peaks then stir into the sugar and passionfruit mix.

If you have an ice-cream maker, lucky you! Follow the instructions and away you go. If you don't, no bother: pour the mix into a plastic container and pop in the freezer for 1 hour. Take the mixture out, give it a good mix and pop back in the freezer. Repeat this every hour for 3–4 hours. Once the gelato is solid, store in the freezer for up to 1 month. Make sure you remove the gelato from the freezer to soften for about 20 minutes before serving, as it is quite dense.

PASSIONFRUIT SKINS

Whole passionfruit jam
MAKES 2 x 300 ML (10 OZ) JARS

We once ran a preserving competition and one of the entries was the most beautiful purple jam. The label said 'Passionfruit Jam', but we were perplexed by the colour, so we rang the maker and she blew our minds when she explained that she used the skins in her jam-making for colour, flavour and pectin. While she didn't share her recipe, we've tried our best to replicate it.

This recipe is for a small batch, using 5–6 passionfruit, but it doubles well, so if passionfruit are cheap, or you or a neighbour are growing them in the garden, make a bigger batch.

Cut 5–6 passionfruit in half and scoop the pulp into a bowl. Put the skins in a medium–large saucepan with 3 cups (750 ml) water and the juice and zest of 1 lemon. Bring to a simmer, then reduce the heat and cook, covered, for 25–30 minutes. During this time the white part of the passionfruit skins should turn purple. Remove from the heat, fish the passionfruit halves out of the pot and allow to cool a little. Scrape out the soft purple pulp from the insides and discard the shells, then return the pulp to the pot and mix well. Add 2 cups (440 g) white (granulated) sugar and place over medium heat, stirring to dissolve, then simmer for 20 minutes, until the jam is thick and glossy. Stir through the passionfruit pulp and cook for another 10 minutes or until the jam reaches setting point (p 503). Pour into clean jars and store in the fridge for up to 6 months, or pour into hot sterilised jars (p 501), and if the seal is good (p 503), store in the pantry for up to 1 year. If you're worried about them keeping through a hot summer or you live in a hot climate, you could heat-process (p 502) your jars for 10 minutes.

Pasta

Some of our most boring food conversations are the most helpful in the kitchen. For about three years now we've been talking about how much pasta is the right amount to cook. We're really fun at parties.

Sometimes you want leftovers, and sometimes leftovers are a pain in the arse that even as you put them in the fridge you know are going to end up in the bin. One of the keys to a low-waste kitchen is not overcooking. Figure out how much your household is going to eat and cook that much, or make enough for another meal, not just a strange left-over amount that no one's going to eat.

Goes with   You don't need to be told what goes with pasta, so instead we'll tell you what doesn't go with pasta: rockmelon (cantaloupe), peanut butter, ice cream and banana. Unless you're 10 years old and having a gross-food competition.

Storage   Our main tip with pasta is to only sauce as much cooked pasta as you're going to eat. A container of left-over cooked pasta without sauce is much more adaptable and versatile than trying to figure out how to turn a weird amount of pesto pasta into another meal. Plain cooked pasta will also last longer in the fridge than sauced pasta. Season left-over cooked pasta with a little oil and salt to stop it turning into a congealed lump, and store in the fridge for up to 5 days. You can also freeze left-over cooked and oiled pasta for up to 3 months. Store uncooked dried pasta in a sealed airtight container in the pantry.

Substitutes   We're not huge fans of pretending something is pasta if it isn't. You're not going to find spiralised zucchini (courgette) spaghetti or grated cauliflower risoni on our tables. Rice, barley and couscous can be served with most pasta sauces, while other wheat noodles, such as udon or soba, will taste different but could be used if the context is right.

How much pasta do you need per person? We can't tell you exactly how much pasta to factor in for each person because every household is different and every stomach is different, but our rule of thumb is 75 g (2¾ oz) uncooked pasta per person and serve your pasta dish with a salad. If this doesn't feel like enough, increase it to 100 g (3½ oz) per person and see if you end up with leftovers. If you want a proper amount of leftovers, get out your calculator (which is actually a very useful tool in the kitchen).

LEFT-OVER COOKED PASTA

If there's not enough pasta for another full pasta meal, use a small amount of cooked pasta in other dishes. Simplest Minestrone Soup (p 36) and Ribollita (p 53) are the usual suspects, or try one of our 'use it up' recipes that follow.

Two-minute cup-a-soup

Who doesn't love a two-minute noodle soup? This is what we have in the fridge when we're trying to encourage the kids to feed themselves something that doesn't come from a packet. It's basically good stock and pre-cooked pasta – all ready to go, with minimal effort. If they're legends they might add some frozen peas.

Teach them to put 1½ cups (375 ml) stock in a saucepan with up to 1 cup (about 175 g) cooked pasta. Add a splash of soy sauce and bring to a simmer. (Side note, this isn't just for kids. We eat it all the time.) Amp it up with kimchi (p 486), chilli, baby spinach or spring onions (scallions).

Head to stock (p 445) for more tips on stock-making and two-minute soup ideas.

'Not from a tin' spaghetti jaffles

This tastes like the tinned spaghetti everyone secretly loves, but better. Turn it into a sealed toasted sandwich and eat it in front of the TV.

For every 1 cup (about 175 g) cooked spaghetti make the quantity of sauce below, scaling the recipe up or down depending on how many jaffles you're making. Combine 2 tbsp tomato paste (concentrated purée), 2 tsp worcestershire sauce, a pinch each of sugar and salt, ¼ tsp garlic powder or ½ finely chopped garlic clove, ¼ tsp dried oregano and 2 tbsp finely grated parmesan. Mix well with a fork then add the cooked spaghetti and stir through, adding a little oil if you need to loosen things up. Butter 2 slices of bread. Lay the first, butter side down, in a sandwich toaster (or jaffle iron), place the spaghetti mixture on top, finish with the second slice of bread, butter side up and close the lid. Cook until toasted to your liking. Feel free to add more cheese, or ham or chilli sauce.

Fried pasta

A good way to heat left-over plain pasta and turn it into something with a bit of wow is to fry it.

Heat 2–3 tbsp oil in a large frying pan over medium heat and sauté something you have in the fridge – sliced button mushrooms, sliced fennel, torn kale, chopped cherry tomatoes (really, anything goes). Once they're starting to soften, add a few sliced garlic cloves and 1 tbsp of something salty and delicious, such as anchovies, chopped olives, capers or preserved lemon. Season with pepper and a little salt, then transfer to a bowl. Add a little more oil to the pan, then fry your left-over cooked pasta, undisturbed, for at least 1 minute. Shake the pan, then leave it undisturbed for another minute. Repeat until the pasta gets a little brown and crunchy. Return the vegetable mix to the pan with the pasta and cook for another 1–2 minutes. Top with cheese or fresh herbs and eat immediately.

Pasta frittata

SERVES 4–6

Now before you skip over this recipe because it sounds a bit ordinary, give this pasta frittata a chance. It's garlicky and parmesany and no one complains when you serve it. It's good for simple minimal-ingredient dinners, cuts well for lunchboxes and reheats for breakfast. And it uses up the strange amounts of cooked pasta in the fridge – penne, shells, even spaghetti. Here we mean cooked pasta with no sauce; a little oil and salt and pepper is okay, but please don't make this with left-over spaghetti bolognese.

Follow the Spanish Potato Omelette recipe (p 150), replacing the potatoes with 1–3 cups (about 175–525 g) cooked pasta; you'll only need to sauté the pasta with the garlic for 1–2 minutes. Before the frittata goes in the oven, top it with extra cheese.

UNCOOKED PASTA

All we've been talking about so far is cooked pasta, mainly because it gets wasted more often than the dried stuff. Dried pasta is best bought in bulk to minimise packaging, and stored in an airtight container in the pantry. You can add a bay leaf to the container to deter weevils.

If you end up with annoyingly small amounts of different pastas, tip them all into one big jar. Over time you'll have enough pasta to use in soup or for a whole meal, and if the sauce is good enough, no one will care that penne and bowties are in the same bowl. Pastas often have different cooking times, so use your common sense – don't mix risoni and jumbo shells in the same jar, for example.

Some simple everyday pasta sauce ideas

* Puttanesca (p 71) to clear out all those half-filled jars in the fridge.
* Fresh Pasta Sauce With Your Eyes Closed (p 462).
* Nothing's in the Cupboard but Chickpeas and Pasta (p 110).
* Egg and Milk Pasta Sauce (p 149).
* Odd-knobs Mac 'n' Cheese (p 101). Not only does it use up all the stray bits of pasta, but it also makes use of all the knobs of cheese in the fridge.

Peaches

When it's peach (or nectarine) season, do yourself a favour and cook them all the ways. Roast them to go with salads, grilled meats, oozy cheeses and good bread using the Savoury Roasted Fruits recipe (p 12). Poach them following the Four Ways to Poach Pears recipe (p 336), or grill them like apricots (p 11), and serve with ice cream and toasted coconut. And don't forget killer Pickled Peaches for fancy cheese plates, to toss through salads or to serve on burgers. Follow the Sweet Mulled Vinegar for Pickling Fruits recipe (p 473).

Go with   They don't say peaches and cream for nothing ... Peaches love dairy products – ice cream, cream, yoghurt, ricotta, mozzarella, parmesan and blue cheese. Pair peaches with most of the other fruits too, especially berries, cherries, oranges and grapes, and with cinnamon, honey and even tomatoes. Nuts, basil, rosemary, black pepper and chilli will add texture and bite.

Storage   Keep underripe peaches on the counter until tender and fragrant. Once ripe, store in the fridge for up to 1 week. Eat peaches raw when they're just ripe and cook with them once they're wrinkled or mushy.

Substitutes   Nectarines, apricots and peaches are like non-identical triplets. Switch them with each other and only their mother would notice. Plums cook in the same way, but have a deeper, spicier flavour. Be sure to turn to apricots (p 10) for more ideas.

Some ideas for transforming a peach or two

* *Peach for lunch* Slice a perfectly ripe peach and pile it on the freshest baguette with blue cheese or ricotta, green leaves and lots of salt and pepper.
* *Peach salsa* Fiery fruit salsa will add bite to tacos, grilled seafood or chicken. Follow the Pineapple Salsa recipe (p 351), using 3–4 not too ripe peaches. »

* ***Savoury peach salad*** Cut a ripe peach, an avocado and a cucumber into 3 cm (1¼ in) dice or similar-sized wedges. Put in a bowl, drizzle with olive oil, salt, pepper and lemon juice, and mix gently. Add plenty of torn herb leaves – coriander (cilantro), mint or basil – then scatter Seedy Salad Mix (p 409) on top.
* ***Peach chicken*** Follow the Apricot Chicken recipe (p 11), replacing the apricots with 2–3 peaches or nectarines, or a mix of all three stone fruits.

Peach iced tea

MAKES ABOUT 3 CUPS (750 ML)

Put 2–3 chopped very ripe peaches (1–2 cups) in a large saucepan and add 3 cups (750 ml) water, ¼ cup (55 g) white (granulated) sugar, and a rosemary sprig or a few strips of lemon peel or a cinnamon stick. Simmer for 10 minutes, then remove from the heat. Add 2 teabags or 1 tbsp black tea leaves in a muslin bag, then leave for at least 10 minutes for the flavours to infuse.

Taste to see if the tea flavour is strong enough for you. When it is, remove the teabags and let the peach infuse a little more, adding up to 1 tbsp honey if you'd like it a little sweeter. Strain, bottle and store in the fridge for 2–3 days. Serve over ice with a squeeze of lemon juice.

Peach crumble

SERVES 4–6

Preheat the oven to 180°C (350°F) and butter a small ovenproof dish. Remove the stones from 4 peaches, then slice thinly and layer in the dish. Drizzle or scatter with 2–3 tbsp maple syrup or brown sugar, sprinkle over a pinch of ground cinnamon or a squeeze of lemon juice, and add a few little dots of butter. Top with a batch of uncooked Oaty Crumble Topping (p 302) and bake for 30 minutes or until golden and bubbling at the edges. Serve with Pouring Custard (p 274) or cream.

Peach jam

The best summer jam – it's both old-fashioned and unexpected, and makes a beautiful breakfast spread or a very handsome gift. Follow the Foolproof Jam recipe (p 389), using 1 kg (2 lb 4 oz) peaches, and limes or oranges instead of lemons.

'What's in the fruit bowl' relish

MAKES 3-4 x 300 ML (10 OZ) JARS

This is for the fruit bowl dregs at the end of the week, or for those peaches you thought you'd turn into a tart and then promptly forgot about. It's the no-guilt waste hack of your dreams, cleaning out the fruit bowl or the crisper in one hit. Go ahead and use those wrinkly apples, overripe pears, the nectarines that have no flavour, or a combination of everything. Think of it as a fruit-salad relish. This is a recipe for a 1 kg (2 lb 4 oz) batch, but feel free to halve or double the quantities depending on whatever fruit, sugar, vinegar and spices you have on hand. Serve at a barbecue, with cured meats, with bread and cheese, on a burger or with fried eggs.

Heat ¼ cup (60 ml) oil of your choice in a frying pan. Sauté 1 sliced onion until soft and translucent. Add your flavours and sauté for another 1–2 minutes. You can choose your own adventure here, but here are some suggestions to get you started:

- 3 tbsp grated fresh ginger, 2 tsp mustard seeds and ½ tsp ground black pepper
- 3 sliced garlic cloves, 1–2 sliced chillies, 2 tsp ground cumin and a pinch of cayenne pepper
- 1 cinnamon stick, 2–3 whole cloves, the zest of 1 lemon or orange and lots of ground pepper.

Add 1 kg (2 lb 4 oz) chopped fruit (no need to peel), and mix well. Pour in 1 cup (250 ml) white vinegar, red wine vinegar or apple cider vinegar, 1½ tsp salt and ½ cup (110 g) white (granulated) sugar. Simmer gently until the relish is glossy and thick. Some fruits have a lower water content, so if the relish is looking dry but the fruit is still hard, add ¼ cup (60 ml) water and keep cooking. Taste and adjust the seasoning, adding more spices, seasoning or citrus zest if needed.

Store in a clean jar or airtight container in the fridge for 2–3 months. Or spoon into sterilised jars (p 501), heat-process (p 502) for 15 minutes and store in the pantry for up to 1 year.

See apricots, cherries and plums for ideas with other stone fruit.

Pears

In our opinion the boring old pear is actually a legend, jumping from breakfast to dinner to dessert, into a lunchbox and cakes, and in and out of the preserving pans. Supermarket pears are often green rocks in the fruit bowl for weeks and then become mushy the second you turn your back. Use unripe green pears in salads, grate them into your sauerkraut, or pickle them and add them to toasties. Once they're fragrant and starting to ripen, poach them, roast them or serve them with hard cheese as a snack. When they've hit the downhill slide towards the compost, turn to chutneys, fruit butters and baked goods.

Go with	Nuts, cheeses, rosemary, sage, apples, quince, lemons, bananas, persimmons, dried fruits, chocolate, celery, beetroot, brussels sprouts, cabbage, daikon, radishes, turnips, pumpkin (squash), silverbeet (Swiss chard), ginger, sunflower seeds, horseradish, cured meats, allspice, cardamom, cinnamon, cloves, star anise, pepper
Storage	If you like pears crunchy, store them in the fridge for 1–2 weeks. If you're after perfectly ripe pears, store them at room temperature until ripe, then pop them in the fridge or leave them where they are and eat them as soon as you can smell their musty perfume.
Substitutes	Firm pears can be replaced with apples and vice versa. Head to apples (p 5) for more recipe ideas. Overripe pears can be mashed like a banana, so if you're overwhelmed by almost rotting pears, turn to bananas (p 24) and have a go at the Black Banana Jam, Simplest Banana Bread or Banana Ketchup, using pears instead. And cooked pears have a similar vibe to cooked quince, so swap them with each other if you want to embrace your inner Maggie Beer.

Some ideas for using up a pear or two

✳ Use pears instead of apples in Jaimee's Apple Bake (p 7) for a simple afternoon tea or dessert.

✳ If your pears are overripe and no one's going to eat them, turn the Simplest Banana Bread (p 27) into Simple Pear Bread. Grate or mash 2 pears and add some ground cinnamon and chopped hazelnuts.

✳ If there's one very soft pear in the fruit bowl, try the Banana Porridge (p 25) with a mashed pear. Add some grated nutmeg and top with yoghurt and honey.

✳ Add thinly sliced pear to a cheese and pickle toastie for a little extra sweetness.

✳ Thinly slice 1 firm pear or cut it into matchsticks, and toss through a cabbage slaw, Basic Brussels Slaw (p 60), bitter greens salad, Raw Grated Beet Salad (p 45) or Whole Fennel Salad (p 158).

✳ Add a sliced or grated nashi pear or firm green pear to Not So Classic Kimchi (p 486).

✳ Add pear to a ham pizza instead of pineapple. All the perks of fruit and cured meat, without the judgement.

Savoury pear salad

SERVES 3–4 AS A SIDE

Salad doesn't always have to be a bowl of greens, and as we keep saying, we're big on the simple salads that highlight one ingredient. So if there are no greens in the house, try either of these mostly pear salads.

Cut 2 firm pears or nashi pears into long, thin strips and place in a bowl. Drizzle with sherry or balsamic vinegar, season with salt and pepper, then mix very gently. Transfer to a flattish serving plate and top with crushed toasted walnuts or hazelnuts, and thyme leaves (or chopped dill leaves or chopped fennel fronds). Add some shavings of parmesan or crumbled blue cheese, if you like, then finish with a drizzle of your best extra virgin olive oil.

Alternatively, dress the pear strips with Lime Dressing (p 253) and top with toasted sesame seeds and plenty of coriander (cilantro) leaves.

Roasted pears

Roasting pears for salads of bitter greens with toasted nuts, to serve with meats, or as a dessert, is a good way of dealing with ageing fruit. Cut pears in half, remove the core, then cut into wedges before roasting. For a savoury version, follow the Savoury Roasted Fruits method (p 12).

Pear and rosemary relish

Turn to the 'What's in the Fruit Bowl' Relish recipe (p 333) and make a pear and rosemary chutney. Flavour with chopped rosemary, the juice and zest of 1 lemon, some ground cinnamon or allspice and plenty of ground black pepper.

Four ways to poach pears (or any other fruit)

Poaching fruits is a classy skill to have up your sleeve. While it's not the answer to managing overripe fruit – firm, ripe fruits are best for poaching – it is a nice way to turn a few pieces of fruit into a simple, elegant dessert, something to add to porridge or muesli, or to serve with cheeses or cakes. You can poach any fruits – try figs, pears, rhubarb, quince, apricots, peaches and cherries.

You can also poach fruit in any liquid – water, wine, juice, tea, vinegar, alcohol – with a sweetener like sugar, honey or maple syrup. Throw in some aromatics, such as whole spices, citrus peel, fresh ginger slices, and/or herbs like rosemary, bay leaf and thyme.

We've included four syrups for you to experiment with: one simple sugar syrup, a tea and honey version, a spiced vinegar syrup and a boozy option. These syrup quantities will poach a small amount of fruit: 2 pears cut into halves or quarters, 4 peeled mandarins or 6 figs. If you'd like to poach more fruit or keep your pears whole, you'll need to double the syrup recipe.

In a small–medium saucepan, bring the poaching syrup of your choice (see opposite) to a simmer, then add the flavours of your choice and the fruit of your choice. If the fruit is floating, cut out a baking paper circle and place it on top to help keep the fruit under the liquid. Cover with the lid, reduce the heat to low, then poach gently until the fruit is very tender but not falling apart. The poaching times will vary depending on size and ripeness. Pears can take up to 90 minutes, depending on their firmness; peeled mandarins take about 30 minutes; and figs and cherries take about 10 minutes. Allow the fruit to sit in the syrup until cool, then store in a jar or airtight container in the fridge for up to 10 days. The more sugar, booze or vinegar in the syrup, the longer the poached fruits will last in the fridge.

SUGAR SYRUP

A simple sugar syrup is equal parts sugar and water. You can reduce or increase the sugar to suit your taste – just remember that the more sugar you use, the longer the fruit and syrup will last in the fridge. For desserts we like 2 cups (500 ml) water and ¾ cup (185 g) white (granulated) sugar, with a vanilla bean and the peel of a lemon, peeled off in strips and avoiding the pith.

TEA AND HONEY POACHING SYRUP

For a light, breakfasty option, poach in tea and honey syrup. This can be used for any fruits, but is especially nice with whole mandarins, whole figs, apricots or dried fruits. Pour 2 cups (500 ml) water into a small saucepan and add 2 teabags or 1 tbsp tea leaves. Bring to a simmer over medium heat, then remove from the heat and leave to steep for 10 minutes. Strain, then return the tea to the saucepan, adding ¼ cup (90 g) honey, 2 tbsp sugar and flavours of your choice. Slices of fresh ginger, cardamom pods and strips of orange peel all work well with tea and honey. It will last in the fridge for 1 week.

SWEET MULLED VINEGAR FOR PICKLING FRUITS

For a sweet pickled option, try poaching fruits in the mixture on p 473. These lightly pickled fruits can be eaten with cheeses and meats, used in place of dried fruits in savoury dishes, or thinly sliced and tossed through salads, slaws and grains.

BOOZY SYRUP

Red wine and pears make some kind of magic – a classic dessert that's classy but not pretentious. Using wine not only adds another layer of flavour, but also acts as an extra layer of preservation, meaning it will store well in the fridge. Make your syrup with 1 cup (250 ml) wine, 1 cup (250 ml) water and ½ cup (110 g) white (granulated) sugar. Warm spices like star anise, black peppercorns, cinnamon sticks and bay leaves are your go-to aromatics. For poaching summer fruits or more fragrant fruits, use white wine, rosé or left-over sparkling wine. Serve chilled.

TO USE EXCESS POACHING SYRUP

Simmer the poaching syrup for another 5–10 minutes to thicken, then pour into a container and store in the fridge for up to 1 month. Drizzle over French Toast (p 51), use to marinate meats or macerate fruit salad, or even add to sparkling water as a cordial.

Some ideas for using up pear scraps

✱ Head to the Apple Scrap Vinegar recipe (p 9) and make pear scrap vinegar.

✱ Follow the Mango Scrap Syrup recipe (p 264), using the pear cores and peel or any old brown half-pears to make a pear syrup that tastes like liqueur. Add a vanilla bean and some lemon peel to the pot. If you want to amp up the flavour, add a generous splash of brandy to the syrup after cooking.

Peas

Sometimes the only greens in the house are half a bag of frozen peas, or two half-opened bags of peas that have frozen into a solid block. Never fear, you can still get greens on the table.

Peas are little legends, grassy but sweet. Even the frozen ones are flavoursome, because they are snap-frozen at the time of harvesting. Add a handful of peas to the Odd-knobs Mac 'n' Cheese (p 101) and you've basically made a salad.

If you're lucky enough to grow peas, or to buy lovely podded peas in spring, make the most of their freshness. Don't overcook them or add them to a pie, just blanch them lightly in boiling salted water or good-quality stock, and add a little butter to the bowl.

Empty pea pods can also be turned into wine. Head to the Broad Bean Pod Wine recipe (p 33) and you'll eventually be able to make a pea-sling.

Go with   Snow peas (mange tout), green beans, carrots, celery, zucchini (courgettes), fennel, potatoes, silverbeet (Swiss chard), parsnips, buckwheat, horseradish, lentils, chilli, curry, mint, basil, tarragon, dill, rosemary, thyme, lemons, pepper, butter, wine, cream, bacon, ham

---

Storage   Remember to seal frozen peas properly so you don't end up with a freezer full of loose peas – it's very annoying. Fresh peas should go straight from the plant to the cooking pot because they deteriorate rapidly. If you buy them from the market, plan to use them that day or the next.

Substitutes   All the other gentle spring greens could replace peas: broad beans, asparagus, snow peas (mange tout) or chopped green beans.

Some ideas for too many peas

* Turn the 'What's in the Fridge' Vegie Pie Filling (p 451) into a curried pea and potato filling for pasties or samosas. Spice it with curry powder and add a hit of fresh chilli or chilli flakes.
* Blanch 1 cup shelled fresh (155 g) or frozen (140 g) peas then add to the green potato salad (see Anything-goes Potato Salad, p 362).
* A simple pea curry served with rice and an Indian-style pickle makes a very cheap and very satisfying dinner. Head to the Really Easy Green Bean Curry (p 40) and replace the beans with fresh or frozen peas.
* You can pickle peas … but not the frozen ones. If you're an enthusiastic gardener, make a jar of pickled peas with garlic, peppercorns and herbs of your choice, following the Basic Vegetable Pickling recipe (p 472).
* ***Pea and mint fritters*** Make a simple and nutritious meal packed with greens and herbs. Serve as is, with eggs, or on a crusty bread roll with mayonnaise and chilli jam. Use the Green Things Fritters recipe (p 439), replacing 1–2 cups of the spinach with lightly mashed peas.
* ***Pea ful medames*** Jaimee makes the most amazing Broad Bean Ful Medames (p 32). Alex loves it, but as she's too lazy to pod all those broad beans she does a cheat's version using only frozen peas. Choose your own adventure based on your personality.

The simplest pea side
SERVES 2

In a small frying pan over medium heat, melt 2–3 tbsp butter or oil with 1 tbsp mustard, and a pinch each of salt and ground pepper. Add 1 cup shelled fresh (155 g) or frozen (140 g) peas and ½ cup (125 ml) water or stock. Bring to a simmer, then reduce the heat to low and cook, covered, until the peas are bright green and tender. Remove the lid, add a handful of chopped herbs (dill, parsley, mint, tarragon), shake the pan and serve with grilled (broiled) fish or Cauliflower Schnitzels (p 81).

Pea soup

Pea soup is a pleasure to eat, especially with great bread and an excellent glass of wine. You can turn the Green Soup (p 440) into pea soup, replacing the spinach with 2 cups shelled fresh (155 g) or frozen (140 g) peas. Use mint or basil as your herb.

Pea mash

MAKES 1½ CUPS (ABOUT 350 G), SERVES 2–3

Blanch 2 cups shelled fresh (310 g) or frozen (280 g) peas in boiling salted water for 2 minutes. Strain and tip into a food processor with 1 roughly chopped garlic clove, a knob of butter, ¼ tsp each salt and ground pepper and 1 tbsp something creamy – sour cream, cream, cream cheese or soy milk. Blitz to a smooth paste and serve warm or as a side with sausages or a vegetarian pie.

Pea pesto

MAKES 2–3 CUPS (ABOUT 500 G), SERVES 3–4 ON PASTA

Blanch 2 cups shelled fresh (310 g) or frozen (280 g) peas in boiling salted water for 2 minutes. Strain and allow to cool and dry. Transfer to a food processor with ¼ cup (40 g) almonds, ¼ cup (25 g) grated parmesan, ½ tsp salt, 2 garlic cloves and 1 large handful of mint, basil or parsley leaves, or a combination. Blitz to a chunky paste then, with the motor running, slowly add ½ cup (125 ml) oil. Serve in wraps, on toast with a fried egg for breakfast, or on hot buttered pasta.

Spring greens medley

SERVES 4

This is a clean-out-the-fridge recipe to use during spring, when all the greens you bought have a short lifespan but you went out for dinner two nights in a row. Use all those greens here – peas, snow peas (mange tout), lettuce, asparagus, silverbeet (Swiss chard), baby spinach, watercress, broccoli florets, chopped green beans. It's light, clean and a perfect springtime meal. Serve as a side with a baked fish, a roast chicken, a frittata or Green Things Fritters (p 439).

You'll need 500 g (1 lb 2 oz) of any spring greens, so get out the scales and empty out the crisper. Thinly slice lettuce, spinach or silverbeet and cut asparagus into bite-sized pieces.

Heat ¼ cup (60 ml) extra virgin olive oil in a frying pan over low heat, then sauté ½ diced brown onion, ½ sliced leek or 2–3 sliced spring onions (scallions) for 2–3 minutes, then add 3 sliced garlic cloves. Add the greens, a generous pinch of salt and ½ cup (125 ml) water, stock or white wine. Simmer gently, covered, for 5–15 minutes, until everything is cooked. Taste and adjust the seasoning with salt and a good grind of black pepper. Transfer to a serving plate, drizzle with a little more oil and top with any chopped herbs that need using. You could also crumble some goat's cheese and/or shave some parmesan on top.

Persimmons

Persimmons come in astringent and non-astringent varieties. Non-astringent persimmons can be eaten in two quite different ways. Firmer fruits are shaved paper-thin and eaten raw in salads, with cheese platters like a pear or an apple, or served with cured meat – like melon and prosciutto. We once made ham, persimmon and rocket (arugula) pizzas and were very pleased with ourselves. These persimmons can also be eaten ripe and turned into jams and pastes, and used in baking. Then there's the astringent variety, which can only be eaten very ripe, when the flesh is sweet and jelly-like. These are best spooned straight from the skin into your mouth, but can also be cooked with, or turned into ice cream. Note that you can eat the skin of non-astringent persimmons.

Go with	Persimmons are used in Chinese, Japanese and Korean cooking, as well as in Portuguese, Mediterranean and Russian kitchens. Hopefully this helps you pair flavours with them accordingly. Like many fruits, they can be eaten in sweet or savoury dishes, and they go well with other fruits, warm spices (ginger, five-spice, nutmeg, cardamom), nuts, coffee, chocolate and dairy products. Try ripe persimmon with mint, basil and bitter greens. Firm, crunchy persimmons suit chilli, fennel, apples, pears, wombok (Chinese cabbage), vinegar, and salty things like olives.
Storage	If you like your persimmons firm, then store them in the coldest part of the fridge, or your crisper, for 1 week. If you want to ripen them, do so at room temperature, then pop them in the fridge for longer storage. The astringent variety needs to stay in the fruit bowl until very soft to the touch. Let them hang out with bananas to help speed up the process. Once ripe, eat right away, or transfer the flesh to a container and keep in the fridge for 2–3 days, or the freezer for 2–3 months.
Substitutes	Persimmons have their own distinct flavour, but you could use very ripe apricots or nectarines, or cooked quince or plums instead. To replace firm, crunchy persimmon, try rockmelon (cantaloupe), green mango or nashi pear.

Some ideas for using a few firm persimmons

✳ Quick-pickle firm persimmons by slicing them paper-thin and using the Quick pickling Melon recipe (p 272). Serve pickled persimmons with cured meats, in a rocket (arugula) salad with toasted nuts, or as a condiment with spicy fish, rice and stir-fried greens.

✳ Cut a firm persimmon into matchsticks and add to Simplest Wombok Slaw (p 485) or Whole Fennel Salad (p 158).

✳ Hard cheese and sliced persimmon on a cracker is the best afternoon-tea snack.

✳ Goat's cheese, sliced persimmon and watercress on delicious bread is the perfect simple picnic lunch.

✳ Sliced green mango, persimmon, coriander (cilantro) and chilli make a refreshing addition to a cold noodle salad.

Some ideas for using a few ripe persimmons

✳ Peel and slice ripe persimmons, mix with mint leaves and a little lemon juice, then serve on top of vanilla ice cream.

✳ Make the Slow-roasted Oven Jam (p 49) with ripe peeled persimmons instead of berries. Serve on scones or French Toast (p 51).

✳ Freeze overripe persimmons in their skins and be wowed by an instant sorbet (this is best done with the astringent variety, where the ripe fruit is almost like jelly).

✳ Slice peeled ripe persimmons and ripe peaches to make Peach Crumble (p 332).

✳ Turn the Fig Crostata (p 163) into a persimmon tart with honey, almonds and nutmeg.

✳ Spoon ripe persimmon on top of porridge, bircher muesli or yoghurt for breakfast.

Persimmon vinegar

Scoop the flesh of a very overripe persimmon into a clean glass jar. Add 1 tsp sugar and 1 cup (250 ml) apple cider vinegar, then cover with muslin and leave at room temperature for at least 1 week. Once the vinegar is orange and tasting exactly like a persimmon, strain into a jar and store in the fridge. This will last well, but it's delicious, so make it the base for your salad dressings for the weeks ahead.

Persimmon paste

Persimmon paste is like quince paste, but secretly better. Serve with cheese and crackers or a ham sandwich. Follow the Quince Paste recipe (p 376), using ripe persimmons.

Roasted persimmon

Follow the Savoury Roasted Fruits recipe (p 12). Serve with roast chicken or pork, or as a side to a wintery green pie (p 412).

Grilled persimmon: for a simple, fancy dessert

Turn the grill (broiler) to high, cut the tops off ripe persimmons and place the fruits in a small baking tray or heatproof dish. Glaze with a drizzle of honey and squeeze of lime juice. Grill until bubbling and golden brown. Serve with cream, mascarpone cheese or your favourite ice cream.

Pesto

Pesto in the fridge calms Alex down. It's the unspoken backup plan when it's seven o'clock and dinner hasn't even been thought about. Pesto pasta is dinner and a salad in one, the meal you make when really you just want to go to bed.

Pesto takes mere moments to make and can take care of so many different greens – basil in the summer months, parsley or kale in cooler months, and you can also try a combination of all the greens that need using up – see p 191 for a classic pesto recipe and p 193 for green sauce ideas. And don't forget to look at Broccoli Pesto (p 56) or Pea Pesto (p 341).

There's also a great range of store-bought pestos out there. Check the chiller section at the deli or greengrocer – just make sure there's nothing nasty on the ingredient list.

Goes with   Pasta, obviously. Also, bread, potatoes, carrots, chicken, tuna, eggs, tomatoes, cauliflower, broccoli, zucchini (courgettes), eggplant (aubergine), green beans, dried beans, lentils, pizza, burgers, olive oil, mayonnaise

---

Storage   Because of its high oil content, pesto will last well in the fridge. Keep your pesto covered in a layer of oil to stop discoloration and it will last for up to 10 days. You can also freeze pesto in ice-cube trays, then pop them in an airtight container and store them in the freezer for about 3 months.

Substitutes   Make a Bright Green Sauce (p 193) if you have some limp herbs lying around. Or chop up some basil or another soft-leaved herb and drizzle with olive oil.

Some non-pesto-pasta ideas for using up that jar

* Add 2–3 tbsp pesto to the butter mix for the Old-school Garlic Bread (p 52) to make green garlic bread. The same pesto garlic butter would be amazing brushed on grilled corn.
* Try a dollop of pesto on top of Simplest Minestrone Soup (p 36), Green Soup (p 440), lentil soup (p 246) or Left-over-chicken Soup (p 106).
* The Green Things Fritters (p 439) can get even greener with 2–3 tbsp pesto added to the mix.
* Add 2 tbsp pesto to ⅓ cup (85 g) Mayonnaise (p 154) with a squeeze of lemon juice, salt and pepper to make a green sauce for burgers and hot chips (fries).
* Pesto and eggs are best mates. Whisk 2–3 tbsp pesto into eggs before scrambling, or add a few spoonfuls of pesto to an omelette (p 150).
* **Pesto dressing** For tomato salads or warm green beans. If you only have a few scrapings of pesto left, add some olive oil, lemon juice, salt and pepper to the jar. Put the lid on, give it a shake and you have a dressing.
* **Green potato salad** Turn Anything-goes Potato Salad (p 362) green with pesto, peas and lots of mint.
* **Nutty pasta sauce** When you have half a jar of pesto and half a jar of tomato passata (puréed tomatoes) in the fridge, combine them for a nutty pasta sauce. Heat the passata as you normally would, then remove from the heat and stir the pesto through it. Add a dash of cream if you have some that needs using.

Pesto roast potatoes
SERVES 2-4

These are yum. Make them as a side for a roast chicken with a big green salad, or with a tomato salad and grilled haloumi.

Preheat the oven to 200°C (400°F). Boil 4 potatoes in salted water until just tender. Drain and allow to dry. Place ¼–½ cup (60–125 g) pesto into a bowl, loosen with a little olive oil, and season with salt and pepper. Put the potatoes into a roasting tin and, using a potato masher or meat tenderiser, smash the potatoes once so they break open a little and flatten. Cover with pesto, drizzling over a little more oil if needed, and roast undisturbed until golden and crispy, about 1 hour.

Pickles

If your fridge looks anything like ours, the top couple of shelves will be heaving with half-full jars of condiments. It's mainly pickles in both our houses, because we serve them with almost every meal. Once jars start falling on you when you open the fridge door, you know it's time for a clear-out. Our top tip is to transfer all the quarter-filled pickle jars into one big jar to make a mixed pickle, ensuring that everything is covered in pickling liquid, then return it to the fridge.

If you're new to pickles, with only the odd jar in the fridge, you may need some ideas on how to start using them in more ways than on burgers or cheese plates. Just a reminder that when we say pickles we don't just mean cucumbers. We're talking about any vegetables or fruit preserved in pickling vinegar. Head to pp 472–73 to learn how to make your own pickles, or look up 'pickle' in the index for more ideas. And never throw away pickling liquid. That stuff is liquid gold. Read on for tips on using left-over pickling liquid.

Go with   We eat pickles multiple times a day. They go with all cheeses, all breads, meats (especially cured meats) and fish. Stir them through yoghurt, sour cream or mayonnaise. Try them in salads, with grains such as barley, lentils and buckwheat, with chilli, tomatoes, avocado, potatoes and soft herbs such as coriander (cilantro), parsley and dill.

Storage   Unopened purchased or home-made pickles can be kept in a cool, dark place for a very long time. Before you throw them away because they've been at the back of the cupboard for years, open them and investigate. If they smell clean like vinegar, look good (they will darken over time) and taste good, then make burgers. Once a jar of pickles is opened, it should be stored in the fridge. As with all condiments and preserves, the proportion of vinegar will determine how long they last, but up to 6 months in the fridge is usually fine.

Substitutes   Pickles bring a salty, sour and sweet element to a dish. Instead of pickles, experiment with a little relish, olives, capers, anchovies, preserved lemon, tomato paste (concentrated purée), miso, kimchi or sauerkraut.

Some ideas for using up that pickle jar

Hint: by adding pickles to everyday meals.

* A favourite breakfast for us is a soft cheese like goat's cheese, cream cheese or ricotta on toast, topped with pickles and ground black pepper.
* Cheese and pickle toasties for lunch. Be extra generous with the pickles – no one ever puts enough pickles on.
* Pickles add zing and bite to simple salads. For example: add ½ cup cucumber (p 128), zucchini (courgettes, p 496) or fennel (p 158) pickles to potato salads (p 362); try pickled grapes, sliced pickled pears or pickled peaches with leafy greens, toasted nuts and parmesan – it's VERY delicious; add chopped pickles to the Best Barley Side (p 29); or include pickled daikon (p 135), ginger (p 175) or radish in the Cold Noodle and Wombok Salad with Pickles (p 487).
* Burgers, hot dogs, salad sandwiches and falafel rolls wouldn't be the same without pickles.
* Add finely chopped pickles to the Curried-egg Sandwich mix (p 149).
* Add a pickled cumquat or grape to a negroni; make an old-fashioned with a pickled cherry; try some pickled celery in a bloody mary; whip up a dirty martini with a slice of Cucumber Pickles (p 128). And don't forget to add a splash of pickling liquid to the cocktail shaker.
* Make a creamy tartare sauce for fish burgers and hot chips (fries). Follow the recipe on p 94, using any chopped green vegetable pickle.
* One of the best green sauces for grilled (broiled) vegetables and meats, Salsa Verde (p 194) uses herbs, garlic and pickles to make a simple bright-green, tangy condiment.

'Clear out the pickle jars' salsa

This salsa is zingy, spicy and excellent on tacos, hot dogs or sliced tomatoes, or with refried beans and guacamole, or grilled (broiled) fish or chicken.

You need 1 cup pickles. Use either one type of pickle or a mix. Finely dice pickles and put them in a bowl. Add ½ finely diced red or brown onion, 1 thinly sliced green or red chilli (more if you want it hot), 1 cup (30 g) coriander (cilantro) leaves, a pinch of salt and a big squeeze of lime juice. Mix together. If you'd like to add diced tomatoes, diced cucumber, corn kernels or diced avocado, by all means do so.

Some ideas for using up pickling liquid

Pickling liquid is often an overlooked ingredient in the kitchen. It's sour, salty and sweet, and full of flavour, adding acidity and intensity to cooked dishes, salads, marinades and drinks.

* Put just-boiled potatoes in a bowl and splash generously with pickling liquid. Cover and leave to cool – the warm potatoes will absorb the liquid, becoming full of flavour. Use the potatoes to make a potato salad (p 362).
* Add a generous splash to marinades; pickling liquid is an excellent meat tenderiser.
* Make a salad dressing. Just add olive oil and mustard and shake.
* Add 1–2 tsp strained pickling liquid to a cocktail.
* Use a dash in place of lemon juice.
* Add a splash to a stir-fry or brothy soup.

Make more pickles

You can reuse pickling liquid for quick-pickling or fridge-pickling. Strain it into a small saucepan and bring to a simmer. Thinly slice vegies, put them in a jar, then cover them with the hot liquid. Allow to cool, then transfer to the fridge. Let them sit for 1 day before eating; they will last for 2–3 weeks in the fridge. Treat them like a quick pickle (p 473).

PICKLING LIQUID REDUCTION

This is a little like brown sauce. If the fridge is full of pickling liquid, strain it into a small saucepan. Bring to the boil, then simmer until thick. The sugar will help make the sauce syrupy, and the vinegar will make it an intensely flavoured condiment to use on eggs, meats or fried noodles.

Pineapple

The Queen of the Tropics, and one of the most consumed and wasted fruits in the kitchen. A pineapple is quite big, and once it's been cut up and the initial craving has been satisfied, it can hang about listlessly until someone takes it to the bin and says, 'Sorry, I just didn't know what to do with you.' Obviously pineapple is highly snackable, but if you want to make sure you get through a whole one, you'll need to have a good range of sweet and savoury recipes on hand. In summer, a pineapple salad or salsa can refresh on the most sweltering days. The trick to not wasting any ingredient is always having options, so when you buy yourself a great big glorious sunny pineapple, lean in to the pineapple week and mix it up.

Goes with   Mango, coconut, papaya, limes, cumquats, banana, kiwi fruit, passionfruit, melons, coconut and macadamias. Good herbs for pineapple are mint and coriander (cilantro), although the aniseed flavour in basil would work too. Try vanilla, cinnamon, star anise, allspice, peppercorns, ginger and honey when preserving or baking; and for savoury pairings, chilli, salt, cured meats and seafood, avocado and mustard. And don't forget that a ripe pineapple is basically a cocktail, so if you've let your pineapple sit for a little too long, get out the blender and put your bikini on.

Storage   Keep pineapple in the fruit bowl until ripe. You'll know it's ripe when its base starts to smell a little boozy. Then either eat it right away, move it to the fridge for a few more days, or cut the skin off, chop up the flesh and store it in a container in the fridge for 3–4 days.

Substitutes   Pineapple is sweet and acidic, so if you're looking to substitute you'll need to find those elements elsewhere. Try mango and lots of lime juice, green apple and lemon juice, banana and kiwi fruit.

Some ideas for when there's a pineapple in the vegie box

✱ Dice a ripe pineapple, add sugar and a splash of a spirit like white rum. Leave to macerate for 1 hour, then serve with coconut ice cream.

✱ Pickle it. You have two options for pickling pineapple. One is quick and very savoury, to serve in salads or on tacos; it should be eaten within 1 week. Follow the Quick-pickled Melon recipe (p 272). The other option is sweeter and deeper in flavour, and would work with cured meats, a celebratory ham, blue cheese or even with not so sweet desserts. Use the Sweet and Sour Cumquats recipe (p 131).

✱ If you want to use the whole thing up in one go, make hot sauce. Follow the Half-a-Melon Hot Sauce recipe (p 271), replacing the melon with pineapple.

✱ Sear wedges of ripe pineapple in a hot dry frying pan until they start to blacken. Squeeze in some lemon or lime juice to get some juices flowing. Pop on a plate and drizzle with honey, salt and chilli flakes.

✱ Go on, make a pizza. We won't tell anyone.

✱ *Pineapple frappé* You may not have heard the word frappé for 20 years, but if there's a ripe pineapple that needs using, it's worth the trip back to the 1990s. In a blender, blitz 1 cup (about 160 g) chopped pineapple with ice, coconut water or a little coconut milk, some fresh mint and some honey or sugar. You could add bananas or mangoes too, if you like.

✱ *Pineapple whip* Follow the Kiwi Fruit Whip recipe (p 227) for an icy tropical snack.

Pineapple salsa
SERVES 4–6 AS A CONDIMENT

This salsa is a good example of how we like to cook – taking one foundation recipe that we can build on, depending on what's in the fridge and how many we are feeding.

Put 2 cups pineapple, diced or cut into small wedges (about 320 g), in a large bowl. Add 1 finely chopped garlic clove, 2 tsp grated fresh ginger, 1–2 tsp sugar, ¼ tsp salt, the zest and juice of ½ lime – and a thinly sliced chilli, if you'd like some heat. You could add a splash of fish sauce or rice wine vinegar too. Leave the salsa to sit for at least 10 minutes, up to 1 hour, then add a few big handfuls of chopped coriander (cilantro). Taste, adjust the seasoning and serve immediately.

TURN THE SALSA INTO A SALAD
Gently mix enough diced avocado, diced tomato, corn kernels, diced cucumber, thinly sliced capsicum (pepper) and thinly sliced red onion to make 2 cups. Add with the coriander (cilantro), along with more salt and lime juice if needed. »

TURN THE SALSA SALAD INTO A MEAL

Gently mix something substantial into the salad – well-seasoned black beans, shredded Spiced Chicken (p 106), spiced pork or grilled flaked fish. Make the Flotsam and Jetsam Flat Breads (p 168) or open a packet of corn chips and dinner is ready.

Pineapple upside-down cake

MAKES 1 x 24 CM (9½ IN) CAKE

So you've probably noticed we're not really bakers, but when the urge hits, or we're feeling guilty about buying yet more muesli bars for the lunchboxes, we can whip something up. The key to stress-free baking is to have a few simple, adaptable recipes up your sleeve that you can switch around to suit whatever you have in the fruit bowl.

Pineapple upside-down cake is like the spring version of Jaimee's Apple Bake (p 7); the method is just a little different. And in summer try this with peaches or apricots.

Cut the top and skin off 1 small pineapple and remove the core. To core a pineapple, stand it upright and put one hand at the centre to steady it. From the top, you'll be able to see the core in the middle. With a sharp knife cut the sides of the pineapple free from the core. You should end up with four pineapple cheeks. (Save the skin and core for Pineapple Skin Syrup, opposite; pineapple scrap vinegar using the Apple Scrap Vinegar recipe, p 9; or Pineapple and Lime Bitters, p 354.) Cut the flesh into thin slices and set aside. In a frying pan or wide saucepan, melt 100 g (3½ oz) unsalted butter, then add ½ cup (110 g) brown sugar and a pinch of salt. Cook over medium heat, stirring often, until the caramel gets a little foamy, then add the pineapple and cook gently for about 10 minutes, until the fruit begins to soften.

Preheat the oven to 170°C (325°F). Line a 24 cm (9½ in) cake tin (not a spring-form tin; it will leak) with baking paper, or use a loaf (bar) tin if that's all you have. Using a slotted spoon, remove the pineapple slices from the pan and arrange them over the bottom of the tin. Allow the caramel to bubble and thicken in the pan for another 2–3 minutes, then pour it over the pineapple. Set aside.

Using an electric mixer, beat 3 eggs with ¾ cup (165 g) caster (superfine) sugar until slightly fluffy, then slowly beat in ½ cup (125 ml) neutral oil, followed by 1 cup (260 g) plain yoghurt and the zest of 1 lemon. In a separate bowl, whisk 1½ cups (225 g) self-raising flour with ½ tsp baking powder, then fold this mixture into the wet ingredients. Pour the batter over the pineapple and bake for 30 minutes or until a skewer inserted in the centre comes out clean. Cool in the tin, then turn out onto a plate so that the pineapple slices are on top.

Home-made 'tinned' pineapple

1 PINEAPPLE MAKES ABOUT 2 x 350 ML (12 OZ) JARS

If you're a pineapple fan, bottle them when they're cheap and fill up the pantry. You'll be shocked how much better home-made bottled pineapple tastes than the tinned supermarket version. Scale up to make as many jars as you'd like to squirrel away.

Heat 3 cups (750 ml) water with 1 cup (220 g) raw or caster (superfine) sugar in a saucepan over low heat and stir to dissolve. Pineapple doesn't need any extra flavour, but if you want to spice things up you can add a few cinnamon sticks, a star anise, some peppercorns or a vanilla pod. Bring the syrup to a simmer.

Cut the top and skin off 1 pineapple. Cut the flesh into 3 cm (1¼ in) wedges, removing the core as you go. (Save the skin and core for Pineapple Skin Syrup, below; pineapple scrap vinegar using the Apple Scrap Vinegar recipe, p 9; or Pineapple and Lime Bitters, over the page.) Add about 500 g (1 lb 2 oz) pineapple to the sugar syrup and simmer for 10 minutes. This removes the air from the pineapple and stops the fruit floating in the jar.

Using clean tongs, pack the pineapple into sterilised jars (p 501), pour over the hot syrup and seal. If you want to include some of the spices in the jar, their flavour will become more pronounced over time. Heat-process (p 502) for 15 minutes, allow to cool, then store in the pantry for up to 1 year.

PINEAPPLE SKIN

Pineapple skin syrup

Don't throw away pineapple skins or cores until you've extracted all their flavour. And once you have, remember to cut the skin into small pieces before composting, as its toughness makes it slow to decompose.

Pineapple skin syrup can be drizzled over cakes, used in sticky marinades and added to cocktails. Follow the Mango Scrap Syrup recipe (p 264), washing the skin well. If you'd like it to be on the sweet *and* savoury side, add a splash of vinegar, a pinch of salt and a big pinch of chilli flakes. Add any left-over pineapple pieces to the pot – they will make it more flavoursome.

Pineapple and lime bitters

Use a 1:1 mixture of pineapple skins and lime skins to make a tropical version of our bitters recipe. Expect the pineapple version to be less bitter but more fruity. Perfect with a splash of tequila and a tiny umbrella. Follow the Grapefruit Skin Bitters recipe (p 180), replacing the grapefruit skin with an equal weight of mixed pineapple skin and lime skin.

Plums

Plums are the dark horses of the stone fruit world, moodier and much more dramatic than peaches and apricots, but just as versatile. There are about a gazillion varieties of plums, each with their own distinct flavour, aroma and use in the kitchen. But we're going to let you off the hook and say a plum is a plum and these recipes will work with whatever you've got.

Go with   Plums like intensity: pepper, ginger, spices, honey, soy sauce, chilli, salt, orange zest, vinegar. They also suit night-time flavours like dark chocolate, red wine, dark spirits and stinky cheeses, as well as rhubarb, poppy seeds, almonds, pistachios and walnuts.

Storage   As for most fruits, store underripe plums at room temperature until tender and fragrant. Once ripe, store in the fridge for up to 1 week. Forgotten plums make delicious simple compotes, jams and sauces, so there's no excuse for throwing them in the bin.

Substitutes   If there are no plums in the house, try peaches, nectarines or apricots, adding a little ground cinnamon and black pepper to match the spiced flavour of plums. For colour, use black grapes, figs, cherries or rhubarb.

Some ideas for using a couple of old plums

* Stewed plums for dessert or breakfast. Place plum halves, cut side up, in a small saucepan. Add a few knobs of butter, the juice and zest of 1 orange and 1–2 tbsp brown sugar, maple syrup or honey. Cook over medium–low heat until soft and stewed, or roast in a 180°C (350°F) oven until the edges start to caramelise.
* Add plum quarters to the Bread and Butter Pudding (p 52), nestling the plum pieces between the slices of bread; or stir into the Baked Rice Pudding (p 392).
* Poach plums in red wine, like the pears on p 336.
* Grill plum halves like the apricots on p 11, and serve with dark chocolate ice cream. »

* Make plum and cinnamon iced tea, following the Peach Iced Tea recipe (p 332).
* Turn the Apricot Chicken (p 11) into a plum, soy and chilli chicken by replacing the apricots with plums and the dijon mustard with soy sauce, and adding 1 tsp chilli flakes.

Plum sauce

MAKES 1 x 250 ML (9 OZ) JAR

Heat 2 tbsp oil in a large saucepan and sauté 1 thinly sliced onion until soft and sweet. Add 1 tbsp grated fresh ginger and 2 cups (about 350 g) chopped ripe plums, stones removed, and cook until the plums are just softened. Add ¼ cup (55 g) brown sugar or honey, 2 tbsp soy sauce and 2 tbsp vinegar of your choice. Cover and cook for 10 minutes, then remove from the heat and allow to cool a little. Blitz using a hand-held blender or in a food processor. Return to the heat and add 2 tsp mixed spices. If you have Chinese five spice, now's the time to get it out of the spice cupboard. Otherwise, use a mix of any of the following ground spices – cloves, star anise, cinnamon, allspice, fennel – and a pinch of chilli powder or cayenne pepper. Season with ½–1 tsp salt and simmer, uncovered, for another 10 minutes. Pour into a clean 250 ml (9 oz) jar and allow to cool. Store in the fridge for 3–4 weeks. Serve with dumplings, noodles, over rice, or with grilled (broiled) meats or tofu.

Plum compote

Plum compote spiced with cinnamon is tart and sweet, and an incredible colour to add to your breakfasts and desserts for the week ahead. Cooking overripe fruit pieces in a liquid – juice, water or wine – with sugar and spices to make a compote gives old fruit a new lease of life. The fruit is left a little chunky and is thick but not set like jam. It can be spooned over ice creams, cakes, muesli and yoghurt, or used in milkshakes. Compotes are less sweet than jam, meaning they won't last as long in the fridge – generally up to 1 week. Or you can bottle and heat-process (p 502) them for 30 minutes for longer storage.

For every 1 kg (2 lb 4 oz) of chopped fruit you put in a saucepan, add ½ cup (110 g) white (granulated) sugar or ⅓ cup (115 g) honey or maple syrup. If you're adding spices, pop them in the pan. Whole spices like cinnamon sticks, star anise and allspice berries can be tied in a piece of muslin or a clean Chux, and you'll need a generous 2 tbsp. If you're using ground spices, throw 1–2 tsp straight into the pot. Add ½ cup (125 ml) liquid of your choice (but if you're using watery fruits like berries or very ripe fruit, halve the water). Cook over low heat, stirring to dissolve the sugar, then bring to a simmer and cook gently, covered, until the fruit is very soft and tender but still holds some shape.

Pickled plums

If you're into pickles, please make some spicy pickled plums. Serve them with a roast, through a barley or brown rice salad or with delicious cheeses. Use the Sweet Mulled Vinegar mix (p 473), adding fresh ginger and chilli, or try another combination.

Drying fruits

When you put plums in a low oven, the hot sun or a dehydrator, they turn into prunes. And when you dry grapes, they turn into sultanas. It's magic. Drying fruits, vegetables and herbs at home is very easy, and a useful technique in a low-waste kitchen. We've tried our hand at drying just about everything, and it's really a case of experimentation to perfect the craft.

Dehydrators make it all very easy and, as with ice-cream makers, you can just follow the manufacturer's instructions. Sun-drying is awesome, low-impact and self-sufficient, but requires the promise of good weather for multiple days, a watchful eye for bugs and birds and, in busy modern lives, is most likely a pipe dream – save it for when you live on a Greek island and have nothing more to do than tend to your rack of drying fruit. We're fond of the oven-drying technique – it takes time, but does all the work itself while you're doing other things.

Preheat the oven as low as it goes – somewhere between 70°C (150°F) and 100°C (200°F) is ideal. The lower the oven, the longer the drying will take, but the more the colour and flavour of the fruit will be preserved. You can thinly slice fruits like apples, citrus fruits, pears and bananas to make fruit chips. You can halve apricots and cherries, quarter peaches and plums or leave things whole. Remember, the bigger the fruit the longer it will take.

As you prepare the fruit, put it in a bowl of water with a squeeze of lemon juice to help the dried fruit maintain its colour. Spread your fruit pieces out on a baking tray lined with baking paper or a wire rack, making sure they're not overlapping, and dry in the oven until the fruit is free from moisture. This may take anywhere from 3 to 12 hours.

Completely dried fruits can be stored in a jar or an airtight container in the pantry.

See apricots, cherries and peaches for ideas with other stone fruit.

Pomegranate

Does anyone really have too many pomegranates? We were unsure if this fruit full of jewels needed to be included in this book, but if you're lucky enough to have a tree in your garden or are panicking because a pomegranate turned up in your vegie box, here are our insights on dealing with them.

Goes with
Walnuts, pine nuts, pistachios, leafy greens, onions, beetroot, purple leaves (radicchio, red cabbage), celery, soft herbs (parsley, mint, dill), most cheeses, olives, other fruits (berries, grapes, rhubarb, oranges), meats, creamy dairy (yoghurt, ice cream)

Storage
Pomegranates look handsome in the fruit bowl and will last for about 1 week. For longer storage, wrap them loosely in a plastic or cloth bag and store in the fridge for 2–3 weeks. The seeds plus their fleshy red bits (commonly referred to together as pomegranate arils), need to be separated from the spongy yellow membrane. They are best used right away, but can be stored in an airtight container in the fridge for up to 1 week, or in the freezer for about 6 months. Defrosted seeds should be cooked, as they will have lost their crunch but not their flavour.

Substitutes
Red grapes, especially if they're pickled (see Preserved Sweet and Sour Grapes, p 182), currants soaked in vinegar, or dried cranberries.

How to extract pomegranate seeds

Bash all over the outside of the fruit with a wooden spoon. Cut the pomegranate in half over a bowl and lots of the seeds will fall out. Continue bashing the outside of the pomegranate to loosen more seeds, then use your fingers to pick out any remaining seeds.

USE POMEGRANATE SEEDS

- On top of a plate of hummus, then drizzle with olive oil and serve with flat breads (p 168).
- Instead of currants in the Pine Nut Sort of Hashweh (p 295).
- On top of the Baked Rice Pudding (p 392) or the chilled Milk Pudding (p 275) when serving.
- Over the Finest Braised Fennel (p 160), with orange zest and chilli flakes.
- On top of the Big Grain Salad (p 379), or toss through the Best Barley Side (p 29).

Some ideas to answer 'What do I do with this thing?'

* ***Walnut and pomegranate side*** A pretty side dish for a shared meal. Mix pomegranate seeds, roughly chopped walnuts, pitted and chopped green olives, roughly chopped parsley and mint, salt, pepper, sumac and a drizzle of olive oil or walnut oil, and something sharp like a little sherry vinegar, Pomegranate Molasses (over the page), lemon juice or pickling liquid. Serve with flat breads (p 168) and meatballs or falafel.
* ***Pomegranate and celery salad*** Paper-thin slices of celery, plenty of chopped parsley, lemon juice, salt and ground black pepper. Top with pomegranate seeds and serve as the fresh element with slow-cooked fatty meats, oily fish, or grilled or creamy cheeses.

TOO MANY POMEGRANATES

Pomegranate juice
1 MEDIUM POMEGRANATE MAKES ⅓–½ CUP (80–125 ML) JUICE

The juice of a pomegranate is sharp like a lemon but complex in its flavour. It makes for a lively ingredient in the kitchen, so when the season is here and pomegranates are cheap, add them to your shopping trolley. If your pomegranate isn't ripe, the juice will taste unpleasantly tannin-y. You can add a little sugar to counterbalance it, but ideally wait until the fruit is ripe. Ripe pomegranates feel heavy and may have a crack in the skin.

There are many ways to juice a pomegranate, so get googling and see what floats your boat. The easiest method is to place the seeds, without attached membranes, in a food processor and blitz briefly. You don't want to pulverise the hard white centre of the seeds too much, or the juice will be bitter. Strain through a fine sieve, pushing down on the pulp to extract as much juice as possible. Use right away or store in a sealed jar or bottle in the fridge for 4–5 days. »

TO MAKE POMEGRANATE VINAIGRETTE

Replace the orange juice in the orange vinaigrette (p 316) with ⅓ cup (250 ml) pomegranate juice. Use on salads, grains or grilled chicken.

POMEGRANATE ICED TEA

Turn the Peach Iced Tea (p 332) into something more elegant. Follow the same steps, using up to 1 cup (250 ml) pomegranate juice instead of whole fruits. This would work with green or black tea. If you like it on the sour side, reduce the sugar. Serve chilled over ice with fresh mint, or add booze for a cocktail.

Sweet pomegranate and orange syrup

This is more for desserts and cocktails than the tart molasses below. Drizzle over cakes (especially chocolate, almond or orange cakes) or fruit salads, or add as a bittersweet element in a cocktail. Follow the Mandarin Syrup recipe (p 258), using all pomegranate juice plus some orange zest, or a combo of orange and pomegranate juice.

Pomegranate molasses

This recipe appeared in our first cookbook. It's a little labour-intensive but it's well worth it, as home-made pomegranate molasses is like nothing you've ever tasted before.

Extract the seeds from 8–10 pomegranates (see previous page), taking care to discard all the bitter yellow membrane. Juice the pomegranate seeds in a juicer. If you don't have a juicer, blitz them briefly in a food processor, then strain the juice through a fine sieve. You need 2 cups (500 ml) juice.

Pour the juice into a small saucepan and add 2 tbsp sugar. Over low heat, slowly bring to a simmer, stirring occasionally. Simmer for 15–20 minutes or until slightly thickened but not too syrupy. Store in clean bottles in the fridge for 2–3 months or pour into sterilised (p 501) bottles, heat-process (p 502) for 15 minutes and store in the pantry for up to 1 year.

Potatoes

Rather than wondering what to do with all those potatoes, we usually feel like there's never enough of them. When there's potatoes in the house you don't have to think very hard about dinner. Jacket potatoes, potato bake, potato rosti, mash, gnocchi, wedges, potato salad – the reliable potato is a reassuring ingredient to have in the kitchen. And they last very well, so they're a good option if you have a tendency to overbuy fresh produce.

Go with   As for pasta and rice, we don't need to tell you all the ingredients that go with potatoes. Potatoes are a worldwide staple, used in different ways in so many different cuisines. We can't even tell you to leave them out of desserts, because potato chocolate cakes and potato donuts are delicious.

Storage   Uncooked potatoes last well stored in a cool, dry and dark place. Light promotes greening and warm temperatures promote sprouting. Don't leave them in a sealed bag, as they need to breathe. Roasted, baked or mashed potato will last for 3–5 days in an airtight container in the fridge. You can freeze mashed potatoes for up to 3 months.

Substitutes   You can easily replace potatoes with other starchy vegetables, such as sweet potato, pumpkin (squash), kohlrabi, swede (rutabaga), celeriac or parsnip. Experiment with cauliflower for soups and mashes, or try grains like couscous, burghul (bulgur) and quinoa.

Some ideas for using up a few potatoes

* If you've got a bit of cream and a few potatoes, make the 'There's Nothing Wrong With That Cream!' Potatoes (p 125). Add a simple salad and a meat or vegetarian option of your choice.
* Grate 1 potato, squeeze out the excess liquid and add to the Flotsam and Jetsam Flat Breads mixture (p 168). Fry the flat breads in a little oil and try not to eat them before they make it to the table. »

* ***Pesto roast potatoes*** Use up that jar to make a green version of roast potatoes (p 346).
* ***Potato rosti*** Follow the Parsnip Rosti recipe (p 323), using about 350 g (12 oz) potatoes instead of parsnips. Serve with fried eggs and chilli jam for breakfast, lunch or dinner.
* ***Potato pizza*** Boil 1 whole potato until just tender, then slice thinly. In a small bowl, mix olive oil, finely chopped garlic, salt, pepper and chopped rosemary, and use instead of tomato sauce to coat a pizza base. Layer the potato slices on top, then season with more salt and pepper, add shavings of an intense-flavoured cheese and cook in a very hot oven (at least 230°C/450°F).

Jude's mum's Hungarian potatoes
SERVES 4 AS A SIDE

Jude, from Alex's family, often shares her mother's Hungarian recipes with us. We keep returning to them because they use minimal ingredients and simple cooking techniques but bring lots of flavour. Dishes like this remind us that you don't need much to get comforting food on the table.

Heat 1 tbsp olive oil in a small saucepan over medium heat, then soften 1 finely chopped onion. Stir in 1½ tsp paprika and sauté for 1–2 minutes. Mix in 3–4 diced potatoes and ½ tsp salt. Add a small amount of water or stock – just enough to cover the bottom of the saucepan. Put the lid on, reduce the heat to very low and cook for 20–30 minutes, until the potatoes are quite soft, shaking the pan occasionally so they don't stick.

Serve as is, or top with a big dollop of sour cream or a generous shaving of parmesan.

Anything-goes potato salad
SERVES 6

Potato salad doesn't have to be drowning in a heavy creamy dressing or contain boiled eggs. By adding different vegetables, herbs, spices and dressings, you can turn the old classic into a meal in itself or a side dish for a barbecue. You can easily halve the quantities, or double them for a party. Use up bits and pieces from the fridge and garden and get creative. If you don't have any pickling liquid, make a half-batch of the quick-pickling liquid on p 473.

Put 1 kg (2 lb 4 oz) potatoes in a stockpot, cover with cold salted water and bring to the boil over medium heat. Reduce the heat and simmer for 25–30 minutes, until tender. Drain well and leave to cool. Cut the potatoes into slices or cubes and mix with ⅓ cup of something thinly sliced from the allium family – spring onions (scallions), chives, onions, the white part of a leek – and plenty of salt and pepper.

In a small saucepan, heat 200 ml (7 fl oz) left-over pickling liquid and pour over the potatoes. Drizzle with a little olive oil, then cover and leave to marinate while you prepare the rest of the meal, or in the fridge overnight. Now you get to choose your own adventure ...

FOR A GREEN POTATO SALAD

Add 2–3 handfuls chopped herbs like dill, parsley, mint or coriander (cilantro) and 1–2 cups green vegetables – blanched and cooled peas or broad beans, thinly sliced cucumbers, shaved fennel, thinly sliced asparagus or even apple matchsticks. Add ½ cup chopped pickles (such as pickled onions, gherkins, pickled celery) or fermented vegetables. Make the Pesto Dressing (p 346) or Classic Mustard Vinaigrette (p 283) and gently mix everything together. Adjust the seasoning as needed and serve.

FOR A SPICED POTATO SALAD

Make the Tarka (p 245) and spoon this over the potatoes, adding 1 bunch of coriander (cilantro) leaves, a few thinly sliced fresh or pickled chillies and 1 cup (200 g) diced tomatoes (optional). Serve with a curry, grilled fish or Spiced Chicken (p 106). Dress with lime juice and more salt.

FOR AN UPDATED CREAMY POTATO SALAD

Make either the Cheat's Caesar Salad Dressing (p 4) or the Russian Dressing (p 418). Add a few big handfuls of chopped dill and celery leaves, 1 cup (about 150 g) thinly sliced celery or apple matchsticks and top with Home-made Bacon Bits (p 23) or fried capers (p 69).

POTATO PEELINGS

Potato peel chips

Put these in the oven while you're preparing dinner. They take 10 minutes and are very nice with a pre-dinner drink. Try this with sweet potato peelings too.

Put potato peelings in a small bowl and add a little oil, salt and smoked paprika. Add a pinch of cayenne pepper if you want a little heat. Mix with your hands. Spread out on a baking tray and bake in a 200°C (400°F) oven for 10–12 minutes, until crispy and crunchy and browned.

LEFT-OVER MASHED POTATO

It's hard to get the maths right on mashed potato – there's always some left over that's not quite enough to do something with. Rule number one to reduce food waste at home is to learn how to cook the right amount of food. Then there will either be no annoying leftovers or enough to actually be helpful as a start to another meal. If you're ever struggling to get your amount right, one idea is to get out your scales, weigh the potatoes before you cook them, notice how much you have left-over and make a note about whether to cook more or less next time.

Potatoes per person for mash

A medium potato is somewhere in the 175–220 g (6–7¾ oz) range. This, with a little added milk or cream, butter and salt, will be enough to serve someone who is averagely hungry. So we recommend about 200 g (7 oz) uncooked potato per person, but if you have multiple big eaters scale up, or small children scale down. When we mash, we multiply the recipe by 1.5, so there's a decent amount left over to make a shepherd's pie, fritters, Fishcakes (p 165) or Colcannon (p 67) the next day.

Some ideas for using left-over mashed potato

* Don't feel weird about bulking out or thickening a soup or stew with mashed potatoes. The potato element in the Leek and Potato Soup (p 236) could be mashed potato if you have some that needs using – remember, it gets blended anyway. We add mash to the Wilted Lettuce Soup (p 248) or to the Green Soup (p 440) for a dairy-free version.
* *Herb, potato and vegetable fritters* Serve these simple and delicious fritters with a green salad and Cheat's Aioli (p 269). Follow the recipe for Pumpkin, Herb and Vegetable Patties (p 370), replacing the pumpkin (squash) with left-over mashed potato. You could also add some cooked flaked fish to the mix to turn them into fishcakes.
* *Colcannon* Old-school Irish fare made with cabbage and mash. Excellent when it's cold outside and you need a hug. Head to p 67 for the recipe.
* *Shepherd's or cottage pie* Go traditional with minced (ground) meat or try any of the pie filling recipes (pp 56, 233, 412, 451). Put the pie filling into a small pie dish, top with mash, brush with milk and grate cheese on top. Bake in a 200°C (400°F) oven for about 20 minutes, until golden and bubbling at the edges.

LEFT-OVER BAKED OR ROAST POTATOES

Cold baked potatoes aren't the most delicious thing to eat. But they can be ...

Some ideas for using left-over baked or roast potatoes

* Add chunks of cooked potato to the 'What's in the Fridge' Vegie Pie Filling (p 451).
  Potatoes work really well in vegetable pies, and using precooked ones mean you can
  mix them with vegies that have a shorter cooking time, like peas, broccoli and spinach.
* *Quick hash* Dice them up small, heat a frying pan, add 1–2 tbsp neutral oil and, once the
  pan is hot, add the potato. Shake the pan every now and then, but not too much – you want
  the potatoes to get really brown and crispy. Add plenty of salt, dried oregano, paprika and
  garlic powder if you have it. Shake again, making sure everything is crispy.
* *Gluten-free minestrone* Add 1–2 cups chopped left-over baked potatoes to a pot
  of minestrone (p 36) instead of cooked pasta.
* *Spanish potato omelette* The recipe on p 150 uses 2 uncooked potatoes, but also works
  with 400 g (14 oz) cooked potatoes. Follow the same method, dicing the cooked potatoes
  instead of thinly slicing, and frying them briefly before adding the eggs.

Preserved lemon

Preserved lemons never go off. There's so much salt in there, they'll just get darker and a little drier. So if you're sick of looking at the preserved lemons that have been in the fridge since 2002, drag them out and get cooking.

Preserved lemons add a salty, citrusy bite to dishes. Remove them from the jar, brush off any excess brine, cut off the salted pulp and finely dice the lemon rind. The pulp is generally thrown away, but have a little taste and see what you think. We add 1–2 tsp to a slow-cooked soup or stew that needs a lift in flavour.

If you're keen to learn how to make your own preserved lemon, head to p 241.

Goes with   Grains, dried beans, green beans, broccoli, cauliflower, fennel, avocado, spinach and silverbeet (Swiss chard), tomatoes, potatoes, capsicum (pepper), eggplant (aubergine), okra, pasta, yoghurt, meatballs, fish and chicken, herbs, chilli, garlic, ginger

---

Storage   Preserved lemons that have been bottled well will last indefinitely. Once opened, store them in the fridge and then leave them in your will.

Substitutes   Plenty of salt, lemon juice and lemon zest make the best substitute for preserved lemon. Otherwise, other salty little bites such as capers, olives, chopped pickles or anchovies will bring a bit of something extra.

Some ideas for using finely diced preserved lemon rind

* Add 1 tbsp to a salsa. Try the Avocado Salsa (p 18), Tomato Salsa (p 461) or Pineapple Salsa (p 351).
* Add to Parsley Pasta Sauce (p 199) for a simple green pasta.
* Mix through gremolata to make a soup topper. Try the Celery Leaf Gremolata With Green Olives (p 88).
* If there are no fresh lemons in the house, make a preserved lemon salad dressing. Replace lemon juice with white wine vinegar and 2–3 tsp very finely chopped preserved lemon rind.

* Add to yoghurt with finely chopped garlic and chopped herbs. Serve with grilled fish, curries or chickpea dishes. Check out the Raita and Tzatziki recipes (both on p 491).
* Add to the Grated Broccoli Salad (p 57), or the Grated Cauliflower version (p 81).
* Make a hummus zesty by adding 2–3 tbsp to the blender for each 200 g (7 oz) tub or home-made batch.
* For a little brightness, add to a lentil soup (p 246), chicken soup (p 106) or Green Soup (p 440).
* Add bite to a potato salad with dill and capers. Head to the Anything-goes Potato Salad (p 362) recipe.
* Add 2–3 tbsp to the Green Things Fritters (p 439) and the Greens Pie Filling (p 412).
* Add extra flavour to grain salads and rice dishes. Try adding 2–3 tbsp to the Best Barley Side (p 29), the Big Grain Salad (p 379) or the Buckwheat Salad (p 63).

Preserved lemon marinade

MAKES ABOUT 150 ML (5½ FL OZ)

This marinade uses up the rest of the jar of preserved lemons, and can be used for chicken thighs, or fish fillets or to coat cauliflower or zucchini (courgettes) before roasting or grilling.

Put ⅓ cup (60 g) chopped preserved lemon rind in a blender or food processor with 4 roughly chopped garlic cloves, 1 cup herb leaves (dill, parsley or coriander/cilantro, or a mix of all three), a big pinch of chilli flakes and 1 tsp ground cumin. Blitz to a rough paste and then, with the motor running, slowly add ¼ cup (60 ml) olive oil, processing until combined. Yoghurt would also work in this mix; stir it through before marinating.

Pumpkin

We advocate buying whole vegetables, rather than portions wrapped in plastic, and then figuring out how to use the whole thing for meals in the week ahead. Try to choose a whole pumpkin (squash) whose size suits your household and won't totally overwhelm you. If you're looking to make your life easier, roast or steam a good whack of it (if not all of it), then store it in the fridge and use it in any of the ways listed in the following pages.

Goes with   All its rooty friends – carrots, parsnips, beetroot, potatoes, sweet potato and swede (rutabaga), other vegetables like cabbage, and soft herbs like chives and parsley. Pumpkin likes sweetness too, so pair it with honey, apples, pears, quince, dried fruits, cinnamon, cloves, nutmeg, ginger and limes. All the woody herbs bring out pumpkin's earthiness – sage, rosemary, thyme – as do lentils, mushrooms, blue cheese, feta, cream, buckwheat, barley, quinoa, nuts, pepitas (pumpkin seeds), coriander seeds, cumin, curry powder, miso, mustard and bacon.

Storage   A whole pumpkin can be stored for a long time in an airy place, but as soon as there's a split or a mushy spot, you'll need to start cooking. Cut pumpkin can be stored, well wrapped in the fridge, for up to 1 week. Cut pumpkin has a tendency to grow mould quickly – carefully cut this off, rather than throwing the whole thing away.

Substitutes   Carrot, sweet potato or regular potato, or a mix of all three, will feel like pumpkin. Add a little parsnip for nuttiness.

LEFT-OVER COOKED PUMPKIN

Some ideas for using left-over cooked pumpkin

✱ Add roasted pumpkin to any of the following dishes to make a little go a bit further: Big Grain Salad (p 379), Simple Lentil Salad (p 244) and Silverbeet Salad (p 411).

✱ *Pumpkin dip* A small amount of cooked pumpkin can be turned into a great dip. Mash with garlic, chickpeas and a little tahini, and you'll have a bright, flavoursome spread for sandwiches or to serve with falafel. Follow the recipe for 'No Food Processor? No Worries' Mashed Hummus (p 109), mashing up to 1 cup (about 250 g) cooked pumpkin with the chickpeas. You'll need to amp up the other flavours, so add a little more tahini, salt and garlic if it needs it. The Most Delicious Almond Dip (p 288) is usually made with roasted capsicum (pepper), but is lovely with roasted pumpkin instead.

✱ *Pumpkin quesadilla* Squish a little roasted pumpkin on a tortilla and scatter some sliced chilli, coriander (cilantro) leaves and grated cheese on top. Cover with another tortilla and dry-fry on both sides until golden. Cut into wedges and add a squeeze of lime juice.

✱ *Pumpkin colcannon* The old-fashioned Irish dish called Colcannon (p 67) uses left-over mashed potato and cabbage to make a comforting and thrifty meal from simple ingredients. You can also make it with left-over cooked pumpkin instead of potato.

✱ *Two-minute cup-a-soup* Make a very quick pumpkin soup with left-over roasted pumpkin, some stock, a little miso paste and chopped spring onions (scallions). See pp 105, 328, 447 for tips on making very quick soups.

Quick pumpkin and ginger relish
MAKES ABOUT 3 CUPS (750 ML)

Sauté 1 sliced onion in some oil until soft and sweet. Add 2 chopped garlic cloves, 2–3 tbsp grated fresh ginger and 2–3 tsp whatever spices you have (ground cumin, ground coriander, mustard seeds, chilli, ground cinnamon, cayenne pepper, sesame seeds). Add 2 cups (about 500 g) cooked pumpkin, ⅓ cup (80 ml) apple cider vinegar, ¼ cup (55 g) sugar of your choice and ¾ tsp salt. Simmer for 10–15 minutes, until thick and glossy.

Serve with fried eggs, a frittata, a chicken sandwich or a cheese and salad wrap. It will last in the fridge for about 3 weeks.

Pumpkin, herb and vegetable patties

MAKES 8

These fritters use left-over cooked pumpkin (squash) or potato, whatever vegetables you have on hand and plenty of herbs. Serve with a salad, with eggs, or on a bread roll with mayonnaise, green leaves and chilli jam.

You'll need about 400 g (14 oz) cooked pumpkin – steamed or baked will both work. Put it in a bowl and mash roughly, adding a splash of milk or cream and a generous amount of salt and pepper. Add 1 cup mixed vegetables (peas, corn, chopped green beans, celery, grated broccoli), ½ cup chopped herbs, 2–3 finely chopped garlic cloves, some finely grated lemon or lime zest, and at least 3 tbsp chopped pickles or capers.

Divide the mixture and shape into 8 patties. To crumb them, whisk 1 egg in a shallow bowl and put 1 cup (60 g) Breadcrumbs (p 51) in another shallow bowl. Coat each patty in egg, then cover with the breadcrumb mix. Heat 100 ml (3½ fl oz) oil in a frying pan over medium heat. Fry the patties in batches until crisp and golden, about 3–4 minutes on each side. Drain on paper towel and serve.

SO THERE'S A PUMPKIN IN THE HOUSE

Some ideas for if you've bought a whole pumpkin

* Make the 'What's in the Fridge' Vegie Pie Filling (p 451), which uses up vegetables in the crisper. A good combination is pumpkin, spinach and cauliflower. You could add some grated fresh ginger for zing.
* For a sweet pie, check out the Sweet Potato Pie With Hazelnut Crust (p 451), replacing the sweet potato with pumpkin.
* Tempura. Head to the recipe on p 153.
* There's a Really Easy Green Bean Curry on p 40. Add some pumpkin if there's a little hanging around that needs a home.
* Head to the potatoes (p 361) and sweet potato (p 449) sections for more ideas.

Pumpkin ratatouille

SERVES 3–4 AS A SIDE

This is based on a recipe from one of our favourite cookbooks, Sam and Sam Clark's *Moro East*. Called pumpkin pisto, it's like a Spanish-style ratatouille. We make this when pumpkins are cheap and in season, so we've taken out the summer vegies – red capsicums (peppers) and tomatoes – to make a winter dish to serve with couscous.

Remove the skin from 500 g (1 lb 2 oz) pumpkin (squash) and chop into small cubes. Heat ¼ cup (60 ml) olive oil in a frying pan over medium heat and sauté 1 sliced brown onion until soft and sweet, about 15 minutes. Add 4 sliced garlic cloves, 1 tbsp chopped herbs (rosemary, thyme or oregano), ½ tsp salt and a good grind of black pepper. Sauté for 1–2 minutes, then add the pumpkin. Reduce the heat to low, then cook, covered, for 10 minutes. Take the lid off, turn the pumpkin and cook for another 10 minutes, or until the pumpkin is tender. Add 1 tbsp red wine vinegar, turn up the heat and cook undisturbed for another few minutes, until the vinegar has evaporated and the pumpkin is a little charred on the bottom, then remove from the heat.

Transfer to a serving plate, crack pepper over the top, cover with toasted pine nuts, pistachios or pomegranate seeds and a huge handful of chopped herbs, and serve.

Miso pumpkin

SERVES 2–3

This makes a great side, and if there are leftovers you can eat them all mashed up on toast the next day.

Preheat the oven to 180°C (350°F). Cut pumpkin (squash) into 3 cm (1¼ inch) thick slices, then lay them in a roasting tin lined with baking paper. Drizzle with oil and bake for 10 minutes. Remove from the oven and baste with Miso Glaze (p 277). Bake for a further 15 minutes, until golden and soft. Scatter toasted sesame seeds on top and serve.

Seedy breakfast muffins

MAKES 8–10

These are the muffins we were very proud of when the kids were small, packed full of wholemeal-y goodness and grated vegetables. We still wish our children preferred these to the white-flour choc-chip version, but alas … The best thing about these is that you can use what you've got – seeds, nuts or grated vegetables – as long as you stick to starchy things like pumpkin (squash), carrots, beets, parsnips or apples. »

Preheat the oven to 180°C (350°F). Grease or line 8–10 holes of a 12-hole muffin tin. In a medium–large bowl, put 1 cup (150 g) wholemeal or white plain (all-purpose) flour, 1½ tsp bicarbonate of soda (baking soda) and ½ tsp salt, then mix well with a whisk. Add 1 cup mixed seeds and/or chopped nuts, ¼ cup something binding like bran, almond meal or desiccated coconut, and 1 tsp ground spices (cinnamon, allspice, nutmeg) or finely grated orange or lemon zest. In another bowl, whisk 2 eggs, then whisk in 1 cup (125 ml) oil, ½ cup (110 g) brown sugar and 2 cups (250 g) grated pumpkin. Fold the wet ingredients into the dry ingredients, taking care not to overmix, then pour into the muffin tin. Sprinkle more seeds on top of each muffin and drizzle with honey. Cook for 20–25 minutes, until a skewer inserted in the centre of a muffin comes out clean. Cool in the tin for 5 minutes, then turn out onto a wire rack to cool completely.

PUMPKIN SKIN AND SEEDS

If you grew a pumpkin or 10, or bought a whole pumpkin, you'll have skins and seeds left over. Here are a few tips for turning them into something more.

Some ideas for using pumpkin skin

* Add washed pumpkin (squash) skin to a batch of End-of-the-week Scrap Stock (p 446). Include roasted onions, rosemary, garlic and pepper.
* Pumpkin skin makes a nice addition to apple jam or orange marmalade. Thinly slice, and soften it by cooking with the apple pieces or citrus skins. Go on, be brave. Give it a go.

Spicy pumpkin seeds

To make your own spicy pepitas (pumpkin seeds), scoop the seeds out of your pumpkin and remove the attached stringy flesh. Rinse in a colander, then place in a bowl of water. Pick out any pumpkin goop and drain the seeds again. Preheat the oven to 120°C (235°F) and spread the seeds out on a baking tray. Bake for 15 minutes. Remove from the oven, then drizzle a little oil of your choice over the seeds and sprinkle them with 1 tsp sea salt, 1 tsp paprika, 1 tsp ground cumin and a pinch of cayenne pepper. Stir to combine. Increase the oven temperature to 160°C (315°F) and bake for a further 15 minutes or until golden. Set aside to cool, then store in an airtight container in the pantry for up to 2 weeks. Serve on soups, salads or risottos, or use as part of a trail mix.

Q

Quince

We call each other quinces as a shorthand for when one of us is getting a bit too fancy for their own good. Although really, to be fair to quinces, they're not that silly at all. Quinces are, in fact, quite rustic for a fruit so floral in fragrance and rich in colour. They need to be slow-cooked to collapsing, and then they lend themselves to simple dishes. It's quite fun to embrace your inner quince and spend a day cooking them to crimson perfection, as if you lived in the South of France and did that sort of thing all the time.

Goes with   Apples, pears, strawberries, rhubarb, dried fruits, carrots, pumpkin (squash), sweet potato, allspice, cinnamon, cloves, star anise, nutmeg, ginger, vanilla, almonds, hazelnuts, walnuts, butter, cream

---

Storage   Do not refrigerate quinces. Keep them in a basket in a single layer and their perfume will fill your kitchen. They will keep this way for about 2 months. As the quince ripens, the skin will become a golden yellow. They don't soften when they're ripe – a soft quince is a rotten quince. Quinces can be frozen whole and will keep in the freezer for 6 months.

Substitutes   In cakes and tarts you can replace quince with strawberry, as they both have a jamminess to them once cooked. Apples and pears have a similar texture to quinces, and you could easily swap a poached quince with a poached pear. But do not eat a quince the way you can eat an underripe pear – the disappointment will be hard to forget.

How to poach quince   Follow the poaching steps for Four Ways to Poach Pears (p 336), using any of the syrups listed. This will be enough syrup to poach 2 quinces, so double it if needed. Be sure to add warm spices like star anise, allspice berries or a cinnamon stick and black peppercorns. To prepare the quinces, wash, peel, quarter and core them. They will take more than 1 hour to soften in the syrup.

TO USE POACHED QUINCE

- Quince makes an incredible stuffing for chickens. Use poached quince instead of the roasted apples in the Roast Apple and Sage Stuffing recipe (p 6). No need to roast the quinces after poaching; just add the rest of the ingredients and away you go.
- Serve poached quince with vanilla ice cream for an elegant and not at all difficult dessert.
- Quince and lamb go beautifully together. Serve sweet pickled quinces (see 'How to Poach Quince' opposite and use the Sweet Mulled Vinegar, p 473) the next time you're roasting lamb, or even with the Spiced Lamb and Chickpea Pie (p 233).
- Poached quince can also just make a humble appearance on your morning porridge. It doesn't need to be fancy at all.

How to slow-cook quince

You can do this in a slow-cooker or an ovenproof dish and the results will be equally delicious. Scrub the fuzz off 3 large quinces, then rinse and dry. Cut them into quarters and remove the core. To oven-cook, preheat the oven to 160°C (315°F). Place the quince pieces in an ovenproof dish so they sit together snugly, and sprinkle them with 300 g (10½ oz) caster (superfine) sugar, 1 cup (250 ml) water, a few bay leaves, the zest and juice of 2 oranges, and a few thyme or rosemary sprigs. Cover with baking paper or foil and cook for 2 hours. Check the quinces, baste them with the juices in the dish and cook, uncovered, for another 2 hours, or until they are deep crimson and the kitchen is filled with their scent. If using a slow-cooker, just bung everything in and cook on the low setting for about 8 hours.

TO USE YOUR SLOW-COOKED QUINCE

- Serve strained slow-cooked quince with aged cheese, toasted walnuts, crackers and a bottle of red for a night when dinner isn't really on the agenda.
- Blitz slow-cooked quince with a splash of port, marsala or red wine to make a sauce to pour over ice cream, puddings or French Toast (p 51), or add a little salt and serve with rich meats.
- **Slow-cooked quince upside-down cake** Replace pineapple with slow-cooked quince in the Pineapple Upside-down Cake recipe (p 352) for an autumnal version.
- **Quince crumble** Yes, please. Put slow-cooked quince in a small buttered ovenproof dish, top with a batch of uncooked Oaty Crumble Topping (p 302) and bake in a 180°C (350°F) oven for 30 minutes.

Quince paste

MAKES ABOUT 4 x 200 ML (7 OZ) JARS OR 2 SMALL TRAYS

Quince paste is the classic preserve to accompany cheese plates, although there are many more ways to use it, so read on for our tips. The short quince season demands that a yearly batch of paste is made, so make it a tradition in your kitchen. For paste-making, choose quinces with a sharp yellow colour because these will have the highest levels of pectin.

Peel and core 1 kg (2 lb 4 oz) quinces and chop roughly. Tie the quince cores and peel in a muslin bag. Put the quince pieces and bag in a saucepan, then barely cover with water. Add the juice and zest of 2 lemons. Simmer over low heat for 30–45 minutes until the quinces are breaking down and pulpy. Remove from the heat and leave to cool.

Push the cooled pulp through a fine-mesh sieve or the fine setting of a food mill, collecting the fruit purée in a bowl or jug. Weigh the purée and pour into a clean saucepan, adding an equal amount of sugar, e.g. 250 g (9 oz) purée + 250 g (9 oz) white (granulated) sugar. Add 4 whole star anise or 6 allspice berries and stir to dissolve the sugar over low heat. Simmer gently, stirring frequently, for about 1 hour. You know your paste is ready when it's thick and glossy, and when you scrape a spoon through the mixture you can see the bottom of the pan for a few seconds.

Once it's ready, pour the hot paste into small sterilised jars (p 501), silicone moulds, a greased muffin tin or two small shallow trays lined with baking paper. Cover and leave at room temperature to set overnight.

Sealed jars can be stored in a cool, dark place for up to 2 years. Ideally, let the paste mature for a few weeks before eating. Paste in a tray or moulds should be covered or wrapped well and will keep in the fridge for a very long time.

TO USE QUINCE PASTE

Whether you've made your own quince paste or three people brought it to your dinner party, you can use it for more than just a cheese plate. The rich flavour of quince paste and its sticky texture can be mixed with other ingredients for nearly endless variations.

- **Quince ketchup** In a small saucepan, warm a generous ½ cup (about 145 g) quince paste with 1 tbsp water, ½ tsp each of salt and pepper, and ¼ tsp ground allspice. While stirring, drizzle in a scant ¼ cup (60 ml) balsamic vinegar, sherry vinegar or apple cider vinegar. Mix it all together until you have a smooth sauce. Allow to cool before using. Use this as you would ketchup. It will keep in the fridge for 1 month.
- **Quince marinade** Makes 200 ml (7 fl oz). In a small saucepan over low heat, melt 100 g (3½ oz) quince paste with a splash of whatever wine is hanging around, the juice of 1 lemon and ¼ cup (60 ml) olive oil. Bring to a simmer, then remove from the heat. Once cooled, use to marinate or roast poultry, or as a glaze for pumpkin (squash) and sweet potato or root vegetables.

- **Quince dressing** Makes 200 ml (7 fl oz). Quince paste makes a truly delicious dressing with a sweet–sour note. It's perfect for warm winter salads like a roasted carrot salad, or for roasted beetroot or brussels sprouts. It would also be lovely on the Winter Parsnip and Hazelnut Salad (p 322). In a small saucepan over low heat, melt ⅓ cup (about 85 g) quince paste with 1 tbsp each of water and red wine vinegar, then slowly add ¼ cup (60 ml) olive oil and mix until combined. Add a pinch each of salt, black pepper and cayenne pepper. Taste and add a little more vinegar or a squeeze of lemon juice if it needs more acid. Allow to cool slightly, then pour over roasted vegetables.
- **Quince dessert sauce** Make vanilla ice cream a bit more fancy by pouring this sauce on top. Also try it with Bread and Butter Pudding (p 52) or pancakes. In a small saucepan over medium–low heat, warm ¼ cup (60 ml) quince paste with ¼ cup (60 ml) strong brewed black tea and a pinch of ground cinnamon. Stir until the quince paste has melted and the sauce is smooth. Taste and add a squeeze of lemon or orange juice if it needs a little acid.

Quinoa

Not a grain, but the seeds of a flowering plant in the amaranth family. In the early 2000s quinoa was hot. So hot, in fact, that its fluctuating prices caused havoc for Andean farmers and consumers. Forget about quinoa being the answer to everything. Diversity in our diets, while also keeping consumer demand in check, is all part of having a sustainable kitchen. Enjoy the nutty flavour of quinoa – it's gluten-free and easily digestible – but just keep it in the mix and not as the main event.

Goes with	In Peru quinoa is usually mixed with rice. It also goes with dried beans, all meats, pumpkin (squash), sweet potato, potatoes, tomatoes, capsicum (pepper), avocado, onions, garlic, ginger, chilli, coriander (cilantro), oregano, cinnamon, coriander seeds and nuts.
Storage	Store uncooked quinoa in the bag it came in, or transfer to an airtight container and store in the pantry for up to 1 year. Store cooked left-over quinoa in an airtight container in the fridge for up to 5 days. Cooked quinoa can be frozen in an airtight container and kept for 1 month.
Substitutes	Rice, couscous, barley, buckwheat and burghul (bulgur) are all suitable substitutes.
How to cook quinoa	Put 1 cup (200 g) uncooked quinoa in a small–medium saucepan and add 2 cups (500 ml) water. Bring to the boil, then reduce the heat to low and cook, covered, for 15 minutes. Remove from the heat and leave, covered, for another 10 minutes. Fluff with a fork. Each 1 cup uncooked quinoa will give you about 3 cups cooked.

Some ideas for using up a bit of left-over quinoa

✱ The Rice, Greens and Half-an-avo Fritters (p 20) works just as well with left-over quinoa as it does with rice.

✱ Use cooked quinoa to crumb meat or veg. Set up your crumbing station as follows: 1 bowl with flour (gluten-free flour works too), 1 bowl with 2–3 whisked eggs, and 1 bowl with ½–1 cup (100–195 g) left-over quinoa. Dip the meat or veg in the flour, then the egg, then the quinoa, and fry in oil over medium heat until crisp and golden.

✱ **Cabbage or silverbeet (Swiss chard) rolls** Make the Best Barley Side (p 29) with quinoa instead of barley and use it as a base for cabbage or silverbeet rolls. The result will be a little lighter and a good option for our gluten-free friends.

✱ **Quinoa porridge** For a great breakfast, add milk of your choice to left-over quinoa and cook to a porridge consistency. Add brown sugar or honey and fruit.

✱ **Quinoa tabouleh** Use Maddie's Grandma's Tabouleh recipe (p 199). Replace the traditionally used burghul (bulgur) with cooked quinoa and it's still the best tabouleh ever.

✱ **Quinoa bircher muesli** Follow the oat Bircher Muesli recipe (p 300), replacing the oats with cooked quinoa.

Big grain salad
SERVES 4 AS A MAIN, 6 AS PART OF A SHARED MEAL

A grain salad is healthy and filling, and you can use this and that from the fridge. Grain salads are great to have under your arm when arriving at a barbecue, they make perfect dinners on hot summer nights, and any leftovers for lunch are always welcome. Add pumpkin (squash) and feta to your grain salad and make like the 1990s – why not?

Start by cooking your grain(s). You'll need 2–3 cups cooked grains: about 390–585 g quinoa, 330–495 g couscous or 290–435 g barley. The trick to this salad is making a flavour base with spiced onions. The onions bring a complementary texture to the grains, as well as flavour, so you don't need to make much of a dressing. Heat ¼ cup (60 ml) oil of your choice in a small frying pan over medium heat then sauté 2 large sliced onions with a pinch of salt until translucent and collapsing. This will take 15 minutes or more. Add 4 finely chopped garlic cloves and continue to sauté. Now add seasoning according to the flavour profile you want. For this quinoa version, we add 1 tsp ground cumin, 1 tsp dried oregano, 1 tsp chilli flakes or powder, and ½ tsp each of salt and pepper. (If using barley or buckwheat, you might want to change this to dill, tarragon and caraway seeds.) Add ¼ cup (40 g) currants and ¼ cup (60 ml) red wine vinegar, then continue to sauté until the onions are very well cooked and browning on the edges. This always takes longer than you think, so keep going. **»**

Remove from the heat and add your 2–3 cups cooked grain(s), mixing well to coat in the pan juices. Transfer to a large mixing bowl and add ½ cup toasted nuts or seeds and 1 large handful of torn herb leaves. Match the herbs to the seasoning you've used. In this version, we like to use a mixture of coriander (cilantro) and mint, but parsley would work well too. Mix all the ingredients together, taste then add more salt and pepper, and a good squeeze of lemon juice or a little more vinegar. Transfer to a serving bowl or platter.

R

Radishes

With a natural heat that ranges from fiery to merely bitey, radishes can bring a lot of flavour to the table for such modest little things. They're mostly eaten raw in salads, and the French serve them with plenty of butter on fresh bread, but they're equally delicious cooked. The whole radish is edible, so don't throw away the green leaves – they have many uses. Radishes are available in the cooler months and are very welcome when there's a scarcity of fresh crunchy produce around.

Go with   Leafy greens, cabbage, silverbeet (Swiss chard), spring onions (scallions), apples, pears, nashi pears, potatoes, pretty much any herb, black pepper, ginger, garlic, sunflower seeds, olive oil, butter, fresh white bread

---

Storage   To make bunches of radishes last longer, remove the stems from unwashed radishes. Wrap the green leaves in a clean damp tea towel (dish towel) or damp paper towel in a reusable plastic bag in the crisper. They will stay fresh for up to 10 days. To store the radishes, remove the little tap root, place them in a reusable plastic bag or lidded container and cover with a dampened tea towel (dish towel) or paper towel. Re-dampen every few days and your radishes will last for 8–10 days.

Substitutes   Daikon (another member of the radish family), thinly sliced kohlrabi or turnip. For a different flavour but similar texture, carrots do the job.

Some ideas for using radishes

* Chuck sliced radish into Not So Classic Kimchi (p 486) or Basic Sauerkraut (p 66).
* Quick-pickle (p 473) sliced radish with coriander seeds and add to tacos.
* A little left-over steak and sliced radish makes a great sandwich combination.

* ***Radish and butter sandwiches*** This classic combination is very French, very civilised picnic fare and very easy. Split a small baguette and spread 2 tbsp softened unsalted butter on each side. Thinly slice 2 radishes and lay on the bottom half. Slice the radish tops very thinly and scatter on top. Add ½ tsp each of salt and pepper. Close the baguette and press down firmly. Slice into 2 sandwiches.
* ***Radish, apple and parsley topping*** Somewhere between a side salad and a gremolata, this goes nicely with grilled meats, potato dishes, and lentil stews and salads. Slice 1–2 radishes and 1 apple into similar-sized matchsticks. Thinly slice ¼ bunch of flat-leaf parsley (or coriander/cilantro, basil, dill, chives, tarragon). Mix the radish, apple and herbs together with a big pinch each of salt and pepper, 1 tsp olive oil and a good squeeze of lemon juice.

Whole radish salad
SERVES 4 AS A SIDE

Use every part of the radish in this crunchy and filling salad. Remove the leaves from 1 bunch of radishes (8–10), then wash and dry well. Slice thinly and set aside. Cut each radish into matchsticks or dice. Slice 4 celery stalks lengthways, then cut into small dice. Combine the celery and radish in a bowl and add 1 cup cooked grain of your choice (about 185 g rice, 165 g couscous, 195 g quinoa, 145 g barley or 190 g buckwheat) and ½ cup chopped toasted nuts. Combine, add the radish leaves and dress with 2 tbsp olive oil and the juice of ½ lemon. Season generously with salt and pepper to taste.

Sauce from tired radishes
MAKES 1½ CUPS (375 ML)

This sauce utilises radishes that have seen better days. It uses a little of this and a little of that, with luxurious-tasting results. Bake a whole fish and serve it on top. It's also delicious with a steak or a big grilled mushroom.

Peel 200 g (7 oz) radishes, keeping the peel. Cut the radish flesh into very thin matchsticks and set aside. Add the radish peel to ½ cup (125 ml) chicken stock, ½ cup (125 ml) cream, 1½ tbsp white wine and a pinch each of salt and pepper. Bring to a simmer and cook gently over low heat for about 10 minutes. Strain the sauce, add ¼ cup (65 g) sour cream and the radish matchsticks, and simmer for 5 minutes to allow the sauce to thicken. Serve immediately.

Roasted radishes

SERVES 4 AS A SMALL SIDE

Roasting radishes takes the bite out of them, making them more savoury, mellow and blushed like a rose. Serve them as you would any roast vegetable, but they're especially good with falafel, koftas or sausages.

Preheat the oven to 200°C (400°F). Cut the leaves off 1 bunch of radishes – you can leave a little bit of the stem on, if you like – and cut them in half. Lay them, cut side down, in a small roasting tin, then drizzle with a little oil and plenty of salt and pepper. Roast for 20 minutes.

Meanwhile, melt 2 tbsp butter in a small saucepan over low heat, then gently sauté 2 finely chopped garlic cloves and 2 tsp caraway seeds for 1 minute. When the radishes are cooked, pour the butter over them and transfer to a serving dish. Serve hot.

RADISH LEAVES

Radish leaves have a very bitter flavour, which works well in mixed vegetable krauts. Add 1–2 cups well-washed then chopped radish leaves to your next batch of sauerkraut (p 66).

Stir-fried sweet and sour radish leaves

SERVES 2

Make this quick side dish with any type of radish leaf – daikon leaves are particularly good.

In a small bowl, combine 1 tbsp soy sauce, 1 tbsp rice wine vinegar, 1 tsp sugar and 1 tsp cornflour (cornstarch) dissolved in 2 tbsp water. Mix to a slurry and set aside. Wash and dry 2 cups (about 20 g) roughly chopped radish leaves. Heat 1 tbsp vegetable oil in a wok over medium heat, then add 1 tbsp finely chopped ginger and 1 thinly sliced green chilli. Stir-fry for no more than 10 seconds. Increase the heat to medium–high, add the radish leaves and 2 finely chopped garlic cloves. Stir-fry for 20 seconds. Add the slurry and stir-fry until the leaves are coated and glossy, no more than 30 seconds. Serve hot.

Relish/chutney

Relish maketh the meal. Well, not quite, but we both feel very strongly that having a jar or two of relish or chutney in the pantry can turn grilled cheese on toast into a meal. In this section we're using relish and chutney interchangeably, but they are different in that relishes are usually cooked for a shorter time and retain more texture and crunch, whereas chutneys are slower-cooked and stickier. If you relish your relishes and chutneys as we do, you no doubt have many nearly empty jars cluttering your fridge. Here are our tips on using every last drop.

To make your own relish or chutney, see the 'What's in the Fruit Bowl' Relish recipe (p 333).

Go with   Relishes and chutneys can be sweet and sticky or bitey and acidic. Eat sweeter relishes with salty foods, and bitey relishes with fatty foods. All relishes and chutneys go with eggs, cheeses, meats, hot chips (fries), potatoes, fritters, salad sandwiches, sour cream, mayonnaise, bread and crackers.

Storage   Unopened relishes and chutneys will keep in a cool, dark place, such as the pantry, for at least 2 years. Once opened, store in the fridge for up to 6 months, perhaps longer. Keep in mind that the more vinegar, salt and sugar in there, the longer it will last. If you accidentally leave the jar in the pantry for a week, don't panic. Just pop it back in the fridge.

Substitutes   It depends on what it's going with, but pickles or sauerkraut can jump into most of the meals you'd serve a relish or chutney with. For deep flavours and stickiness, use caramelised onions with a little brown sugar and mustard.

Some ideas for using up the last bit of relish in the jar

* Make a dip. Mix whatever relish or chutney you have with mayonnaise, sour cream or yoghurt, and use as a dip, condiment or sandwich spread.
* Every time you make fritters, pile relish on top. »

* Use onion- or tomato-based relishes and chutneys as a base for savoury pies and tarts. Thinly spread the last scraping in the jar over the pastry base of a pie or tart. Don't use too much or the bottom will be soggy, but make sure it's enough for extra flavour.

* Relishes and chutneys are so full of flavour that thinning them out and adding some oil turns the dregs into a great sauce. Mix equal parts relish and oil of your choice, then thin out with a little water if necessary. Add salt and pepper and use to dress vegetables before roasting for extra flavour and caramelisation.

* Cheddar and chutney make the perfect toasted sandwich. Or replace the jam in the Brie and Jam Fried Sandwich (p 91) with whichever chutney or relish needs using.

* Get used to including chutney in more meals. Whenever you're cooking eggs, make sure you get the chutney out of the fridge.

* Add a scraping of relish to any sandwich, especially curried egg (p 149) or chicken and mayonnaise.

* If you're out of tomato paste (concentrated purée), add some tomato- or onion-based relish instead.

* **Savoury muffins** Add a few spoonfuls of relish or chutney to the Whatever-cheese Eggy Muffins recipe (p 93). Don't mix it in too much, just spoon it in and give it a light swirl so the relish doesn't get lost in the batter.

* **Relish chilli con carne** Follow the Chilli Con Carne recipe (p 36) and replace the tomato paste (concentrated purée) with left-over relish or chutney.

Relish clean-out sauce – for meatloaf, burgers and fries
MAKES ABOUT ½ CUP (150 G)

In the 1980s meatloaf was generally glazed with tomato sauce (ketchup). Tomato sauce is sweet and salty and hey, so are relishes. So we thought why not go one better than tomato sauce and use up all the random relish jars to make an uber relish sauce? You can definitely use this to glaze a meatloaf, or just on burgers or pies, or wherever you would use a brown sauce. We also use it for dipping hot chips (fries) or deep-fried cauliflower.

Scrape out all the quarter-filled relish and chutney jars in the fridge – you want about ½ cup (about 140 g) altogether. Using a hand-held blender or small food processor, blitz to a smooth paste. To this add 2 tbsp of something very savoury, such as worcestershire sauce, soy sauce or tomato paste (concentrated purée). Blitz again. You may need to add 1 tbsp water to loosen it and get the consistency you want. It should be saucy and full of flavour.

Store in a clean jar or airtight container in the fridge for up to 1 month.

Rhubarb

So you bought a bunch of rhubarb, it doesn't fit in the fridge and now you're regretting the impulse buy. Don't worry, Alex raised her children on rhubarb and is happy to share her wisdom. The big news is that rhubarb is actually a vegetable that fakes being a fruit, but it can't be eaten raw and needs a ton of sweetness to make it palatable. It has a tart flavour and the most intense colour, and it's a staple in the preserver's kitchen as it makes the most delicious old-fashioned jams, sauces, ketchups and relishes. We've included manageable, small-batch recipes that use up a bunch or two.

And a little reminder – while we're advocates for using all parts of fruits and vegetables, rhubarb leaves should never be eaten. They are toxic to humans.

Goes with
Rhubarb needs sweetness, so try the sugar of your choice, maple syrup or honey. Rhubarb also likes pepper, ginger, rosemary, juniper berries and warm spices like cinnamon, cloves and allspice. Other fruits (apples, berries, plums, cherries, oranges, quince, pomegranate), work with rhubarb, as do dried fruits and dairy products (vanilla ice cream, yoghurt, fresh cheeses like ricotta and goat's curd).

Storage
Cut the leaves off and discard. Wrap stems in a tight bundle in a clean cloth or reusable plastic bag with the ends exposed, and store in the fridge for up to 2 weeks.

Substitutes
If you don't have rhubarb, try plums or quince, as they're both sweet and tart.

Some ideas for using up rhubarb

* Add a few rhubarb stems to the Simple Stewed Apples (p 7). Up the sweetness a little to balance the tartness. Eat with your morning muesli.
* Rhubarb in baked goods has a nice old-fashioned afternoon tea vibe. Try the Pineapple Upside-down Cake (p 352) with 1 bunch of rhubarb (6–8 stalks), chopped into 5 cm (2 in) lengths instead of the pineapple.
* **Roasted rhubarb** Very delicious, it's almost like a quick cheat's relish. Follow the Savoury Roasted Fruits recipe (p 12), adding a little more brown sugar, ground pepper, ground ginger and red wine vinegar. Serve with grilled meats, on burgers or with roasted beetroot.
* **Rhubarb compote** For porridge or crumbles, or to serve with old-fashioned desserts like Bread and Butter Pudding (p 52), Baked Rice Pudding (p 392) or Baked Custard (p 151). Follow the Plum Compote recipe (p 356), increasing the sugar a little. Finely grated orange zest and/or slices of fresh ginger make a nice flavour match with rhubarb.

Rhubarb fizz
MAKES 6 CUPS (1.5 LITRES)

Alex has been making this version of Australian preserving hero Sally Wise's sparkling rhubarb drink for many moons. This is a small-batch version, using a bunch of rhubarb and some fresh ginger. Scale up to make many bottles if you love it as much as we do.

Roughly chop 1 bunch of washed rhubarb (6–8 stalks), weigh it and put it in a big jar, jug, food-grade bucket or even a very clean vase. Cover with an equal weight of sugar and add a clean, unpeeled chopped lemon or orange, 100 g (3½ oz) sliced fresh ginger, 2½ tbsp apple cider vinegar and 6 cups (1.5 litres) water. Cover with a clean tea towel (dish towel) or cloth and leave at room temperature for 1 week. Strain and pour into sterilised (p 501) or very clean bottles, seal and store in the refrigerator. This fizz takes a while to carbonate – at least a week – so keep an eye on it. Open bottles tentatively, over the sink or outside, and don't wear white. Drink over the next few weeks.

Foolproof jam

MAKES 2–3 x 300 ML (10 OZ) JARS

Jam is jam is jam. Once you know how to make jam you don't need a recipe; you can eyeball the fruit and the pot and know what it needs. This is a base recipe to turn whatever fruit you have into jam. It's not a big-scale recipe and it may not win you first prize at the country show or fair, but it's a delicious, humble home-made jam you'll spread liberally on toast, cakes and scones, and it will be even more delicious because you cleared out the fruit bowl to make it. Feel free to halve the recipe if you only have a few pieces of fruit.

We're not going to get into the science of jam-making here. Just keep in mind that jam needs pectin to set, some fruits have more pectin than others, and the higher the pectin the firmer the set. If your fruit is low in pectin, add extra citrus juice and zest or be happy with a softer-set jam – it will still taste delicious. Also check out the kitchen-scrap Pectin Stock (p 9). You can use this instead of water to help your jam set.

Rhubarb jam is especially delicious, so we're using rhubarb as the example here. Replace it with whatever fruit you have on hand and use the aromatics you enjoy.

Trim off the leaves from 1–2 bunches of rhubarb (6–16 stalks), wash the stalks and chop them into 3 cm (1¼ in) lengths – you need 1 kg (2 lb 4 oz) chopped fruit. Place in a wide saucepan or jam pan and add 2 cups (500 ml) water or pectin stock, the zest and juice of 2 lemons or oranges and the aromatics of your choice. Tie any spices you're using in a square of muslin or a clean Chux. With this jam, 6 slices fresh ginger and 1 tsp allspice berries is very nice.

Gently cook over low heat until the fruit is soft and pulpy. Once it resembles runny stewed fruit, carefully transfer it to a large bowl and weigh. To preserve the jam properly, you'll need a weight of sugar that's 60 per cent that of the fruit pulp – i.e. for 1 kg (2 lb 4 oz) pulp, you need at least 600 g (1 lb 5 oz) white (granulated) sugar. Return the pulp to the pan, add the sugar and stir in until dissolved. Increase the heat to medium and simmer (but don't let it be a volcano), stirring every now and then to prevent sticking, for up to 30 minutes or until the jam reaches setting point (p 503).

For fridge jam, remove the jam from the heat, allow it to cool slightly, then fill 2–3 clean jars, seal and, once cool, store in the fridge for up to 6 months. For pantry jam, fill hot sterilised jars (p 501), check the seal (p 503), then store in the pantry for up to 1 year. If you're worried about them keeping through a hot summer or you live in a hot climate, you could heat-process (p 502) your jars for 10 minutes.

Rice

What a grain! The most consumed staple food in the world, and perhaps the most versatile because of its many varieties and infinite preparations. Rice is breakfast, dinner and dessert; it's the support act for a fiery curry and the foundation of a comforting pudding. Yet for all its versatility, rice is one of the most wasted foods. Using rice up is actually quite easy; you just need to commit to the leftovers as you're putting them in a container for storage in the fridge or freezer. Read our suggestions and consider the next night's dinner.

Goes with	As a staple on nearly every continent on the planet, there's little that rice doesn't go with. It will complement almost anything you have in the cupboard or fridge.
Storage	Uncooked rice can be stored indefinitely in an airtight container if kept free from moisture. Pop in a bay leaf to keep the creepy crawlies out. The greatest of care needs to be taken when storing and reheating cooked rice, to prevent the growth of harmful bacteria. Left-over cooked rice must be cooled quickly in an airtight container in the fridge, then reheated quickly and thoroughly. Before you start, check online for the most reliable up-to-date guidelines on the safe storage, and in particular reheating, of rice. In Australia, see the Food Safety Information Council site, foodsafety.asn.au. Cooked rice that has been stored correctly should not be kept in the fridge for longer than 3 days or the freezer for 1 month. If left-over takeaway rice has been left out too long before refrigerating or freezing, it won't be safe to reheat.
Substitutes	Other grains and pseudo-grains, such as couscous, barley, buckwheat, quinoa, wild rice and freekeh.

How to cook rice, once and for all

We don't need a million ways to cook rice, as there is one way and this is it. Unless of course you're cooking brown rice, which is different. Or you have a rice cooker, in which case follow the manufacturer's instructions.

For white rice, whether it's short-grain, medium-grain or long-grain (such as basmati), begin by rinsing the rice several times until the water runs clear. Place the drained rice in a saucepan. No matter how much rice you have, you need to add enough water so it covers the rice and when you poke your index finger into the pan and it just touches the surface of the rice, the water level comes up to your first knuckle. Cover the saucepan and bring the rice to the boil. Immediately reduce the heat to low and cook, covered, until fluffy, generally 10 minutes. Remove from the heat and leave to stand for 5 minutes.

For brown rice, the general rule is 2 cups (500 ml) water for each 1 cup (200 g) rice and follow the same method as above, but cook for 30–45 minutes.

If you've made rice ahead of time, you can keep it hot for up to 30 minutes if you wrap the whole saucepan in a hand or bath towel, but don't be tempted to leave it for any longer.

LEFT-OVER COOKED RICE

There's *always* left-over rice after a meal. Since cooked rice needs to be used quite quickly, consider the leftovers as being halfway to your next meal.

Some ideas for using left-over cooked rice

* Make the Best Barley Side (p 29) and replace the barley with rice. Use it to stuff Cabbage Rolls (p 68) or capsicums (peppers; p 75), or eat it as a side.
* Add ¼–½ cup (45–95 g) cooked rice to soups to make them heartier. Add to the Egg Drop Soup (p 148) before you add the eggs, make the Simplest Minestrone Soup (p 36) with rice instead of pasta, or simply add it to a very flavoursome broth.
* A quick rice porridge makes a nice break from oats and is a good way to use up last night's left-over rice. Follow the same steps as for the Left-over-buckwheat Porridge (p 63).
* Add 2–3 tbsp rice to Tasty Meatballs (p 54), Vegie Burgers (p 111) or fritters; it will help stretch the other ingredients further.
* The obvious decision for dinner when you have left-over rice is fried rice. We cook extra rice so we know what's for dinner tomorrow night. Follow the Green Eggy Fried Rice recipe (p 57).
* If you only have a little cooked brown rice, make the Rice, Greens and Half-an-avo Fritters (p 20). You can also use left-over white rice or other grains.

Brown rice, mushroom and spinach soup

SERVES 3-4

Wholesome much? Sometimes brown rice can taste like carpet, but mix it with other earthy flavours and it's the dinner equivalent of a long bushwalk on a crisp day. If you have left-over brown rice, bring it together with these complementary ingredients. This soup can also be made with left-over white rice. The result is lighter but just as nourishing.

Heat 2 tbsp neutral oil in a heavy-based saucepan over medium heat and sauté 1 diced onion until translucent. While the onion is cooking, slice 300 g (10½ oz) mushrooms and set aside. Add 2 finely chopped garlic cloves and 1–2 tbsp grated fresh ginger to the onion and sauté for about 20 seconds more. Gradually add the sliced mushrooms and allow them to sweat down and release some of their liquid. When all the mushrooms are in, add 1 cup (185 g) cooked brown rice and 1 cup of a chopped leafy green such as spinach, kale or silverbeet (Swiss chard). Sauté for another 5 minutes or so, until the greens have wilted and flavours combined. Add 1–2 tbsp soy sauce and ½ tsp pepper. Cover with 4 cups (1 litre) chicken or vegetable stock and bring to the boil, then reduce the heat to low and simmer, covered, for 10 minutes. Taste and adjust the seasoning, adding a squeeze of lemon juice or splash of kimchi brine. Serve with a good scattering of toasted sesame seeds or a few drops of sesame oil on top.

Baked rice pudding

SERVES 6

Eating rice pudding is like being tucked into bed and read a story. This version fast-tracks the comfort by starting with left-over rice. But if you don't have left-over rice, it's worth cooking some rice just for this. Serve it after a roast dinner for old-fashioned hospitality, or make it and drop it off to someone who's in need of being tucked into bed.

Preheat the oven to 180°C (350°F). Put 2½ cups (465 g) cooked rice in a large saucepan with 4 cups (1 litre) milk of your choice and a pinch of salt. If you want, add up to ⅓ cup chopped dried fruit now. Cook over medium–low heat for 30 minutes, stirring often. Once the mixture is well thickened, remove from the heat. Generously grease an ovenproof dish with butter. If using poached, roasted or stewed fruits, stir these into the rice mixture now, along with ½ cup (125 ml) maple syrup or honey and ½ tsp ground cinnamon. Spoon the rice into the ovenproof dish and if you have thick (double) cream in the fridge that needs using, pour ½ cup (125 ml) over the top. Bake for 30 minutes so the creamy top browns and gets bubbly. Remove from the oven and leave to set for 10–15 minutes before serving, sprinkled with ground cinnamon or grated nutmeg. You can also serve this cold.

Baked rice pie

SERVES 4

Okay, this is truly the kind of thing you make to use up the left-over rice. It's a simple meal with a salad, a snack or something for the lunchbox. It's light but really moreish, and this trick of pulling all the leftovers together, mixing them with egg and baking is well worth knowing because it always works.

Preheat the oven to 180°C (350°F). Put 2 cups (370 g) cooked rice in a mixing bowl and add up to 1 large handful of chopped soft herb leaves. If you have some left-over shredded chicken or flaked fish, cooked lentils or chopped vegetables, you could add up to ¾ cup. Mix everything together. In a small separate bowl, whisk 4 eggs with ½ cup (130 g) plain yoghurt, 1 tsp oil, ¼ cup of something delicious and salty like chopped olives or capers, 1–2 tsp spices, such as crushed fennel seeds, ground allspice or sumac, ¾ tsp salt and plenty of ground black pepper. Pour this wet mixture into the rice mix and combine well. Grease a 20 cm (8 in) pie tin or ovenproof dish with oil or butter and press in the rice mixture. Bake for 30 minutes. Allow to cool for about 5 minutes before serving. The pie will keep in the fridge for 2 days.

A LITTLE RICE IN THE PANTRY

Even a small amount of uncooked rice can feed many mouths. Everything depends on how you prepare it and what you add to it to make the most of what you have. There's a saying in China that the rich ate rice and the poor ate congee, because boiling the rice in a large volume of water or stock could make a handful of rice feed the whole family. Overcooking a small amount of rice to a thick, porridge-like consistency is a technique that appears all over the world, from India to Portugal. We've included a simple Congee recipe (over the page) that will satisfy both the soul and the pocket.

Making dinners that use up a bit of this and a bit of that is our favourite way to clean out the fridge. Rice is a most excellent staple for bringing other ingredients together into a whole meal. Rice, vegetables, beans, some protein – whatever is around can always be turned into something to feed a whole family. The beauty of using rice in this way is that you don't have to have much of anything, but bring them all together and you're in business.

Congee
SERVES 4

Pure comfort. This is a recipe for lots of stock and a little rice. In the long cooking process the individual rice grains burst open. This method of cooking was a clever way to stretch out only a small amount of rice. Congee can be very simple, even just rice cooked in water, or it can be made into more of an occasion, with the best-quality stock and lots of condiments. We lean towards the latter.

Rinse ¾ cup (150 g) white rice until the water runs clear. Transfer to a medium–large heavy-based saucepan or stockpot and cover with 8 cups (2 litres) stock of your choice. Cover the pot and bring to the boil over medium heat. Reduce the heat to low and simmer for 2 hours. Stir and scrape the bottom of the pot every 20–30 minutes to prevent sticking. After 1 hour, remove the lid so the congee can thicken. It will thicken even more as it cools. Spoon into bowls, season with sesame oil, soy sauce and 1 tsp grated fresh ginger, and add any or many of the following.

TO ADD FLAVOUR TO CONGEE
- Not So Classic Kimchi (p 486)
- Wilted spinach
- Home-made Bacon Bits (p 23)
- Left-over shredded chicken
- Japanese-style Sesame Greens (p 40)
- Tomatoes sautéed in ginger and garlic
- Pickled Eggs (p 151)
- Stir-fried Snow Pea Shoots (p 416) or Celery (p 87)
- Mandarin peel powder salt (p 260)

Anything-goes rice
SERVES 4

This staple dish is very forgiving. It combines the vegetables in the fridge with rice and stock, and is an absolutely 'Do not go to the shops, we'll sort this out together' kind of recipe. Serve it alongside meatballs or grilled fish, or with braised vegetables, or even just pop a fried egg on top.

Preheat the oven to 180°C (350°F). Heat ¼ cup (60 ml) olive oil in a flameproof casserole dish over medium heat, and sauté an onion, leek or 1 cup thinly sliced fennel or silverbeet (Swiss chard) stalks for 5 minutes or until soft and sweet. Add 2–3 finely chopped garlic cloves and 1–2 cups thinly sliced vegetables – cabbage, fennel, capsicum (pepper), silverbeet (Swiss chard), grated carrot or even grated broccoli – and sauté until tender. Add the zest of 1 lemon and 1 tsp of your favourite dried herb or spice. Sauté for a few more seconds, then add 1¼ cups (250 g) white rice, 2¼ cups (560 ml) stock of your choice and ½ tsp salt – if your stock is store-bought and very salty, add less salt. Stir, bring to a simmer, then put on the lid and cook in the oven for 15 minutes. Remove from the oven, give the rice a quick fluff with a fork, then replace the lid and leave to sit for 10 minutes. Top with 1 large handful of chopped herbs before serving.

Cheat's paella

SERVES 3-4

Paella is a lovely dish, isn't it? But would anyone be bothered to make it when they've walked through the door at 6 pm? No, they would not. Our super cheat's version is a very reasonable option when you don't have 2 hours to make this Spanish classic. Serve with a salad or barbecued corn.

If you have it, soak ¼ tsp saffron threads in 1 tbsp warm water. If you don't, no sweat. In your biggest frying pan with a lid, heat 2 tbsp oil over medium heat. Gently sauté 1 diced small onion until soft and sweet. Add 3 chopped garlic cloves, ½ tsp each of salt and smoked paprika and a pinch of cayenne pepper, then sauté for another 2–3 minutes. Add 1 cup (220 g) paella rice and stir well, so all the rice is coated. Add 400 g (14 oz) tinned tomatoes, 2 cups (500 ml) stock and the saffron and its soaking water if using. Add lots of ground pepper and stir well. Bring to a simmer, then reduce the heat to low and cook, covered, for 20 minutes. Remove the lid and add 1 cup vegetables (frozen peas, sliced green beans, roasted capsicum/pepper). And if you have left-over cooked fish, shredded chicken or sliced cooked sausage, add ½–1 cup. Cover and cook for 5 minutes, then remove the lid, mix everything together and cook for another 5 minutes or so.

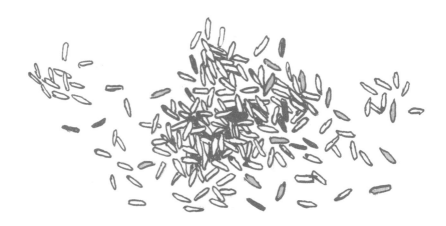

S

Sauerkraut

Sauerkraut – fermented cabbage – has been around for thousands of years, though it's only recently hit the big time, thanks to a fermenting revival. Jaimee is especially pleased to see sauerkraut in people's kitchens, as she grew up with a Russian grandmother who seemed to serve it with every meal. Check out our recipe for Basic Sauerkraut (p 66) to find out how easy it is to make. And if not, there are so many delicious variations available from markets and even supermarkets these days that you're spoilt for choice. The question we're frequently asked is how to eat sauerkraut. Often it's bought with enthusiasm and then lies idle in the fridge. You need to eat that stuff! We'll show you how.

Goes with	Onions, carrots, tomatoes, potatoes, beetroot, mushrooms, kale, kohlrabi, horseradish, juniper berries, mustard, beef, bacon, eggs, rice and other grains, rye bread, butter, sour cream, cheese, dill, parsley, tarragon
Storage	As a live fermented product, even unopened sauerkraut needs to be refrigerated to slow down fermentation. Sauerkraut will last up to 6 months in the fridge. If you've bought pasteurised sauerkraut from the supermarket shelf rather than the chiller section, it will last unopened in the pantry for 1 year. Once opened, refrigerate and keep for up to 6 months.
Substitutes	If you don't have any sauerkraut you can use chopped pickles or capers for a similar sour–salty flavour. Cooked cabbage is a good substitute for texture.

Some ideas for finishing the sauerkraut jar

* Add kraut to soups and stews. Try adding ¼–½ cup (about 35–75 g) to borscht, the Brown Rice, Mushroom and Spinach Soup (p 392) or a lentil stew (p 246).
* Pile kraut on burgers and hot dogs. The Vegie Burgers recipe (p 111) takes well to 1–2 heaped tbsp sauerkraut. »

* Add ½ cup (about 75 g) to the Best Barley Side (p 29).
* Make the creamy version of the Anything-goes Potato Salad (p 362) with ½ cup (about 75 g) sauerkraut mixed through. Nothing acts as a foil to rich ingredients the way fermented cabbage does.
* Serve sauerkraut with the Parsnip Rosti (p 323) or Green Things Fritters (p 439).
* A fried egg on toast with lots of kraut on top is an excellent way to start the day. If you make your own bacon and egg rolls, add sauerkraut to help balance the richness.
* **Kraut two-minute cup-a-soup:** Melt a little butter in a small saucepan and sauté some finely chopped dill, a bit of sliced or shredded left-over chicken or ¼ cup (55 g) left-over mashed potato, and 2–3 tbsp sauerkraut. Cover with 1 cup (250 ml) stock and when it's hot, the soup is ready.
* **Reuben sandwich** Fresh bread, pastrami, Russian Dressing (p 418), Swiss cheese and sauerkraut. Best sandwich in the business.
* **Quick kraut salad** Combine 1 cup (about 150 g) sauerkraut, 1 grated carrot, ¼ thinly sliced onion and whatever herbs you have around. Dress with 2 tbsp neutral oil, a big squeeze of lemon juice, and salt and pepper.

Sautéed sauerkraut
SERVES 2–3 AS A SIDE

Many people think sauerkraut is to be eaten raw and only raw, but sauerkraut in cooked food adds depth of flavour, and sautéed sauerkraut makes a soul-fortifying side to baked potatoes, sausages, chops, lentil stews (p 246), dumplings and other comfort foods.

In a frying pan over medium heat, melt 2 tbsp butter or oil and sauté 1 large diced onion until translucent. Add 3 chopped garlic cloves and, if you'd like, 3 chopped bacon rashers or some chopped speck. Stir until the bacon or speck is crisp. Now add 2 cups (about 300 g) strained sauerkraut and 1 tsp mustard or ½ tsp mustard powder. Stir, then cook for about 10 minutes. Add ¼ cup (60 ml) cream and cook for another few minutes.

Some ideas for using sauerkraut brine

Don't throw the juice away. Sauerkraut brine has all the flavour of the kraut itself, and if it comes from an unpasteurised jar then it's also full of live cultures.

* Knock back a shot to benefit from its microbial goodness.
* Use it as the base of a salad dressing. Add some olive oil and salt, and that's it.
* Add a splash to soup. The brine's acidity and depth of flavour will give the soup a lift.
* It's a good replacement for lemon juice if you've run out of lemons. Splash a little on barbecued greens such as asparagus or zucchini (courgettes) or grilled (broiled) fish.
* Use it instead of pickling liquid in the Anything-goes Potato Salad (p 362).
* Add a splash to a bloody mary or a vegetable juice.

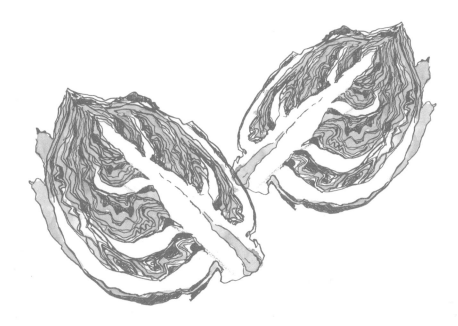

Seeds

So much goodness in such a little package. Seeds are the most consumed part of plants – given that cereals, dried beans, chickpeas and pulses such as lentils are actually seeds, and most of what we think of as nuts (p 285) are also seeds, not to mention some spices (p 419). In short, we're eating seeds all the time. Here we're using the supermarket classification system (not a real thing) and including what are commonly called seeds in domestic kitchens – chia seeds, linseeds (flaxseeds), pepitas (pumpkin seeds), poppy seeds, sesame seeds and sunflower seeds. While seeds are highly nutritious and flavoursome, and can be used widely, they do tend to get wasted – but there's always room to sneak in a seed or 200.

Storage	Like nuts, seeds are high in oils, which makes them vulnerable to light and oxygen. If not stored properly, seeds will quickly go rancid. Buy seeds whole and chop or grind them as you go. Always store seeds in an airtight container, and preferably in the fridge. If you plan to go through them quickly, the pantry is fine, but anything longer than a month or two and they will need to stay cold. In the fridge, seeds will stay fresh for 1 year, and in the freezer for 2 years.
How to toast seeds	Toasting seeds brings out their depth of flavour and can also make their nutrients easier for our bodies to absorb. On a day when you don't have too much to do and feel like being organised, you can toast seeds, let them cool and then store them in an airtight container ready for use. Because seeds are small, we usually toast them in a dry frying pan, where we keep an eye on them so they don't burn. Place the pan over low heat and add the seeds. Stir frequently and hover about. The smaller the seed the faster they will toast, so sesame seeds might take 3–5 minutes, depending on how many you're doing, whereas pepitas (pumpkin seeds) might take 7–10 minutes. Your nose is the best guide. When they smell toasty and nutty, they're done. Just don't walk away.

CHIA SEEDS

Chia seeds have been considered a staple food in South America since Aztec times. In Australia they're something of a novel food that first came into fashion through health-food circles. Chia seeds have a very subtle nutty flavour that's versatile for sweet and savoury cooking. Remember that they need to absorb liquid before being consumed, so *don't* sprinkle them dry over cereal or else the swelling and thickening will happen in your stomach. Soak them in any liquid overnight. We find that chia seeds are one of those purchases that are motivated by good intentions and then ignored, but they make great puddings and porridge.

Go with   Fruits, nut milks, oats, cereals, other seeds, tahini

Substitutes   Chia seeds are unique. If you want to make puddings, then try tapioca. For no-sugar jams, try gelatine.

Some ideas for finishing the chia seed packet

* Add 2 tsp chia seeds to Overnight Yoghurt Oats (p 301).
* Stir soaked chia seeds through stewed fruits (p 7) and top with granola or nuts.
* Chia seeds would work in Baked Rice Pudding (p 392), Left-over-buckwheat Porridge (p 63) or even the Pantry-strays Slice (p 302) or Simple Oat Cookies (p 303).
* *Little chia pud* Serves 2. We use coconut milk here, but macadamia milk (p 292), almond milk or cow's milk are also great. In a food processor, or with a hand-held blender, blitz 1 cup (250 ml) coconut milk with 2 tbsp honey or maple syrup and 1 banana to a smoothie consistency. Add ¼ cup (about 45 g) chia seeds and pulse quickly to disperse seeds evenly. Pour this mixture into 2 ramekins or a bowl and set in the fridge overnight.

No-cook jam

MAKES 1 x 250 ML (9 OZ) JAR

This is such a good little recipe. The jam sets in the fridge and must be kept there – remember, there's no sugar, so it's not preserved and won't last very long. You can spread it on your morning toast, combine it with nut milk for a milkshake or stir it into yoghurt. »

In a food processor, or using a hand-held blender, blitz 250 g (9 oz) hulled strawberries (or other berries) and mix in 1 tbsp honey or maple syrup. Pour this mixture into a clean jar and stir in ¼ cup (about 45 g) chia seeds. Refrigerate for 2 hours or until thick. Use within 1 week.

LINSEEDS (FLAXSEEDS)

These seeds come from the flax plant, which also produces flaxseed oil and linen. Linseeds are high in omega-3 fatty acids, which are said to be anti-inflammatory. Whole linseeds are stable, but you should avoid buying ground linseed that's been kept at room temperature, as its shelf life is very short and it will often already be rancid. Use whole linseeds to boost nutrition and give texture to baked goods and your morning cereal.

Go with   Chia seeds, sesame seeds, allspice, cinnamon, woody herbs, nuts, breads, cakes, biscuits, oats, dried fruits, yoghurt, honey

----

Substitutes   Swap linseeds with sesame seeds or crushed almonds.

Some ideas for finishing the linseed packet

* Add a handful to the Seedy Breakfast Muffins (p 371) for extra fibre.
* Sneak them into the Simplest Banana Bread (p 27) to make it more nutritious, then pack it in the kids' lunchboxes.
* Make your own ground linseed, sunflower seed and almond mix, and stop buying ready-made LSA. Using a spice grinder or small food processor, grind whole linseeds. Store in an airtight container in the fridge for up to 4 months.
* Use them as an egg replacer. For each egg, mix 1 tbsp ground linseeds with ¼ cup (60 ml) water. Soak until they develop a gooey texture, then use as a binding agent in cookie, pancake or cracker recipes. Note, however, that this isn't a very reliable option in cake recipes.
* Where there's an oat, there may also be a linseed. Look in the oats section (p 300) and feel free to finish off a packet of linseeds by adding them liberally to any of the recipes.

Linseed crackers

MAKES 12–15

These are the perfect crackers to eat with cheese or dips. And the real beauty is that you can flavour them however you want. They're like the fancy expensive ones, only cheaper and better.

Preheat the oven to 180°C (350°F). Blitz 1 cup (about 180 g) whole linseeds in a high-powered blender or spice grinder. Tip the ground linseeds into a bowl and add 2 tbsp whole linseeds, ½ tsp salt, 1–2 tsp dried herbs or spices such as dried oregano or rosemary, paprika, chilli flakes or curry powder. Slowly mix in ½ cup (125 ml) water until the mixture comes together. Tear off a 30 cm (12 in) sheet of baking paper, lay it on a clean benchtop and transfer the mix to it. Smooth the dough out and place another sheet of baking paper on top. Using a rolling pin, roll out the dough evenly to form a 20 cm (8 in) square or disc about 5 mm (¼ in) thick. Carefully remove the top sheet of baking paper, then transfer the bottom sheet with the rolled dough on it to a baking tray. Bake for 45–50 minutes. Allow to cool completely before breaking into smaller pieces. Store in an airtight container in the fridge for up to 1 week.

PEPITAS (PUMPKIN SEEDS)

One of the best-tasting seeds; raw or toasted, they have a sweet nutty flavour. They're also a good source of potassium and magnesium, and are used regularly in Mexican cooking – in sauces, as a snack food or as a garnish. Try all of these options. Pepitas are great in savoury cooking and in salads, while in sweet baking they can add a savoury note that feels very wholesome. And don't throw away the seeds next time you're making pumpkin soup. Toast your own pepitas using the method on p 372.

Go with   Almonds, walnuts, chia seeds, sunflower seeds, raw zucchini (courgettes), cabbage, green beans, broccoli, pumpkin (squash), potatoes, corn, salad greens, tomatoes, avocado, apples, pears, tahini

---

Substitutes   Sunflower seeds have a similar sweet nuttiness and make a versatile substitute.

Some ideas for finishing the pepita packet

✳ Add pepitas to Bircher Muesli (p 300), Banana Porridge (p 25) or Left-over-buckwheat Porridge (p 63).

✳ Use pepitas instead of nuts in the Classic Basil Pesto (p 191).

✳ Add pepitas to your next batches of Maple Granola (p 303), Pantry-strays Slice (p 302), Dried Fruit Tea Loaf (p 140) or Seedy Breakfast Muffins (p 371).

✳ Pepitas would be delicious in Pistachio Nut Bars (p 297) or Peanut Brittle (p 294).

✳ Toast them and use to top salads and salsas, such as a Green Potato Salad (p 363), Avocado Salsa (p 18), Basic Brussels Slaw (p 60) or Big Grain Salad (p 379).

✳ To use up the last of the packet, add them to the Seedy Salad Mix (p 409). You can keep a jar of this on hand and add to avocado on toast or simple green salad for added texture and nutrients.

Pepita seed mole

MAKES ABOUT 2 CUPS (350 G)

Despite what you might previously have encountered with moles, they don't have to have chocolate in them – think *guaca*-mole. This one is based on a recipe from one of our best-loved books, *Healing Spices* by Bharat B. Aggarwal, and has become a firm favourite. It's fiery, green and nutty, and warms your whole body; and it's delicious poured over grilled (broiled) chicken or fish, brushed onto pumpkin (squash) before roasting, or served with rice or tortillas.

In a hot frying pan over medium heat, toast 1 cup (155 g) pepitas (pumpkin seeds) until dry. Allow to cool, then blitz to crumbs in a food processor or using a mortar and pestle. Set aside. In the food processor, combine 3 roughly chopped long red chillies, 1 generous cup (about 10 g) roughly chopped coriander (cilantro) leaves and stems, 1 roughly chopped small brown onion, 2 roughly chopped garlic cloves, 2 tsp dried oregano, 1 tsp ground cumin, 1 tsp salt and the pepita seed crumbs. Blitz to a paste and then, with the motor running, drizzle in 2 tbsp olive oil.

Store the mole in a jar or airtight container in the fridge for up to 1 week. To use, empty into a saucepan over medium heat, add 1–2 cups (250–500 ml) vegetable or chicken stock, simmer to thicken, and serve.

POPPY SEEDS

Poppy seeds are so tiny that you might not even realise they're kidney-shaped. A single gram of poppy seeds is made up of thousands of individual seeds. They are the micro-beauties of the kitchen, with a nutty bittersweet taste that's deeply appreciated in Eastern European, Jewish and Indian cooking. Whether ground and mixed with sugar to fill pastries, used as a thickener for curries, or sprinkled over cakes and breads, wherever poppy seeds go they add charm, colour and crunch.

Go with   Hazelnuts, almonds, chia seeds, rye bread, butter, dried fruits, eggs, carrots, potatoes, spinach, sweet potato, buttery baked goods, oranges, lemons, cherries, plums

---

Substitutes   For savoury dishes you could replace them with mustard seeds, keeping in mind that mustard seeds are a bit more intense. Use sesame seeds in sweet recipes.

Some ideas for finishing the poppy seed packet

✱ Poppy seeds would be lovely in the Seedy Breakfast Muffins (p 371); try them with grated pumpkin (squash) or pear and plenty of cinnamon.

✱ Poppy seeds add a pop of colour to sweet grain dishes. Add 1–2 tbsp to Baked Rice Pudding (p 392) or Banana Porridge (p 25).

✱ ***Poppy seed potatoes*** Parboil 400 g (14 oz) potatoes until cooked through. Drain and cut into cubes. Heat 2 tbsp ghee or your favourite oil in a medium–large frying pan and add the potatoes, a pinch each of salt and ground turmeric, and 1–2 tbsp poppy seeds. Fry until the potatoes are golden.

✱ ***Quick egg noodles for two*** Cook 150 g (5½ oz) egg noodles (or egg pasta) according to packet directions. In a medium–large frying pan, melt 2 tbsp butter with ¼ tsp each of salt and pepper, 1 tsp paprika and 1 tbsp poppy seeds until the butter begins to brown. Remove from the heat. Drain the egg noodles and mix into the poppy seed butter.

✱ ***Poppy seed and orange dressing*** Use this for dark, bitter salad leaves like radicchio or rocket (arugula), roasted beetroot, a fennel salad or a raw grated carrot salad. In a small jar, combine the juice and zest of 1 small orange, 2 tsp freshly grated horseradish or ginger, 2 tbsp olive oil, ½–1 tbsp red wine vinegar, ¼–½ tsp salt, 1 tsp orange jam or marmalade, 2 tsp dijon mustard and 2 tsp poppy seeds. Shake to emulsify. Store in the fridge for up to 1 week.

Savoury poppy seed spread
MAKES ABOUT ½ CUP (165 G)

This spread is like having a bagel. Spread it on toast or crackers and add a pickle.

In a small bowl, combine ½ cup (120 g) cream cheese, 2 tbsp poppy seeds, 2 tbsp finely chopped chives, and a pinch each of salt and pepper. Mash with a fork to really get everything well combined. Keep in the fridge for up to 1 week.

Sweet poppy seed spread
MAKES ABOUT 1⅓ CUPS (250 G)

This is a sweet filling for cakes, pastries or biscuits. It can also be used as a spread on your morning toast, with waffles or in crepes. It will last in the fridge for 1 week.

Start by grinding ½ cup (80 g) poppy seeds as finely as you can using a spice grinder, high-powered blender or mortar and pestle. In a small saucepan, combine ½ cup (125 ml) milk, the ground poppy seeds and 1 tbsp caster (superfine) sugar, then simmer for 5 minutes until you have a thick paste. You will need to stir constantly. Remove from the heat and add 2 tbsp butter and ½ tsp vanilla extract. Refrigerate for 30 minutes or until the spread has set.

SESAME SEEDS
One of the oldest crops known to humans, sesame seeds are used in cooking from Africa to Japan. They're a good source of vitamin B, calcium and zinc, and are generally available in black or white seeds. The black seeds have the stronger flavour, but the rich nutty flavour of both is stronger when they've been lightly toasted. Mix them together to use them up – it will be very pretty. Sesame seeds come either hulled or unhulled. Unhulled seeds are slightly more bitter in flavour, while hulled seeds taste nuttier.

Go with	Eggplant (aubergine), green beans, asparagus, carrots, cucumber, daikon, cabbage, broccoli, kale, kohlrabi, salad greens, pumpkin (squash), sweet potato, garlic, ginger, apples, other seeds, cashews, tahini of course, tofu, chicken, beef, coriander (cilantro), mint, coconut, honey, chocolate, coffee
Substitutes	Poppy seeds can be used as a garnish in place of sesame seeds. To replicate sesame's rich flavour, try toasted peanuts.

Some ideas for finishing the sesame seed packet

* Make the Japanese-style Sesame Greens (p 40). The nutty flavour comes from smashed sesame seeds.
* Add sesame seeds to the Kimchi Pancakes (p 225).
* Pumpkin (squash) and sesame seeds are lovely together. Add 2–3 tbsp sesame seeds to the Quick Pumpkin and Ginger Relish (p 369), or scatter them over Miso Pumpkin (p 371). Really, sesame seeds would work in any of the recipes in the pumpkin section.
* A nice version of the Seedy Breakfast Muffins (p 371) is sesame and carrot. Use ½ cup (75 g) sesame seeds and ½ cup chopped nuts, along with the grated carrot. Perfect sustenance on a bushwalk.
* Make a sesame mayonnaise mix to spread on fish burgers, or to serve with fritters or fried chicken. Add a good splash of sesame oil to ½ cup (120 g) mayonnaise, along with 2–3 tbsp toasted sesame seeds and a pinch of salt.
* Sesame seeds add flavour, texture and protein to salads. Add a generous handful of toasted sesame seeds to a slaw with a spicy dressing, or to Raw Carrot Salad (p 77), Daikon Salad (p 135) or Apple Salad (p 6).
* Don't forget to add sesame seeds to bread or cookie doughs, especially the Flotsam and Jetsam Flat Breads (p 168).
* Add sesame seeds to the Seedy Salad Mix (p 409).
* Lots of toasted sesame seeds on top of dan dan noodles (p 454) gives both texture and the perfect finish.
* We add toasted sesame seeds to the Creamy Tahini Dressing (p 455) and pour it over koftas or falafel.
* ***Home-made tahini*** Toast 1 cup (145 g) white sesame seeds until fragrant and golden. Tip into a high-powered blender or food processor and begin to blend. To make it easier for the seeds to form a paste, add 2 tbsp olive oil and keep blending. Blend past the crumbly stage and past the sticky stage until you have a smooth, thick paste. Keep in a jar in the fridge for up to 4 months.

Everyday dukkah

MAKES 1 x 200 ML (7 OZ) JAR

Originating in Egypt, this spiced seed and nut blend has long been used as a genius way of adding protein to even the simplest meal of bread and olive oil. Dukkah comes from an Arabic word that means 'to pound', giving you a clue as to what kind of texture you want – neither whole seeds and spices, nor a paste. Use dukkah to accompany bread dipped in oil, as well as on top of soups or hummus, or sprinkled over avocado or tomato on toast.

In a dry frying pan, toast (pp 285–86) ¼ cup (40 g) sesame seeds, with 2–3 tbsp stray nuts if you have them (but don't worry about it if you don't), 1 tbsp chilli flakes, 2 tsp fennel seeds, 1 tsp cumin seeds, ¼ tsp ground warm spices (e.g. allspice or cinnamon) and a generous pinch each of salt and pepper. Toast until the seeds are beginning to turn golden, stirring often to prevent them burning. Add the juice of ½ lemon and continue to toast until the lemon juice has been absorbed and the mixture is dry again. Remove from the heat and allow to cool, then pound using a mortar and pestle until the seeds are breaking down but remain crunchy. Or you can very briefly pulse in a food processor, taking care not to over-process. Store the dukkah in an airtight container in the fridge for up to 2 weeks.

SUNFLOWER SEEDS

Sunflower seeds (technically speaking, not seeds but fruits) are available in their black and grey striped husks or as edible hulled kernels. The kernels are a good source of vitamin E and magnesium. Raw sunflower seeds have the typical grassy flavour of many seeds; once toasted, they release a deeper, nuttier flavour.

Go with   Almonds, sesame seeds, pine nuts, walnuts, hazelnuts, chia seeds, pepitas (pumpkin seeds), oats, coconut, dried fruits, apples, pears, avocado, beetroot, radishes, cabbage, broccoli, kale, kohlrabi, lettuces, tahini

---

Substitutes   Pepitas (pumpkin seeds) and sesame seeds can replace sunflower seeds, as can pine nuts.

Some ideas for finishing the sunflower seed packet

* Add sunflower seeds to the Best Barley Side (p 29). The barley and sunflower seeds are a similar size, and combine to give great texture and earthiness.
* Avocado on rye toast with pickles, sprouts and a sprinkling of sunflower seeds is a seriously good breakfast when you've got a big day ahead.
* Sunflower seeds are great in vegie burgers, adding extra flavour and helping to bind the patties. In the Vegie Burgers recipe (p 111), replace the ½ cup (60 g) breadcrumbs with ½ cup (75 g) toasted sunflower seeds, roughly blitzed in a food processor.
* Add sunflower seeds to the Pantry-strays Slice (p 302). We use this recipe as a way to finish off daggy old stale Weetbix and add sunflower seeds for some extra nutrition.
* ***Sunflower seed and corn salad*** Toast ½ cup (75 g) sunflower seeds and set aside to cool. Blanch the kernels from 4 corn cobs in boiling water for 5 minutes, then drain and allow to cool and dry. In a bowl, combine the corn kernels and sunflower seeds and season with salt and pepper. Chop up 2–3 pickled chillies, throw in a small handful of oregano leaves, and dress with the juice of 1 lime and plenty of sunflower or olive oil.

Seedy salad mix
MAKES ABOUT ⅔ CUP (120 G)

This salad mix is one of the best things you can have on hand to make some boring lettuce a bit more of a show-off. It gives not only a mean flavour boost, but a nutritional boost too.

Preheat the oven to 150°C (300°F) and line a baking tray with baking paper. In a small bowl, combine ½ cup (75 g) sunflower seeds with 2 tbsp of another seed, such as sesame seeds or pepitas (pumpkin seeds), and ½ tsp salt. Drizzle with a little oil, and add 2 tsp dried herbs or spices (paprika, ground cumin, oregano, rosemary, fennel seeds, nigella seeds) and a pinch of cayenne pepper. Mix well. Spread out the seeds on the baking tray and toast them in the oven for 5–7 minutes, until golden and crunchy. Set a timer to make sure you move the seeds around every 2–3 minutes so they toast evenly.

Once cool, store in an airtight container in the pantry. They will stay fresh for about 1 week. If they're a little stale, give them another 3–5 minutes in the oven to revive them.

Silverbeet

Big glossy ruffly silverbeet (also known as Swiss chard) – just buying it feels virtuous. And then you have it, and there's just so much, and what was the plan for it anyway? Used wisely, a whole bunch of silverbeet can be your main vegetable for a few days. Raw and cooked, leaves and stems will give you many options for mains and side dishes. Our advice is not to get overwhelmed by silverbeet's considerable size and just work your way through it, one leaf at a time. Or if you want to use that thing in one hit, make the Greens Pie Filling on p 412.

Goes with	Onions, leeks, spinach, potatoes, mushrooms, tomatoes, radishes, apples, pears, figs, pomegranate, lemons, dried beans, lentils, chickpeas, tofu, bacon, cheeses, eggs, butter, cream, barley, miso, hazelnuts, pine nuts, almonds, allspice, nutmeg, cumin, paprika, mustard seeds
Storage	To make storage easier, remove the stems from the leaves. Bundle them together, wrap in a slightly damp clean tea towel (dish towel) or clean Chux, and keep in a reusable plastic bag or cloth bag in the crisper. Silverbeet is very robust and should stay fresh for at least 1 week.
Substitutes	For the most part, spinach and silverbeet can be swapped in most recipes. Kale is also a good substitute, as is cavolo nero.

Some ideas for how to deal with silverbeet

* The Green Things Fritters (p 439) work very well with silverbeet leaves sliced into ribbons. Don't add the stems; keep them for the Sautéed Silverbeet Stems (p 413).
* **Green rice** Turn the Anything-goes Rice (p 394) green with silverbeet. Sauté the stems instead of onion and slice the leaves. Add extra lemon juice and a pinch of chilli flakes.

* **Wilted silverbeet** A very easy side that uses half a bunch. Heat ¼ cup (60 ml) olive oil in a frying pan and add the very thinly sliced stems of ½ bunch (about 500 g/1 lb 2 oz) of silverbeet. Sauté for 10 minutes, then add 2 finely chopped garlic cloves and 1 tbsp diced preserved lemon or finely grated lemon zest. Now add the silverbeet leaves, torn into large pieces. Sauté for 5 minutes, until wilted. Stir through a handful each of currants and pine nuts, then season with salt and pepper.
* **The tastiest bunch of silverbeet** Four recipes in one. Follow The Tastiest Bunch of Kale recipe on p 221, replacing the kale with 1 bunch (about 1 kg/2 lb 4 oz) of silverbeet.
* **Creamed silverbeet with plenty of garlic** Remove the stems from 1 bunch (about 1 kg/ 2 lb 4 oz) of silverbeet and save for another meal. Roughly tear the leaves. Melt 1 tbsp butter in a frying pan over medium–low heat and add 5 finely chopped garlic cloves. Sauté for only 1 minute. Add the silverbeet leaves, ½ tsp salt and some pepper, and sauté until the silverbeet wilts. Add ¼ cup (60 ml) cream or plain yoghurt and cook for another 2–3 minutes.

Silverbeet quesadillas
MAKES 2

Shred the leaves from 1 bunch (about 1 kg/2 lb 4 oz) of silverbeet. (Keep the stems for the Sautéed Silverbeet Stems, p 413). In a frying pan, heat 1 tbsp neutral oil. Add to the pan with 2–3 chopped garlic cloves, 1 sliced chilli, ½ tsp each of ground cumin and paprika, and a good pinch of salt. Sauté for 2–3 minutes. This mix will be enough to make 2 large quesadillas. If you're feeding more people, add some shredded chicken, cooked minced (ground) meat or 400 g (14 oz) tinned black beans to the silverbeet mix to stretch it out.

Place the silverbeet mixture on tortillas and top with plenty of grated cheddar. Add a little more salt and pepper, close the quesadilla with another tortilla and cook on both sides in a dry frying pan, until the cheese has melted and the outside is golden. Serve with sour cream or guacamole and hot sauce.

Silverbeet salad
SERVES 4–6 AS A SIDE SALAD

Raw silverbeet leaves can be fibrous, depending on their size, but shred them finely and they make a great winter salad that's as pretty as it is substantial. Keep the stems for another dish.

Wash and dry the leaves from 1 bunch (about 1 kg/2 lb 4 oz) of silverbeet. Shred them into long ribbons and place them in a bowl. Thinly slice either 1 small fennel bulb or 1 red onion and add to the bowl. Season with a generous pinch each of salt and pepper and toss together. »

Add any of the following to give the salad some extra oomph:

- 3–4 diced boiled eggs and 1 bunch chopped dill
- 1 grated beetroot and a handful of toasted hazelnuts
- about 8 thinly sliced radishes and 2 tbsp drained capers
- 1 thinly sliced apple or pear, some toasted sunflower seeds and a few handfuls of torn herb leaves of your choice
- 1 cup (160 g) cooked or tinned chickpeas, lightly sautéed with garlic and caraway seeds, then cooled
- roast pumpkin (squash), toasted pine nuts and crumbled feta.

Dress with a creamy dressing, such as the Blue Cheese Dressing (p 90), Cheat's Caesar Salad Dressing (p 4), Creamy Tahini Dressing (p 455) or Orange Vinaigrette (p 316). Top generously with toasted seeds or nuts.

Silverbeet rolls
SERVES 4

The large crinkly leaves of the silverbeet are perfect for stuffing. Between the green of the silverbeet and the heartiness of the stuffing, you don't need anything else. You'll need to make a batch of the Best Barley Side (p 29) or some spiced sautéed minced (ground) meat.

Wash and dry the leaves from 1 bunch (about 1 kg/2 lb 4 oz) of silverbeet. Bring a saucepan of salted water to the boil. Blanch the silverbeet leaves for 4 minutes, until softened. Drain and allow to cool. Preheat the oven to 180°C (350°F). Lightly oil an ovenproof dish and, working one at a time, lay a leaf out flat on a clean benchtop. Put 3 tbsp of the filling about three-quarters of the way down the leaf. Fold in the sides of the leaf, then roll up the leaf from bottom to top, enclosing the stuffing completely. Place in the ovenproof dish and repeat until all your filling is used up. Pour 400 g (14 oz) tinned chopped tomatoes or 1 cup (250 ml) stock of your choice over the rolls. Cover and bake for 30–45 minutes, until the sauce is rich and glossy.

Greens pie filling
SERVES 4-6

This pie mix can be used to make smaller pies or triangles, or a single large pie. You can use a thinly rolled shortcrust or filo pastry, or Sour Cream Pastry (p 418). Here we call for silverbeet, but really any green leaf (kale, rocket/arugula, spinach) will do, and if you're a gardener or forager, make it with a mix of everything from dandelion leaves to warrigal greens. Don't be afraid to use limp old greens for this recipe; once it hits the table, no one will notice.

Bring a saucepan of salted water to the boil. Wash and dry 1 bunch (about 1 kg/ 2 lb 4 oz) of silverbeet and separate the stems from the leaves. Blanch the leaves in the boiling water for about 4 minutes, then drain and leave to cool. When cool enough to handle, wring out each leaf as if you were doing the laundry. Do this well, because you want to get as much of the water out as you can. Finely chop the wrung-out leaves and set aside.

Thinly slice the silverbeet stems and 1 onion. Heat ¼ cup (60 ml) oil of your choice in a large frying pan over medium heat and sauté the onion and stems until translucent. Add 4–5 sliced garlic cloves and sauté again for 1–2 minutes. Add the silverbeet leaves, 3 tbsp fresh oregano leaves (or 1 tbsp dried), and 1 tsp each of salt and ground pepper, then sauté for another 5 minutes.

Remove from the heat and allow to cool until the silverbeet is only warm, then transfer to a medium bowl. In a small bowl, whisk 4 eggs, then mix them with the silverbeet. Add 200 g (7 oz) grated cheddar (or any other cheese you fancy or have in the fridge). Mix everything together well, then assemble your pie.

SILVERBEET STEMS

Sautéed silverbeet stems
SERVES 2–3 AS A SIDE

The flavours of a gratin with none of the waiting.

In a large frying pan over medium heat, melt 1 tbsp butter with a little splash of oil. Sauté 1 finely diced onion for about 5 minutes. Thinly slice the stems of 1 bunch (about 1 kg/2 lb 4 oz) of silverbeet (or use stems left-over from another dish), add them to the pan and sauté for 10 minutes. Add ½ cup (125 ml) cream and 50–100 g (1¾–3½ oz) cheddar or blue cheese, turn to the lowest heat and cook for another 10 minutes. Serve with plenty of ground black pepper.

Lemon and chilli silverbeet stems

Heat ¼ cup (60 ml) olive oil in a large frying pan over medium heat and sauté 1 finely diced onion, 1 sliced long red chilli and ½ tsp salt for about 5 minutes. While they're cooking, cut the stems from 1 bunch (about 1 kg/2 lb 4 oz) of silverbeet (or use stems left-over from another dish) and slice thinly. Add them to the pan and sauté for 10 minutes. Add the juice of 1 lemon, turn to the lowest heat and cook for another 10 minutes. Add plenty of ground black pepper to serve.

Snow peas

These lovely things are so tender and crisp that it seems a shame to cook them. But if you don't, snow peas (mange tout) become tough and stringy before you can say 'stir-fry'. At their best, eat them raw in salads or quick-pickle them. When they've been kicking around longer, give them a flash stir-fry and marvel at how they come good instantly.

Go with   Asparagus, peas, carrots, celery, spring onions (scallions), broccoli, Asian greens, ginger, garlic, lemon, chilli, chives, coriander (cilantro), mint, peanuts, cashews, butter, eggs, chicken, pork, beef, tofu

---

Storage   Do not wash snow peas before storing them. Keep them in a reusable plastic bag, cloth bag or airtight container for up to 4 days. If you want to freeze them, give them a quick blanch in boiling water for a few seconds. Drain, cool and dry, then store them in an airtight container in the freezer for up to 3 months. To refresh limp snow peas, soak them in really cold water for 15–30 minutes.

Substitutes   Sugar snap peas are same same, but green beans will also do just fine, as will the plain old pea. Broccoli stems, thinly sliced lengthways, make a great snow pea stand-in.

Some ideas for using up a few snow peas

* Cut snow peas (mange tout) into matchsticks and add to the Cold Noodle and Wombok Salad With Pickles (p 487) or a cabbage slaw.
* Sauté snow peas (mange tout) lightly and eat with Congee (p 394). The crunchy snow peas and soft warming congee are opposites that attract.
* Add snow peas (mange tout) to brothy soups. Ditch the spinach in the Brown Rice, Mushroom and Spinach Soup (p 392), and add sliced snow peas instead; or add them to the Left-over-chicken Soup (p 106), along with corn kernels, sliced chilli and some noodles.

* If you've neglected the bag of snow peas (mange tout) in the fridge, don't beat yourself up; the Spring Greens Medley (p 341) revives all sad greens. While making it, add the last few green beans and even the ¼ cos lettuce that has seen better days.
* **Quick-pickled snow peas** Follow the recipe on p 473 and have snow peas (mange tout) ready in time for dinner. Remove their string and cut them on the diagonal. Serve with rice paper rolls, grilled (broiled) fish or a noodle salad.
* **Green potato salad** Add snow peas (mange tout) to the Anything-goes Potato Salad (p 362). Slice them on the diagonal into thin strips and add plenty of chives and mint.

Little snow pea salad

SERVES 1-2

This delicate salad would be nice with a poached egg for lunch or as a side with dinner. It's crunchy and spring-greeny.

Thinly slice 200 g (7 oz) snow peas (mange tout) lengthways into matchsticks and place in a small bowl. Add 1 handful each of snow pea shoots (or other small green leaves such as baby spinach or rocket/arugula) and mint leaves. If you want to add a few seeds or nuts that would be nice. We add toasted pepitas (pumpkin seeds) or pistachios to keep everything green. Dress this salad lightly with salt, white pepper, 1 tbsp neutral oil and a big squeeze of lemon or lime juice.

Snow pea stir-fry

If your snow peas have been forgotten in the depths of the fridge, use the Stir-fried Celery recipe on p 87, replacing the celery with 200 g (7 oz) stringed snow peas (mange tout) and cooking them only until they turn bright green and are a little tender.

Lemony snow pea sauté

SERVES 4 AS A SIDE

Melt 2 tbsp butter in a saucepan over low heat and add 1 smallish onion or ½ onion very finely diced. Cover and cook for 5 minutes so the onion sweats but doesn't brown. Add 300 g (10½ oz) stringed snow peas (mange tout) with the juice and zest of ½ lemon, ¼ cup (60 ml) water and a good pinch each of salt and pepper. Allow to simmer over very low heat for another 5 minutes. Transfer to a serving bowl and garnish with another squeeze of lemon juice and plenty of torn mint leaves or chopped chives.

SNOW PEA SHOOTS

If you grow snow peas (mange tout), you'll be lucky enough to have snow pea shoots. If not, they're often available from Asian food markets in the early spring. Their texture is crunchy and light, and they make a great change from standard salad leaves. Add them to delicate white bread sandwiches. The Snow Pea Salad on the previous page also uses snow pea (mange tout) shoots.

Stir-fried snow pea shoots

SERVES 2 AS A SIDE

Heat 1 tbsp neutral oil in a wok over high heat and add 2–3 cups (about 150 g) snow pea shoots. Stir-fry them for about 1 minute. Add a little salt and pepper, ¼ cup (60 ml) stock, 1 tbsp rice wine vinegar and 1 tbsp sesame oil. Stir-fry for another minute, then serve hot with any rice dish (it's particularly good with Congee, p 394).

Sour cream

Sour cream is exactly what it says it is – soured cream. It's tangy and tart, yet also creamy and rich. We have a lot of taco Tuesdays in our houses, so we often end up with a third of a tub of sour cream left over, which isn't quite enough for another meal. As dairy is resource-heavy to produce, we've come up with some simple ideas to ensure this valuable ingredient doesn't end up in the bin.

Goes with	Sour cream adds richness to mushrooms, spinach, silverbeet (Swiss chard), cucumber, beetroot, carrots, potatoes, cabbage, apples, pears, berries, minced (ground) meat, beans, eggs, garlic, horseradish and chocolate.
Storage	Store in the fridge in the original container until its use-by date, but after that take a whiff. Chances are it will still be okay for 7–10 days after.
Substitutes	Yoghurt is the best substitute as it has a similarly tangy, albeit lighter, flavour. You can also use fresh ricotta.

Some ideas for using up the rest of the sour cream

* Use a generous dollop of sour cream instead of the cream in the Wilted Lettuce Soup (p 248), the lentil soup from the Simple Lentil Base Four Ways (p 245), or the Green Soup (p 440). It's the easiest way to make sure the whole tub gets used up.
* Sour cream is the secret ingredient in the Minty Green Goddess Sauce (p 197).
* It's the sour cream that makes Jaimee's Apple Bake (p 7) luscious.
* Use a little sour cream instead of eggs when crumbing chicken, fish or cauliflower schnitzels.
* Use 1 tbsp sour cream to help bind meatballs and fritters. The Parsnip Rosti (p 323) could include a little sour cream instead of cream.
* Top jacket potatoes or Jacket Sweet Potatoes (p 450) with left-over Chilli Con Carne (p 36), Quick-pickled Corn (p 118) and the rest of the tub of sour cream.
* Make the Flotsam and Jetsam Flat Breads (p 168), using sour cream thinned with a little water as your dairy option.

Sour cream pastry
MAKES ABOUT 550 G (1 LB 4 OZ)

This is our standby pastry recipe for sweet and savoury baking. The sour cream gives the pastry its lovely flaky texture, similar to puff pastry but nowhere near as fiddly. Use it with the Fig Crostata (p 163), or any of the pie fillings.

Combine 1⅔ cups (250 g) plain (all-purpose) flour and 1 tsp salt in a food processor. Add 200 g (7 oz) cubed cold unsalted butter and pulse until the mixture is crumbly and resembles sand. With the motor running, add 120 g (4¼ oz) sour cream and mix until everything just comes together and forms a ball. Wrap the dough in a beeswax or plastic wrap and refrigerate for at least 30 minutes before using.

Well wrapped, this pastry dough will keep in the fridge for 2–3 days. You can freeze it for up to 1 month.

Sour cream gravy
MAKES ABOUT 1⅓ CUPS (330 ML)

So decadent and rich, eating this feels like being under a thick quilt on a cold night. Pour it over pork meatballs, a steak, mashed potatoes or roasted mushrooms.

In a small saucepan over medium heat, melt 2 tbsp butter and whisk in 2 tbsp plain (all-purpose) flour. Stir until lightly browned, then whisk in ¾ cup (185 ml) stock and ½ tsp each of salt and pepper. Continue whisking until thickened. Remove from the heat, whisk in ⅓ cup (85 g) sour cream, then taste and adjust the seasoning if needed. Stir chopped chives or parsley through the gravy and serve.

Russian dressing
MAKES ABOUT ½ CUP (130 G)

For a Russian-Style Celery and Potato Salad (p 86), Reuben Sandwich (p 398) or even wedges of cold iceberg lettuce, don't forget the Russian Dressing. It's an old standard. Know it. Make it.

In a small bowl, mix ¼ cup (65 g) sour cream, ¼ cup (60 g) mayonnaise, 1 tbsp tomato sauce (ketchup), 2 tsp worcestershire sauce, 1 finely chopped garlic clove, 1 tbsp lemon juice, and salt and pepper to taste.

See cheese, cream, milk, whey and yoghurt for ideas with other dairy products.

Spices

We cooks would be lost without spices. They give a recipe its character. Sometimes they're subtle and sometimes bold. So much depends on spices that wars have been fought over them, boats have set sail in pursuit of them, cities have been founded and cultures destroyed in the wake of their trade; much of the world as we know it is a consequence of the love of spices. Today, the spice trade is still fraught with global issues of poor labour conditions, environmental degradation and long supply chains. While it can be difficult to find ethical, single-origin spices (they're out there, though), wasting any spices is not an option. Treat them as the precious elements they are and treasure them in your cooking.

We've included only the most common spices here. But we haunt spice shops as a hobby, and know full well that there are many more. What we hope to offer in this short section is a way of thinking about spices that gets you using them all and not letting them lurk in the cupboard, just waiting for the yearly clean-out.

- -

Storage　　You'll get more flavour from your spices by buying them whole and grinding them as you need them. Whole spices have a long shelf life, lasting well for a few years. Ground spices only stay fresh for up to 6 months before their flavour starts to deteriorate. Store both whole and ground spices in airtight glass jars or containers in a cool, dark place.

Everyday spice blends
MAKE ABOUT 50 G (1¾ OZ) EACH

Reliable spice blends have saved us from eating bland meals, no matter how tired or 'could not be bothered' we feel. A good spice blend can be the base of a stew, or the seasoning on top of avocado on toast, that will make good cooking effortless. We make them in relatively small batches so they stay fresh, and store them in labelled jars in the pantry.

They're also a good way to get kids and new cooks confident with using spices. A little ready-made spice blend from one jar makes everything very easy.

SPICE MIX 1: THE PIZZA AND PASTA BLEND

2 tbsp dried oregano

1 tbsp dried thyme

1 tbsp paprika

½ tsp ground allspice

½ tsp ground black pepper

SPICE MIX 2: THE CURRIES BLEND

1 tbsp ground coriander

1 tbsp ground cumin

1 tbsp ground turmeric

1 tbsp whole fennel seeds

1 tbsp whole mustard seeds

1 tbsp ground black pepper

SPICE MIX 3: FOR KOFTAS, SPINACH PIES AND RICE DISHES

2 tbsp ground cumin

2 tbsp ground coriander

1 tbsp ground cinnamon

1 tsp whole fennel seeds

SPICE MIX 4: FOR TACOS, SALSAS, BEAN DISHES OR SHREDDED MEATS

2 tbsp dried oregano

2 tbsp paprika

1 tbsp ground cumin

1 tsp chilli flakes

¼ tsp cayenne pepper

pinch of sugar

SPICE MIX 5: WARM SPICES FOR BAKING, COOKING FRUITS AND PUDDINGS

2 tbsp ground cinnamon

2 tbsp ground allspice

1 tsp ground cloves

½ tsp ground nutmeg

pinch of ground black pepper

SPICE MIX 6: FOR PICKLING

2 tbsp whole mustard seeds

1 tbsp whole fennel seeds or dill seeds

1 tbsp black peppercorns

1 tsp chilli flakes (optional)

½ tsp ground allspice or cloves

Sticky chai blend

MAKES ABOUT 400 ML (14 FL OZ)

A sticky chai is a celebration of all the spices. This is our own blend, using common spices. Feel free to play around with the quantities.

With a large mortar and pestle, pound 16 cardamom pods, 8 star anise, 6 whole cloves, ¼ tsp grated nutmeg, 2 tsp ground allspice, 1 tsp black peppercorns and 4 cinnamon sticks until the whole spices are broken into small pieces but not reduced to a powder. Transfer to a small heatproof bowl and mix with 1 cup (85 g) black tea leaves and 4 tbsp (about 65 g) grated fresh ginger.

In a small saucepan over low heat, warm ½ cup (175 g) honey, 2 tbsp lemon juice and ½ tsp vanilla extract, stirring to combine. Pour the warm honey mixture over the tea and spice mix, and stir well to combine. Allow to cool, then store in a clean, dry airtight container in the fridge for up to 3 months.

TO MAKE THE BEST CHAI

In a small saucepan, combine 1 cup (250 ml) milk of your choice with 2 tbsp sticky chai blend. Simmer for 5 minutes, then strain to serve.

Chilled mulled wine

MAKES ABOUT 4 CUPS (1 LITRE)

Considering a southern hemisphere Christmas can be upwards of 35°C (95°F), it's a bit silly to be drinking toasts with steaming cups of mulled wine. Our chilled, southern hemisphere version is both festive and refreshing.

In a small saucepan over medium–low heat, bring ½ cup (125 ml) water, ½ cup (175 g) honey, 10 whole cloves, 4 allspice berries, 4 whole star anise, 2 cinnamon sticks and 1 vanilla pod to a simmer, then reduce the heat to low and simmer for 2–3 minutes.

Remove from the heat, add a 750 ml (25 oz) bottle of white or rosé wine and mix well. Refrigerate and allow the flavours to infuse overnight. Strain through a sieve lined with muslin and serve over ice, with a cherry or a slice of peach in each glass.

ALLSPICE

Allspice has the perfect name, as it tastes and smells like all the spices. It's commonly mistaken for a mix of ground spices, but is in fact its own little reddish-brown berry that comes from the pimento tree.

Often confused with cloves, allspice also has nutmeg, cinnamon and black pepper vibes. It's sweet and warm, and can be used in both sweet and savoury dishes. Allspice gives jerk chicken and pork its jerkiness and mulled wine (p 421) its pungent aroma. Use allspice in curries, meaty stews and spice rubs; in pickles, jams and baked goods; and when poaching fruits or making anything mulled.

Goes with   Chocolate, nuts, cinnamon, cloves, nutmeg, star anise, coriander seeds, fennel seeds, turmeric, cumin, pepper, bay leaves, onions, sweet potato, silverbeet (Swiss chard), garlic, chilli, ginger, chicken, seafood, pork, rice and couscous dishes, oats, linseeds (flaxseeds), dried fruits, apples, pears, grapes, quince, citrus fruits, pineapple, persimmons, rhubarb, custard

Substitutes   If you're out of ground allspice, replace it with a mix of ground cinnamon, cloves and nutmeg. Use cinnamon sticks, or whole cloves or star anise, instead of allspice berries.

Some ideas for using allspice

* Add ground allspice to cakes, gingerbread, banana bread and apple or pumpkin pies.
* Add 1 tsp ground allspice to your next chocolate cake.
* Sprinkle a little ground allspice and cayenne pepper over pumpkin (squash) or sweet potato before baking.
* Ground allspice helps give home-made ketchups and barbecue sauces their distinct sweet–spicy flavour. Add it to the Quince Paste (p 376) or Banana Ketchup (p 26).
* We love allspice in our pickles for a little warmth. Add 3–4 whole berries to each jar, along with your other spices.
* Add ½ tsp allspice berries to a soup or stew – especially good with slow-cooked meats.
* Add 4 allspice berries to mulled wine (p 421) or cider.
* Poach pears, quinces or plums in red wine and raw sugar with allspice berries and some strips of orange peel. See p 336 for poaching tips.

BLACK PEPPER

If there's only one spice in the house, let it be pepper. As the most widely used spice in the world, it's indispensable in the kitchen. A little pepper on the table is used as a subtle seasoning, but a lot of pepper used in cooking is a not so subtle spice. Black pepper will keep its robust flavour when added towards the end of cooking, but it can become bitter if added too early. The good news is that time is on your side when getting through black pepper, as thoroughly dried peppercorns will last indefinitely.

Goes with   Everything. Seriously. Depending on how you're using it, black pepper goes with yoghurt (think tzatziki); berries (a little black pepper gives some edge to strawberry jam); and all the vegetables, dairy products, meats and legumes you can think of.

Substitutes   This is a bit tough, because black pepper is unique. If you're after the heat, add some chilli in place of black pepper. If you're after the musty notes of ground pepper, try mustard powder.

Some ideas for using black pepper

* If you can stand it, go hard and use black pepper as the main flavour in a stir-fry. Yotam Ottolenghi made this technique famous with his black pepper tofu in *Plenty*. This light version could be used when stir-frying anything. Follow the stir-fry method on p 87, adding 2–3 tbsp ground pepper, 2 tbsp soy sauce and 1 tsp caster (superfine) sugar, and hold on to your hat.
* If you use whole black peppercorns when you're pickling or fermenting, they will soften over time and lend the liquid not only their heat but great texture too. All pickling jars are improved by ½ tsp peppercorns.
* Black pepper added to the Whatever-cheese Eggy Muffins (p 93) is a good, sharp foil to the cottage cheese or ricotta.
* Please make the Orange Pepper (p 318). It brings flair to everything it touches.
* Pepper and fruit, together forever. Add ground pepper to any of the recipes in berries (p 47); make a batch of Pear and Rosemary Relish (p 336), using a little rosemary and plenty of ground black pepper; or add peppercorns to the Home-made 'Tinned' Pineapple (p 353).

CINNAMON

Most of the time when we think we're sprinkling cinnamon, it's actually cassia. It's confusing, we know, but both spices are the bark from closely related trees, one native to Sri Lanka and the other to China, and have a very similar flavour profile. Here we discuss cinnamon, knowing full well that we might be cooking with cassia. The beauty of these spices is that their versatility is nearly unparalleled. From apple pie to pho, cinnamon is a key ingredient for complexity and sweet spiciness. It's one of the essential spices to have in your pantry.

Goes with   Chocolate, coffee, honey, cream, nuts, oats, quinoa, linseeds (flaxseeds), cloves, allspice, nutmeg, star anise, cumin, turmeric, ginger, lemongrass, chilli, mint, bay leaves, thyme, bananas, stone fruits, apples, pears, grapes, quince, citrus fruits, rhubarb, pineapple, persimmons, dried fruits, parsnips, carrots, cucumber, tomatoes, pumpkin (squash), sweet potato, mushrooms, anchovies, chicken, beef, pork

----

Substitutes   If you're out of cinnamon, substitute an equal amount of ground allspice.

Some ideas for using cinnamon

* If you use a stovetop espresso maker, add a little pinch of cinnamon to the ground coffee.
* Apple and cinnamon are made for each other. Add cinnamon to Jaimee's Apple Bake (p 7), the Apple Pie Filling (p 8) or Simple Stewed Apples (p 7).
* Use cinnamon in the Anchovy Butter (p 3).
* Make a tomato raita by dicing 2 tomatoes, mixing in a good pinch of cinnamon and salt, and adding ¼ cup (70 g) plain yoghurt. See p 491 for yoghurt condiment ideas.
* A little ground cinnamon should be the secret ingredient in your bolognese sauce.
* A cinnamon stick is very important to the Chilli Con Carne on p 36.
* Add cinnamon to Chilli Oil (p 113) for depth.
* Stir your black tea with a cinnamon stick for subtle added flavour. Let it dry and reuse it.
* ***Hot cinnamon butter rum*** In a small saucepan, melt 1 tbsp butter with 2 tsp sugar and 2 cinnamon sticks. Heat until the sugar dissolves. Pour this mixture into 1 cup (250 ml) rum, mix and divide between 4 small glasses.
* ***Cinnamon sugar*** Mix ½ cup (110 g) caster (superfine) sugar with 2 tbsp ground cinnamon and store in a jar for easy cinnamon toast, rolling donuts in or to sprinkle on top of porridge.

CLOVES

It's beginning to smell a lot like Christmas ... Seriously, though, there's more to cloves than ham and pudding. Cloves are used in cooking the world over for their pungent, sweet and woodsy taste. The most important thing to know about cloves is that a little goes a very long way. Add only a few for aroma and depth, because it's very easy for them to overpower a dish so it ends up tasting like you've been to the dentist. For this reason, be extra careful with ground cloves. And if using them whole, remember to fish them out before serving, as biting into a whole clove is quite the experience.

Go with   Allspice, cardamom, cumin, ginger, nutmeg, cinnamon, turmeric, fennel seeds, bay leaves, chocolate, apples, pears, quince, grapefruit, oranges, mandarins, cherries, grapes, rhubarb, plums, cumquats, persimmons, dried fruits, oats, pickles of all kinds (including egg), onions, cabbage, pumpkin (squash), sweet potato, parsnips, mushrooms, sardines

---

Substitutes   The next best thing if you're out of cloves would be to use allspice, as it's similarly pungent – but you can be slightly heavier-handed with allspice.

Some ideas for using cloves

✳ Well, of course, ham. Score and stud a ham with cloves and brush with your favourite glaze. Cloves bring Christmas to ham like nothing else.

✳ A pinch of ground cloves lends a musty sweet note to the Sweet Potato Pie With Hazelnut Crust (p 451).

✳ A mere ¼ tsp ground cloves over roasted plums is delicious. Follow the method for Savoury Roasted Fruits on p 12.

✳ Include ground cloves in your spice mix for Banana Ketchup (p 26), for authentic flavour.

✳ Add a pinch of cloves to Beautiful Braised Onions (p 313).

✳ Put 3 whole cloves in the saucepan when cooking rice, to give it a little something extra.

✳ Suck on a clove as a traditional soother for toothache.

✳ Try the Mandarin Jam (p 258) with cloves rather than star anise.

✳ Put a clove in each pickle jar for a little warmth, or in the Home-made 'Tinned' Pineapple jar (p 353) for a touch of spiciness. »

* **Clove gargle** Add 1 tbsp whole cloves to a small saucepan of water and simmer for 5 minutes. Remove from the heat and add 1 tsp salt. Allow to cool completely before using as a gargle to help soothe a scratchy throat or as a mouthwash.

CORIANDER SEEDS

Coriander seeds have a pleasant citrusy, floral flavour and are used in Mexican, Indian, Moroccan, Greek and French cuisines, to name a few. A stash of coriander seeds can help get many a meal off the ground. We recommend keeping your coriander seeds whole and grinding them with a mortar and pestle or spice grinder as you go. Crushed coriander seeds in slow cooking add a nice pop of texture to the final meal. Coriander is also a great balancing spice, so if you've added too much clove or chilli, for instance, you can add the same amount of coriander seeds to balance out the flavours. It's a culinary band-aid.

Goes with Cumin, allspice, cardamom, fennel seeds, mustard seeds, turmeric, ginger, apples, citrus fruits, blueberries, bananas, dried fruits, coconut, coriander (cilantro) leaves, bay leaves, lemongrass, potatoes, pumpkin (squash), sweet potato, eggplant (aubergine), capsicum (pepper), okra, mushrooms, peanuts, lentils, dried beans, chickpeas, chicken, pork

Substitutes Out of coriander seeds? A little mixture of lemon juice and ground fennel seeds will do the trick.

Some ideas for using coriander seeds

* The Chilli Pickled Okra (p 307) has lots of coriander seed flavour.
* Add a whole lot of coriander seeds to Fermented Chilli (p 114), or add to the jar when pickling chillies, so they can offer more than just fire.
* If you've bought some rather ordinary-tasting olives, sprinkle them with a mixture of whole and ground coriander seeds. They will immediately become much tastier. See p 309 for how to fancy up olives by marinating them.
* If you want to make a slightly more exotic apple pie, add 1 tsp ground coriander, along with the cinnamon, to the Apple Pie Filling on p 8.
* Mix coriander seeds with peppercorns and use them in the pepper mill.

* Sprinkle ground coriander over steamed rice or couscous.
* Make a rub for meat by mixing butter, ground coriander, crushed garlic and paprika.
* Add a few coriander seeds to the One-punnet Berry Vinegar (p 48).
* Coriander seeds have a very citrusy note, so they will be right at home in any of the citrus preserving recipes in this book, such as Salt-preserved Lemons (p 241), Sweet Pickled Limes (p 254) and Sweet and Sour Quick Mandarin Relish (p 259).
* We use ground coriander for a more savoury variation of the Macadamia Biscuits on p 292.

CUMIN

Take a whiff of cumin. Some people loathe it, some love it. To say it's earthy isn't quite right; it's more bodily, animal even, on the nose. Once the whole or ground seeds hit the frying pan or saucepan, their flavour is transformed into something roasted, nutty and essential to so many dishes. Cumin is almost a prerequisite of Mexican cooking, but is also widely used in Indian, Middle Eastern and North African cooking, making it indispensable in the kitchen.

Goes with   Allspice, caraway seeds, cinnamon, cloves, chilli, fennel, coriander seeds, mustard seeds, star anise, turmeric, chocolate, apricots, cumquats, dried fruits, ginger, garlic, onions, avocado, carrots, cauliflower, green beans, eggplant (aubergine), zucchini (courgettes), capsicum (pepper), tomatoes, potatoes, pumpkin (squash), silverbeet (Swiss chard), spinach, okra, dried beans, chickpeas, lamb, lemons, parsley, bay leaves, oregano

----

Substitutes   As a stand-in for cumin, try half the amount of caraway seeds mixed with a little ground turmeric.

Some ideas for using cumin

* Very lightly toast cumin seeds and add to the Flotsam and Jetsam Flat Breads recipe (p 168), then serve with curry.
* Cumin is a star player in the Ful Medames on p 32.
* Add cumin seeds or ground cumin to potatoes, sweet potatoes or pumpkin (squash) before roasting. As the vegetables roast, the cumin will toast.
* Toasted cumin seeds in the Everyday Dukkah (p 408) are a very good idea. »

* Make a little dressing by combining 2 tbsp orange juice, 1 tbsp olive oil, a pinch of salt and ½ tsp cumin seeds or ground cumin.
* Sauté 1 onion, 2 finely chopped garlic cloves and 2–3 tsp ground cumin until the onion is starting to caramelise a little. Use this mix on top of cooked lentils.
* Cumin is crucial to any salsa or guacamole. Even just adding a good pinch of ground cumin to smashed avo makes it taste more like a Mexican cantina.
* Cumin is excellent in preserving. Add ½ tsp whole seeds to a jar of preserved lemons with some chilli flakes or to a jar of pickled green beans.

CURRY POWDER

What even is curry powder? It's kind of an undefined mix of whatever. There's an old-fashioned quaintness about curry powder, and it shares an English–Indian heritage with chutneys and pickles, for which we obviously have great affection. There's nothing at all wrong with curry powder, but it does seem to be something people keep forgetting they've already bought, and then they end up with a few packets or little tins. Because it's a bit generic in flavour you can use it in a lot of places – even in dishes that weren't expecting a visit from the curry powder fairy at all.

Goes with   Almost everything! Including potatoes, pumpkin (squash), tomatoes, peas, peanuts, coconut, coconut milk, chicken, beef, pork, fish, eggs, lentils, chickpeas and mayonnaise.

Substitutes   Curry mixes are usually a blend of turmeric, ground cumin, ground coriander, ground ginger, mustard powder and chilli. So make a combo with whatever you have in the pantry. If you want a recipe, try spice mix 2 (p 420).

Some ideas for using curry powder

* Turn the 'What's in the Fridge' Vegie Pie Filling (p 451) into a classic curry pie. Use potatoes, peas and 1 tbsp curry powder.
* A Curried-egg Sandwich (p 149) is perfect for a packed lunch or picnic.
* Kedgeree. If you've got left-over fish, rice and a tin of curry powder, dinner is pretty much organised. See the recipe on p 166.
* **Cheat's tarka** Tarka is a fried spice mix served over dal (p 244) and other dishes. This very quick one is for dinner in a hurry. Melt 1 tbsp butter or ghee (you can also use oil) and sauté 1–2 diced tomatoes. Add 1 tsp curry powder and a pinch of salt.
* **Japanese curry rice** This is a version of a street-food favourite. The first step is to make a curry roux by melting 2 tbsp butter in a small saucepan over medium heat, and mixing in 2 tsp plain (all-purpose) flour and 2 tsp curry powder. Now slowly add 1 cup (250 ml) stock, stirring until you have a thick sauce. Add ½ tsp honey and mix thoroughly. Season with salt and pepper. Serve over plain rice, with some steamed carrots and cabbage if you'd like.
* **Cheat's curry aioli** Serve with hot chips (fries), grilled (broiled) fish and pickles. Mix ¼ cup (60 g) mayonnaise, ½ tsp curry powder and a big pinch of salt.

Curried sausage

SERVES 3–4 WITH RICE

Yup. A classic of the English kitchen and a secret comfort food for many. This recipe may have fallen out of fashion, but it's worth revisiting.

Melt 1 tbsp butter in a frying pan over medium heat. Add 1 sliced onion and sauté until translucent. Add 2 finely chopped garlic cloves and 2 tsp curry powder and continue to sauté until fragrant and well mixed. Now add 3 sausages and fry until cooked through. Cut the cooked sausages into bite-sized pieces, return to the pan and stir to coat in the spices. Stir in ⅓ cup (80 ml) cream. Serve over rice or mashed potato.

FENNEL SEEDS

The aniseed flavour of fennel seeds is similar to that of the bulb. This aniseed/licorice taste is not to everyone's liking, but fennel seeds seem to break down barriers and can be very convincing when they're in a dish. Jaimee, who is no fan of licorice, loves fennel seeds in Italian cooking and in breads, so go figure. Fennel seeds are a great addition to any spice blend; they travel well across many cuisines and span the sweet and savoury spectrum. Leaving fennel seeds whole adds texture to dishes and a pop of flavour. Occasionally we grind the seeds so their flavour can be more evenly dispersed. Head to fennel (p 157) for ways to use fennel bulb.

Go with	Garlic, chilli, pepper, allspice, cloves, coriander seeds, mustard seeds, star anise, turmeric, coriander (cilantro), bay leaves, rosemary, thyme, tomatoes, fennel, eggplant (aubergine), zucchini (courgettes), potatoes, mushrooms, cabbage, cauliflower, okra, green beans, onions, leeks, citrus fruits, lentils, chickpeas, fish, sausages, chicken, hard cheeses, goat's cheese
Substitutes	You can swap fennel seeds and aniseed. Lemon zest will also fill in the citrusy gaps if you don't have any fennel seeds in the house, or try finely chopped fennel fronds.

Some ideas for using fennel seeds

* If you have some wrinkly zucchinis (courgettes), make the quick Zucchini Mash (p 496), adding 1 tbsp fennel seeds. The match is truly dreamy.
* When making 'Clear Out the Fridge' Pizza (p 97), sprinkle fennel seeds over even the plainest combination for a flavoursome result. They're especially good on a potato pizza.
* Add fennel seeds to the Basic Sauerkraut (p 66).
* Make a dip by warming olive oil with fennel seeds and serving with bread for snacking during a long Italian lunch.
* Add 1–2 tsp fennel seeds to lemon (p 240) or lime marmalade (p 253) for an interesting savoury bite.
* Try adding fennel seeds to the Herby Vinegar (p 202).
* In the Savoury Orange Salad (p 316), fennel seeds scattered over the orange slices is a beautiful pairing.
* Add fennel seeds to the Oregano Salt (p 207) and use for seasoning potatoes, salads and fish.

Breath freshener

MAKES ABOUT ⅔ CUP (30 G)

Fennel seeds contain an antibacterial compound that can help fight bad breath, as well as increase saliva production. Serve this at the end of a rich or spicy meal to freshen your breath and aid digestion.

In a dry frying pan over low heat, gently toast 5 tbsp fennel seeds. Stir in 1 tbsp caster (superfine) sugar, allowing the sugar to coat the seeds and dissolve. Add 2 tbsp desiccated coconut and toast very lightly. Remove from the heat and cool completely. Keep the cooled fennel seed mix in a small bowl on the table in case you want to kiss your guests after dinner.

JUNIPER BERRIES

Squeeze open a juniper berry and surely you can smell a gin and tonic. Juniper is, after all, one of the main aromatics used in distilling gin. Tragically, many people think that's where its application ends. So if you find yourself with juniper berries and are at a loss as to what to do with them – read on. Don't throw whole berries into your cooking as they won't impart much flavour; the piny fresh scent and flavour can only be released by crushing the berries first. Juniper is famous for cutting through fatty flavours and complementing sharp ones. Use it in slow-cooked meat dishes and long fermentations.

Go with   Caraway seeds, bay leaves, parsley, thyme, sage, nutmeg, garlic, cabbage, mushrooms, olives, citrus fruits, rhubarb, sauerkraut, pickled vegetables, hard cheeses, pork, chicken, fish

---

Substitutes   Out of juniper? Adding 1 tsp gin for every few berries will do the job (even if you're fermenting sauerkraut).

Some ideas for using juniper berries

* Juniper berries are the classic flavour in sauerkraut. See p 66 for the Basic Sauerkraut recipe.
* Add some crushed juniper berries to Finest Braised Fennel (p 160).
* Add 1 tbsp crushed juniper berries to Roast Apple and Sage Stuffing (p 6).
* Squish a juniper berry between your fingers and add it to a cocktail. »

* Juniper and grapefruit bring out the best in each other. Add juniper berries to Grapefruit Marmalade (p 179) for a mocktail treat on your morning toast, or make a batch of Grapefruit Skin Bitters (p 180).
* Roast a whole fish and stuff it with juniper berries and lemon. Serve with a fennel salad.
* Mushrooms and juniper are unusual friends. Add crushed juniper berries to Mushroom Pâté (p 280) or add a few juniper berries to the jar when you're pickling mushrooms.

MUSTARD SEEDS AND MUSTARD POWDER

For such tiny things, mustard seeds are responsible for big culinary staples. Prepared mustard (p 282), pickling spices and Indian tarka all begin with mustard seeds. As for variety, the rule of thumb is that the smaller and darker the seed, the hotter it is. Commonly, mustard powder is made from yellow mustard seeds, as are most prepared mustards. Keep both yellow and brown mustard seeds in your pantry if you can. Fried mustard seeds add a crunchy texture to a dish, but be careful not to overcook them, or they will become bitter. Buy whole mustard seeds and make your own mustard powder if you have a spice grinder; it's far more fragrant than store-bought. If not, try to have both whole and ground on hand.

Go with   Cumin, cardamom, curry leaves, star anise, coriander seeds, fennel seeds, ginger, turmeric, garlic, cucumber, cabbage, potatoes, cauliflower, kohlrabi, silverbeet (Swiss chard), dried beans, lentils, tomatoes, fruits in savoury dishes

------

Substitutes   Use twice as much dijon or wholegrain mustard as mustard powder in recipes. For mustard seeds, substitute another flavoursome seed, such as fennel or cumin.

Some ideas for using mustard seeds and mustard powder

* Make Dal (p 244) and Tarka (p 245). The fried mustard seeds in the tarka give the most incredible texture when used to top dal. They pop and simmer in the mouth.
* Whip up a Classic Mustard Vinaigrette (p 283), using 1 tsp mustard powder instead of dijon mustard.

* Melt 2 tbsp butter in a frying pan and add 1 tbsp yellow or brown mustard seeds or a mixture and 1 tsp grated fresh ginger. Fry until the seeds start to pop, then use to top roast vegetables, such as potato, pumpkin (squash) or cauliflower.
* If you really want to use up mustard seeds, get pickling. Mustard seeds give pickles bite, so add 1 tsp to each jar. Or see spice mix 6 on p 421. Chutneys and relishes, especially fruit relishes, also love mustard seeds for texture and flavour. Try making a fruit chutney (see 'What's in the Fruit Bowl' Relish, p 333), using plenty of mustard seeds, grated fresh ginger and a pinch of cayenne pepper.
* *Quick home-made mustard* This isn't the sort of mustard you keep in the pantry for a long time – it's meant to be eaten right away, but will last for 1 week in the fridge. Mix 4 tbsp mustard powder, 2 tbsp milk, 1 tsp honey, a pinch of salt and another flavour, such as some fennel seeds or very finely chopped dill. Allow the mustard to sit for 10 minutes before serving.

NUTMEG

Another classic warm spice that hints of rich stews, baked custards and mulled wines. As with cloves and allspice, you only need a small amount to flavour a whole dish. Buy whole nutmeg and grate it as you go – ground nutmeg in a packet or jar has only a fraction of its complexity. The sophistication of nutmeg counters overly sweet desserts, so if you've gone too far with the sugar you may be able to rescue things with a generous grating of nutmeg. It's also commonly used in creamy savoury dishes, such as Bechamel Sauce (p 274). The smallest amount of nutmeg will often give an unexpected layer of flavour that will convince people that you're a very good cook indeed.

Goes with   Cinnamon, cloves, allspice, juniper berries, star anise, persimmons, quince, dried fruits, bay leaves, carrots, cauliflower, potatoes, sweet potato, pumpkin (squash), parsnips, spinach, silverbeet (Swiss chard), nuts, peanuts, oats, butter, feta, ricotta, cream, milk puddings and custards, honey, eggs, mushrooms, bolognese sauce

---

Substitutes   A mixture of cinnamon and cloves will do the trick if you don't have any nutmeg in the house.

Some ideas for using nutmeg

✱ Grate a little nutmeg over Sautéed Cabbage (p 67).

✱ Any of the pudding recipes will be enhanced by grated nutmeg – Baked Custard (p 151), Bread and Butter Pudding (p 52), Baked Rice Pudding (p 392) or Milk Pudding (p 275).

✱ Add a little nutmeg to the Apple Pie Filling (p 8).

✱ 'There's Nothing Wrong With That Cream!' Potatoes (p 125) and Creamed Silverbeet (p 411) will both do well with grated nutmeg.

✱ Mushrooms and nutmeg are the earthiest combination. It will remind you that you're part of nature. Head to the mushrooms section (p 278) and embrace it.

✱ **Roast baby carrots with nutmeg** Cut the tops off baby carrots. Wash and thoroughly dry the tops and set aside. Preheat the oven to 180°C (350°F). Toss the carrots in a little oil with a pinch of salt and plenty of grated nutmeg. Roast for 15–20 minutes. Place carrots on a serving plate and sprinkle with a little more salt. Chop the carrot tops and scatter on top of the carrots. Serve.

PAPRIKA

Whether it's sweet, smoked or hot, we're never without paprika in our kitchens. This vibrant spice comes from a variety of capsicum (pepper) that's dried and ground several times until it's almost silky. Smoked paprika is most often associated with Spanish cuisine, while sweet paprika is used liberally in Hungarian dishes. We use both with abandon. Smoked paprika gives a meaty body to vegetarian dishes, while sweet paprika is a little less bitter and gives a full-bodied flavour to almost any dish. You can sprinkle paprika over finished dishes, but really the flavour is at its best when it has been cooked into a dish.

Goes with	Bay leaves, thyme, oregano, basil, garlic, chilli, onions, tomatoes, potatoes, eggplant (aubergine), capsicum (pepper), silverbeet (Swiss chard), chicken, pork, seafood, rice, lentils, chickpeas, dried beans, almonds
Substitutes	If you're after hot paprika's kick, you could add a pinch of cayenne pepper as a stand-in. If you want to make a paprika-heavy casserole but you're out of paprika, try using well-sautéed or roasted diced capsicum (pepper) or tomato and a little chopped bacon or speck.

Some ideas for using paprika

✱ Paprika is essential to the Cheat's Paella (p 395).

✱ Don't make Jude's Mum's Hungarian Potatoes (p 362) without paprika.

✱ Smoked paprika in most things will be a very good substitute for bacon, prosciutto or speck. For a variation, you could add 1–2 tsp smoked paprika to Baked Beans (p 37).

✱ Make bacon taste more bacon-y by sprinkling it with smoked paprika before cooking in a 180°C (350°F) oven. See Home-made Bacon Bits (p 23) for more tips.

✱ Add paprika to capsicum (pepper) dishes to emphasise their flavours. Try the Most Delicious Almond Dip (p 288) or the Smooth and Silky Capsicum (p 75).

✱ Add plenty of paprika to Crispy Spiced Cauliflower (p 82). Serve it with a mayonnaise-based dipping sauce.

Bravas sauce
MAKES ABOUT 1 CUP (250 ML)

This tapas sauce is deliciously heavy on the paprika. Serve it on roast potatoes.

In a frying pan, heat 2 tbsp olive oil and sauté 1 diced onion until translucent. Add 4 finely chopped garlic cloves and continue to sauté for 2–3 minutes. Now add 1 tbsp smoked paprika, a few fresh thyme or oregano leaves, ½ tsp salt and a pinch of sugar. Add 3–4 diced tomatoes (or 400 g/14 oz tinned diced tomatoes) and simmer for 10 minutes. Halfway through the cooking time, add 1 tbsp sherry vinegar or red wine vinegar. Remove from the heat and cool. Transfer to a food processor or use a hand-held blender to blitz to a smooth sauce.

STAR ANISE

How could a spice be so pretty? These eight-pointed stars with a sweet and woody licorice flavour are so important to Chinese and Vietnamese cooking. The whole spice itself is not edible, so do pull it out after cooking unless you want its decorative qualities. A little star anise goes a long way. Usually 1–2 stars are more than enough to flavour a whole dish. Too much star anise and the bitter compounds will overwhelm your cooking. Ground star anise can of course be eaten, but remember to go easy. When you grind a whole star, know that the flavour is in the star and not so much the seeds inside, so grind the whole thing. Use star anise in sweet and savoury dishes, and if you only have one or two hanging around, chuck them into your next stock.

Goes with	Allspice, cardamom, chilli, cinnamon, black pepper, cumin, curry leaves, nutmeg, mustard seeds, fennel seeds, coriander (cilantro), mint, ginger, garlic, celery, green beans, onions, eggplant (aubergine), mushrooms, chicken, beef, tofu, citrus fruits (especially oranges, mandarins and cumquats), pears, plums, pineapple, quince

----

Substitutes	Swap star anise with other warm spices, such as allspice, cinnamon and cloves. Add a little fennel seed or aniseed for the licorice notes.

Some ideas for using star anise

* When making a stock or broth, such as chicken or beef, add 1 star anise at the start of simmering. It will infuse the whole stock with such warmth that it will need little else when you come to use it.
* When braising onions (as on p 313), add 1–2 star anise.
* Star anise adds sweetness and depth of flavour to preserves. Pop a star anise on top of each jar of plum jam before putting the lid on. It will be a pretty surprise when the jar is opened. Use 1–2 star anise when making cocktail syrups – like the Mandarin Syrup (p 258) or the Pineapple Skin Syrup (p 353). Or add a star anise to pickling jars; this is especially delicious when pickling beetroot or onions, or in sweet pickled pears.
* Make a cheat's worcestershire sauce by mixing 1 cup (250 ml) malt vinegar, 3 tbsp molasses or brown sugar, 4–5 star anise, 2–3 generous tbsp spices (mustard seeds, grated fresh ginger, cinnamon sticks), a little cayenne pepper and 1 tsp salt, then simmering until slightly thickened.

TURMERIC

Don't let anyone call turmeric poor man's saffron. The only thing these two spices have in common is their intense colour. Turmeric is a member of the ginger family and shares a similar sharp spiciness. Fresh turmeric, which is becoming easier to buy, has a hint of eucalyptus to it, while dried ground turmeric is earthier. Turmeric is the most widely used spice in Indian cooking, but don't be shy about using it in other cuisines. It adds a beautiful golden colour to rice, pickling liquids and broths. Turmeric is also very rich in curcumin, which is said to have health-promoting and medicinal properties.

Goes with	Black pepper, cinnamon, allspice, cloves, coriander seeds, fenugreek, curry leaves, cumin, fennel seeds, mustard seeds, lemongrass, ginger, garlic, coconut, coconut milk, tomatoes, eggplant (aubergine), potatoes, onions, chilli, limes, curries, lentils, fish, rice, cauliflower, peanuts, cashews

Substitutes	If you're out of ground turmeric, try an equal quantity of mustard powder, but expect more bite.

Some ideas for using turmeric

* Add a pinch of ground turmeric to pickling liquid (pp 472–73) to liven up the colour a little.
* Use turmeric when cooking Dal (p 244) for extra flavour and so it doesn't look insipid.
* Turmeric has been used as a dye since ancient times. If you have half a packet of turmeric hanging around and it's unlikely you're going to cook with it, you could have a bit of fun and try using it to dye natural fibres a beautiful rich golden colour. Wet the fabric (we suggest something small, like pillow slips) thoroughly, then dissolve ¼ cup ground turmeric in 2 cups (500 ml) hot water. Add the fabric and leave overnight. Drain, rinse and dry in the shade, as sunlight can make the colour fade to a pale brown. Turmeric dye can run, so dyed items need to be washed separately.
* A little ground turmeric in your scrambled tofu makes it a sunny yellow.
* A little turmeric in a spiced potato salad (p 362) will bring the party to the table.
* Use turmeric to give colour to relishes. Try the Chow Chow recipe (p 120) to make something bright and bitey for sandwiches and burgers.
* *Golden tea* An easy and delicious way to ingest turmeric's antioxidants. Pour 2 cups (500 ml) cold water into a small saucepan and add 2 tsp ground turmeric and 1 tsp black peppercorns. Bring to a simmer, then remove from the heat just before it boils. Add up to 2 tbsp honey, to taste. Strain before drinking.

Spinach

From fresh leaves to sea monster in the blink of an eye, spinach is often wasted if it isn't used rather quickly. Buy it with intention and prepare for two days of loving spinach. Luckily for you, it's one of the most versatile vegetables: we can't think of a single cuisine that doesn't have a plethora of ways to use spinach. Even on its deathbed, spinach can still be sautéed and make it to the table.

Goes with   Onions, garlic, ginger, tomatoes, zucchini (courgettes), mushrooms, potatoes, sweet potato, asparagus, silverbeet (Swiss chard), figs, pomegranate, basil, coriander (cilantro), chicken, ham, dried beans, chickpeas, tofu, poppy seeds, mustard, butter, cream, yoghurt, coconut milk, soft cheeses, parmesan, barley, miso, nutmeg, pepper

Storage   Do not wash spinach before storing it. For a bunch of spinach, if there's a rubber band or string holding it together, untie it, wrap the bunch in a clean tea towel (dish towel), then place in a reusable plastic bag or cloth bag and store in the fridge for a few days. To freeze spinach, blanch in boiling water for 30 seconds, then submerge in iced water for 1 minute or until the heat is completely out of the spinach. Squeeze dry and pop into an airtight container in little fistfuls. Frozen spinach can be kept for 3 months. We generally avoid buying baby spinach that comes in a plastic bag because of the packaging, but you can store unopened bags in the fridge until the use-by date. Once opened they will only last about 1 day, so get cooking.

Substitutes   The other green things are good substitutes: silverbeet (Swiss chard), kale, cavolo nero and, in a salad, rocket (arugula).

Some ideas for spinach that needs using

* Try the Silverbeet Quesadillas (p 411) with spinach.
* Make creamed spinach, following the Creamed Silverbeet recipe on p 411. Wilted spinach *really* reduces, of course, so the resulting dish will be perfect for 1–2 people.
* **Spinach salad** Toss torn spinach leaves with ½ thinly sliced red onion, ½ cup (45 g) thinly sliced button mushrooms and a handful of toasted pine nuts. Season with salt and pepper, then dress with olive oil and red wine vinegar or Classic Mustard Vinaigrette (p 283).
* **Green dip** Blitz a few spinach leaves with some green olives and plain yoghurt for a lively dip. Season to taste with salt, pepper and some chilli flakes.

Margi's green sauce
MAKES ABOUT 200 ML (7 OZ)

This great sauce from our friend Margi appeared in *Use It All*, but it's too good to leave out here. Add it to scrambled eggs for green eggs.

Steam ½ bunch (about 175 g/6 oz) spinach, stems and all, until wilted. Remove from the heat and allow to cool. Transfer to a food processor with ½ chopped garlic clove, 1½ tbsp olive oil, ½ tsp flour and a pinch each of salt and pepper. Blitz until smooth, then add a little dash of milk or cream. If it doesn't look smooth enough, add a little more oil and blitz again.

Green things fritters
MAKES 5–6

Long live the fritter. Could there be a more forgiving and useful trick up your sleeve? When in doubt, make fritters. When the fridge needs a clear out, make fritters. When the vegie patch is looking like it could do with a tidy-up, make fritters. Here's a green fritter recipe for all of the above. Use Spinach, silverbeet (Swiss chard), zucchini (courgettes), kale, celery leaves, peas, herbs, or a mix of what you have.

Finely chop 1 bunch (about 350 g/12 oz) spinach. You can include the stems, but make sure to chop them small (you'll need about 3 firmly packed cups in all). Put the spinach (or other greens) in a bowl with 1 cup picked fresh herbs of your choice, ½ cup grated or crumbled cheese (haloumi and strained feta cheese work well), ¼ cup (35 g) plain (all-purpose) flour and 3 eggs beaten with ½ tsp salt. Mix all the ingredients very well. Heat 2 tbsp oil in a frying pan over medium–high heat and pour in ½ cupfuls of the green mix, cooking 2–3 fritters at a time for 3 minutes on each side.

Serve the fritters warm, but they're also great the next day for a packed lunch.

Green soup

SERVES 4

This recipe is about using up every green thing ever, so feel free to swap ingredients. Different greens will have different cooking times, so you'll need to make adjustments here and there depending on what you're using. We've made this with spinach, peas, asparagus, silverbeet (Swiss chard), kale, broccoli and zucchini (courgettes), and they all work slightly differently.

Heat 2 tbsp olive oil in a large saucepan or stockpot over medium heat, then add one of the following: 2–3 sliced celery stalks, 1 onion, ½ diced small fennel bulb or 6 sliced spring onions (scallions). Sauté for about 7 minutes. Add 3 roughly chopped garlic cloves and sauté for 2–3 minutes. Add 3 cups of your chosen greens. Tender greens such as spinach and peas will only take 2–3 minutes to cook. More fibrous vegetables such as asparagus, kale and broccoli will take longer, perhaps 5 minutes. Once the vegetables begin to soften, season with 1 tsp salt (less if you're going to be using shop-bought stock, which is quite salty already), plenty of pepper and 1 tbsp red wine vinegar. Cover with 3 cups (750 ml) stock and bring the boil, then reduce the heat and simmer, covered, for 10 minutes or until the vegetables are tender. Add 1 large handful of herbs such as parsley or basil leaves, and cook for a further 2 minutes. Allow to cool slightly, then blend using a hand-held blender or a food processor until very smooth.

Serve as is or add ¼ cup plain yoghurt (70 g) or cream (60 ml) and blend again. If the soup is feeling a little thin, or you're making a dairy-free option, add ¼ cup left-over mashed potatoes and blend. Taste for seasoning, adding more salt and pepper if needed. A squeeze of lemon or a splash of sauerkraut brine will brighten things further. Serve hot or cold. We recommend making this soup ahead of time and leaving in the fridge overnight, as it's even better the next day.

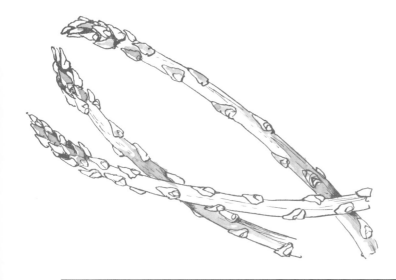

Palak paneer

SERVES 4

This vegetarian dish is one of the most popular Indian curries for good reason. Palak is Hindi for spinach and paneer is a type of Indian fresh cheese that can be found readily but does vary in quality. Go for one that's on the softer side, or find a recipe online and make your own if you have extra milk you need to use up. This version of the dish is quite mild, but if you want to increase the heat or intensity just add more chilli and more garlic.

Start by placing 1 bunch of washed spinach (about 350 g/12 oz), with the stems, in a bowl and covering it with boiling water. Leave for 1 minute, then transfer to a bowl of iced water. Once the heat is completely out of the spinach, drain really well and chop roughly. Rinse a 200 g (7 oz) block of paneer (it can be quite salty), then pat dry, cut into 2 cm (¾ in) cubes and set aside.

In a large frying pan over medium heat, melt 2 tbsp ghee or butter and add 1 finely diced onion, 2 tbsp grated fresh ginger, 4 roughly chopped garlic cloves, 1 chopped green chilli, 1 diced tomato, ½ tsp salt, 3 tsp ground cumin, 3 tsp ground coriander and 2 tsp garam masala (or replace these three spices with 2 tbsp spice mix 2, p 420). Sauté for 2–3 minutes.

Carefully transfer everything in the pan to a food processor and blitz. Add the spinach and blitz again, until you have a bright-green purée. You may need to add a splash of water. Return the purée to the frying pan and gently heat through. Mix in ¼ cup (60 ml) cream and add the paneer, then heat the paneer through for about 2 minutes. Serve hot over rice or with the Flotsam and Jetsam Flat Breads (p 168).

Spring onions

The confusing array of names for these things – spring onions, scallions, shallots – it never ends. In *Use It All* we decided to go with spring onion as the name of the long tubular onion sold in bunches, and we're sticking to that here. To use up a big bunch of spring onions, use them as you would any other allium (onions, leeks, shallots). Spring onions have a mild and sweet flavour, so when cooking them as the base of a recipe, use more than you would brown or red onions. They're very tender, so they cook much faster. Ultra versatile, they can be used raw, cooked or like a herb in place of chives.

Go with	Asparagus, leafy greens, radishes, carrots, potatoes, wombok (Chinese cabbage), snow peas (mange tout), green beans, tomatoes, leeks, garlic, ginger, chilli, limes, mango, chicken, tofu, rice, eggs, peanuts
Storage	Remove the rubber band, wrap the bunch in a clean tea towel (dish towel) and pop in a reusable plastic bag or cloth bag. Spring onions are at their best for a few days and then they start to wilt. If any of the bunch has gone slimy, just discard that one or use your judgement and cut that portion off.
Substitutes	In cooking, any onion can replace spring onions. If using raw, red onion, leek or chives work well.

Some ideas for using half a bunch of spring onions

* Try quick-pickling spring onions (p 473). Use them in noodle salads and to top dumplings.
* Add the lot to a potato salad. Spring onion and potato are such a good combination. In a potato salad they act like chives but are more substantial. Head to the Anything-goes Potato Salad (p 362) and use spring onions in any of the versions.
* Add any lonely spring onions to your next batch of Odd-knobs Ginger Paste (p 175), for curries and stir-fries, or to the End-of-the-week Vegie Stock Paste (p 447).
* If you bought a whole bunch of spring onions and only used one, thinly slice the rest and sauté in a little oil with a few chopped garlic cloves and a big pinch of salt until soft. You can store this in the fridge for up to 5 days, ready to use as the base for soups and sautéed dishes. It will save you sautéing an onion when you get home from work late.
* Spring onions make a delicious fritter, and the Green Things Fritters (p 439) call for 3 cups of green things – make a portion of those thinly sliced spring onions.
* Add thinly sliced spring onions to your next batch of Not So Classic Kimchi (p 486) instead of onion.
* Add 1–2 thinly sliced spring onions to the Whatever-cheese Eggy Muffins (p 93).
* Pop 1–2 sliced spring onions into your next batch of Chimichurri (p 193). It adds zing and is perfect with fish.
* Thinly sliced spring onions are a classic garnish. Use on the Agedashi Tofu (p 458) to give more body and extra flavour to the soup, on Japanese-style Sesame Greens (p 40), Cold Noodle and Wombok Noodle Salad With Pickles (p 487) or Snow Pea Stir-fry (p 415), or simply toss through leafy greens with toasted sesame seeds.
* *Spring onion omelette* Thinly slice 1–2 spring onions and mix with 1 tsp grated fresh ginger and ½ diced tomato or a few diced cherry tomatoes. Follow the Two-egg Omelette recipe (p 150), using the spring onion mix as your filling.

Spring onion sauce from a wilting bunch
MAKES ABOUT 1 CUP (250 ML)

Quick, the spring onions (scallions) are turning to seaweed before your very eyes! Don't panic, this sauce will save them. Spoon it over fish or chicken, add it to fried rice or noodle recipes, or just use it to gussy up plain rice with a fried egg.

Finely chop ½–1 bunch (about 100 g/3½ oz) spring onions. To do this, halve them lengthways, then dice them. Heat ¼ cup (60 ml) neutral oil in a frying pan over medium–low heat. Add 1 tbsp finely chopped or grated fresh ginger (more if you love ginger) and fry for 2–3 seconds, then add the spring onions and ½ tsp salt and sauté for about 5 minutes. Taste and add another ¼ tsp salt if needed. Transfer to a small bowl and cover with 1 tbsp sesame oil. Store in the fridge for up to 4 days.

Spring onion pancakes
MAKES 12 SMALL PANCAKES

These are a very lazy version of spring onion pancakes. Eat them with a soft-boiled egg and Not So Classic Kimchi (p 486), with Congee (p 394) or with fish and sautéed greens.

Use the Flotsam and Jetsam Flat Breads (p 168) recipe, replacing the seeds with 4 thinly sliced spring onions (scallions). After the dough has rested, divide it into 12 balls. Flatten each ball, then roll it out to a circle about 10 cm (4 in) across. Heat ¼ cup (60 ml) neutral oil in a frying pan over medium heat. Fry each pancake for 3 minutes on each side or until golden.

See garlic, leeks and onions for ideas with other alliums.

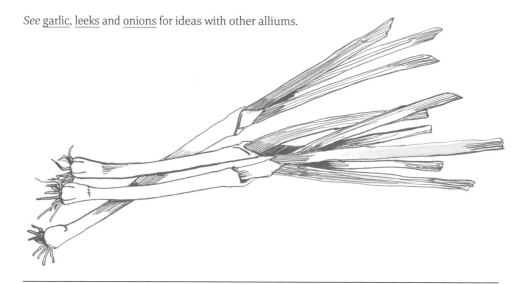

Stock

Stock is a *big* part of our lives. It sounds boring, but it's true. We make it, cook with it, swap it or talk about it almost daily. Good stock brings simple ingredients together, adding a depth of flavour you can't get using quick cooking methods. Add a quarter-cup of excellent stock to a simple stir-fry and it's instantly elevated; use a cup of stock when making a rice or grain dish and everyone asks for the recipe; braise vegetables in nothing more than stock and herbs and the plate will be licked clean. You'll find many of the recipes in this book suggest a little stock. We use this instead of fancy ingredients or complicated cooking techniques. Keep a container of stock in the fridge for the week and splash it into everything.

Now please don't think we're making 48-hour bone broth every week. On occasion we do fill up the freezer like smug little squirrels, but most of the time we make small batches of quick stocks (see over the page), using up vegetables, fridge scraps and bones left over from meals in the previous week.

And when we're too tired to think about making stock, we'll buy a good-quality one from the supermarket or, even better, from our local butcher.

Storage

For unopened store-bought stock, check the use-by date and keep in the fridge or pantry as directed. Once opened, store in the fridge in an airtight container for up to 1 week. Store home-made stock in an airtight container in the fridge for up to 1 week, but if it has a healthy layer of fat on top, it will probably keep for a few days more. Our best advice is to freeze stock, storing lighter-style stocks in larger quantities. For stocks with deep, intense flavour, freeze in ice-cube trays and, once frozen, transfer to a container in the freezer. Grab one whenever your dish needs a boost of flavour.

Substitutes

We always have miso paste on hand to use as an emergency stock replacement. If a recipe calls for a small amount of stock, you can use water and something flavoursome like a little Vegemite or worcestershire sauce, or half water and half white wine, or soak a parmesan rind or some dried mushrooms or sun-dried tomatoes in boiling water and use that. Don't forget to try the home-made stock paste (p 447) when you have no stock.

Quick stocks

These are our go-to stocks that make the most of the parts of vegetables, herbs, bones or cheese that often end up in the bin. We make these in small batches – no more than 4 cups (1 litre) water, sometimes even just 2 cups (500 ml). Use these stocks for small-batch meals, for braising, or to make a simple soup with noodles and vegies:

- Woody Asparagus End Stock (p 16)
- Corn Cob Stock (p 120)
- chicken stock (see Left-over-chicken Soup, p 106)
- Parmesan Rind Stock (p 99)
- Leek and Herb Broth (p 235)
- Roasted Mushroom Broth (p 281)
- Fish Stock (p 166).

End-of-the-week scrap stock

Open up the fridge and see what needs to go. Bendy carrots, squishy tomatoes, dried-out herbs ... into the pot with all of them. Turn these overlooked wallflowers into next week's star attraction. We've listed everything we'd be happy for you to add. If it's not on the list, enter at your own risk.

Ingredients can go into the pot washed and raw, or if you really want to intensify the flavour of your stock, then roast your vegetables with a little oil first, until they're brown at the edges. The best stocks have an underlying sweet element; roasting not only brings out the sweetness of vegetables but will also give your stock a rich colour.

- **For the stockpot** Onion (skin on will deepen the colour), leek, celery, carrot, parsnip, tomato, capsicum (pepper), mushrooms, spring onions (scallions), corn cobs, pumpkin (squash) skin, a cabbage core, broccoli stems (not too many), any left-over bones or scraps from a roast, or a chicken carcass
- **Woody herbs** Bay, thyme, a little rosemary or oregano
- **Soft herbs to add a little later** Basil or parsley stems, or celery leaves
- **Extra flavour** Parmesan rind, dried mushrooms or sun-dried tomatoes.

Place your raw or roasted ingredients in a large stockpot with at least 4 bruised garlic cloves (just give them a bash), 1 tsp black peppercorns, and any woody herbs you're using. Cover, but don't drown, your ingredients in water and bring to a simmer. Add any extra umami flavours, such as parmesan rind, dried mushrooms or sun-dried tomatoes. Once simmering, reduce the heat and simmer very gently for 30–60 minutes, depending on the size of your stock. In the last 15 minutes of cooking, add the stems from soft herbs if you have any. Remove from the heat and let the stock stand for 30 minutes. While the stock is resting, taste and see what else it needs, adding soy sauce and/or miso paste for extra flavour. Make sure you season your stock very well – the salty note brings it to life.

Carefully strain and allow to cool before refrigerating. Keep in the fridge for 4–5 days or freeze for up to 3 months.

End-of-the-week vegie stock paste
MAKES 1 x 300 ML (10 OZ) JAR

This recipe is a great way to quickly preserve a few scraps from the crisper. It's heavy on the salt to preserve and draw out the flavour. To use this paste, add 1–2 tsp for every 2 cups (500 ml) water.

You'll need 250 g (9 oz) vegie scraps such as: onions (no skins), leek tops, spring onions (scallions), garlic (no skin), fennel stems and fronds, carrots and their leafy tops, celery and its leaves, parsley stems, coriander (cilantro) stems and roots, sun-dried tomatoes or even the odd preserved lemon.

Roughly chop everything to make sure all the scraps are about the same size, add 65 g (2½ oz) salt and blitz in a food processor to form a paste. Pack into a very clean jar and seal. Store in the fridge for up to 1 year.

Two-minute cup-a-soup
SERVES 1

Sometimes we just want fast food, as in food that's ready immediately. Our compromise is home-made fast food. Having stock in the house means a cup of soup can be made in no time. Sometimes even our teenagers make it, often to perk up packet ramen.

Keep it simple with cooked noodles, broth and soy sauce for a vegetable-free two-minute noodle soup. Or add shredded chicken and corn kernels to hot broth with a little knob of butter for a quick, nutritious snack.

If you want to step it up a notch but still feed yourself quickly, in a small saucepan heat a little oil and add any of the following:
- frozen peas, a little leek and some mint
- some crushed garlic, half a diced tomato and lots of chopped herbs
- 1–2 thinly sliced asparagus spears and a sprinkle of Home-made Bacon Bits (p 23)
- ½ cup (about 125 g) diced left-over roast pumpkin (squash) and 1 tsp miso paste for a quick pumpkin soup »

- Not So Classic Kimchi (p 486), 1 thinly sliced radish or 2–3 snow peas (mange tout) cut into matchsticks, and ½ cup (95 g) left-over cooked rice
- sauerkraut (p 66) and brown rice
- some left-over white beans, diced tomato and a little tomato paste (concentrated purée)
- left-over meatballs and a handful of spinach.

Sauté for 1 minute, then add 1 cup (250 ml) stock, turn the heat up and warm through for another minute. Season well with salt, pepper and lemon juice. Voilà, two-minute soup.

Sweet potato

Tasting like a cross between a pumpkin (squash) and a potato, but related to neither, the sweet potato is one of the most useful vegetables in the kitchen. They have a long season and are generally affordable. Sweet potatoes are so widely used around the world that they've lent themselves to every kind of recipe imaginable. Sometimes they're called kumara and sometimes yams, so keep that in mind when you're lost in international recipe-blogging waters. If you grow sweet potatoes, you'll find that their leaves are edible and delicious. Sadly, they're hard to come by when shopping. Eat sweet potatoes baked, boiled, fried and in desserts; they're a true and flexible friend in the kitchen.

Goes with	Potatoes, pumpkin (squash), spinach, tomatoes, cauliflower, cabbage, corn, carrots, ginger, chickpeas, quince, dried fruits, coriander (cilantro), chives, rosemary, sage, allspice, cinnamon, cloves, nutmeg, coriander seeds, poppy seeds, coconut, rice, quinoa, miso, brown sugar, maple syrup, honey, chicken, bacon
Storage	Sweet potatoes keep for 2–4 weeks in a cool, dark place such as a basket in the pantry. The fridge will make sweet potatoes spoil faster, but if it's very hot for a few days, we suggest putting them in the crisper compartment of the fridge. Store cooked sweet potato in an airtight container in the fridge for 3–5 days, or in the freezer for up to 3 months.
Substitutes	Potatoes and pumpkin (squash) are interchangeable with sweet potatoes for most things. Carrots also make a passable substitute.

Some ideas for what to do with one sweet potato

✱ The Pumpkin Ratatouille (p 371) is equally good with sweet potato.

✱ Change the flavour of Anything-goes Rice (p 394) by adding 1 cup (140 g) diced sweet potato instead of green capsicum (pepper), 2 tbsp toasted pistachios and ½ tsp each of ground cinnamon and ground allspice.

✱ **Sweet potato rosti** Follow the Parsnip Rosti recipe (p 323), grating about 350 g (12 oz) raw sweet potato and adding some chopped rosemary.

✱ **Sweet potato wedges** Preheat the oven to 180°C (350°F). Cut sweet potatoes into wedges and toss with plenty of neutral oil to coat well. Sprinkle with salt, finely chopped rosemary and paprika or spice mix 4 (p 420). If you add some garlic powder these will taste like you're at the pub. Bake for 40 minutes. They make a great alternative to fries on burger night.

✱ **Tempura sweet potato** Using a mandoline or sharp knife, very thinly slice sweet potato and use the Tempura-style Egg White Batter (p 153), then deep-fry (p 82).

✱ **Maple-syrup-glazed sweet potato** Cook thinly sliced sweet potato in the Bacon and Maple Syrup (p 23). It's sweet and salty, and good enough to be a main.

Jacket sweet potatoes

This is a great way to make smaller sweet potatoes a main meal.

Preheat the oven to 200°C (400°F). Rub unpeeled sweet potatoes with a little oil, season with a sprinkle of salt and bake whole for 45–50 minutes. They should be crisp on the outside and tender inside. Split them lengthways and stuff them with whatever you have on hand. The beauty of this is that it can become more elaborate with beans or lentils piled on top, or kept simple with a dollop of sour cream and some chopped chives.

Serve with Minty Green Goddess Sauce (p 197) and a salad for an easy vegetarian dinner.

'What's in the fridge' vegie pie filling
SERVES 4-6 AS A FINISHED PIE

If the fridge needs a clean-out, make a pie filling. We often cook this filling when we have vegies that really need to be used, and then store it in the fridge or freezer to keep on hand when there's a big week ahead and time is going to be tight. Either make our easy Sour Cream Pastry (p 418) or pick up store-bought on your way home. See also Greens Pie Filling (p 412) and Spiced Lamb and Chickpea Pie Filling (p 233).

In a frying pan, heat ¼ cup (60 ml) oil and sauté a chopped onion, or any other allium you have (leek, spring onions/scallions, shallots) for 5 minutes until soft and sweet. Add 4 chopped garlic cloves and 1–2 sweet potatoes (about 500 g/1 lb 2 oz), cut into 2 cm (¾ in) cubes, then sauté for 10 minutes. Add about 700 g (1 lb 9 oz) roughly chopped (if necessary) vegies – peas, carrots, cauliflower and pumpkin (squash) all work well. Add ½ cup (125 ml) stock, ½ cup (125 ml) cream or coconut cream, 1 tsp salt, ½ tsp pepper and 1 tbsp of one of the spice blends on p 420. Mix well. Sprinkle in 1 tbsp plain (all-purpose) flour and mix again. Cook for 5 minutes, until the sauce has thickened slightly.

Allow to cool, then use to make a whole family pie or individual vegie pasties. Bake at 180°C (350°F) for 45–60 minutes, depending on the thickness of your pastry.

Sweet potato pie with hazelnut crust
SERVES 6-8

This classic pie is very American, the kind of thing eaten in 'the fall'. We love to make it in cooler weather too, but as it's served at room temperature and is very good with vanilla ice cream, it can finish a special meal at any time of year.

Cut 2 cups (280 g) scrubbed sweet potato into cubes and boil until tender. Drain and cool, then mash. Preheat the oven to 180°C (350°F). To make the filling, whisk the mashed sweet potato with ⅓ cup (75 g) brown sugar, 3 eggs, 1 cup (250 ml) coconut milk, 1 tbsp cornflour (cornstarch), a pinch of salt and either ¼ tsp each of ground cinnamon, ground allspice and grated fresh ginger with a pinch of ground cloves, or 1 tsp spice mix 5 (p 420). Mix very well. Pour the sweet potato mix into the Simple Sweet Hazelnut Crust (p 291) or a sweet shortcrust pastry tart shell and bake for 50 minutes. The mixture should be set but still have a little wobble to it. Allow to cool in the tin before serving.

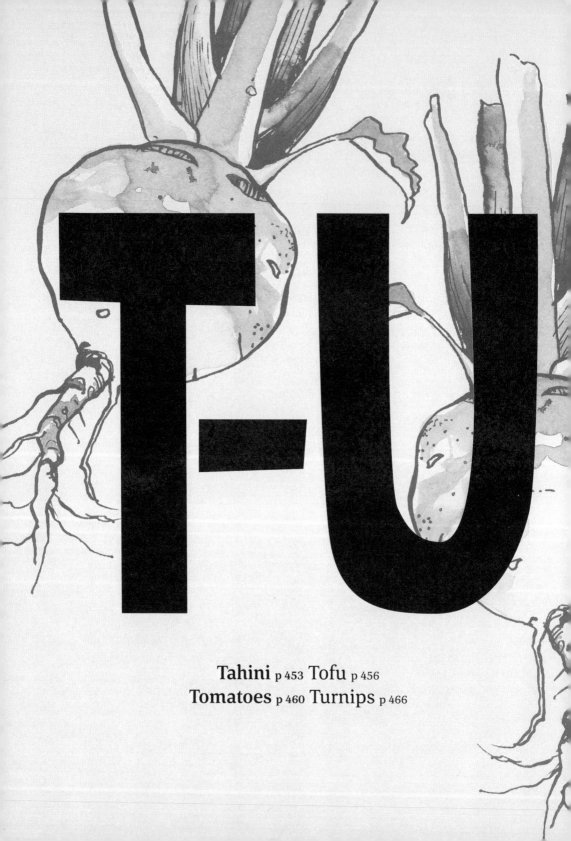

T-U

Tahini

Did you buy a jar of tahini for an Ottolenghi recipe and now you're stuck as to what to do with it? Well, drag it out and put it to work. There are many uses. Tahini is a paste made from ground sesame seeds and is a mainstay of Middle Eastern cooking, featuring in condiments like hummus and baba ghanoush. Sesame seed paste (basically tahini, although sesame seed paste is made from toasted seeds) is also used in Japanese and Chinese cooking. The two varieties of tahini are hulled and unhulled: hulled tahini is lighter in colour and flavour, while unhulled is darker, more bitter and contains more calcium. The two are interchangeable in recipes.

Often tahini is mixed with other liquids to make dips, dressing and sauces. Note that when a small amount of lemon juice, vinegar or water is added, tahini will seize (become thicker and quite stiff), but as you add more liquid it will begin to loosen again.

Goes with	Green beans, beetroot, cauliflower, kale, eggplant (aubergine), capsicum (pepper), tomatoes, cucumber, crunchy lettuces, okra, capsicum (pepper), chickpeas, black beans, kidney beans, lentils, apples, lemons, oranges, cumquats, honey, chocolate, miso, nuts, seeds
Storage	Although tahini is high in fat, sesame seeds are quite stable and tahini can therefore be kept in the pantry or cupboard. Generally tahini can be stored for up to 1 year. If the oil has separated, just give it a stir good to recombine.
Substitutes	Nut butters, like almond or macadamia, make good substitutes for tahini in baking and sauces – add some extra neutral oil to get the right consistency. Sprinkle your dish with sesame seeds if you're after a similar flavour.

Some ideas for using up the rest of the tahini jar

✳ Use tahini in the Pantry-strays Slice (p 302). It's a great binding agent for muesli bars and cookies. It also gives a nutty flavour without the nut.

✳ Try the 'No Food Processor? No Worries' Mashed Hummus (p 109). Better than hummus from the supermarket – very easy, no plastic tub and no extra clean-up. Winning.

✳ Add 1–2 tbsp tahini to your vegie burger mix to hold everything together. Check out our Vegie Burgers recipe (p 111) for a classic family-friendly burger.

✳ Mash left-over roasted pumpkin (squash) or sweet potato with some tahini, salt and pepper for a quick dip or sandwich filling.

✳ Add 1 tbsp toasted sesame seeds to 2–3 tbsp tahini for texture, then drizzle over steamed green beans.

✳ *Yoghurt and tahini sauce* Make a quick condiment for koftas, falafel or grilled vegetables by adding 3 tbsp tahini, 1 crushed garlic clove, ½ tsp ground cumin, the juice of ½ lemon and 1 tsp salt to 1 cup (260 g) plain yoghurt. Mix until you have a creamy sauce. Keep in the fridge for up to 1 week.

✳ *Green tahini* In a food processor, combine ½ cup (135 g) tahini, 1 cup herb leaves of your choice (coriander/cilantro or parsley is good), 1 finely chopped garlic clove, 2 tbsp lemon juice and a pinch of salt. Blitz until smooth and pale green. Use as a spread or as the base of a dressing.

✳ *Tahini-baked fish* Next time you're roasting a whole fish or fillets, make this sauce and spoon over the fish before baking. Mix ¼ cup (65 g) tahini with ¼ cup (60 ml) lemon juice, 4 finely chopped garlic cloves, ½ tsp ground coriander, ½ tsp fennel seeds and ¼ tsp salt. Stir vigorously to combine.

Dan dan noodle sauce our way
SERVES 2

We're not winning any awards for authenticity here, but as lovers of Chinese cooking and spicy sauces, we couldn't resist making a pantry version of this Sichuanese classic.

Mix ¼ cup (65 g) tahini, 1 tbsp rice vinegar, 1 tsp brown sugar and ½ tsp ground sichuan pepper (or ground black pepper) until thick and combined. Add ¼ cup (60 ml) chilli oil (see p 113 for a version using fresh chillies) and ½ cup (125 ml) hot stock, whisking until smooth. Put 1 handful of hot noodles into each bowl and pour the sauce over the top. Garnish with toasted sesame seeds, browned minced (ground) meat, stir-fried tofu or a pile of wilted greens.

Creamy tahini dressing
MAKES ABOUT 1¾ CUPS (435 ML)

Drizzle this creamy dairy-free dressing over Silverbeet Salad (p 411), roasted eggplant (aubergine) or cauliflower, or a cabbage slaw. We use the dressing as is throughout the book, but you can add more ingredients to take it in other directions (see below).

In a food processor or using your big muscles and a whisk, combine 1 cup (270 g) tahini, 2 finely chopped garlic cloves, ½ cup (125 ml) lemon juice, ¼ cup (60 ml) olive oil and a pinch of salt. Remember that the tahini will seize at first, but keep adding the liquid and it will reach the consistency you want. Blitz or mix until very smooth. Adjust the flavours as you see fit – a little more salt, a little more lemon. Make it your own.

FOR EXTRA FLAVOUR, ADD
- ½ avocado to the food processor and combine
- ½ tsp cayenne pepper, for a spicy version
- 1 finely diced cucumber and some chopped mint after blending, to serve with koftas and eggplant (aubergine) dishes
- some miso paste instead of the lemon juice and neutral oil instead of olive oil; use as a dipping sauce for dumplings and rice paper rolls
- ¼ cup (90 g) honey instead of olive oil, garlic and salt; drizzle over roasted plums or figs.

'Use up that jar' cookies
MAKES ABOUT 24

We've used tahini here, which makes a nutty shortbread-esque cookie, but you can replace it with peanut butter or Nutella to make the kids happy, or try marmalade instead.

In a food processor, whiz 180 g (6 oz) softened butter with ½ cup (110 g) caster (superfine) sugar or raw sugar until light and creamy – this will take less than a minute. Scrape down the sides every now and then if needed. With the motor running, add 1 egg, then 4 tbsp tahini (or another spread), and mix until combined. Add 1⅔ cups (250 g) plain (all-purpose) flour and 1 tsp baking powder, then pulse until a soft, thick, mousse-like dough forms.

Spread two sheets of baking paper on the benchtop and divide the dough between them. Knead each piece of dough briefly, then shape into a log in the middle of the paper. Wrap in the paper, twisting the ends to secure. Chill in the fridge for 2–3 hours or freeze for up to 3 months.

When ready to bake, preheat the oven to 160°C (315°F). Slice the dough log into 1 cm (½ in) rounds and lay on baking trays lined with baking paper. Bake for 20 minutes, until golden, then cool on the trays.

Tofu

Delicate bean curd has the mildest of tastes itself, and yet this is precisely what makes tofu so appealing, as it will take up any flavour, in any application and in any cuisine.

There are two common types of tofu: firm and silken. Firm tofu has a lower water content and is best used in longer-cooked dishes or for deep-frying as its texture holds up well. Silken tofu has a higher water content and is silky smooth. Use it in gently simmered soups or blitz it to make creamy desserts and sauces. Take advantage of tofu's simplicity and versatility, and add it to the list of ingredients that are at home in your kitchen – you won't regret it.

Goes with   Leafy greens, broccoli, asparagus, onions, leeks, spring onions (scallions), green beans, mushrooms, tomatoes, seaweed, miso, soy sauce, coriander (cilantro), mint, parsley, chives, ginger, chilli, star anise, cashews, sesame seeds, kimchi, rice, noodles, eggs, pork, chicken

---

Storage   Store opened tofu in an airtight container with enough water to cover it and a pinch of salt for up to 4 days, changing the water daily. Left-over cooked tofu can be stored in the fridge in an airtight container for 4 days.

Substitutes   If you're looking for other plant-based proteins, try tempeh (although the texture and flavour are very different). Chicken, seafood and egg have a similarly light flavour to tofu, and will work in some tofu recipes.

Some ideas for using tofu

* ***Creamy dressing*** This makes a dairy-free creamy salad dressing to pour over a green salad or potato salad (p 362). In a small bowl, combine ½ cup (100 g) silken tofu, 1 tsp white wine vinegar, 1 tsp dijon mustard, 1 tbsp olive oil and a generous pinch each of salt and pepper. You could add a pinch of cayenne pepper too. Use a blender, hand-held blender or hand-held electric beaters to obtain a creamy consistency. Keep in a jar in the fridge for up to 1 week.

* ***Curried tofu*** The Curried Sausage recipe (p 429) works really well with 300 g (10½ oz) firm tofu cut into cubes.

* ***Stir-fry*** Add sliced firm tofu to a vegetable stir-fry to make a more complete meal. Try adding it to the Stir-fried Celery (p 87) before the celery.

* ***Miso-glazed tofu*** If you're grilling or barbecuing tofu, brush on the Miso Glaze (p 277) towards the end of cooking. This is a sticky, salty–sweet, lip-smacking way to eat tofu.

* ***Grilled tofu with chimichurri*** Cut firm tofu into long strips, brush all over with a neutral oil and sprinkle with salt. Pop under the grill (broiler) and cook for 2 minutes, then turn and cook the other side for 2 minutes. Once grilled, place tofu on a plate and spoon Chimichurri (p 193) on top. This makes a good starter at a barbecue.

* ***Deep-fried tofu*** Deep-fried is probably the best way to eat tofu – crisp on the outside, soft on the inside. Drain and pat dry 300 g (10½ oz) firm tofu and cut into bite-sized cubes. Follow the deep-frying method on p 82.

Scrambled tofu
SERVES 1 HUNGRY PERSON, OR 2 AS A LIGHT MEAL

Heat 2 tbsp neutral oil in a non-stick frying pan over medium heat. Sauté ½ finely diced onion until translucent, then add 1 finely chopped garlic clove with a pinch each of salt, pepper and ground turmeric. Now add 150 g (5½ oz) firm tofu cut into small pieces or crumbled, and stir-fry. Splash in 2–3 tbsp nut milk (or cow's milk if you're not cooking for vegans), for moisture and to create a bit of a sauce. Cook until some of the liquid has evaporated. Serve on toast or in soft-shell tacos.

You can season this scramble according to the direction you want to take it. Make it herby with 1 handful of chopped herbs, or spicy by adding some sliced chilli when you sauté the onion.

Agedashi tofu

SERVES 4 AS A LIGHT STARTER, OR 2 AS A SIMPLE MAIN

Lightly fried tofu in a dashi broth: the simplicity of this dish, which brings together crisp and pillowy tofu and a nurturing broth, is its triumph. It can be served as a starter to a meal or as a light meal in itself.

Begin well ahead by soaking 3 dried shiitake mushrooms in ¾ cup (185 ml) cold water for at least 2 hours, or overnight. Drain and pat dry 300 g (10½ oz) firm tofu (silken tofu is traditionally used, but it can be tricky to work with). Cut the tofu into 3 cm (1¼ in) cubes and set aside. Make a dashi broth by straining the shiitake soaking liquid into a small saucepan, really squeezing the mushrooms to get as much liquid as possible (keep the mushrooms for another use, such as thinly sliced in a stir-fry). Add 2 cups (500 ml) water and ¼tsp salt, then bring to a gentle simmer.

Meanwhile, heat a heavy-based frying pan over medium–high heat and add ½ cup (125 ml) neutral oil. Put ⅓–½ cup (40–60 g) potato starch or cornflour (cornstarch) on a flat plate. Toss the tofu cubes in the starch to coat well. Fry in batches of four until all sides are a light golden. Divide between the bowls and pour ½ cup (125 ml) dashi broth into each bowl. Top with thinly sliced spring onion (scallion) or grated daikon.

Tofu and kimchi stew

SERVES 4

This stew is fiery with chilli, slick with sesame oil, salty and sour with kimchi and fragrant with ginger. It's warming right to the bones.

Drain and pat dry 300–400 g (10½–14 oz) firm or silken tofu, cut into cubes and set aside. Heat 2 tbsp neutral oil and 1 tbsp sesame oil in a medium–large saucepan over medium heat. Sauté 1 brown onion, sliced lengthways (or a small sliced leek), for 3 minutes. Add 2 finely chopped garlic cloves and 1 tbsp grated fresh ginger. Sauté everything until soft and fragrant. Add 2 thinly sliced small red chillies and sauté for 2–3 seconds until fragrant. Add ¼ cup (60 ml) soy sauce and about ½ cup diced daikon (about 45 g) or ½ cup diced carrot (80 g), then pour in 4 cups (1 litre) chicken or vegetable stock. Simmer for 15 minutes, until the daikon or carrot is cooked through. Add 1 cup (about 150 g) kimchi and the tofu, then simmer for another 10 minutes. Taste, adding a pinch of salt if it needs it. Serve in soup bowls and drizzle a few drops of sesame oil on top.

Mapo tofu, of sorts

SERVES 4

Another Sichuanese standard we've adapted. This dish usually has minced (ground) pork in it – we've omitted it here, but feel free to add it back in if you'd like. Sichuan pepper is the vital ingredient for its numbing smoky heat. This is the perfect meal for the darkest winter night.

Heat a wok over medium–high heat and add ¼ cup (60 ml) chilli oil if you have it, or neutral oil. Add 4–6 roughly chopped dried chillies or 2–3 tbsp chilli flakes and sauté for 2–3 seconds, making sure they don't burn. Quickly add 1 tbsp crushed sichuan pepper, ¼ cup (about 50 g) grated fresh ginger, ½ tsp salt and 6 small or 3 large finely chopped garlic cloves. Stirring constantly to ensure nothing burns, cook until fragrant. If you want to use minced (ground) pork, add 200 g (7 oz) now and fry until browned all over.

Add 1 tbsp black bean sauce (or miso paste or oyster sauce, if that's what you have) and ⅔ cup (170 ml) chicken or vegetable stock (or even water, if you're out of stock) and let this all simmer for 2–3 minutes. In a small bowl, mix 1½ tsp cornflour (cornstarch) with ¼ cup (60 ml) water. Stir the cornstarch mixture into the wok and cook for 1–2 minutes to thicken the sauce. Now add 300–500 g (10½ oz – 1 lb 2 oz) silken tofu, cut into cubes, and stir through – it will break up in the sauce. Allow everything to cook and heat through for 5 minutes. Mix in ¼ tsp caster (superfine) sugar and ½ tsp sesame oil, then serve over plain white rice.

Tomatoes

When tomatoes are good, they're really good, and when they're not ... well, what's the point? Tomatoes are for summer eating. Winter tomatoes are anaemic, floury things that aren't worth spending your money on. But when tomatoes are cheap and really good, or the garden is heaving with them, bring them to the centre of your cooking.

The thing about tomatoes is that the unripe, the ripe and the overripe all have something to offer a cook, so you can seize any moment in their life cycle and make the most of it. A green tomato is tart, crunchy and wonderful in salads, fried or to pickle or ferment. A ripe tomato can be used everywhere, raw or cooked, diced or blitzed. And an overripe squishy tomato, oozing its juice at the lightest touch, is still a good tomato – just cut out any mouldy bits, season and cook the bejesus out of it. Going to the effort of peeling tomatoes for sauces and soups will give you much smoother results, but we'd rather you cook them with the skins on than have them end up in the bin.

Go with	Cucumber, avocado, lettuces, corn, zucchini (courgettes), capsicum (pepper), eggplant (aubergine), fennel, kale, spinach, silverbeet (Swiss chard), sweet potato, okra, onions, spring onions (scallions), green beans, lentils, dried beans, chickpeas, garlic, ginger, horseradish, basil, chives, dill, coriander (cilantro), basil, chives, mint, parsley, bay leaves, thyme, oregano, rosemary, sage, lemongrass, chilli, cinnamon, cumin, curry, turmeric, fennel seeds, mustard seeds, paprika, capers, olives, pepitas (pumpkin seeds), peanuts, cashews, tahini, anchovies and other oily fish, beef, pork, ham, tofu, cheeses, mayonnaise, quinoa, pasta, strawberries, cherries, watermelon, figs, peaches
Storage	Fridge or counter is our ongoing debate. In a hot summer kitchen, we find that keeping tomatoes at room temperature until ripe, then moving them into the fridge buys us the most time.
Substitutes	Buy good-quality tinned tomatoes (local, if you can) for the winter, or bottle your own.

Some ideas for using tomatoes

* Add a lone halved tomato when making stock. Tomatoes give stocks colour, flavour and a little acid, which helps to keep the liquid clear. Acid also draws out the gelatin in bones. See End-of-the-week Scrap Stock (p 446) or Left-over-chicken Soup (p 106). If you've let tomatoes get really wrinkly (but not mouldy or oozy), try the Parmesan Rind Stock (p 99).

* If you have a whole heap of tomatoes, try the Oven-baked Ratatouille (p 498) or add them to the Simple Chickpea Stew (p 110) instead of tinned tomatoes.

* If you have three or four tomatoes that need using, try Maddie's Grandma's Tabouleh (p 199) or Perugu Pachadi (p 492).

* Put some tomatoes on fresh bread. White bread, good butter, flavoursome tomatoes, salt and pepper. There's nothing better.

* *Tomato salsa* Salsa is essential when you're serving tacos, nachos or Chilli Con Carne (p 36). Follow the recipe for Pineapple Salsa (p 351), replacing the pineapple with tomato.

* *Spiced tomato and parsley fry-up* The best way to use a few tired tomatoes. Heat 1–2 tbsp oil in a frying pan over medium heat. Stir in 2–3 roughly chopped tomatoes, 1 tsp ground cumin, a generous pinch each of chilli flakes and salt, and 1–2 big handfuls of chopped parsley. Cook over high heat for 2–3 minutes, until the tomatoes are soft and glossy. Delicious served with barbecued meats or vegetables, or spread on toast and topped with an egg.

Tomato and peach salad with herbs and sumac

SERVES 4–6

This is the perfect simple summer salad when tomatoes and stone fruit are ripe, delicious and abundant. The sumac adds a sour tang to the fruit, while the tarragon gives a savoury bite.

In a bowl, combine 400 g (14 oz) ripe tasty tomatoes, cut into wedges, with 2 sliced peaches or nectarines (or plums or ripe figs), the zest and juice of ½ lemon and a pinch of salt. Set aside for 5–15 minutes to marinate. Add a splash of olive oil, a pinch of sumac and a handful of tarragon or dill leaves. Toss to combine. Spread out on a serving platter, and serve immediately. You could add some dollops of ricotta or labneh if you'd like a little creaminess.

Pickled green tomatoes

Red tomatoes don't make crunchy pickles, but green ones are wonderful fried and incredible pickled. Green tomatoes are available at the very beginning and very end of the tomato season. They're not a separate variety of tomato but simply unripe tomatoes, which have their own fresh, almost citrusy flavour. To pickle green tomatoes, use the Basic Vegetable Pickling recipe (p 472). Cut the tomatoes into quarters and fill a jar, then pour the pickling liquid over them, being sure to submerge everything. Add a few peeled garlic cloves, bay leaves and whole allspice berries. Store in the fridge for up to 3 months, or heat-process (p 502) and store in the pantry for up to 1 year.

The best way to cook wrinkled cherry tomatoes

When the cherry tomatoes have been forgotten at the back of the fridge, or rejected from school lunchboxes, give this a go. Heat the oven to 180°C (350°F) and place the tomatoes in a smallish roasting tin. Drizzle with olive oil and a little sherry vinegar or balsamic vinegar, and sprinkle generously with pepper, salt and dried oregano or thyme. Roast for 10–15 minutes, until the tomatoes have collapsed and caramelised.

Serve as a side with grilled (broiled) meats, roasted vegetables or an omelette (p 150), or squish onto burger buns instead of ketchup.

Fresh pasta sauce with your eyes closed

Salting overripe tomatoes draws out the flavoursome juices, creating a quick no-cook sauce. This is our go-to recipe when we need to make dinner quickly and we have tomatoes that need using.

Finely dice a couple of tomatoes and put them in a bowl. Add 2 finely grated garlic cloves, lots of salt and pepper, and plenty of olive oil. Mix together and leave to sit while the pasta boils, then toss through the hot pasta and grate whatever cheese you have in the fridge over the top.

Quick stovetop pasta sauce
MAKES 2 CUPS (500 ML)

The best pasta sauces take time to cook slowly, developing flavour as they simmer. This super-quick version takes only as long as it takes to boil pasta. When you're cooking quickly, remember to beef up the seasonings and flavours, given that they won't have time to intensify as they do over longer cooking times.

Slowly heat a generous amount (about ¼ cup/60 ml) of extra virgin olive oil or butter (or a combo of both) in a medium saucepan over low heat. Add 4 finely chopped garlic cloves and sauté very gently for a few minutes, being careful not to let them burn. Add 4–6 (about 650 g/ 1 lb 7 oz) finely diced ripe tomatoes, mix well, then simmer, covered, for about 15 minutes. Remove the lid and add ½ tsp each of salt and sugar, lots of ground black pepper and any chopped herbs you have on hand (thyme, oregano, basil – fresh or dried). Turn up the heat a little and simmer for 10 minutes, until slightly thickened. Feel free to stir through chopped olives, capers, finely grated lemon zest and/or chilli flakes, if you like.

TO TURN IT INTO A QUICK TOMATO SOUP

Add 2–3 cups (500–750 ml) home-made or good-quality stock (p 446) with the salt and sugar. At the end of cooking, remove from the heat, allow to cool slightly, then blend carefully, adding a little cream or sour cream if you want. Serve with garlic bread or cheese toasties.

Madame Lee's famous four-tomato and pork soup

SERVES 6 AS A STARTER, 3-4 AS A LIGHT MEAL

A delicious and comforting soup from the mother of a family friend.

Heat 1–2 tbsp vegetable oil in a saucepan over medium–low heat. Gently sauté 3 chopped garlic cloves, being careful not to burn them. Add 4 chopped tomatoes and let them cook in their own juices for 5 minutes, until soft. Add 250 g (9 oz) minced (ground) pork (this soup works best with fattier meat), and let it cook for a few minutes with the tomatoes. Add 2–2½ cups (500–625 ml) stock or water and simmer for 2–3 minutes until the pork is cooked. Season with 1–2 tbsp sugar, 1 tsp salt and a little pepper. If you have oyster sauce or soy sauce, add 1 tbsp of that too. Taste and balance the flavours as needed. Leave the soup chunky or blitz with a hand-held blender for a smoother consistency. Crack 1 egg into a small bowl and whisk with a fork. Stir the soup to create a whirlpool and pour in the egg, then remove from the heat and add a drizzle of sesame oil, some ground black pepper and thinly sliced spring onions (scallions).

Tomato jam

MAKES 2 x 375 ML (13 OZ) JARS

Treat this as a savoury jam and use it on sandwiches, burgers or cheese scones, or eat it with ham. Or melt 2–3 tbsp over low heat to use as a marinade for sticky chicken wings, ribs or tofu.

Heat 100 ml (3½ fl oz) oil in a shallow, wide, heavy-based pan over medium heat. Add 1 thinly sliced onion and sauté until soft and sweet but not browned, about 15 minutes. **»**

Add 1 tsp warm spices (ground cinnamon, allspice, cloves or ginger), ½ tsp salt, ¼ tsp ground black pepper and 1 kg (2 lb 4 oz) diced red or green tomatoes, then reduce the heat to low and cook for 15 minutes to soften the tomatoes and release their juices. Add ½ cup (125 ml) water and 1 cup (250 ml) apple cider vinegar or white wine vinegar, increase the heat to medium, and simmer for 5 minutes.

Remove from the heat and add 400 g (14 oz) caster (superfine) or raw sugar, stirring to dissolve. Return to medium heat and cook for 20–30 minutes, stirring occasionally to prevent the mixture from sticking.

Check for setting point (p 503). When it's ready, remove from the heat and let it cool for a few minutes. Carefully fill hot sterilised jars (p 501) with hot jam. Remove any air bubbles by carefully inserting a clean butter knife or chopstick to push them out or burst them, then seal immediately. Cool on the benchtop, then store in a cool, dark place for up to 1 year. Once opened, store in the fridge for up to 3 months, or you could heat-process (p 502) your jars for 10 minutes for longer storage.

TOMATO PASTE (CONCENTRATED PURÉE)

Bloody tomato paste. You buy a jar or tub, use half, it goes mouldy, you throw it away and then you put it on the shopping list again. Tomato paste is just concentrated tomatoes, and as it's without salt, vinegar or sugar, it doesn't last as long as you think it might. If you've got half a jar or tub that needs using, plan a dish for later that week that will use up the other half, or get liberal with it and start spreading it on your grilled cheese sandwiches instead of butter. You could also try buying tomato paste in a tube, which ensures less exposure to oxygen.

Some ideas for using up tomato paste (concentrated purée)

The trick to getting the most flavour out of tomato paste is to cook it in oil or fat over highish heat before adding it to your dish. This takes away its raw tomato taste and replaces it with a much deeper intensity. Once you start cooking with tomato paste like this, it's unlikely to become fossilised at the back of the fridge.

* Use it as the base of your next bolognese sauce, stew, ragu, tomatoey soup or pizza sauce. Heat 2–3 tbsp oil in a small frying pan over medium heat. Dump the tomato paste from the fridge (up to ⅓ cup/90 g) in the pan, add 2 crushed garlic cloves, and simmer for 2–3 minutes.

* Next time you sauté onions, add 2–3 tbsp tomato paste about 10–15 minutes into cooking. Let it darken and caramelise at the bottom of the pan, then serve with sausages in crusty bread rolls.
* The Green Beans and Grains (p 41) will use up the tired green beans in the fridge as well as the last 2–3 tbsp tomato paste.
* Replace the tomato sauce in cocktail sauce or Russian Dressing (p 418) with a little tomato paste and a pinch of sugar.
* Add a little tomato paste, worcestershire sauce and dried oregano to minced (ground) meat when making sausage rolls.
* Turn rice red. Add 2 tbsp tomato paste to the base of the Anything-goes Rice (p 394) for a quick tomato rice to serve with salad and meatballs, fried eggs or smoky beans and tacos.

Shaken barbecue marinade
MAKES ABOUT ¾ CUP (185 ML)

In an almost empty tomato paste (concentrated purée) jar, combine 2–3 tbsp oil, 2–3 tbsp apple cider vinegar, 2–3 tbsp something sweet like brown sugar, honey, maple syrup or molasses, 1 crushed garlic clove, ¼ tsp cayenne pepper, and 1 tsp each of ground black pepper, salt and smoked paprika. Shake to emulsify, then use to marinate chicken wings, a piece of pork, tofu slices or eggplant (aubergine).

Turn tomato paste into dinner
SERVES 2

When there's not much in the fridge but opened tomato paste (concentrated purée), make this. It's a simple spiced base for chickpeas or white beans, browned chicken or roasted eggplant (aubergine). Pair with rice or couscous, and dinner is served.

Heat 2–3 tbsp olive oil or butter in a frying pan. Add 2–3 tbsp tomato paste, 1 tsp paprika, 2 finely chopped garlic cloves, a good few pinches of dried oregano, chilli flakes, crushed fennel seeds or similar, and ¼ tsp salt. Cook for 1 minute, then add 1 cup (250 ml) water or stock and 400 g (14 oz) drained tinned or cooked brown lentils or chickpeas, a few browned chicken thighs or a cubed and roasted eggplant (aubergine). Simmer for 2–3 minutes, then taste, season as needed and serve.

Turnips

A bit of an old-fashioned vegetable that's still popular in the United States and France, but is hardly piled sky-high in Australian supermarkets or farmers' markets. Usually they turn up in vegie boxes and become the last vegetable standing after everything else has been put to good use. It's a bit of a shame, because turnips are good. They're related to radishes and mustard greens, but are the mild-mannered cousin of the family. Eat them raw or roasted, sautéed or mashed. If you can, buy them with their tops still on, as the leaves have an excellent peppery taste. The smaller the turnip the sweeter the flavour, so use these ones raw. Larger turnips can be a little bitter, so opt for cooked recipes.

Go with
Potatoes, kohlrabi, carrots, cabbage, onions, leeks, green beans, brussels sprouts, cauliflower, apples, pears, lemons, parsley, thyme, mint, chives, tarragon, garlic, black pepper, mustard, nutmeg

---

Storage
If your turnips have come with their green tops, remove and wrap them in a clean damp tea towel (dish towel) and store in a cloth bag with the rest of your herbs and leafy greens. Store the roots in the crisper section of the fridge for up to 3 weeks.

Substitutes
Potatoes have a similar texture and can be used to replace cooked turnips, but they are starchier. Or try the other underrated vegetable that's related to turnip – swede (rutabaga).

Some ideas for when a turnip turns up

* Use turnips in place of any of the root vegetables in Wally Rath's Barley Vegetable Soup (p 30). It's old-fashioned and comforting.
* Roast them as you would a potato or any other root vegetable. They go particularly well with roasted carrots. The peppery turnip and the sweet carrots make for contrast as well as balance.

* *Turnip and leek soup* For something a little different, replace the potatoes in the Leek and Potato Soup (p 236) with turnips.
* *Turnip slaw* Raw turnip is peppery and makes an excellent slaw. If your knife skills are up to it, cut 500 g (1 lb 2 oz) turnips into very fine matchsticks. If not, coarsely grate them. Follow the Basic Brussels Slaw recipe (p 60), adding lots of chopped parsley and chives.
* *Mashed turnip* A bit of a change from ol' mashed potato. Follow the steps for Mashed Kohlrabi (p 229). If you have left-over mashed turnip, follow the Pumpkin, Herb and Vegetable Patties recipe (p 370), using the turnip instead of the pumpkin (squash).
* *Turnip rostis* Yes, they are delicious. Follow the Parsnip Rosti recipe (p 323), but use raw grated turnip instead of parsnip.

Pink fermented turnips
MAKES 2 x 500 ML (18 OZ) JARS

Jaimee's all-time favourite fermented pickle. This is based on a Lebanese style of pickling turnips with beetroot so they turn hot-pink. Eat these with your eyes *and* your mouth. Serve with koftas or falafel, or chop finely and add to tabouleh. You can also go rogue and add them to egg and mayonnaise sandwiches or potato salad (p 362), or chop them finely and stir through yoghurt with a little honey for a quick dip.

Make a brine by dissolving 10 g (¼ oz) salt in 2 cups (500 ml) water: boil the water and salt, then allow the brine to cool completely before using. Wash and scrub 1 kg (2 lb 4 oz) turnips and cut into wedges about 2 cm (¾ in) thick. In each jar, place 1 tsp black peppercorns, a small piece of peeled raw beetroot and the wedges of turnip. Fill the jars with the cooled brine, making sure all the ingredients are well covered. Seal the jars and place in a cool, dry place for 4 days. Over this time, the colour will be leached from the beetroot and the turnips will turn hot pink. Your turnips will bubble and some juice may escape. Simply wipe the jar down. After 4 days, place the jars in the fridge. The turnips may be eaten immediately but will improve with time (we suggest waiting at least 1 week). Once open, store in the fridge for up to 6 months. See also the fermenting tips on p 504.

Turnip tartiflette

SERVES 4

Sounds fancy? Relax, it's not. This simple, rustic French dish is usually made with potato and a soft rind cheese called reblochon, but in this version we're using turnips and brie. If you want to use potatoes instead, by all means do. What makes this dish so delicious is that it's made up of layers and, as they cook, all the ingredients succumb to the wine they're cooked in to create the cheesy, salty, carby spoonful of heaven that is tartiflette. Serve this with a salad of bitter greens and a few pickles to counter the richness.

In a flameproof casserole dish over medium heat, melt 2 tbsp butter and sauté 1 very finely diced large onion until translucent. Add 1 finely chopped garlic clove, 4 diced bacon rashers (unless you want the dish to be vegetarian) and ½ tsp each of salt and pepper. Sauté until the bacon is cooked through. Remove from the heat and transfer to a bowl, leaving all the seasoning on the bottom of the casserole dish. Preheat the oven to 200°C (400°F). Very thinly slice 500–750 g (1 lb 2 oz – 1 lb 10 oz) turnips. Arrange the turnip slices in a single layer on the bottom of the casserole dish, season with a little salt and spread half the onion and bacon mixture over the top. Add another layer of turnip slices and spread the remaining onion and bacon mix on top. Add a final layer of turnip slices and 150 g (5½ oz) sliced brie. Pour in ⅔ cup (170 ml) white wine, then add a good grind of black pepper and another pinch of salt. Cover the casserole dish and cook in the oven for 45 minutes.

Pickled turnip

MAKES ABOUT 1 CUP (125 G)

We have adapted this beautiful pickle recipe from our friend Nancy Singleton Hachisu's book *Preserving the Japanese Way*. This pickling technique uses salt rather than vinegar. It also uses yuzu, a Japanese citrus with a floral fragrance, but if you find it hard to come by, use lemon instead, as we do. Serve with steamed rice and vegetables.

Wash and peel 1 turnip, keeping its greens on if they are attached. Cut the turnip into bite-sized pieces and place in a small airtight container or a clean reusable plastic bag. Add the zest of 1 lemon, 2 tsp chilli flakes and 1 tbsp salt, then mix everything together well using clean hands. Seal the bag or container and refrigerate overnight. The next day, remove the turnip pieces you want to use and squeeze them thoroughly to remove excess moisture and salt. You may even need to give them a rinse, but bear in mind that they're meant to be salty and zesty. They will last in the fridge for 3 days but will become saltier over time, so use them up soon.

TURNIP LEAVES

Turnip leaves are peppery and tasty. Use them as you would any other strongly flavoured green. Try the Basic Sauerkraut recipe (p 66) using turnip leaves.

Turnip leaf and dandelion leaf salad
SERVES 4 AS A SIDE

For those who love their bitter greens. This salad requires a little foraging adventure to your garden or local park. Most of us can identify dandelion leaves – they are jagged and grow in a rosette formation, and of course in spring they have a sunny-yellow, single-stemmed flower growing from their centre. If you're not the foraging type, or you live somewhere with no dandelions around, then use any bitter green leaves for this salad.

Thoroughly wash 1 cup torn turnip leaves and 1 cup torn dandelion leaves (about 60 g of each) and leave to dry well. Place 1 unpeeled potato in a small saucepan of water and add 1 tsp caraway seeds. Boil until tender. Drain and allow to cool completely. Hard-boil 3 eggs, then drain and cool. Peel the eggs and the potato. Place the turnip and dandelion leaves in a bowl and grate the potato on top. Roughly chop the eggs and add to the salad. Season with a pinch of salt and pepper, then gently mix all the ingredients together. Dress with the Poppy Seed and Orange Dressing (p 405) or the Classic Mustard Vinaigrette (p 283).

V

Vinegar p 471

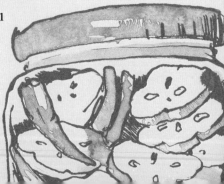

Vinegar

You probably already have a bottle of one of the great secret weapons in cooking sitting in your pantry cupboard. Not demanding too much attention but quietly confident that you will reach for it soon, vinegar is as much a staple as oil, sugar and salt. While we all know that vinegar creates the balancing act that is salad dressing, vinegar's sharp elbow in the ribs will bring brightness and contrast to many dishes. You can get very excited about all the fancy vinegars out there and by all means become a connoisseur, but for everyday cooking you really only need a vinegar for salad dressings and a vinegar that you can use for cooking as well as pickling. If you have white distilled vinegar in the house, we will politely suggest that you keep it under the sink, to be used only for cleaning. In the kitchen you need decent vinegars – not expensive, but not something that will take the lining off your oesophagus.

Depending on what we're cooking or pickling, we use apple cider vinegar, white or red wine vinegar, rice wine vinegar, malt vinegar, sherry vinegar and fruit vinegars. For preserving, make sure your vinegar has at least 5 per cent acidity (most supermarket vinegars do). Don't use balsamic and aged vinegars for pickling – they're best used in cooking and salads.

You'll never waste vinegar once you know how much it will do for your cooking. It offers balance to overly sweet or fatty foods, it rounds out the flavour of a stock, and a dash can bring a soup to life.

Storage   Vinegar can be stored indefinitely; its high acidity means it won't go off. It can, however, be affected by light and atmospheric humidity, which may make it appear a little cloudy. Vinegar might also get darker over time, with more sediment. This is all harmless and doesn't affect the vinegar quality. If the 'mother' – the acetic acid bacteria that make the vinegar – grows too big or there's too much sediment, simply strain the vinegar before use.

Substitutes   If you need to give a lift to a dish or need an acidic base for a dressing or salsa and you're out of vinegar, use lemon, lime or orange juice, or check the fridge for a mostly eaten jar of pickles and use the pickling liquid. A splash of wine might also give the contrast needed. Alas, none of these can take vinegar's place in preserving – that's a job for the serious acid of vinegar.

Basic vegetable pickling

You can use this simple pickle recipe to pickle any of your favourite vegetables or fruits. The great thing is that it uses a ratio of 4:2:1 – that is, 4 parts vinegar to 2 parts water to 1 part sugar – so you can scale it up or down, according to how many vegetables you're going to pickle.

Prepare the vegetables by washing and leaving whole, or slicing thinly, or cutting into batons or wedges. Sturdy vegetables and fruit, such as carrots, beetroot, green beans, okra, peas and rhubarb, can be cut and go straight into the jar raw. Produce with a high water content, such as cucumber, zucchini (courgettes), green tomatoes, onions and green mango, need to be salted before pickling. To do this, slice the vegies, sprinkle with pure salt (i.e. with no additives) in the ratio of 1 tbsp salt to 1 kg produce, and let them sit for 1–4 hours. Drain and then start pickling.

Make the pickling liquid by combining 4:2:1 vinegar, water and sugar, along with salt to taste, in a saucepan over low heat. For 1 kg (2 lb 4 oz) vegetables in 4 × 400 ml (14 oz) jars, you'll need about 2 cups (500 ml) vinegar, 1 cup (250 ml) water, ½ cup (110 g) white (granulated) sugar and at least 1 tsp salt. Stir to dissolve the sugar and salt. Increase the heat, bring to simmering point, then remove from the heat. Put up to 1 tbsp whole spices in each jar to complement your produce: consult the list at the beginning of each ingredient. Try spice mix 6 (p 421), or experiment with woody herbs, garlic, ginger, chillies and lemon peel.

Pack vegetables into sterilised jars (p 501) using small clean tongs or clean hands. Cover with brine until the vegetables are submerged. Remove air bubbles by carefully inserting a clean butter knife or chopstick to push them out or burst them. Wipe the rim of the jar with a clean tea towel (dish towel) or paper towel and seal. Store in the fridge for up to 3 months, or heat-process (p 502) for 15 minutes and store in the pantry for up to 1 year. These pickles get better over time, so let them sit for at least a few weeks before eating. If you're looking for instant pickles, see opposite.

Quick-pickling

MAKES ABOUT 1¾ CUPS (375 ML)

An instant pickling liquid is for the impatient, the time-poor preservers and the waste warriors. These pickles are light, mellow and ready for the table almost immediately. Use this recipe to make quick pickles from the odds and ends left in the fridge – half an onion, one corn cob, a few radishes, celery sticks, the last carrot or beetroot or even broccoli stems.

Combine 1 cup (250 ml) very hot water, ½ cup (125 ml) vinegar (white wine, red wine, apple cider or rice), ¼ cup (55 g) caster (superfine) sugar and 1 tsp salt in a jug. Stir until the salt and sugar are dissolved. In an airtight container or clean jar, put 1 cup thinly sliced vegetables and 1 tsp spices of your choice (mustard seeds, fennel seeds, dill seeds, chilli flakes, peppercorns) or a few slices of fresh ginger or a bay leaf. Pour the hot brine over the vegetables and leave to sit for at least 20 minutes before eating. Once cool, cover and store in the fridge for up to 2 weeks.

Sweet mulled vinegar for pickling fruits

Poaching fruits in a sweet, spiced vinegar mix turns average-tasting fruits – disappointing apricots or unripen-able pears – into something special. This mulled vinegar lightly pickles the fruits and they can then be eaten with cheeses and meats, used in place of dried fruits in savoury dishes, or thinly sliced and tossed through salads and grain dishes. You could even serve them with a not so sweet dessert. Never throw away the syrup – it can be the base of a marinade or dressing, or you could add a splash to a fancy cocktail.

In a saucepan, heat equal parts sugar, water, and apple cider or wine-based vinegar: try 1 cup (250 ml) of each for 4 or more pieces of fruit. Stir to dissolve the sugar, then add spices of your choice. Mulling spices, like spice mix 5 on p 420, work well, as do strips of citrus peel, slices of fresh ginger and woody herbs like thyme, rosemary or bay leaves. Add whole or sliced pieces of firm fruit, then simmer gently until just tender – you want the fruit to keep its shape and some texture.

Keep your spiced fruits in an airtight container or a jar in the fridge for many months, or bottle them in sterilised jars (p 501), heat-process (p 502) for 15 minutes and keep in the pantry for up to 1 year.

How to flavour vinegars

Would you like a pantry of your own fancy vinegars to dress up a salad, or to add flavour to dips, salsas, soups and sauces? You don't need to spend a fortune. All you need is a decent vinegar and some herbs, spices or citrus peel. The best bit is that you're making use of scraps and little bits of left-over ingredients to create a useful and delicious new ingredient in the kitchen. Flavoured vinegars also look so pretty in bottles and make lovely gifts.

Simply put your ingredients in a clean jar or bottle and cover with white wine vinegar, rice wine vinegar, apple cider vinegar or red wine vinegar. If you want to add a little sugar and salt to balance out the acidity, pop it in along with the other ingredients. Leave to infuse for 3–4 weeks. During this time, keep tasting the vinegar until you're happy with the flavour, and one day you'll know it's ready. Strain, then return the flavoured vinegar to the bottle and store in the pantry or fridge. It will last for up to 2 years.

Always match your ingredients to your vinegar, and don't go overboard. We find one or two flavours are the most successful – you'll want 3 tbsp flavour for each 300 ml (10½ fl oz) vinegar. Here's a short guide to get you started – remember to use only one or two aromatics, not everything suggested:

- **White wine vinegar** Strips of lemon peel, black peppercorns, rosemary, thyme, chilli, peeled garlic, slices of ginger
- **Red wine vinegar** Horseradish, black peppercorns, peeled garlic, tarragon, a cinnamon stick, star anise
- **Apple cider vinegar** Sage, thyme, strips of orange peel, ginger, rosemary
- **Rice wine vinegar** Pierced chillies, bashed lemongrass stems, peeled garlic, slices of ginger, turmeric, strips of lime peel, bashed coriander (cilantro) roots.

W-X

Watermelon

Here are some ideas for you and your watermelon, so you can buy a whole one and go plastic-free. First, choose a watermelon that's a suitable size for your household. Second, cut up the watermelon as soon as you get it home, then walk around the house offering slices to everyone. This should deal with a good portion. Once everyone has had enough of you and your plates of watermelon, you can get stuck into our ideas. Consider it the week of the watermelon and luxuriate in this remarkable if bulbous fruit. And don't forget to check out melon (p 270) for more ideas.

Goes with	Watermelon is perfect on its own, but you can tart it up with limes, chilli, salt, pepper, salty black olives, feta, mozzarella, haloumi, cashews, ham, pickled red onions or vodka. Watermelon also likes cucumber, tomatoes, pineapple, grapes, mango, other melons, strawberries, cherries, lemons, mint, coriander (cilantro) and sumac.
Storage	Watermelons are best kept in the fridge. A whole one will last at room temperature for 2–3 days, but if the weather is warm, make room in the fridge. Once cut, seal the cut side tightly with a beeswax wrap, plastic wrap or a reusable plastic bag.
Substitutes	You can swap any melon with another. Just remember that watermelon has a much higher water content than rockmelon (cantaloupe) or honeydew melon. Cucumber matches watermelon's cool crunch.

Some ideas for having some watermelon

* ***Watermelon whip*** This is an easy way to use up the watermelon and turn it into something new. Follow the Kiwi Fruit Whip recipe (p 227), using about 200 g (7 oz) chopped and frozen watermelon instead of kiwi fruit.

* ***A slushy, but for the grown-ups*** Blitz 2 cups (about 350 g) chopped watermelon, seeds removed, in a blender with 1 cup (about 130 g) ice cubes, 1 tbsp icing (confectioners') sugar, a pinch of salt and ¼ cup (60 ml) vodka or gin.

* ***Watermelon and tomato salsa*** Use the Pineapple Salsa (p 351) recipe, with 2 cups (about 350 g) cubed watermelon or a combination of watermelon and diced tomato.

* ***Watermelon lemonade*** Make the Berry Berry Good Lemonade (p 49), replacing the berries with 2 cups (about 350 g) chopped watermelon.

* ***All-the-red-fruit salad*** This is so pretty and much more refined than your average fruit salad. Place 2 cups (about 350 g) watermelon, cut into small cubes on the diagonal, in a shallow serving bowl. Scatter in 1 cup (150 g) sliced strawberries and ½ cup (180 g) pitted and sliced cherries. Sprinkle with 2 tsp caster (superfine) sugar and top with a dollop of the Almond Cream on p 287 or plain yoghurt.

Watermelon bloody mary
MAKES 6 CUPS (1.5 LITRES) OR 6 DRINKS

In a blender or food processor, combine 4 chopped tomatoes, ¼ chopped fairly large watermelon (about 1 kg/2 lb 4 oz) and 100 ml (3½ fl oz) lemon juice. Blitz very well, then pass through a sieve – you want about 4 cups (1 litre) liquid. Taste and season with salt and pepper. Put lots of ice in tall glasses and pour in the bloody mary mix. Add a dash of worcestershire sauce and 30 ml (1 fl oz) vodka per serving. Or you can keep it booze-free if you'd like a virgin mary.

Salted watermelon salad
SERVES 4 AS A SIDE

Mix up your salad-making game with this salted watermelon combination. Serve with grilled haloumi or sardines and pretend you're on holiday.

Cut 600 g (1 lb 5 oz) watermelon into chunks or slices, with the rind removed, and arrange on a serving plate. Add 2–3 large handfuls of mint leaves, a generous sprinkling of salt and 1 tbsp sumac. Drizzle with 2 tbsp lemon juice and 1 tbsp olive oil. If you want a little something extra, some Quick-pickled Red Onion (p 312) or thinly sliced black olives would be very welcome.

Watermelon granita

SERVES 6–8

This very simple dessert is perfect on a very hot day. It's like shaved ice without the lurid colours and additives. This one is inspired by the flavours of Mexico, but would be excellent to serve after any rich meal.

Cut 1 kg (2 lb 4 oz) watermelon into cubes and remove the seeds, then blitz in a food processor with ½ cup (110 g) caster (superfine) sugar and the zest and juice of 1 lime. If you're making this for adults who like to live a little, add a pinch of cayenne pepper. Pour into an airtight container and freeze for at least 4 hours. During this time, set your timer, and every 40 minutes or so scrape and break up the freezing granita so it doesn't form one big ice block – it's supposed to have the texture of snow. Once frozen, the granita will keep in the freezer for 10 days.

Watermelon rind pickle

MAKES 1 x 500 ML (18 OZ) JAR

Watermelon rind fills compost bins in summer, but this pickle recipe is a delicious way to get through the waste. You can thinly slice the pickled rind and toss it through a green salad or a slaw. Add it to a grainy salad for some bite, or eat with sharp cheddar on rye bread.

In this recipe, we're just pickling the white rind. Remove the green skin from about 250 g (9 oz) rind using a sharp knife, then cut the white rind into thin strips. Sprinkle generously with salt and let it sit for at least 1 hour, or overnight. Make a pickling liquid by simmering 1 cup (250 ml) apple cider vinegar, ½ cup (125 ml) water and ½ cup (110 g) white (granulated) sugar with a big pinch of chilli, ½ tsp black peppercorns and something warm like a few slices of fresh ginger, ½ tsp allspice berries, a cinnamon stick, some juniper berries or a few star anise. Rinse the salt off the rind, put into a jar or airtight container and cover with the spiced pickling liquid. Allow to cool, then seal and store in the fridge for up to 1 month.

Whey

If you make your own labneh (p 493) or you eat a lot of yoghurt, you'll probably find yourself with left-over whey. In which case you're very lucky indeed, because whey can be extremely useful in the kitchen. Whey is the liquid part of curdled milk – curds being the solid or semi-solid part. The taste of whey is slightly salty and acidic; even a tablespoon of the stuff (such as might be making a pool on the top of your yoghurt) can be put to good use, thanks to its high protein content and live bacterial cultures (the kinds we use in fermentation).

Goes with	All fruits if you want to add whey to a smoothie. Use whey to cook meats, or add it to soups with dried beans, chickpeas or lentils. It can also be used to cook rice and potatoes.
Storage	Store whey in a clean jar or airtight container in the fridge for up to 3 weeks. You can also freeze whey in ice-cube trays and keep for 3 months.
Substitutes	None really.

Some ideas for going *all the wheys*

* The whey from yoghurt is full of the friendly bacteria that fermented it. When making Basic Sauerkraut (p 66), add 1 tbsp whey to the cabbage with the salt and seasoning. It will help speed up the fermentation process, while ensuring that no nasties take hold.
* The *whey to go* for slow-cooked meat for dinner. If you have lots of whey, add it to your lamb shanks, to help tenderise the meat and bring out a unique complexity.
* Use whey as a dressing base. Mix 3 tbsp whey, 1 generous tbsp neutral oil, 2 tsp very finely chopped herbs and salt and pepper to taste. Use this to dress soft lettuce leaves.
* Use whey in baking in place of water or skim milk. It's low in fat, so keep that in mind and don't use it to replace full-fat milk or cream.
* Whey is a very nice face treatment – it makes your skin feel soft and is lightly exfoliating. Pat it on in the evening and leave overnight, then rinse off in the morning.

Whey caramel
MAKES 200 ML (7 FL OZ)

This caramel is semi-sweet with a malt flavour. Stir it through softened ice cream and refreeze; use it to make milkshakes; or drizzle it over cakes and puddings.

Strain 2 cups (500 ml) whey through a sieve into a saucepan. Add 125 g (4½ oz) caster (superfine) sugar and stir over medium heat to dissolve. Slowly bring the mixture to the boil, then reduce the heat to as low as possible and simmer, uncovered, for 1 hour, or until a golden caramel has formed. Remove from the heat and let it cool for a few minutes. You can store this caramel in a jar or airtight container in the fridge for up to 2 weeks. It will thicken in the fridge. To warm and make it runny again, simply sit the container in hot water for 10 minutes and give the caramel a good stir.

Whey soda
MAKES ABOUT 6 CUPS (1.5 LITRES)

This is a kind of fermented lemonade. It's lightly carbonated and, once refrigerated, very refreshing. The whey activates the fermentation by introducing good bacteria that will convert the sugar to lactic acid and produce carbonation. Think of this recipe as fermentation 'lite', as it's very easy and you get all the gut-nourishing benefits of a beverage that's alive with healthy bacteria.

In a very clean jar (at least 6 cups/1.5 litres capacity, or 2 smaller jars), pour 4 cups (1 litre) room-temperature water. Add ¼ cup (55 g) caster (superfine) sugar and stir vigorously to dissolve. Add ¼ cup (60 ml) strained whey and the juice of 3 lemons, plus 1 tsp freshly grated nutmeg or ground cinnamon.

Give all the ingredients a very good stir and seal the jar tightly. Leave out of direct sunlight at room temperature for 2–3 days, depending on how warm the weather is. You may notice a foaminess developing on the surface of the soda; just skim it off and replace the lid. Put it in the fridge for another day and then the soda is ready to drink. Keep refrigerated for up to 1 week.

See cheese, cream, milk, sour cream and yoghurt for ideas with other dairy products.

Wine

Yes, yes, we know, there's no such thing as left-over wine. Except sometimes there is. Like after a dinner party, or if you live alone, or if you bought a wine that turned out to be not very nice for drinking. Unlike spirits and fortified wines, which can hang around for years, an opened bottle of wine or prosecco must be dealt with one way or another. If it's not for drinking, then put wine to use in other ways, as its acidity will work in much the same way as vinegar, and its aromatics will add a depth of flavour to sauces, soups, braises and cooked fruit.

Goes with	In cooking, wine cuts through fats, so use it when cooking meats, or let it add its mellow notes to slow-cooked dried beans, chickpeas and lentils. Wine adds sophistication to desserts such as poached pears, and matches very well with berries of all kinds.
Storage	Keep unopened wine out of direct light, and don't store it above 20°C (70°F). If there's any wine left in a bottle, replace the cap or put the cork back in, stained end down, and pop in the fridge for up to 2 days.
Substitutes	To replace wine's acidity, use a splash of vinegar, sauerkraut brine or pickling liquid, or a squeeze of lemon juice.

Some ideas for using the wine dregs

* Use instead of stock. Half wine, half water, a knob of butter and a generous amount of salt can make a good substitute for stock at a pinch. This is helpful if you forget the stock or need to use up the wine when you're making risotto, or your dish needs a small amount of stock.
* Half a bottle (about 1½ cups/375 ml) of left-over red or white wine can be put to extremely good use when poaching fruit (see the Boozy Syrup on p 337). It's especially good for poaching pears, cherries and quinces.
* Add wine to the stockpot. A splash of red or white wine in stock towards the end of cooking will add acidity and liveliness. »

* Wine for braises. Left-over wine is perfect to use the next day when making a braise. Read the instructions on turning tired vegetables into Velvety Braised Vegetables (p 159) and be glad you didn't pour the last bit of wine down the sink.
* Make vinegar. Possibly the best use for left-over wine is to make your own vinegar. Here's a simple ratio: 3 parts left-over wine (red, white, even champagne or beer) to 1 part vinegar (use a vinegar that has a 'mother'). Combine in a very clean jar, cover loosely and leave out of direct sunlight for 1–6 months. The vinegar will get better the longer you leave it. As it ferments, it will develop its own 'mother'; strain it out before using the vinegar.

White wine mussels
SERVES 4

The easiest dinner-party meal. Just add crusty bread and open some more wine.

Heat ¼ cup (60 ml) olive oil in a large saucepan over medium heat and sauté 1 sliced onion or ½ very thinly sliced fennel bulb until soft. Add 2–3 sliced garlic cloves and sauté until fragrant. Add ½ bunch of chopped parsley, a big squeeze of lemon juice and ½ tsp each of salt and pepper. You could also throw in any cherry tomatoes that need using, or sliced chilli. Pour in up to 2 cups (500 ml) white wine, bring to a simmer, cook for a few minutes, then taste the winey stock to make sure you're happy with the flavour. Adjust the seasoning and acidity (with more lemon juice) if necessary.

Scrub 1–2 kg (1 lb 2 oz – 2 lb 4 oz) mussels and pull out the hairy beards, discarding any broken mussels, and any open ones that don't close when tapped on the bench, then rinse well. Add them to the pot, then put on the lid and steam the mussels until they open, about 5 minutes. Discard any that haven't opened during cooking. Put the pot on the table with a loaf of bread and plenty of good butter.

Drunken spaghetti
SERVES 4

This is the way to use half a bottle of red, if there ever was one. Cook 300 g (10½ oz) spaghetti for half the time it says on the packet. Meanwhile, melt 2 tbsp butter in a frying pan, add 2 finely chopped garlic cloves and cook for 2–3 seconds, then add 1½ cups (375 ml) red wine. Strain the pasta and add to the wine, then cover the pan and cook for 6 minutes or until the pasta is al dente. Season with salt and ground black pepper, then serve with plenty of grated parmesan and more vino.

Prosecco and mustard chicken

Jaimee makes this when there's a bit of flat prosecco left over. Serve with the Spring Greens Medley (p 341).

Brown chicken thighs in butter or oil in a frying pan over medium–high heat. Season with salt and pepper and smear dijon mustard over the skins. Once the chicken is brown, pour ¼ bottle (about ¾ cup/185 ml) prosecco over it, then cover, reduce the heat to medium–low and cook for 10–15 minutes. Remove the lid, baste the chicken with the sauce and cook for another 5 minutes.

Wombok

The cabbage with many names: Chinese cabbage, Chinese leaf, napa cabbage, celery cabbage, the list goes on. Ah, but a cabbage by any other name ... takes up just as much room in the fridge. If there's one thing about a wombok, it's that it's big. So big that some avoid it altogether or waste the half they haven't used. But wombok is actually very versatile; it can be cooked or eaten raw. Its high water content means it will take up flavours very well, whether it's the heat of kimchi or a delicate splash of soy sauce and sesame oil. If you find yourself in the kitchen with a big wombok, rejoice, as there's more than one way to eat a Chinese cabbage.

Goes with	Onions, carrots, daikon, spring onions (scallions), green beans, mushrooms, ginger, garlic, tofu, chicken, beef, pork, fish, eggs, miso, chilli, chives, coriander (cilantro), mint, lemongrass, Thai basil, sesame seeds, nashi pears, green apple, green mango, soy sauce
Storage	Wrap wombok in a clean damp tea towel (dish towel) and it will stay fresh for a week. As you cut into it, keep rewrapping the unused portion. When you're down to the last portion, shred it and keep it in an airtight container with a few drops of water and use it within 1–2 days.
Substitutes	Plain old cabbage will do just fine. Because wombok has very wide and fibrous ribs, you can also substitute thinly sliced daikon in salads.

Some ideas for getting through a whopping big wombok

* If you're making the simple Egg Drop Soup (p 148) or Left-over-chicken Soup (p 106), throw in a few handfuls of shredded wombok and drop a little sesame oil on top.
* **Soy-pickled wombok** Follow the steps for the Japanese-style Soy-pickled Cucumber (p 128), replacing the cucumber with wombok. Have it on hand for a quick dinner with rice and a fried egg.
* **Stir-fried wombok on the side** Follow the recipe for Stir-fried Celery (p 87), tearing the leaves into large pieces. Add some grated fresh ginger with the garlic.
* **Simplest wombok slaw** Shred whatever amount of wombok you have, cut a nashi pear or green apple into matchsticks, add a big handful of coriander (cilantro) leaves, and season with salt and pepper. Lightly dress with a little sesame oil and some rice wine vinegar. Top with toasted sesame seeds if you have them.

Wrap a whole chicken
SERVES 4–6

Peel 12 leaves off a wombok and blanch them quickly in boiling water. Cool in iced water and gently squeeze out the excess water.

Preheat the oven to 180°C (350°F). Stuff a chicken with garlic, lemon and ginger, then wrap it in the wombok leaves. Put the wrapped chicken in an ovenproof dish with ½ cup (125 ml) water, 2 tbsp soy sauce, 2–3 star anise and a pinch of salt. Cover with foil and bake for 90 minutes.

Pull off the wombok leaves, chop them roughly and douse them with sesame oil. Cut the chicken into pieces and serve everything with plain rice.

Grilled wombok salad

Serve this with tofu dishes or grilled (broiled) fish, or as a side with dumplings.

Lightly oil a barbecue or chargrill pan and set the heat to medium–high. In a small bowl, mix 2 tbsp fish sauce, the juice of 1 lime, 1 tbsp grated fresh ginger, 1 crushed garlic clove and 1 tbsp caster (superfine) sugar. Mix until the sugar dissolves, then set aside.

Cut 1 wombok into quarters or eighths, depending on its size, or just use half of it, and brush all over with a neutral oil. Place on the barbecue or chargrill pan and cook until the wombok is beginning to soften and the outer leaves are well charred, about 3 minutes on each side. Arrange on a platter. Scatter thinly sliced red chilli and toasted sesame seeds or peanuts over the wombok and pour the dressing over the lot.

Not so classic kimchi

MAKES ABOUT 2 x 1 LITRE (35 OZ) JARS

This recipe makes use of a whole wombok. Depending on how much kimchi you eat, you'll have yourself stocked up for a while. Or, divide it up and give some to your friends. There are many 'classic' recipes for kimchi – there are as many variations as there are Korean households. Jaimee learnt how to make kimchi through trial and error, and from Korean students and friends along the way. A very influential book for her is *Kimchi* by Byung-Hi Lim and Byung-Soon Lim. This book not only helped her to refine her kimchi recipe, but showed her how to eat kimchi, from adding it to stews to making a kimchi martini. Have a look at the kimchi section (p 224) for ideas.

Cut the wombok in half and place the halves, cut side up, in a large bowl. Salt the leaves, layer by layer, with 250 g (9 oz) salt and cover with water. You may need to weigh the wombok down with a plate. Leave to stand at room temperature overnight.

The next day, drain the water and taste the wombok for saltiness. If it isn't very salty, you may want to add salt to your chilli paste.

In a food processor, put 300 g (10½ oz) daikon, cut into smallish pieces, 1 roughly chopped brown onion, 50 g (1¾ oz) roughly chopped fresh ginger, 10 peeled garlic cloves, 2 tbsp fish sauce, 1 tbsp caster (superfine) sugar and 50 g (1¾ oz) Korean chilli powder (gochugaru) or, to replicate the distinctively smoky heat of gochugaru, 2 tbsp chilli flakes, 1 tbsp smoked paprika and 1 tsp cayenne pepper. Blitz to a paste. You can also do the mixing by hand if you grate the daikon and onion and crush the ginger and garlic.

Cut each wombok half into quarters or even eighths and rub the paste between the leaves.

Fit the wombok into the very clean containers of your choice: 1–2 large glass jars, an airtight plastic container or a ceramic fermenting crock. Press the ingredients down firmly to release as much liquid as possible. Seal and leave to ferment at room temperature for 24–48 hours (see p 504 for more fermenting tips), then place in the fridge for 7–10 days before eating. Your kimchi will last for several months refrigerated. Cut into smaller slices to serve.

Cold noodle and wombok salad with pickles

SERVES 3–4

This dish is about texture as much as flavour. Crunchy and light, it's also adaptable – you can make it for meat-eaters or vegans, or make it gluten-free. Add pickles or fermented vegetables for more texture and as a balance to the sweet and spicy dressing.

First make the dressing. In a small bowl, combine 1 tbsp chilli flakes or powder (or to taste), 2 tbsp rice wine vinegar, 1 tbsp soy sauce, 1 tbsp honey, 1 tbsp sesame oil and 1 tbsp toasted sesame seeds. Mix and set aside. Heat 1 tbsp peanut oil in a wok or large frying pan over high heat and stir-fry 250 g (9 oz) minced (ground) chicken or pork, or chopped tofu. Season with salt and pepper, then stir until cooked through. Remove from the heat, cool thoroughly and drain off any excess liquid.

Now put 250 g (9 oz) vermicelli in a bowl, pour boiling water on top and set aside for 3–5 minutes. While the noodles are soaking, prepare 2 cups (90 g) thinly sliced wombok, 5–6 thinly sliced spring onions (scallions) and about ¼ cup (about 60 g) Vietnamese-style Daikon Pickles (p 135), Fermented Carrots (p 78) or Soy-pickled Lettuce (p 250).

Drain the noodles and rinse in cold water until completely cool. Shake the colander well to get rid of any excess water. Place the noodles in a big serving bowl and prettily arrange your sliced vegetables, minced (ground) meat or tofu and pickled daikon on top. Drizzle with the dressing.

Wombok dumplings

MAKES 24

A fresh and light dumpling filling means you can eat more dumplings. The high water content of wombok makes the filling soupy and delicious. Make these spicy, if you like, by adding sliced chilli. Serve with Chilli Oil (p 113) or Mandarin and Soy Dressing (p 257).

In a small bowl, mix 1½ tbsp shaoxing wine, sherry or mirin, 1½ tbsp grated fresh ginger, 5 sliced garlic cloves, 1 tsp black pepper and 1½ tsp sesame oil and set aside. In another bowl, sprinkle 3 cups (about 180 g) shredded wombok with ½ tsp salt and gently massage until the wombok breaks down. Squeeze out the excess water and discard. Pour the sauce over the wombok and combine well.

Lay a dumpling wrapper on a clean benchtop. Place 2 tsp of the wombok filling to one side of the wrapper, then fold the wrapper in half and seal by pinching the sides together with damp fingers. Repeat for the remaining filling. Cook according to the directions on the wrapper packet.

See broccoli, brussels sprouts, cabbage, cauliflower, kale and kohlrabi for ideas with other brassicas.

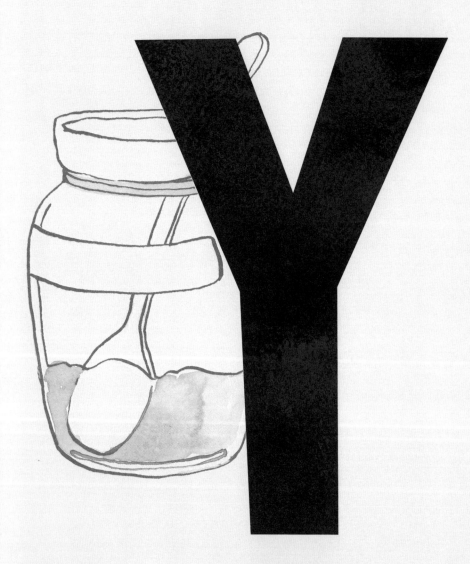

Yoghurt p 489

Yoghurt

Yoghurt is perhaps the most familiar fermented product in the kitchen. It's produced by culturing milk with different strains of bacteria. The milk thickens and becomes acidic, giving yoghurt its distinctive tangy taste. In our houses, yoghurt is bought or made (p 274) by the kilo. It goes with the muesli in the morning and is made into sides and dips, marinades and cheese, drinks and dinner and dessert, and, and, and ... Even the last scraping of yoghurt is always good for something. What's not so versatile is sweetened fruit yoghurt. Our advice is to buy or make plain yoghurt and sweeten or add fruit yourself. That way you can be flexible with the way you use up the yoghurt in the fridge.

Goes with   Fruits (especially bananas, berries, lemons), rhubarb, eggplant (aubergine), zucchini (courgettes), coconut, honey, nuts, oats, pasta, olive oil, garlic, spinach, crunchy lettuces, chilli, pepper, mint, parsley, coriander (cilantro), tarragon, dill, lamb, chicken, fish, dried beans, chickpeas, couscous

---

Storage   Store yoghurt in the coldest place in your fridge. This is usually not those compartments on the inside of the door but on the shelves. Use the best-before stamp as a guide and then your senses as the ultimate decider. Most yoghurt will be fine for a few more days after the use-by date – it just gets more sour – but stick your nose in there and have a smell. If it's off, you'll know it. Home-made yoghurt will keep for about 2 weeks.

Substitutes   Out of yoghurt? Depending on the recipe, sour cream or cream can make a good substitute. If you need more tang, add a squeeze of lemon juice or a splash of vinegar.

Some ideas for using up a tub of yoghurt

* If you only have a little bit of yoghurt to use up, Green Things Fritters (p 439) or Parsnip Rosti (p 323) can make good use of it. They both call for a little dairy, so simply use yoghurt.
* Make Jaimee's Apple Bake (p 7) with yoghurt instead of sour cream. The result is a little lighter.
* For a simple breakfast, try a small bowl of yoghurt topped with Plum Compote (p 356) or Quick Berry Compote (p 48).
* Make the Overnight Yoghurt Oats (p 301) for a healthy and filling breakfast.
* For simple yoghurt flat breads, follow the Flotsam and Jetsam Flat Breads recipe on p 168.
* **Green chicken or fish marinade** Alex's mum taught us this quick dinner a million years ago and we still make it when we have yoghurt and herbs to use up. In a food processor, blitz 1–2 bunches of herbs – stalks and all – with 3 roughly chopped garlic cloves. Mix through ½ cup (130 g) plain yoghurt and season with salt and pepper. It should be quite green. Marinate chicken thighs or breasts or fish fillets in this mixture for 1 hour before grilling.
* **Mango lassi** Go to the recipe on p 262; it uses 1 cup (260 g) plain yoghurt to make a sweet and tangy drink.
* **Matilda's frozen yoghurt** A friend of ours taught us this trick. It makes a very quick dessert that's additive-free and as good as any frozen yoghurt from the shops. In a high-powered blender or food processor, combine 2 cups (250 g) frozen berries, 1–3 tbsp honey, sugar or maple syrup, 1 cup (260 g) plain yoghurt and ½ cup (125 ml) cream. Blitz to a smooth frozen dessert with the consistency of soft serve. If you want it firmer, refreeze for 2–3 hours.

Yoghurt pasta

SERVES 4

We learnt the basic idea of this recipe from *Moro*, by Sam and Sam Clark. At first we weren't sure, but it proved so delicious that it's been a family favourite in both our houses for more than ten years.

Melt 2 tbsp butter in a large frying pan over medium–low heat and add 2 tbsp pine nuts or roughly chopped almonds and 2 finely chopped garlic cloves. Fry until the nuts are lightly golden. Mix the nuts and butter through ¾ cup (200 g) plain yoghurt seasoned with ¼ tsp ground allspice and a pinch of ground cinnamon. Cook 300 g (10½ oz) short pasta shapes according to the packet directions, then drain and mix through the yoghurt. Serve immediately – it can get a bit gluggy if it hangs around too long.

Basic yoghurt condiments

MAKES ABOUT 1½ CUPS (390 G)

Across the globe, yoghurt condiments sit beside main dishes ready to cool, soothe, complement or balance a meal. Their sourness and creaminess make them the perfect support act for rich or spicy foods as well as perfect as dips and spreads. If you're serving grilled (broiled) meat or a fiery curry, make sure you have a yoghurt sauce or two up your sleeve to complete the meal. Of course, there are subtle and not so subtle differences between many of the yoghurt sauces served with different cuisines, but you can use this adaptable recipe to make raitas, tzatziki or perugu pachadi with a simple swap of a herb and switch of a vegetable.

YOGHURT BASE

Mix 1 cup (260 g) plain yoghurt, ¼ tsp salt and 1 tbsp lemon juice or 1 tsp white wine vinegar. Turn this mixture into any of the condiments below.

TZATZIKI

Dice 2 cucumbers, removing the seeds if they're very big and wet. Sprinkle the cucumber with a pinch of salt. Leave for 20 minutes, then drain off the excess liquid. Mix into the yoghurt base with 1 crushed garlic clove and a handful of torn mint leaves. Season with ground black pepper and a glug of olive oil. Serve with koftas, falafel and flat breads (p 168).

RAITA

In a small frying pan, heat 1 tbsp neutral oil and fry 2 tsp ground cumin, 1 tbsp brown mustard seeds and 1 tbsp grated fresh ginger, taking care not to burn the spices. Once the mustard seeds pop, remove from the heat and add to the yoghurt base. Add 1 sliced green chilli, if you like, and a big handful of chopped coriander (cilantro) leaves. Raitas tend to have quite a thin consistency, so add a splash of water if the yoghurt is very thick. Serve with curries or spicy grilled meats.

GARLIC YOGHURT SAUCE

Crush or very finely chop 4 garlic cloves and mix into the yoghurt base. Season with ground black pepper or a big pinch of paprika. Use this sauce to marinate chicken, fish or lamb, or drizzle it over Grilled Zucchini (p 497), Roasted Eggplant (p 144) or a chickpea salad with flat breads.

TAHINI YOGHURT SAUCE

Mix 3 tbsp tahini, the zest of 1 small lemon and a generous pinch of ground cumin into the yoghurt base. Top with toasted pine nuts. Serve with grilled cauliflower, or on the side of the Big Grain Salad (p 379). »

PERUGU PACHADI

This is a tomato yoghurt chutney from southern India. Heat 2 tbsp neutral oil in a frying pan over medium heat, then fry 1 small diced onion with ½ tsp mustard seeds, 1 tsp cumin seeds and 1 tsp ground turmeric, until the onions are translucent. Add 2–3 good-sized diced tomatoes and cook for 6 minutes. Remove from the heat and allow to cool, then stir into the yoghurt base and top with chopped coriander (cilantro) leaves, if you have them. Serve with curries and flat breads.

Yoghurt soup

SERVES 4

Many Middle Eastern countries have versions of yoghurt soup. Some are made with dried yoghurt and some with fresh. We have played around with a few versions and think this is not only delicious but yoghurt-soup-novice-friendly.

In a bowl, whisk ½ cup (130 g) plain yoghurt with 1 egg yolk, ¼ tsp each of salt and ground pepper and 1 tbsp cornflour (cornstarch) until there are no lumps. Set aside.

In a medium frying pan over medium heat melt 2 tbsp butter and gently fry 2 finely chopped garlic cloves for 2–3 seconds, then add 400 g (14 oz) drained tinned chickpeas, 1 tsp chilli flakes and ¼ tsp ground allspice. Cook for 10 minutes.

Yoghurt donuts

MAKES 12

Okay, so this is an internet sensation that we couldn't resist because it has only two ingredients and everyone loves donuts. We love donuts even more when there isn't much faffing about. Self-raising flour means you get a light fluffy donut without waiting around for yeast, and the plain yoghurt gives flavour.

In a medium–large bowl, mix 160 g (5¾ oz) self-raising flour and ⅔ cup (190 g) plain yoghurt. Knead until you have a smooth dough. If it still feels tacky, add a little more flour. Cover with a clean tea towel (dish towel) and set aside at room temperature for 10 minutes. Turn the dough out onto a floured surface, then using a rolling pin, roll the dough out to about 1 cm (½ in) thick. Using a small cookie-cutter, or indeed a donut-cutter if you have one, cut out 12 donuts and set aside.

In a large heavy-based saucepan or very stable wok, heat 2 cups (500 ml) frying oil (rice bran oil is good) to 160°C (315°F). You can test the oil by throwing in a little piece of bread and seeing if it quickly goes golden. Using metal tongs, carefully drop one of the donuts into the oil. Fry for

1 minute. When it's ready, the donut will float to the surface and turn golden. Using tongs or a slotted spoon, remove the donut from the oil and drain on paper towel. Repeat for the remaining donuts. You will probably be able to fry 2 donuts at a time.

Dust the cooked donuts with Cinnamon Sugar (p 424), or fill them with jam by putting 2–3 tbsp in a piping bag, pushing the nozzle into the donut and squeezing the piping bag.

To reuse the frying oil, see the tips on p 83.

Labneh

The simplest cheese you can make, labneh is yoghurt strained of all the whey, leaving you a soft, fresh and delicious curd cheese. We love it for two reasons: you can make as little or as much as you like to use up yoghurt close to its use-by date, and you can add the last half bunch of herbs or finish a jar of spices to make a good thing even better.

Use a clean piece of muslin or clean Chux to line a colander and place over a bowl. In another bowl, mix the amount of yoghurt you want to use – we recommend 1–2 cups (260–520 g) – with a good pinch of salt and up to ½ bunch of fresh chopped herbs or 1 tbsp spices, such as fennel seeds, chilli flakes or powder, caraway seeds or paprika. Spoon this yoghurt mixture into your lined colander, folding over the edges of the muslin or Chux to cover the yoghurt. Place the colander and bowl in the fridge and leave overnight.

The next day, the whey will have gathered in the bowl. Don't throw this away! See whey (p 479) for how to put it to good use. Unwrap the labneh and serve with flat breads (p 168), grilled (broiled) meats and vegetables, meatballs, falafel, salads and pickles. Labneh will keep in an airtight container in the fridge for up to 1 week.

See cheese, cream, milk, sour cream and whey for ideas with other dairy products.

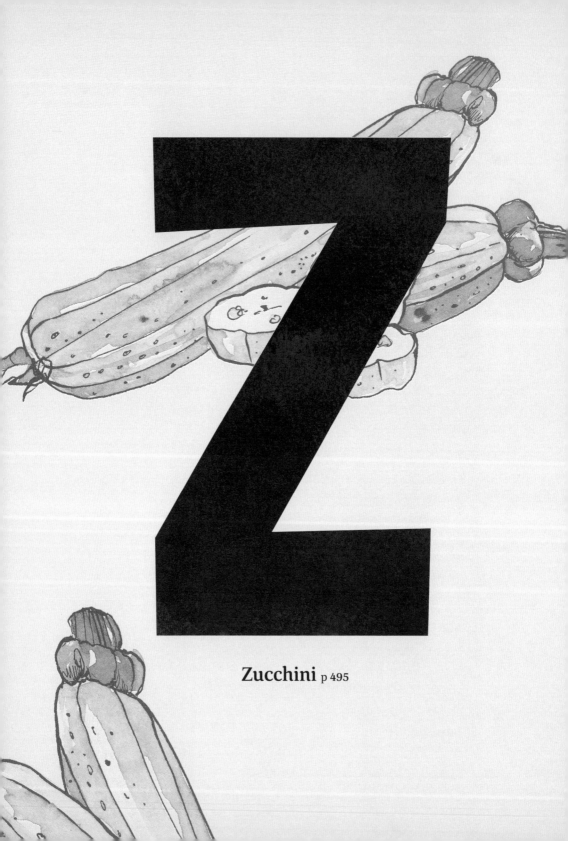

Zucchini p 495

Zucchini

In summer there are always more zucchini (courgettes) than you need. Either the garden is full of them, your vegie box has too many, or you bought them because they were cheap and now you're over them. We're guessing most households have a couple of zucchini in varying states of decay in the fridge. We hope this section will help you embrace and enjoy the zucchini glut. Keep in mind that small zucchini are best for eating raw and preserving; they're sweeter and have lower water content. Big old waterlogged guys, or the very neglected versions, are best kept for long slow cooking.

Go with   Zucchini is mild-mannered and plays well with most other vegetables, particularly eggplant (aubergine), tomatoes, capsicum (pepper), corn, onions, green beans and spinach, and herbs such as basil, chives, mint, dill, parsley and oregano. To give it some edge, choose sharp flavours like feta, vinegar, lemons, garlic, chilli, capers, parmesan, currants and anchovies. It also goes with other cheeses, dried beans, lentils, peas, cumin and fennel seeds.

Storage   Store zucchini in a bag of some sort in the fridge: paper with the top open, mesh or cloth. They need a little air or they'll turn to slime.

Substitutes   For cooked zucchini dishes, use capsicum (pepper) or eggplant (aubergine). For raw, cool dishes, substitute cucumber.

Some ideas for using up zucchini

* If there's only one zucchini (courgette) that needs using, add it to the Spring Greens Medley (p 341), or the 'What's in the Fridge' Vegie Pie filling (p 451). Grate it, squeeze out the excess moisture and add it to the Whatever-cheese Eggy Muffins (p 93) or the Seedy Breakfast Muffins (p 371).
* Add zucchini (courgette) to the Green Soup (p 440). It uses 3 cups of greens; you can make it all zucchini or, if you just have half a zucchini rolling around, mix it with spinach and dill. »

* The simplest way to cook a solo zucchini (courgette) is to heat a little butter and oil in a frying pan until just brown, then add 1 thinly sliced zucchini and a pinch of salt and ground black pepper. Fry until cooked, then scatter herbs over the top to serve.
* **Chow chow** Chow chow is a go-to mustardy relish for turning excess vegetables into a simple preserve with zing. We generally make it with corn, but it also works well with zucchini (courgettes). You may need a little extra cooking time, as zucchini have a higher water content than corn, but other than that the recipe is the same. You'll find the steps on p 120.
* **Zucchini mash** Grate as many zucchini (courgettes) as you have. Heat plenty of olive oil in a large frying pan and add 1 finely chopped garlic clove per zucchini, cooking gently for 30 seconds. Add the grated zucchini, plus plenty of salt, finely grated lemon zest and lemon juice, and ground black pepper to taste. Cook until it becomes a beautiful glossy mash – this will take quite a while. Spread on toast, toss through hot pasta, or use in an omelette (p 150).
* **Pickled zucchini** Zucchini (courgettes) make the best pickles. They just need to be salted beforehand to prevent sogginess. Slice them thinly, sprinkle with salt and leave to sit for about 1 hour. Shake off the excess moisture. For pickles fast, add the Quick-pickling liquid (p 473). If you have lots of zucchini, follow the Basic Vegetable Pickling recipe (p 472), putting ½ tsp each of chilli flakes, fennel seeds and mustard seeds in each jar.
* **Zucchini fritters** The Green Things Fritters (p 439) can also be made with zucchini (courgettes). Grate 3 zucchini and give them a good squeeze to remove the excess liquid. Use instead of the spinach and add plenty of chopped herbs.

Raw zucchini, chilli and sesame salad

SERVES 4

Small zucchini (courgettes) are sweet and tender and don't need cooking. This salad combines the coolness of zucchini with the heat of chilli to make a light summer salad.

Shave 2–3 small zucchini into ribbons with a vegetable peeler or mandoline. Thinly slice 1–2 red chillies and gently mix with the zucchini ribbons in a bowl. Sprinkle with salt and pepper and a splash of white wine vinegar or rice wine vinegar, then set aside for about 5 minutes. In a small bowl, whisk 2 tbsp soy sauce, 1 tbsp sesame oil and ¼ tsp sugar, then drizzle over the salad. Add a handful of coriander (cilantro) or mint leaves and either toasted peanuts or sesame seeds to serve.

Garlicky parsley zucchini
SERVES 2-3 AS A SMALL SIDE

Cut 2-3 zucchini (courgettes) into cubes. Heat 2-3 tbsp olive oil in a frying pan over medium heat, add the zucchini and fry for 3-4 minutes. Add 4-6 finely chopped garlic cloves, ½ tsp fennel seeds and a big pinch of salt, then cook until the garlic smells delicious. Once the zucchini has started to soften, add 2-3 large handfuls of finely chopped parsley and a squeeze of lemon juice, and fry for another 30 seconds or so. Top with ground black pepper and serve.

Grilled zucchini four ways

Grilling zucchini (courgettes) is an excellent way to hide imperfections. Cut zucchini lengthways into 5 mm (¼ in) thick strips and put into a bowl. Drizzle with olive oil, and sprinkle with salt and pepper. Heat a barbecue or chargrill pan and grill the strips for 3 minutes on each side. You want the zucchini to be charred a little and to soften without getting soggy.

Now choose your own adventure from the options below.

GRILLED ZUCCHINI SALAD
Lay the grilled zucchini on a platter. Drizzle with more oil and with lemon juice, then scatter parsley, toasted nuts, plenty of ground black pepper and shavings of parmesan cheese on top.

GRILLED ZUCCHINI GHANOUSH
Just like baba ghanoush, only green. Put 3 cooled grilled zucchini in a food processor with 2 tbsp tahini, 1 tbsp lemon juice, ¼ tsp salt and 1 crushed garlic clove. Give all the ingredients a good blitz, taste, adjust the seasoning and serve with flat breads (p 168) and charred asparagus spears.

MARINATED CHILLI ZUCCHINI
Somewhere between antipasto and a pickle, these are equally good with cheese and fancy wine and on toast for breakfast. Follow the Blistered Marinated Capsicum recipe (p 74), using grilled zucchini instead. Add extra chilli flakes or sliced fresh chilli to the mix.

GRILLED ZUCCHINI PASTA
Season hot pasta well with olive oil, salt and pepper. Toss with torn grilled zucchini and plenty of finely chopped preserved lemon, basil leaves and toasted pine nuts or crushed walnuts. Top with grated parmesan.

Oven-baked ratatouille for wrinkly summer vegetables
SERVES 4–6

When the garden or fridge is full of ageing summer vegetables, make ratatouille. This oven-baked version chars the vegetables first to intensify their flavour – and the high heat will hide all the vegetables' imperfections. Serve ratatouille with eggs, stirred through pasta, with sausages, on toast or with grilled (broiled) fish.

Preheat the oven to 200°C (400°F). In a roasting tin, put 1 kg (2 lb 4 oz) roughly chopped summer vegetables – a mix of zucchini (courgettes), eggplant (aubergine), capsicum (pepper), and red or brown onion. Drizzle ¼ cup (60 ml) olive oil over everything and sprinkle with salt, then roast for 30–40 minutes, until soft and starting to char on the edges.

Meanwhile, lightly oil 4 large tomatoes (about 650 g/1 lb 7 oz) and place in a separate roasting tin. Add to the oven and blacken for about 30 minutes. Once they're jumping out of their skins, remove from the oven and allow to cool a little.

Reduce the oven temperature to 180°C (350°F). Roughly chop the tomatoes, remove any big bits of tough skin or core, and add to the charred vegetables with 2 tsp crushed coriander seeds or crushed fennel seeds, ½ tsp salt, lots of ground black pepper and another 2 tbsp oil. Mix everything together and return to the oven for 15–30 minutes, depending on how tender you like your ratatouille. Taste and add more salt and pepper if needed. Serve hot or cold.

Zucchini slice

SERVES 6 AS A MEAL, OR MORE FOR A PICNIC

This is served every Christmas at Alex's house. It was a staple in her house growing up and has now reached legendary status. Based on Stephanie Alexander's recipe, this is a very stripped-back, minimal-ingredient version that's really easy to make and can help you get through a heap of zucchini if the garden is overloaded.

Preheat the oven to 180°C (350°F). Grate 1 kg (2 lb 4 oz) zucchini (courgettes) and squeeze out the excess moisture with clean hands. Put the squeezed zucchini in a big bowl with 3 cups (300 g) grated parmesan, 1⅔ cups (250 g) self-raising flour and lots of salt and pepper. Add 6–7 lightly beaten eggs and ½ cup (125 ml) extra virgin olive oil. Gently combine everything and pour into a 20 × 30 cm (8 × 12 in) baking tin lined with oiled baking paper. Smooth down with the back of a spoon and bake for 30–40 minutes until firm to the touch. Allow to cool, then cut into squares and serve with a tomato relish.

PRESERVING GUIDE

You'll notice a lot of preserving recipes in all the Cornersmith cookbooks. It's true, we're obsessed with preservation, not just because we love the flavour of preserved foods and condiments, but for its important role in a low-waste kitchen. We use preservation techniques every day. This doesn't mean we're bottling boxes of fruit and vegetables all the time – in fact, lots of cooks are preserving without even realising it. Covering pesto with oil is a short-term preservation method to stop your green sauce deteriorating from exposure to oxygen. Drying herbs in the sun is preservation, as you're removing the moisture that mould needs to grow.

If you know what you're doing, you can preserve a cucumber in vinegar or an apricot in sugar syrup for many years. The earlier Cornersmith books will give you more in-depth knowledge about the craft and science of longer-term preserving. In this book, we want to give you some simple traditional preserving techniques as a way to combat food waste. We've chosen easy recipes that we both make in our home kitchens: adaptable jams for what's in the fruit bowl, pickles for the oversized daikon you accidentally bought, syrups for fruit scraps and so on.

Preserving doesn't always mean sterilisation, fancy jars and hours spent hunched over pots of boiling water. Sterilising jars and heat-processing are really important if you're looking to store your preserves out of the fridge for long periods of time. This is a good skill to have if you're making four or more jars of something and you don't want to fill up the fridge, or if you don't think you'll be able to eat them over the next few months. A lot of the recipes you'll find here only fill one clean (rather than sterilised) jar or container to be stored in the fridge. This might be, for example, a quick pickle, a kraut, or an infused vinegar. We'll let you know which recipes you need to be more careful with, and which ones you can bung in an old (clean) takeaway container.

Sterilising jars and bottles

It sounds like a big mystery, but sterilising your jars and bottles is pretty easy.

CHECKING YOUR JARS AND BOTTLES

When you're starting out, just use what you have in the kitchen cupboard. Second-hand jars are fine to reuse, as long as there are no cracks or chips in the glass that could harbour microorganisms or cause the jar to break when heated. Second-hand metal (but not plastic) lids are okay too, if they're in good condition. Make sure there's no rust, and that the white acid-proof coating inside the lids is intact. Also check that the lids aren't misshapen or dented, as both of these can interfere with the seal.

HOW TO STERILISE YOUR JARS AND BOTTLES

Wash them in hot soapy water and rinse well, then place upright in an ovenproof dish in a cold oven. Heat the oven to 110°C (225°F). Once it has reached temperature, leave the jars in the oven for 10–15 minutes or until completely dry, then remove them carefully. Pour a hot mixture straight into hot jars; when packing cold pickles or preserves, wait for the jars to cool down first.

To sterilise the lids, place them in a large saucepan of boiling water and leave for 5 minutes, then drain and dry with clean paper towel, or sit them on a wire rack to air dry. Make sure they are completely dry before using.

Filling your jars

This information is if you're looking for long storage times. For quick pickling or one jar of jam, just store it in the fridge and eat it! Remember that hot jams or chutneys need hot jars, and cool pickles need cool jars, otherwise the heat shock could break the glass.

FILLING JAM JARS

Carefully pour the hot jam into your hot sterilised jars, leaving a 5 mm (¼ in) gap at the top of the jar. Wipe the rims of the jars with paper towel or a clean damp cloth and seal immediately. Store unopened jars of jam and marmalade in a cool, dark place; once opened, they should be kept in the fridge and used within 2–3 months. If you want to make a bigger batch and keep it for longer, heat-process (p 503) your jars before storing them.

PACKING PICKLES INTO JARS

We usually cold-pack our pickles, packing the raw vegetables and spices directly into cooled sterilised jars to help maintain their colour and crunch. Occasionally we'll give hard vegetables, such as whole baby beetroot or brussels sprouts, a quick blanch in boiling water first.

Packing fruit or vegetables perfectly into jars takes practice. You want to get in as much as possible without squashing or bruising them, or bursting their skins, so you need a firm hand but a gentle touch. Aim to fill the jars to just below the rim, leaving enough room for the vegetables to be completely covered in pickling liquid without them touching the lid.

Slowly pour the liquid over the vegetables, making sure they're completely submerged (anything left uncovered will discolour and deteriorate, and could potentially go mouldy). It's important to get rid of any air bubbles from the jars before sealing them or the pickles may spoil, because the oxygen in the bubbles enables microorganisms to thrive. To do this, gently tap each jar on the bench and slide a clean butter knife or chopstick around the inside of the jar to release any hidden air pockets – you'll see bubbles being released from between the pickles. You may need to add more vegetables or brine afterwards.

You need to leave a gap of 5–15 mm (¼–⅝ in) between the liquid and the lid – this is called the headspace, and it allows the vegetables to expand as they absorb the liquid. Keep in mind that smaller and sliced vegetables will absorb less liquid than larger ones, so adjust the headspace accordingly.

Heat-processing

This process uses heat to stop the growth of bacteria, remove oxygen from the jar and vacuum-seal the lid, making your preserves safe to store in the pantry for long periods rather than the fridge. We generally recommend heat-processing in the following instances:

- You're making big batches of preserves and will be storing them in the pantry for more than 1 year.
- You're making jam and you've reduced the sugar content to lower than 60 per cent. Each 1 kg (2 lb 4 oz) of softened fruit needs at least 600 g (1 lb 5 oz) of white (granulated) sugar to preserve it safely out of the fridge.
- You live in a very hot climate, or your pantry gets very hot. Heat can affect your preserves if they're not properly sealed.

- You've put cold preserves in a cold jar. Jars require heat to form a vacuum seal. If you put hot chutney into a hot sterilised jar, the lid will seal itself. If you're cold-packing your preserves, the jar won't seal and will still have oxygen inside. This means there is no guarantee that it will stay mould-free.
- You're a nervous Nellie. Heat-processing is like a security blanket.

HOW TO HEAT-PROCESS

Get the biggest pan you have, such as a stockpot, and put it on the stovetop. Lay a folded tea towel (dish towel) in the bottom of the pan, then sit your filled, lidded jars on the tea towel. Make sure your lids aren't on too tight! Roughly match the water temperature to the temperature of the jars (to help prevent breakages from thermal shock), then pour in enough water to cover the jars, either completely or at least until three-quarters submerged. Bring to the boil over medium heat. The heat-processing times are given in the recipes and start from the moment the water reaches boiling point.

At the end of the processing time, carefully remove the hot jars from the water using preserving clamps or a very thick cloth. Line your jars up on your benchtop and let them sit overnight. As they cool, a vacuum will form inside each jar and suck down the lid, sealing them securely. In the morning, the lids should be concave, meaning they're sealed. These jars can be safely stored in the pantry for up to 2 years. If you have concerns about the seal of any of your jars (sometimes a couple of jars fail to seal correctly), store them in the fridge and use their contents within 2–3 weeks.

Jam setting point

There are many ways to test for setting point, but we find the easiest way is to put several small saucers in the freezer before you start.

Once the sugar is in the pan and your jam has been bubbling away for 20 minutes (or 15 minutes for marmalade), get one of the saucers out of the freezer and drop a small spoonful of your jam onto it. Let it sit for a minute or so, then run your finger through it: if your finger leaves a clear line that stays put, your jam or marmalade has reached setting point. You can test multiple times, but once you get close to your jam being ready, take it off the heat while you test, as it's a very fine line between nicely set and overcooked jam. Other signs that your jam is ready include a thick texture, glossy surface and bubbles that are heavy and slow, unlike the fast bubbles at the beginning of cooking.

As soon as setting point is reached, turn off the heat. If any 'scum' has formed on the surface of the jam, either stir it in or remove it with a slotted spoon – it's perfectly harmless, but some people prefer to skim it off for aesthetic reasons.

If your jam or marmalade refuses to cooperate, don't throw it away. Unset jam is great on ice cream, in smoothies or in ice blocks (popsicles). Overcooked jam can be used in marinades and glazes.

Fermentation

Lacto-fermentation is the method of fermentation used in this book to make sauerkraut (p 66), kimchi and pickles. During lacto-fermentation, lactobacillus bacteria present on the surface of fruit and vegetables convert carbohydrates into lactic acid. This lactic acid not only preserves produce, but also gives fermented food its distinctive sour flavour. For successful lacto-fermentation, all you need are clean jars, the produce you want to ferment, pure salt (i.e. with no additives), and in some cases water. During the fermentation process, you need to store your jar out of direct sunlight and somewhere you'll remember to check on it. Fermentation will begin immediately, but the flavour of fermented foods takes some time to develop. We recommend between 2 days and 2 weeks, depending on the weather (food will ferment more quickly in warmer months), and how punchy you like things to taste. Try your ferments after a few days and see what you think. One of the by-products of fermentation is carbon dioxide, which will build up inside a sealed jar. Release the carbon dioxide by opening the jar every few days. Once you're happy with the flavour of your ferments, pop them in the fridge and they'll last a few months.

Once fermentation is underway, the environment in the jar is hostile to harmful bacteria, so relax. Very rarely does anything go wrong, but if any black mould develops on your ferment, throw the contents of that jar away. If a little white mould is visible on the surface, carefully scoop it off and check underneath: the rest of the ferment might be fine.

Always trust your instincts, though, especially when you first start fermenting, and if something doesn't smell or taste right, discard it.

ACKNOWLEDGEMENTS

This book is a beast! It took many minds to get it out of our heads and onto the pages.

Thank you, as always, to the wonderful team at Murdoch Books. It's a pleasure to work with so many excellent women – Jane Morrow, Virginia Birch, Megan Pigott, Sue Bobbermein, Nicola Young, Alison Cowan and Jacqui Porter.

A big thankyou to our friends and colleagues who tested and ate recipes for us. There are so many recipes in the book, we couldn't have gotten through them without you. Shauna Greyerbiehl, you are a legend and one of the best cooks we know. Maddy Dobbins, Clare Barnes, Estelle Cuiuli and Leanne Stevenson, thank you.

And finally, thank you to our families who have eaten so many strange combinations and endured weeks of eating a single ingredient. We know the turnip week was asking a bit much.